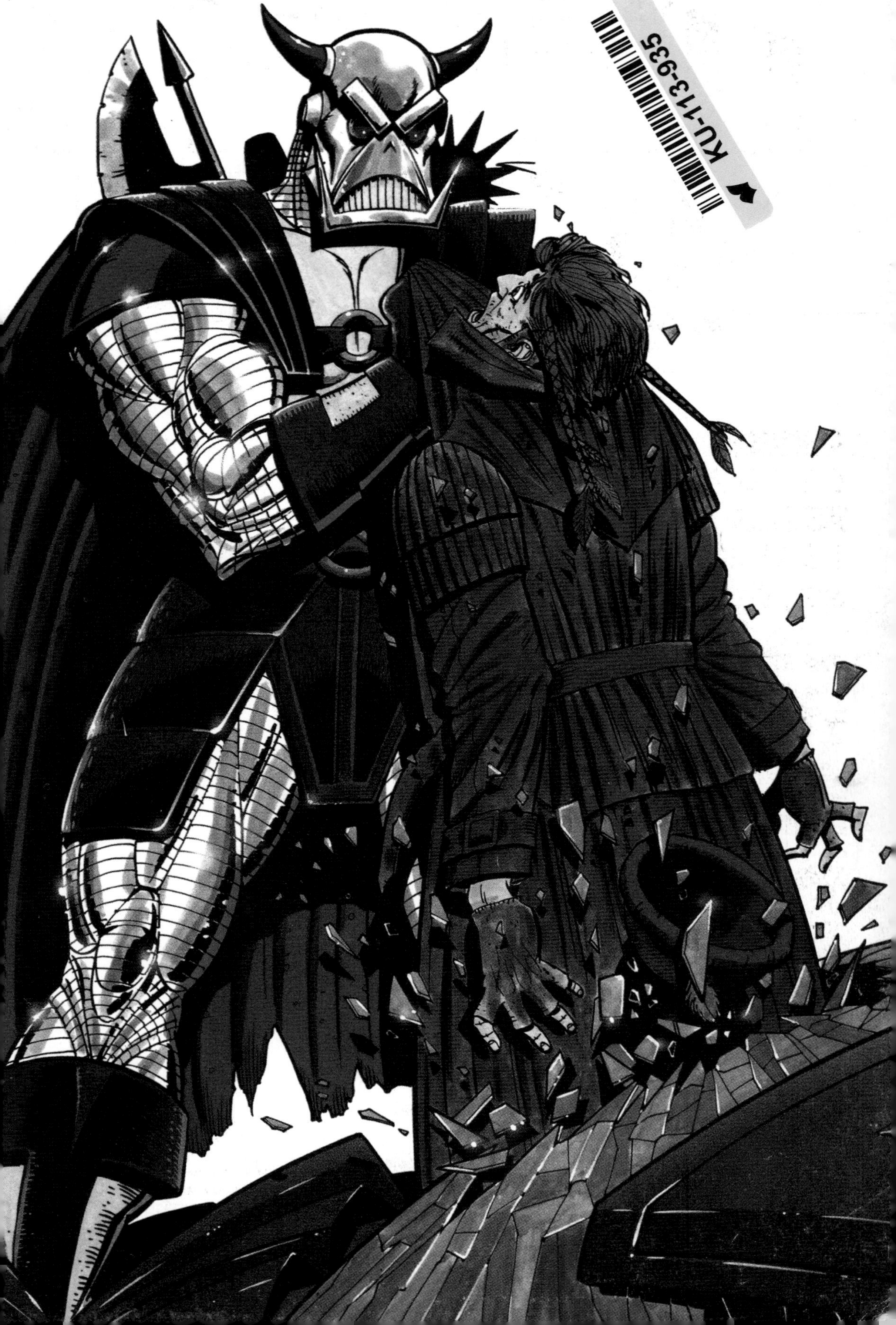

FREELANCE PEACEKEEPING AGENT BACK IN BUSINESS, YES?

(OR THE RISE AND FALL – AND RISE AGAIN – OF DEATH'S HEAD)

One way or another, it's taken 20 years to get Death's Head collected. Complete. Properly. It's not for want of trying, though. Back in 1990, Marvel (UK) gathered together selected chunks of the original 10-issue Death's Head series under the title **The Life and Times of Death's Head**. However, much (indeed, whole issues) was omitted for the sake of the 146 pages allotted to that slender single volume, and the result was rather unsatisfying (to me at least). A better stab at reprinting/repackaging the Death's Head series came with **The Incomplete Death's Head**. This 12-issue maxi-series, published throughout 1993, was essentially a reprint title, but with new originated/linking segments featuring DH's successor, **Death's Head II**. All in all, it did a pretty good job of gathering DH's various appearances and stringing them together into a new narrative, but it wasn't a collected edition, and it was, indeed, incomplete.

So here we are, at last. Over the course of this collection and a first volume (still available in bookstores), every bruising bit of bounty-hunting badness has been gathered, dusted off and reprinted/repackaged for your delectation. The first volume (which, I may have mentioned, is still to be had) guided us through first appearances and crossovers with the likes of **Doctor Who** and **Dragon's Claws** and on into seven issues of **Death's Head** itself. We join things here with **Death's Head #8** and something of a curiosity. For a second time Death's Head crosses paths with the nomadic Time Lord, the Doctor, but on this occasion their meeting is handled, script-wise, by someone other than me (which didn't happen an awful lot with Death's Head).

While I got on with supplying scripts for both **Geoff Senior** (#9) and **Bryan Hitch** (#10), **Steve Parkhouse (Night Raven, The Bojeffries Saga)** stepped in to pen #8's 'Time Bomb.' Hey, I was writing **Death's Head, Dragon's Claws** and **Transformers...** and working full time at Marvel UK in an editorial capacity. I'm only human! Steve, who certainly knew his Doctor, was the perfect choice for the fill-in issue, and artist **Art Wetherell** adds his own distinctive flourish. The central villain, Josiah W. Dogbolter, had previously appeared in **Doctor Who Monthly** (#84, #85-86 in a story entitled 'The Moderator'), also written by Steve.

MARVEL
DEATH'S HEAD
9
IT'S CLOBBERIN' TIME, YES?

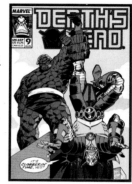

Steve kindly left Death's Head where I needed him for issue #9, specifically atop Four Freedoms Plaza (home, back then, to the Fantastic Four). The story was notable for two things. It was the first-ever Marvel UK/US crossover, something that was to happen a whole lot the next time Marvel UK started producing its own originated characters/titles, and sported a superb cover by acclaimed writer/artist **Walt Simonson (Thor, X-Factor)**, who'd taken a liking to the character. Walt, apart from pencilling the cover to the Death's Head original graphic novel, **The Body in Question**, would go on to guest-star Death's Head during his run on **Fantastic Four** (an issue collected herein). And then, in #10, not content with having held his own against the Fantastic Four, Death's Head took on the Iron Man of 2020 (a future version of the classic Marvel character introduced in the superb **Tom DeFalco/Barry Windsor-Smith Machine Man** series).

That, as it turned out, was it for the Death's Head series. This was well before UK comics were distributed widely in the US by Diamond, and on UK newsstands the comic tended to get lost, swamped by standard (larger-format) UK comics. Sales just couldn't support continuing the series and so (in late 1989) it was truncated rather abruptly. However, Death's Head would return. One year later I was reunited with Death's Head co-creator Geoff Senior on **The Body in Question,** an original graphic novel in the oversized album format. A story thread (revolving around a psychotic hitman with a king-sized grudge named Big Shot) from **Death's Head #7** was picked up and spun into an honest-to-gosh origin for the 'freelance peacekeeping agent.' It was also serialized (at or around the same time) in **Strip**, Marvel UK's anthology magazine. Cue another mouth-watering cover from Walt Simonson.

SSPPLLAHHAMMM!
CAN BEGIN SPEED SEARCH NOW FOR TARGET!
HRM. CURIOUSER AND CURIOUSER. WHOLE EARTH STOPPED!

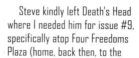

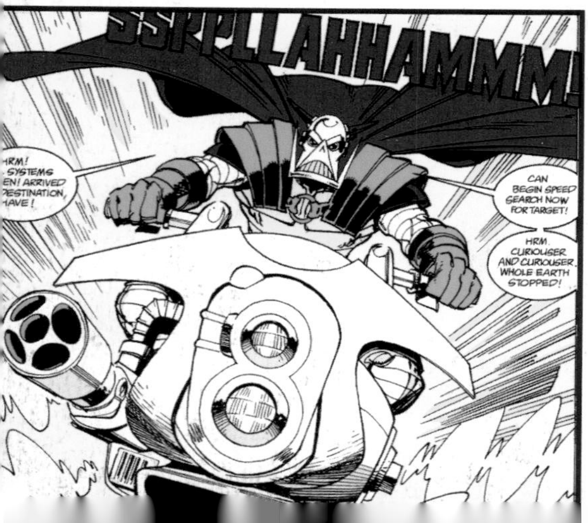

Next, Death's Head made the crossover to Marvel US proper, featuring in both **She-Hulk #24** and (in an 8-page self-contained story) **Marvel Comics Presents #76**, both stories drawn by Bryan Hitch, who was at the time making a big name for himself in the States. However, despite these and the aforementioned guest appearance in **Fantastic Four** (#376), courtesy of Walt Simonson, Death's Head never quite made the transition to the big leagues. At the time, Marvel UK were gearing up for a second assault on the

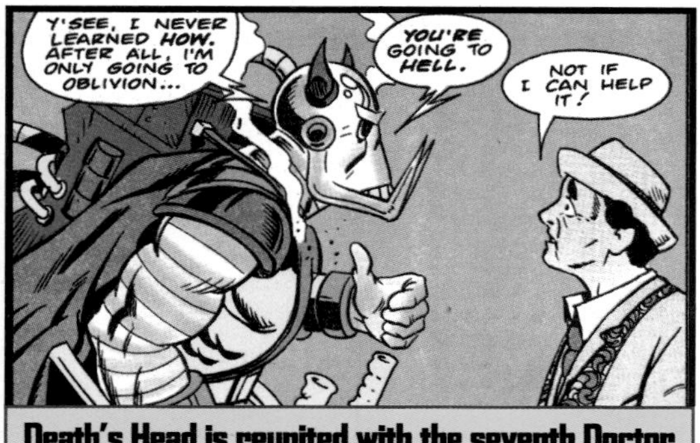
Y'SEE, I NEVER LEARNED HOW. AFTER ALL, I'M ONLY GOING TO OBLIVION...
YOU'RE GOING TO HELL.
NOT IF I CAN HELP IT!

Death's Head is reunited with the seventh Doctor.

wider US (format) comics market, and Death's Head was recalled to lead the charge. However, this move would precipitate great changes for the character, and (for a time at least) the end of my involvement with Death's Head.

In 1992, a new Death's Head series, written by myself and with art by Geoff Senior, was begun (in terms of the creative processes of script and art) and then abruptly canned in favour of a complete reinvention of the character as **Death's Head II**. N sew Marvel UK editor-in-chief **Paul Neary** arrived with a new broom and the intended series went out with the trash. Oh, how I wish I still had some of the amazing art Geoff had delivered up to that point! A new creative team of writer **Dan Abnett** and artist **Liam Sharp** came in and turned the character into something else. Not necessarily worse, it just wasn't Death's Head any more. Busy over at Marvel US on the likes of **Robocop** and **Alpha Flight**, I wasn't involved at all in that first wave of second-generation Marvel UK titles (though I would later pen **Death Metal**, a DHII spin-off series). I assumed that was the end of the original Death's Head. Again, I was wrong.

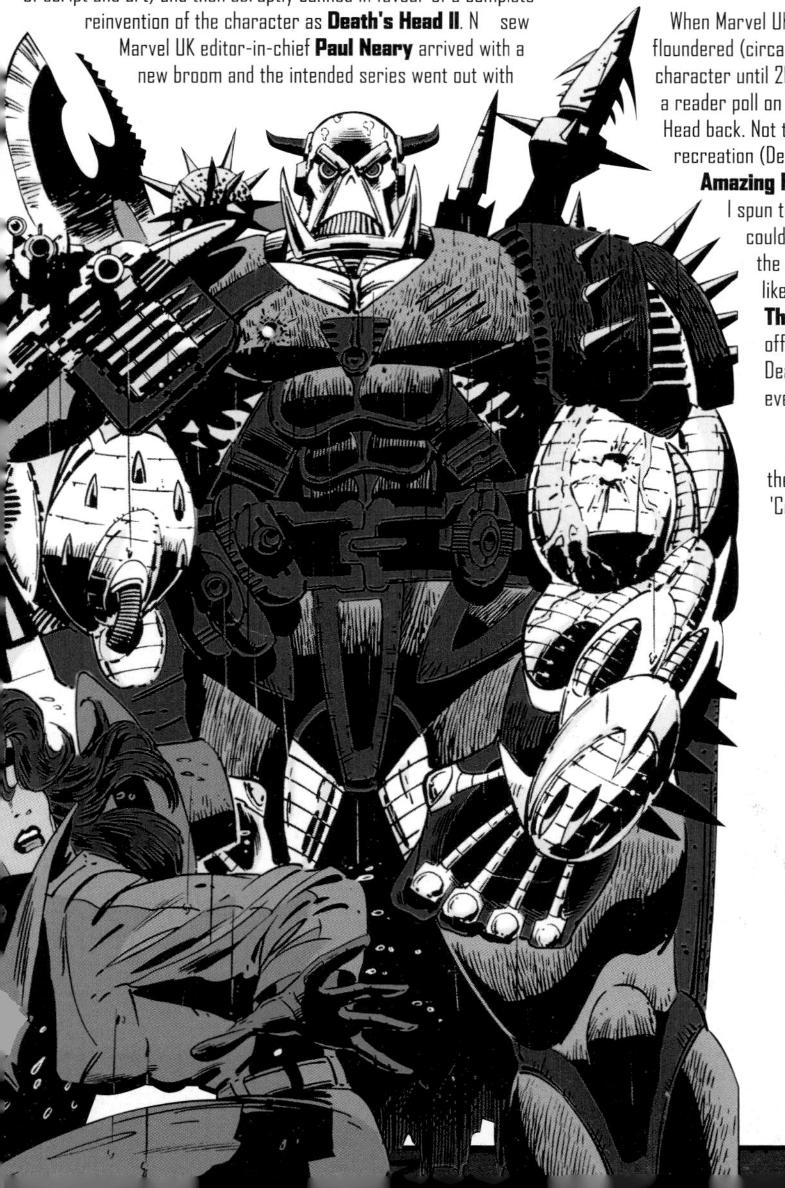

A year or so later, I got a chance to literally re-write history. I was writing (on an on-off basis) Marvel US's **What If?** series, in which classic storylines are revisited and turned on their head, a new story spinning out from a pivotal moment. Editor **Rob Tokar** was a great fan of the original Death's Head and suggested a last hurrah for the character. I was happy to oblige. And so, along with Geoff, I set about spinning my own take on the first meeting between Minion (the artificial being that would 'evolve' into Death's Head II) and Death's Head (in **What If? #54**). Though not a person to bear grudges, it was, I confess, a deeply satisfying and cathartic experience.

When Marvel UK's second wave of US-format titles floundered (circa 1995), that was pretty much it for the character until 2005, when I was asked (as the result of a reader poll on Marvel US's website) to bring Death's Head back. Not the classic, unfortunately, but another recreation (Death's Head 3.0), that graced the pages of **Amazing Fantasy (vol 2) #16-20**. However, I spun the story in such a way that, effectively, it could serve as a prequel; an earlier version of the classic. Should I ever get the chance, I'd like to close that loop (taking into account **The Body In Question** along the way), and offer the definitive origin/timeline of Death's Head. Who knows, one day I may even get to do that.

In the meantime, sit back and savour the 'complete' Death's Head. I know I will. 'Complete' **Dragon's Claws**, anyone?

Simon Furman
London - 2007

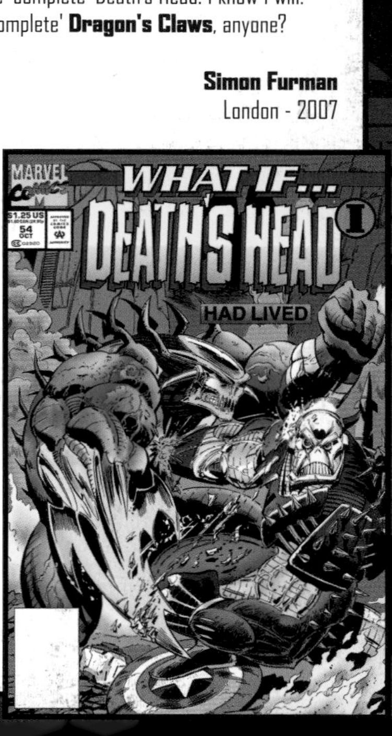
MARVEL COMICS
WHAT IF...
DEATH'S HEAD I
HAD LIVED
$1.25 US
54
OCT

Stan Lee presents:

DEATH'S HEAD™

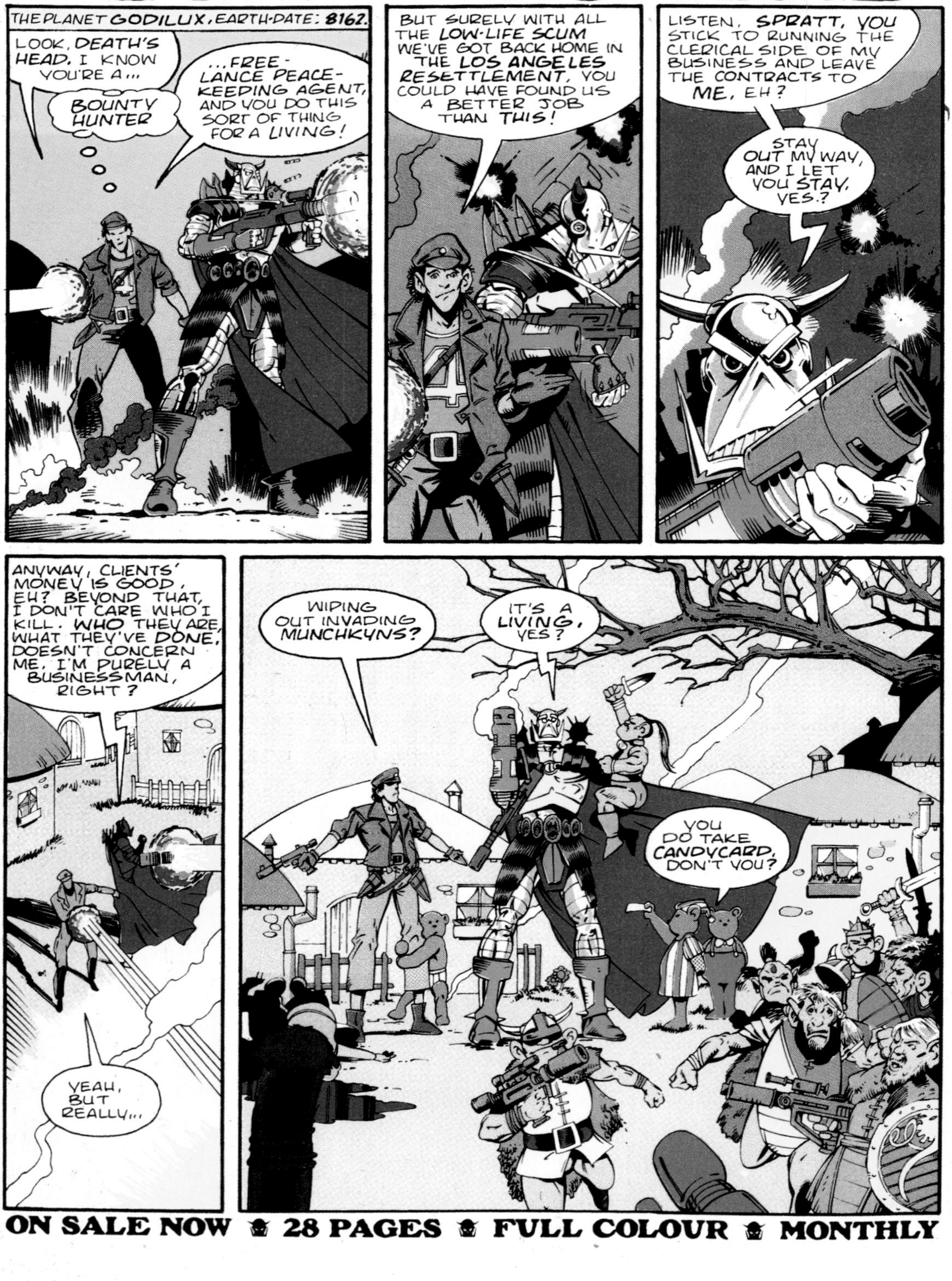
THE PLANET GODILUX, EARTH-DATE: 8162.
LOOK, DEATH'S HEAD, I KNOW YOU'RE A...
BOUNTY HUNTER
...FREE-LANCE PEACE-KEEPING AGENT, AND YOU DO THIS SORT OF THING FOR A LIVING!
BUT SURELY WITH ALL THE LOW-LIFE SCUM WE'VE GOT BACK HOME IN THE LOS ANGELES RESETTLEMENT, YOU COULD HAVE FOUND US A BETTER JOB THAN THIS!
LISTEN, SPRATT, YOU STICK TO RUNNING THE CLERICAL SIDE OF MY BUSINESS AND LEAVE THE CONTRACTS TO ME, EH?
STAY OUT MY WAY, AND I LET YOU STAY, YES.?
ANYWAY, CLIENTS' MONEY IS GOOD, EH? BEYOND THAT, I DON'T CARE WHO I KILL. WHO THEY ARE, WHAT THEY'VE DONE, DOESN'T CONCERN ME. I'M PURELY A BUSINESSMAN, RIGHT?
YEAH, BUT REALLY...
WIPING OUT INVADING MUNCHKYNS?
IT'S A LIVING, YES?
YOU DO TAKE CANDYCARD, DON'T YOU?

ON SALE NOW ☗ 28 PAGES ☗ FULL COLOUR ☗ MONTHLY

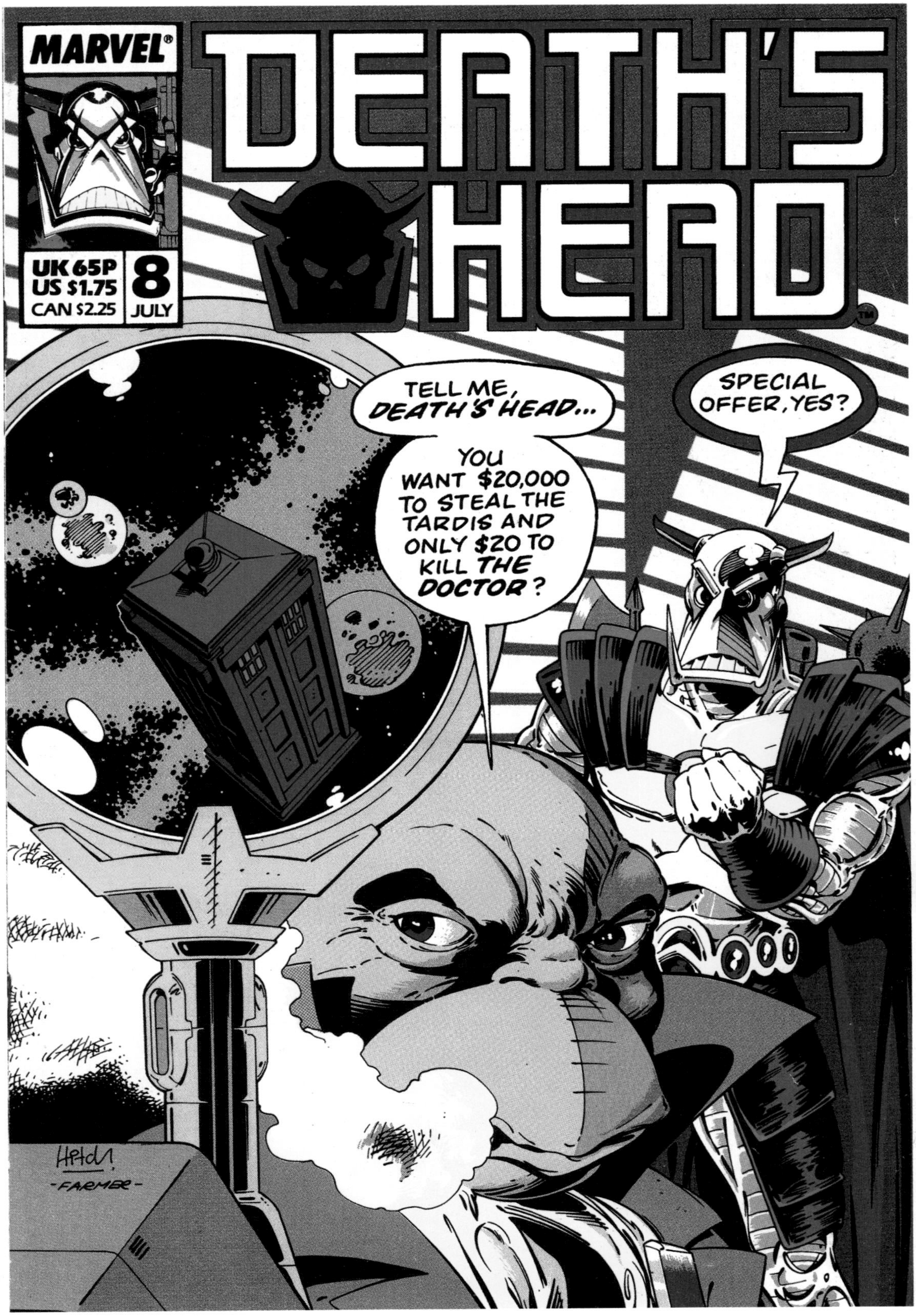
MARVEL
DEATH'S HEAD
UK 65P
US $1.75
CAN $2.25
8
JULY
TELL ME, DEATH'S HEAD...
YOU WANT $20,000 TO STEAL THE TARDIS AND ONLY $20 TO KILL THE DOCTOR?
SPECIAL OFFER, YES?
-FARMER-

Stan Lee presents:

DEATH'S HEAD™

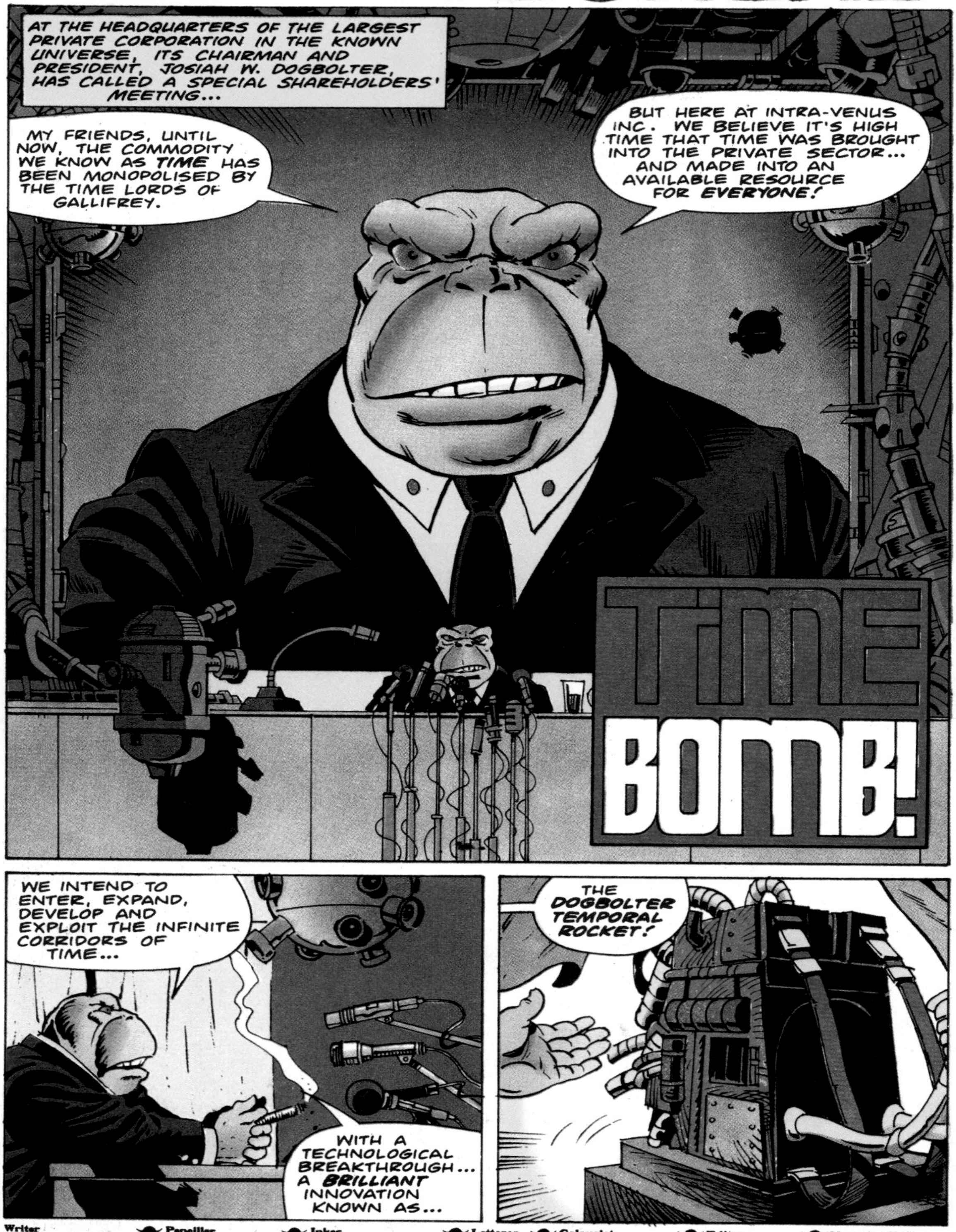
AT THE HEADQUARTERS OF THE LARGEST PRIVATE CORPORATION IN THE KNOWN UNIVERSE, ITS CHAIRMAN AND PRESIDENT, JOSIAH W. DOGBOLTER, HAS CALLED A SPECIAL SHAREHOLDERS' MEETING...
MY FRIENDS, UNTIL NOW, THE COMMODITY WE KNOW AS TIME HAS BEEN MONOPOLISED BY THE TIME LORDS OF GALLIFREY.
BUT HERE AT INTRA-VENUS INC. WE BELIEVE IT'S HIGH TIME THAT TIME WAS BROUGHT INTO THE PRIVATE SECTOR... AND MADE INTO AN AVAILABLE RESOURCE FOR EVERYONE!
TIME BOMB!
WE INTEND TO ENTER, EXPAND, DEVELOP AND EXPLOIT THE INFINITE CORRIDORS OF TIME...
WITH A TECHNOLOGICAL BREAKTHROUGH... A BRILLIANT INNOVATION KNOWN AS...
THE DOGBOLTER TEMPORAL ROCKET!

Writer STEVE PARKHOUSE · Penciller ART WETHERELL · Inker STEVE PARKHOUSE · Letterer ANNIE H · Colourist LOUISE CASSELL · Editor STEVE WHITE · Managing Editor JENNY O'CONNOR

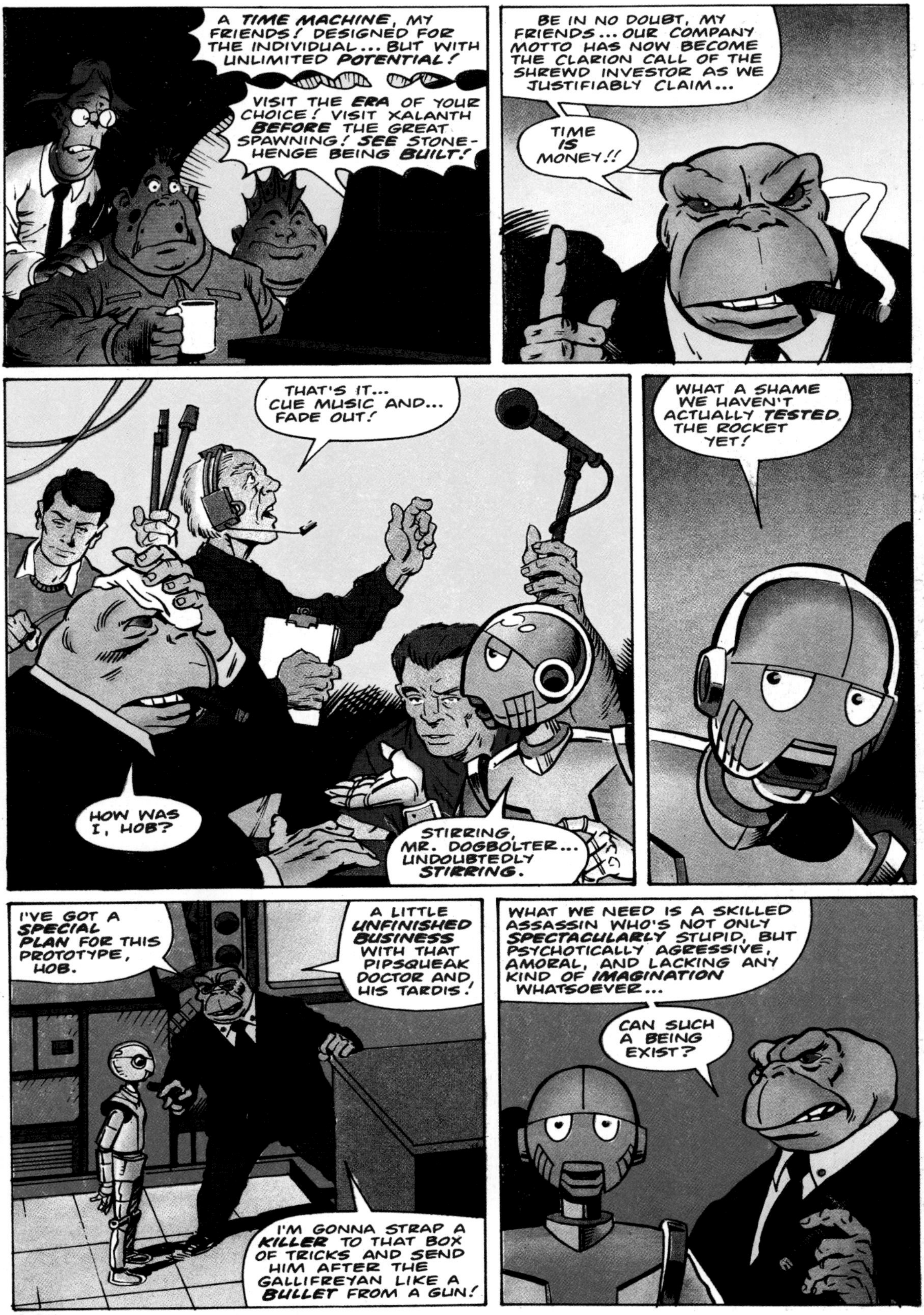
A TIME MACHINE, MY FRIENDS! DESIGNED FOR THE INDIVIDUAL... BUT WITH UNLIMITED POTENTIAL!
VISIT THE ERA OF YOUR CHOICE! VISIT XALANTH BEFORE THE GREAT SPAWNING! SEE STONE-HENGE BEING BUILT!
BE IN NO DOUBT, MY FRIENDS... OUR COMPANY MOTTO HAS NOW BECOME THE CLARION CALL OF THE SHREWD INVESTOR AS WE JUSTIFIABLY CLAIM...
TIME IS MONEY!!
THAT'S IT... CUE MUSIC AND... FADE OUT!
HOW WAS I, HOB?
STIRRING, MR. DOGBOLTER... UNDOUBTEDLY STIRRING.
WHAT A SHAME WE HAVEN'T ACTUALLY TESTED THE ROCKET YET!
I'VE GOT A SPECIAL PLAN FOR THIS PROTOTYPE, HOB.
A LITTLE UNFINISHED BUSINESS WITH THAT PIPSQUEAK DOCTOR AND HIS TARDIS!
I'M GONNA STRAP A KILLER TO THAT BOX OF TRICKS AND SEND HIM AFTER THE GALLIFREYAN LIKE A BULLET FROM A GUN!
WHAT WE NEED IS A SKILLED ASSASSIN WHO'S NOT ONLY SPECTACULARLY STUPID, BUT PSYCHOTICALLY AGRESSIVE, AMORAL, AND LACKING ANY KIND OF IMAGINATION WHATSOEVER...
CAN SUCH A BEING EXIST?

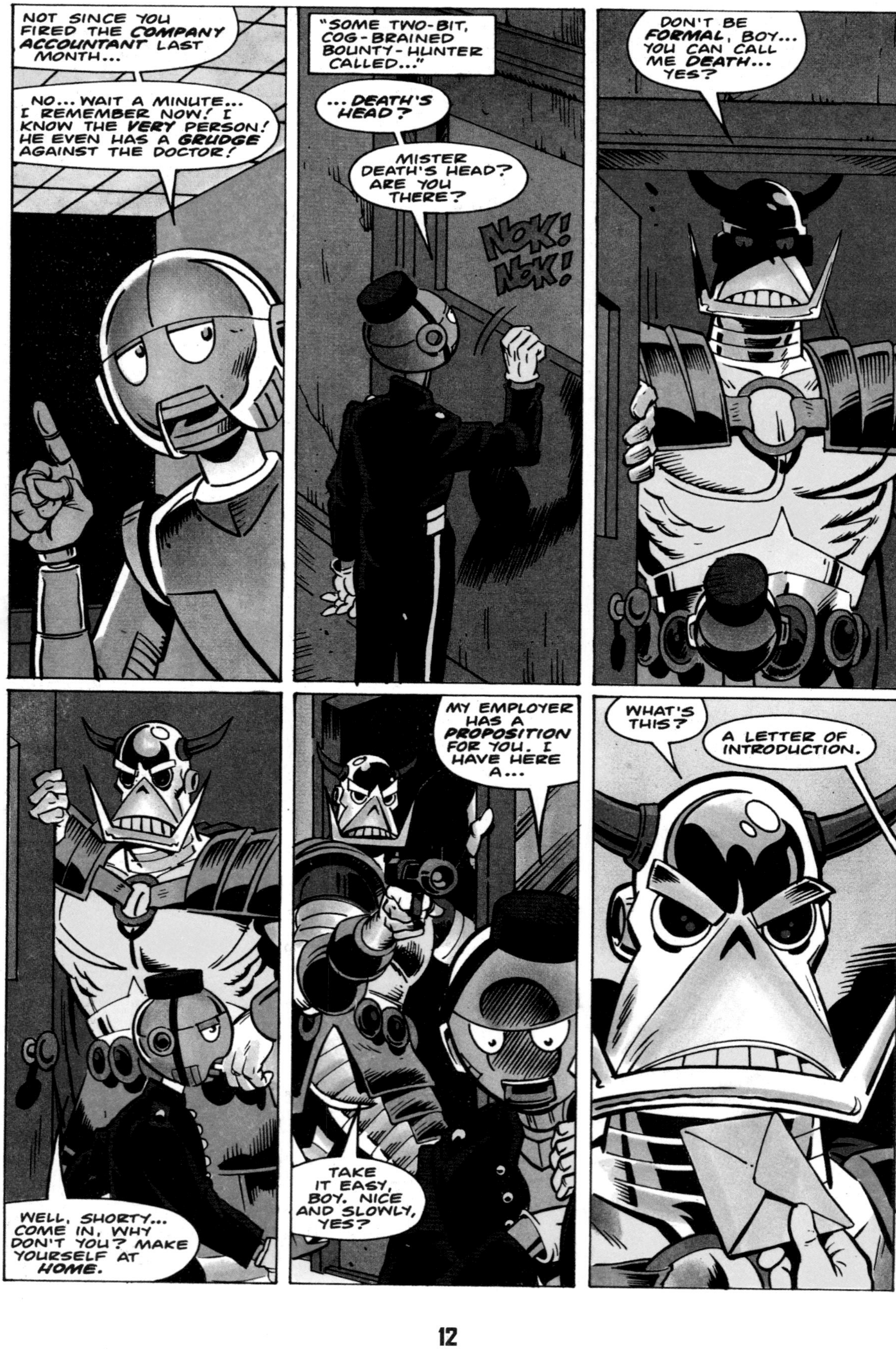
NOT SINCE YOU FIRED THE COMPANY ACCOUNTANT LAST MONTH...
NO... WAIT A MINUTE... I REMEMBER NOW! I KNOW THE VERY PERSON! HE EVEN HAS A GRUDGE AGAINST THE DOCTOR!
"SOME TWO-BIT, COG-BRAINED BOUNTY-HUNTER CALLED..."
...DEATH'S HEAD?
MISTER DEATH'S HEAD? ARE YOU THERE?
NOK! NOK!
DON'T BE FORMAL, BOY... YOU CAN CALL ME DEATH... YES?
WELL, SHORTY... COME IN, WHY DON'T YOU? MAKE YOURSELF AT HOME.
MY EMPLOYER HAS A PROPOSITION FOR YOU. I HAVE HERE A...
TAKE IT EASY, BOY. NICE AND SLOWLY, YES?
WHAT'S THIS?
A LETTER OF INTRODUCTION.

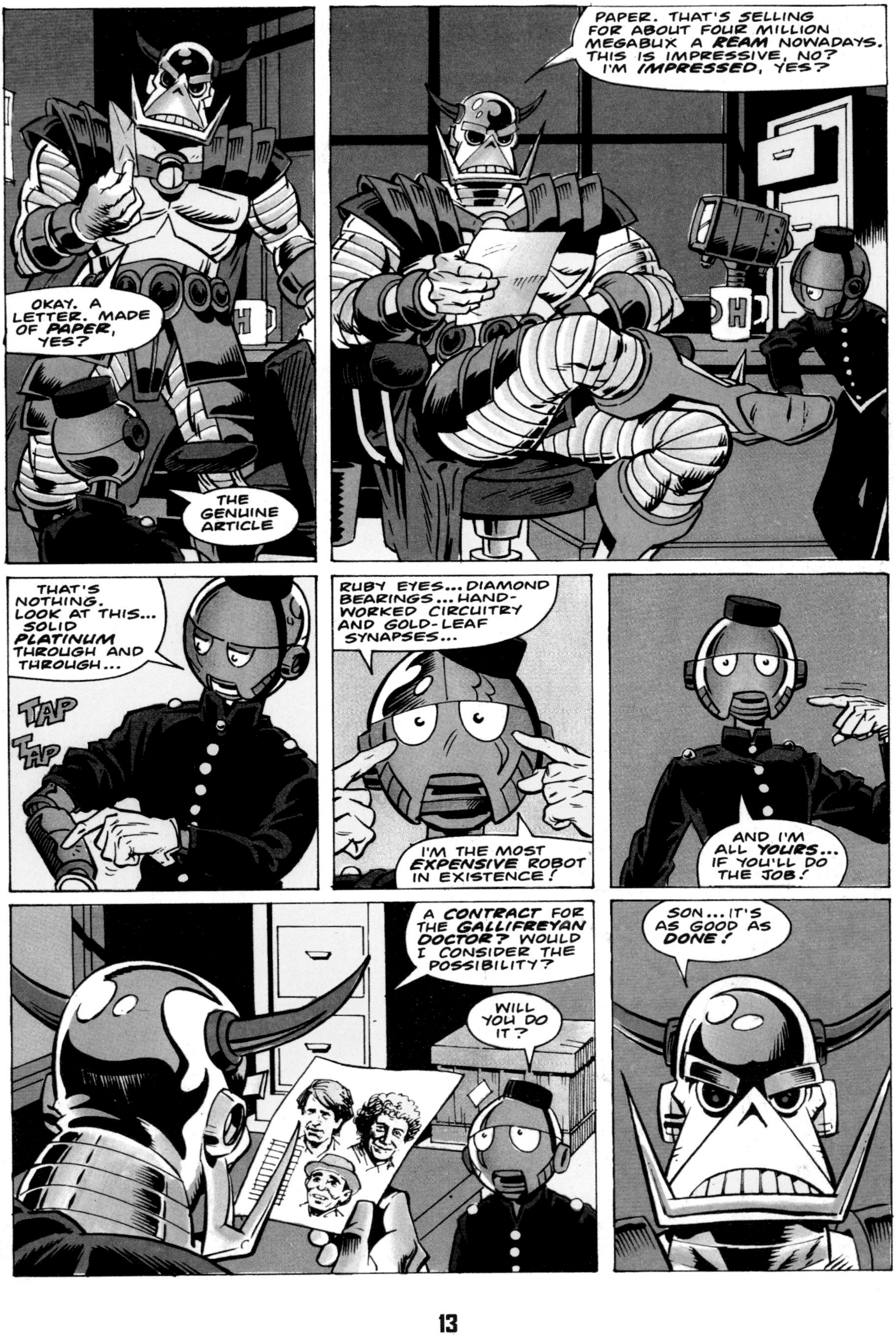
OKAY. A LETTER. MADE OF PAPER, YES?
THE GENUINE ARTICLE
PAPER. THAT'S SELLING FOR ABOUT FOUR MILLION MEGABUX A REAM NOWADAYS. THIS IS IMPRESSIVE, NO? I'M IMPRESSED, YES?
THAT'S NOTHING. LOOK AT THIS... SOLID PLATINUM THROUGH AND THROUGH...
TAP
TAP
RUBY EYES... DIAMOND BEARINGS... HAND-WORKED CIRCUITRY AND GOLD-LEAF SYNAPSES...
I'M THE MOST EXPENSIVE ROBOT IN EXISTENCE!
AND I'M ALL YOURS... IF YOU'LL DO THE JOB!
A CONTRACT FOR THE GALLIFREYAN DOCTOR? WOULD I CONSIDER THE POSSIBILITY?
WILL YOU DO IT?
SON... IT'S AS GOOD AS DONE!

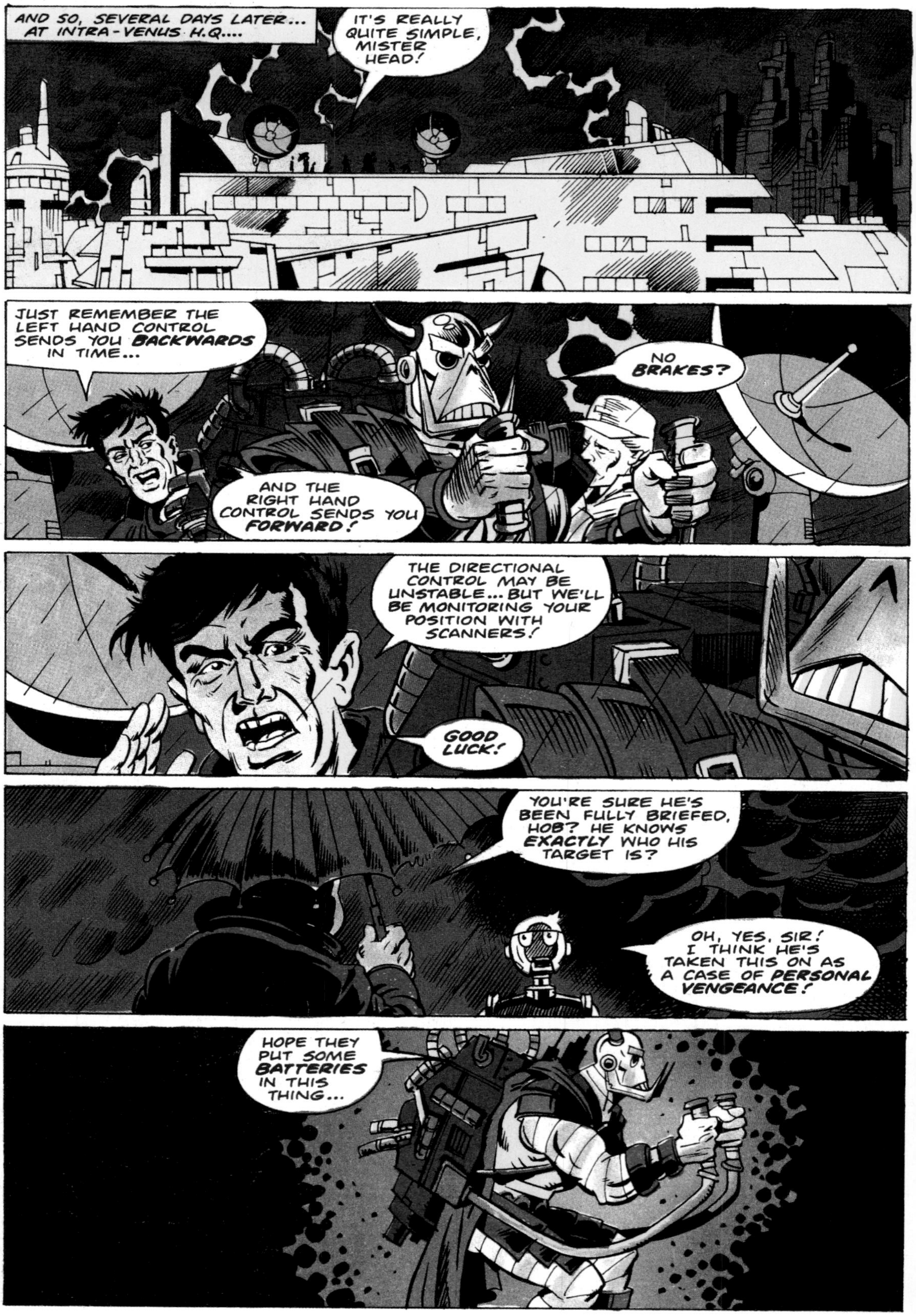
AND SO, SEVERAL DAYS LATER... AT INTRA-VENUS H.Q....
IT'S REALLY QUITE SIMPLE, MISTER HEAD!
JUST REMEMBER THE LEFT HAND CONTROL SENDS YOU BACKWARDS IN TIME...
NO BRAKES?
AND THE RIGHT HAND CONTROL SENDS YOU FORWARD!
THE DIRECTIONAL CONTROL MAY BE UNSTABLE... BUT WE'LL BE MONITORING YOUR POSITION WITH SCANNERS!
GOOD LUCK!
YOU'RE SURE HE'S BEEN FULLY BRIEFED, HOB? HE KNOWS EXACTLY WHO HIS TARGET IS?
OH, YES, SIR! I THINK HE'S TAKEN THIS ON AS A CASE OF PERSONAL VENGEANCE!
HOPE THEY PUT SOME BATTERIES IN THIS THING...

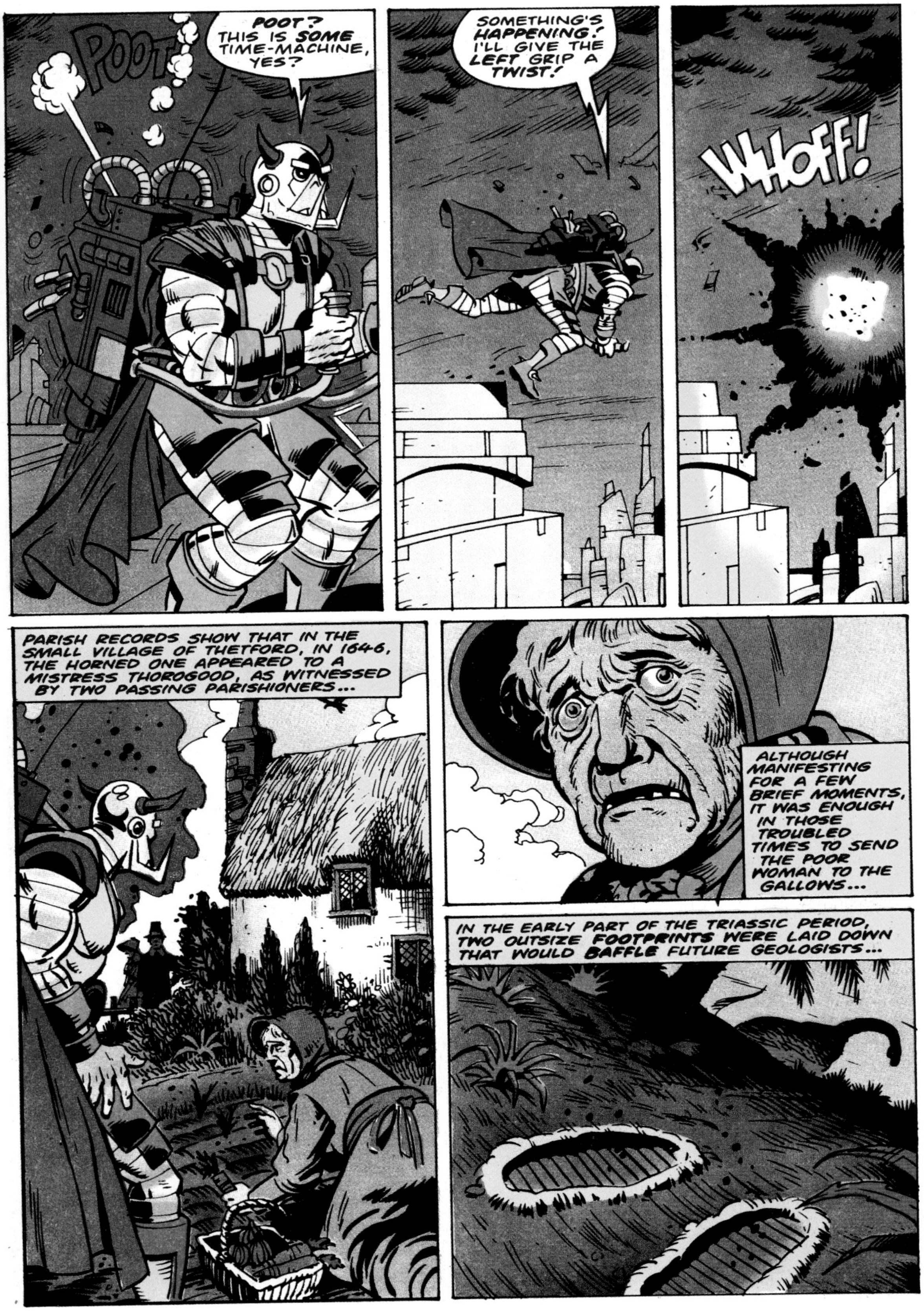
POOT!
POOT? THIS IS SOME TIME-MACHINE, YES?
SOMETHING'S HAPPENING! I'LL GIVE THE LEFT GRIP A TWIST!
WHOFF!
PARISH RECORDS SHOW THAT IN THE SMALL VILLAGE OF THETFORD, IN 1646, THE HORNED ONE APPEARED TO A MISTRESS THOROGOOD, AS WITNESSED BY TWO PASSING PARISHIONERS...
ALTHOUGH MANIFESTING FOR A FEW BRIEF MOMENTS, IT WAS ENOUGH IN THOSE TROUBLED TIMES TO SEND THE POOR WOMAN TO THE GALLOWS...
IN THE EARLY PART OF THE TRIASSIC PERIOD, TWO OUTSIZE FOOTPRINTS WERE LAID DOWN THAT WOULD BAFFLE FUTURE GEOLOGISTS...

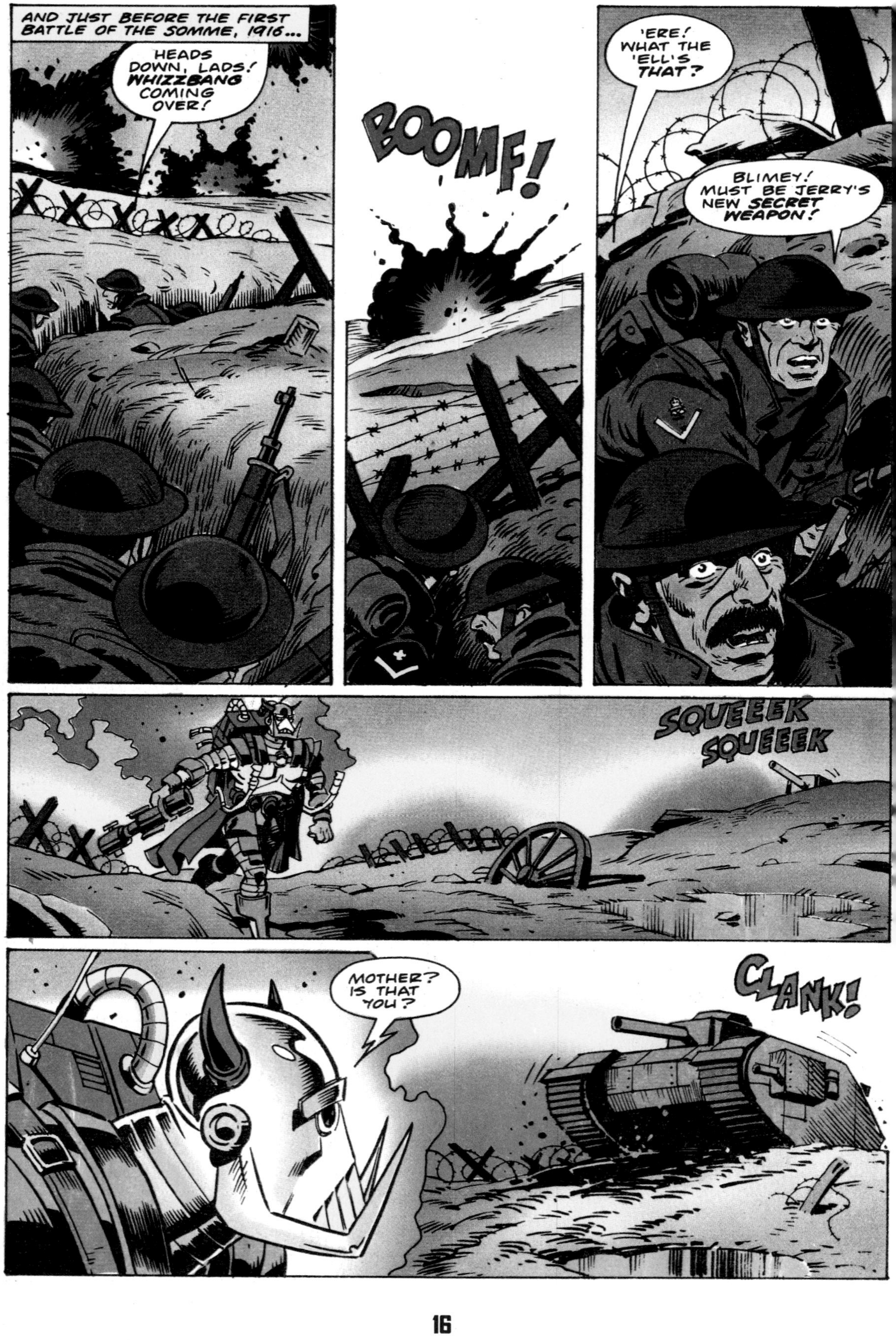
AND JUST BEFORE THE FIRST BATTLE OF THE SOMME, 1916...
HEADS DOWN, LADS! WHIZZBANG COMING OVER!
BOOMF!
'ERE! WHAT THE 'ELL'S THAT?
BLIMEY! MUST BE JERRY'S NEW SECRET WEAPON!
SQUEEEK SQUEEEK
MOTHER? IS THAT YOU?
CLANK!

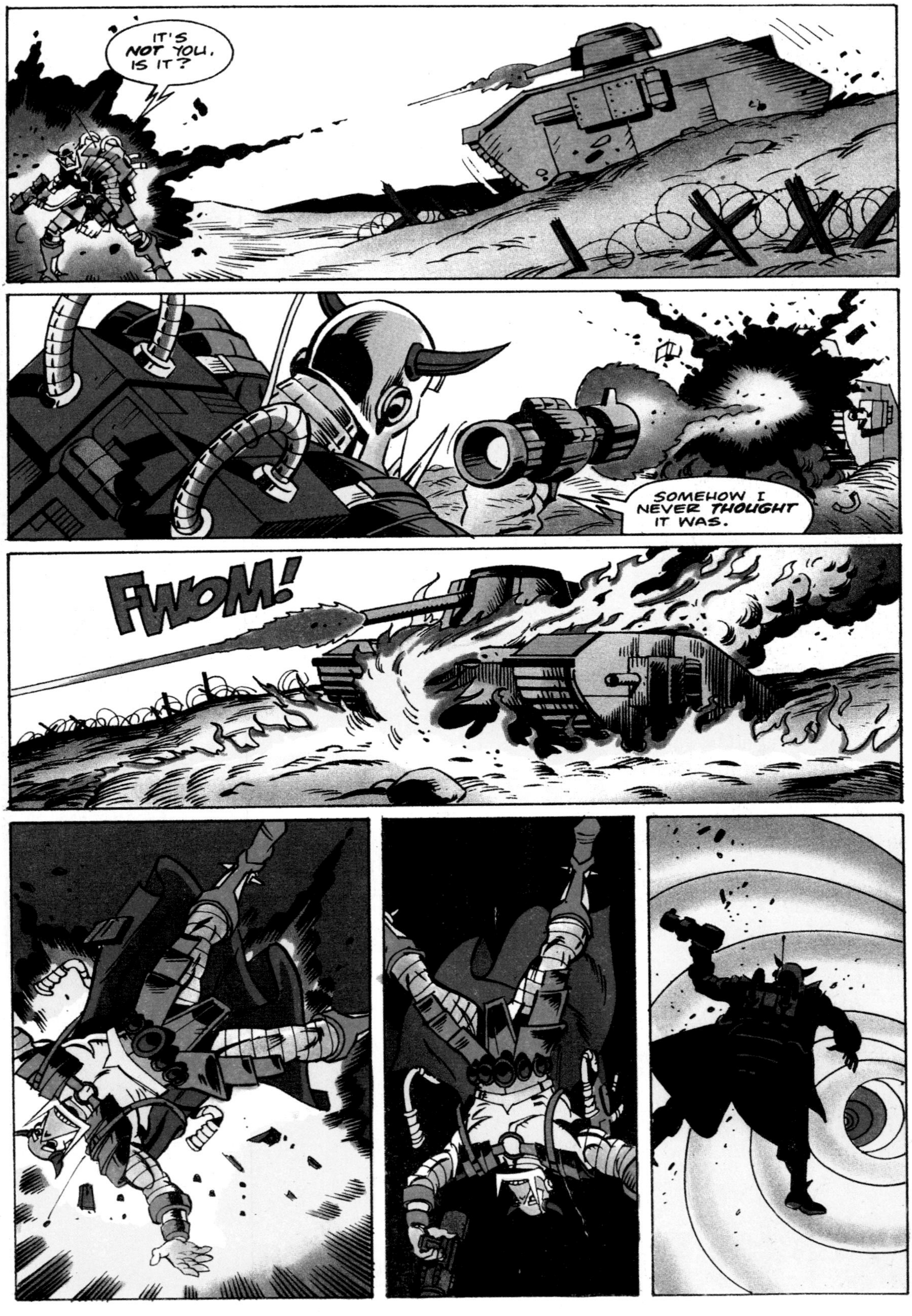
IT'S NOT YOU, IS IT?
SOMEHOW I NEVER THOUGHT IT WAS.
FWOM!

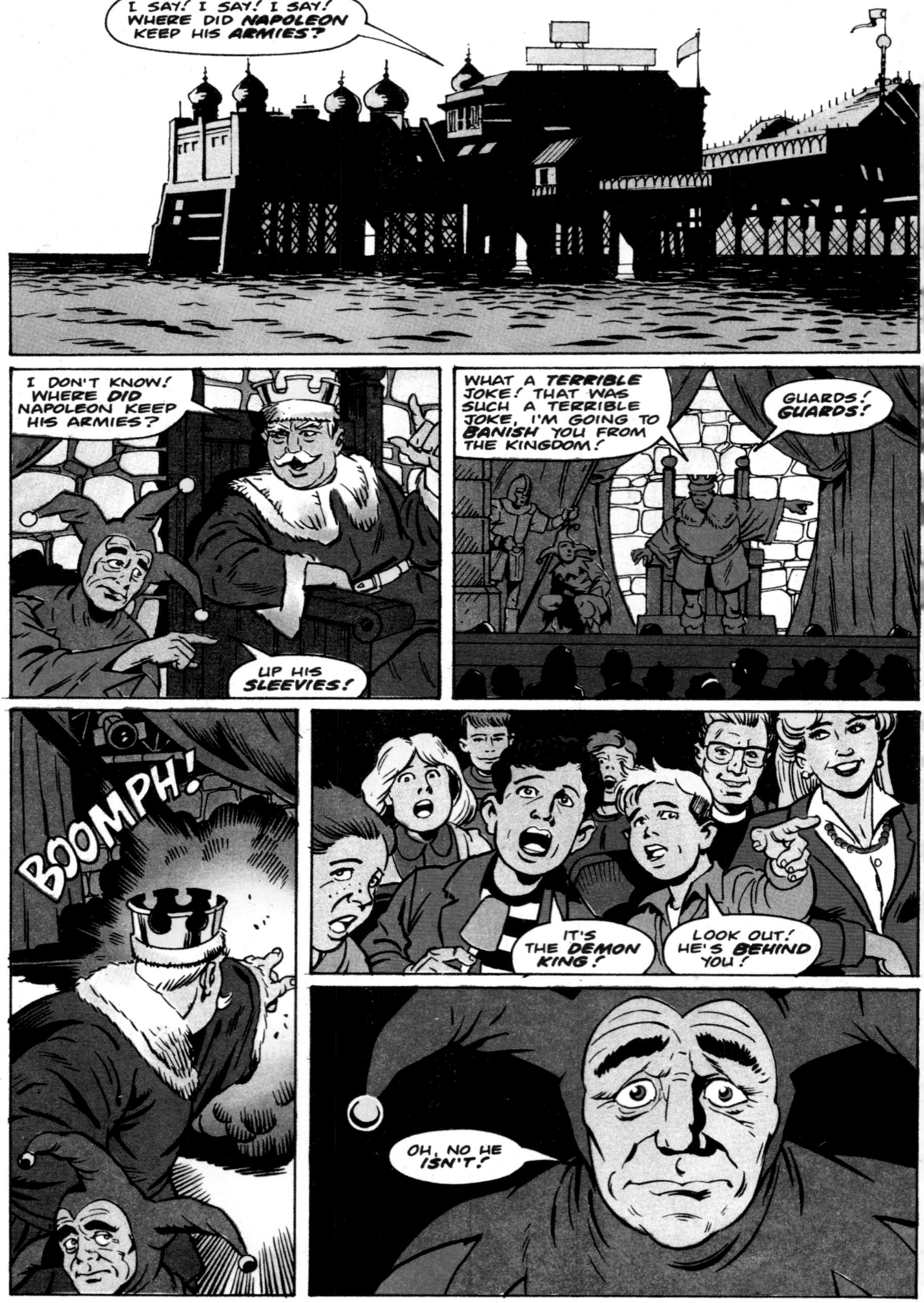
I SAY! I SAY! I SAY! WHERE DID NAPOLEON KEEP HIS ARMIES?
I DON'T KNOW! WHERE DID NAPOLEON KEEP HIS ARMIES?
UP HIS SLEEVIES!
WHAT A TERRIBLE JOKE! THAT WAS SUCH A TERRIBLE JOKE, I'M GOING TO BANISH YOU FROM THE KINGDOM!
GUARDS! GUARDS!
BOOMPH!
IT'S THE DEMON KING!
LOOK OUT! HE'S BEHIND YOU!
OH, NO HE ISN'T!

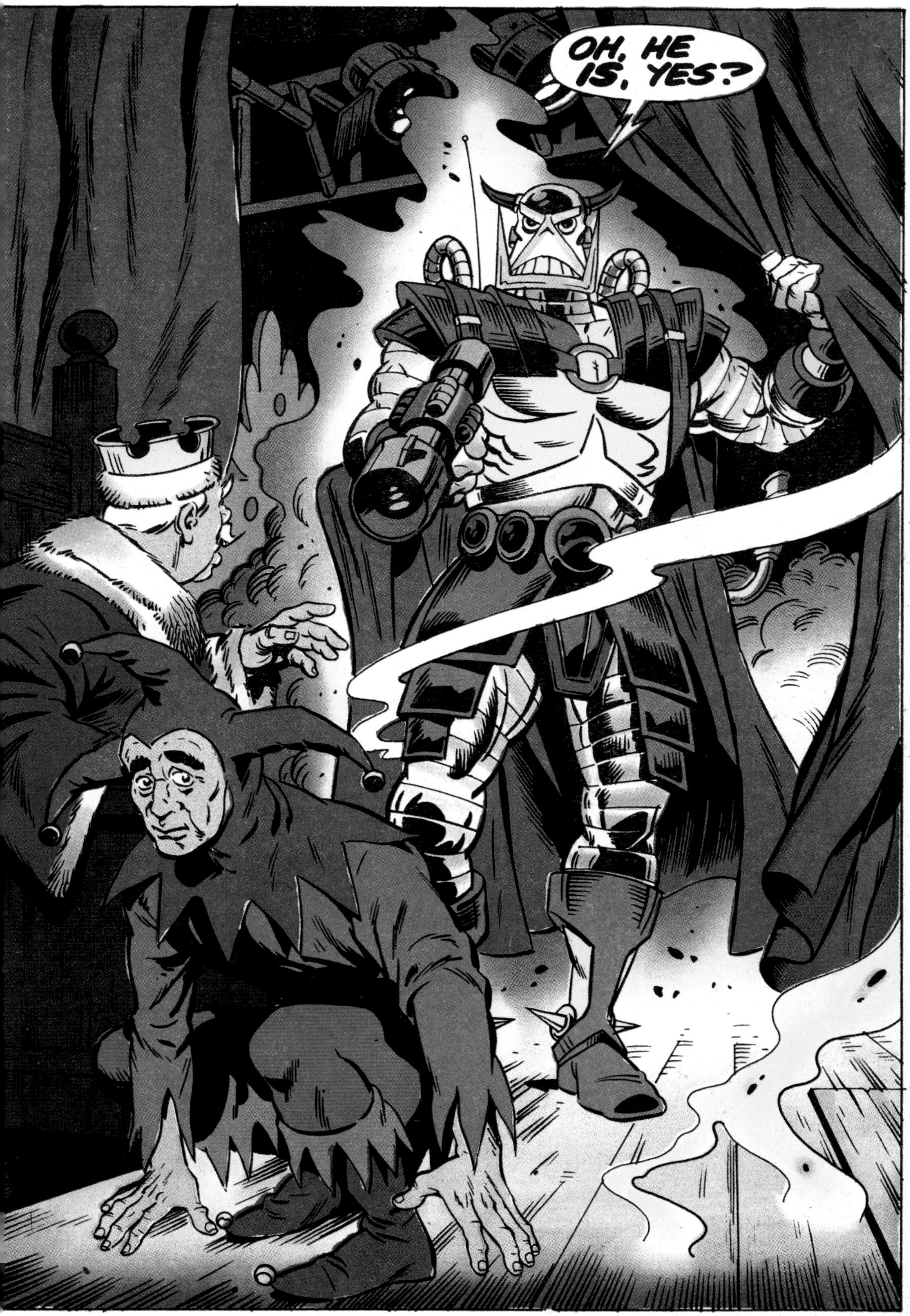
OH, HE IS, YES?

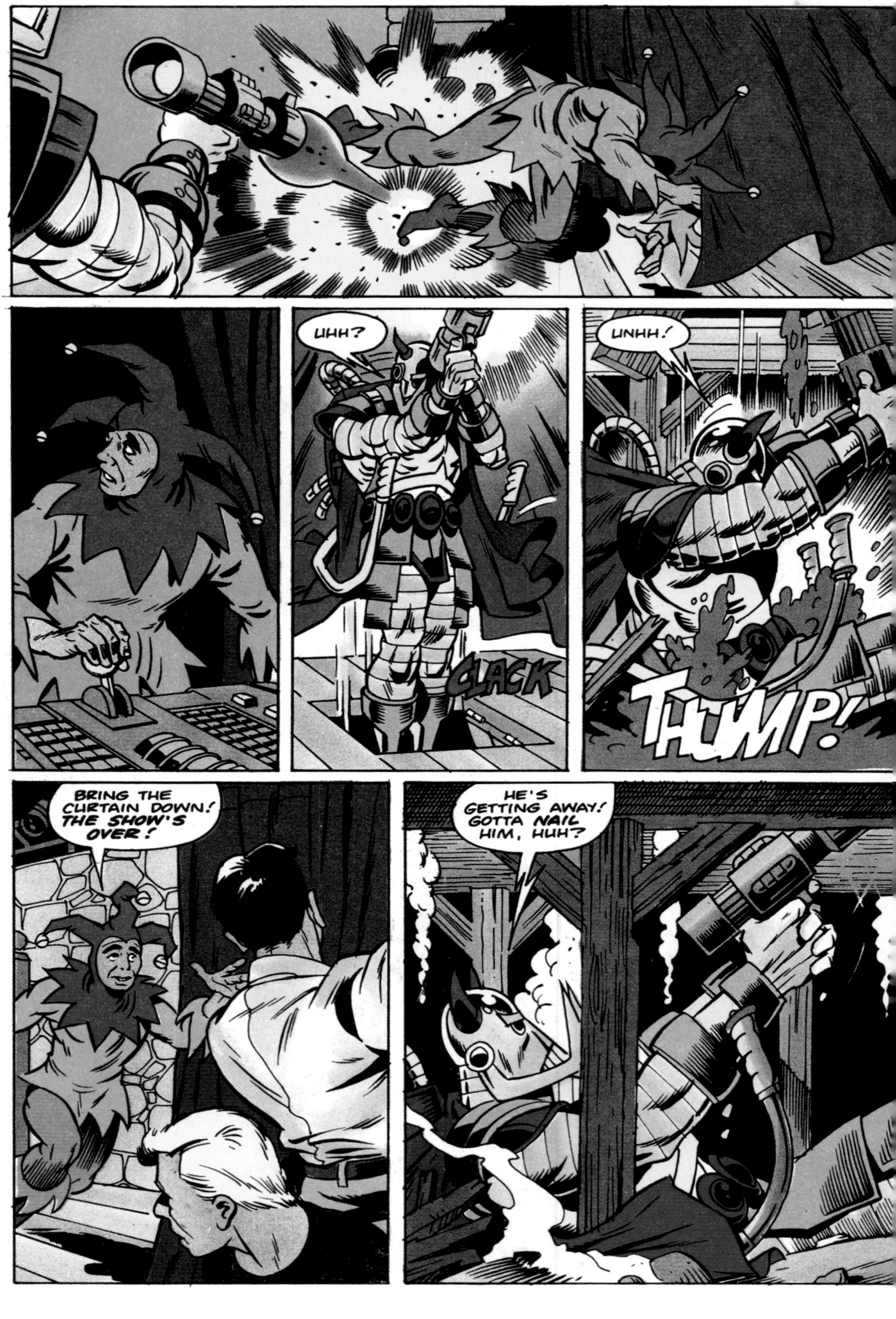
UHH?
CLACK
UNNH!
THUMP!
BRING THE CURTAIN DOWN! THE SHOW'S OVER!
HE'S GETTING AWAY! GOTTA NAIL HIM, HUH?

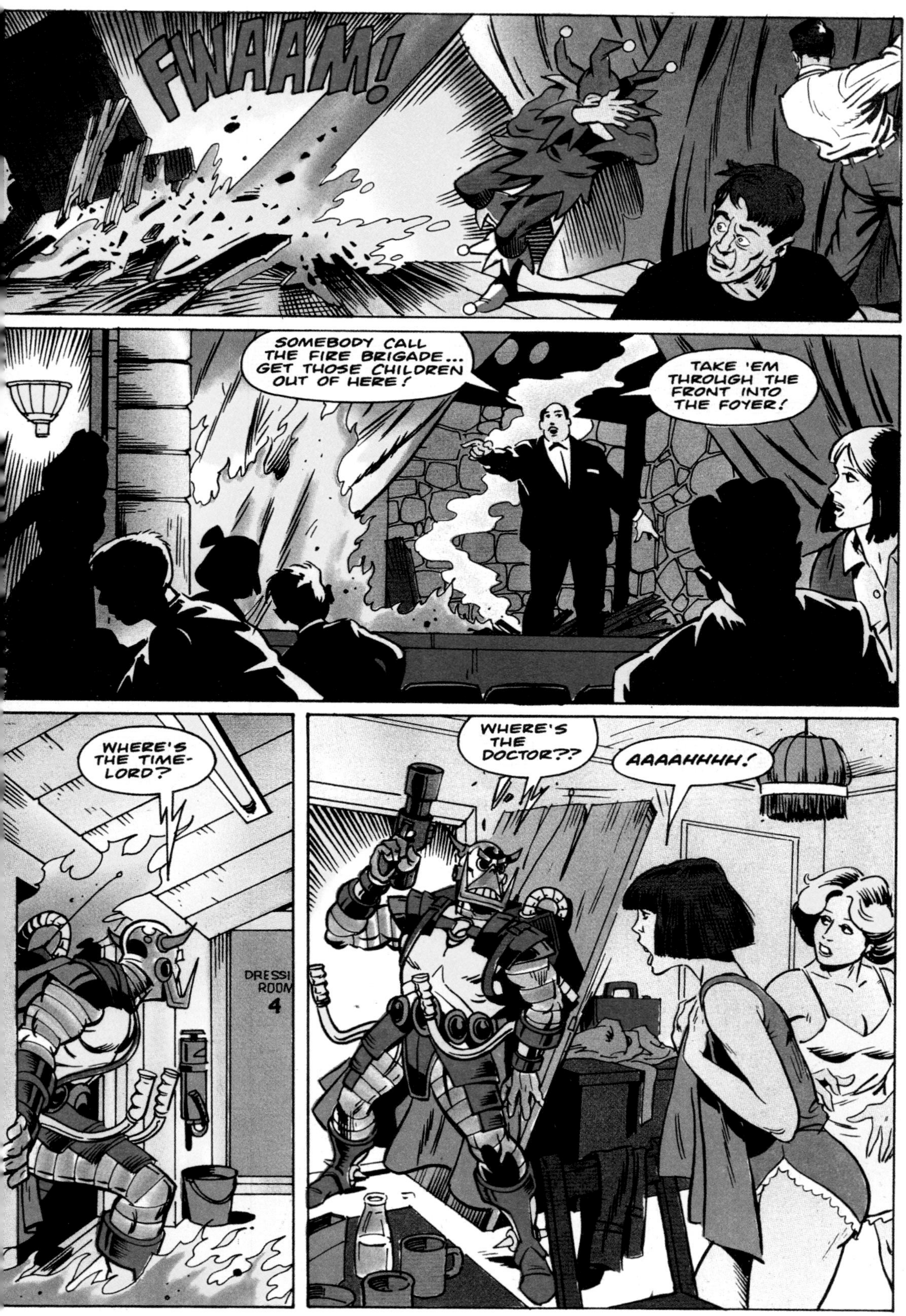
FWAAM!
SOMEBODY CALL THE FIRE BRIGADE... GET THOSE CHILDREN OUT OF HERE!
TAKE 'EM THROUGH THE FRONT INTO THE FOYER!
WHERE'S THE TIME-LORD?
DRESSI ROOM 4
WHERE'S THE DOCTOR??
AAAAHHHH!

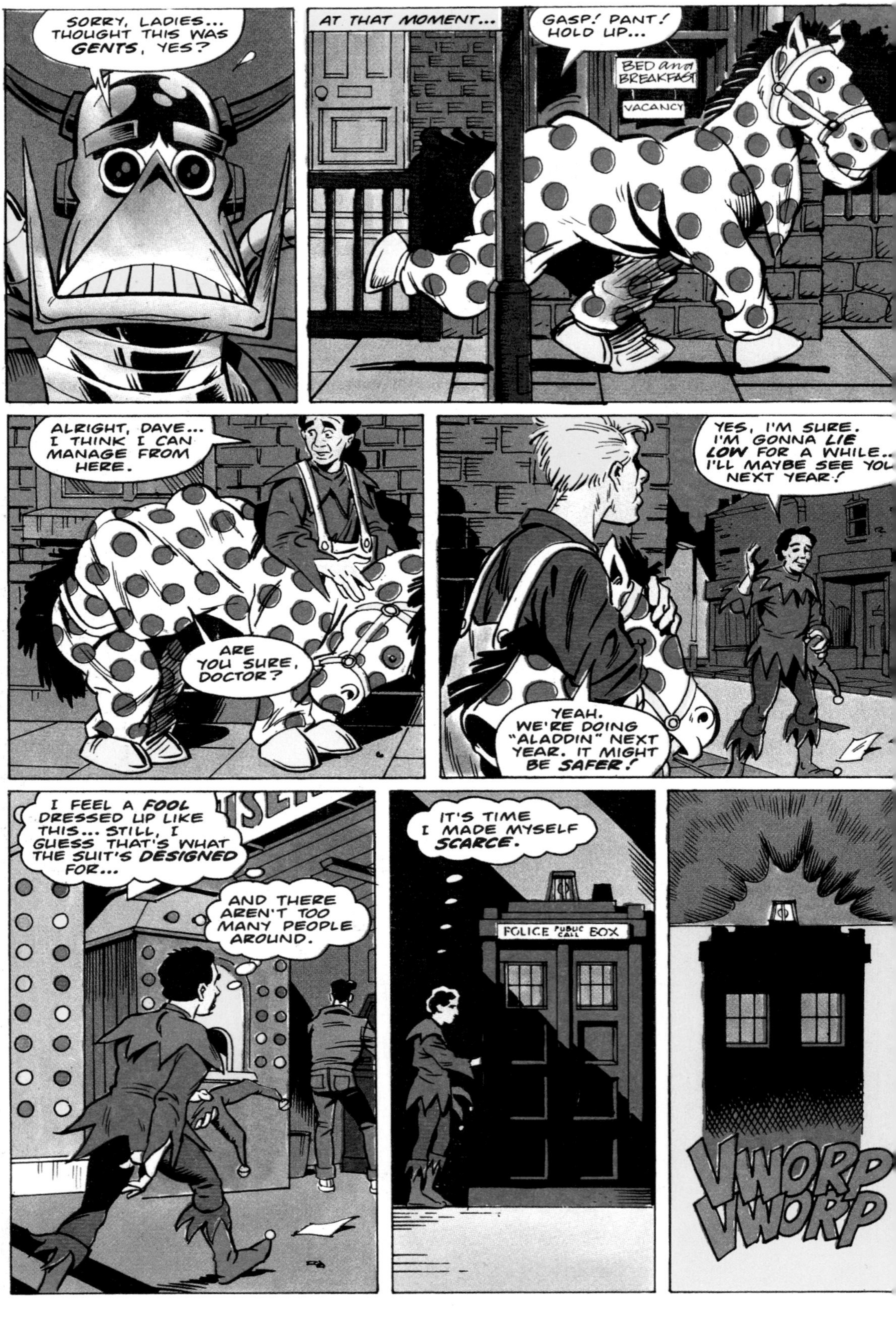
SORRY, LADIES... THOUGHT THIS WAS GENTS, YES?
AT THAT MOMENT...
GASP! PANT! HOLD UP...
BED and BREAKFAST
VACANCY
ALRIGHT, DAVE... I THINK I CAN MANAGE FROM HERE.
ARE YOU SURE, DOCTOR?
YES, I'M SURE. I'M GONNA LIE LOW FOR A WHILE... I'LL MAYBE SEE YOU NEXT YEAR!
YEAH. WE'RE DOING "ALADDIN" NEXT YEAR. IT MIGHT BE SAFER!
I FEEL A FOOL DRESSED UP LIKE THIS... STILL, I GUESS THAT'S WHAT THE SUIT'S DESIGNED FOR...
AND THERE AREN'T TOO MANY PEOPLE AROUND.
IT'S TIME I MADE MYSELF SCARCE.
POLICE PUBLIC CALL BOX
VWORP VWORP

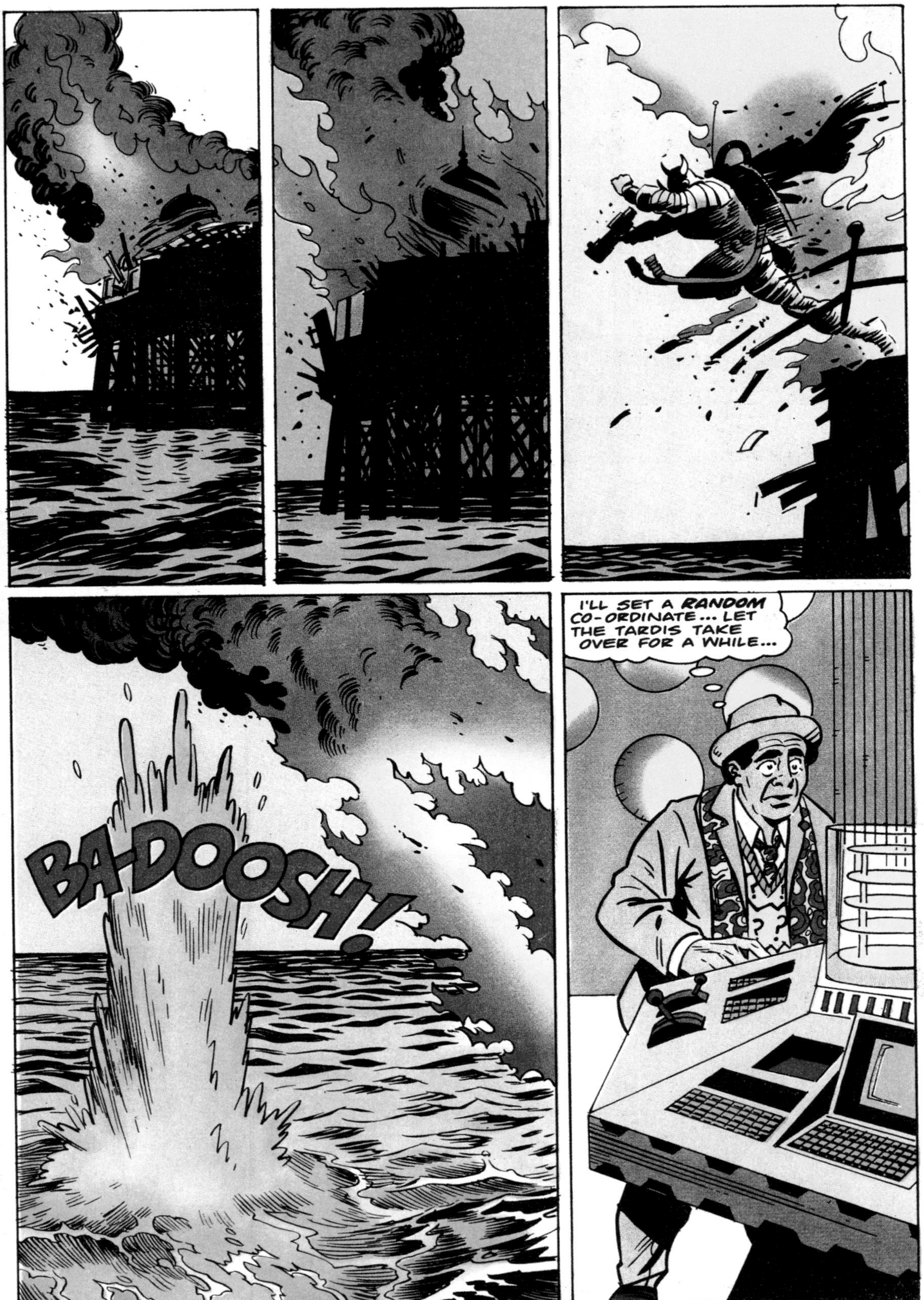
BA-DOOSH!
I'LL SET A RANDOM CO-ORDINATE... LET THE TARDIS TAKE OVER FOR A WHILE...

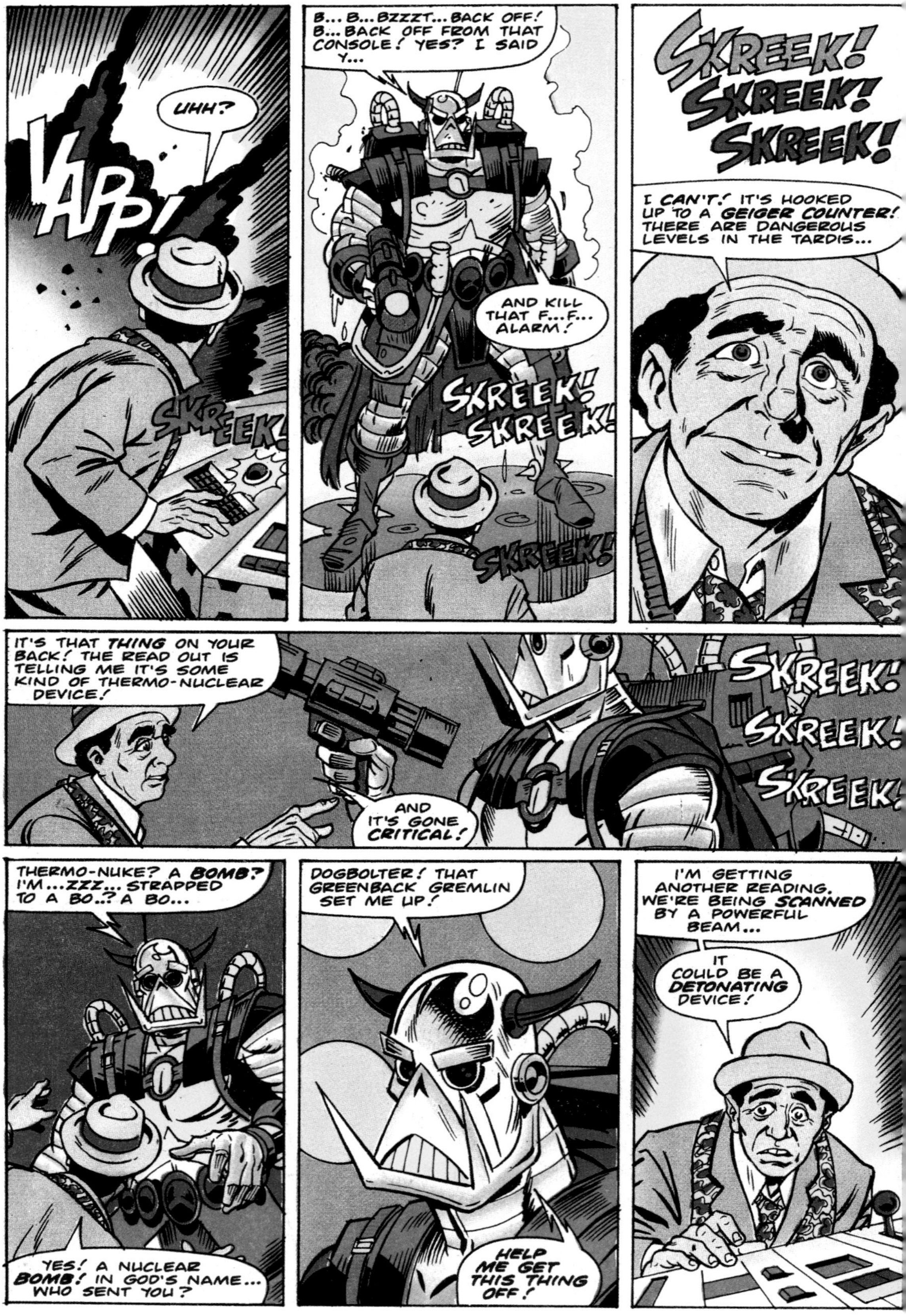
VAPP!
UHH?
SKREEEK!
B... B...BZZZT...BACK OFF! B...BACK OFF FROM THAT CONSOLE! YES? I SAID Y...
AND KILL THAT F...F... ALARM!
SKREEK! SKREEK!
SKREEK!
SKREEK! SKREEK! SKREEK!
I CAN'T! IT'S HOOKED UP TO A GEIGER COUNTER! THERE ARE DANGEROUS LEVELS IN THE TARDIS...
IT'S THAT THING ON YOUR BACK! THE READ OUT IS TELLING ME IT'S SOME KIND OF THERMO-NUCLEAR DEVICE!
AND IT'S GONE CRITICAL!
SKREEK! SKREEK! SKREEK!
THERMO-NUKE? A BOMB? I'M...ZZZ... STRAPPED TO A BO..? A BO...
YES! A NUCLEAR BOMB! IN GOD'S NAME... WHO SENT YOU?
DOGBOLTER! THAT GREENBACK GREMLIN SET ME UP!
HELP ME GET THIS THING OFF!
I'M GETTING ANOTHER READING. WE'RE BEING SCANNED BY A POWERFUL BEAM...
IT COULD BE A DETONATING DEVICE!

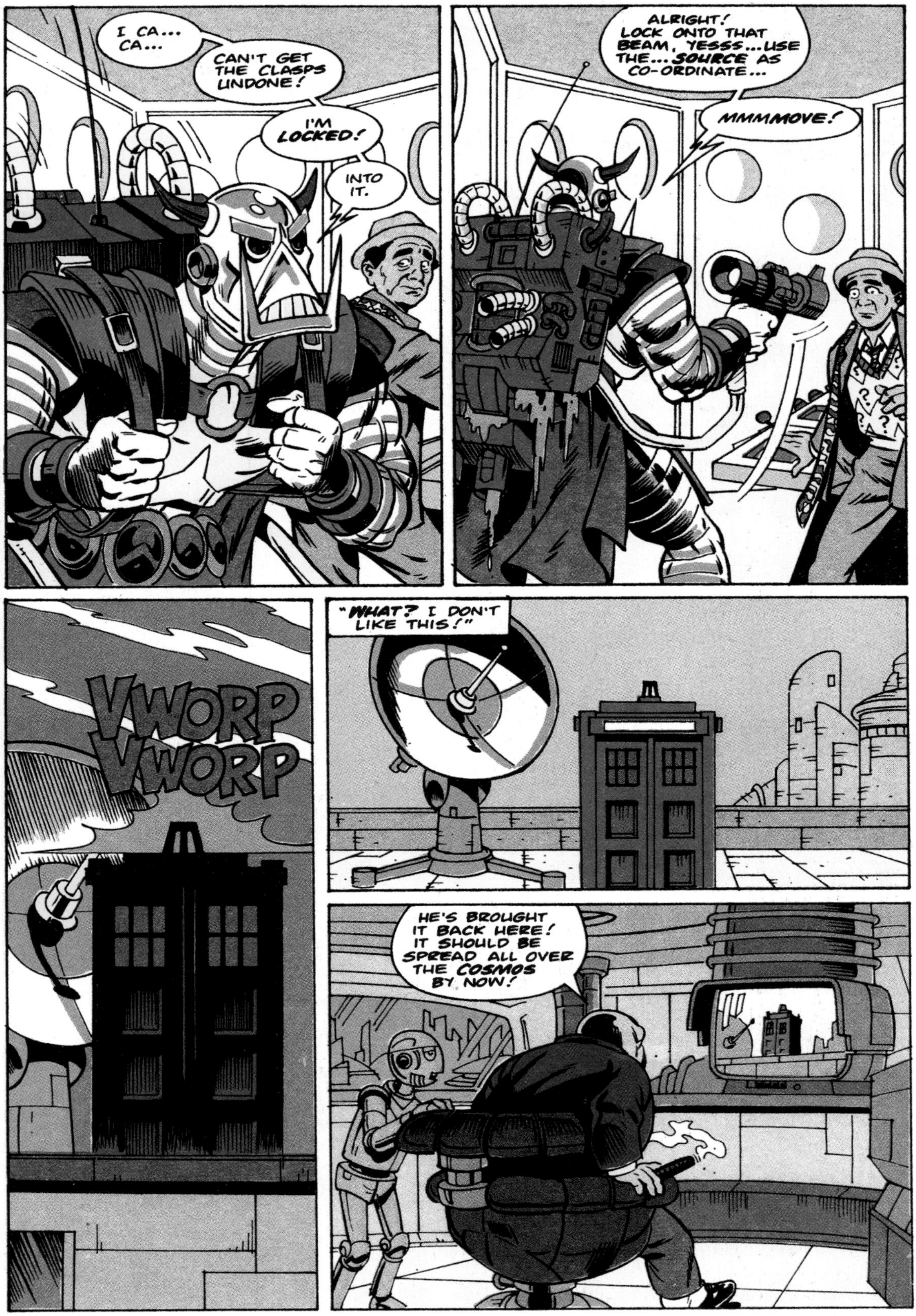
I CA... CA...
CAN'T GET THE CLASPS UNDONE!
I'M LOCKED!
INTO IT.
ALRIGHT! LOCK ONTO THAT BEAM, YESSS...USE THE...SOURCE AS CO-ORDINATE...
MMMMOVE!
VWORP VWORP
"WHAT? I DON'T LIKE THIS!"
HE'S BROUGHT IT BACK HERE! IT SHOULD BE SPREAD ALL OVER THE COSMOS BY NOW!

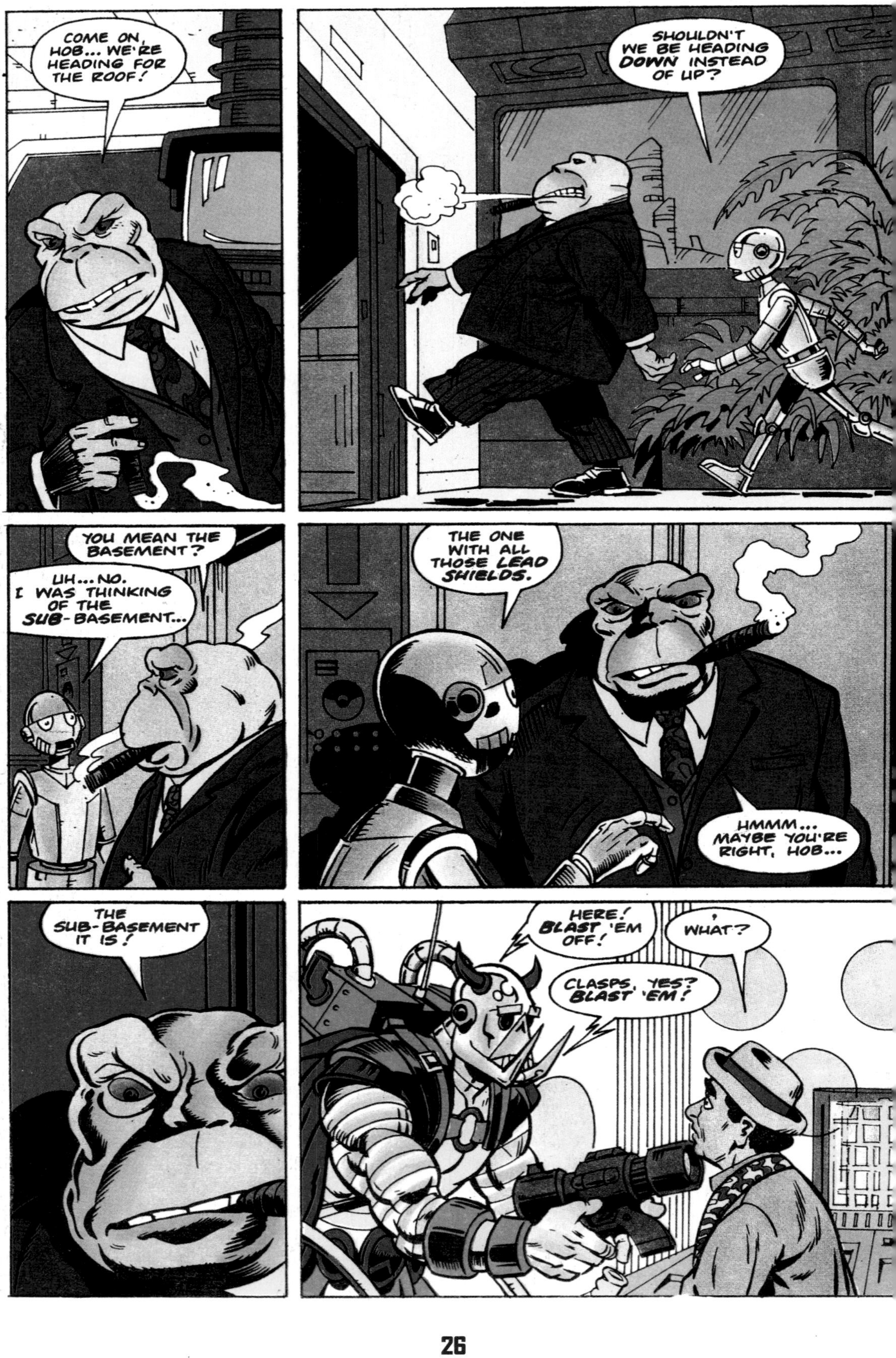
COME ON, HOB... WE'RE HEADING FOR THE ROOF!
SHOULDN'T WE BE HEADING DOWN INSTEAD OF UP?
YOU MEAN THE BASEMENT?
UH... NO. I WAS THINKING OF THE SUB-BASEMENT...
THE ONE WITH ALL THOSE LEAD SHIELDS.
HMMM... MAYBE YOU'RE RIGHT, HOB...
THE SUB-BASEMENT IT IS!
HERE! BLAST 'EM OFF!
WHAT?
CLASPS, YES? BLAST 'EM!

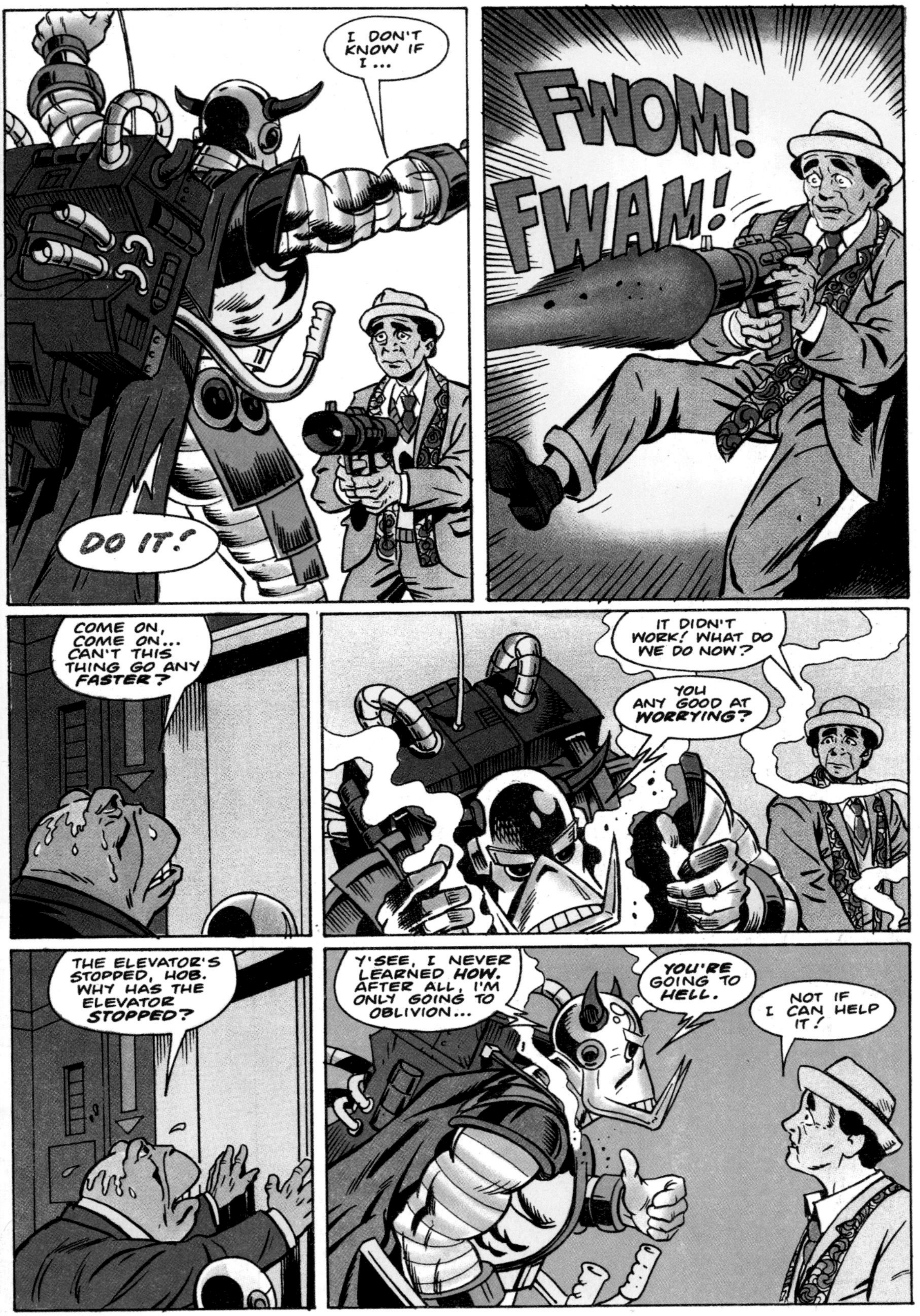
I DON'T KNOW IF I ...
DO IT!
FWOM!
FWAM!
COME ON, COME ON... CAN'T THIS THING GO ANY FASTER?
IT DIDN'T WORK! WHAT DO WE DO NOW?
YOU ANY GOOD AT WORRYING?
THE ELEVATOR'S STOPPED, HOB. WHY HAS THE ELEVATOR STOPPED?
Y'SEE, I NEVER LEARNED HOW. AFTER ALL, I'M ONLY GOING TO OBLIVION...
YOU'RE GOING TO HELL.
NOT IF I CAN HELP IT!

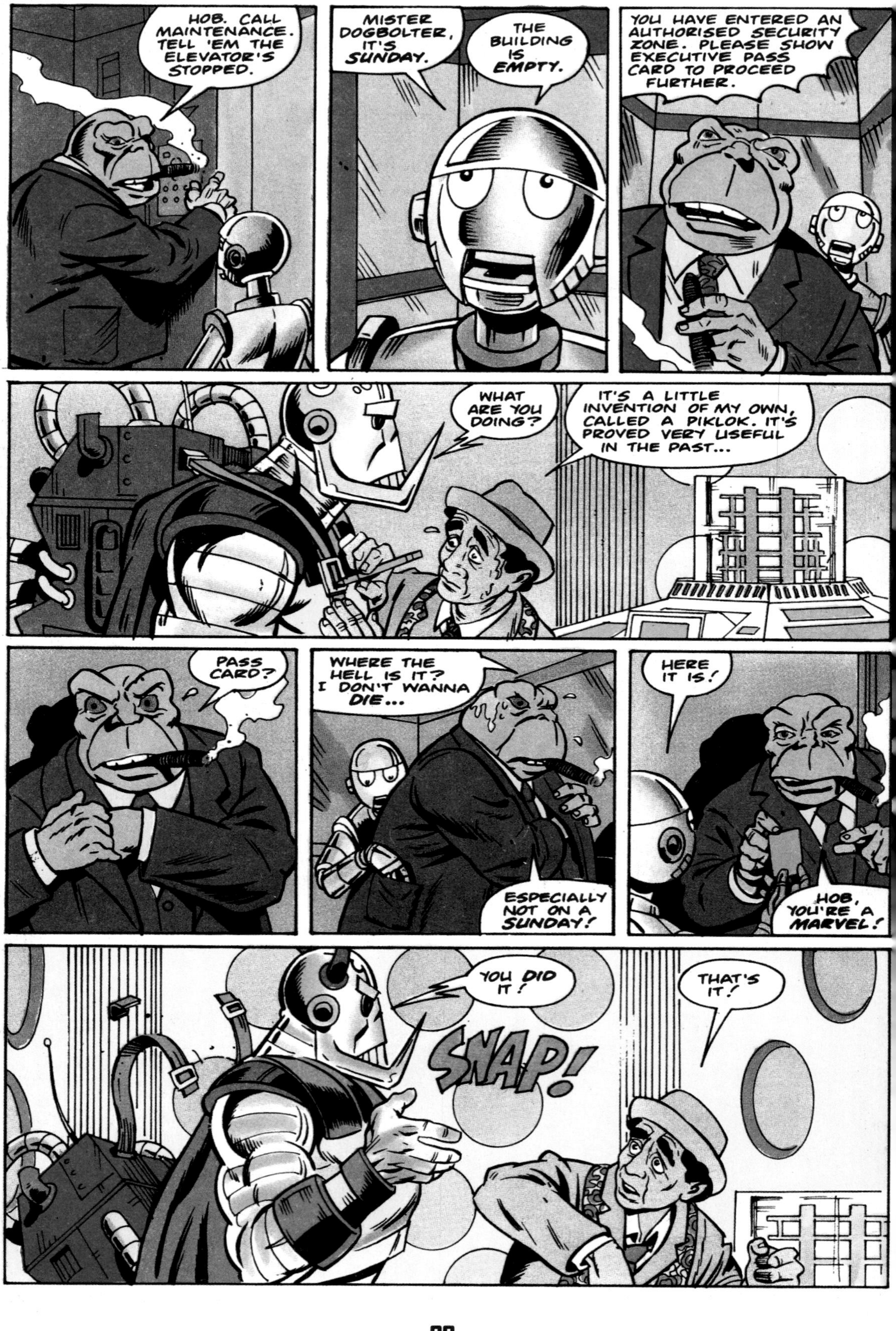
HOB. CALL MAINTENANCE. TELL 'EM THE ELEVATOR'S STOPPED.
MISTER DOGBOLTER, IT'S SUNDAY.
THE BUILDING IS EMPTY.
YOU HAVE ENTERED AN AUTHORISED SECURITY ZONE. PLEASE SHOW EXECUTIVE PASS CARD TO PROCEED FURTHER.
WHAT ARE YOU DOING?
IT'S A LITTLE INVENTION OF MY OWN, CALLED A PIKLOK. IT'S PROVED VERY USEFUL IN THE PAST...
PASS CARD?
WHERE THE HELL IS IT? I DON'T WANNA DIE...
ESPECIALLY NOT ON A SUNDAY!
HERE IT IS!
HOB, YOU'RE A MARVEL!
YOU DID IT!
SNAP!
THAT'S IT!

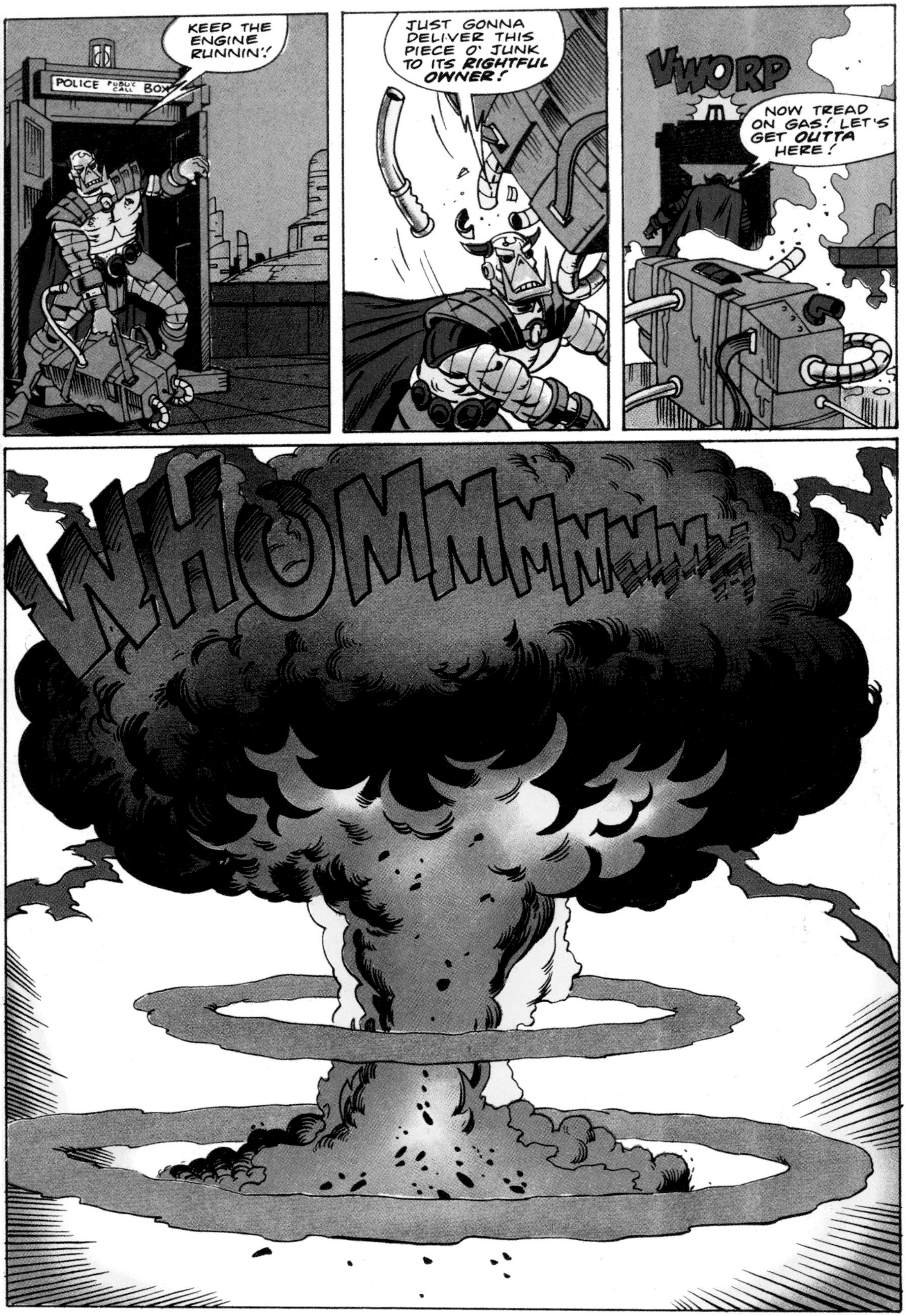
KEEP THE ENGINE RUNNIN'!
POLICE PUBLIC CALL BOX
JUST GONNA DELIVER THIS PIECE O' JUNK TO ITS RIGHTFUL OWNER!
VWORP
NOW TREAD ON GAS! LET'S GET OUTTA HERE!
WHOMMMMMM

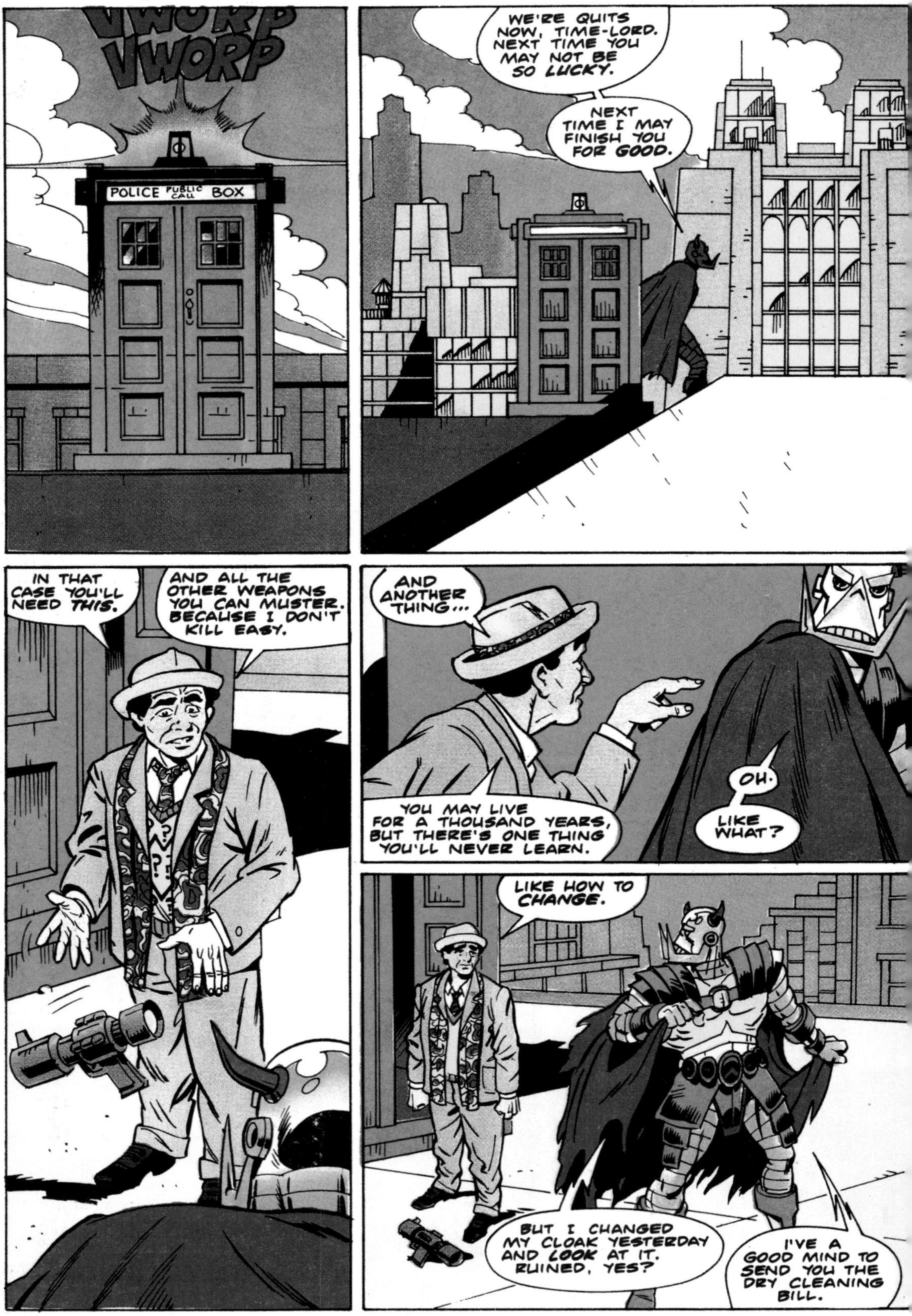
VWORP VWORP
POLICE PUBLIC CALL BOX
WE'RE QUITS NOW, TIME-LORD. NEXT TIME YOU MAY NOT BE SO LUCKY.
NEXT TIME I MAY FINISH YOU FOR GOOD.
IN THAT CASE YOU'LL NEED THIS.
AND ALL THE OTHER WEAPONS YOU CAN MUSTER. BECAUSE I DON'T KILL EASY.
AND ANOTHER THING...
YOU MAY LIVE FOR A THOUSAND YEARS, BUT THERE'S ONE THING YOU'LL NEVER LEARN.
OH.
LIKE WHAT?
LIKE HOW TO CHANGE.
BUT I CHANGED MY CLOAK YESTERDAY AND LOOK AT IT. RUINED, YES?
I'VE A GOOD MIND TO SEND YOU THE DRY CLEANING BILL.

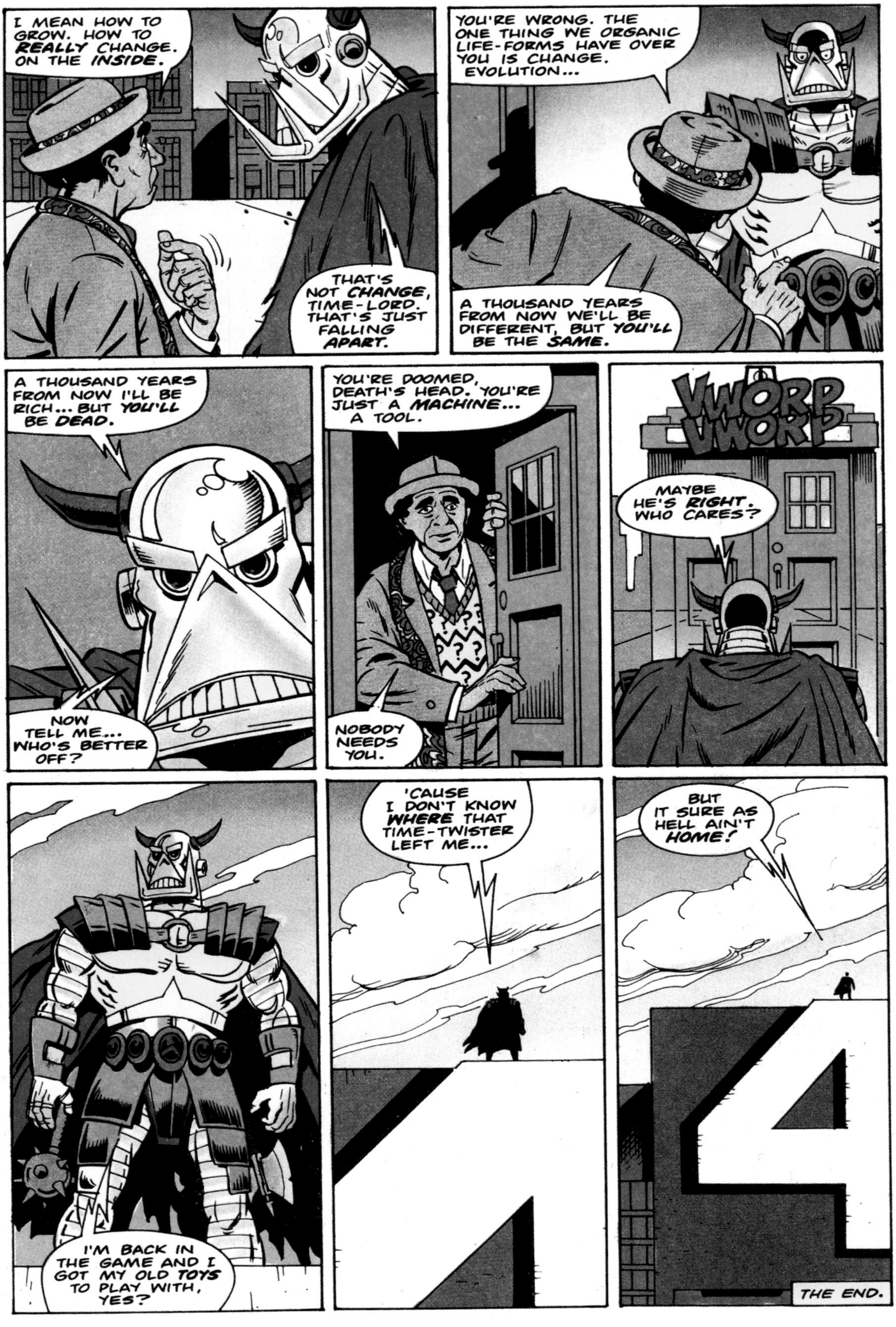
I MEAN HOW TO GROW. HOW TO REALLY CHANGE. ON THE INSIDE.
THAT'S NOT CHANGE, TIME-LORD. THAT'S JUST FALLING APART.
YOU'RE WRONG. THE ONE THING WE ORGANIC LIFE-FORMS HAVE OVER YOU IS CHANGE. EVOLUTION...
A THOUSAND YEARS FROM NOW WE'LL BE DIFFERENT, BUT YOU'LL BE THE SAME.
A THOUSAND YEARS FROM NOW I'LL BE RICH... BUT YOU'LL BE DEAD.
NOW TELL ME... WHO'S BETTER OFF?
YOU'RE DOOMED, DEATH'S HEAD. YOU'RE JUST A MACHINE... A TOOL.
NOBODY NEEDS YOU.
VWORP VWORP
MAYBE HE'S RIGHT. WHO CARES?
I'M BACK IN THE GAME AND I GOT MY OLD TOYS TO PLAY WITH, YES?
'CAUSE I DON'T KNOW WHERE THAT TIME-TWISTER LEFT ME...
BUT IT SURE AS HELL AIN'T HOME!
THE END.

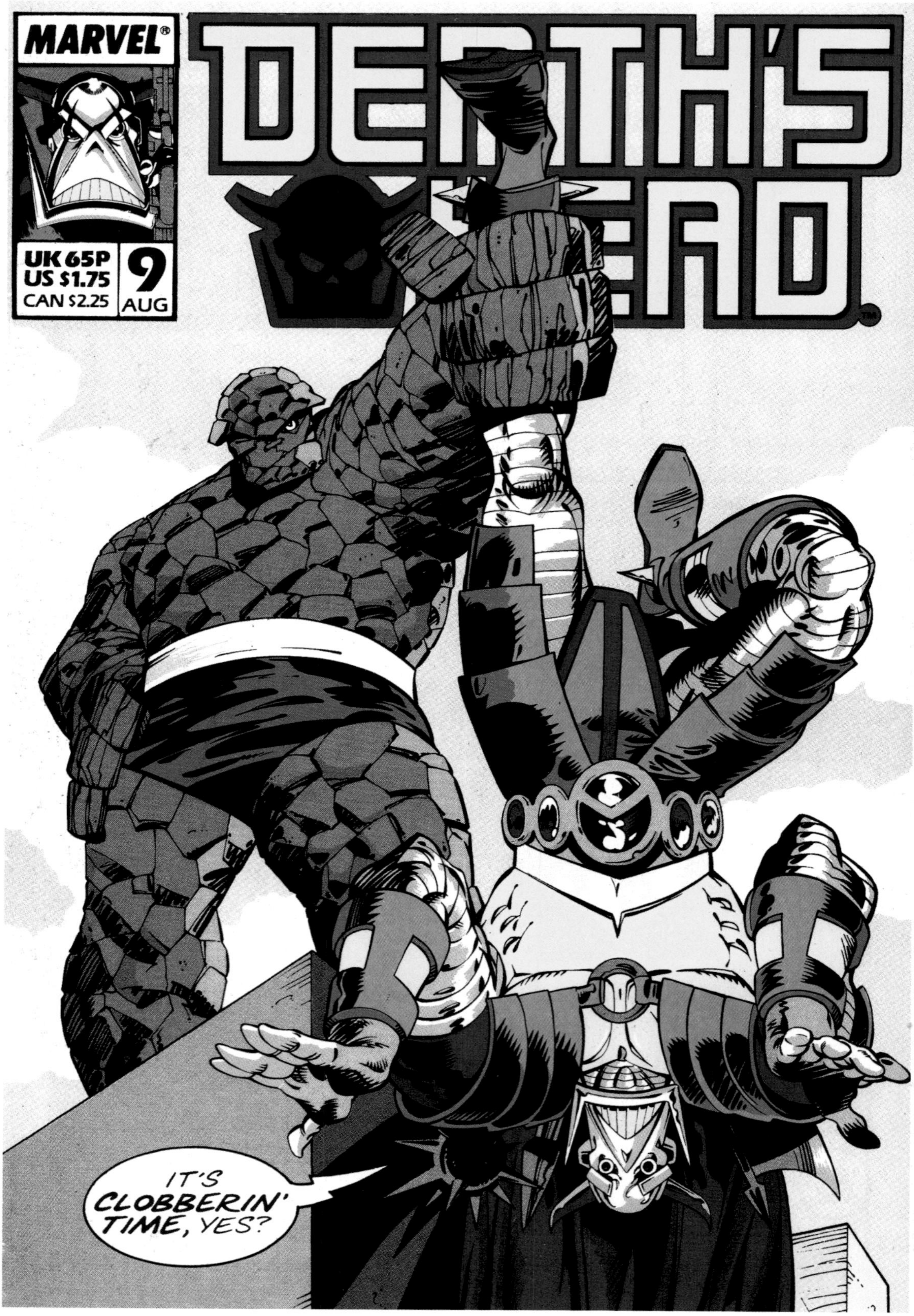
MARVEL
DEATH'S HEAD
UK 65P
US $1.75
CAN $2.25
9
AUG
IT'S CLOBBERIN' TIME, YES?

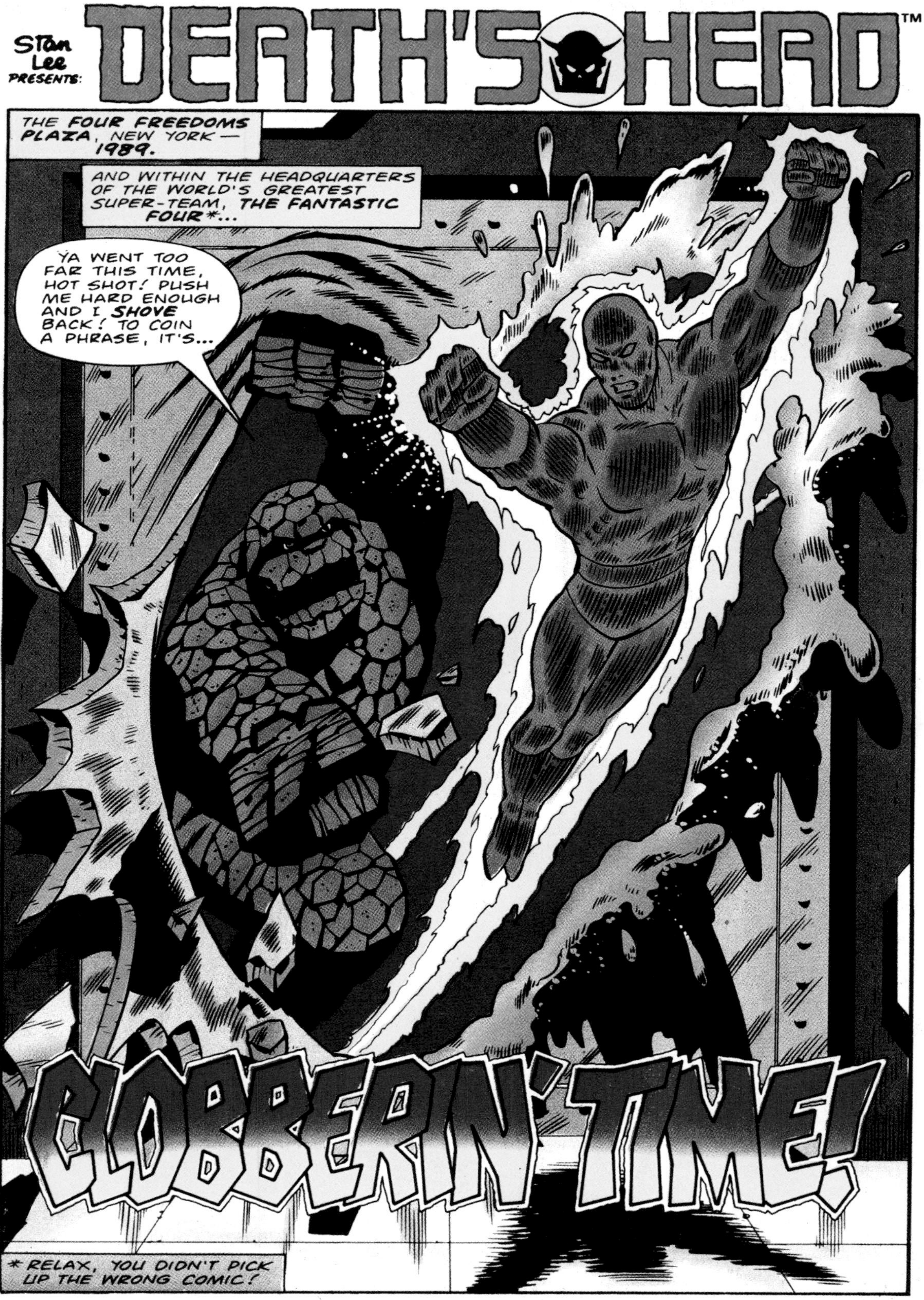
STAN LEE PRESENTS:
DEATH'S HEAD™
THE FOUR FREEDOMS PLAZA, NEW YORK — 1989.
AND WITHIN THE HEADQUARTERS OF THE WORLD'S GREATEST SUPER-TEAM, THE FANTASTIC FOUR*...
YA WENT TOO FAR THIS TIME, HOT SHOT! PUSH ME HARD ENOUGH AND I SHOVE BACK! TO COIN A PHRASE, IT'S...
CLOBBERIN' TIME!
* RELAX, YOU DIDN'T PICK UP THE WRONG COMIC!

Writer SIMON FURMAN · Artist GEOFF SENIOR · Colourist LOUISE CASSELL · Letterer ANNIE H · Editor STEVE WHITE · Managing Editor JENNY O'CONNOR

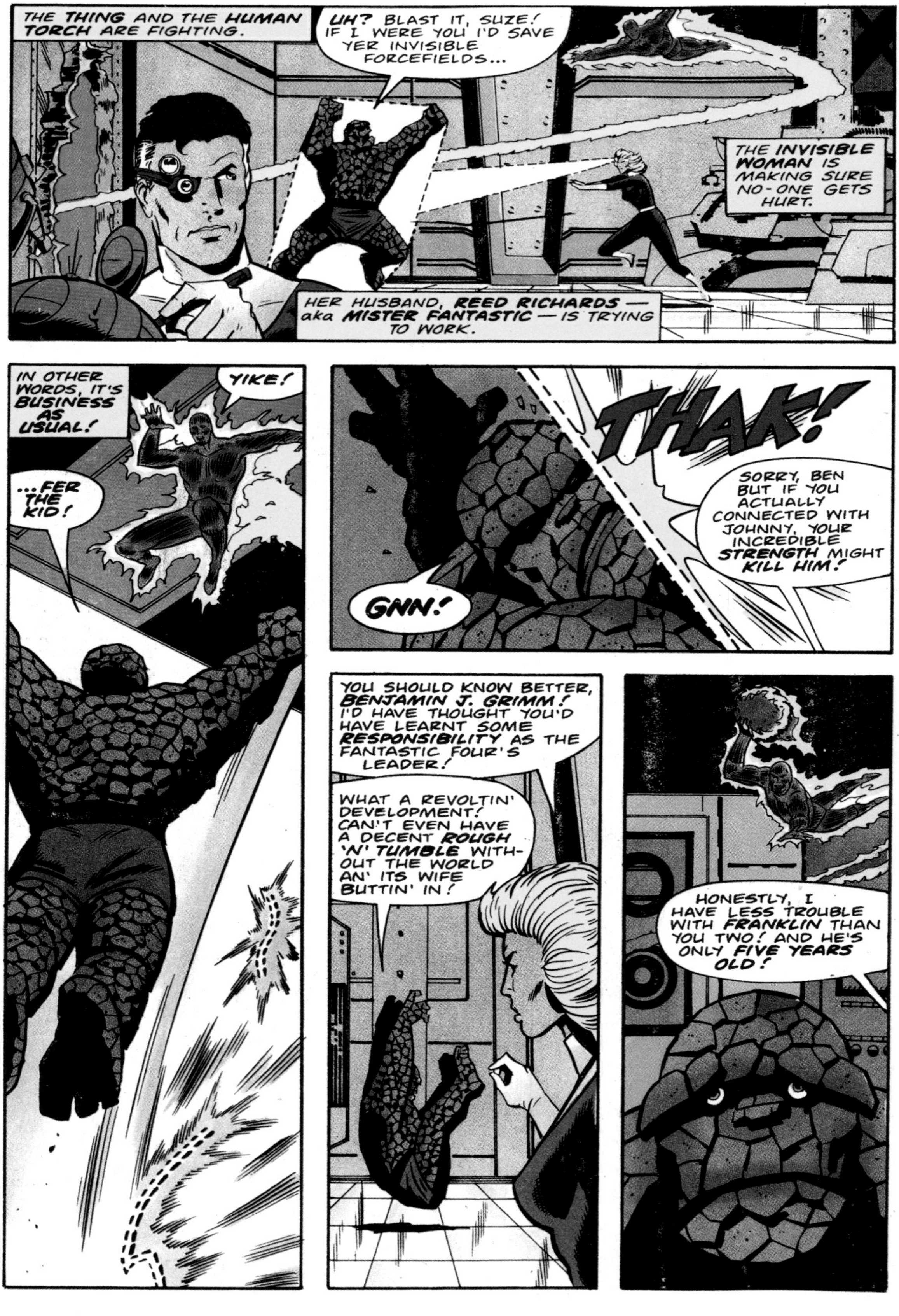
THE THING AND THE HUMAN TORCH ARE FIGHTING.
UH? BLAST IT, SUZE! IF I WERE YOU I'D SAVE YER INVISIBLE FORCEFIELDS...
THE INVISIBLE WOMAN IS MAKING SURE NO-ONE GETS HURT.
HER HUSBAND, REED RICHARDS — aka MISTER FANTASTIC — IS TRYING TO WORK.
IN OTHER WORDS, IT'S BUSINESS AS USUAL!
YIKE!
...FER THE KID!
THAK!
SORRY, BEN BUT IF YOU ACTUALLY CONNECTED WITH JOHNNY, YOUR INCREDIBLE STRENGTH MIGHT KILL HIM!
GNN!
YOU SHOULD KNOW BETTER, BENJAMIN J. GRIMM! I'D HAVE THOUGHT YOU'D HAVE LEARNT SOME RESPONSIBILITY AS THE FANTASTIC FOUR'S LEADER!
WHAT A REVOLTIN' DEVELOPMENT! CAN'T EVEN HAVE A DECENT ROUGH 'N' TUMBLE WITH-OUT THE WORLD AN' ITS WIFE BUTTIN' IN!
HONESTLY, I HAVE LESS TROUBLE WITH FRANKLIN THAN YOU TWO! AND HE'S ONLY FIVE YEARS OLD!

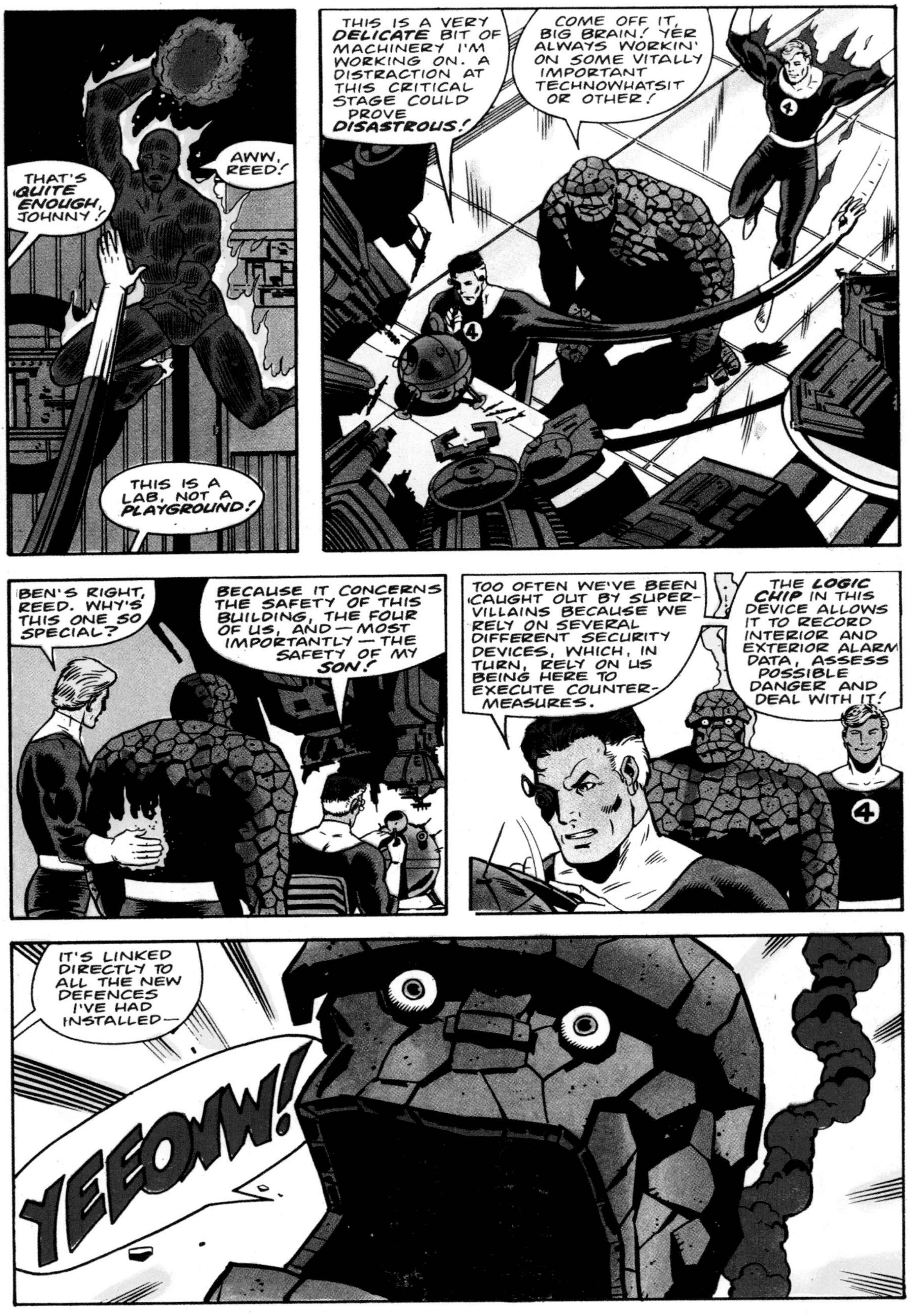
AWW, REED!
THAT'S QUITE ENOUGH, JOHNNY!
THIS IS A LAB, NOT A PLAYGROUND!
THIS IS A VERY DELICATE BIT OF MACHINERY I'M WORKING ON. A DISTRACTION AT THIS CRITICAL STAGE COULD PROVE DISASTROUS!
COME OFF IT, BIG BRAIN! YER ALWAYS WORKIN' ON SOME VITALLY IMPORTANT TECHNOWHATSIT OR OTHER!
BEN'S RIGHT, REED. WHY'S THIS ONE SO SPECIAL?
BECAUSE IT CONCERNS THE SAFETY OF THIS BUILDING, THE FOUR OF US, AND—MOST IMPORTANTLY—THE SAFETY OF MY SON!
TOO OFTEN WE'VE BEEN CAUGHT OUT BY SUPER-VILLAINS BECAUSE WE RELY ON SEVERAL DIFFERENT SECURITY DEVICES, WHICH, IN TURN, RELY ON US BEING HERE TO EXECUTE COUNTER-MEASURES.
THE LOGIC CHIP IN THIS DEVICE ALLOWS IT TO RECORD INTERIOR AND EXTERIOR ALARM DATA, ASSESS POSSIBLE DANGER AND DEAL WITH IT!
IT'S LINKED DIRECTLY TO ALL THE NEW DEFENCES I'VE HAD INSTALLED—
YEEOWW!

I DON'T BELIEVE IT! THE LITTLE PUNK DID IT TO ME *AGAIN!*

REEEEE

INTRUDER ALERT— SECTOR THREE. INITIATING COUNTER- MEASURES.

WHAT? BUT I DIDN'T ACTIVATE— WAIT, SECTOR THREE...

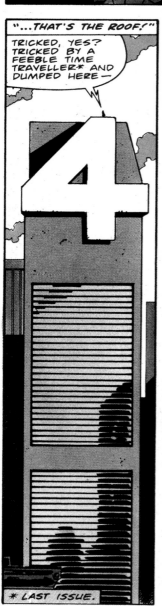

"...THAT'S THE ROOF!"

TRICKED, YES? TRICKED BY A FEEBLE TIME TRAVELLER* AND DUMPED HERE—

4

* LAST ISSUE.

HRM. FEELING OF *DEJA VU,* YES?

SERIOUSLY CONSIDERING RELAXING 'NEVER KILL FOR REVENGE' RULE, HUH? GETTING SO YOU CAN'T *TURN YOUR BACK* ON ANY—

FLMM

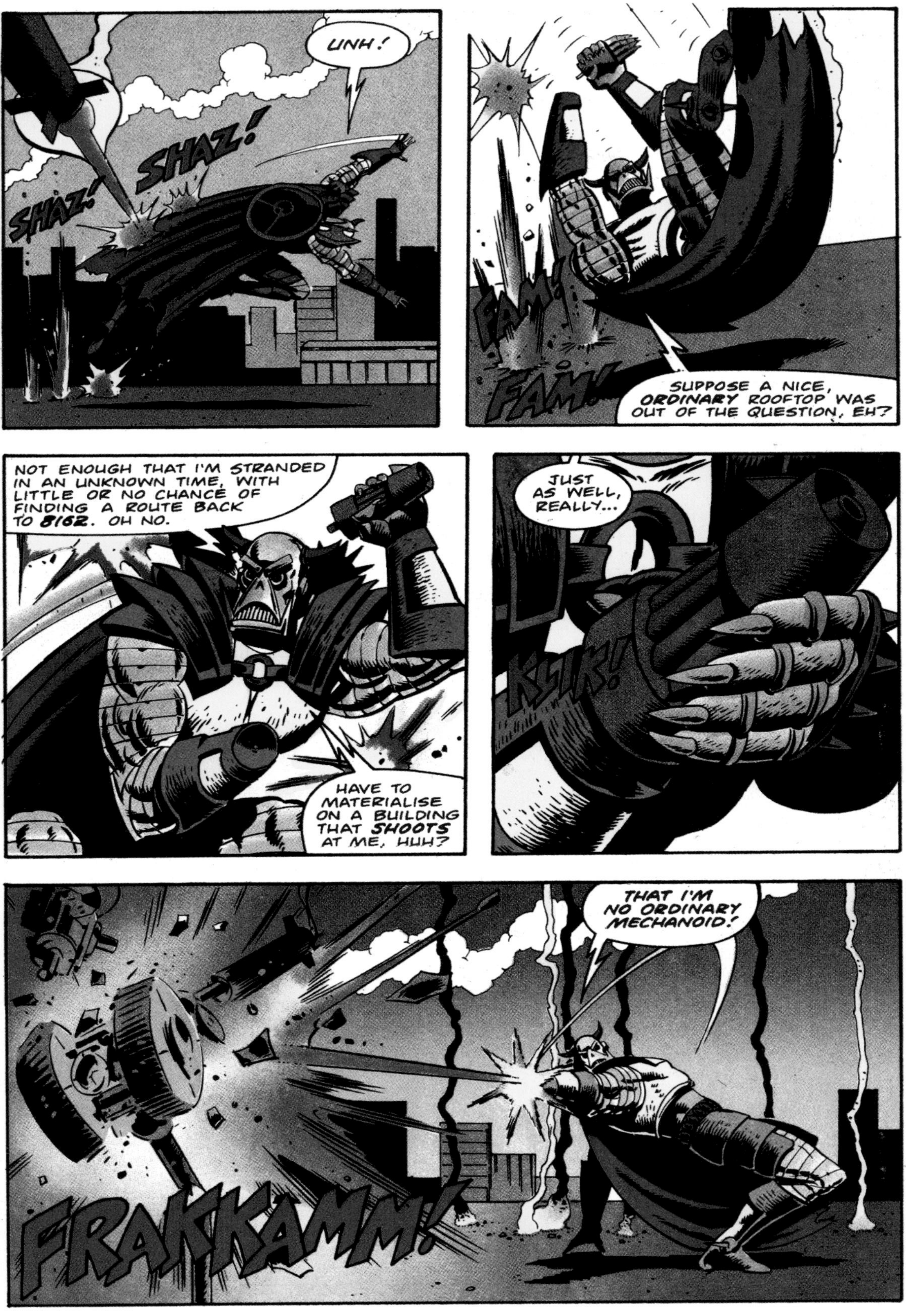
UNH!
SHAZ!
SHAZ!
FAM!
FAM!
SUPPOSE A NICE, ORDINARY ROOFTOP WAS OUT OF THE QUESTION, EH?
NOT ENOUGH THAT I'M STRANDED IN AN UNKNOWN TIME, WITH LITTLE OR NO CHANCE OF FINDING A ROUTE BACK TO 8162. OH NO.
HAVE TO MATERIALISE ON A BUILDING THAT SHOOTS AT ME, HUH?
JUST AS WELL, REALLY...
KLIK!
THAT I'M NO ORDINARY MECHANOID!
FRAKKAMM!

NO PROBLEM, HUH? THE DAY A *FREELANCE PEACE-KEEPING AGENT* OF MY CALIBRE CAN'T HANDLE A LITTLE GUN LIKE THAT—

KITCH! FWOOSH! KA-KITCH! RICHUT! BRRROA! EENK! AK-TANG!

Sigh.

TIME TO GO, YES?

KABOOM!

UNF! THOUGH PERHAPS NOT QUITE *THIS FAR*, EH?

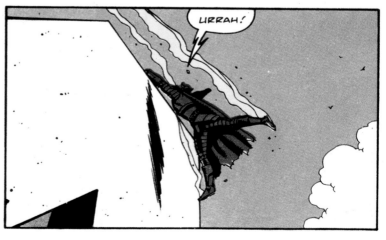

URRAH!

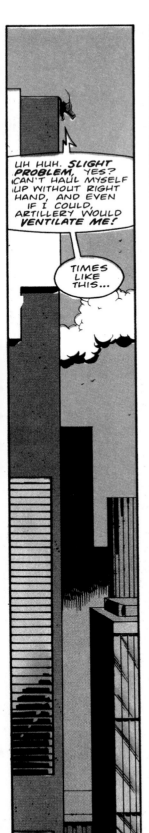

UH HUH. *SLIGHT PROBLEM*, YES? CAN'T HAUL MYSELF UP WITHOUT RIGHT HAND, AND EVEN IF I COULD, ARTILLERY WOULD *VENTILATE ME!*

TIMES LIKE THIS...

...I'M GLAD *BOOT JETS* WERE AN *OPTIONAL EXTRA!*

BYE NOW. LIKE TO STOP AND CHAT, BUT I'M AFRAID I MUST *FLY*, YES?

4

HRM.

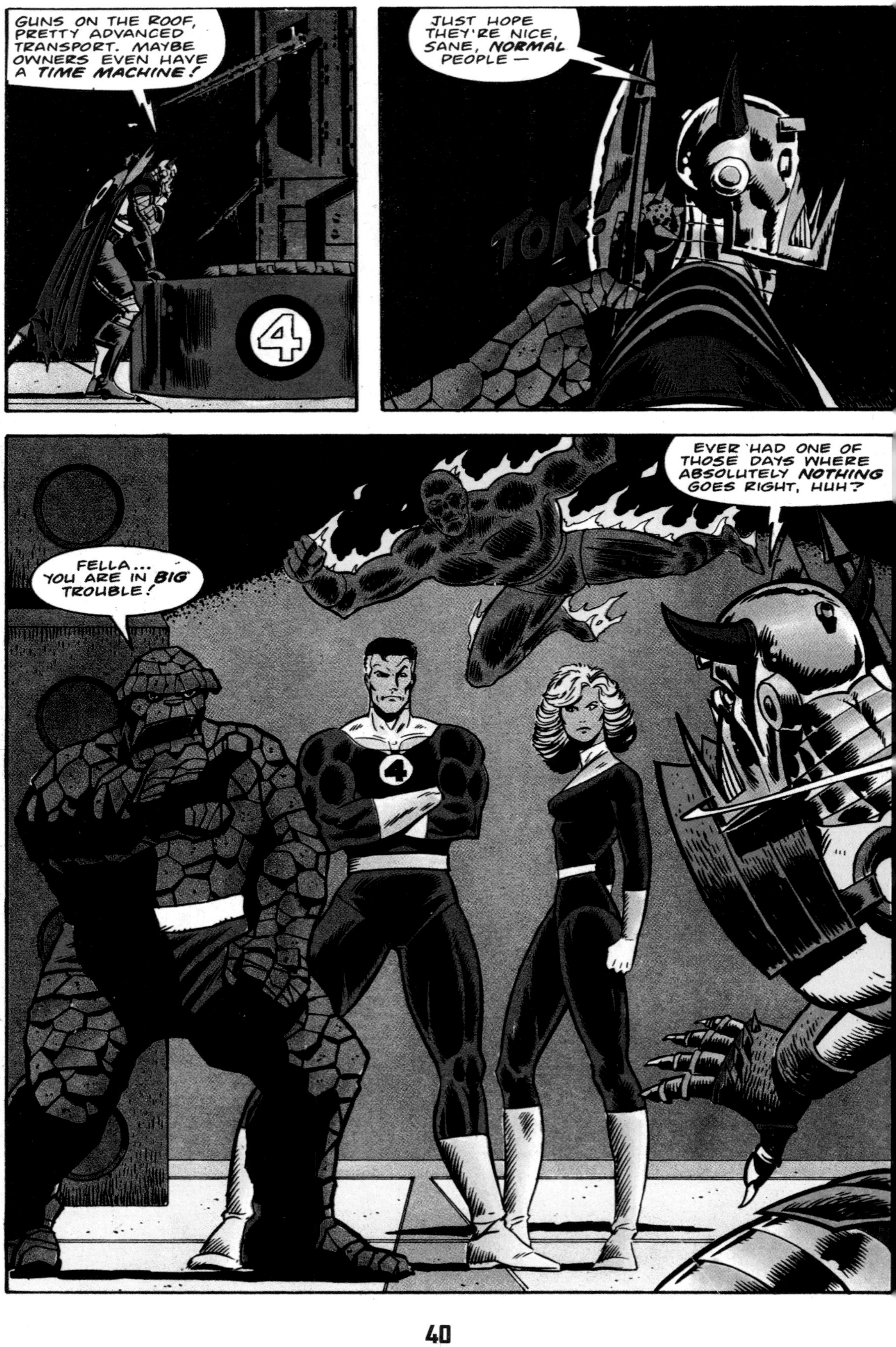
GUNS ON THE ROOF, PRETTY ADVANCED TRANSPORT. MAYBE OWNERS EVEN HAVE A TIME MACHINE!
JUST HOPE THEY'RE NICE, SANE, NORMAL PEOPLE —
TOK!
EVER HAD ONE OF THOSE DAYS WHERE ABSOLUTELY NOTHING GOES RIGHT, HUH?
FELLA... YOU ARE IN BIG TROUBLE!

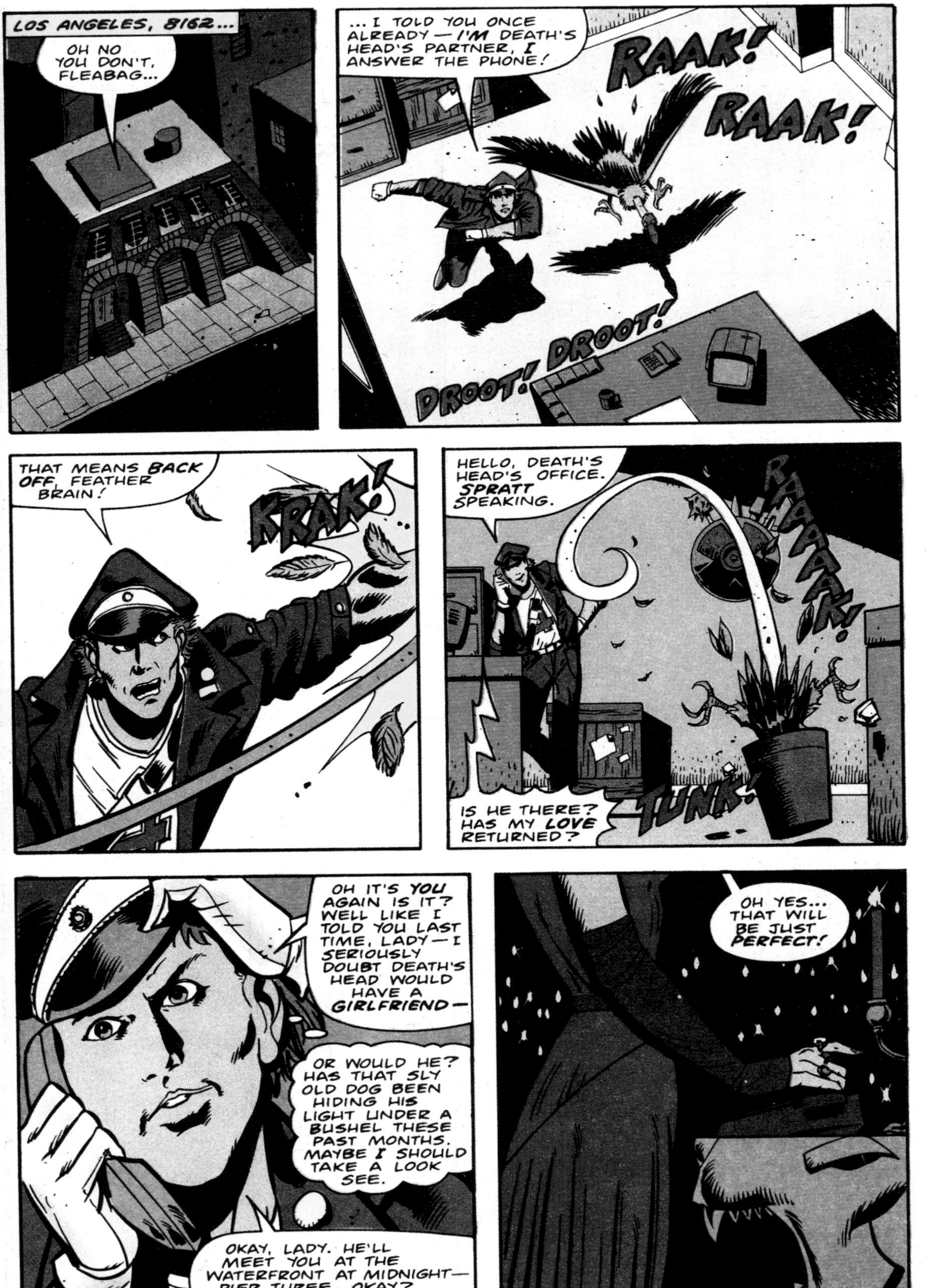

LOS ANGELES, 8162...
OH NO YOU DON'T, FLEABAG...
...I TOLD YOU ONCE ALREADY — I'M DEATH'S HEAD'S PARTNER, I ANSWER THE PHONE!
RAAK! RAAK!
DROOT! DROOT!
THAT MEANS BACK OFF, FEATHER BRAIN!
KRAK!
HELLO, DEATH'S HEAD'S OFFICE. SPRATT SPEAKING.
RAAAAAK!
TUNK!
IS HE THERE? HAS MY LOVE RETURNED?
OH IT'S YOU AGAIN IS IT? WELL LIKE I TOLD YOU LAST TIME, LADY — I SERIOUSLY DOUBT DEATH'S HEAD WOULD HAVE A GIRLFRIEND—
OR WOULD HE? HAS THAT SLY OLD DOG BEEN HIDING HIS LIGHT UNDER A BUSHEL THESE PAST MONTHS. MAYBE I SHOULD TAKE A LOOK SEE.
OKAY, LADY. HE'LL MEET YOU AT THE WATERFRONT AT MIDNIGHT— PIER THREE. OKAY?
OH YES... THAT WILL BE JUST PERFECT!

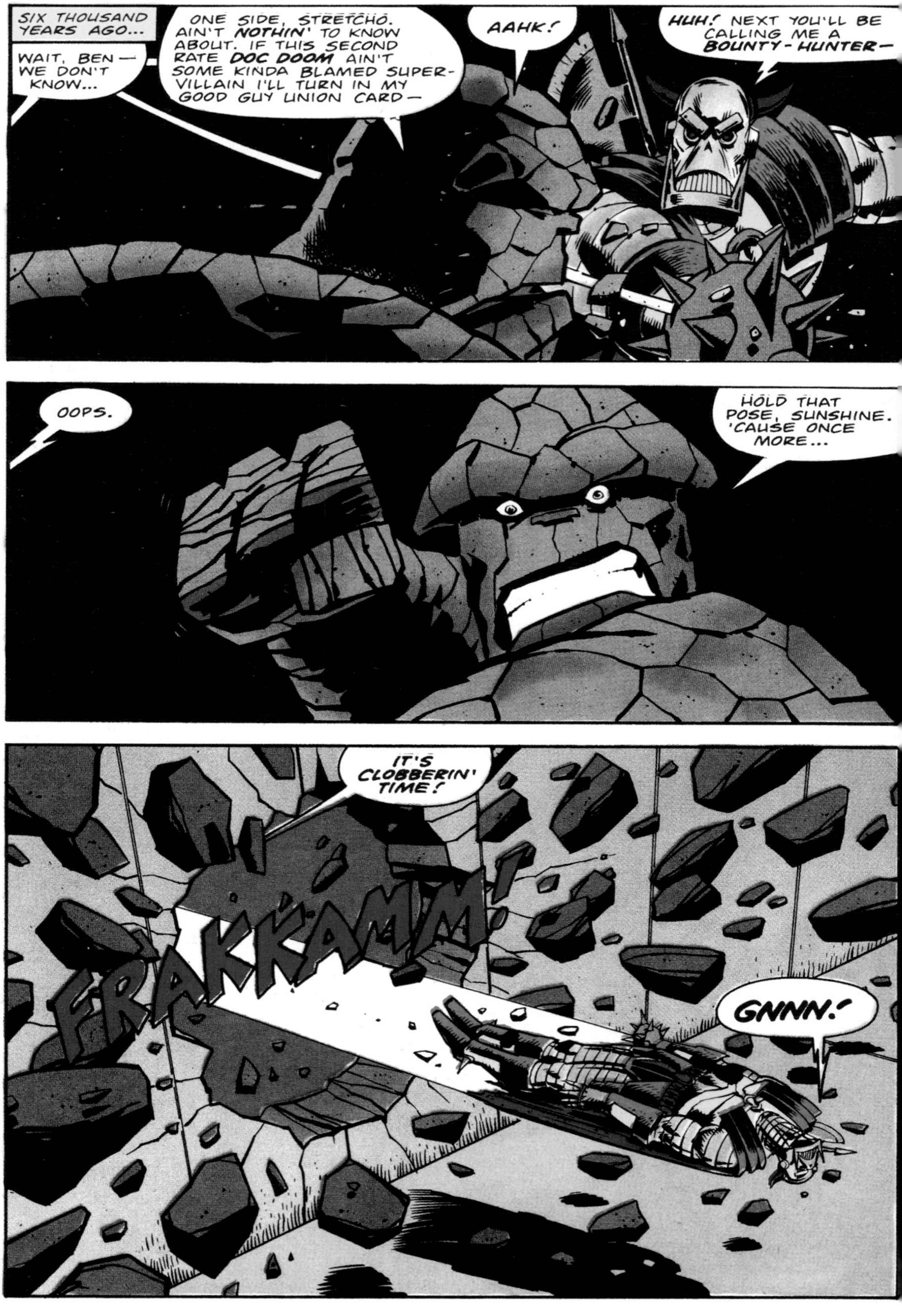
SIX THOUSAND YEARS AGO...
WAIT, BEN — WE DON'T KNOW...
ONE SIDE, STRETCHO. AIN'T NOTHIN' TO KNOW ABOUT. IF THIS SECOND RATE DOC DOOM AIN'T SOME KINDA BLAMED SUPER-VILLAIN I'LL TURN IN MY GOOD GUY UNION CARD —
AAHK!
HUH! NEXT YOU'LL BE CALLING ME A BOUNTY-HUNTER —
OOPS.
HOLD THAT POSE, SUNSHINE. 'CAUSE ONCE MORE...
IT'S CLOBBERIN' TIME!
FRAKKAMM!
GNNN!

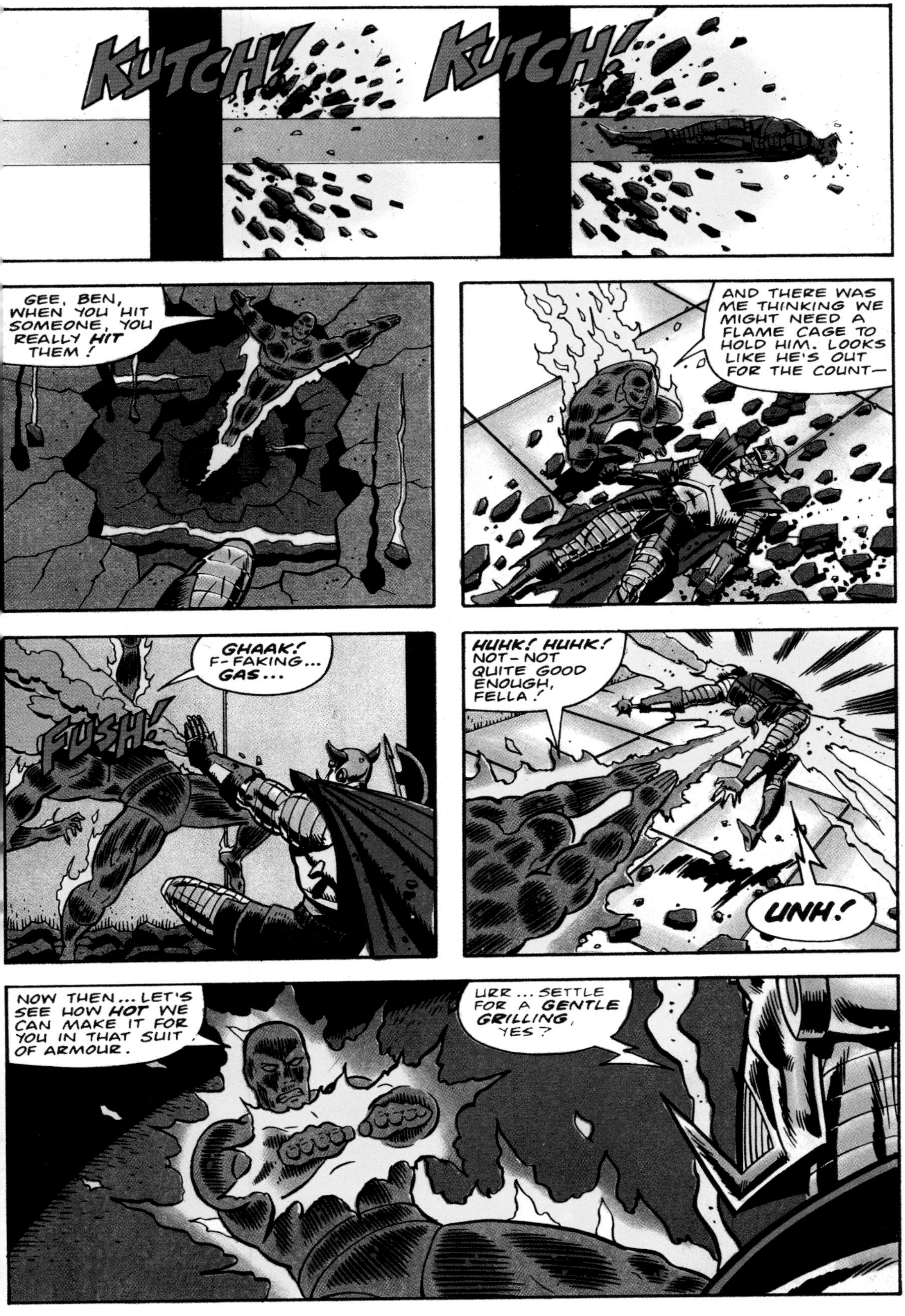
KUTCH! KUTCH!
GEE, BEN, WHEN YOU HIT SOMEONE, YOU REALLY HIT THEM!
AND THERE WAS ME THINKING WE MIGHT NEED A FLAME CAGE TO HOLD HIM. LOOKS LIKE HE'S OUT FOR THE COUNT—
GHAAK! F-FAKING... GAS...
FUSH!
HUHK! HUHK! NOT-NOT QUITE GOOD ENOUGH, FELLA!
UNH!
NOW THEN... LET'S SEE HOW HOT WE CAN MAKE IT FOR YOU IN THAT SUIT OF ARMOUR.
URR... SETTLE FOR A GENTLE GRILLING, YES?

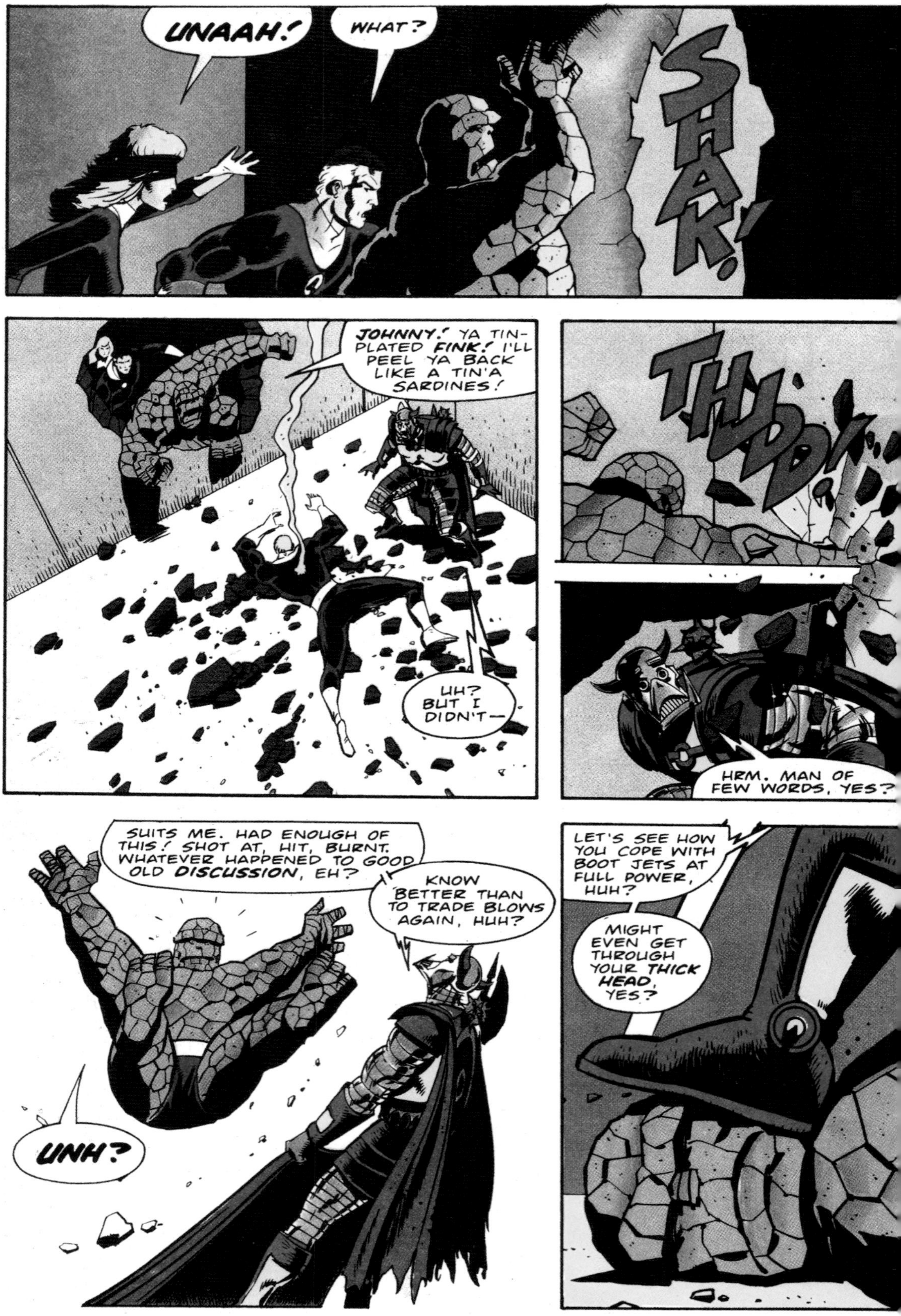
UNAAH!
WHAT?
SHAK!
JOHNNY! YA TIN-PLATED FINK! I'LL PEEL YA BACK LIKE A TIN'A SARDINES!
UH? BUT I DIDN'T—
THUDD!
HRM. MAN OF FEW WORDS, YES?
SUITS ME. HAD ENOUGH OF THIS! SHOT AT, HIT, BURNT. WHATEVER HAPPENED TO GOOD OLD DISCUSSION, EH?
KNOW BETTER THAN TO TRADE BLOWS AGAIN, HUH?
UNH?
LET'S SEE HOW YOU COPE WITH BOOT JETS AT FULL POWER, HUH?
MIGHT EVEN GET THROUGH YOUR THICK HEAD, YES?

LET'S **NOT** FIND OUT, MY FRIEND. SUE, READY WITH—

SHEEAH!

REED!

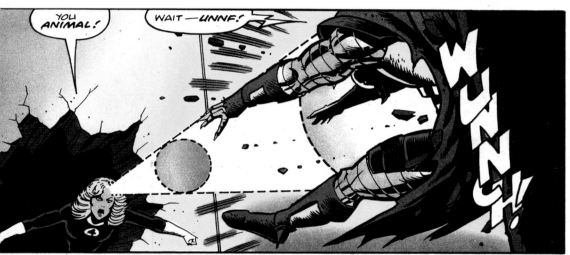

YOU ANIMAL!

WAIT—UNNF!

WUNN!

NNNN! NOT ME. CAME FROM...

TH-THE FLOOR...

HE'S TELLING THE TRUTH. IT DIDN'T COME FROM HIM.

THEN **WHAT**?

UNDERFLOOR CURRENT... PART-PART OF THE BUILDING'S... DEFENCES!

45

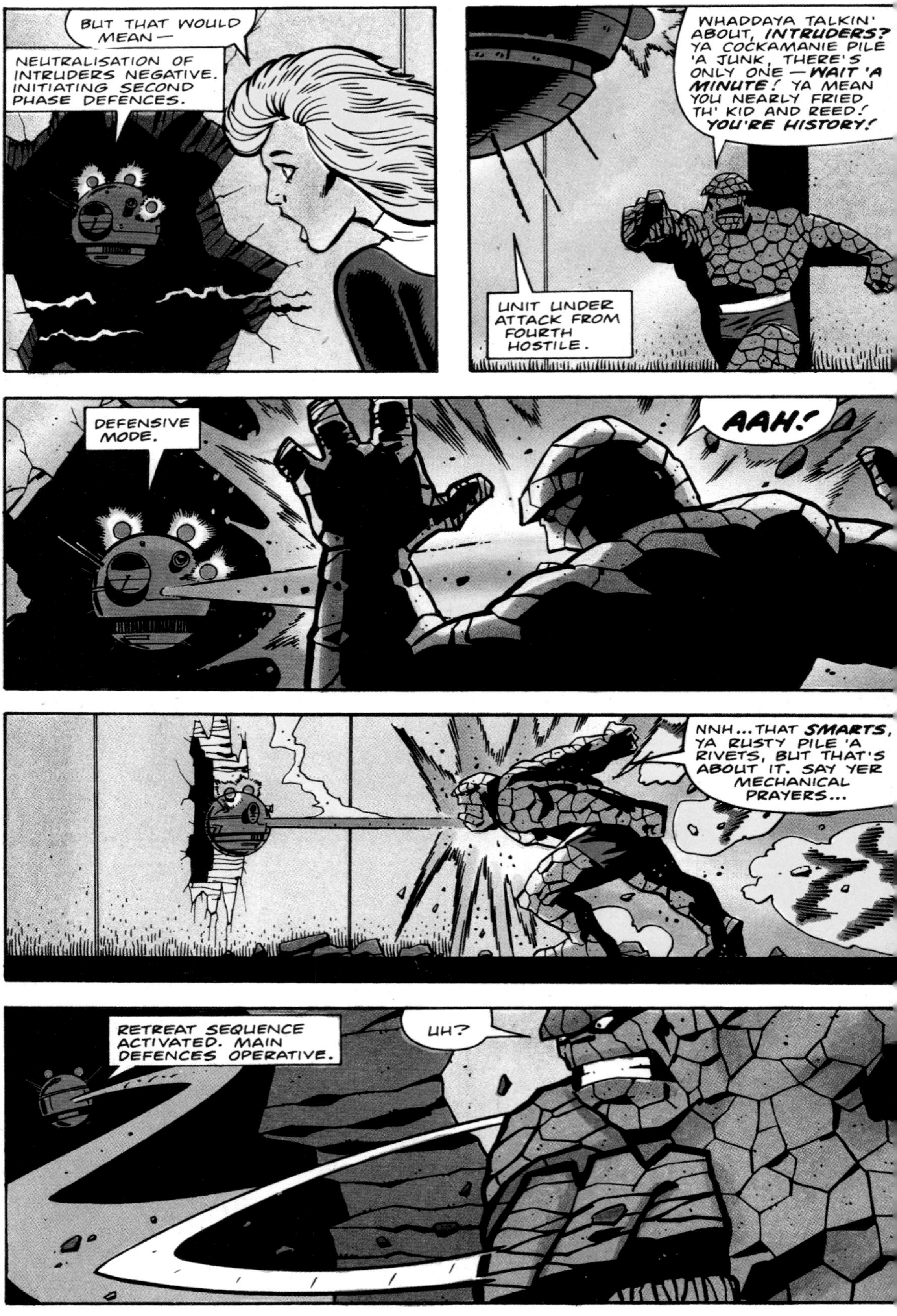
BUT THAT WOULD MEAN—
NEUTRALISATION OF INTRUDERS NEGATIVE. INITIATING SECOND PHASE DEFENCES.
WHADDAYA TALKIN' ABOUT, INTRUDERS? YA COCKAMANIE PILE 'A JUNK, THERE'S ONLY ONE—WAIT 'A MINUTE! YA MEAN YOU NEARLY FRIED TH' KID AND REED! YOU'RE HISTORY!
UNIT UNDER ATTACK FROM FOURTH HOSTILE.
DEFENSIVE MODE.
AAH!
NNH...THAT SMARTS, YA RUSTY PILE 'A RIVETS, BUT THAT'S ABOUT IT. SAY YER MECHANICAL PRAYERS...
RETREAT SEQUENCE ACTIVATED. MAIN DEFENCES OPERATIVE.
UH?

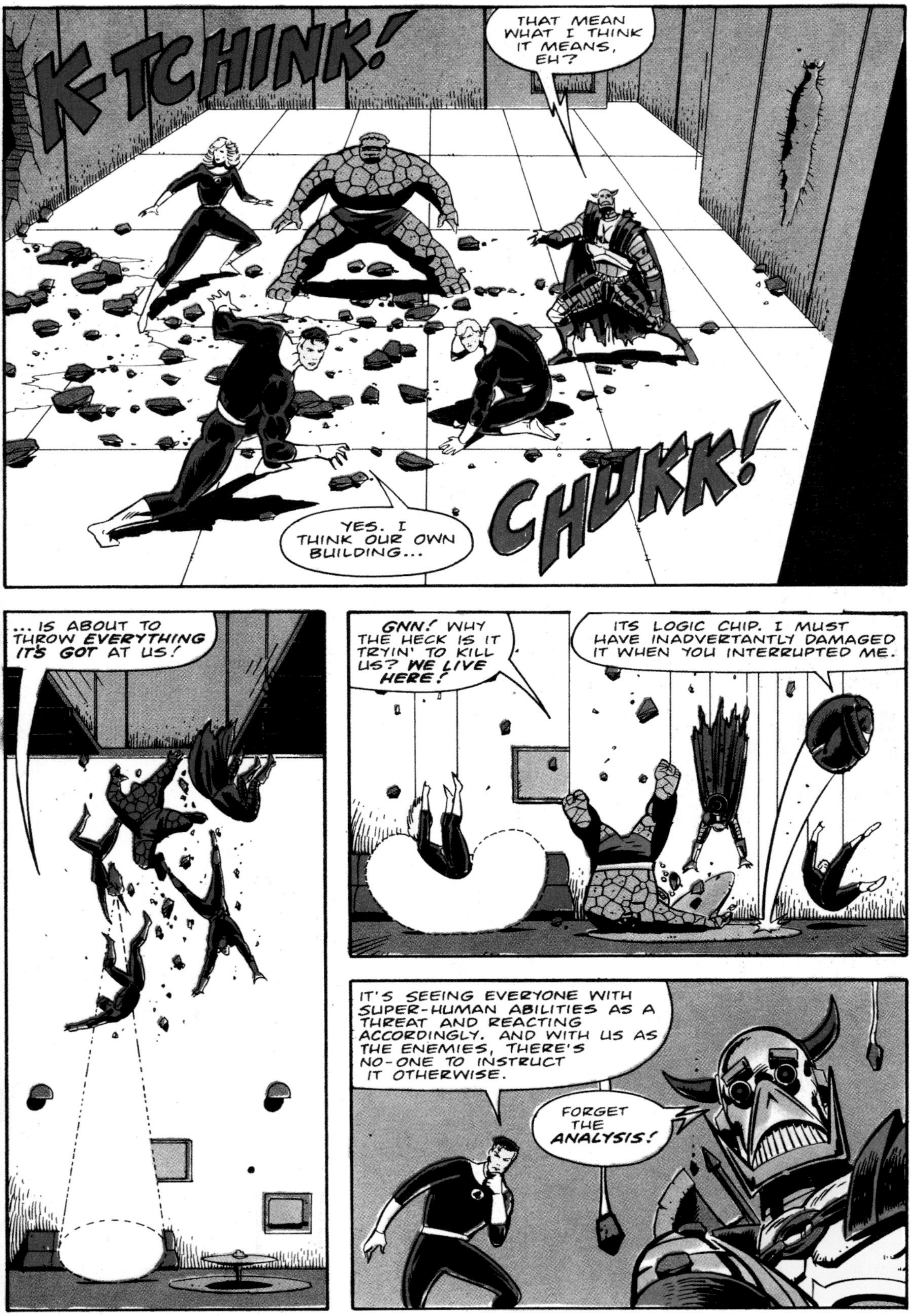
K-TCHINK!
THAT MEAN WHAT I THINK IT MEANS, EH?
YES. I THINK OUR OWN BUILDING...
CHUKK!
...IS ABOUT TO THROW EVERYTHING IT'S GOT AT US!
GNN! WHY THE HECK IS IT TRYIN' TO KILL US? WE LIVE HERE!
ITS LOGIC CHIP. I MUST HAVE INADVERTANTLY DAMAGED IT WHEN YOU INTERRUPTED ME.
IT'S SEEING EVERYONE WITH SUPER-HUMAN ABILITIES AS A THREAT AND REACTING ACCORDINGLY. AND WITH US AS THE ENEMIES, THERE'S NO-ONE TO INSTRUCT IT OTHERWISE.
FORGET THE ANALYSIS!

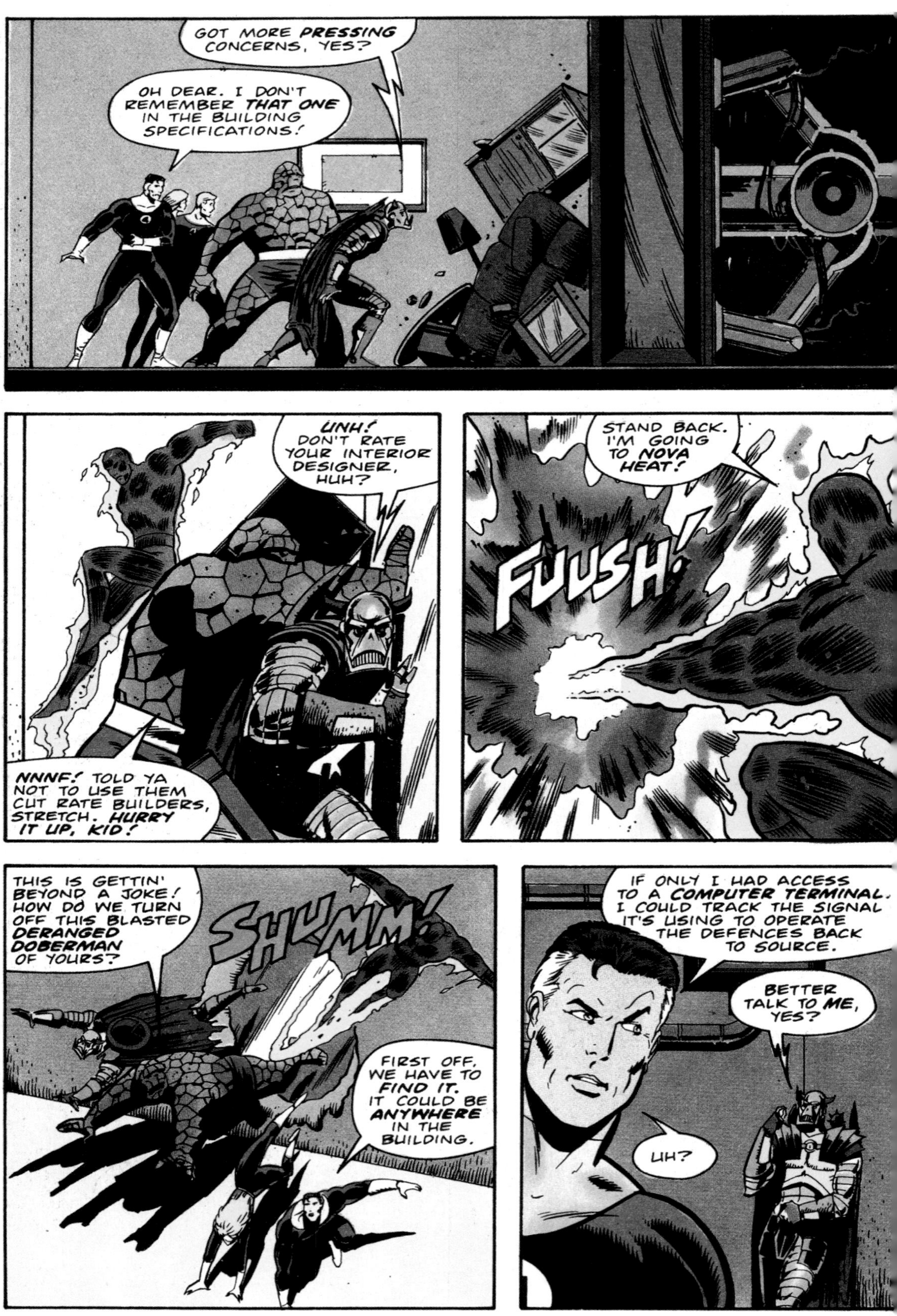
OH DEAR. I DON'T REMEMBER THAT ONE IN THE BUILDING SPECIFICATIONS!
GOT MORE PRESSING CONCERNS, YES?
UNH! DON'T RATE YOUR INTERIOR DESIGNER, HUH?
NNNF! TOLD YA NOT TO USE THEM CUT RATE BUILDERS, STRETCH. HURRY IT UP, KID!
STAND BACK. I'M GOING TO NOVA HEAT!
FUUSH!
THIS IS GETTIN' BEYOND A JOKE! HOW DO WE TURN OFF THIS BLASTED DERANGED DOBERMAN OF YOURS?
SHUMM!
FIRST OFF, WE HAVE TO FIND IT. IT COULD BE ANYWHERE IN THE BUILDING.
IF ONLY I HAD ACCESS TO A COMPUTER TERMINAL. I COULD TRACK THE SIGNAL IT'S USING TO OPERATE THE DEFENCES BACK TO SOURCE.
BETTER TALK TO ME, YES?
UH?

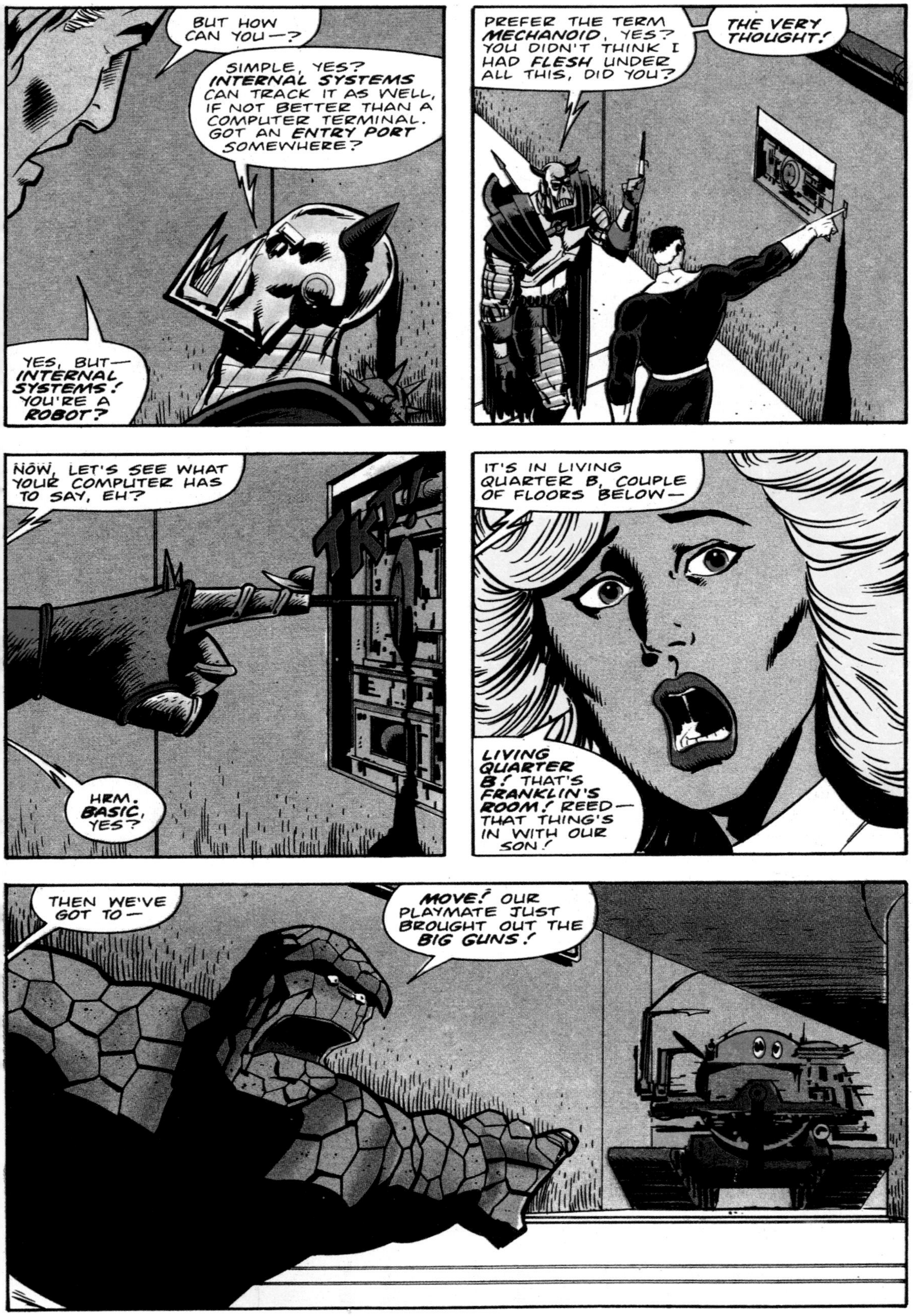
BUT HOW CAN YOU—?
SIMPLE, YES? INTERNAL SYSTEMS CAN TRACK IT AS WELL, IF NOT BETTER THAN A COMPUTER TERMINAL. GOT AN ENTRY PORT SOMEWHERE?
YES, BUT— INTERNAL SYSTEMS! YOU'RE A ROBOT?
PREFER THE TERM MECHANOID, YES? YOU DIDN'T THINK I HAD FLESH UNDER ALL THIS, DID YOU?
THE VERY THOUGHT!
NOW, LET'S SEE WHAT YOUR COMPUTER HAS TO SAY, EH?
TKT!
HRM. BASIC, YES?
IT'S IN LIVING QUARTER B, COUPLE OF FLOORS BELOW—
LIVING QUARTER B! THAT'S FRANKLIN'S ROOM! REED— THAT THING'S IN WITH OUR SON!
THEN WE'VE GOT TO—
MOVE! OUR PLAYMATE JUST BROUGHT OUT THE BIG GUNS!

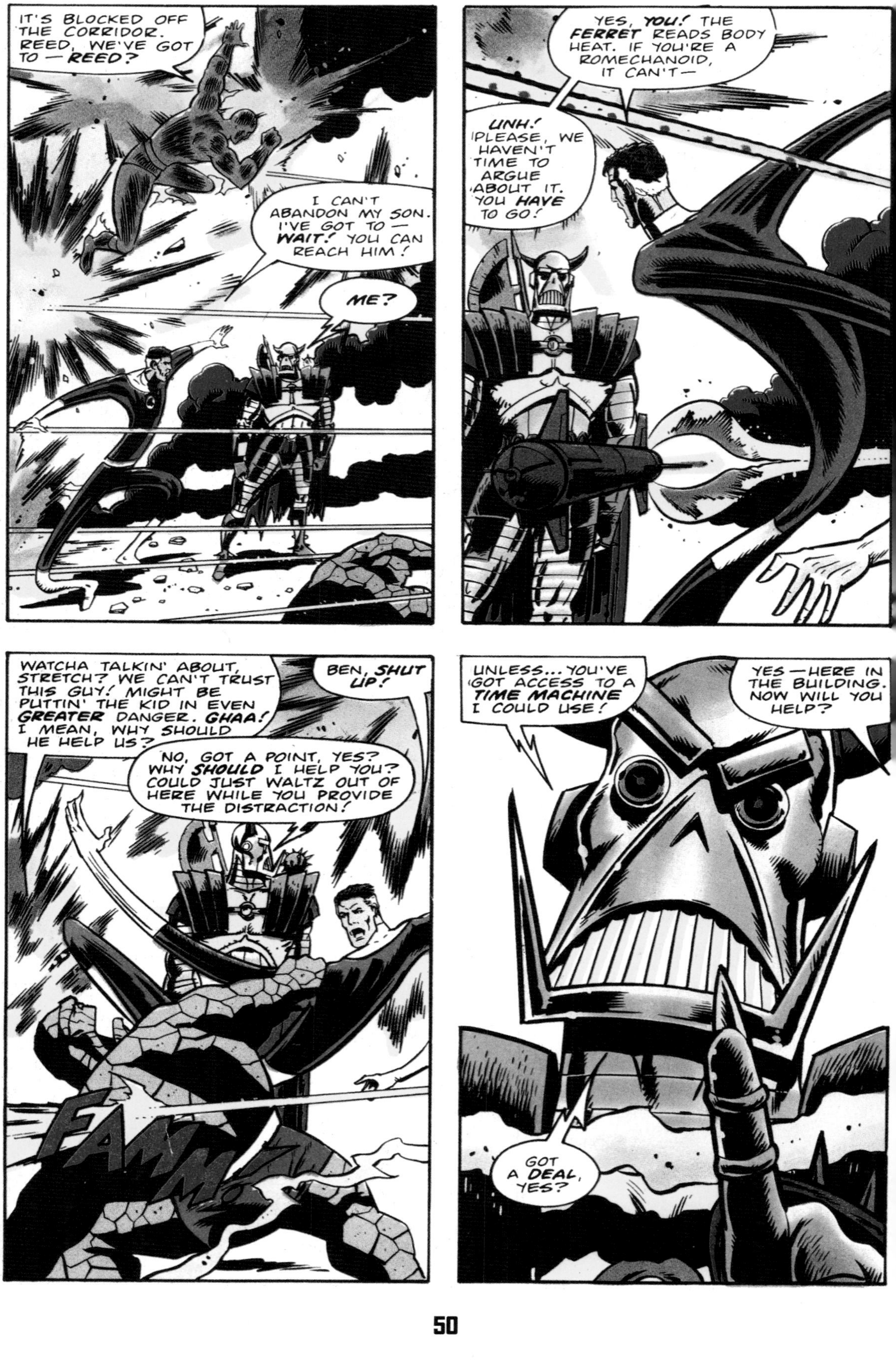
IT'S BLOCKED OFF THE CORRIDOR. REED, WE'VE GOT TO — REED?
I CAN'T ABANDON MY SON. I'VE GOT TO — WAIT! YOU CAN REACH HIM!
ME?
YES, YOU! THE FERRET READS BODY HEAT. IF YOU'RE A ROMECHANOID, IT CAN'T—
UNH! PLEASE, WE HAVEN'T TIME TO ARGUE ABOUT IT. YOU HAVE TO GO!
WATCHA TALKIN' ABOUT, STRETCH? WE CAN'T TRUST THIS GUY! MIGHT BE PUTTIN' THE KID IN EVEN GREATER DANGER. GHAA! I MEAN, WHY SHOULD HE HELP US?
BEN, SHUT UP!
NO, GOT A POINT, YES? WHY SHOULD I HELP YOU? COULD JUST WALTZ OUT OF HERE WHILE YOU PROVIDE THE DISTRACTION!
FAMM
UNLESS... YOU'VE GOT ACCESS TO A TIME MACHINE I COULD USE!
YES — HERE IN THE BUILDING. NOW WILL YOU HELP?
GOT A DEAL, YES?

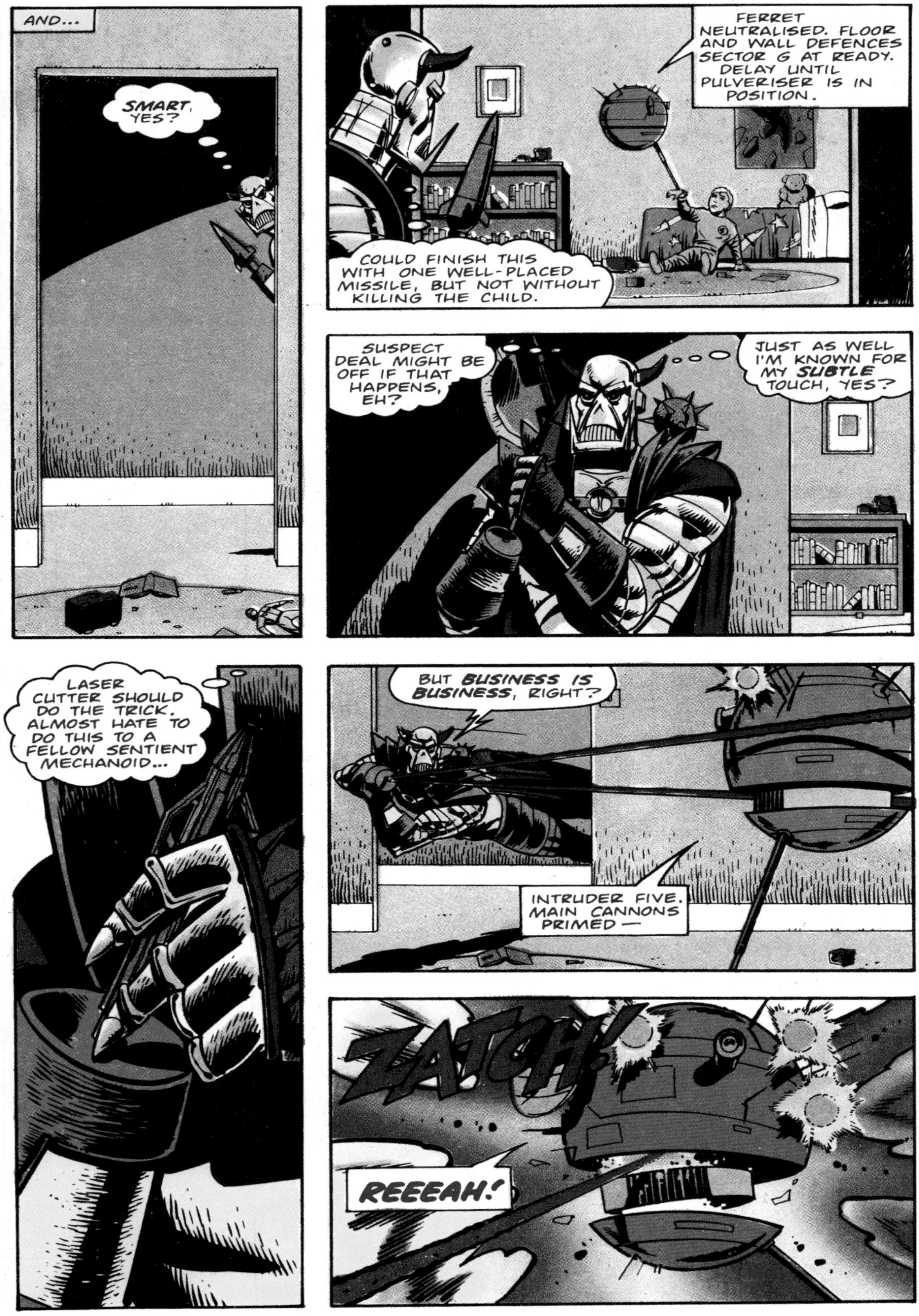

AND...
SMART, YES?
FERRET NEUTRALISED. FLOOR AND WALL DEFENCES SECTOR G AT READY. DELAY UNTIL PULVERISER IS IN POSITION.
COULD FINISH THIS WITH ONE WELL-PLACED MISSILE, BUT NOT WITHOUT KILLING THE CHILD.
SUSPECT DEAL MIGHT BE OFF IF THAT HAPPENS, EH?
JUST AS WELL I'M KNOWN FOR MY SUBTLE TOUCH, YES?
LASER CUTTER SHOULD DO THE TRICK. ALMOST HATE TO DO THIS TO A FELLOW SENTIENT MECHANOID...
BUT BUSINESS IS BUSINESS, RIGHT?
INTRUDER FIVE. MAIN CANNONS PRIMED—
ZATCH!
REEEAH!

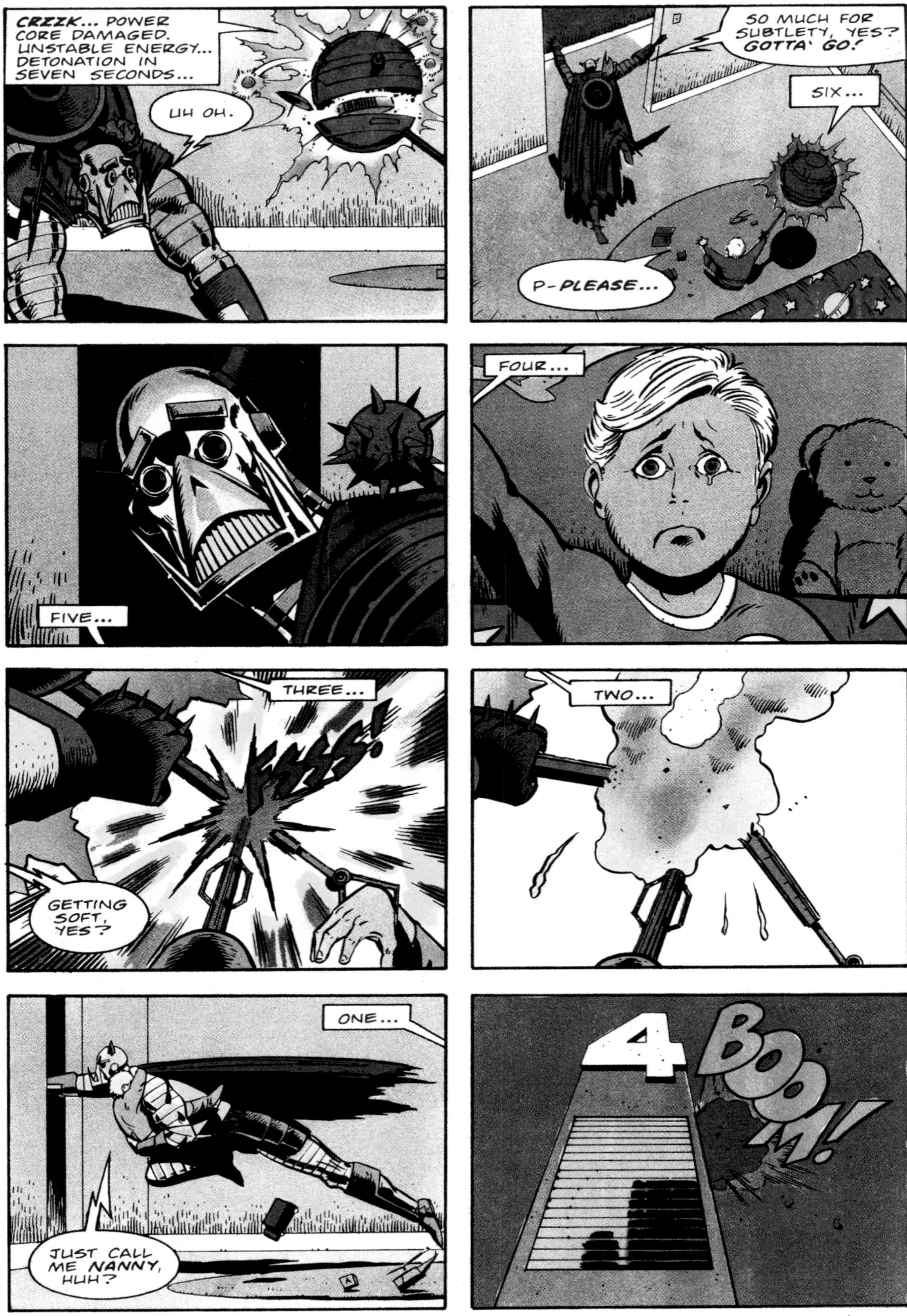
CRZZK... POWER CORE DAMAGED. UNSTABLE ENERGY... DETONATION IN SEVEN SECONDS...
UH OH.
SO MUCH FOR SUBTLETY, YES? GOTTA' GO!
SIX...
P-PLEASE...
FIVE...
FOUR...
THREE...
FSSS!
GETTING SOFT, YES?
TWO...
ONE...
JUST CALL ME NANNY, HUH?
4
BOOM!

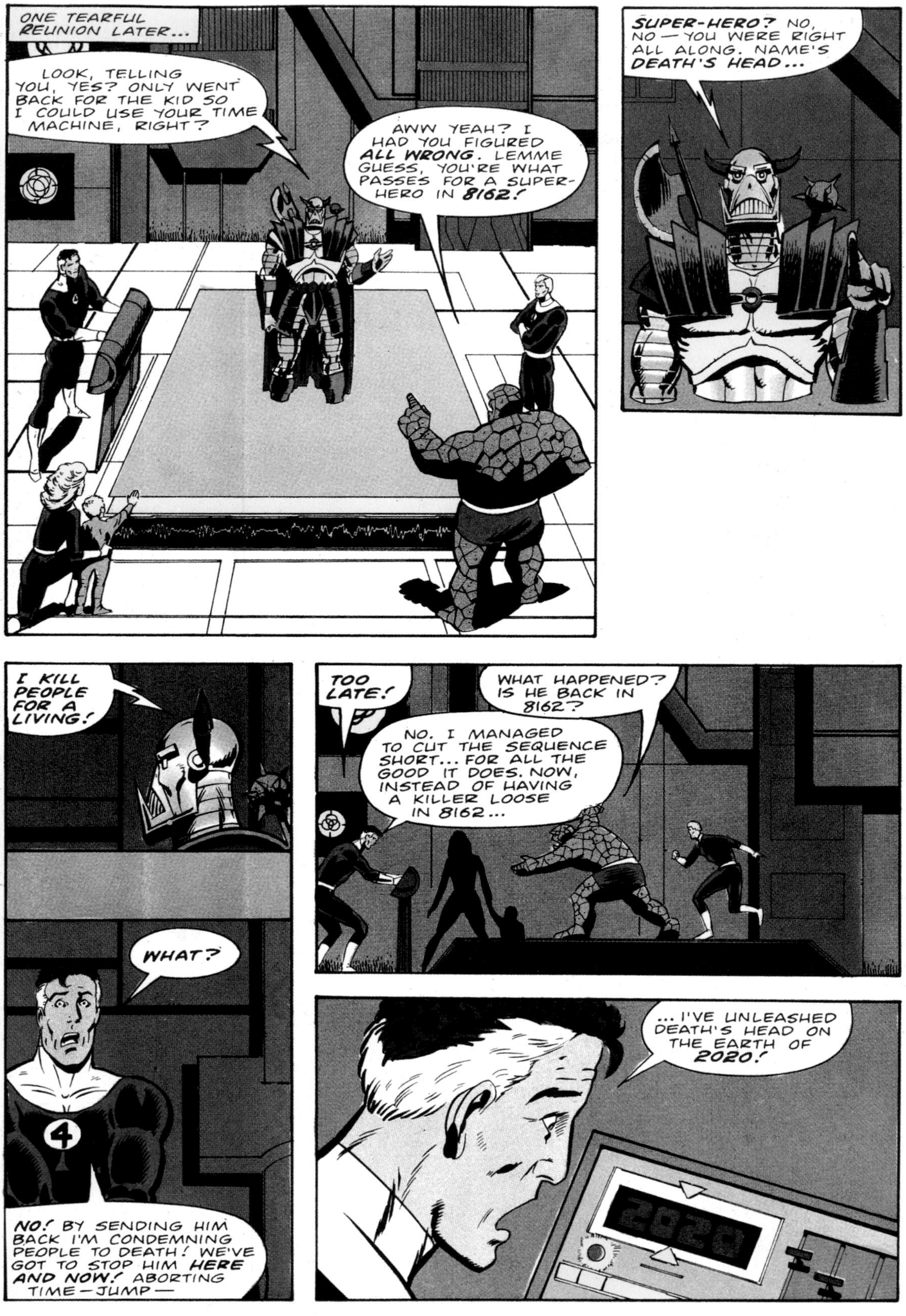
ONE TEARFUL REUNION LATER...
LOOK, TELLING YOU, YES? ONLY WENT BACK FOR THE KID SO I COULD USE YOUR TIME MACHINE, RIGHT?
AWW YEAH? I HAD YOU FIGURED ALL WRONG. LEMME GUESS, YOU'RE WHAT PASSES FOR A SUPER-HERO IN 8162!
SUPER-HERO? NO, NO — YOU WERE RIGHT ALL ALONG. NAME'S DEATH'S HEAD...
I KILL PEOPLE FOR A LIVING!
WHAT?
NO! BY SENDING HIM BACK I'M CONDEMNING PEOPLE TO DEATH! WE'VE GOT TO STOP HIM HERE AND NOW! ABORTING TIME-JUMP—
TOO LATE!
WHAT HAPPENED? IS HE BACK IN 8162?
NO. I MANAGED TO CUT THE SEQUENCE SHORT... FOR ALL THE GOOD IT DOES. NOW, INSTEAD OF HAVING A KILLER LOOSE IN 8162...
...I'VE UNLEASHED DEATH'S HEAD ON THE EARTH OF 2020!
2020

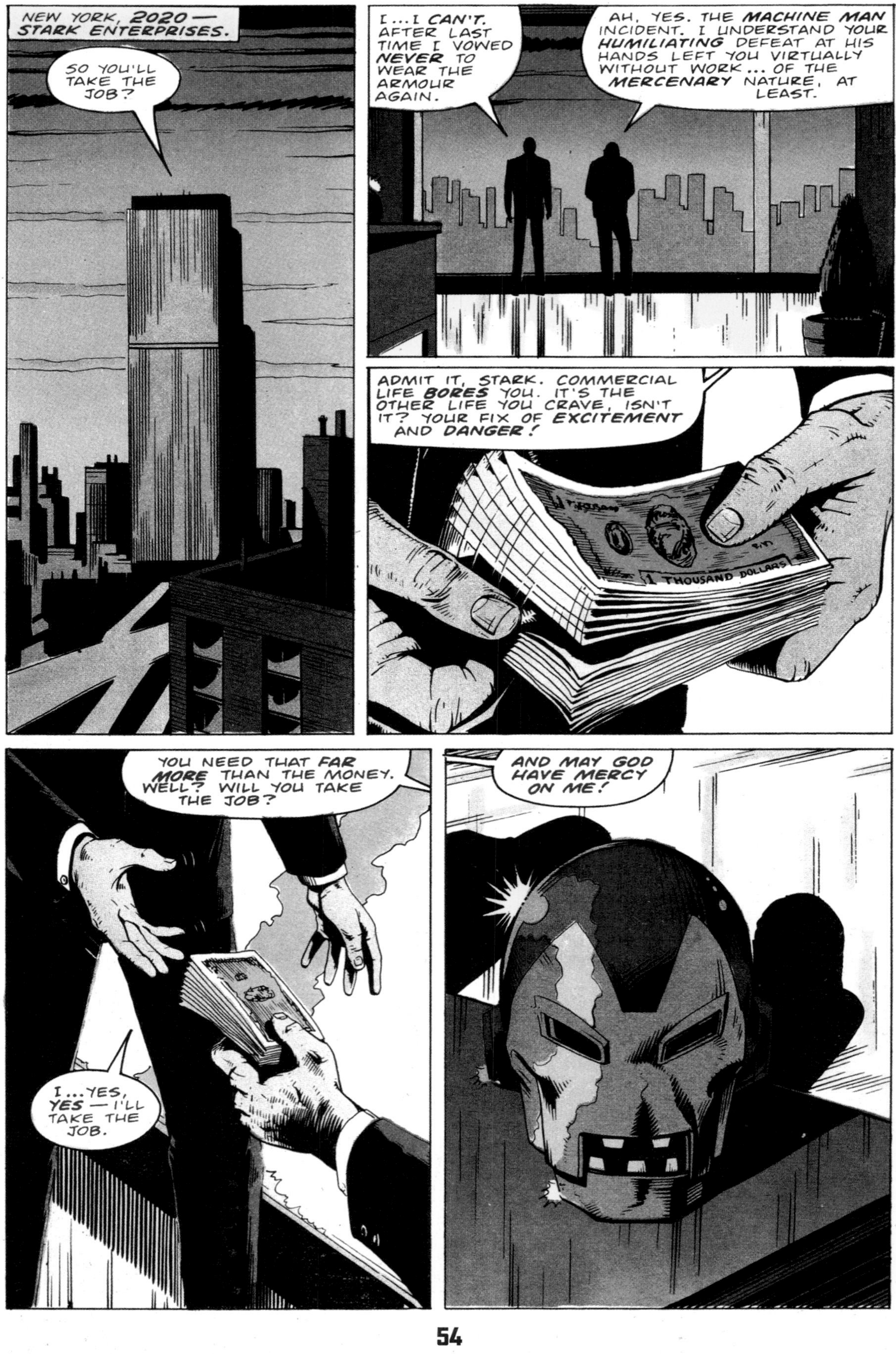
NEW YORK, 2020 — STARK ENTERPRISES.
SO YOU'LL TAKE THE JOB?
I...I CAN'T. AFTER LAST TIME I VOWED NEVER TO WEAR THE ARMOUR AGAIN.
AH, YES. THE MACHINE MAN INCIDENT. I UNDERSTAND YOUR HUMILIATING DEFEAT AT HIS HANDS LEFT YOU VIRTUALLY WITHOUT WORK... OF THE MERCENARY NATURE, AT LEAST.
ADMIT IT, STARK. COMMERCIAL LIFE BORES YOU. IT'S THE OTHER LIFE YOU CRAVE, ISN'T IT? YOUR FIX OF EXCITEMENT AND DANGER!
1 THOUSAND DOLLARS
YOU NEED THAT FAR MORE THAN THE MONEY. WELL? WILL YOU TAKE THE JOB?
I...YES, YES — I'LL TAKE THE JOB.
AND MAY GOD HAVE MERCY ON ME!

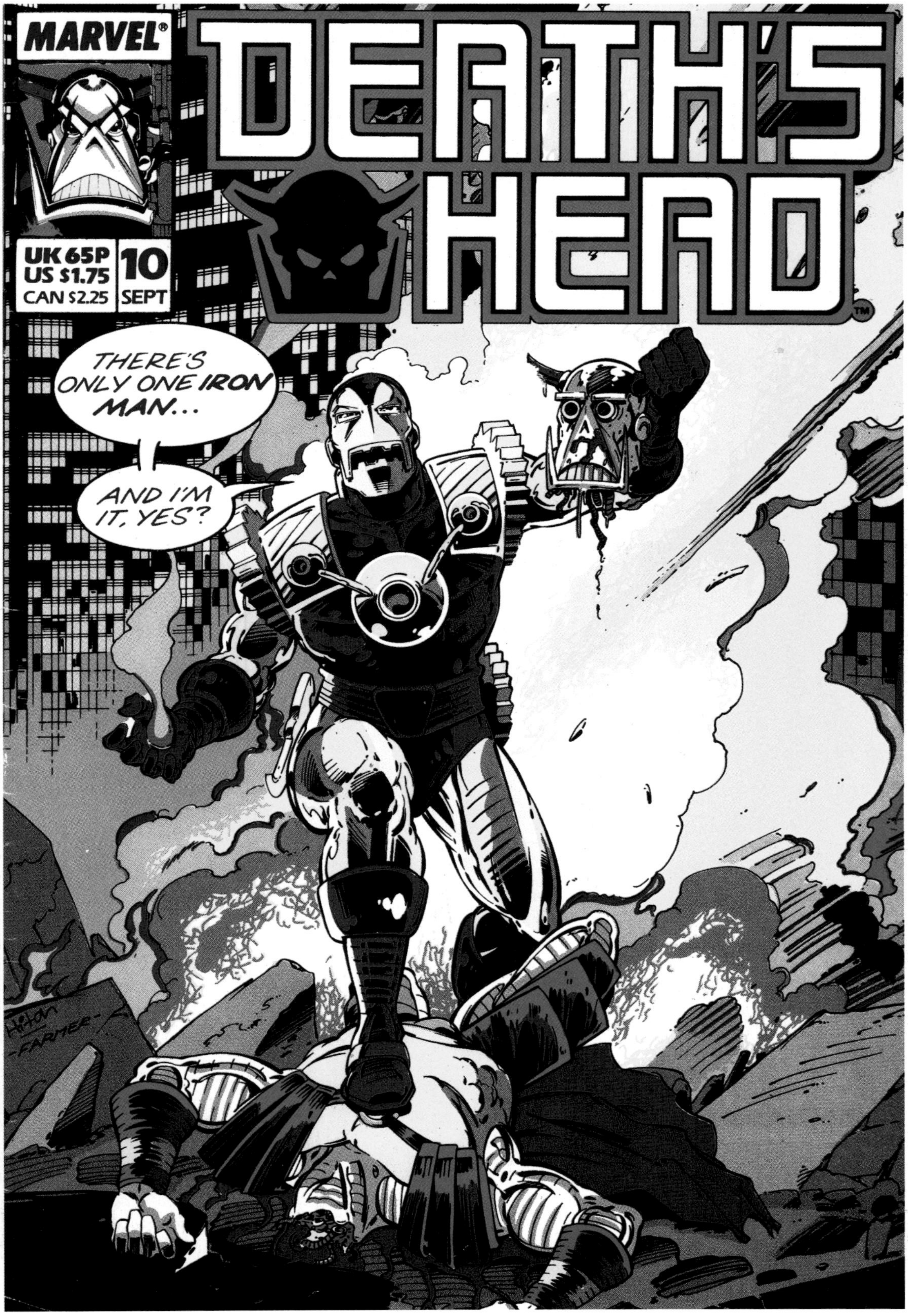
MARVEL
DEATH'S HEAD
UK 65P
US $1.75
CAN $2.25
10
SEPT
THERE'S ONLY ONE IRON MAN...
AND I'M IT, YES?
Hilton
FARMER

Stan Lee presents:

DEATH'S HEAD™

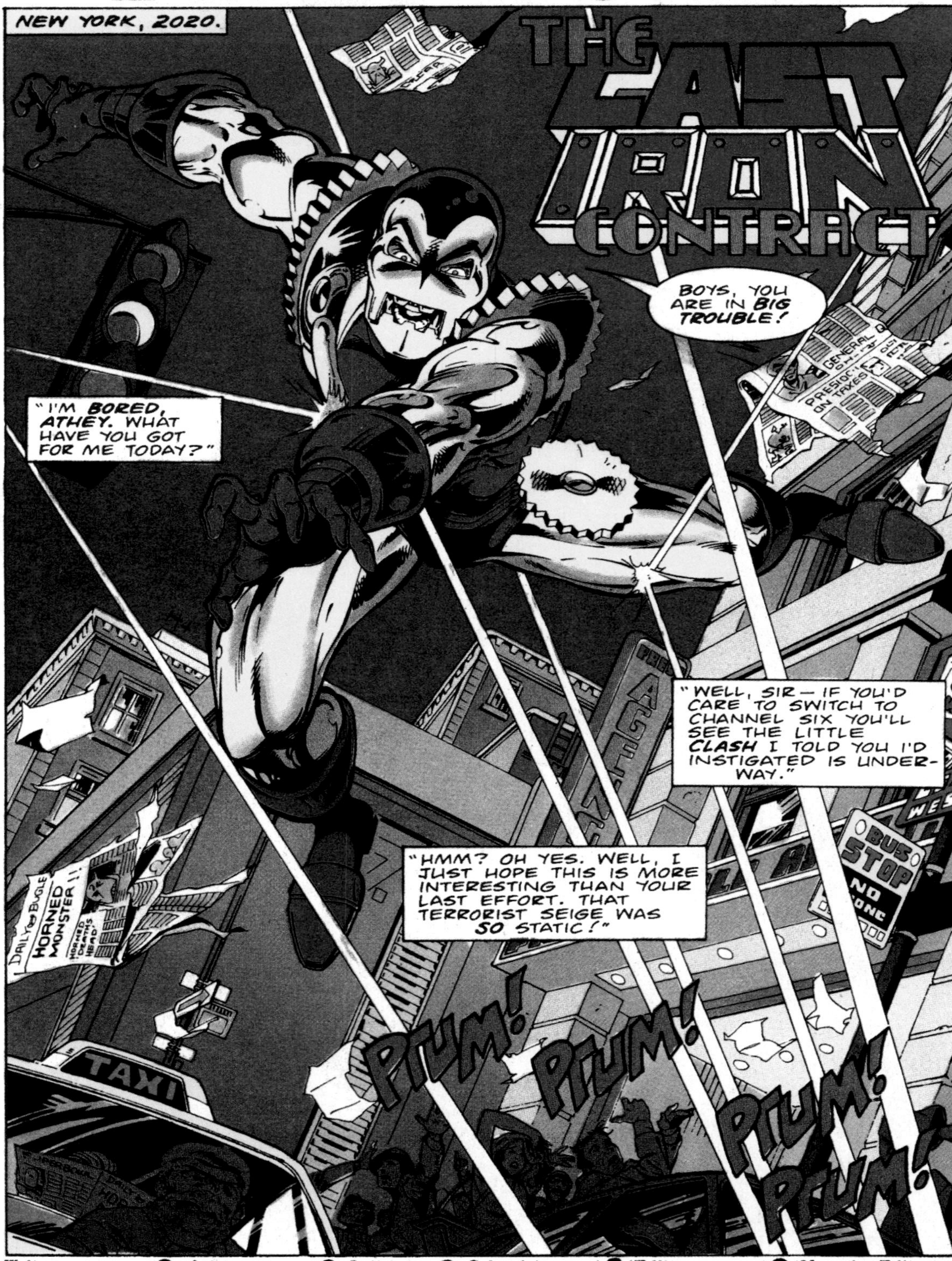
NEW YORK, 2020.
THE CAST IRON CONTRACT
BOYS, YOU ARE IN BIG TROUBLE!
"I'M BORED, ATHEY. WHAT HAVE YOU GOT FOR ME TODAY?"
"WELL, SIR— IF YOU'D CARE TO SWITCH TO CHANNEL SIX YOU'LL SEE THE LITTLE CLASH I TOLD YOU I'D INSTIGATED IS UNDER-WAY."
"HMM? OH YES. WELL, I JUST HOPE THIS IS MORE INTERESTING THAN YOUR LAST EFFORT. THAT TERRORIST SEIGE WAS SO STATIC!"
DAILY BUGLE
HORNED MONSTER!!
BUS STOP
TAXI
PTUM! PTUM! PTUM! PTUM!

Writer SIMON FURMAN · Art BRYAN HITCH · Letterer ANNIE H · Colourist EVAN PETERS · Editor STEVE WHITE · Managing Editor JENNY O'CONNOR

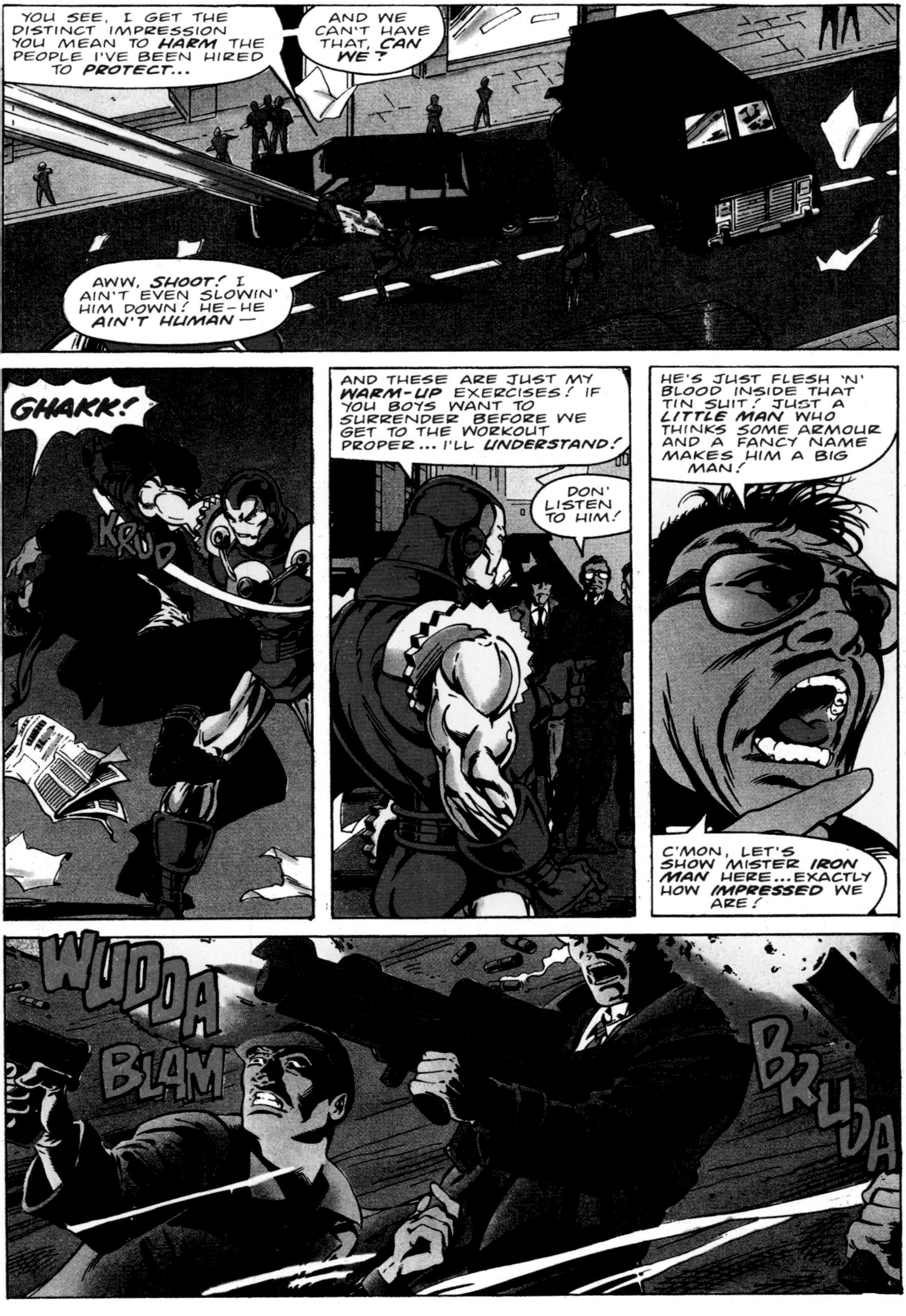

YOU SEE, I GET THE DISTINCT IMPRESSION YOU MEAN TO HARM THE PEOPLE I'VE BEEN HIRED TO PROTECT...
AND WE CAN'T HAVE THAT, CAN WE?
AWW, SHOOT! I AIN'T EVEN SLOWIN' HIM DOWN! HE-HE AIN'T HUMAN—
GHAKK!
KRUD
AND THESE ARE JUST MY WARM-UP EXERCISES! IF YOU BOYS WANT TO SURRENDER BEFORE WE GET TO THE WORKOUT PROPER... I'LL UNDERSTAND!
DON' LISTEN TO HIM!
HE'S JUST FLESH 'N' BLOOD INSIDE THAT TIN SUIT! JUST A LITTLE MAN WHO THINKS SOME ARMOUR AND A FANCY NAME MAKES HIM A BIG MAN!
C'MON, LET'S SHOW MISTER IRON MAN HERE... EXACTLY HOW IMPRESSED WE ARE!
WUDDA
BLAM
BRUDA

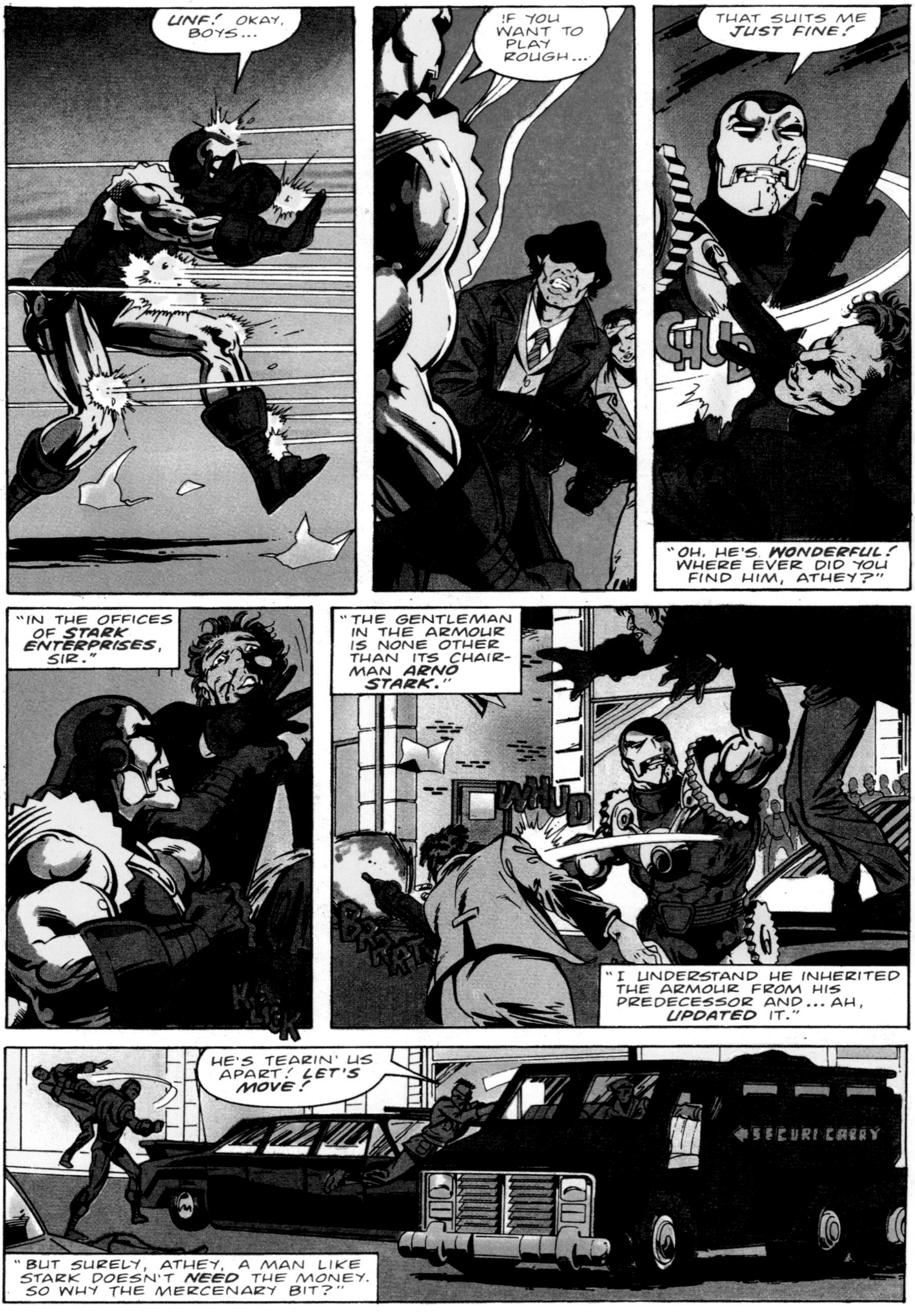
UNF! OKAY, BOYS...
!F YOU WANT TO PLAY ROUGH...
THAT SUITS ME JUST FINE!
CHUD
"OH, HE'S WONDERFUL! WHERE EVER DID YOU FIND HIM, ATHEY?"
"IN THE OFFICES OF STARK ENTERPRISES, SIR."
KLICK
"THE GENTLEMAN IN THE ARMOUR IS NONE OTHER THAN ITS CHAIRMAN ARNO STARK."
WHUD
"I UNDERSTAND HE INHERITED THE ARMOUR FROM HIS PREDECESSOR AND... AH, UPDATED IT."
HE'S TEARIN' US APART! LET'S MOVE!
SECURI-CARRY
"BUT SURELY, ATHEY, A MAN LIKE STARK DOESN'T NEED THE MONEY. SO WHY THE MERCENARY BIT?"

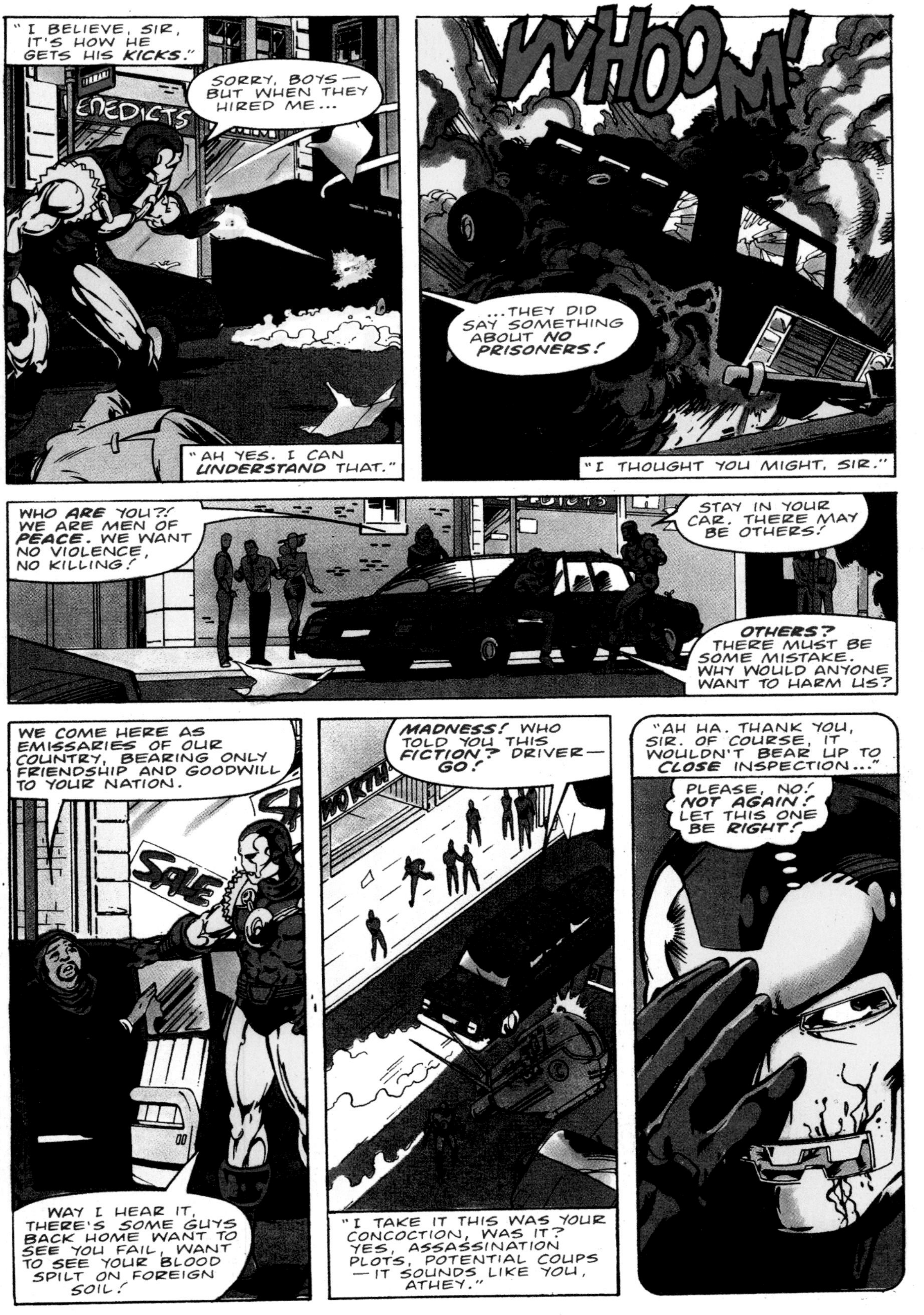
"I BELIEVE, SIR, IT'S HOW HE GETS HIS KICKS."
SORRY, BOYS— BUT WHEN THEY HIRED ME...
"AH YES. I CAN UNDERSTAND THAT."
WHOOOM!
...THEY DID SAY SOMETHING ABOUT NO PRISONERS!
"I THOUGHT YOU MIGHT, SIR."
WHO ARE YOU?! WE ARE MEN OF PEACE. WE WANT NO VIOLENCE, NO KILLING!
STAY IN YOUR CAR. THERE MAY BE OTHERS!
OTHERS? THERE MUST BE SOME MISTAKE. WHY WOULD ANYONE WANT TO HARM US?
WE COME HERE AS EMISSARIES OF OUR COUNTRY, BEARING ONLY FRIENDSHIP AND GOODWILL TO YOUR NATION.
SALE
WAY I HEAR IT, THERE'S SOME GUYS BACK HOME WANT TO SEE YOU FAIL, WANT TO SEE YOUR BLOOD SPILT ON FOREIGN SOIL!
MADNESS! WHO TOLD YOU THIS FICTION? DRIVER— GO!
"I TAKE IT THIS WAS YOUR CONCOCTION, WAS IT? YES, ASSASSINATION PLOTS, POTENTIAL COUPS —IT SOUNDS LIKE YOU, ATHEY."
"AH HA. THANK YOU, SIR. OF COURSE, IT WOULDN'T BEAR UP TO CLOSE INSPECTION..."
PLEASE, NO! NOT AGAIN! LET THIS ONE BE RIGHT!

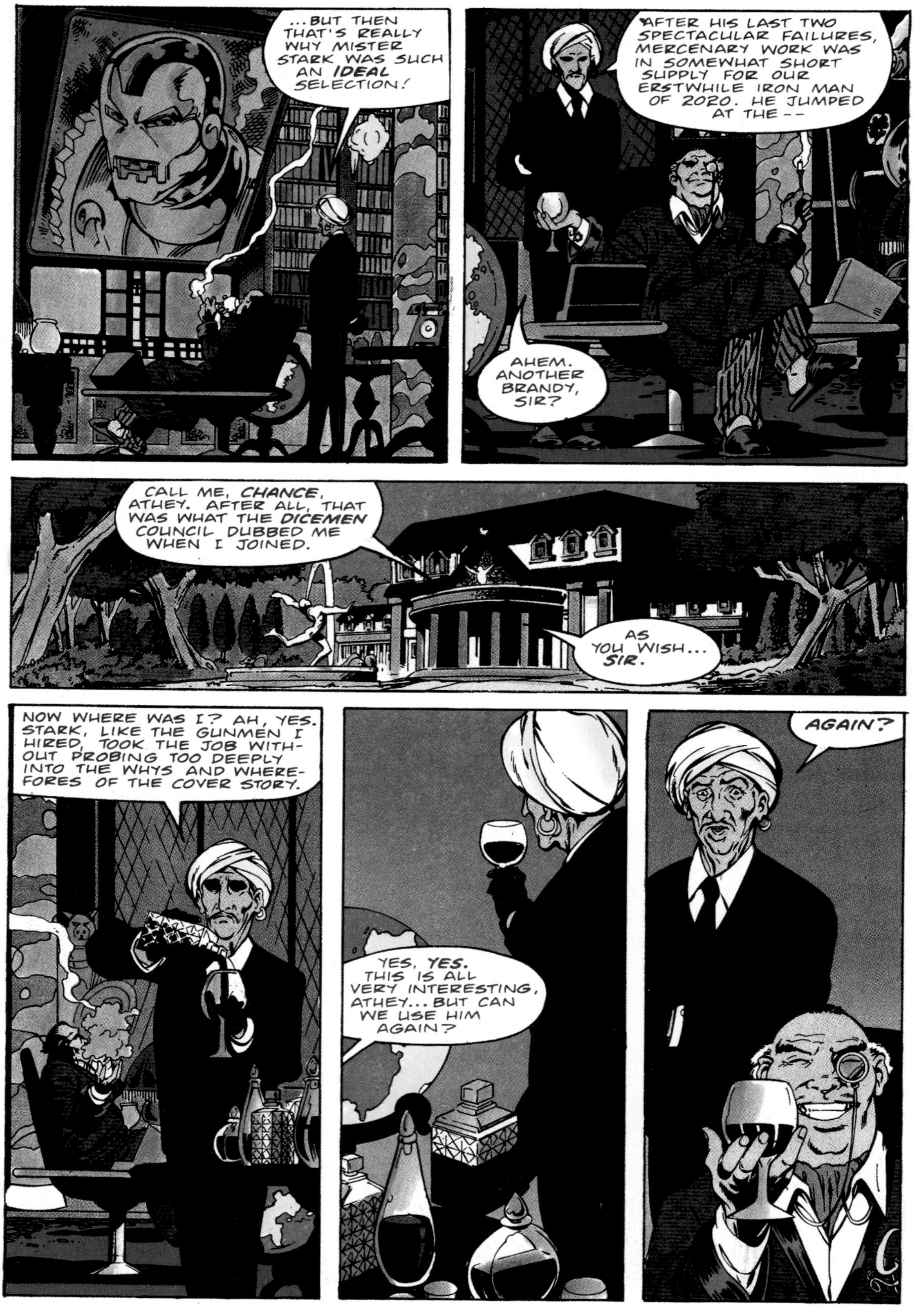
...BUT THEN THAT'S REALLY WHY MISTER STARK WAS SUCH AN IDEAL SELECTION!
AFTER HIS LAST TWO SPECTACULAR FAILURES, MERCENARY WORK WAS IN SOMEWHAT SHORT SUPPLY FOR OUR ERSTWHILE IRON MAN OF 2020. HE JUMPED AT THE --
AHEM. ANOTHER BRANDY, SIR?
CALL ME, CHANCE, ATHEY. AFTER ALL, THAT WAS WHAT THE DICEMEN COUNCIL DUBBED ME WHEN I JOINED.
AS YOU WISH... SIR.
NOW WHERE WAS I? AH, YES. STARK, LIKE THE GUNMEN I HIRED, TOOK THE JOB WITHOUT PROBING TOO DEEPLY INTO THE WHYS AND WHEREFORES OF THE COVER STORY.
YES, YES. THIS IS ALL VERY INTERESTING, ATHEY... BUT CAN WE USE HIM AGAIN?
AGAIN?

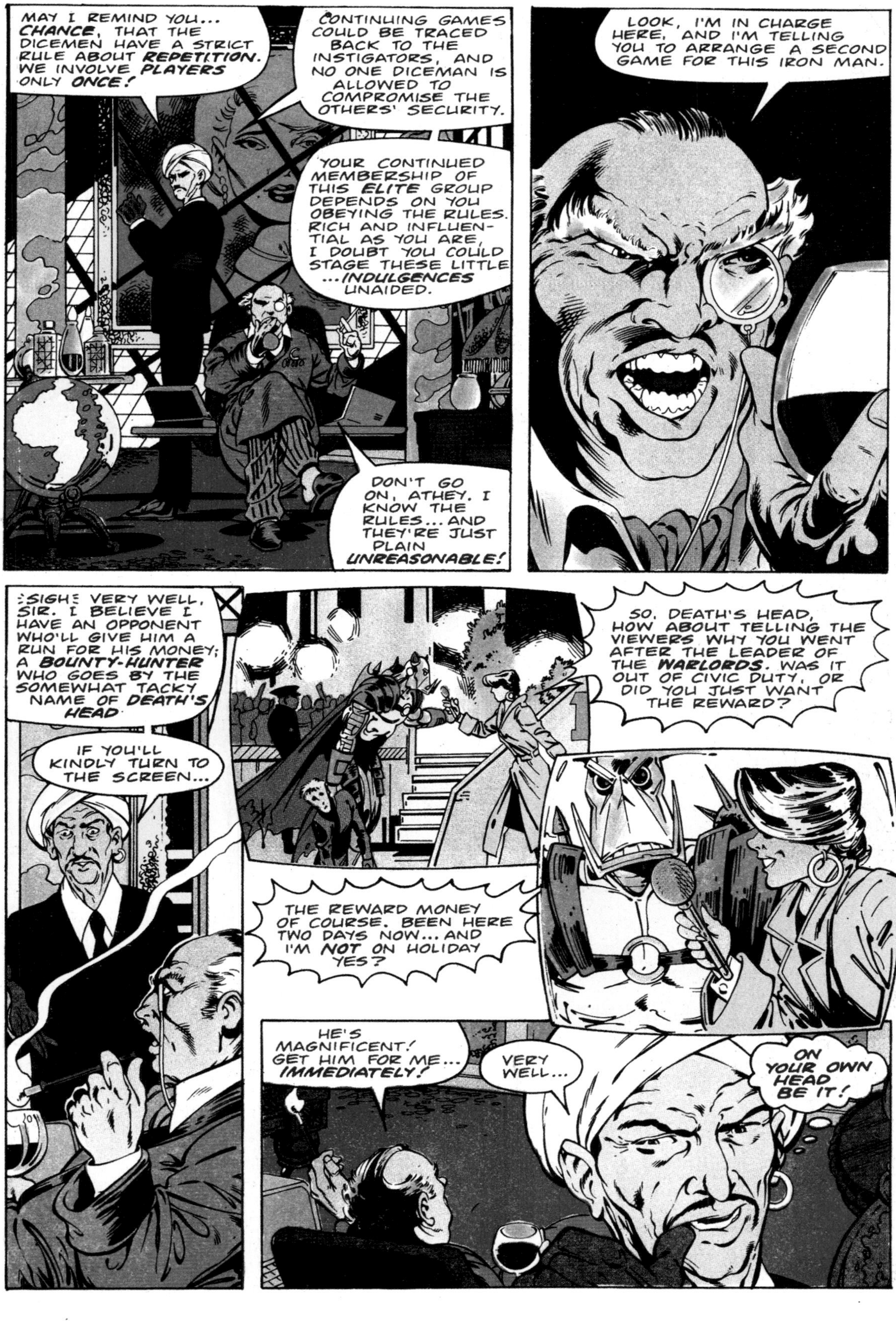
MAY I REMIND YOU... CHANCE, THAT THE DICEMEN HAVE A STRICT RULE ABOUT REPETITION. WE INVOLVE PLAYERS ONLY ONCE!
CONTINUING GAMES COULD BE TRACED BACK TO THE INSTIGATORS, AND NO ONE DICEMAN IS ALLOWED TO COMPROMISE THE OTHERS' SECURITY.
YOUR CONTINUED MEMBERSHIP OF THIS ELITE GROUP DEPENDS ON YOU OBEYING THE RULES. RICH AND INFLUENTIAL AS YOU ARE, I DOUBT YOU COULD STAGE THESE LITTLE ...INDULGENCES UNAIDED.
DON'T GO ON, ATHEY. I KNOW THE RULES... AND THEY'RE JUST PLAIN UNREASONABLE!
LOOK, I'M IN CHARGE HERE, AND I'M TELLING YOU TO ARRANGE A SECOND GAME FOR THIS IRON MAN.
:SIGH: VERY WELL, SIR. I BELIEVE I HAVE AN OPPONENT WHO'LL GIVE HIM A RUN FOR HIS MONEY; A BOUNTY-HUNTER WHO GOES BY THE SOMEWHAT TACKY NAME OF DEATH'S HEAD
IF YOU'LL KINDLY TURN TO THE SCREEN...
SO, DEATH'S HEAD, HOW ABOUT TELLING THE VIEWERS WHY YOU WENT AFTER THE LEADER OF THE WARLORDS. WAS IT OUT OF CIVIC DUTY, OR DID YOU JUST WANT THE REWARD?
THE REWARD MONEY OF COURSE. BEEN HERE TWO DAYS NOW... AND I'M NOT ON HOLIDAY YES?
HE'S MAGNIFICENT! GET HIM FOR ME... IMMEDIATELY!
VERY WELL...
ON YOUR OWN HEAD BE IT!

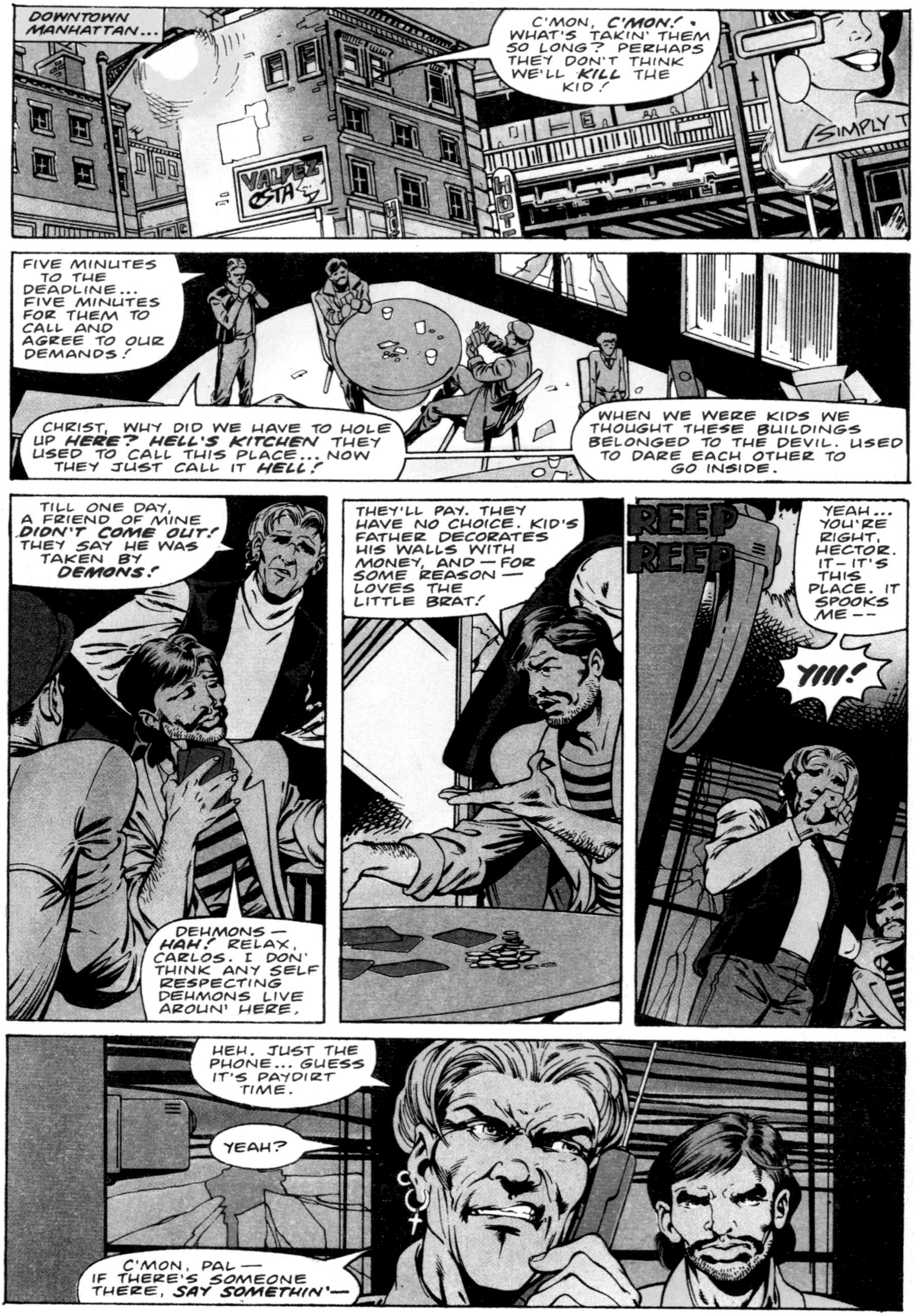
DOWNTOWN MANHATTAN...
C'MON, C'MON! WHAT'S TAKIN' THEM SO LONG? PERHAPS THEY DON'T THINK WE'LL KILL THE KID!
VALDEZ
SIMPLY T
FIVE MINUTES TO THE DEADLINE... FIVE MINUTES FOR THEM TO CALL AND AGREE TO OUR DEMANDS!
CHRIST, WHY DID WE HAVE TO HOLE UP HERE? HELL'S KITCHEN THEY USED TO CALL THIS PLACE... NOW THEY JUST CALL IT HELL!
WHEN WE WERE KIDS WE THOUGHT THESE BUILDINGS BELONGED TO THE DEVIL. USED TO DARE EACH OTHER TO GO INSIDE.
TILL ONE DAY, A FRIEND OF MINE DIDN'T COME OUT! THEY SAY HE WAS TAKEN BY DEMONS!
DEHMONS— HAH! RELAX, CARLOS. I DON' THINK ANY SELF RESPECTING DEHMONS LIVE AROUN' HERE.
THEY'LL PAY. THEY HAVE NO CHOICE. KID'S FATHER DECORATES HIS WALLS WITH MONEY, AND — FOR SOME REASON — LOVES THE LITTLE BRAT!
REEP REEP
YEAH... YOU'RE RIGHT, HECTOR. IT– IT'S THIS PLACE. IT SPOOKS ME --
YIII!
HEH. JUST THE PHONE... GUESS IT'S PAYDIRT TIME.
YEAH?
C'MON, PAL — IF THERE'S SOMEONE THERE, SAY SOMETHIN'—

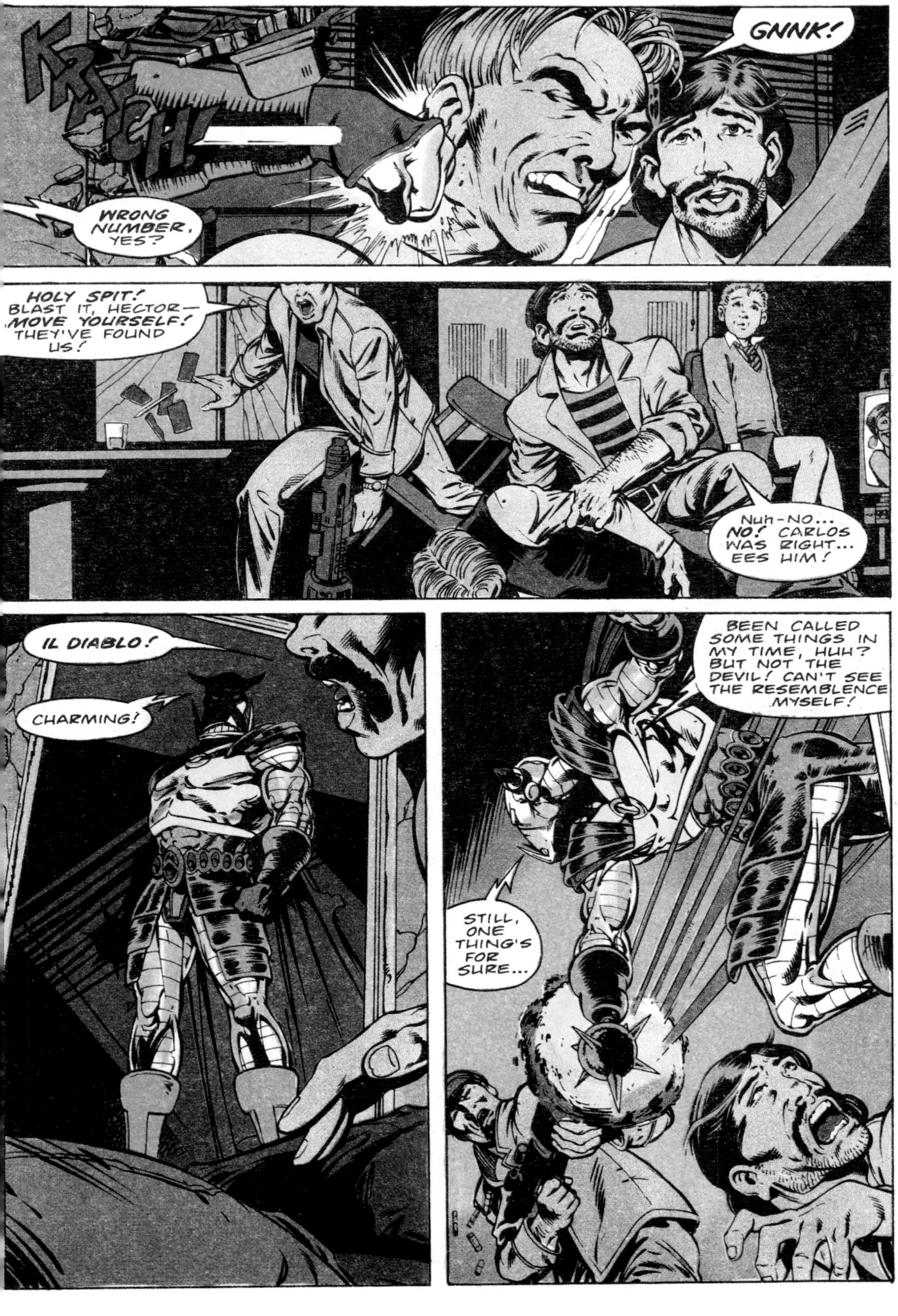
KRASCH!
GNNK!
WRONG NUMBER, YES?
HOLY SPIT! BLAST IT, HECTOR— MOVE YOURSELF! THEY'VE FOUND US!
Nuh-NO... NO! CARLOS WAS RIGHT... EES HIM!
IL DIABLO!
CHARMING!
BEEN CALLED SOME THINGS IN MY TIME, HUH? BUT NOT THE DEVIL! CAN'T SEE THE RESEMBLENCE MYSELF!
STILL, ONE THING'S FOR SURE...

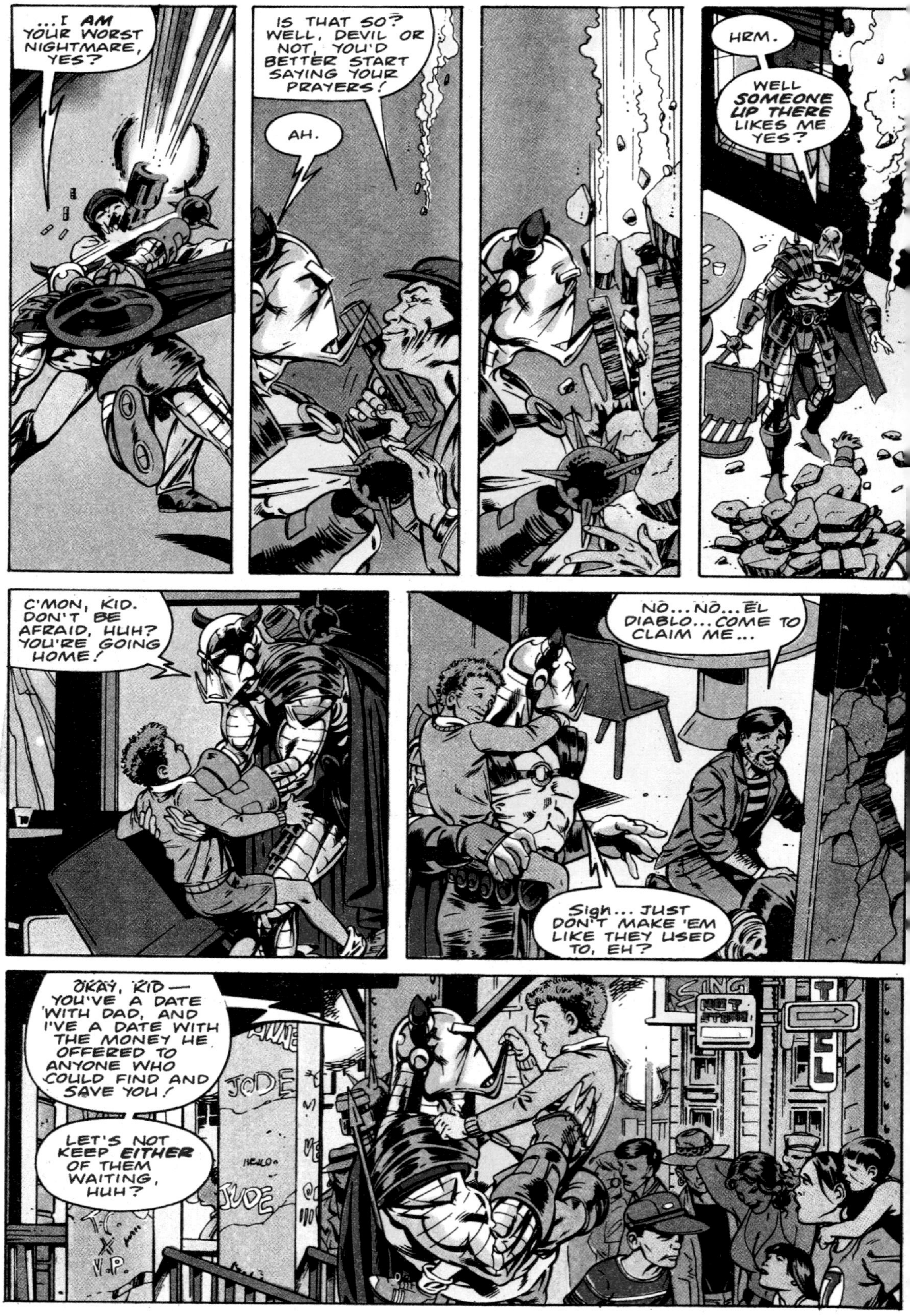
...I AM YOUR WORST NIGHTMARE, YES?
IS THAT SO? WELL, DEVIL OR NOT, YOU'D BETTER START SAYING YOUR PRAYERS!
AH.
HRM.
WELL SOMEONE UP THERE LIKES ME YES?
C'MON, KID. DON'T BE AFRAID, HUH? YOU'RE GOING HOME!
NO...NO...EL DIABLO...COME TO CLAIM ME...
Sigh... JUST DON'T MAKE 'EM LIKE THEY USED TO, EH?
OKAY, KID— YOU'VE A DATE WITH DAD, AND I'VE A DATE WITH THE MONEY HE OFFERED TO ANYONE WHO COULD FIND AND SAVE YOU!
LET'S NOT KEEP EITHER OF THEM WAITING, HUH?

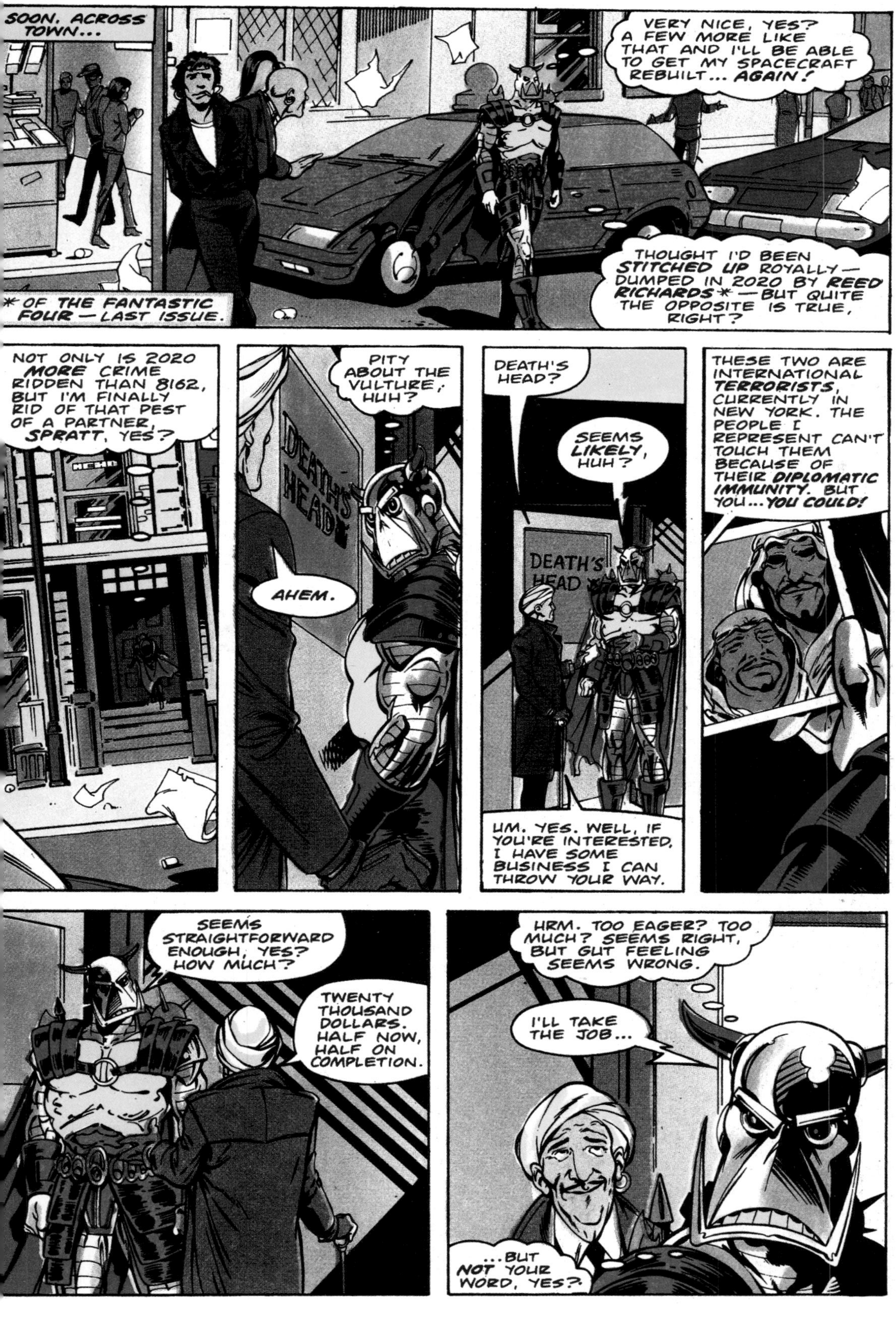
SOON. ACROSS TOWN...
VERY NICE, YES? A FEW MORE LIKE THAT AND I'LL BE ABLE TO GET MY SPACECRAFT REBUILT... AGAIN!
THOUGHT I'D BEEN STITCHED UP ROYALLY — DUMPED IN 2020 BY REED RICHARDS* — BUT QUITE THE OPPOSITE IS TRUE, RIGHT?
*OF THE FANTASTIC FOUR — LAST ISSUE.
NOT ONLY IS 2020 MORE CRIME RIDDEN THAN 8162, BUT I'M FINALLY RID OF THAT PEST OF A PARTNER, SPRATT, YES?
PITY ABOUT THE VULTURE, HUH?
DEATH'S HEAD
AHEM.
DEATH'S HEAD?
SEEMS LIKELY, HUH?
DEATH'S HEAD
UM. YES. WELL, IF YOU'RE INTERESTED, I HAVE SOME BUSINESS I CAN THROW YOUR WAY.
THESE TWO ARE INTERNATIONAL TERRORISTS, CURRENTLY IN NEW YORK. THE PEOPLE I REPRESENT CAN'T TOUCH THEM BECAUSE OF THEIR DIPLOMATIC IMMUNITY. BUT YOU... YOU COULD!
SEEMS STRAIGHTFORWARD ENOUGH, YES? HOW MUCH?
TWENTY THOUSAND DOLLARS. HALF NOW, HALF ON COMPLETION.
HRM. TOO EAGER? TOO MUCH? SEEMS RIGHT, BUT GUT FEELING SEEMS WRONG.
I'LL TAKE THE JOB...
...BUT NOT YOUR WORD, YES?

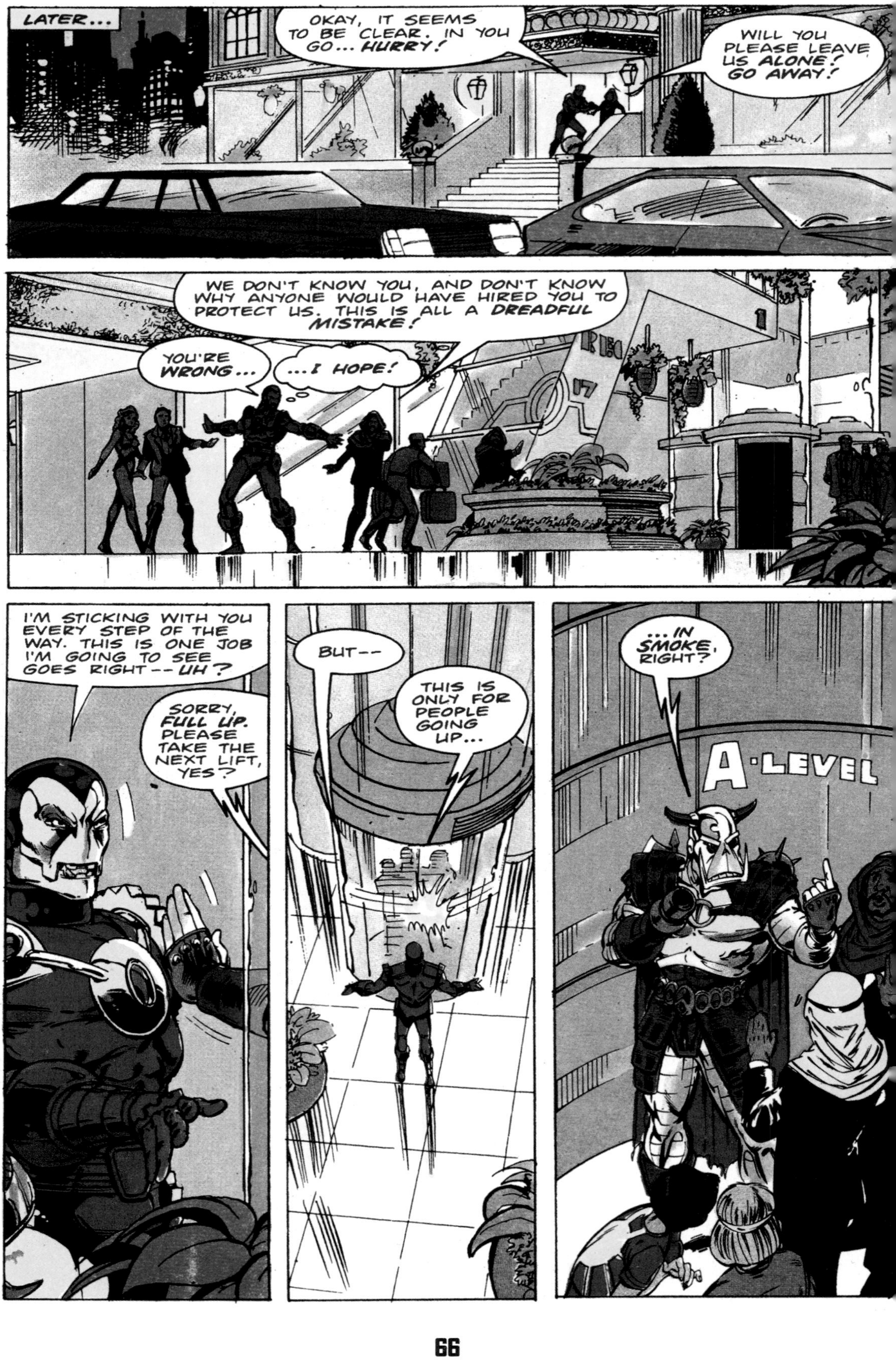
LATER...
OKAY, IT SEEMS TO BE CLEAR. IN YOU GO... HURRY!
WILL YOU PLEASE LEAVE US ALONE! GO AWAY!
WE DON'T KNOW YOU, AND DON'T KNOW WHY ANYONE WOULD HAVE HIRED YOU TO PROTECT US. THIS IS ALL A DREADFUL MISTAKE!
YOU'RE WRONG...
...I HOPE!
I'M STICKING WITH YOU EVERY STEP OF THE WAY. THIS IS ONE JOB I'M GOING TO SEE GOES RIGHT--UH?
SORRY, FULL UP. PLEASE TAKE THE NEXT LIFT, YES?
BUT--
THIS IS ONLY FOR PEOPLE GOING UP...
...IN SMOKE, RIGHT?
A·LEVEL

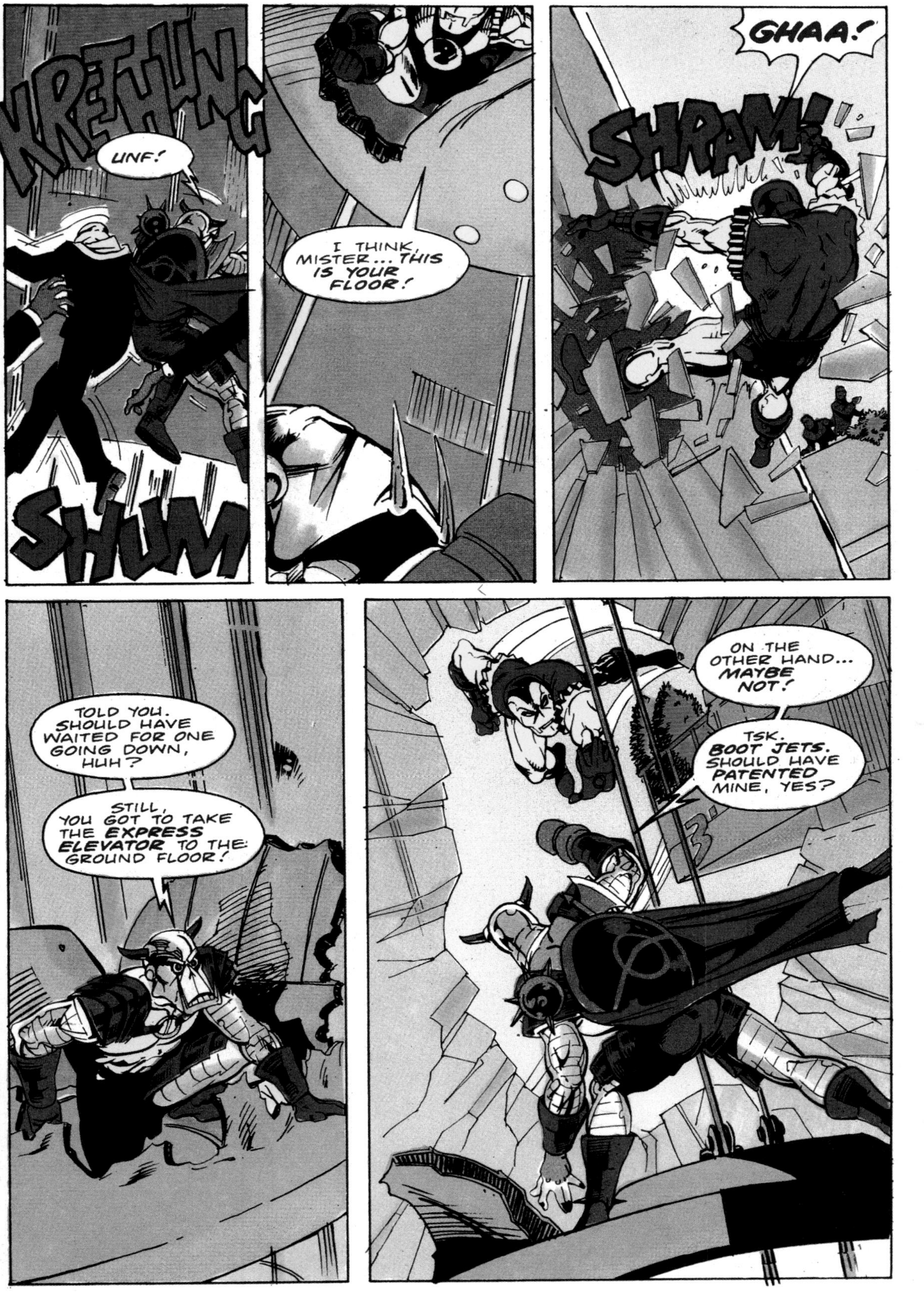
KRETHUNG
UNF!
SHUM
I THINK, MISTER... THIS IS YOUR FLOOR!
GHAA!
SHRAM!
TOLD YOU. SHOULD HAVE WAITED FOR ONE GOING DOWN, HUH?
STILL, YOU GOT TO TAKE THE EXPRESS ELEVATOR TO THE GROUND FLOOR!
ON THE OTHER HAND... MAYBE NOT!
TSK. BOOT JETS. SHOULD HAVE PATENTED MINE, YES?

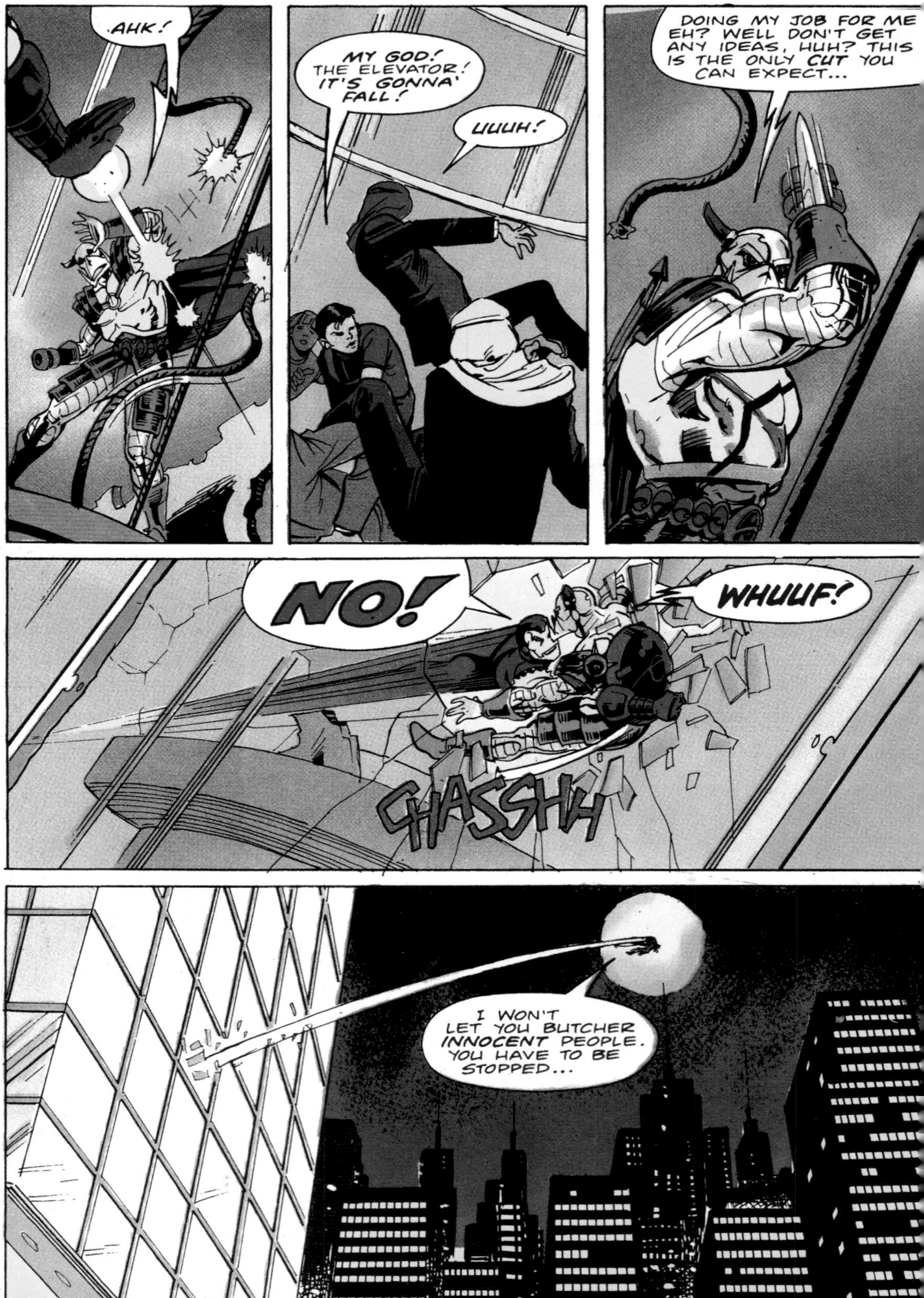
AHK!
MY GOD! THE ELEVATOR! IT'S GONNA' FALL!
UUUH!
DOING MY JOB FOR ME EH? WELL DON'T GET ANY IDEAS, HUH? THIS IS THE ONLY CUT YOU CAN EXPECT...
NO!
WHUUF!
CHASSHH
I WON'T LET YOU BUTCHER INNOCENT PEOPLE. YOU HAVE TO BE STOPPED...

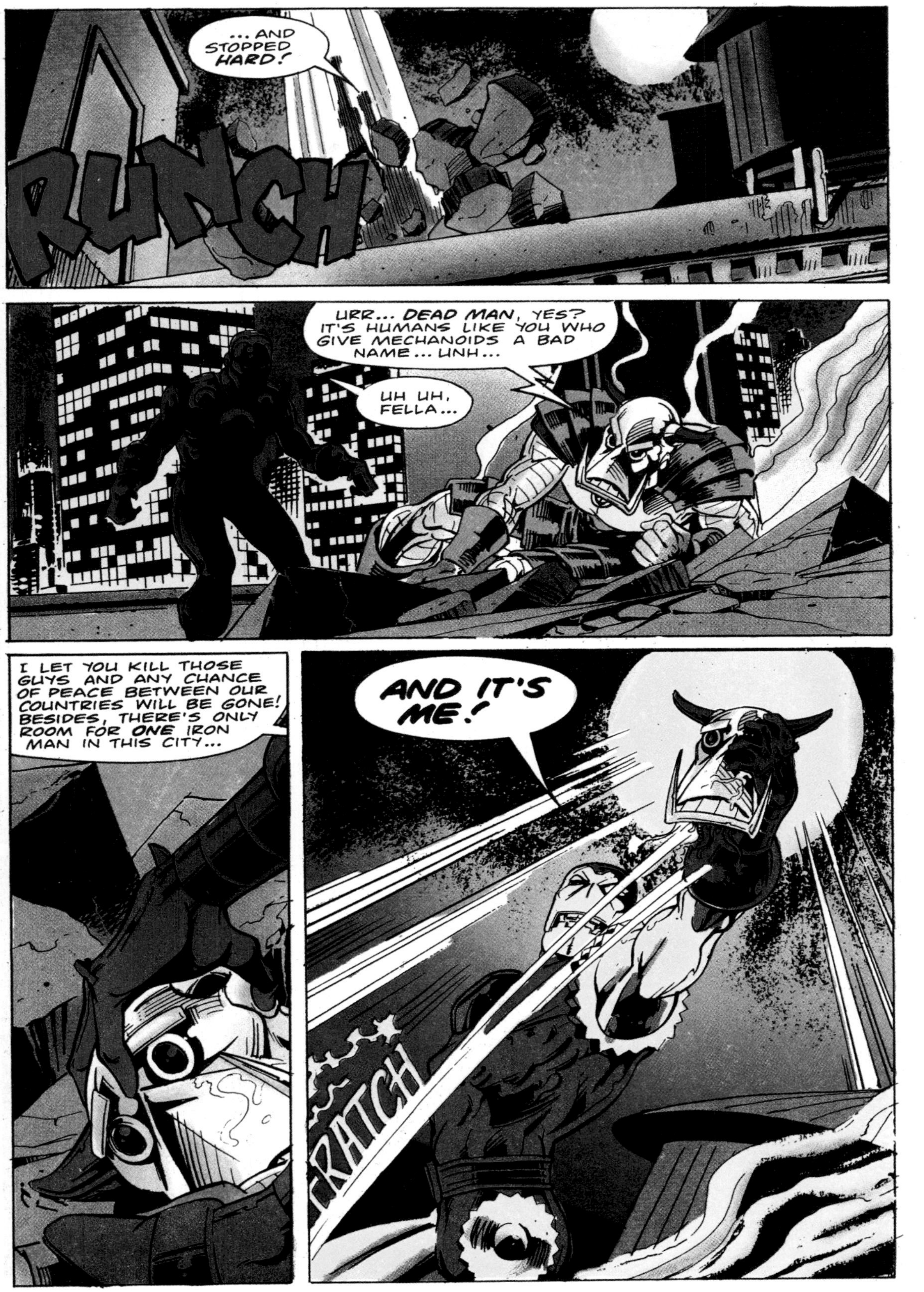
...AND STOPPED HARD!
RUNCH
URR... DEAD MAN, YES? IT'S HUMANS LIKE YOU WHO GIVE MECHANOIDS A BAD NAME... UNH...
UH UH, FELLA...
I LET YOU KILL THOSE GUYS AND ANY CHANCE OF PEACE BETWEEN OUR COUNTRIES WILL BE GONE! BESIDES, THERE'S ONLY ROOM FOR ONE IRON MAN IN THIS CITY...
AND IT'S ME!
RATCH

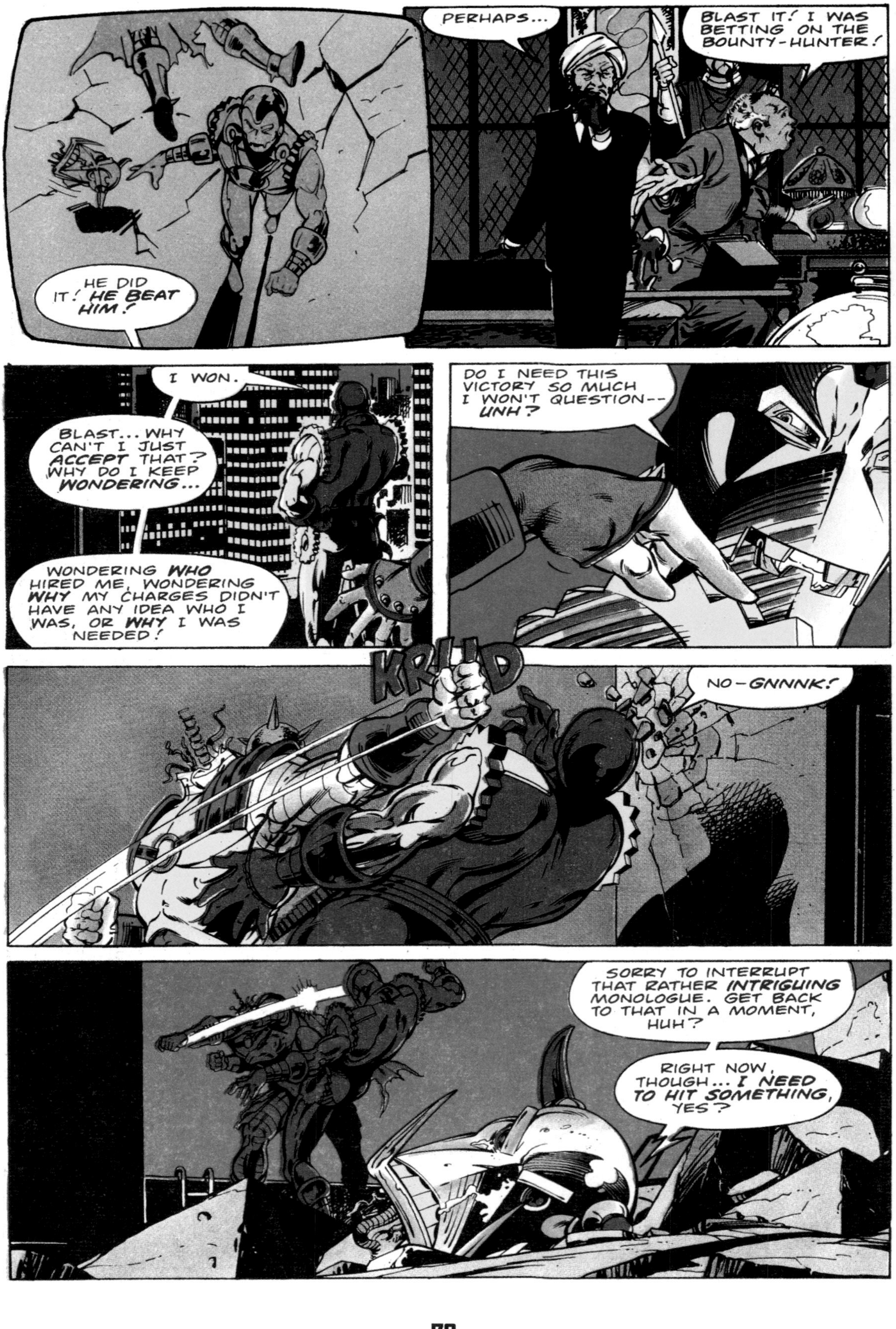
HE DID IT! HE BEAT HIM!
PERHAPS...
BLAST IT! I WAS BETTING ON THE BOUNTY-HUNTER!
I WON.
BLAST... WHY CAN'T I JUST ACCEPT THAT? WHY DO I KEEP WONDERING...
WONDERING WHO HIRED ME, WONDERING WHY MY CHARGES DIDN'T HAVE ANY IDEA WHO I WAS, OR WHY I WAS NEEDED!
DO I NEED THIS VICTORY SO MUCH I WON'T QUESTION-- UNH?
KRUD
NO-GNNNK!
SORRY TO INTERRUPT THAT RATHER INTRIGUING MONOLOGUE. GET BACK TO THAT IN A MOMENT, HUH?
RIGHT NOW, THOUGH... I NEED TO HIT SOMETHING, YES?

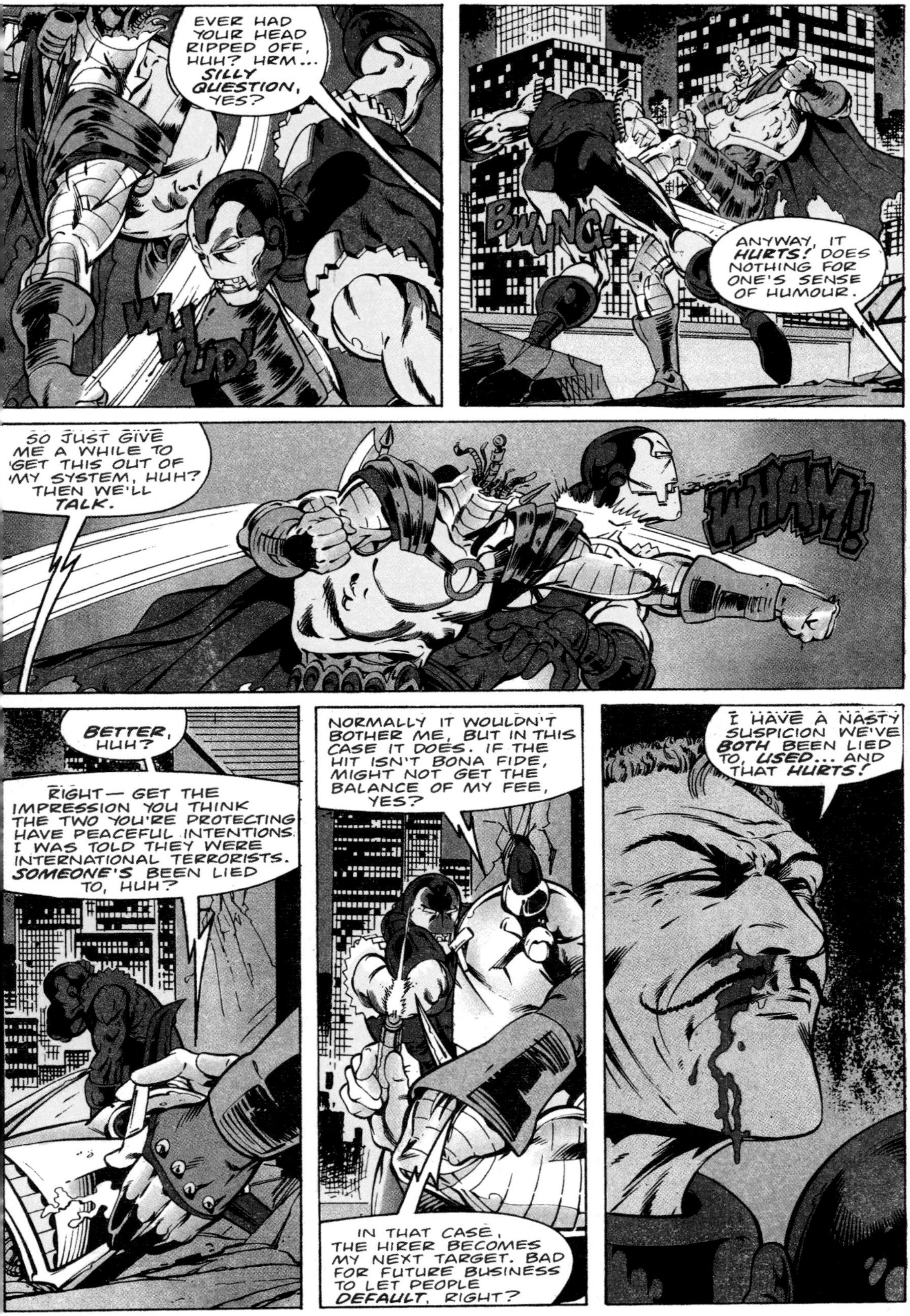
EVER HAD YOUR HEAD RIPPED OFF, HUH? HRM... SILLY QUESTION, YES?
WHUD!
BWUNG!
ANYWAY, IT HURTS! DOES NOTHING FOR ONE'S SENSE OF HUMOUR.
SO JUST GIVE ME A WHILE TO GET THIS OUT OF MY SYSTEM, HUH? THEN WE'LL TALK.
WHAM!
BETTER, HUH?
RIGHT— GET THE IMPRESSION YOU THINK THE TWO YOU'RE PROTECTING HAVE PEACEFUL INTENTIONS. I WAS TOLD THEY WERE INTERNATIONAL TERRORISTS. SOMEONE'S BEEN LIED TO, HUH?
NORMALLY IT WOULDN'T BOTHER ME, BUT IN THIS CASE IT DOES. IF THE HIT ISN'T BONA FIDE, MIGHT NOT GET THE BALANCE OF MY FEE, YES?
IN THAT CASE, THE HIRER BECOMES MY NEXT TARGET. BAD FOR FUTURE BUSINESS TO LET PEOPLE DEFAULT, RIGHT?
I HAVE A NASTY SUSPICION WE'VE BOTH BEEN LIED TO, USED... AND THAT HURTS!

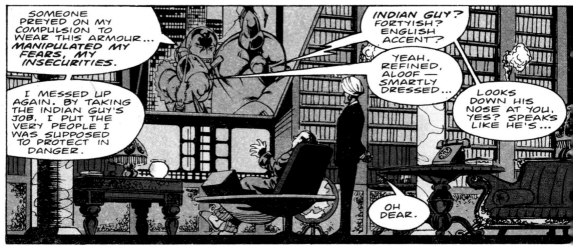

SOMEONE PREYED ON MY COMPULSION TO WEAR THIS ARMOUR... *MANIPULATED MY FEARS*, MY INSECURITIES.

INDIAN GUY? FORTYISH? ENGLISH ACCENT?

YEAH. REFINED, ALOOF — SMARTLY DRESSED...

LOOKS DOWN HIS NOSE AT YOU, YES? SPEAKS LIKE HE'S ...

I MESSED UP AGAIN. BY TAKING THE INDIAN GUY'S JOB, I PUT THE VERY PEOPLE I WAS SUPPOSED TO PROTECT IN DANGER.

OH DEAR.

IT'S THE SAME GUY. BUT *WHY?*

ATHEY — *DO* SOMETHING?

I — I...

IT'S LIKE... WE WERE SET UP TO FIGHT EACH OTHER. LIKE COMPETITORS...

...ON TV, YES? A CAMERA... SOMEWHERE. MUST BE CLOAKED. SCANNING...

ATHEY--

TOO LATE, I FEAR. THE MONITOR WASN'T BUILT FOR SPEED— JUST STEALTH.

JUDGING BY HOW EASILY THEY LOCATED IT, I IMAGINE ITS *RECEIVING SIGNAL* ...

C-CAN THEY USE IT... TO FIND US?

72

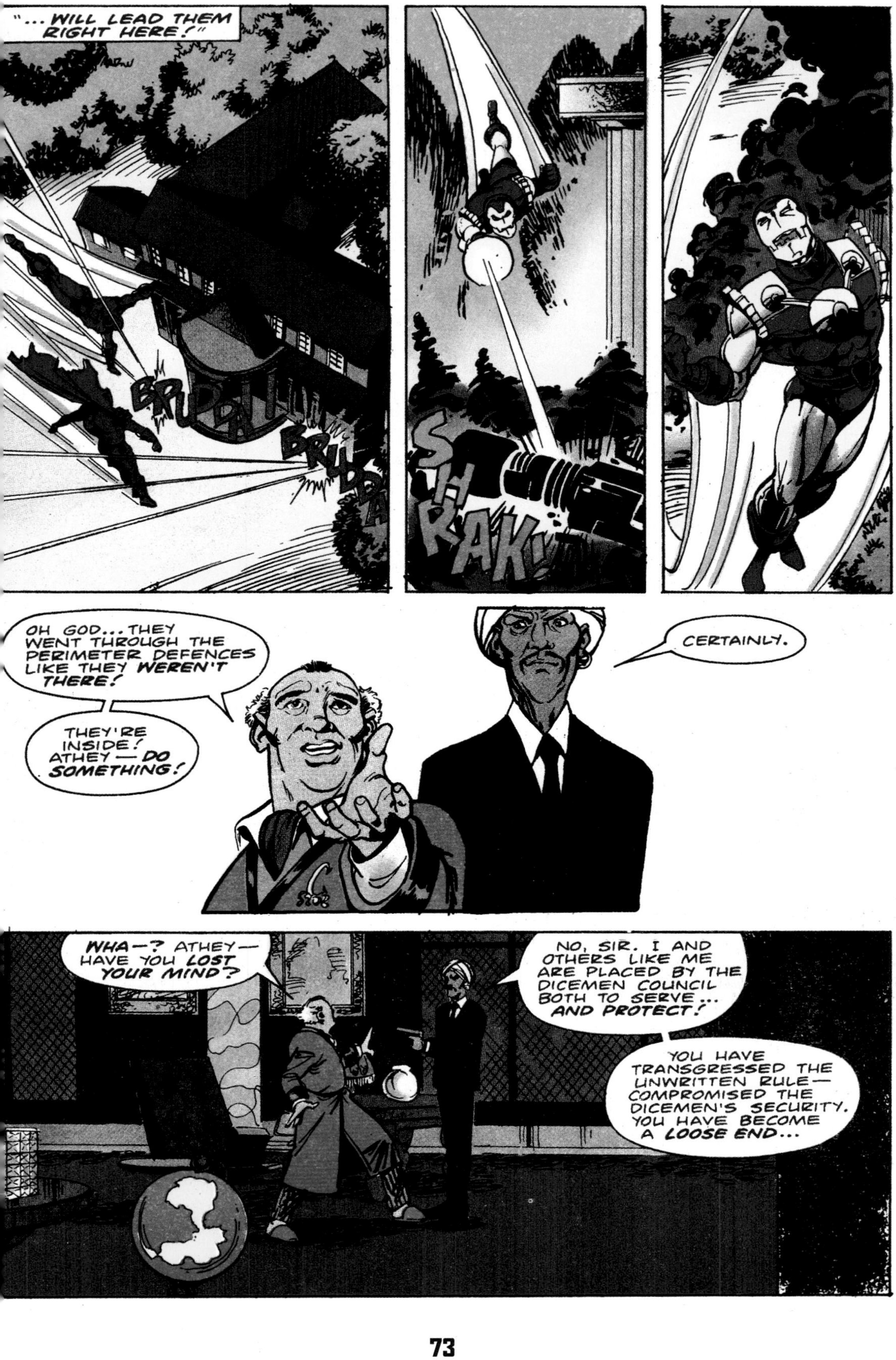
"... WILL LEAD THEM RIGHT HERE!"
BRUDDA
BRUDDA
SHHRAK!
OH GOD... THEY WENT THROUGH THE PERIMETER DEFENCES LIKE THEY WEREN'T THERE!
THEY'RE INSIDE! ATHEY — DO SOMETHING!
CERTAINLY.
WHA—? ATHEY— HAVE YOU LOST YOUR MIND?
NO, SIR. I AND OTHERS LIKE ME ARE PLACED BY THE DICEMEN COUNCIL BOTH TO SERVE... AND PROTECT!
YOU HAVE TRANSGRESSED THE UNWRITTEN RULE— COMPROMISED THE DICEMEN'S SECURITY. YOU HAVE BECOME A LOOSE END...

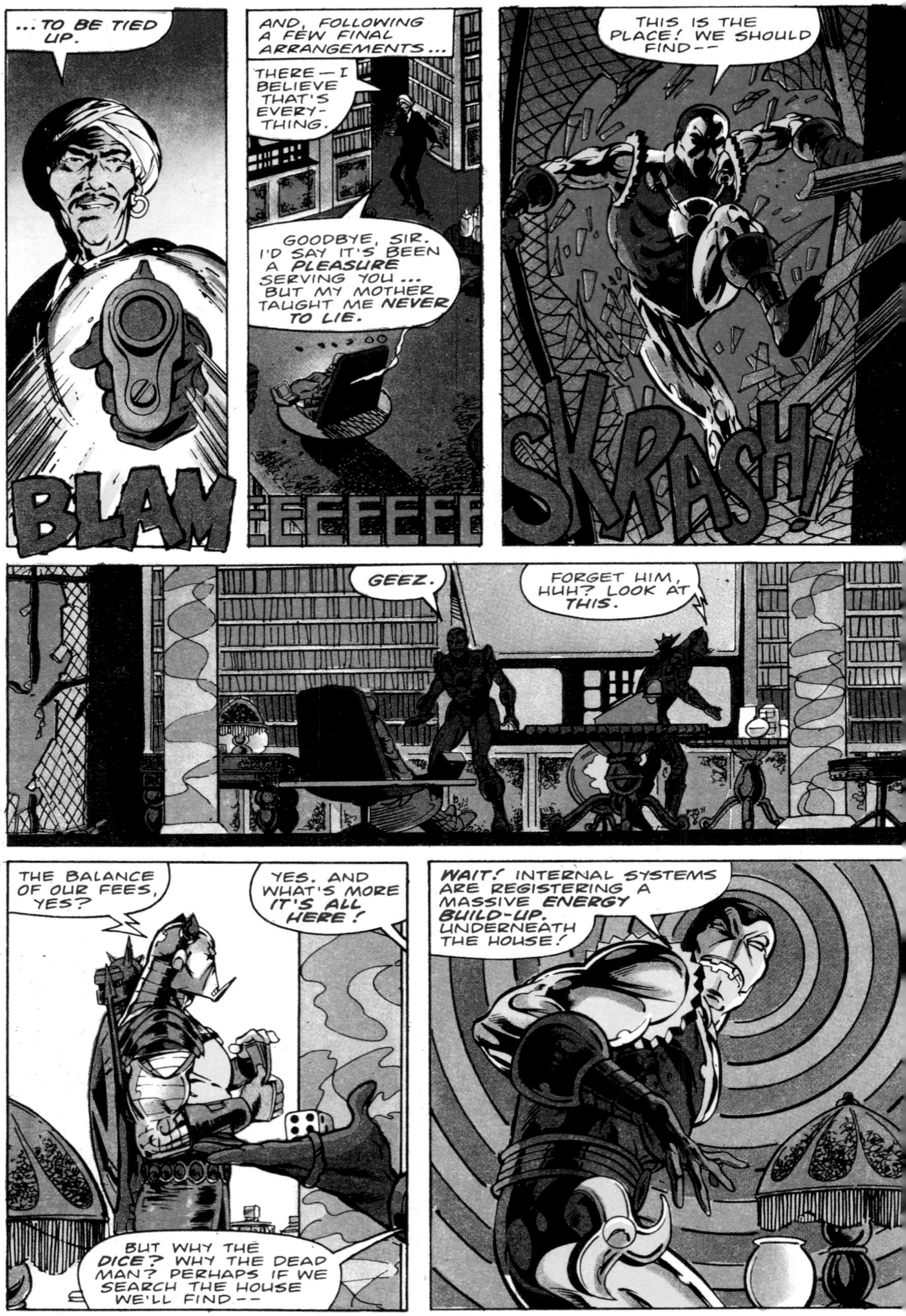

...TO BE TIED UP.
BLAM
AND, FOLLOWING A FEW FINAL ARRANGEMENTS...
THERE—I BELIEVE THAT'S EVERY-THING.
GOODBYE, SIR. I'D SAY IT'S BEEN A PLEASURE SERVING YOU... BUT MY MOTHER TAUGHT ME NEVER TO LIE.
EEEEEEE
THIS IS THE PLACE! WE SHOULD FIND--
SKRASH!
GEEZ.
FORGET HIM, HUH? LOOK AT THIS.
THE BALANCE OF OUR FEES, YES?
YES. AND WHAT'S MORE IT'S ALL HERE!
BUT WHY THE DICE? WHY THE DEAD MAN? PERHAPS IF WE SEARCH THE HOUSE WE'LL FIND--
WAIT! INTERNAL SYSTEMS ARE REGISTERING A MASSIVE ENERGY BUILD-UP. UNDERNEATH THE HOUSE!

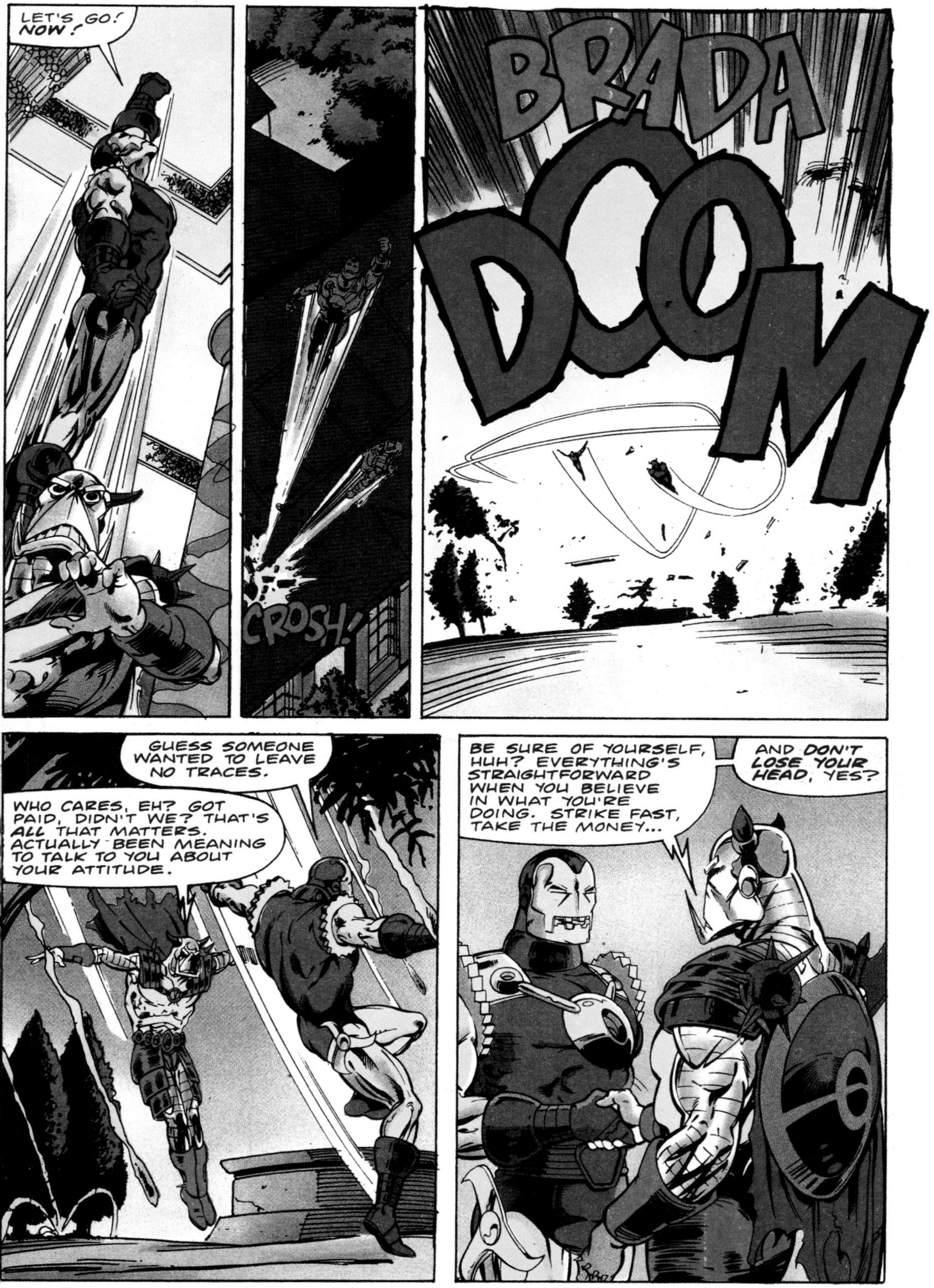
LET'S GO! NOW!
CROSH!
BRADA DOOM
GUESS SOMEONE WANTED TO LEAVE NO TRACES.
WHO CARES, EH? GOT PAID, DIDN'T WE? THAT'S ALL THAT MATTERS. ACTUALLY BEEN MEANING TO TALK TO YOU ABOUT YOUR ATTITUDE.
BE SURE OF YOURSELF, HUH? EVERYTHING'S STRAIGHTFORWARD WHEN YOU BELIEVE IN WHAT YOU'RE DOING. STRIKE FAST, TAKE THE MONEY...
AND DON'T LOSE YOUR HEAD, YES?

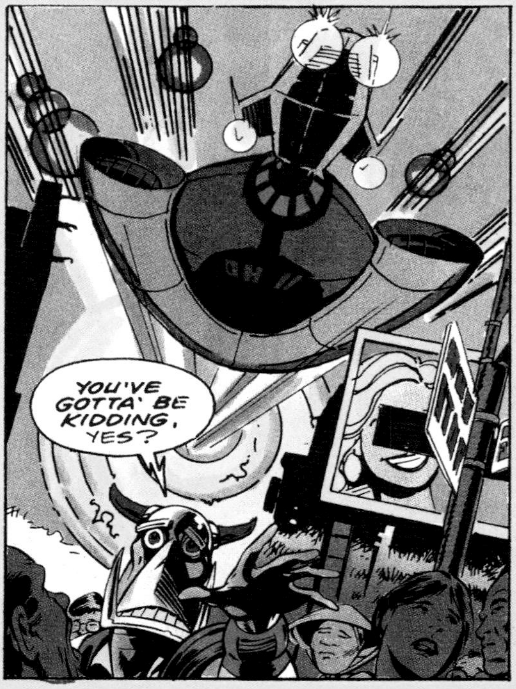
YOU'VE GOTTA' BE KIDDING, YES?

ON HIS WAY, DEATH'S HEAD WAS ***MODERATELY*** SURPRISED TO SEE HIS SPACECRAFT FLY OUT OF A DIMENSIONAL PORTAL.

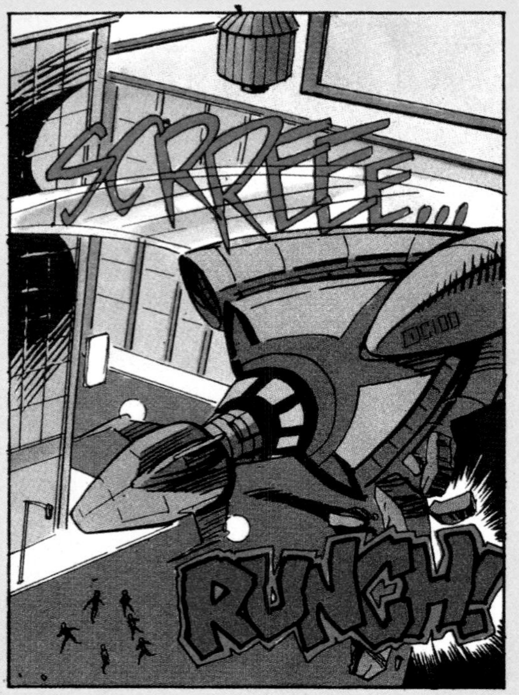
SCRREEE...
RUNCH!

HE WAS RELIEVED TO SEE THAT THE PILOT BROUGHT THE CRAFT IN FOR A GRACEFUL, CONTROLLED LANDING.

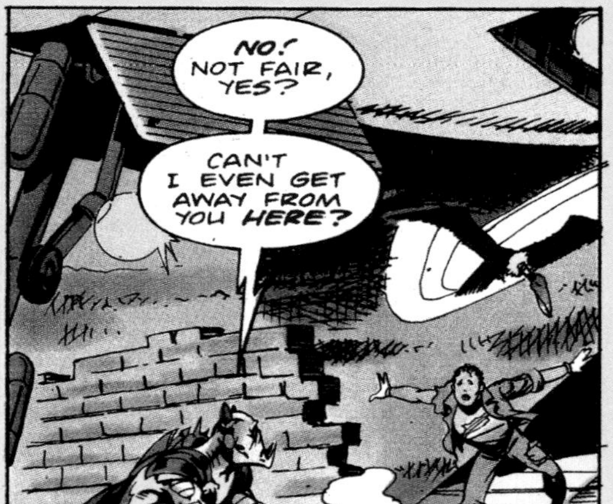
NO! NOT FAIR, YES?
CAN'T I EVEN GET AWAY FROM YOU ***HERE?***

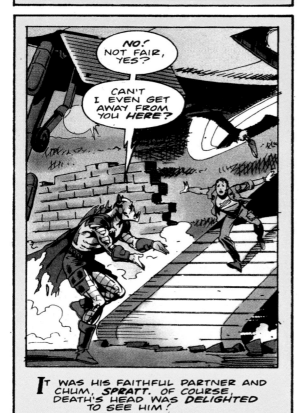

IT WAS HIS FAITHFUL PARTNER AND CHUM, ***SPRATT.*** OF COURSE, DEATH'S HEAD WAS ***DELIGHTED*** TO SEE HIM!

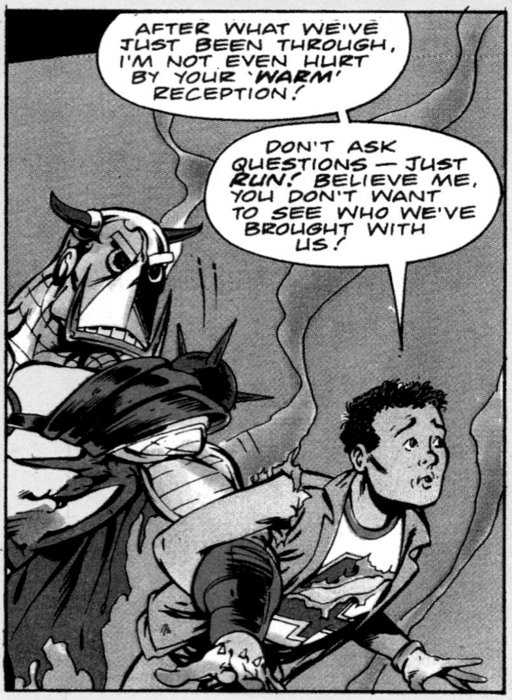
AFTER WHAT WE'VE JUST BEEN THROUGH, I'M NOT EVEN HURT BY YOUR '***WARM***' RECEPTION!
DON'T ASK QUESTIONS — JUST ***RUN!*** BELIEVE ME, YOU DON'T WANT TO SEE WHO WE'VE BROUGHT WITH US!

THERE WAS JUST SO MUCH FOR THE CHUMS TO TALK ABOUT, THAT IN THEIR HASTE TO BE AWAY, THEY FORGOT THEIR ***OTHER*** FRIEND...

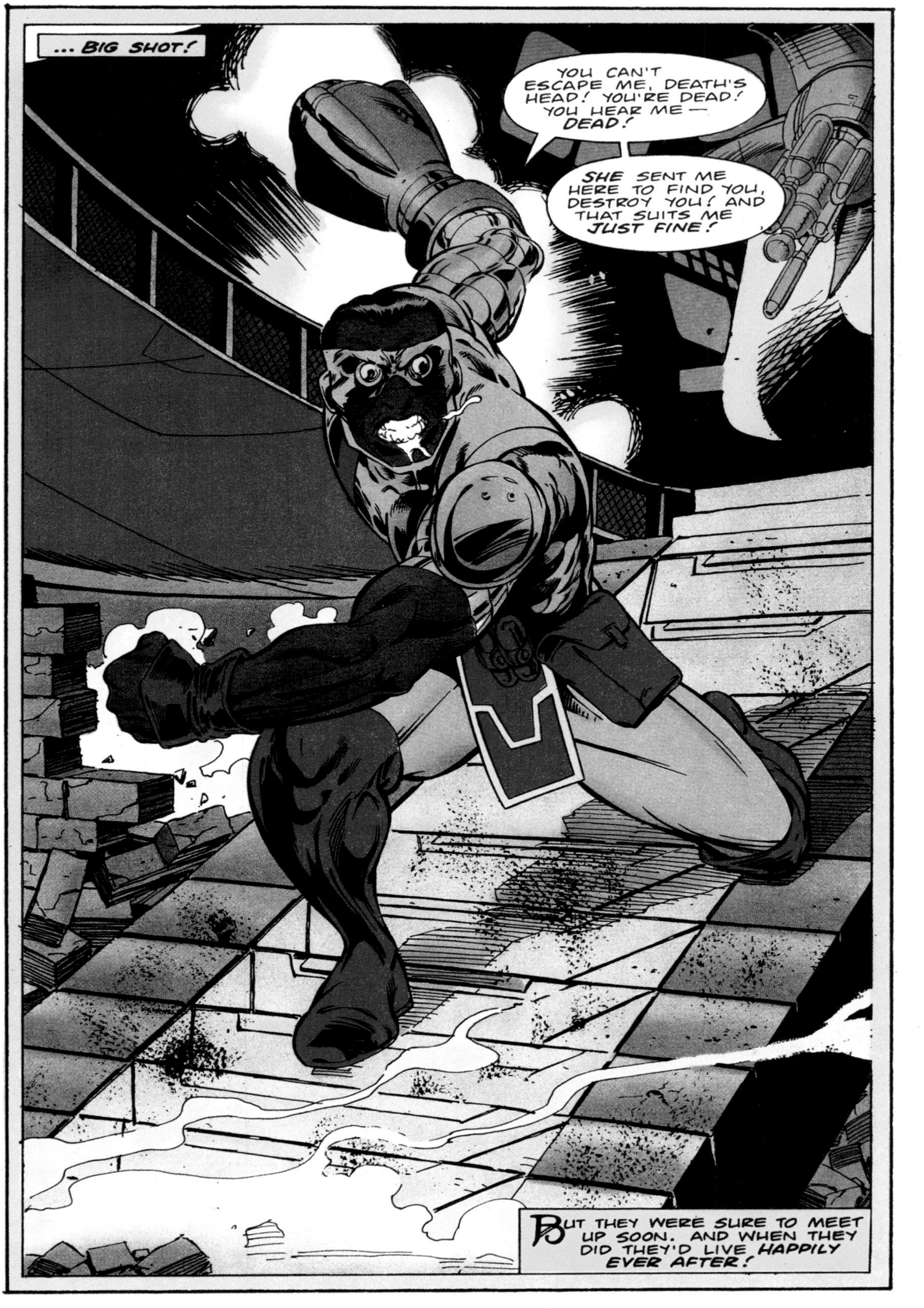
... BIG SHOT!
YOU CAN'T ESCAPE ME, DEATH'S HEAD! YOU'RE DEAD! YOU HEAR ME — DEAD!
SHE SENT ME HERE TO FIND YOU, DESTROY YOU! AND THAT SUITS ME JUST FINE!
BUT THEY WERE SURE TO MEET UP SOON. AND WHEN THEY DID THEY'D LIVE HAPPILY EVER AFTER!

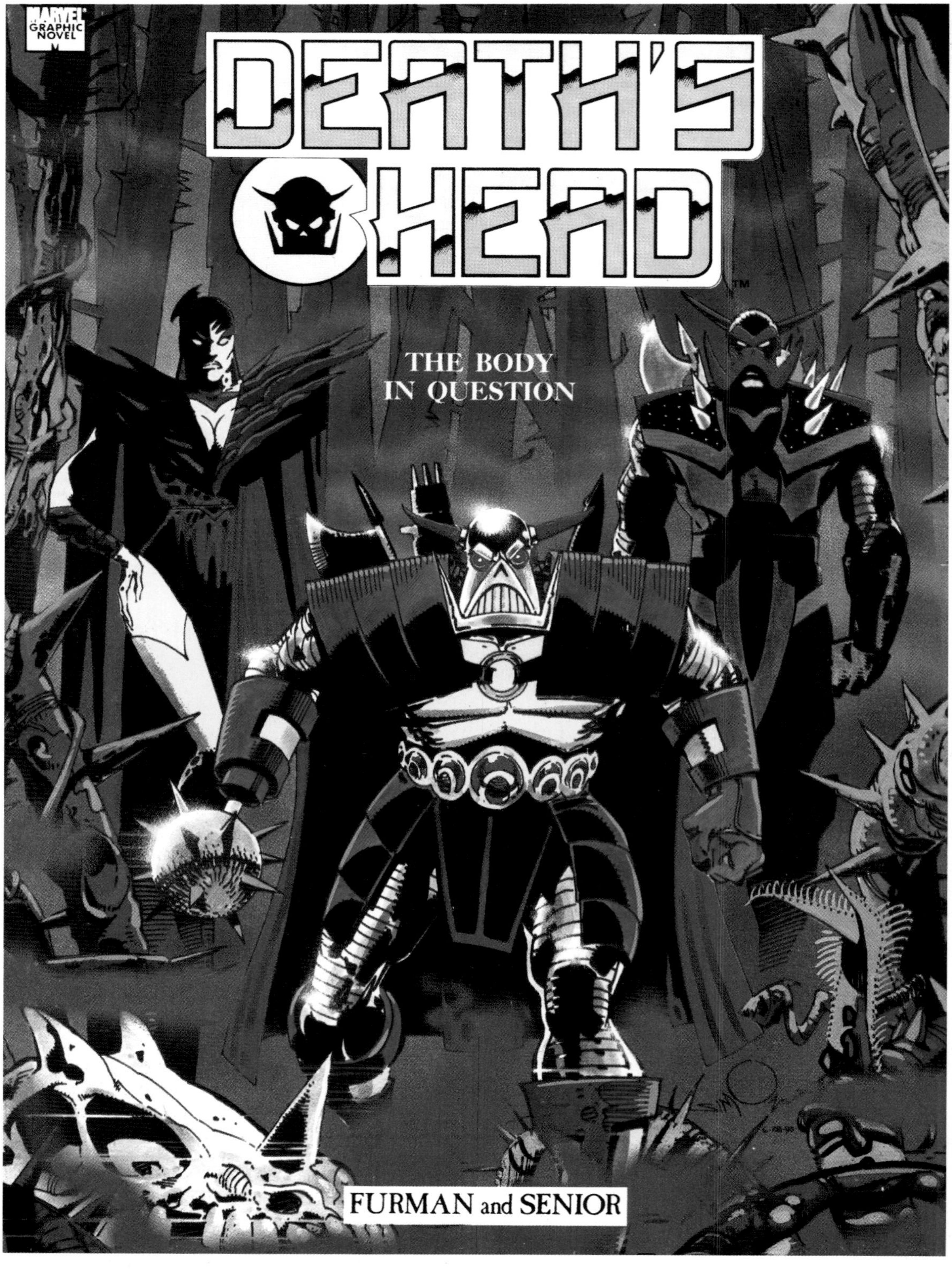
MARVEL GRAPHIC NOVEL
DEATH'S HEAD
TM
THE BODY IN QUESTION
FURMAN and SENIOR

HEAD TO HEAD ... AN INTRODUCTION

by **Irwin Micklethwaite Poster**

I was on the way to one of the most bizarre interviews I've ever conducted! Not only was I to meet and talk to comic book writer, **Simon Furman,** I was actually going to meet – in person (if you can describe it that way!) – his greatest creation . . . **DEATH'S HEAD!**

You're sceptical. Well, to be honest, so was I. But, on entering a modest and comfortable house on the outskirts of Carlisle, I was greeted by (on the one hand) 5′10″ of bearded human and (on the other hand) 6′10″ of sinewed steel mechanoid. This was going to be no ordinary after-tea chat – that, at least was, certain!

IMP: Simon, perhaps you can start us off by explaining how Death's Head came about. Cheese and kippers just before bedtime, perhaps?

DH: Watch it, yes?

SF: Well, we needed a bounty-hunting –

DH: Freelance Peacekeeping.

SF: Ah ha. Yes. We needed a freelance peacekeeping character for a story in Marvel UK's TRANSFORMERS comic – a disposable one we could conveniently bump off at the end.

DH: – should let Death's Head answer this, right? Right? No – one – least of all him – gave me a personality. It was just there, eh? I only kill for profit, never for sport or revenge. I always see a job through and I play no favourites. If they pay, I'll slay, yes?

IMP: But what about this habit of yours of making every statement a question?

DH: I don't do that, huh?

IMP: Right. Anyway, Simon – how about giving us a brief rundown of Death's Head appearances to date.

SF: After his third appearance in TRANSFORMERS, Death's Head went (via a bridging story in DOCTOR WHO MAGAZINE) into issue #5 of DRAGON'S CLAWS. From there it was straight into his own series, which ran for ten issues.

IMP: And now into a Graphic Novel, right?

DH: Strange habit you've got – ending statements with questions.

SF: Yes, yes – that's right. THE BODY IN QUESTION is due out in September. It's 59 pages, written by me and painted by Geoff, with a cover by Walt Simonson.

IMP: And it deals with the origin of Death's Head – who created him and why.

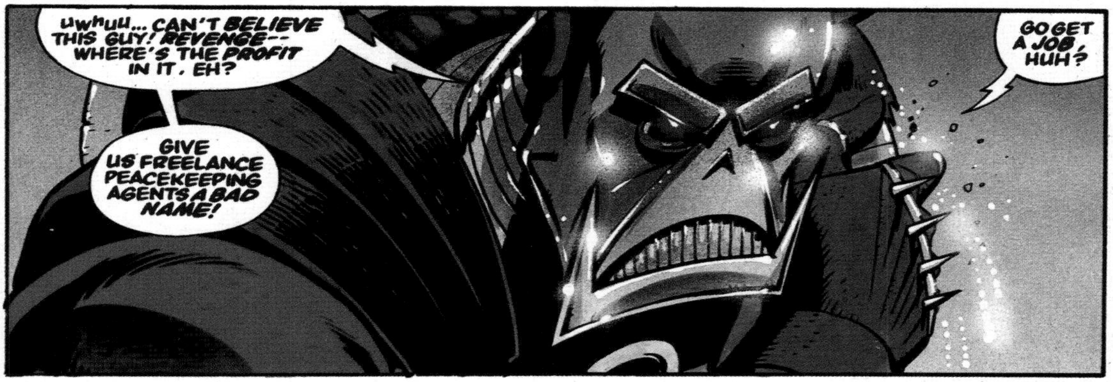

UWHUU... CAN'T BELIEVE THIS GUY! REVENGE-- WHERE'S THE PROFIT IN IT, EH?
GIVE US FREELANCE PEACEKEEPING AGENTS A BAD NAME!
GO GET A JOB, HUH?

DH: Charming, yes?

SF: Only Geoff Senior's character sketches were so . . . inspiring, I decided there and then that Death's Head was destined for greater things.

DH: It took you that long?

(SF clears his throat noisily)

SF: As I was saying, we decided Death's Head was destined for greater things, so I fleshed out the character and – while Geoff was busy with the TRANSFORMERS/DEATH'S HEAD storyline – prepared an introductory one-page story that Bryan Hitch then drew.

IMP: But what about the character himself – his mannerisms and outlook on life?

SF: Well I –

SF: Yep. You could say he actually meets his maker.

(laughter)

IMP: Which, if you think about it, is what he's doing now!

(more laughter)

DH: Look, think I should take over here, yes? When I *allowed* this person to be my biographer, I made it clear that it was to be done carefully, *respectfully.* Understand? In fact, there are one or two things in the graphic novel I'd like to take issue with, huh?

IMP: I'm sure there'll be time for that later. Simon, you mentioned Walt Simonson earlier. There's quite a bit of interest been shown in Death's Head in the States, hasn't there?

SF: That's right, Irwin. Simonson himself featured

LET THE MECHANOID GO AND *STAYAWAY!* YOU'RE UNDER ARREST!

Death's Head in issue #338 of FANTASTIC FOUR, and – in addition to an 8-page story in MARVEL COMICS PRESENTS – he's scheduled to appear in SHE-HULK #24, drawn by former Death's Head artist, Bryan Hitch.

DH: It's the scenes where he shows me being beaten up, huh? Just didn't happen that way!

IMP: I'm sure the readers would like to know a bit about you and Geoff, Simon – how you started, what you've been working on recently.

DH: I mean, do you see any bits missing, eh? Both horns are still here, all my weaponry, armour's intact!

SF: Let's see, I started scripting about six years ago, for a comic called SCREAM. After that I moved to Marvel UK, working editorially and scripting for the likes of TRANSFORMERS, ACTION FORCE and THUNDERCATS. Since then I've gone from DRAGON'S CLAWS to DEATH'S HEAD and am currently working on TRANSFORMERS and BRUTE FORCE (for Marvel US).

DH: Really, as if that Big Shot could actually harm me! He's just a human with a gun! And as for Lupex –

SF: Geoff started off working for Marvel UK, beginning on good old TRANSFORMERS. From there, the prolific Mr. Senior went on to do hundreds of pages, spanning TRANSFORMERS, THUNDERCATS, ACTION FORCE and DOCTOR WHO MAGAZINE. He drew the whole 10-issue run of DRAGON'S CLAWS and has done four issues of Marvel US's TRANSFORMERS.

DH: Hello? Is anyone listening to me, huh?

IMP: But Geoff always seemed to come back to Death's Head, huh?

DH: You're doing it again!

SF: Yeah, that's right. Both Geoff and I share a sort of paternal affection for the character, and we're always looking for opportunities to work together on him.

DH: Look. I've been very patient, yes? Will you listen to me now!

IMP: So where next? Where do you, Geoff and Death's Head go from here?

(Death's Head unlocks his right hand)

SF: Hopefully into a new limited series.

(Death's Head selects his axe attachment and locks it into place)

SF: I'm sure there's life in the old dog yet!

(Furman playfully thumps Death's Head on the back)

SHHHHLLK!

IMP: Oh god! I thought you only killed for profit.

DH: I make the odd exceptions, yes?

At this point, with Death's Head enquiring about a new biographer, I chose to make my discreet exit. The serialisation of THE BODY IN QUESTION begins right here, and the graphic novel comes out in September. Read it at your peril . . !

The Body In Question is by:

Simon Furman
writer

Geoff Senior
artist

Helen Stone
lettering

Steve White
story editor

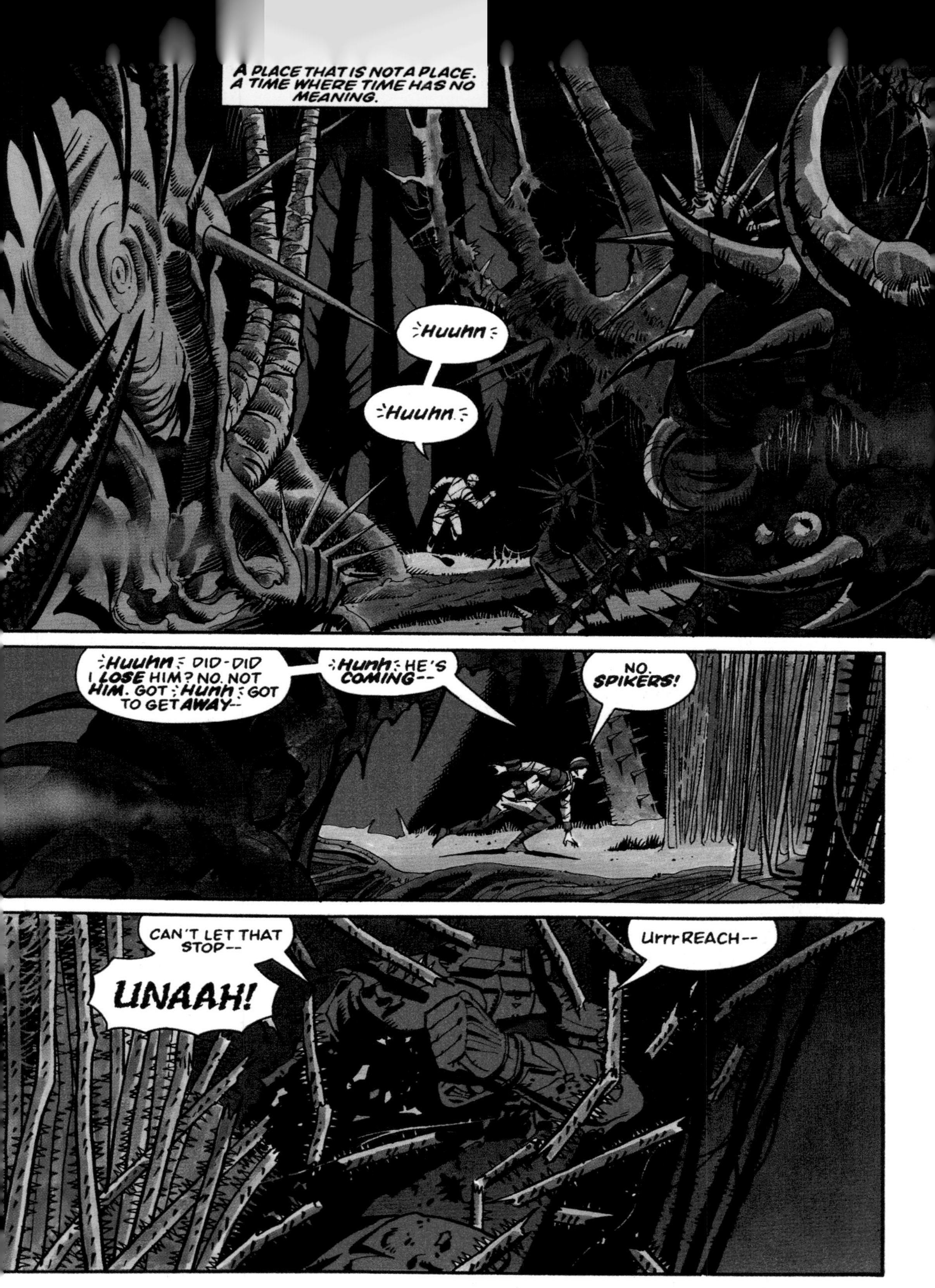
A PLACE THAT IS NOT A PLACE. A TIME WHERE TIME HAS NO MEANING.
Huuhn
Huuhn
Huuhn DID-DID I LOSE HIM? NO. NOT HIM. GOT Hunh GOT TO GET AWAY--
Hunh HE'S COMING--
NO. SPIKERS!
CAN'T LET THAT STOP--
UNAAH!
Urrr REACH--

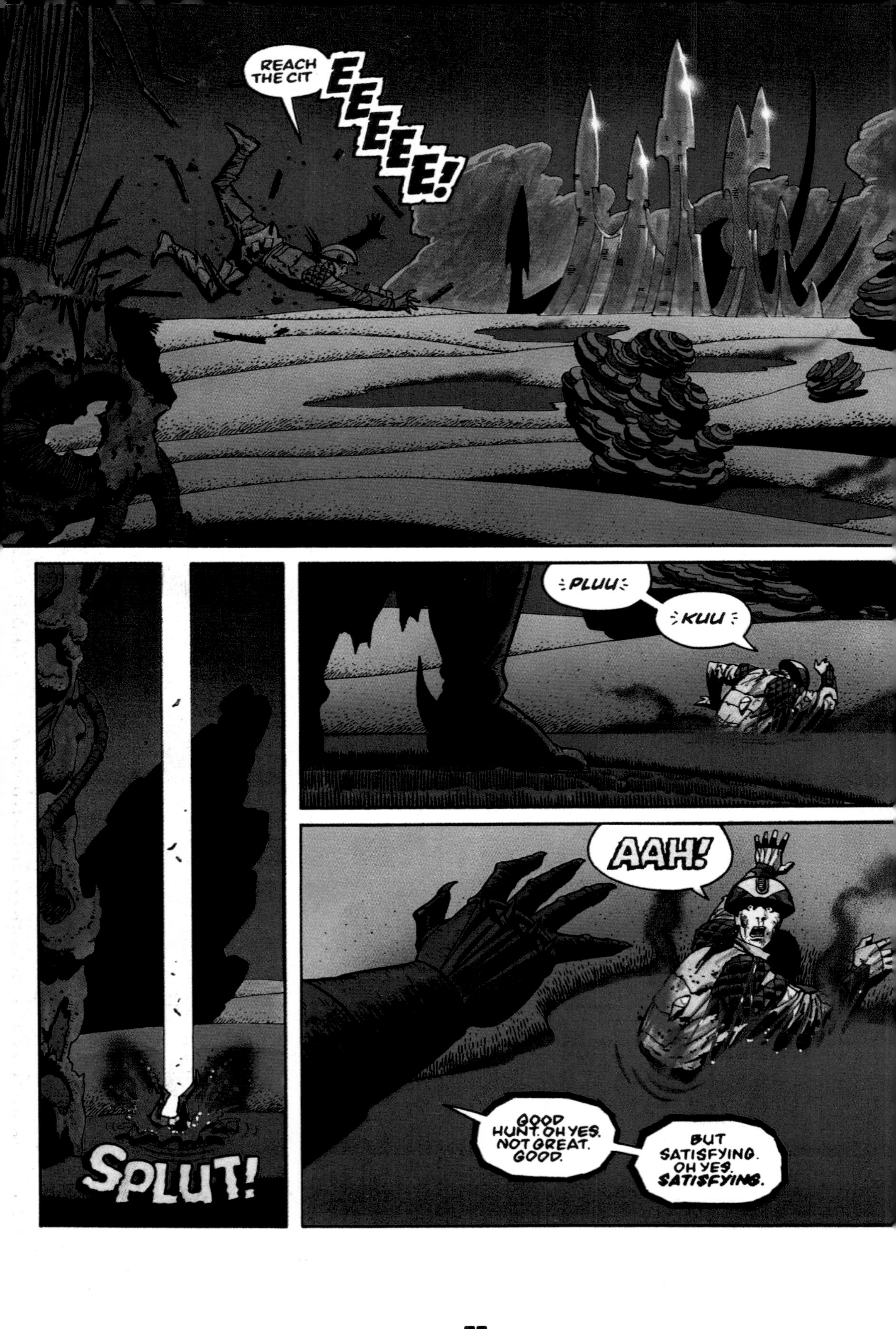
REACH THE CIT
EEEEE!
SPLUT!
PLUU
KUU
AAH!
GOOD HUNT. OH YES. NOT GREAT. GOOD.
BUT SATISFYING. OH YES. SATISFYING.

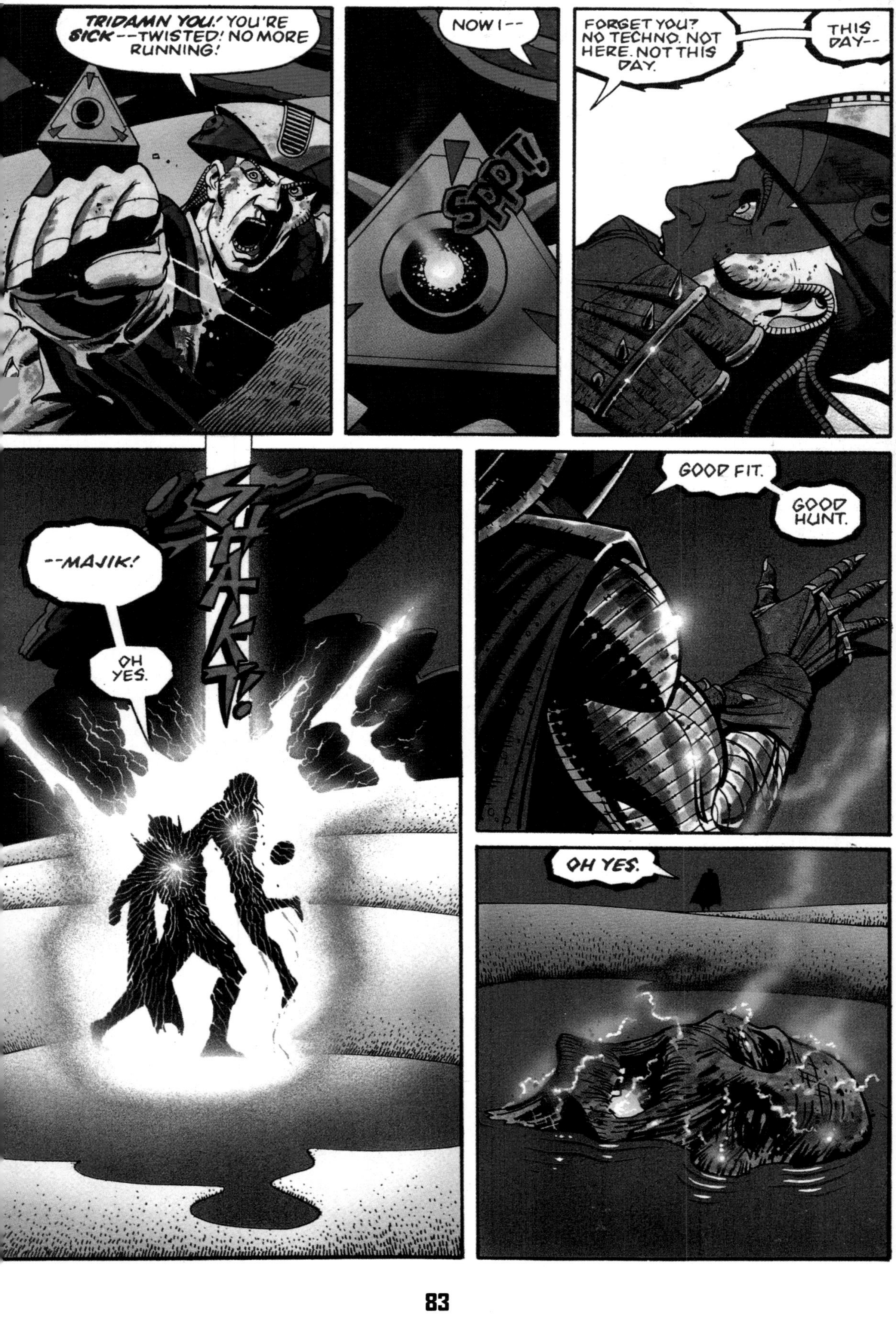
TRIDAMN YOU! YOU'RE SICK--TWISTED! NO MORE RUNNING!
NOW I--
SPPT!
FORGET YOU? NO TECHNO. NOT HERE. NOT THIS DAY.
THIS DAY--
--MAJIK!
OH YES.
SHAKT!
GOOD FIT.
GOOD HUNT.
OH YES.

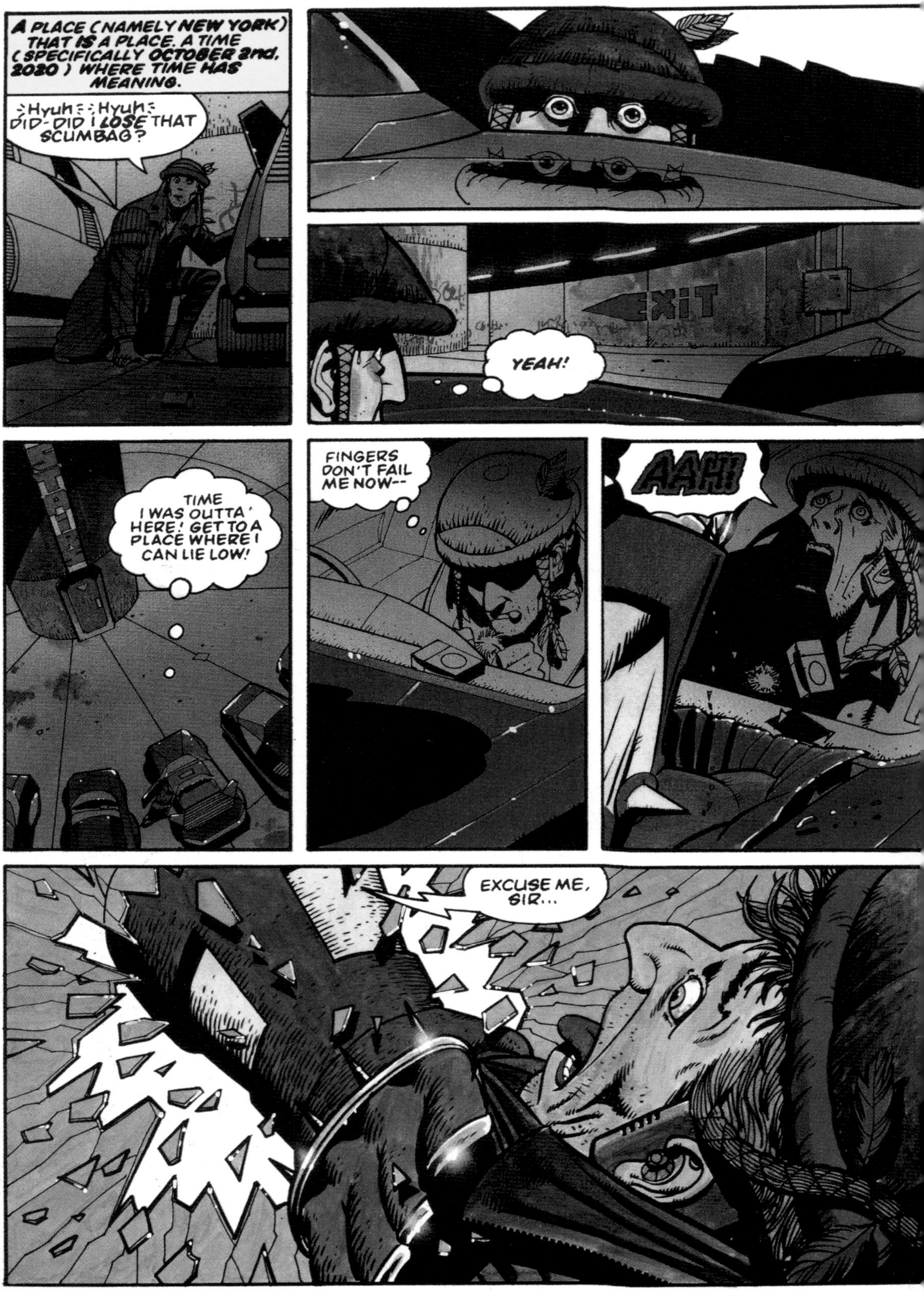
A PLACE (NAMELY NEW YORK) THAT IS A PLACE. A TIME (SPECIFICALLY OCTOBER 2nd, 2030) WHERE TIME HAS MEANING.
Hyuh Hyuh DID-DID I LOSE THAT SCUMBAG?
EXIT
YEAH!
TIME I WAS OUTTA' HERE! GET TO A PLACE WHERE I CAN LIE LOW!
FINGERS DON'T FAIL ME NOW--
AAH!
EXCUSE ME, SIR...

BOOK ONE
HUNTERS

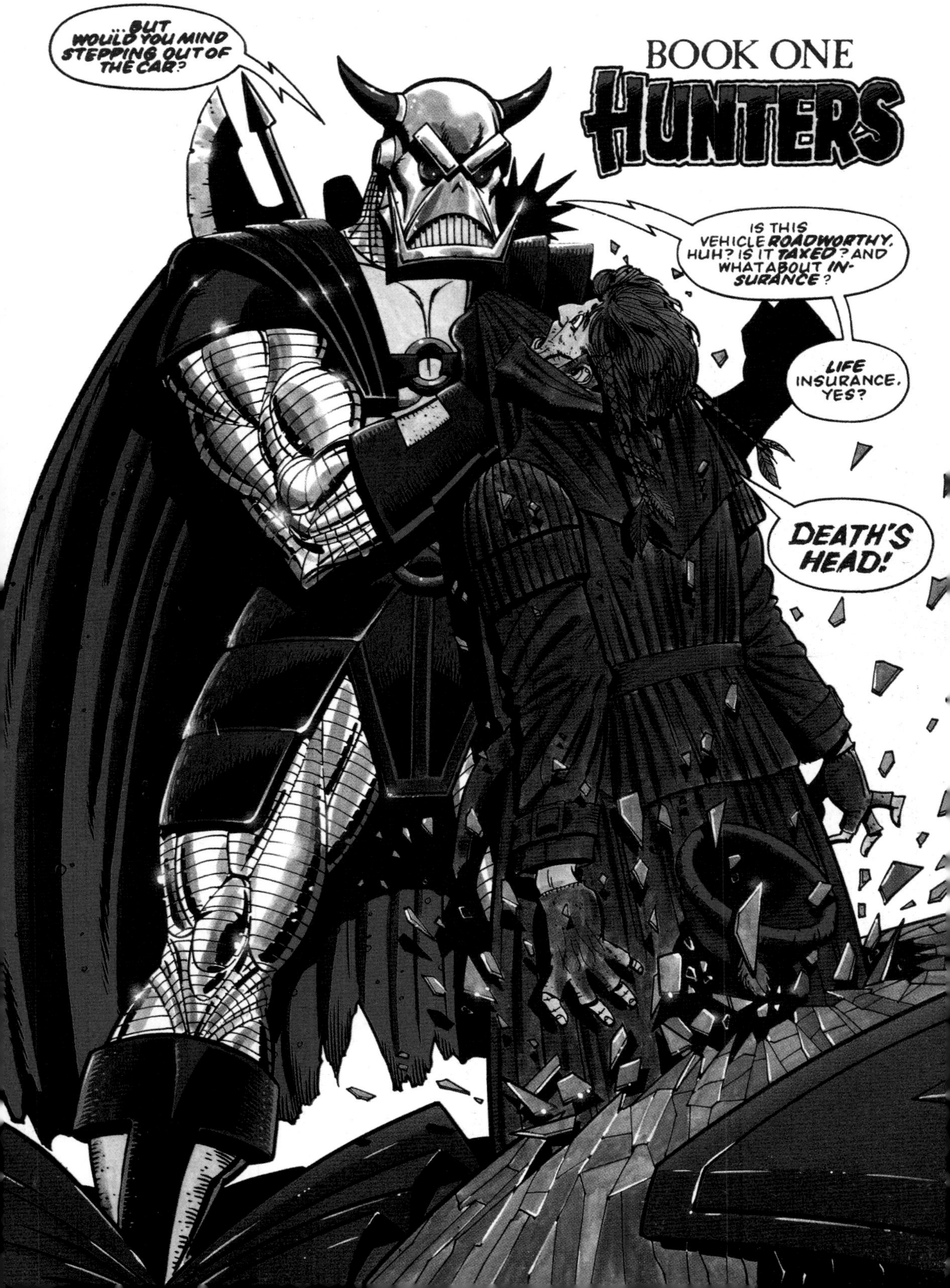

...BUT WOULD YOU MIND STEPPING OUT OF THE CAR?
IS THIS VEHICLE ROADWORTHY, HUH? IS IT TAXED? AND WHAT ABOUT INSURANCE?
LIFE INSURANCE. YES?
DEATH'S HEAD!

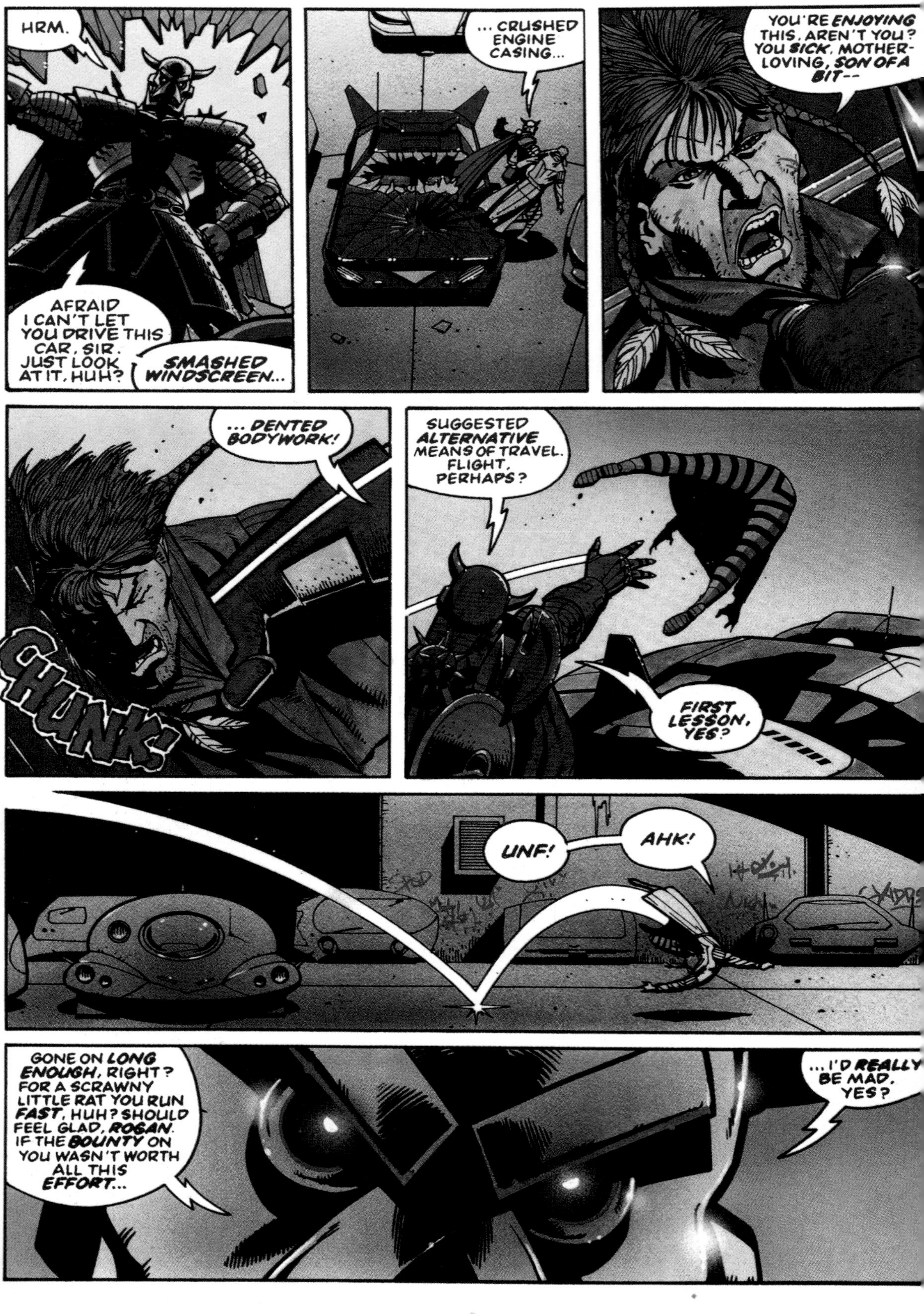
HRM.
AFRAID I CAN'T LET YOU DRIVE THIS CAR, SIR. JUST LOOK AT IT, HUH?
SMASHED WINDSCREEN...
... CRUSHED ENGINE CASING...
YOU'RE ENJOYING THIS, AREN'T YOU? YOU SICK, MOTHER-LOVING, SON OF A BIT--
... DENTED BODYWORK!
CHUNK!
SUGGESTED ALTERNATIVE MEANS OF TRAVEL. FLIGHT, PERHAPS?
FIRST LESSON, YES?
UNF!
AHK!
GONE ON LONG ENOUGH, RIGHT? FOR A SCRAWNY LITTLE RAT YOU RUN FAST, HUH? SHOULD FEEL GLAD, ROSAN. IF THE BOUNTY ON YOU WASN'T WORTH ALL THIS EFFORT...
... I'D REALLY BE MAD, YES?

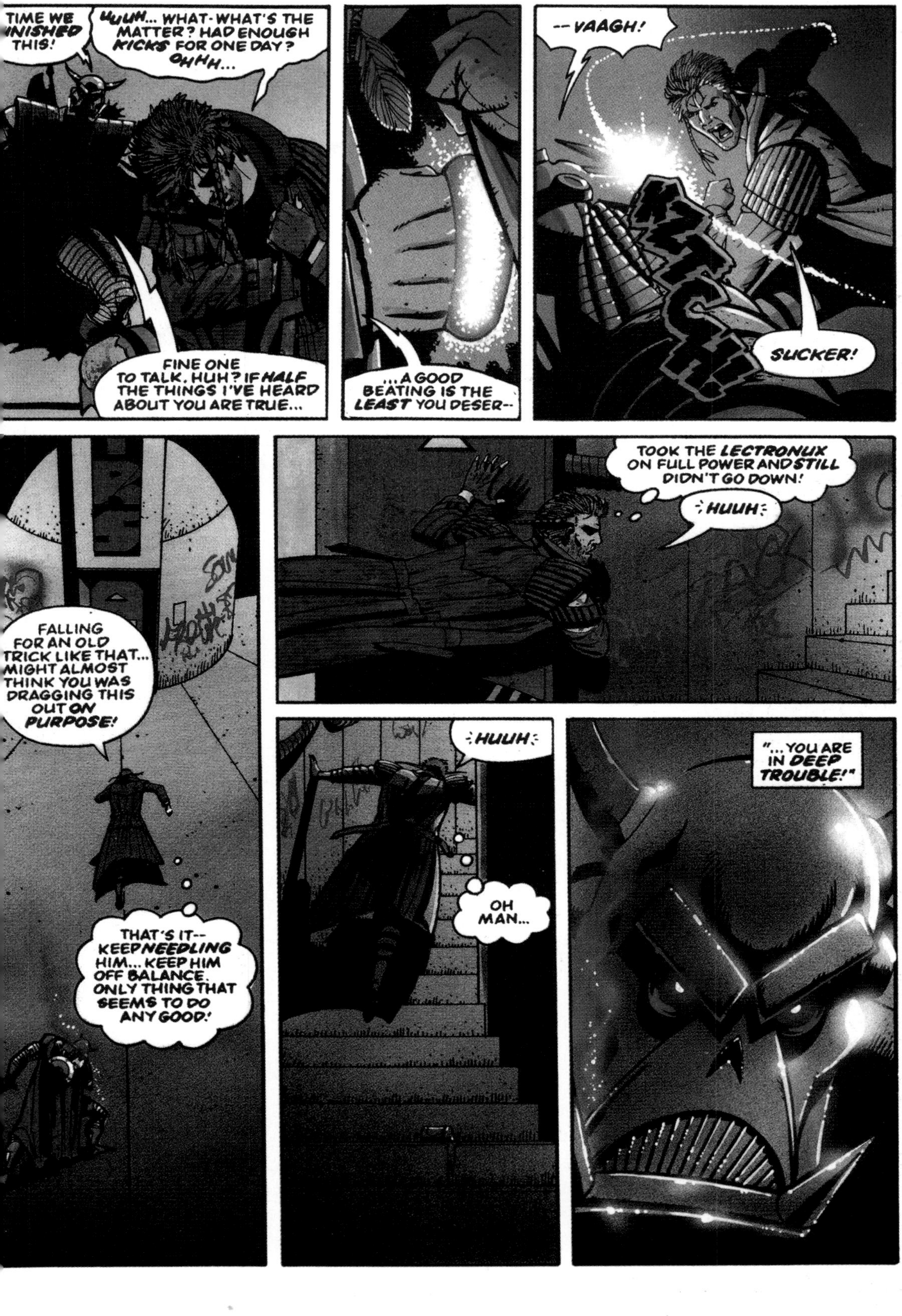
TIME WE FINISHED THIS!
UUUH... WHAT-WHAT'S THE MATTER? HAD ENOUGH KICKS FOR ONE DAY? OHHH...
FINE ONE TO TALK. HUH? IF HALF THE THINGS I'VE HEARD ABOUT YOU ARE TRUE...
...A GOOD BEATING IS THE LEAST YOU DESER--
--VAAGH!
KZZSH
SUCKER!
TOOK THE LECTRONUX ON FULL POWER AND STILL DIDN'T GO DOWN!
HUUH
FALLING FOR AN OLD TRICK LIKE THAT... MIGHT ALMOST THINK YOU WAS DRAGGING THIS OUT ON PURPOSE!
THAT'S IT-- KEEP NEEDLING HIM... KEEP HIM OFF BALANCE. ONLY THING THAT SEEMS TO DO ANY GOOD!
HUUH
OH MAN...
"...YOU ARE IN DEEP TROUBLE!"

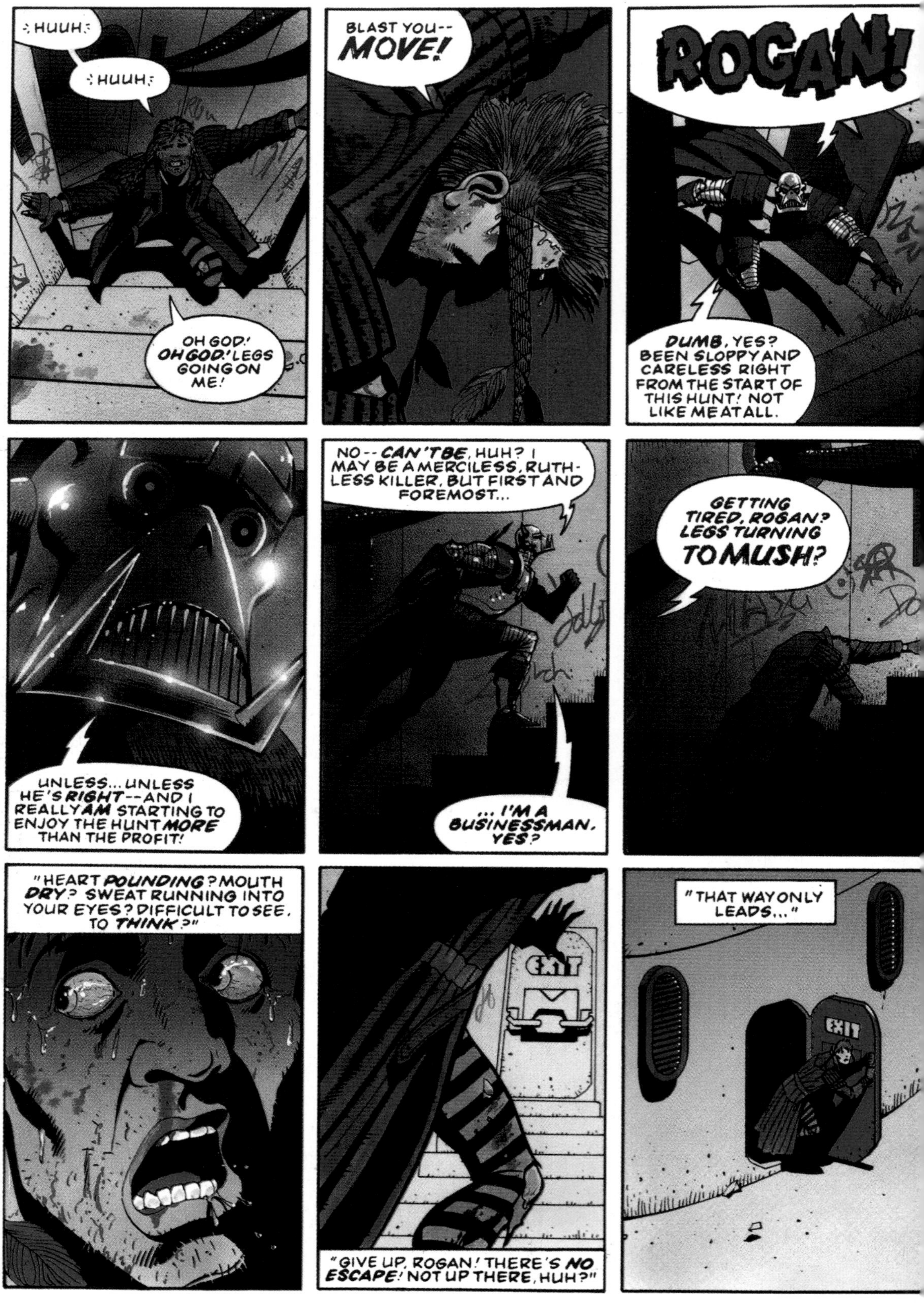
HUUH
HUUH
OH GOD! OH GOD! LEGS GOING ON ME!
BLAST YOU-- MOVE!
ROGAN!
DUMB, YES? BEEN SLOPPY AND CARELESS RIGHT FROM THE START OF THIS HUNT! NOT LIKE ME AT ALL.
UNLESS... UNLESS HE'S RIGHT--AND I REALLY AM STARTING TO ENJOY THE HUNT MORE THAN THE PROFIT!
NO-- CAN'T BE, HUH? I MAY BE A MERCILESS, RUTHLESS KILLER, BUT FIRST AND FOREMOST...
... I'M A BUSINESSMAN, YES?
GETTING TIRED, ROGAN? LEGS TURNING TO MUSH?
"HEART POUNDING? MOUTH DRY? SWEAT RUNNING INTO YOUR EYES? DIFFICULT TO SEE, TO THINK?"
EXIT
"GIVE UP, ROGAN! THERE'S NO ESCAPE! NOT UP THERE, HUH?"
"THAT WAY ONLY LEADS..."
EXIT

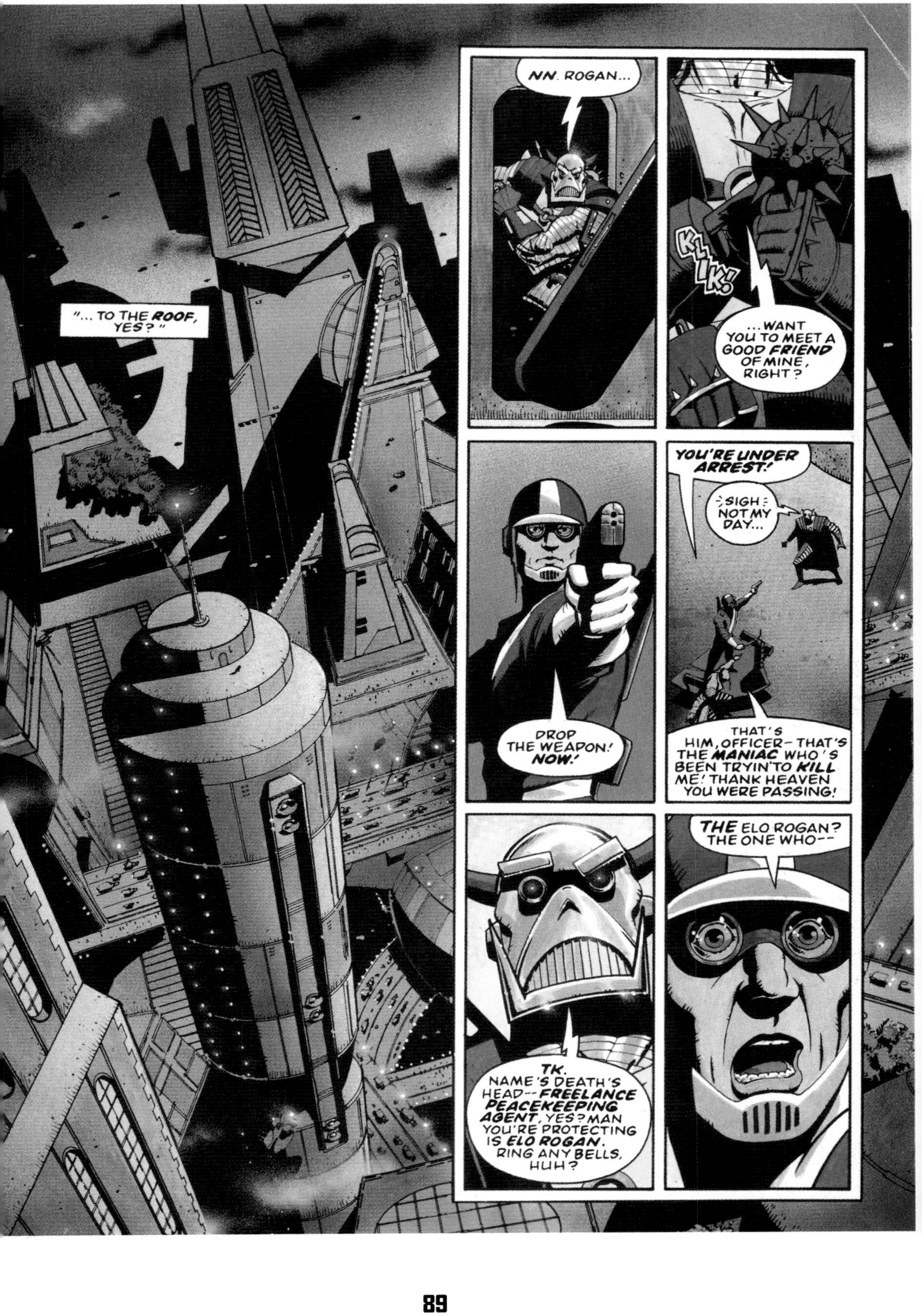
"... TO THE ROOF, YES?"
NN. ROGAN...
KLIK!
...WANT YOU TO MEET A GOOD FRIEND OF MINE, RIGHT?
DROP THE WEAPON! NOW!
YOU'RE UNDER ARREST!
SIGH NOT MY DAY...
THAT'S HIM, OFFICER-- THAT'S THE MANIAC WHO'S BEEN TRYIN' TO KILL ME! THANK HEAVEN YOU WERE PASSING!
TK. NAME'S DEATH'S HEAD-- FREELANCE PEACEKEEPING AGENT, YES? MAN YOU'RE PROTECTING IS ELO ROGAN. RING ANY BELLS, HUH?
THE ELO ROGAN? THE ONE WHO--

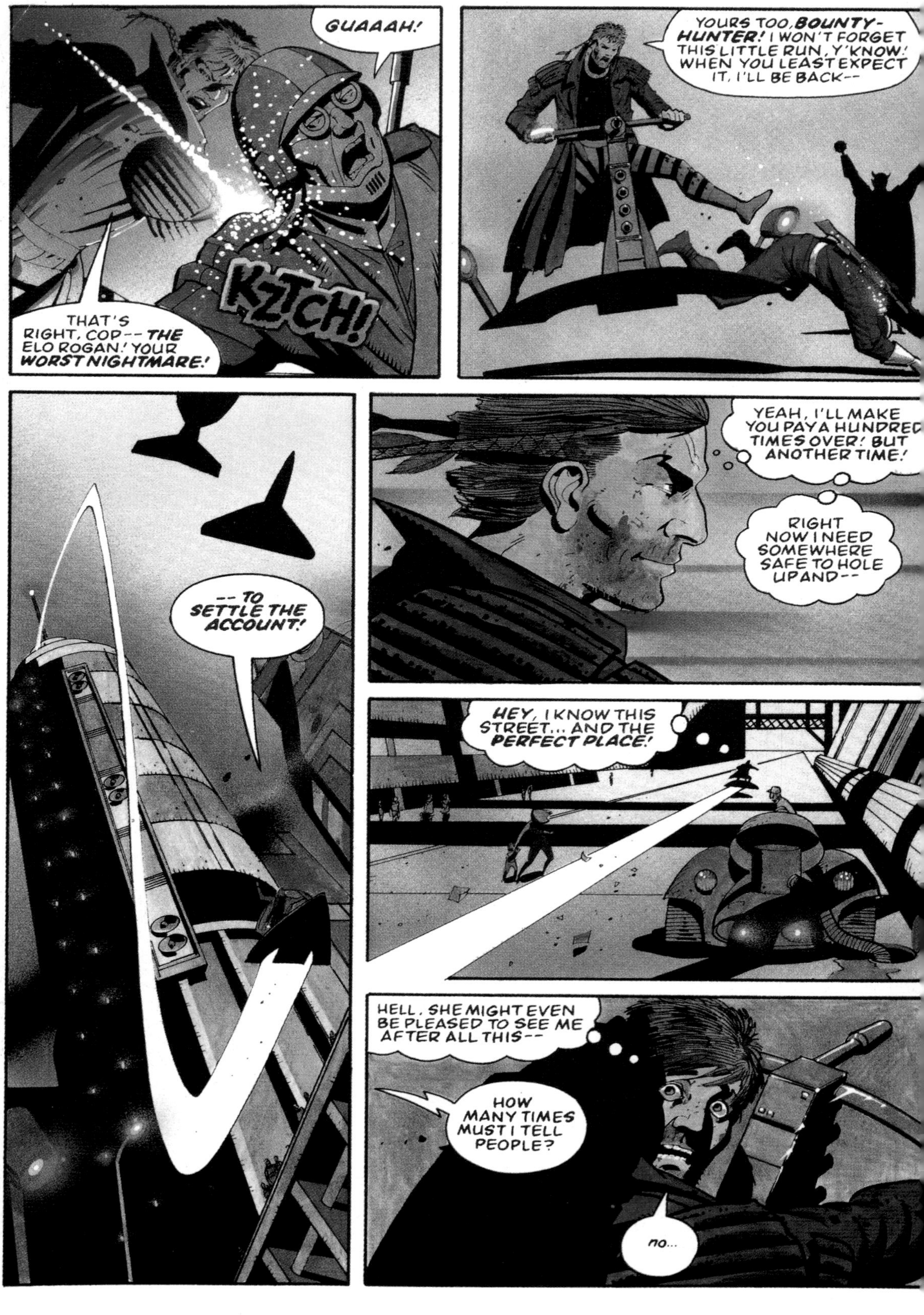
GUAAAH!
KZTCH!
THAT'S RIGHT, COP-- THE ELO ROGAN! YOUR WORST NIGHTMARE!
YOURS TOO, BOUNTY-HUNTER! I WON'T FORGET THIS LITTLE RUN, Y'KNOW! WHEN YOU LEAST EXPECT IT, I'LL BE BACK--
-- TO SETTLE THE ACCOUNT!
YEAH, I'LL MAKE YOU PAY A HUNDRED TIMES OVER! BUT ANOTHER TIME!
RIGHT NOW I NEED SOMEWHERE SAFE TO HOLE UP AND--
HEY, I KNOW THIS STREET... AND THE PERFECT PLACE!
HELL, SHE MIGHT EVEN BE PLEASED TO SEE ME AFTER ALL THIS--
HOW MANY TIMES MUST I TELL PEOPLE?
no...

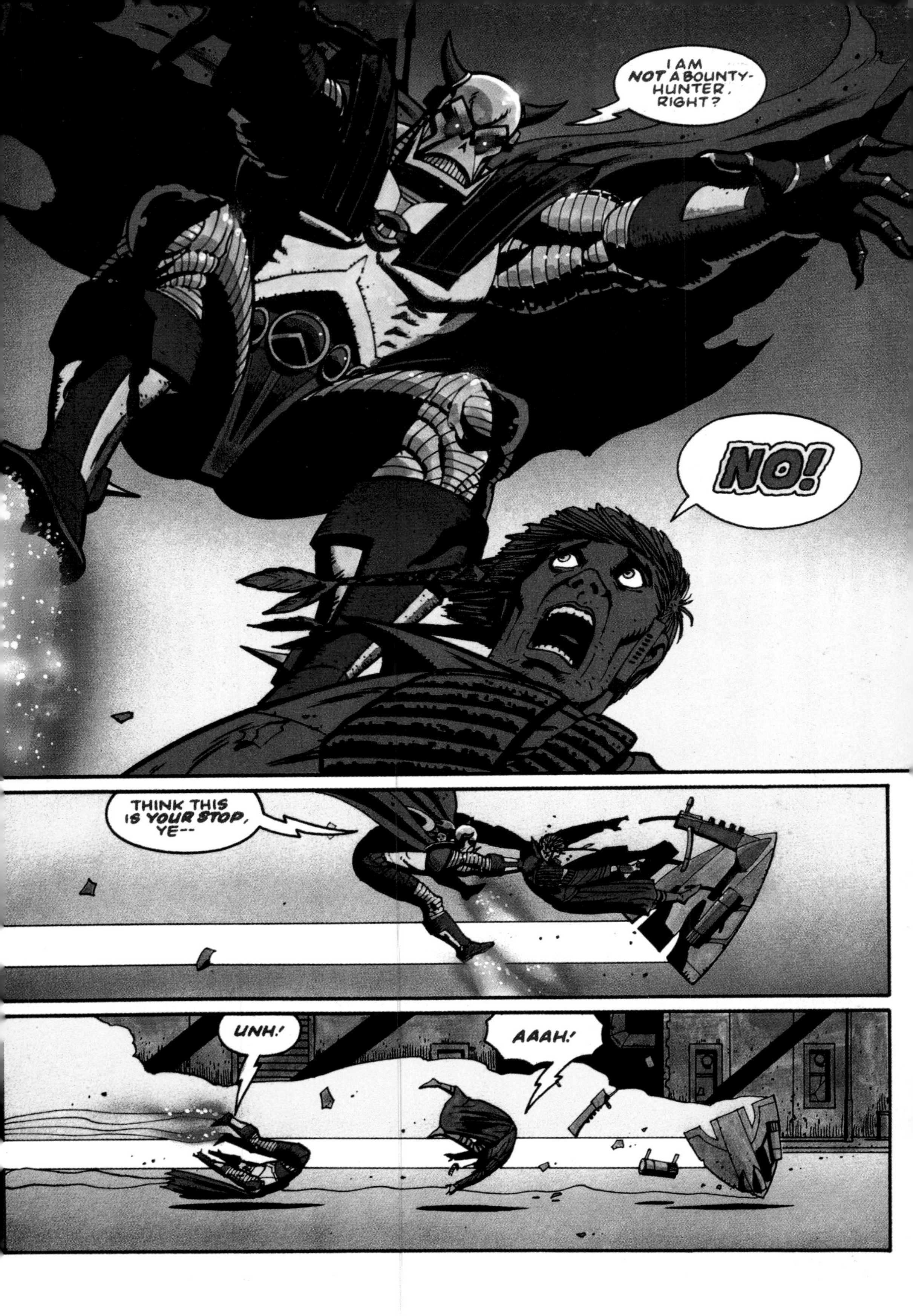
I AM NOT A BOUNTY-HUNTER, RIGHT?
NO!
THINK THIS IS YOUR STOP, YE--
UNH!
AAAH!

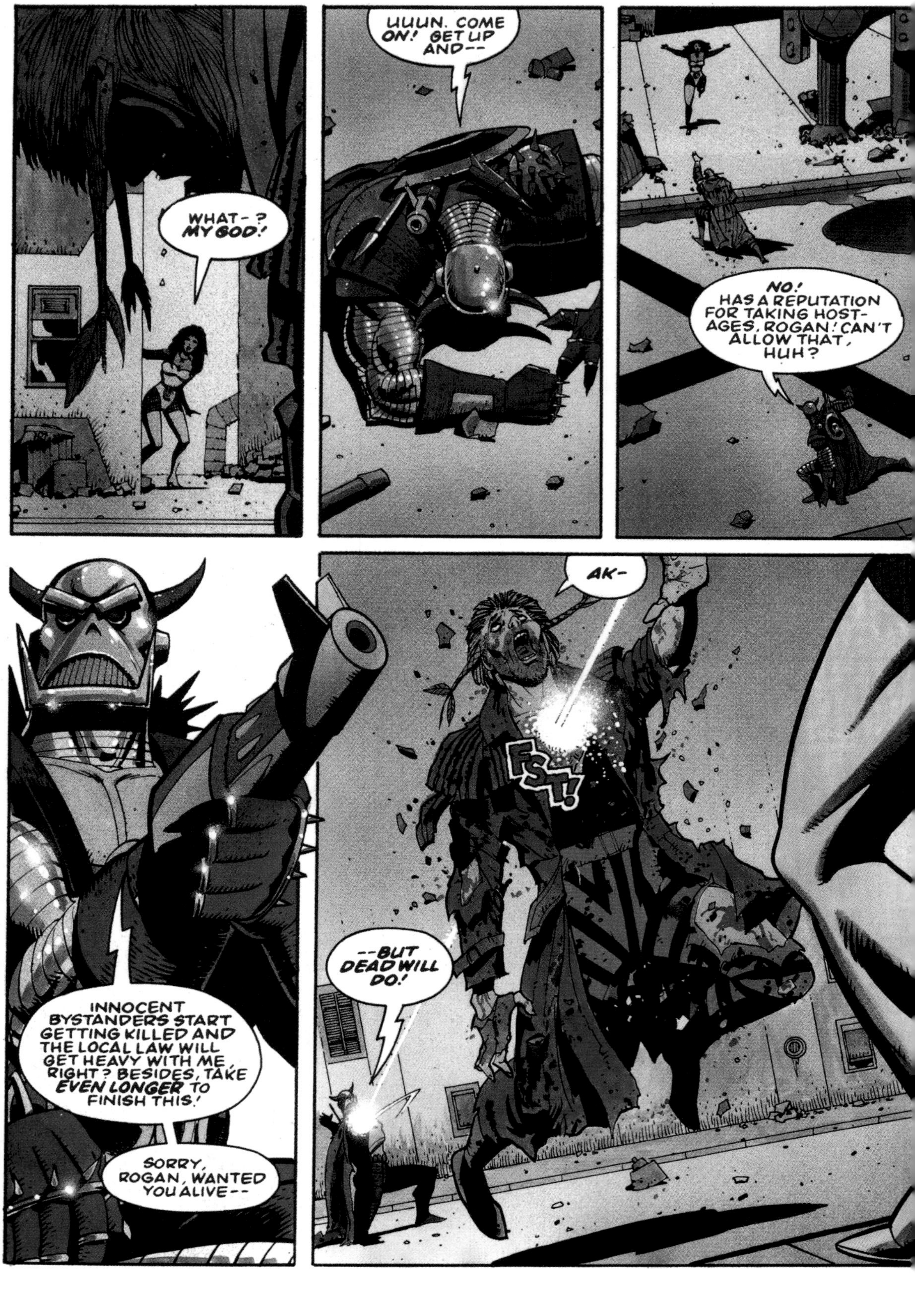
WHAT-? MY GOD!
UUUN. COME ON! GET UP AND--
NO! HAS A REPUTATION FOR TAKING HOST-AGES, ROGAN! CAN'T ALLOW THAT, HUH?
INNOCENT BYSTANDERS START GETTING KILLED AND THE LOCAL LAW WILL GET HEAVY WITH ME, RIGHT? BESIDES, TAKE EVEN LONGER TO FINISH THIS!
SORRY, ROGAN, WANTED YOU ALIVE--
AK-
FSST!
--BUT DEAD WILL DO!

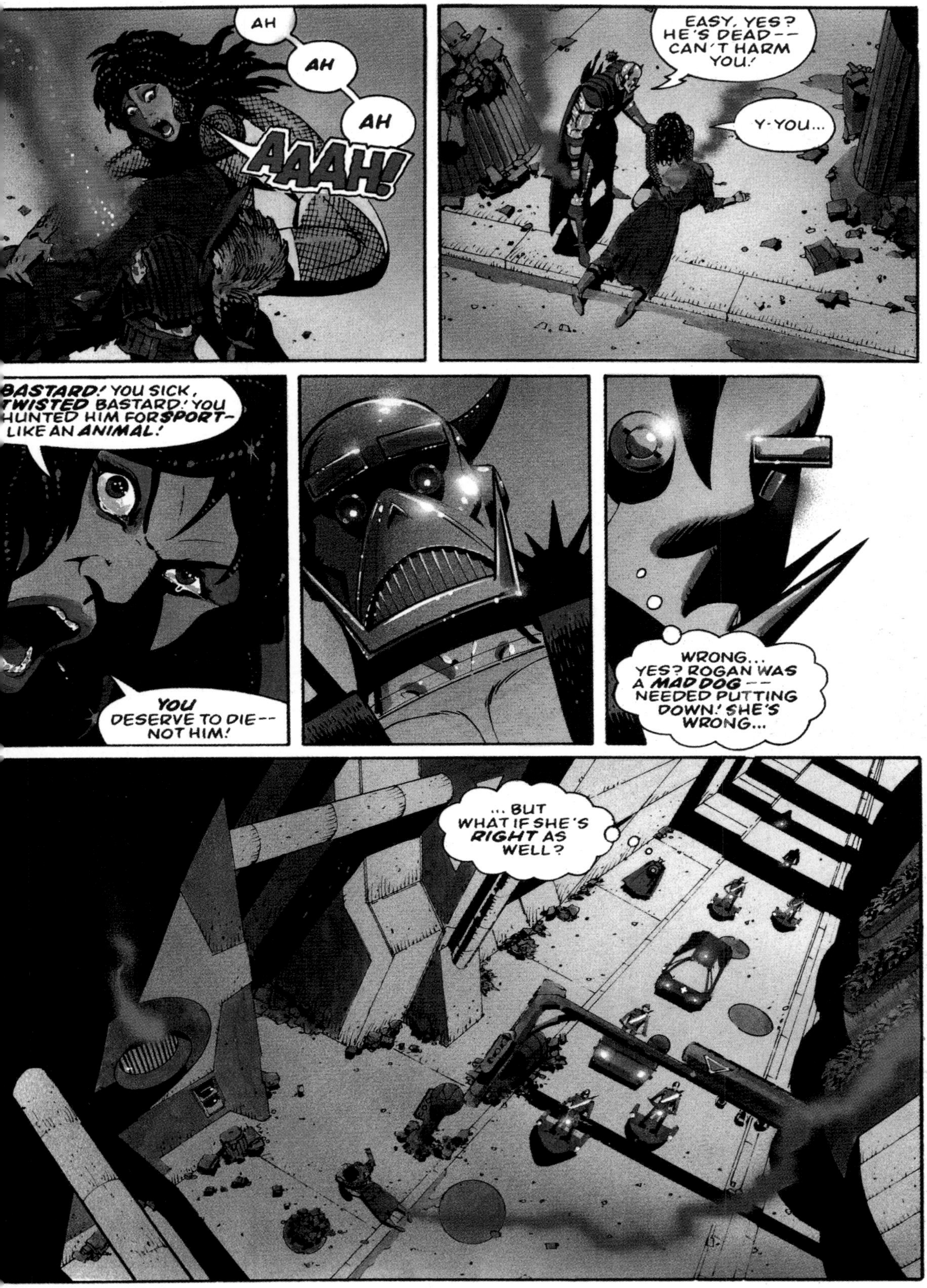
AH
AH
AH
AAAH!
EASY, YES? HE'S DEAD-- CAN'T HARM YOU!
Y-YOU...
BASTARD! YOU SICK, TWISTED BASTARD! YOU HUNTED HIM FOR SPORT- LIKE AN ANIMAL!
YOU DESERVE TO DIE-- NOT HIM!
WRONG... YES? ROGAN WAS A MAD DOG -- NEEDED PUTTING DOWN! SHE'S WRONG...
... BUT WHAT IF SHE'S RIGHT AS WELL?

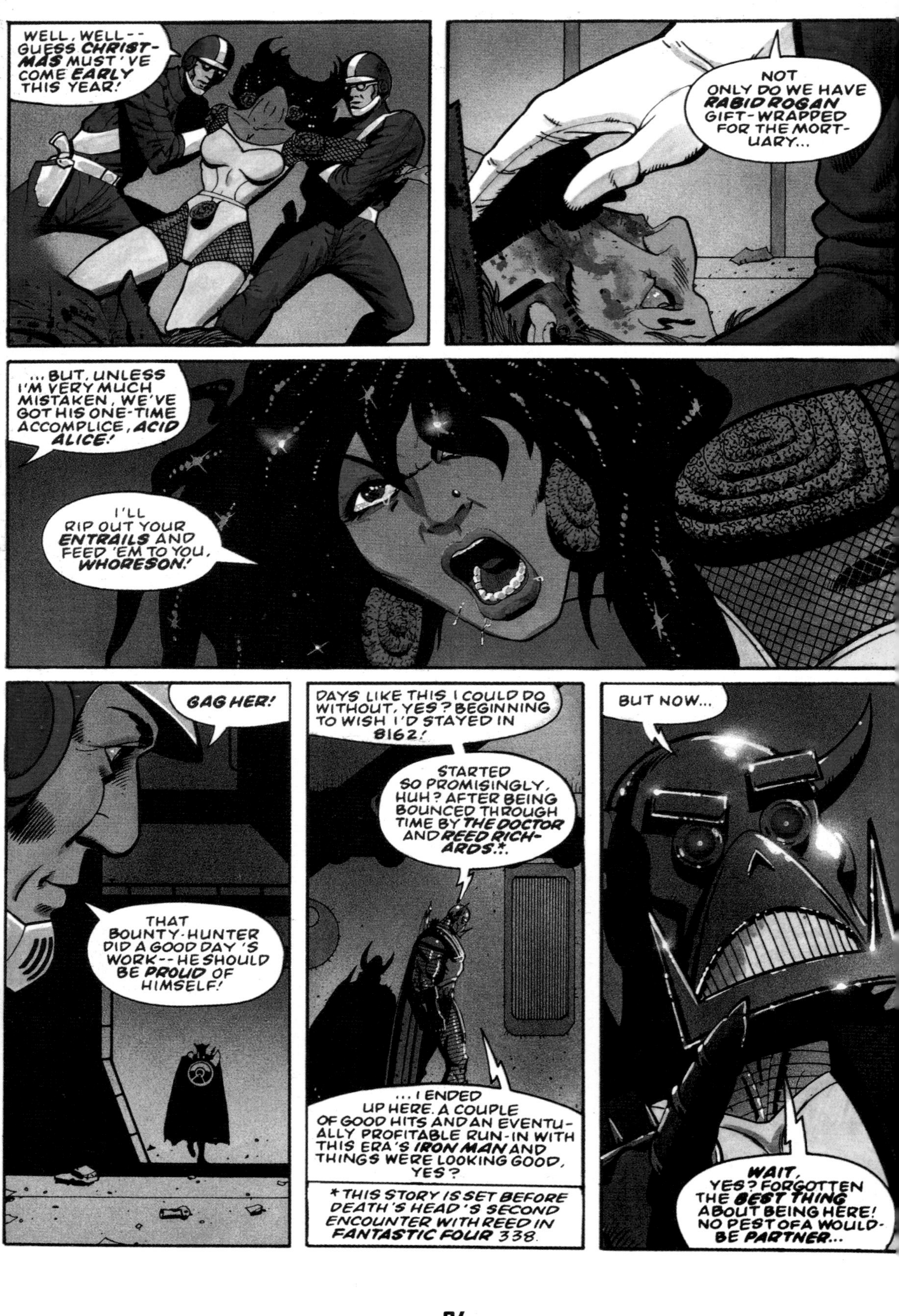

WELL, WELL-- GUESS CHRISTMAS MUST'VE COME EARLY THIS YEAR!
NOT ONLY DO WE HAVE RABID ROGAN GIFT-WRAPPED FOR THE MORTUARY...
...BUT, UNLESS I'M VERY MUCH MISTAKEN, WE'VE GOT HIS ONE-TIME ACCOMPLICE, ACID ALICE!
I'LL RIP OUT YOUR ENTRAILS AND FEED 'EM TO YOU, WHORESON!
GAG HER!
THAT BOUNTY-HUNTER DID A GOOD DAY'S WORK--HE SHOULD BE PROUD OF HIMSELF!
DAYS LIKE THIS I COULD DO WITHOUT, YES? BEGINNING TO WISH I'D STAYED IN 8162!
STARTED SO PROMISINGLY, HUH? AFTER BEING BOUNCED THROUGH TIME BY THE DOCTOR AND REED RICHARDS.*.
...I ENDED UP HERE. A COUPLE OF GOOD HITS AND AN EVENTUALLY PROFITABLE RUN-IN WITH THIS ERA'S IRON MAN AND THINGS WERE LOOKING GOOD, YES?
* THIS STORY IS SET BEFORE DEATH'S HEAD'S SECOND ENCOUNTER WITH REED IN FANTASTIC FOUR 338.
BUT NOW...
WAIT, YES? FORGOTTEN THE BEST THING ABOUT BEING HERE! NO PEST OF A WOULD-BE PARTNER...

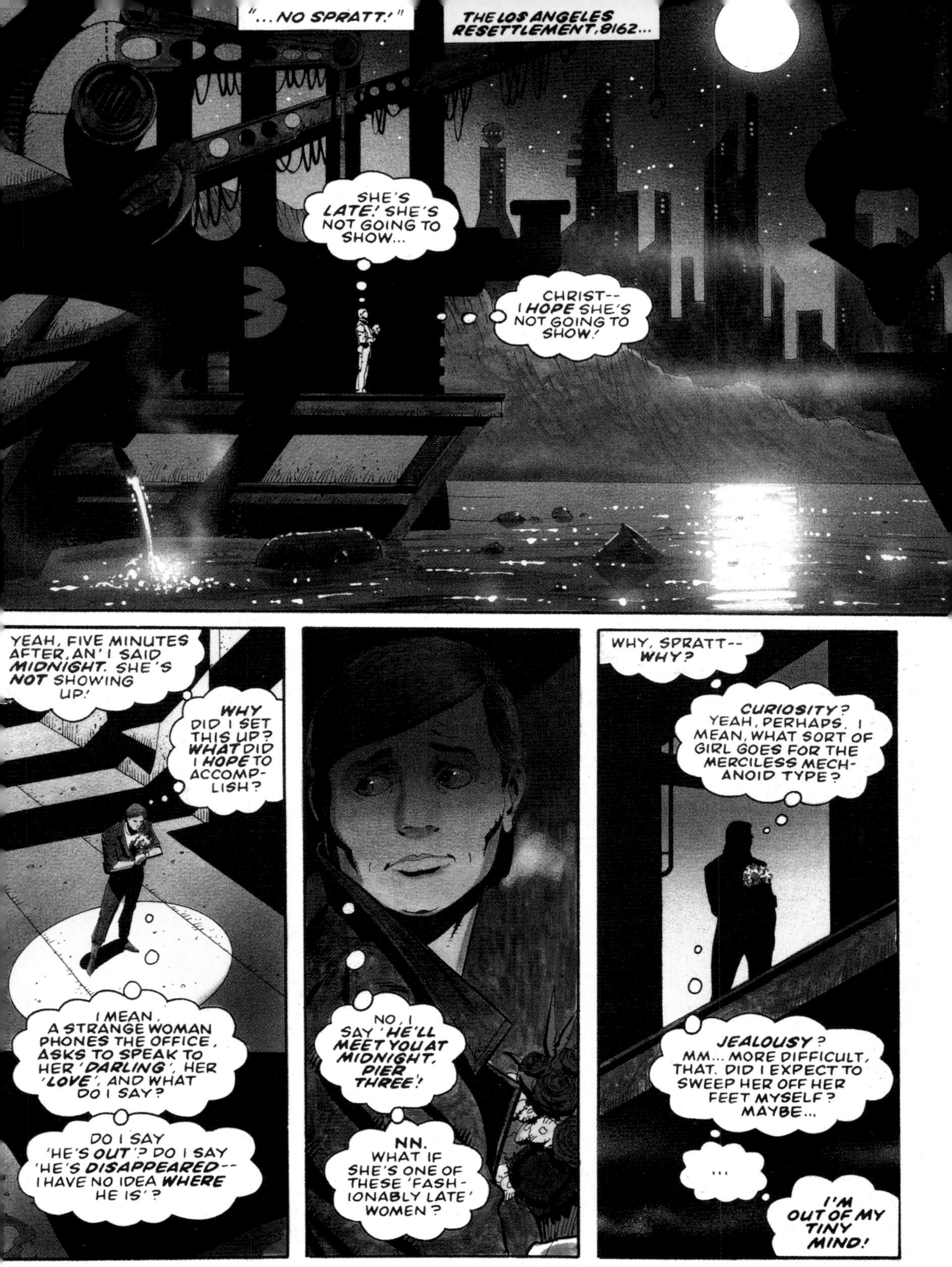
"... NO SPRATT.'"
THE LOS ANGELES RESETTLEMENT, 8162...
SHE'S LATE! SHE'S NOT GOING TO SHOW...
CHRIST-- I HOPE SHE'S NOT GOING TO SHOW!
YEAH, FIVE MINUTES AFTER, AN' I SAID MIDNIGHT. SHE'S NOT SHOWING UP!
WHY DID I SET THIS UP? WHAT DID I HOPE TO ACCOMP-LISH?
I MEAN, A STRANGE WOMAN PHONES THE OFFICE, ASKS TO SPEAK TO HER 'DARLING', HER 'LOVE', AND WHAT DO I SAY?
DO I SAY 'HE'S OUT'? DO I SAY 'HE'S DISAPPEARED-- I HAVE NO IDEA WHERE HE IS'?
NO, I SAY 'HE'LL MEET YOU AT MIDNIGHT, PIER THREE'!
NN. WHAT IF SHE'S ONE OF THESE 'FASH-IONABLY LATE' WOMEN?
WHY, SPRATT-- WHY?
CURIOSITY? YEAH, PERHAPS. I MEAN, WHAT SORT OF GIRL GOES FOR THE MERCILESS MECH-ANOID TYPE?
JEALOUSY? MM... MORE DIFFICULT, THAT. DID I EXPECT TO SWEEP HER OFF HER FEET MYSELF? MAYBE...
...
I'M OUT OF MY TINY MIND!

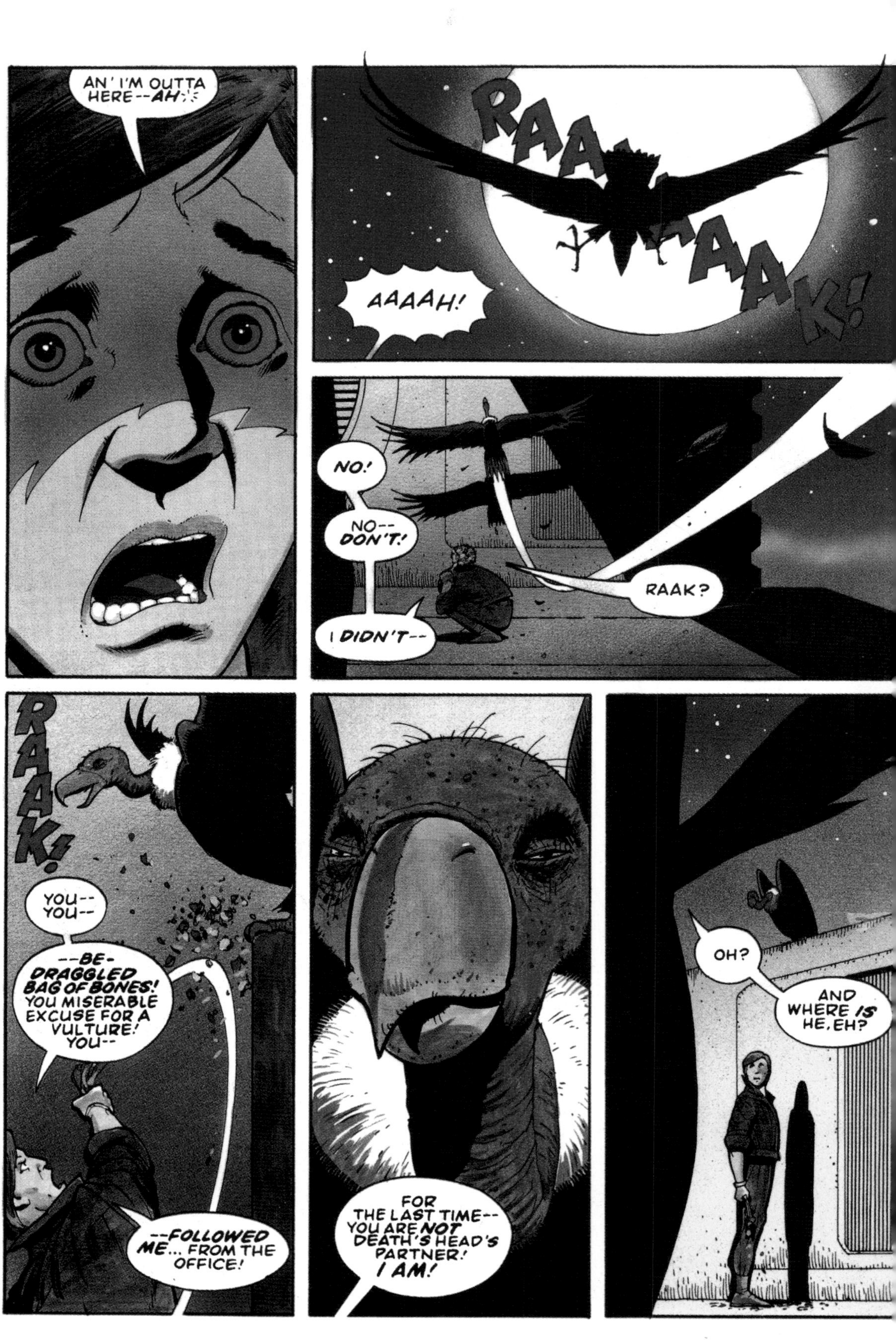
AN' I'M OUTTA HERE--AH--
RAAAAAAK!
AAAAH!
NO!
NO-- DON'T!
I DIDN'T--
RAAK?
RAAAK!
YOU-- YOU--
--BE-DRAGGLED BAG OF BONES! YOU MISERABLE EXCUSE FOR A VULTURE! YOU--
--FOLLOWED ME... FROM THE OFFICE!
FOR THE LAST TIME-- YOU ARE NOT DEATH'S HEAD'S PARTNER! I AM!
OH?
AND WHERE IS HE, EH?

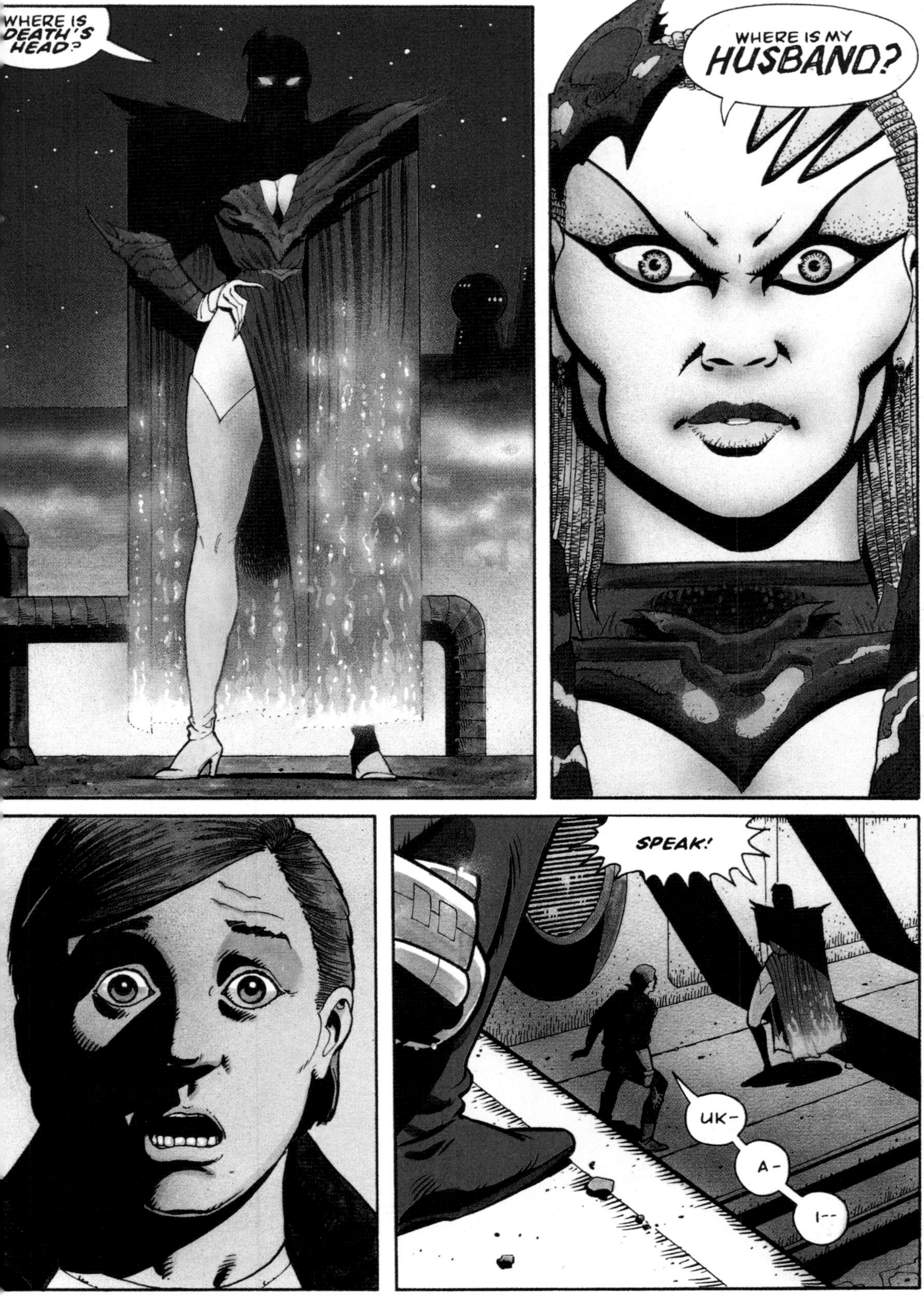
WHERE IS DEATH'S HEAD?
WHERE IS MY HUSBAND?
SPEAK!
UK-
A-
I--

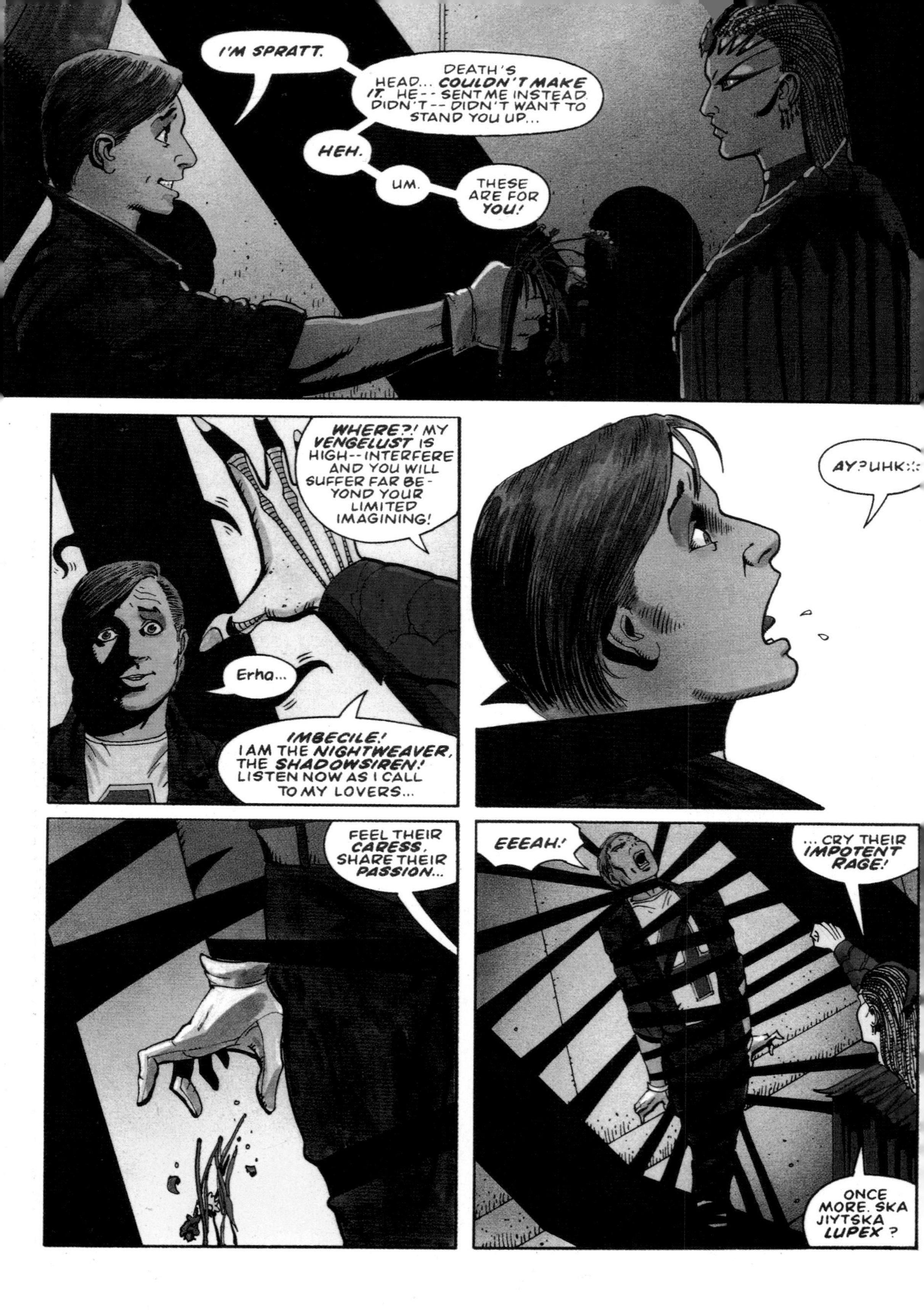
I'M SPRATT.
DEATH'S HEAD... COULDN'T MAKE IT. HE-- SENT ME INSTEAD. DIDN'T -- DIDN'T WANT TO STAND YOU UP...
HEH.
UM.
THESE ARE FOR YOU!
WHERE?! MY VENGELUST IS HIGH--INTERFERE AND YOU WILL SUFFER FAR BE-YOND YOUR LIMITED IMAGINING!
Erha...
IMBECILE! I AM THE NIGHTWEAVER, THE SHADOWSIREN! LISTEN NOW AS I CALL TO MY LOVERS...
AY?UHK::
FEEL THEIR CARESS, SHARE THEIR PASSION...
EEEAH!
...CRY THEIR IMPOTENT RAGE!
ONCE MORE, SKA JIYTSKA LUPEX?

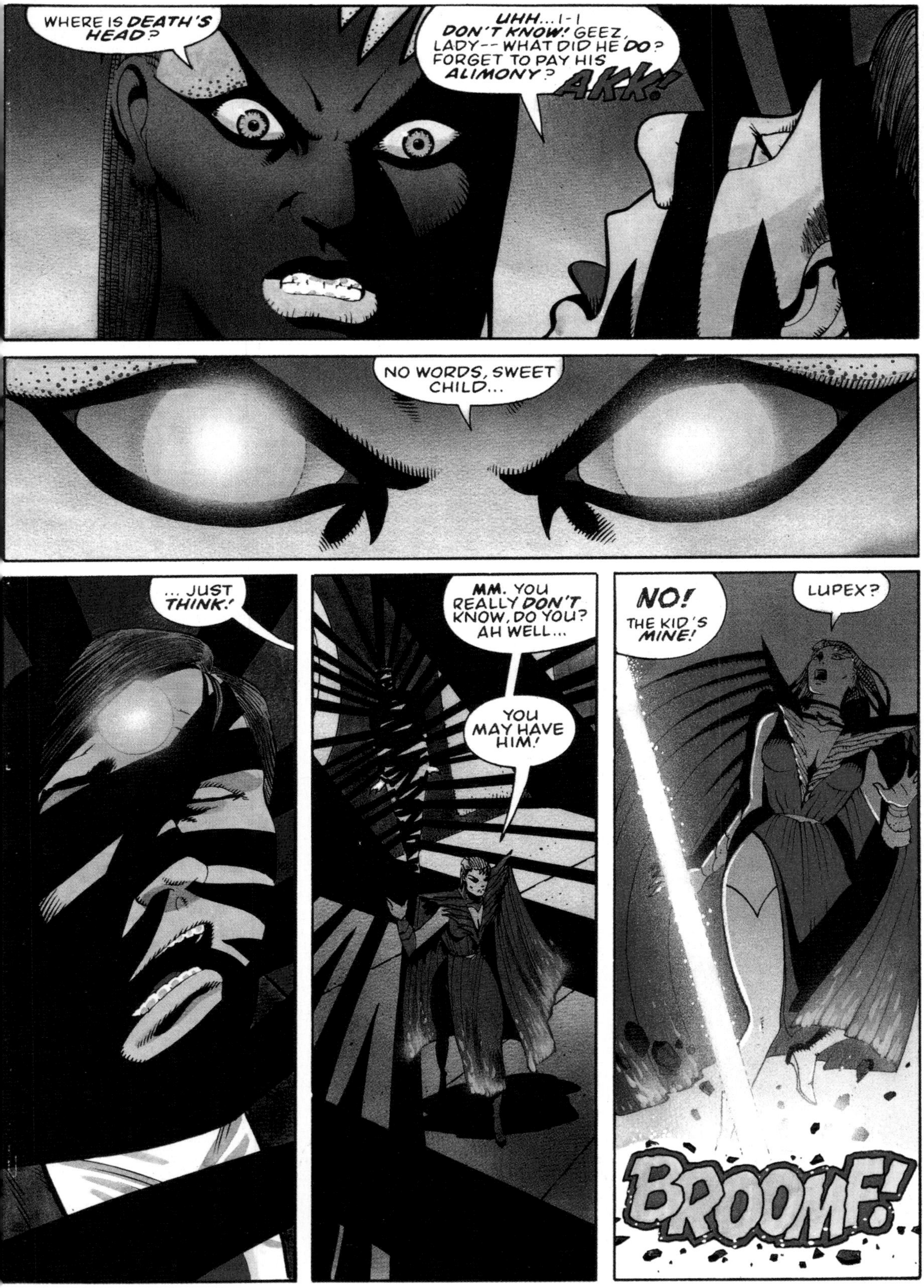
WHERE IS DEATH'S HEAD?
UHH...I-I DON'T KNOW! GEEZ, LADY-- WHAT DID HE DO? FORGET TO PAY HIS ALIMONY?
AKK!
NO WORDS, SWEET CHILD...
...JUST THINK!
MM. YOU REALLY DON'T KNOW, DO YOU? AH WELL...
YOU MAY HAVE HIM!
NO! THE KID'S MINE!
LUPEX?
BROOMF!

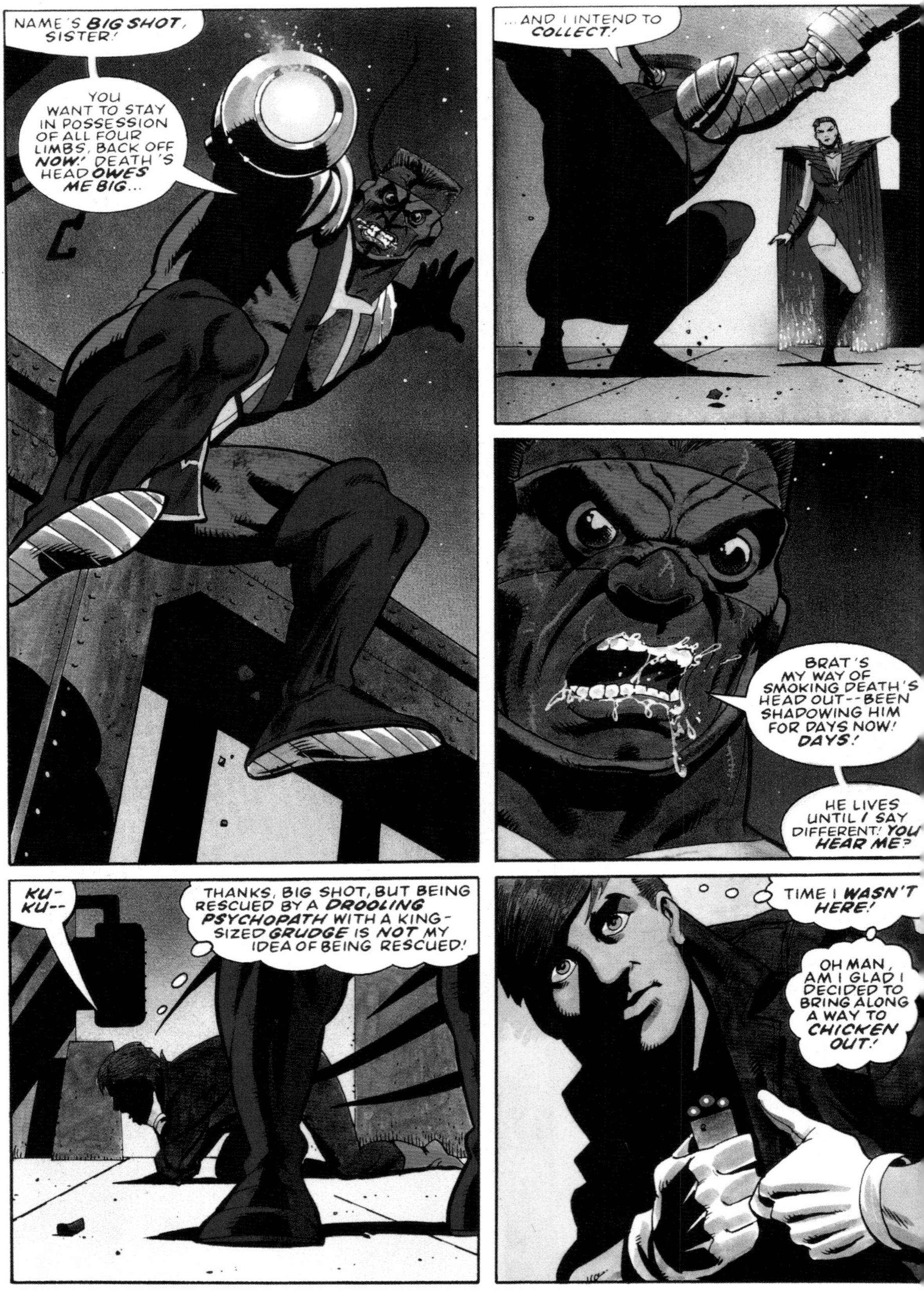

NAME'S BIG SHOT, SISTER!
YOU WANT TO STAY IN POSSESSION OF ALL FOUR LIMBS, BACK OFF NOW! DEATH'S HEAD OWES ME BIG...
...AND I INTEND TO COLLECT!
BRAT'S MY WAY OF SMOKING DEATH'S HEAD OUT--BEEN SHADOWING HIM FOR DAYS NOW! DAYS!
HE LIVES UNTIL I SAY DIFFERENT! YOU HEAR ME?
KU-KU--
THANKS, BIG SHOT, BUT BEING RESCUED BY A DROOLING PSYCHOPATH WITH A KING-SIZED GRUDGE IS NOT MY IDEA OF BEING RESCUED!
TIME I WASN'T HERE!
OH MAN, AM I GLAD I DECIDED TO BRING ALONG A WAY TO CHICKEN OUT!

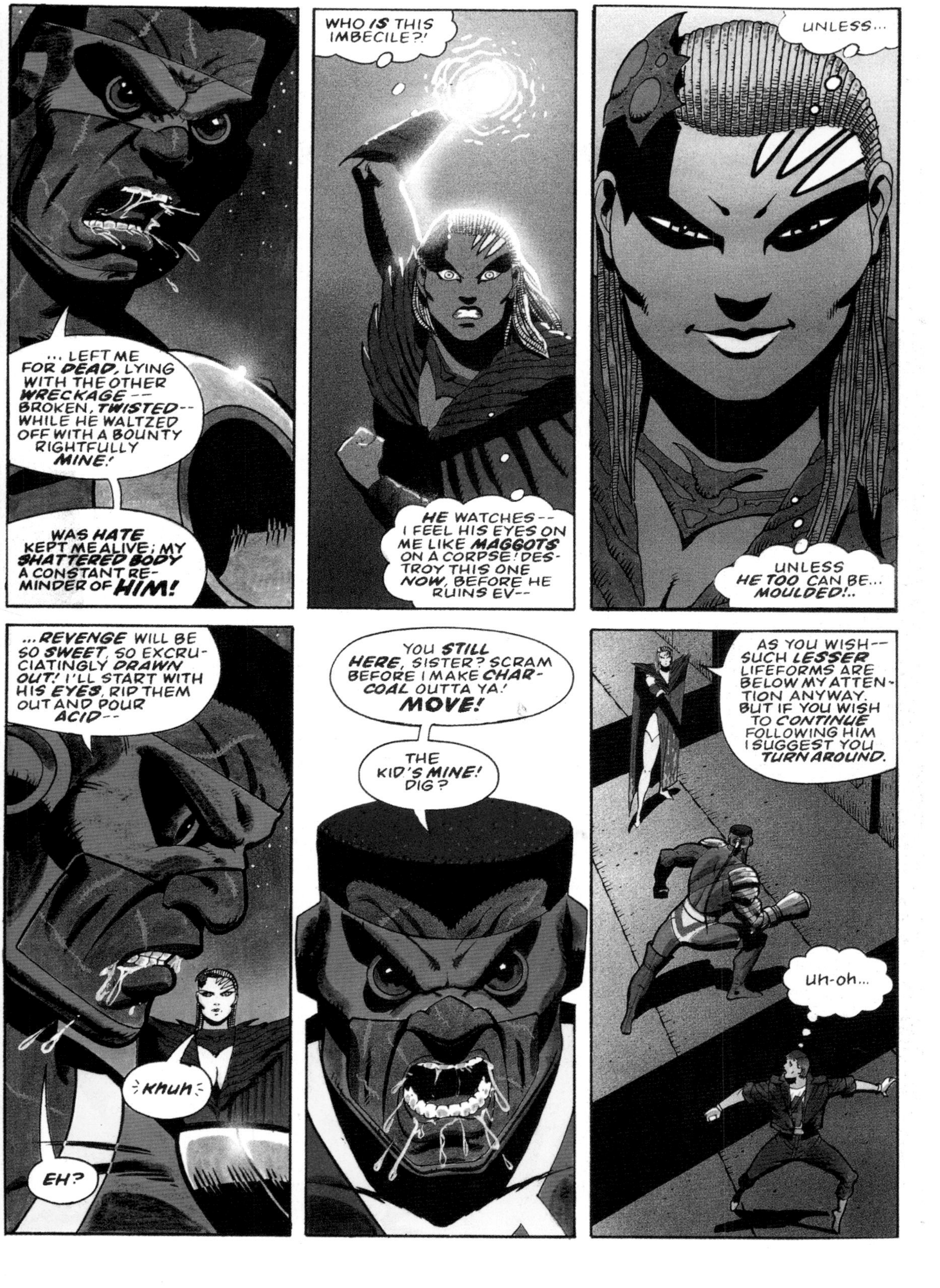

... LEFT ME FOR DEAD, LYING WITH THE OTHER WRECKAGE -- BROKEN, TWISTED -- WHILE HE WALTZED OFF WITH A BOUNTY RIGHTFULLY MINE!
WAS HATE KEPT ME ALIVE; MY SHATTERED BODY A CONSTANT RE-MINDER OF HIM!
WHO IS THIS IMBECILE?!
HE WATCHES -- I FEEL HIS EYES ON ME LIKE MAGGOTS ON A CORPSE! DES-TROY THIS ONE NOW, BEFORE HE RUINS EV--
UNLESS...
UNLESS HE TOO CAN BE... MOULDED!..
... REVENGE WILL BE SO SWEET, SO EXCRU-CIATINGLY DRAWN OUT! I'LL START WITH HIS EYES, RIP THEM OUT AND POUR ACID--
KHUH
EH?
YOU STILL HERE, SISTER? SCRAM BEFORE I MAKE CHAR-COAL OUTTA YA! MOVE!
THE KID'S MINE! DIG?
AS YOU WISH -- SUCH LESSER LIFEFORMS ARE BELOW MY ATTEN-TION ANYWAY. BUT IF YOU WISH TO CONTINUE FOLLOWING HIM I SUGGEST YOU TURN AROUND.
uh-oh...

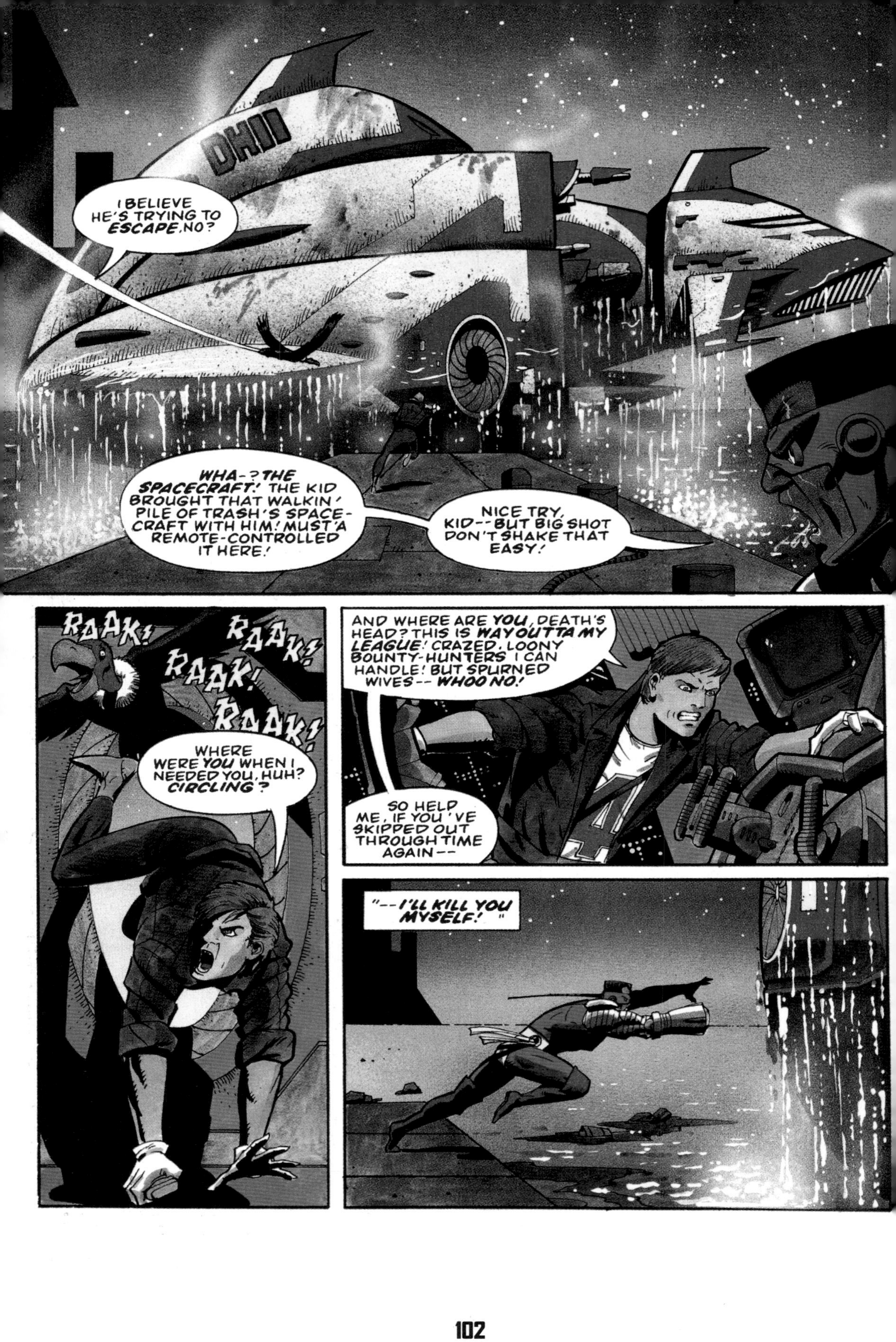
I BELIEVE HE'S TRYING TO ESCAPE, NO?
WHA-? THE SPACECRAFT! THE KID BROUGHT THAT WALKIN' PILE OF TRASH'S SPACE-CRAFT WITH HIM! MUST'A REMOTE-CONTROLLED IT HERE!
NICE TRY, KID--BUT BIG SHOT DON'T SHAKE THAT EASY!
RAAK! RAAK! RAAK! RAAK!
WHERE WERE YOU WHEN I NEEDED YOU, HUH? CIRCLING?
AND WHERE ARE YOU, DEATH'S HEAD? THIS IS WAY OUTTA MY LEAGUE! CRAZED, LOONY BOUNTY-HUNTERS I CAN HANDLE! BUT SPURNED WIVES--WHOO NO!
SO HELP ME, IF YOU'VE SKIPPED OUT THROUGH TIME AGAIN--
"--I'LL KILL YOU MYSELF!"

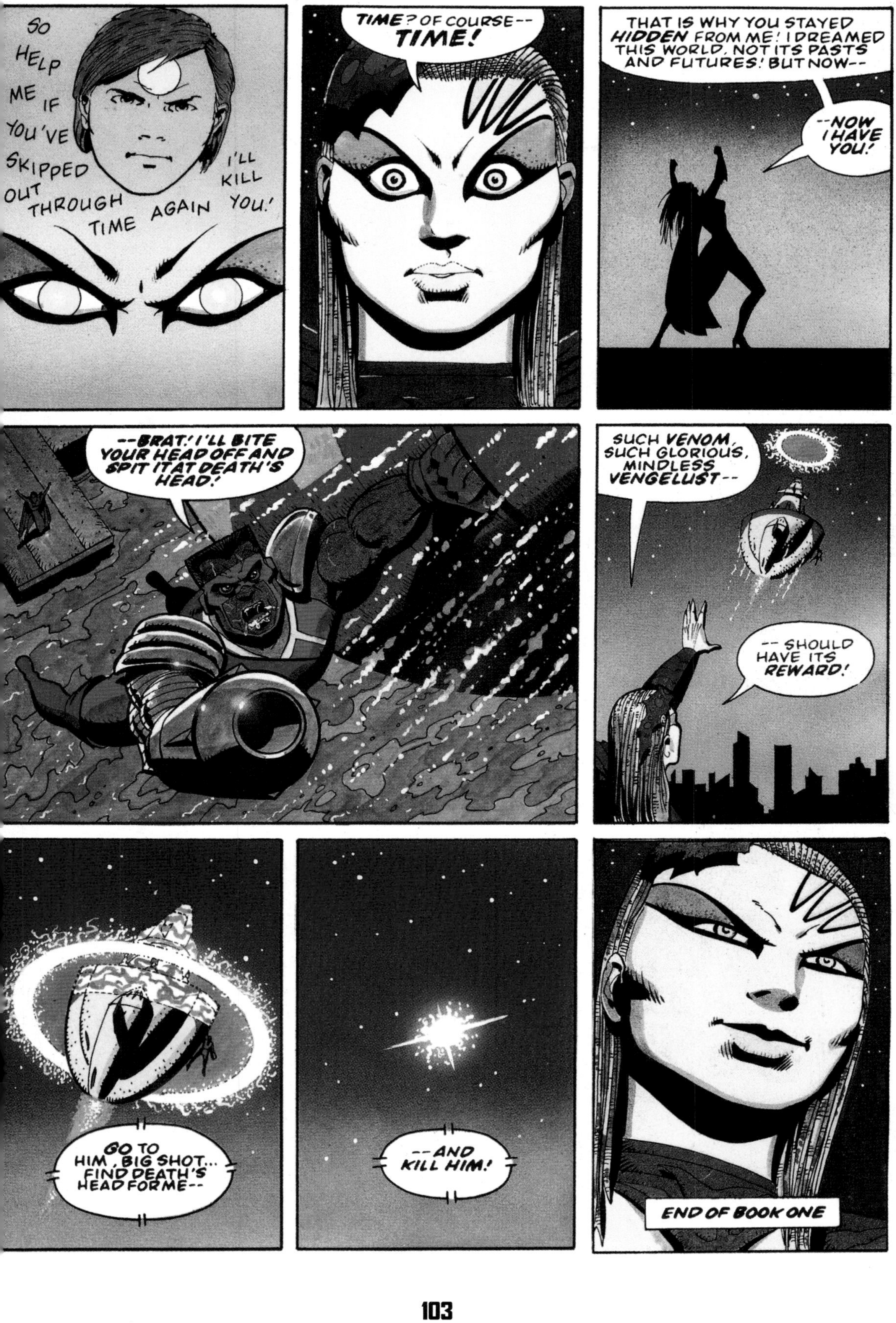

SO HELP ME IF YOU'VE SKIPPED OUT THROUGH TIME AGAIN I'LL KILL YOU!
TIME? OF COURSE-- TIME!
THAT IS WHY YOU STAYED HIDDEN FROM ME! I DREAMED THIS WORLD, NOT ITS PASTS AND FUTURES! BUT NOW--
--NOW I HAVE YOU!
--BRAT! I'LL BITE YOUR HEAD OFF AND SPIT IT AT DEATH'S HEAD!
SUCH VENOM, SUCH GLORIOUS, MINDLESS VENGELUST--
-- SHOULD HAVE ITS REWARD!
GO TO HIM, BIG SHOT... FIND DEATH'S HEAD FOR ME--
--AND KILL HIM!
END OF BOOK ONE

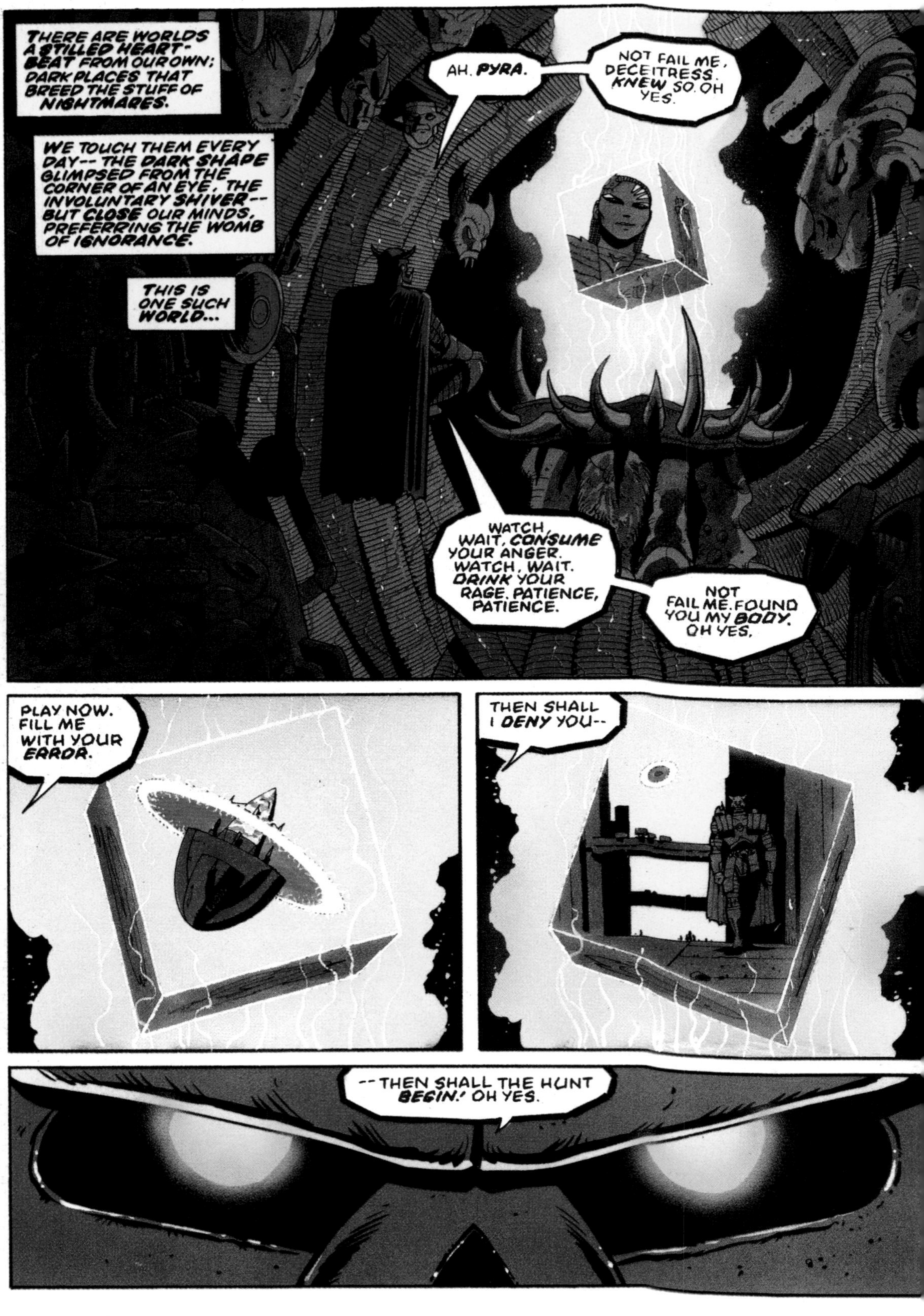
THERE ARE WORLDS A STILLED HEART-BEAT FROM OUR OWN; DARK PLACES THAT BREED THE STUFF OF NIGHTMARES.
WE TOUCH THEM EVERY DAY-- THE DARK SHAPE GLIMPSED FROM THE CORNER OF AN EYE, THE INVOLUNTARY SHIVER-- BUT CLOSE OUR MINDS, PREFERRING THE WOMB OF IGNORANCE.
THIS IS ONE SUCH WORLD...
AH. PYRA.
NOT FAIL ME, DECEITRESS. KNEW SO. OH YES.
WATCH WAIT, CONSUME YOUR ANGER. WATCH, WAIT. DRINK YOUR RAGE, PATIENCE, PATIENCE.
NOT FAIL ME. FOUND YOU MY BODY. OH YES.
PLAY NOW. FILL ME WITH YOUR ERROR.
THEN SHALL I DENY YOU--
--THEN SHALL THE HUNT BEGIN! OH YES.

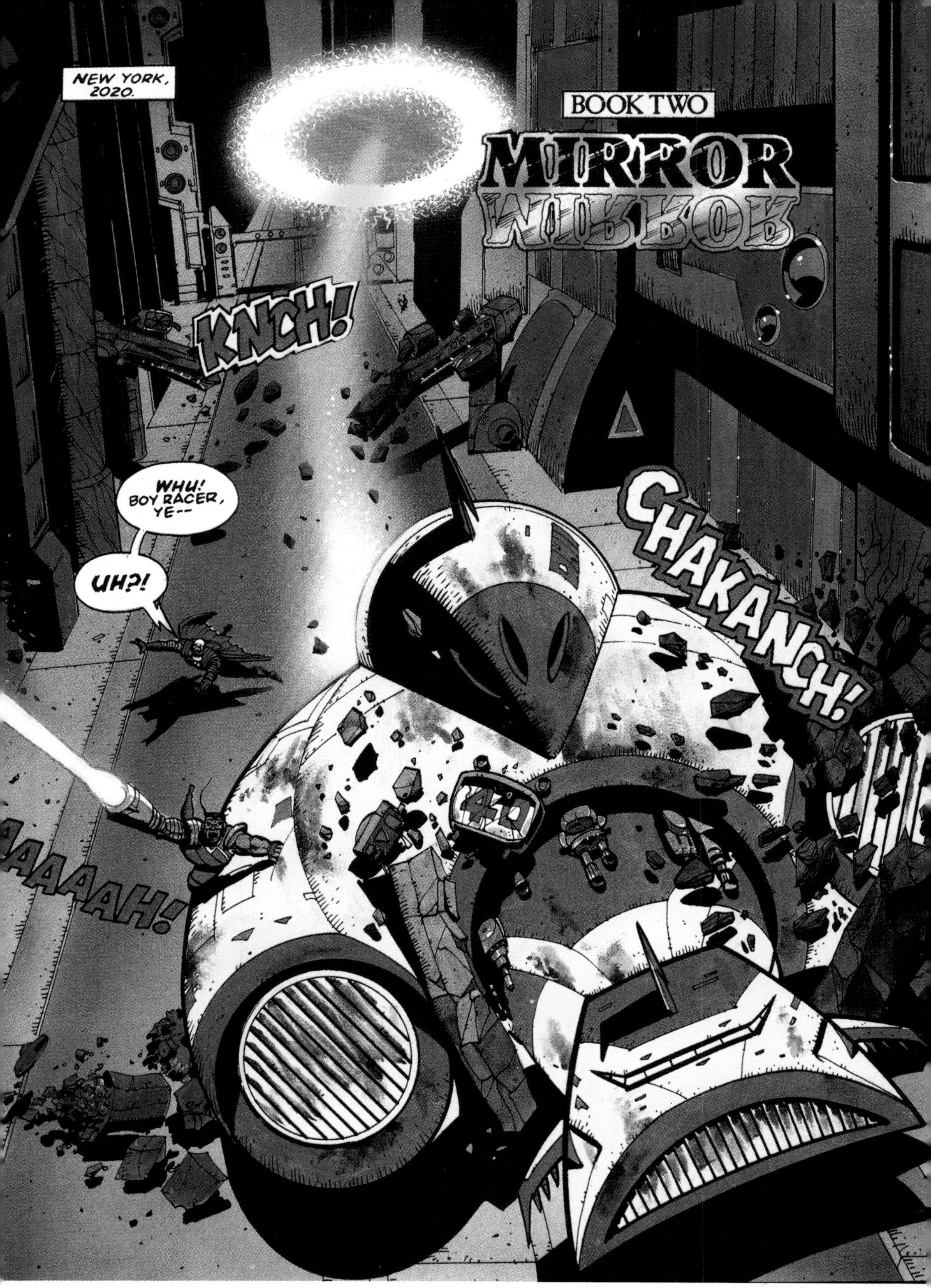
NEW YORK, 2020.
BOOK TWO
MIRROR
WIKKOK
KNCH!
WHU! BOY RACER, YE--
UH?!
CHAKANCH!
AAAAAH!

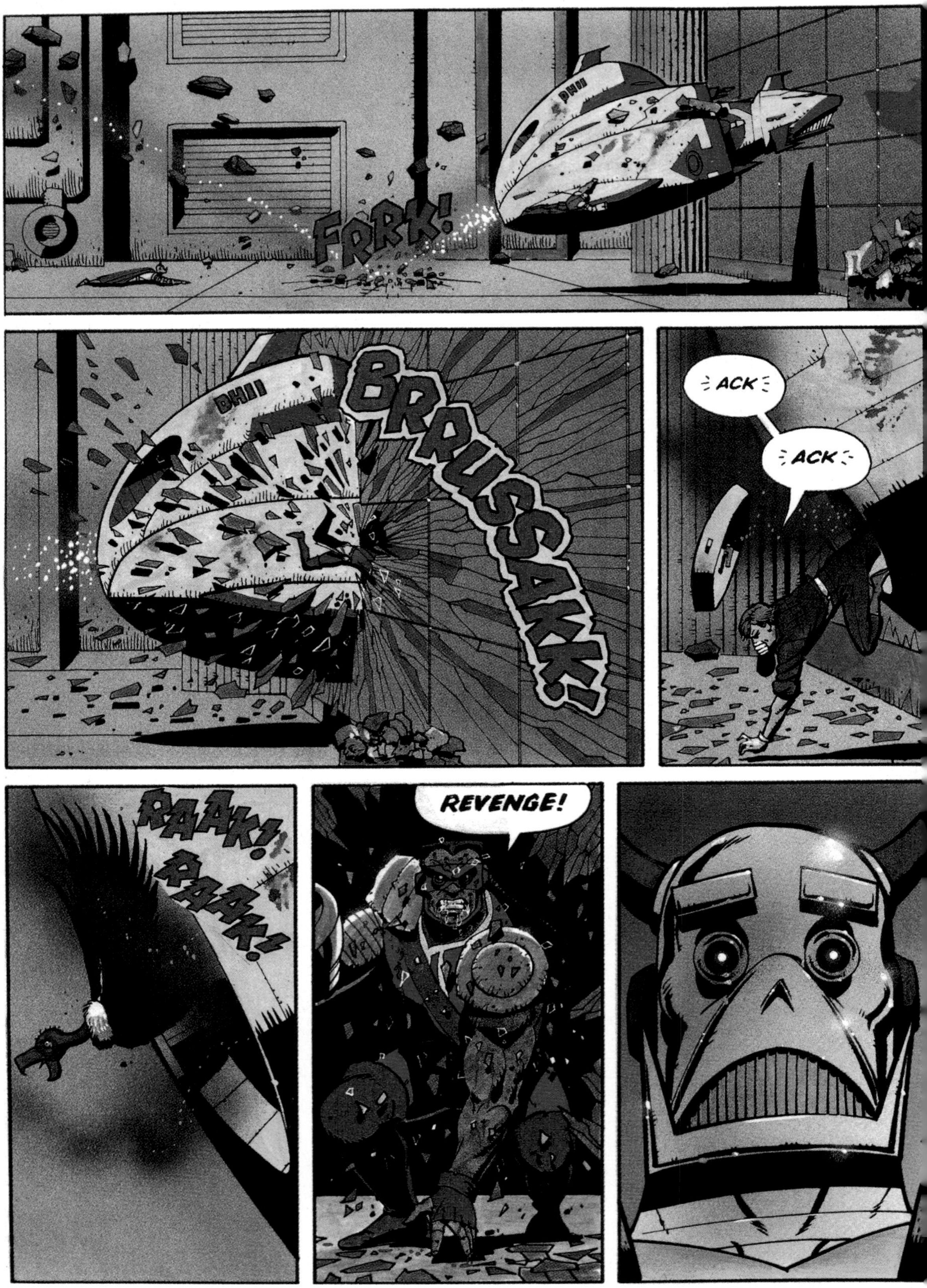
FRRK!
BRRUSSAKK!
ACK
ACK
RAAK! RAAK!
REVENGE!

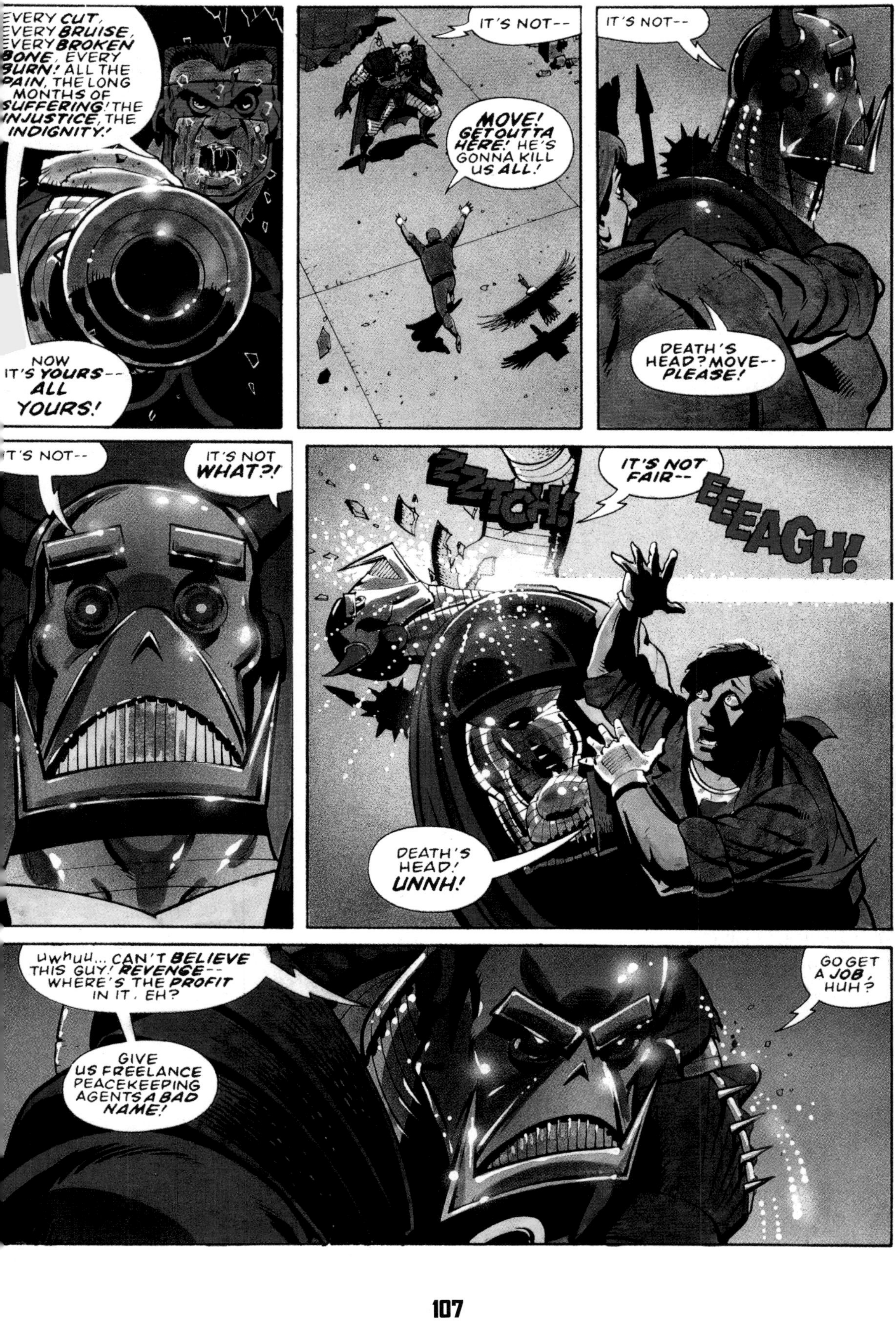
EVERY CUT, EVERY BRUISE, EVERY BROKEN BONE, EVERY BURN! ALL THE PAIN, THE LONG MONTHS OF SUFFERING! THE INJUSTICE, THE INDIGNITY!
NOW IT'S YOURS-- ALL YOURS!
IT'S NOT--
MOVE! GET OUTTA HERE! HE'S GONNA KILL US ALL!
IT'S NOT--
DEATH'S HEAD? MOVE-- PLEASE!
IT'S NOT--
IT'S NOT WHAT?!
ZZZTCH!
IT'S NOT FAIR--
EEEAGH!
DEATH'S HEAD! UNNH!
UWHUU... CAN'T BELIEVE THIS GUY! REVENGE-- WHERE'S THE PROFIT IN IT, EH?
GIVE US FREELANCE PEACEKEEPING AGENTS A BAD NAME!
GO GET A JOB, HUH?

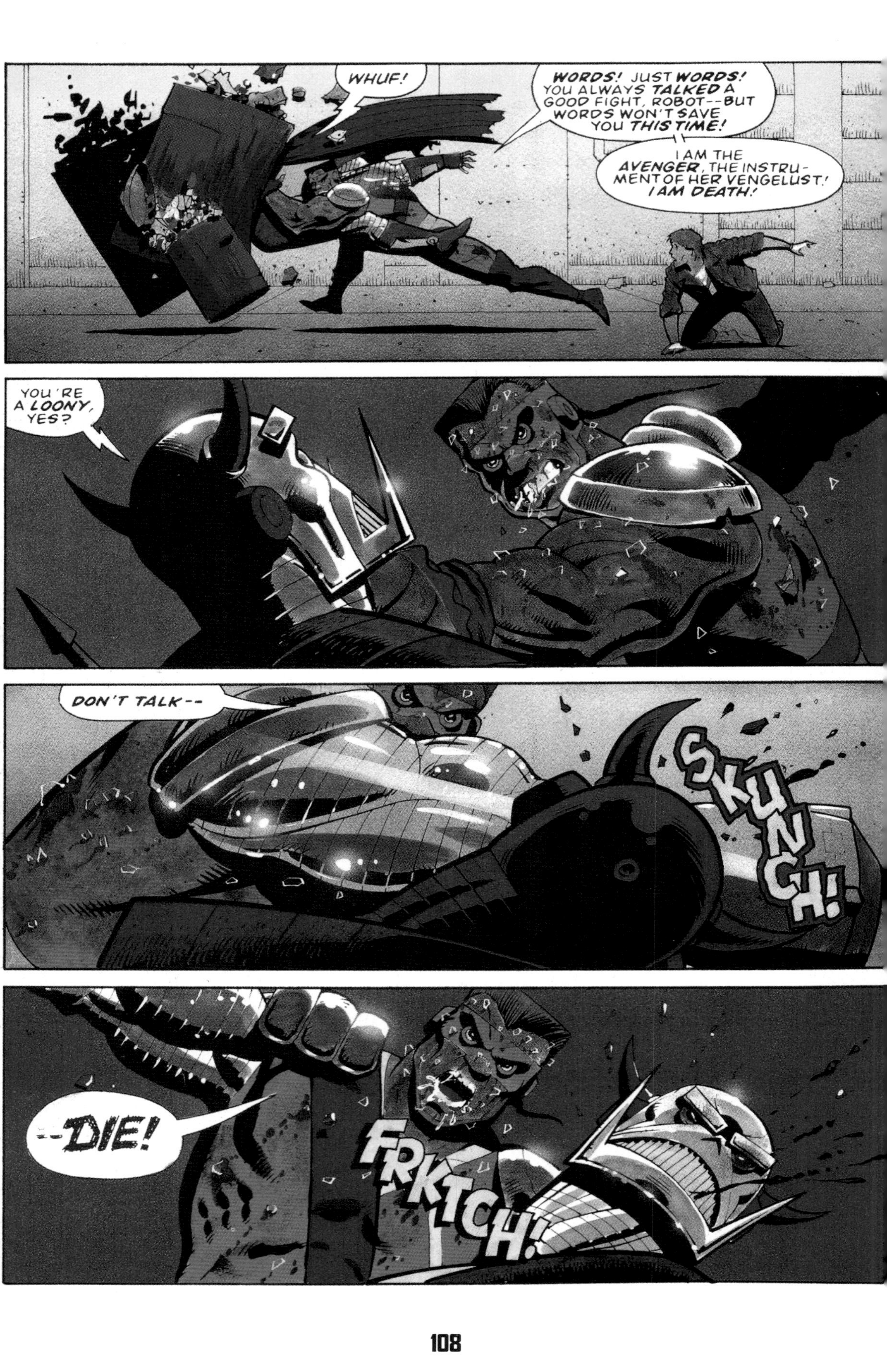
WHUF!
WORDS! JUST WORDS! YOU ALWAYS TALKED A GOOD FIGHT, ROBOT--BUT WORDS WON'T SAVE YOU THIS TIME!
I AM THE AVENGER, THE INSTRUMENT OF HER VENGELUST! I AM DEATH!
YOU'RE A LOONY, YES?
DON'T TALK--
SKUNCH!
--DIE!
FRKTCH!

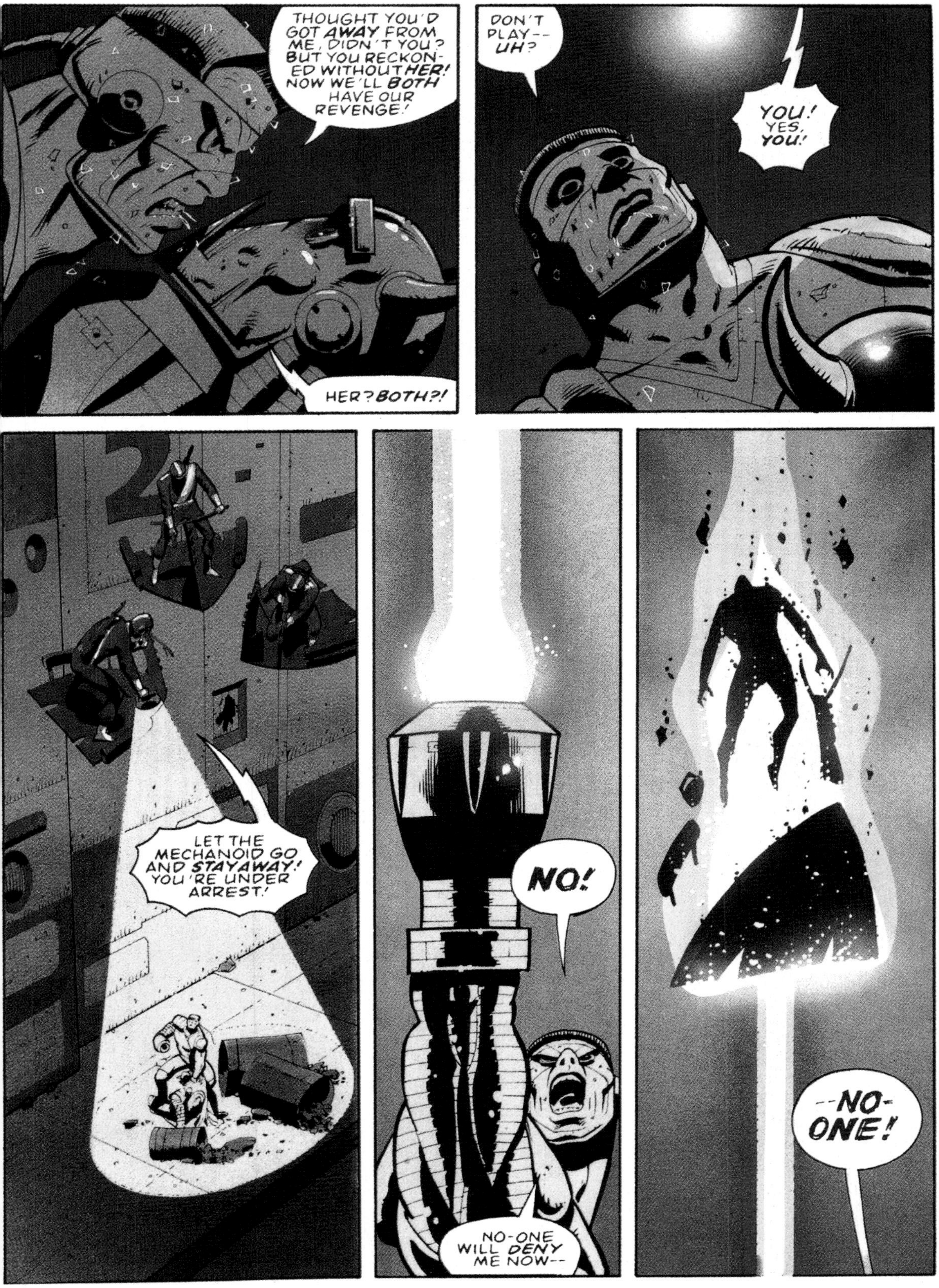
THOUGHT YOU'D GOT AWAY FROM ME, DIDN'T YOU? BUT YOU RECKONED WITHOUT HER! NOW WE'LL BOTH HAVE OUR REVENGE!
HER? BOTH?!
DON'T PLAY-- UH?
YOU! YES, YOU!
LET THE MECHANOID GO AND STAY AWAY! YOU'RE UNDER ARREST!
NO!
NO-ONE WILL DENY ME NOW--
--NO-ONE!

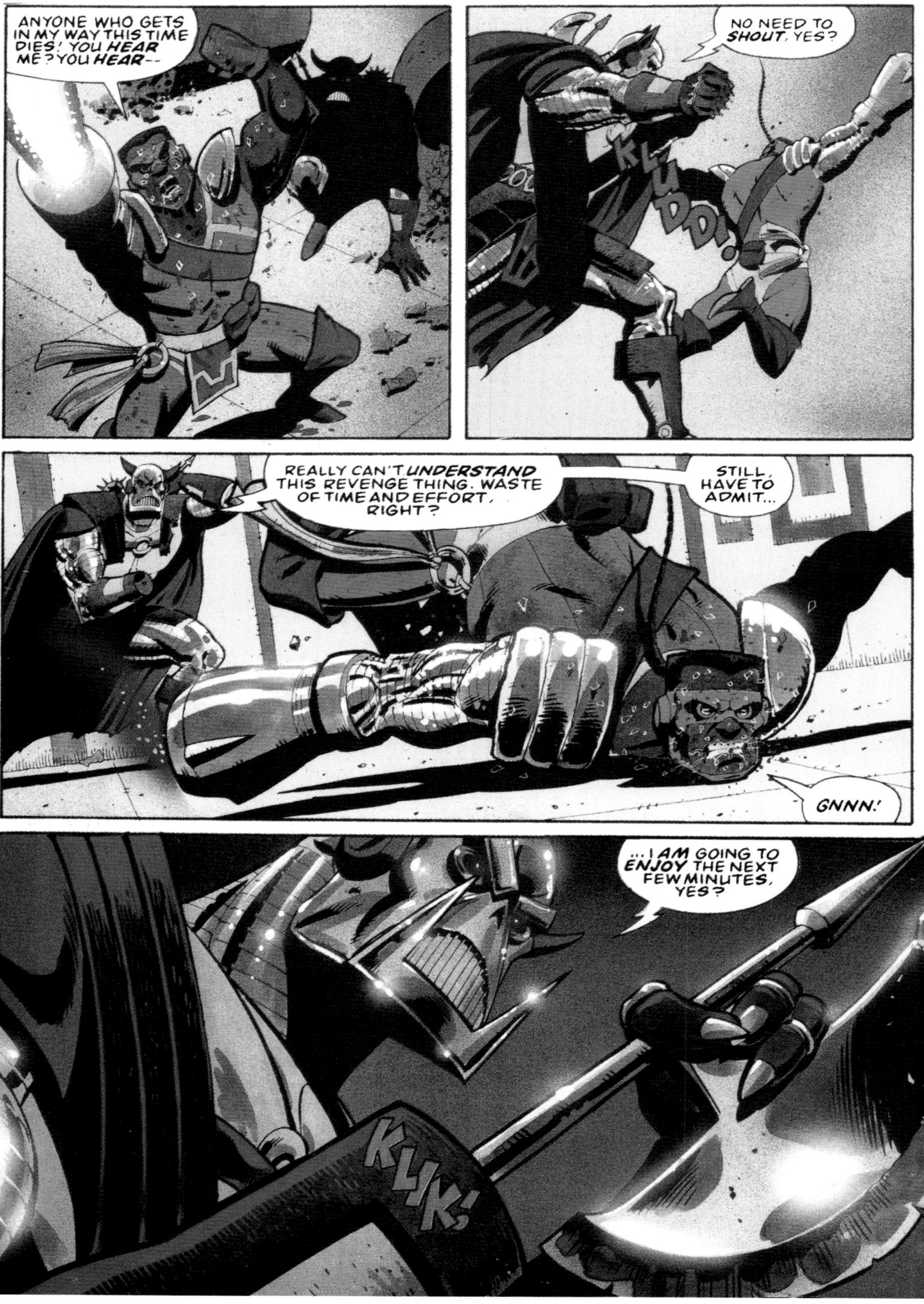
ANYONE WHO GETS IN MY WAY THIS TIME DIES! YOU HEAR ME? YOU HEAR--
NO NEED TO SHOUT, YES?
KLUDD!
REALLY CAN'T UNDERSTAND THIS REVENGE THING. WASTE OF TIME AND EFFORT, RIGHT?
STILL, HAVE TO ADMIT...
GNNN!
...I AM GOING TO ENJOY THE NEXT FEW MINUTES, YES?
KLIK!

--AND *BARBECUE* THEM SLOWLY OVER *HOT COALS!* OR REACH DOWN HIS THROAT AND PULL HIS *LUNGS* OUT THROUGH HIS NOSE! OR...

HRM. CHOPPED INTO *LITTLE PIECES* AND MARINATED IN *WHITE WINE* IS MY *FAVOURITE,* YES?

AH.

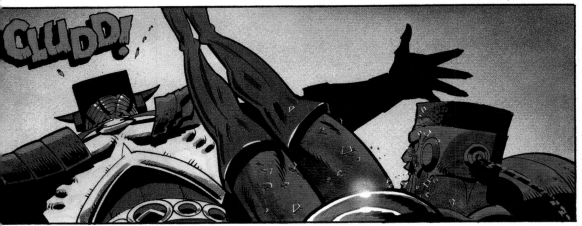

CLUDD!

JUST MAKING MATTERS *WORSE* FOR YOURSELF, HUH?

HAH!

YOU THINK YOU'RE SO BLASTED *SUPERIOR,* DON'T YOU? YOU'RE JUST LIKE THE *REST OF US!*

WE'RE *ALL* BOUNTY-HUNTERS, *ALL* PAID KILLERS--

--HACK HIS GUN OFF AND STICK IT--

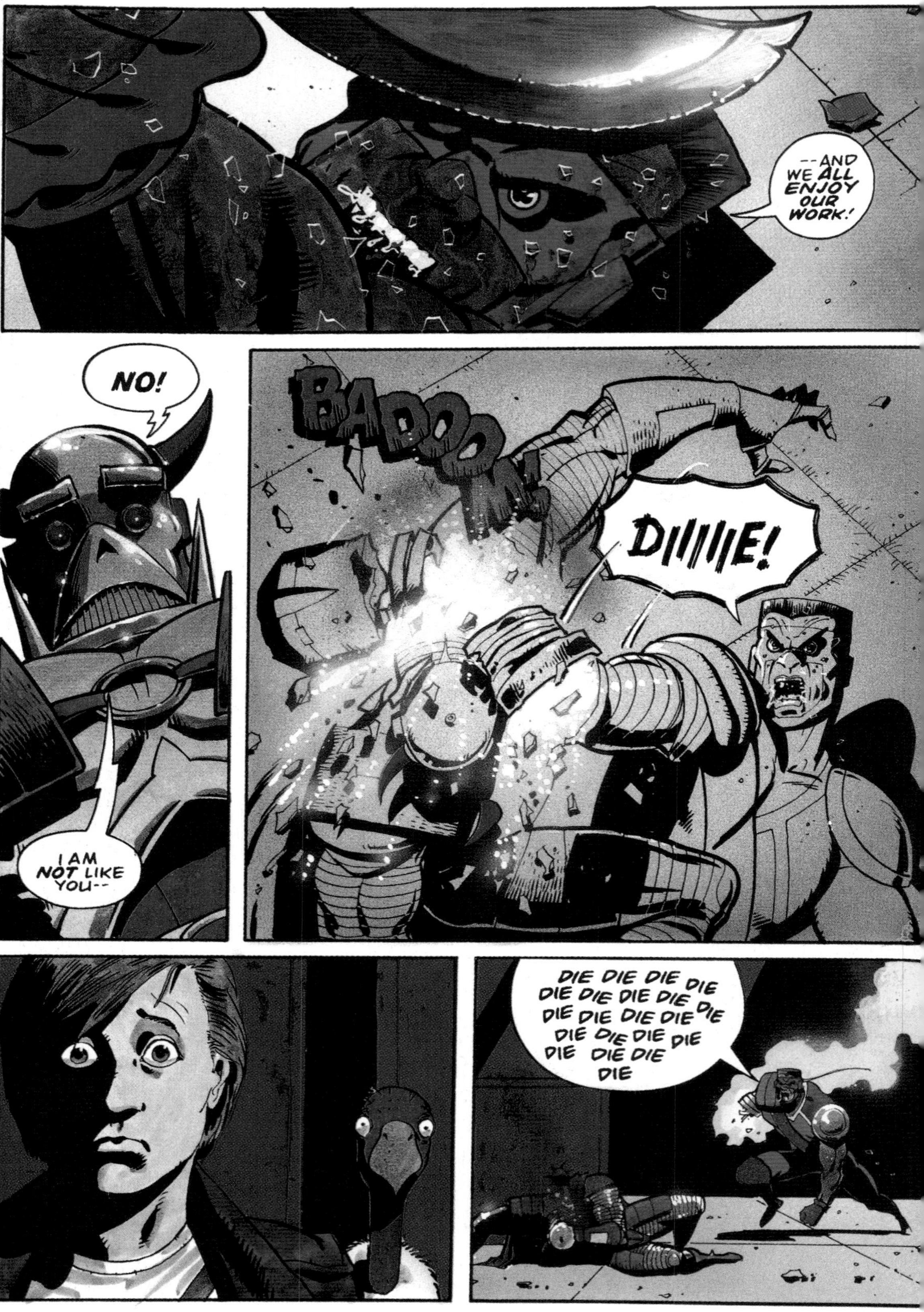
--AND WE ALL ENJOY OUR WORK!
NO!
I AM NOT LIKE YOU--
BADOOM!
DIIIIE!
DIE DIE DIE DIE DIE DIE DIE DIE DIE DIE DIE DIE DIE DIE DIE DIE DIE DIE DIE DIE DIE DIE DIE DIE

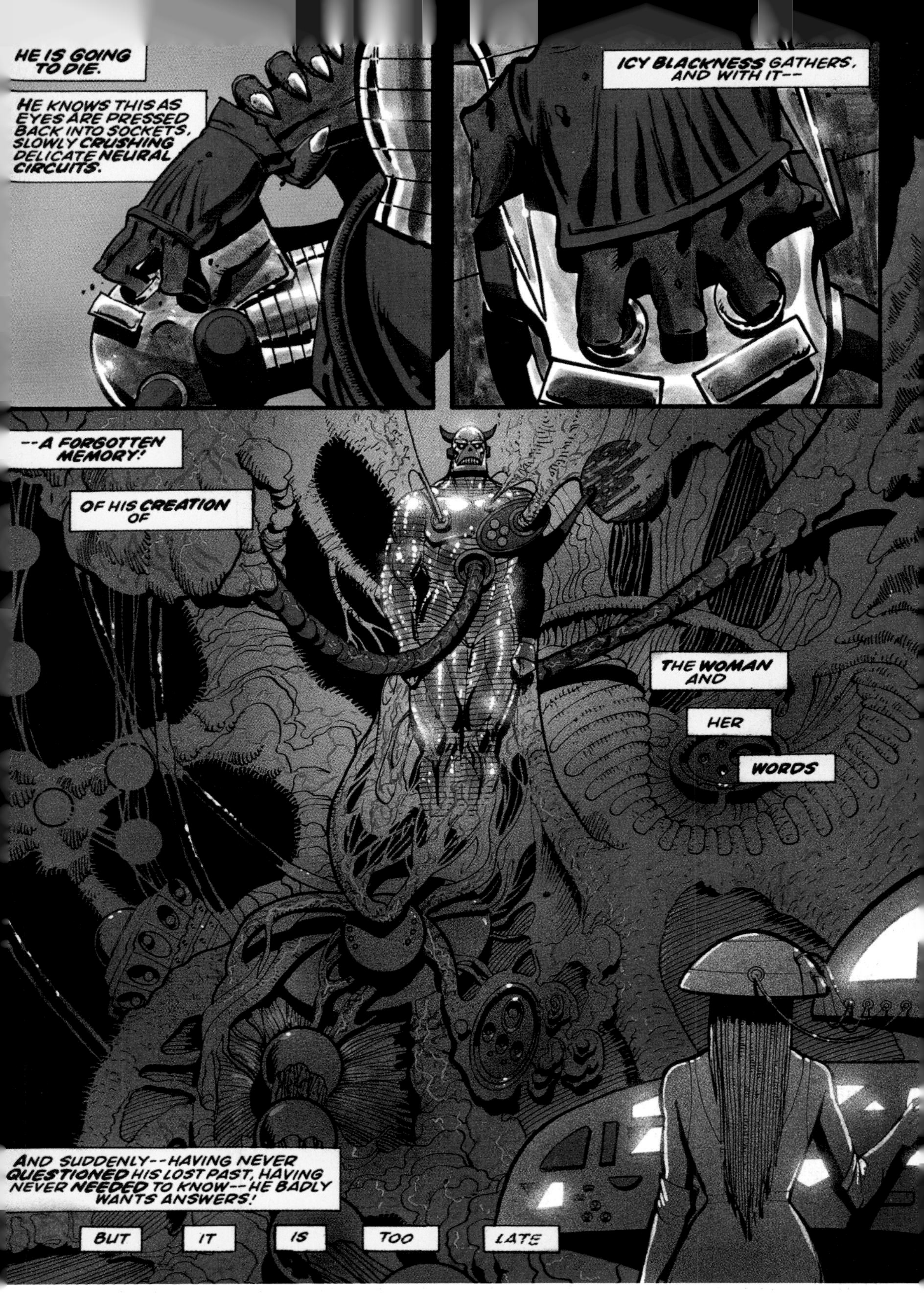
HE IS GOING TO DIE.
HE KNOWS THIS AS EYES ARE PRESSED BACK INTO SOCKETS, SLOWLY CRUSHING DELICATE NEURAL CIRCUITS.
ICY BLACKNESS GATHERS, AND WITH IT--
--A FORGOTTEN MEMORY!
OF HIS CREATION OF
THE WOMAN AND
HER
WORDS
AND SUDDENLY--HAVING NEVER QUESTIONED HIS LOST PAST, HAVING NEVER NEEDED TO KNOW--HE BADLY WANTS ANSWERS!
BUT
IT
IS
TOO
LATE

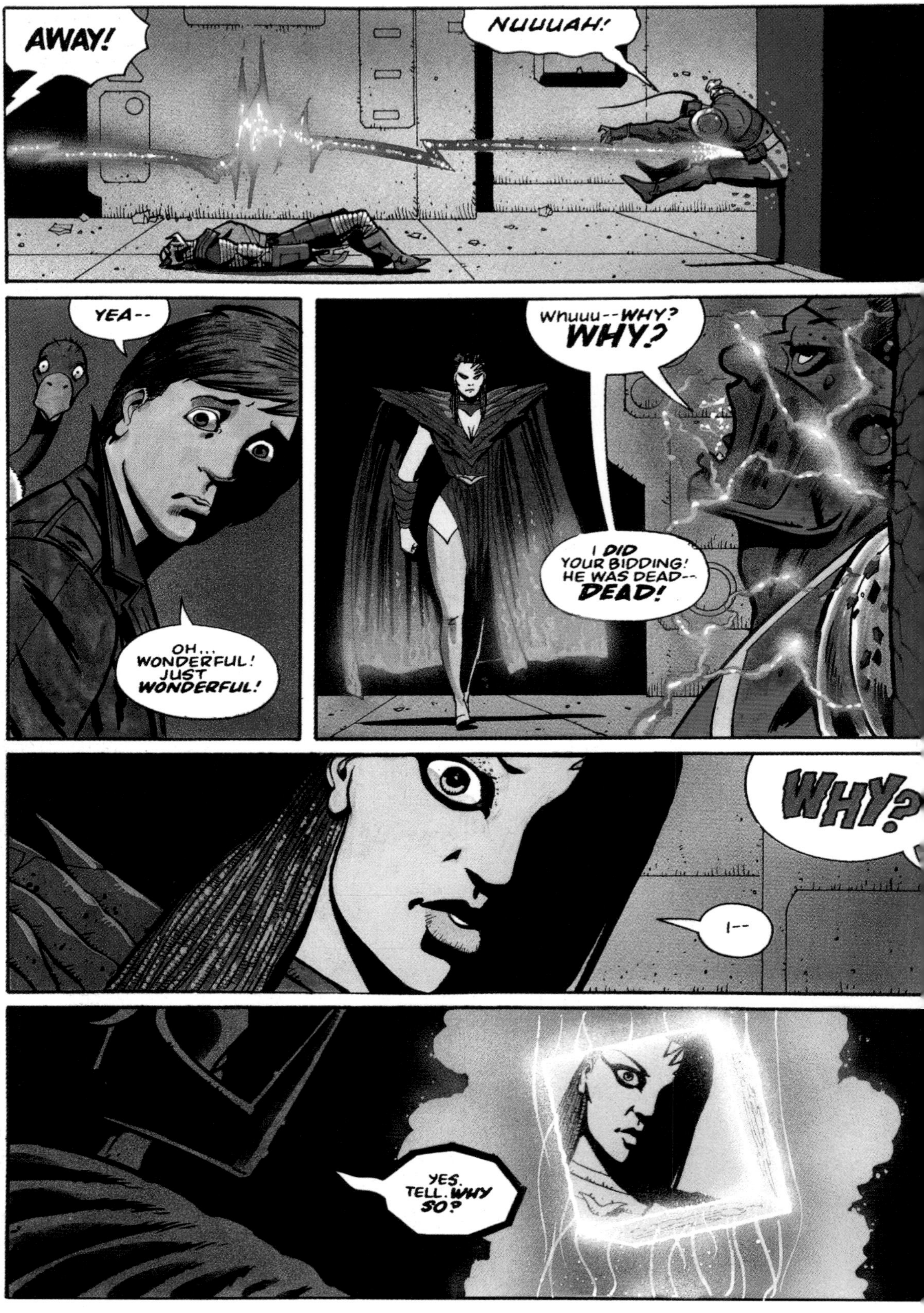
AWAY!
NUUUAH!
YEA--
OH... WONDERFUL! JUST WONDERFUL!
Whuuu--WHY? WHY?
I DID YOUR BIDDING! HE WAS DEAD--DEAD!
WHY?
I--
YES. TELL. WHY SO?

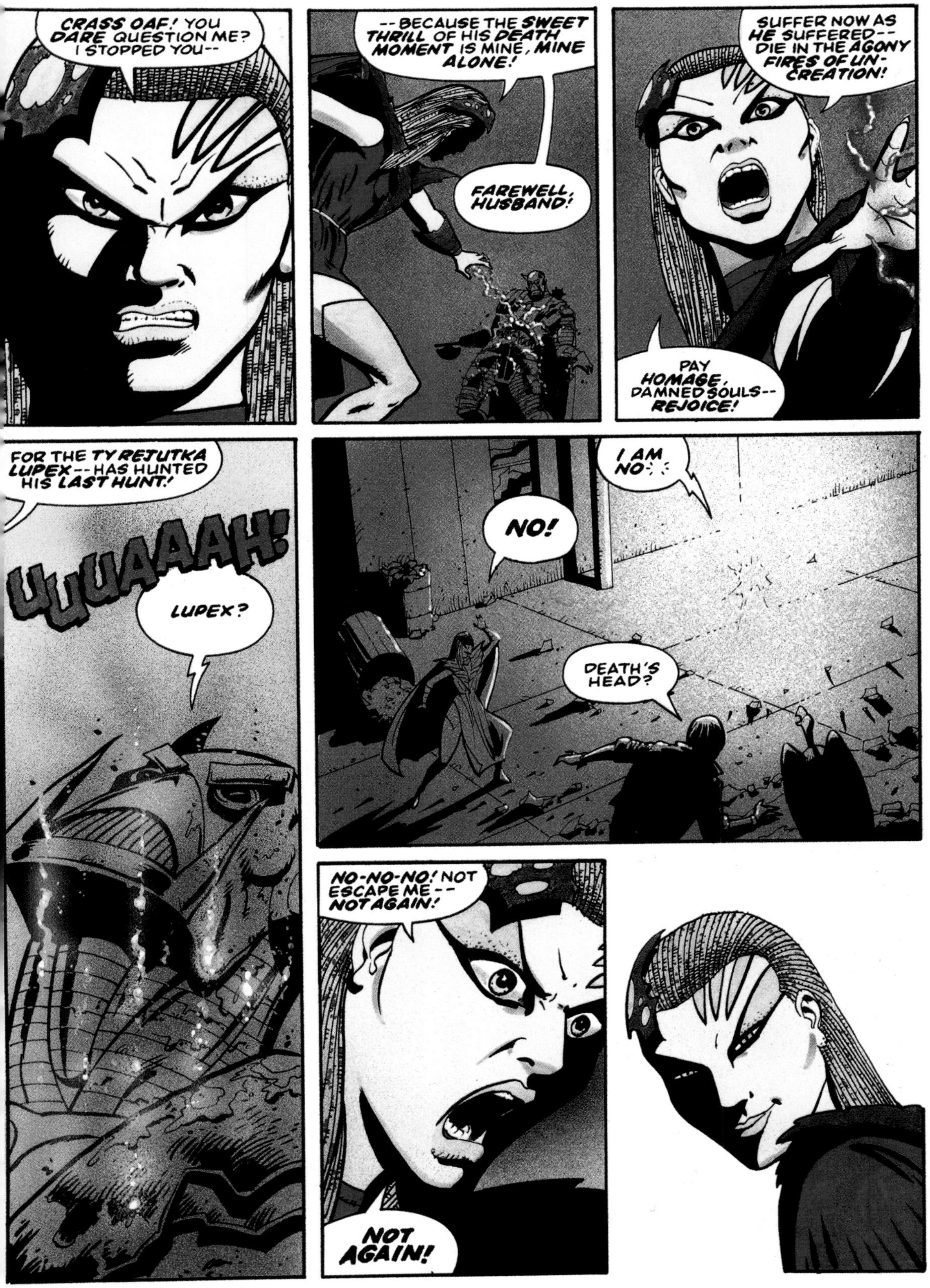
CRASS OAF! YOU DARE QUESTION ME? I STOPPED YOU--
--BECAUSE THE SWEET THRILL OF HIS DEATH MOMENT IS MINE, MINE ALONE!
FAREWELL, HUSBAND!
SUFFER NOW AS HE SUFFERED-- DIE IN THE AGONY FIRES OF UN-CREATION!
PAY HOMAGE, DAMNED SOULS-- REJOICE!
FOR THE TY REJUTKA LUPEX--HAS HUNTED HIS LAST HUNT!
UUUAAAAH!
LUPEX?
I AM NO··
NO!
DEATH'S HEAD?
NO-NO-NO! NOT ESCAPE ME-- NOT AGAIN!
NOT AGAIN!

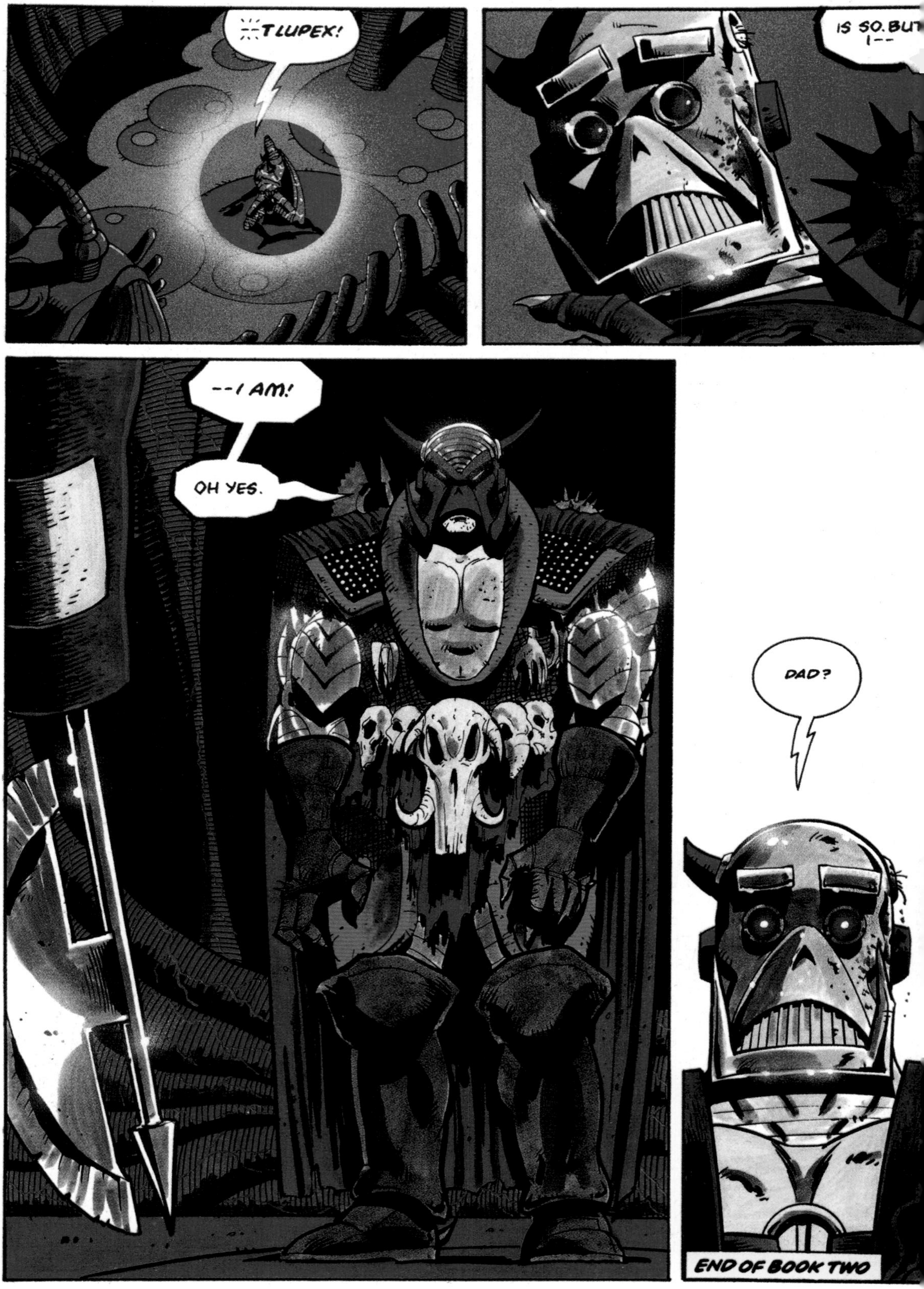
--TLUPEX!
IS SO. BUT I--
--I AM!
OH YES.
DAD?
END OF BOOK TWO

A CIRCUIT FUSES.

A HYDRAULIC MUSCLE STIFFENS AND LOCKS.

A SERVO MOTOR SPUTTERS AND DIES.

A FINAL RESERVE POWER SYSTEM EBBS AND FADES.

A MASTERPIECE OF ADVANCED LIVING ROBOTIC TECHNOLOGY--

--BECOMES DEAD METAL WEIGHT!

...EX-EXCELLENT PARTY... SUPERB FOOD BUT... BUT BUTBUT--

THINK!

...MUST FLY YOUR MOTH...ERS NEVER TEACH YOU TO...

BABBLING. LOSING IT. THINK! SOMETHING--

...KNOCK YOUR INTERIOR DESIGNERERR...

--HE SAID. LUPEX. IN--

--THE NEST. YES, THE NEST. THINK!"

"ABOUT THIS PLACE. HE SAID-- TIME. NEED MORE--"

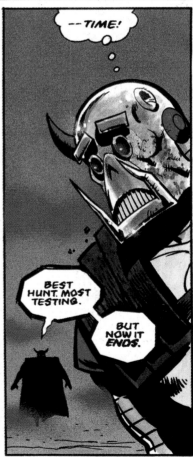

--TIME!

BEST HUNT. MOST TESTING.

BUT NOW IT ENDS.

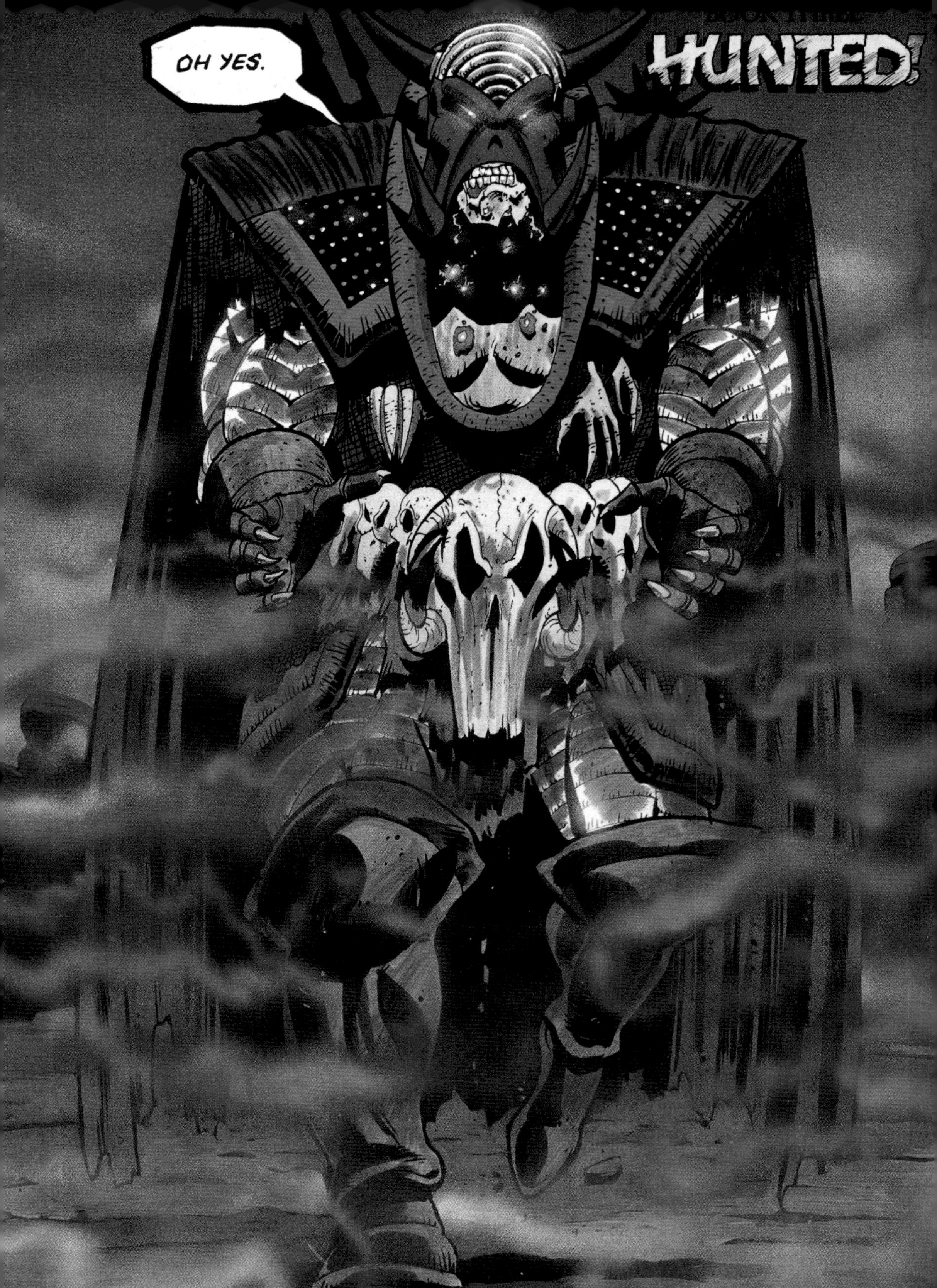
OH YES.
HUNTED!

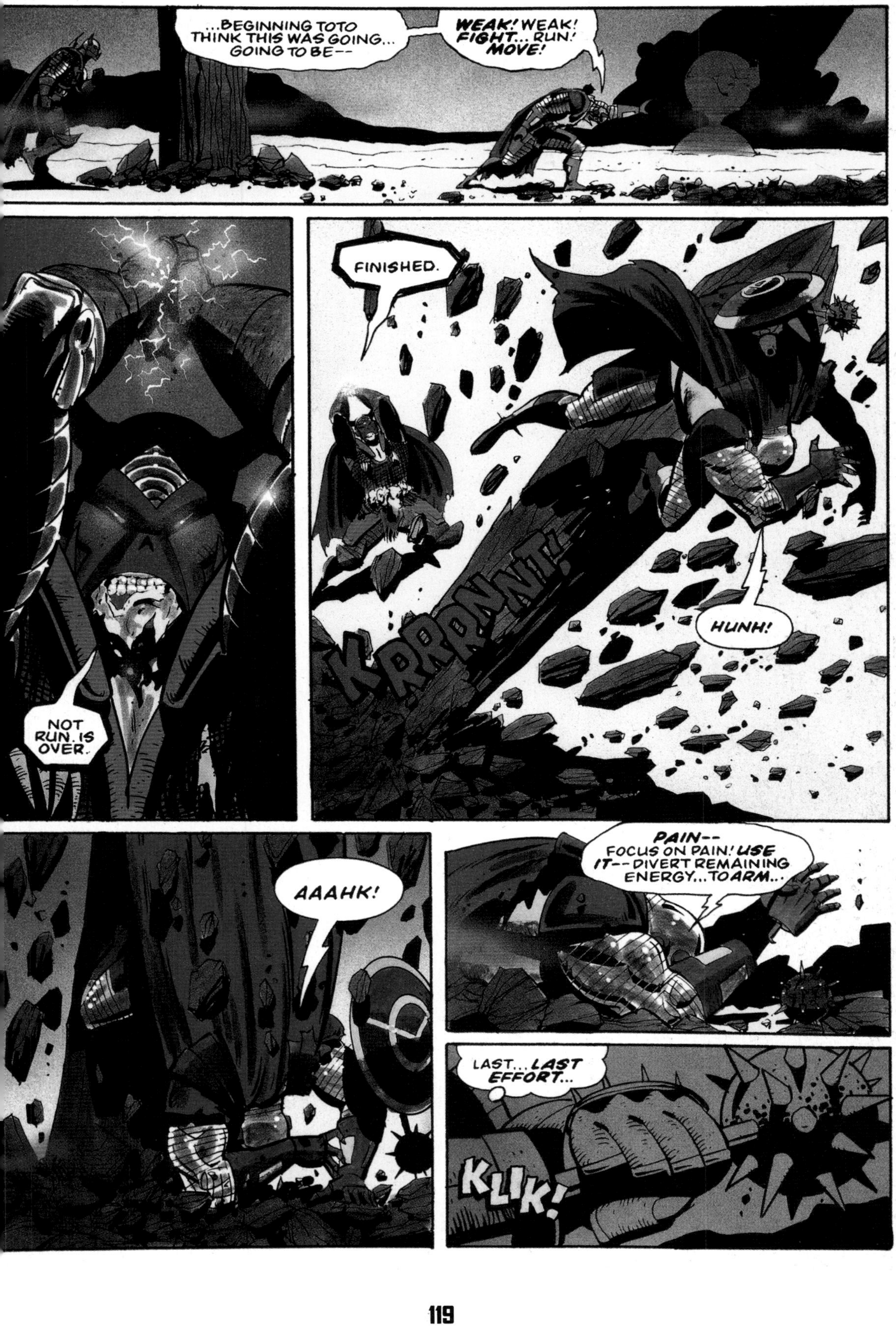
...BEGINNING TO TO THINK THIS WAS GOING... GOING TO BE--
WEAK! WEAK! FIGHT... RUN! MOVE!
NOT RUN. IS OVER.
FINISHED.
KRRRNNNT!
HUNH!
AAAHK!
PAIN-- FOCUS ON PAIN! USE IT-- DIVERT REMAINING ENERGY... TO ARM...
LAST... LAST EFFORT...
KLIK!

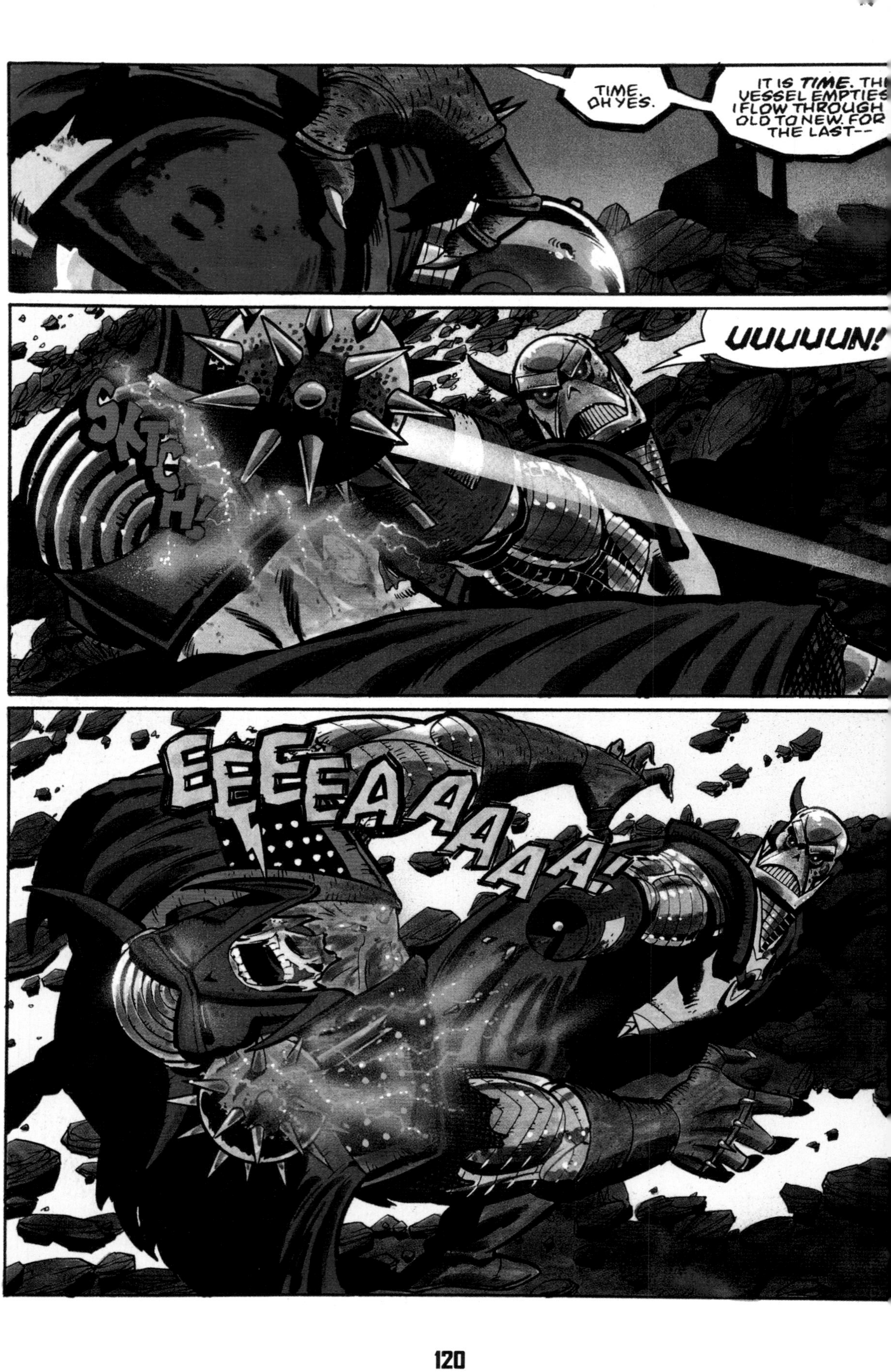
TIME. OH YES.
IT IS TIME. THE VESSEL EMPTIES I FLOW THROUGH OLD TO NEW. FOR THE LAST--
UUUUUN!
SKTCH!
EEEEAAAAAA!

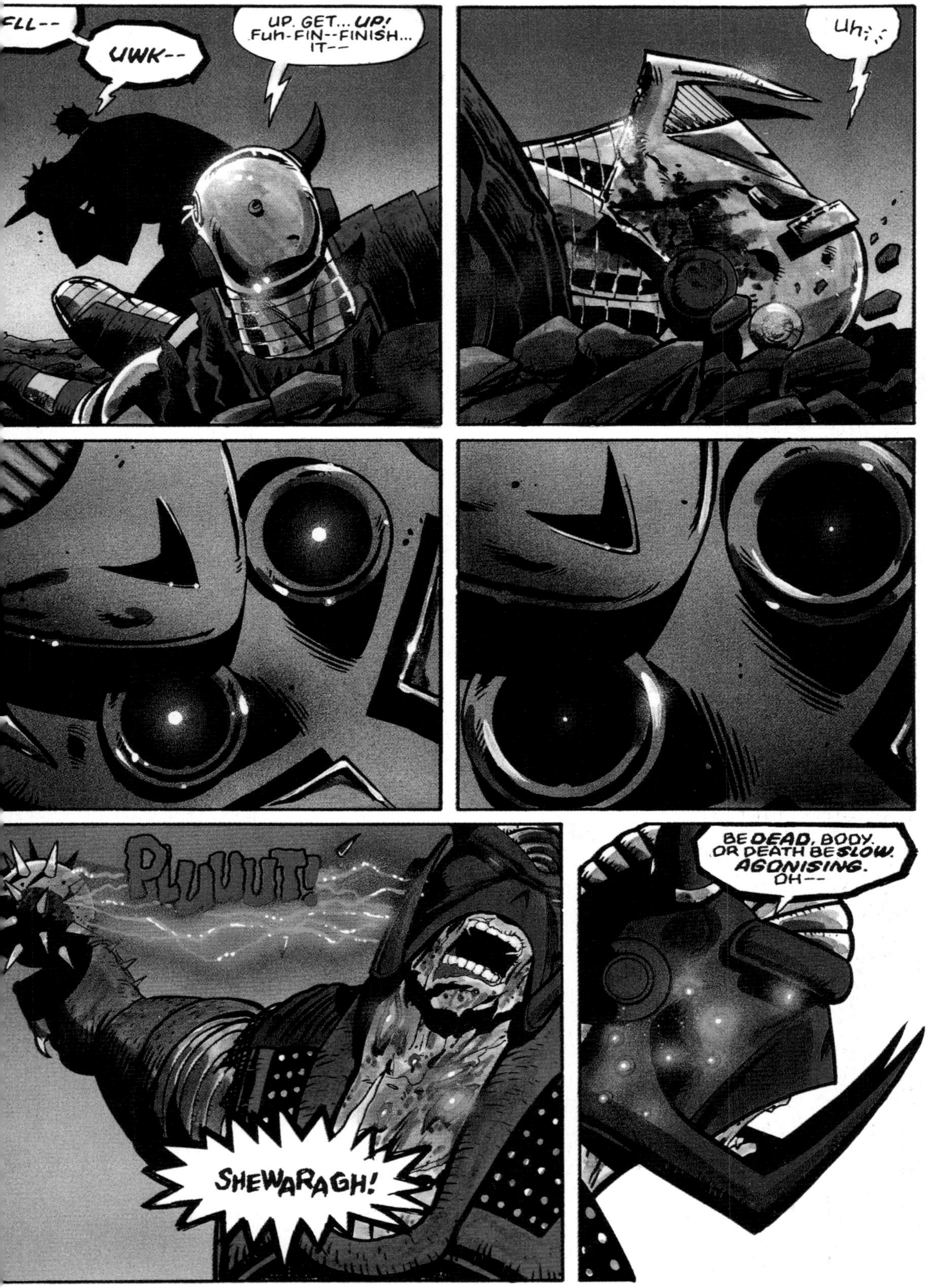
FLL--
UWK--
UP. GET... UP! Fuh-FIN--FINISH... IT--
Uh;
PLUUUT!
SHEWARAGH!
BE DEAD, BODY. OR DEATH BE SLOW. AGONISING. OH--

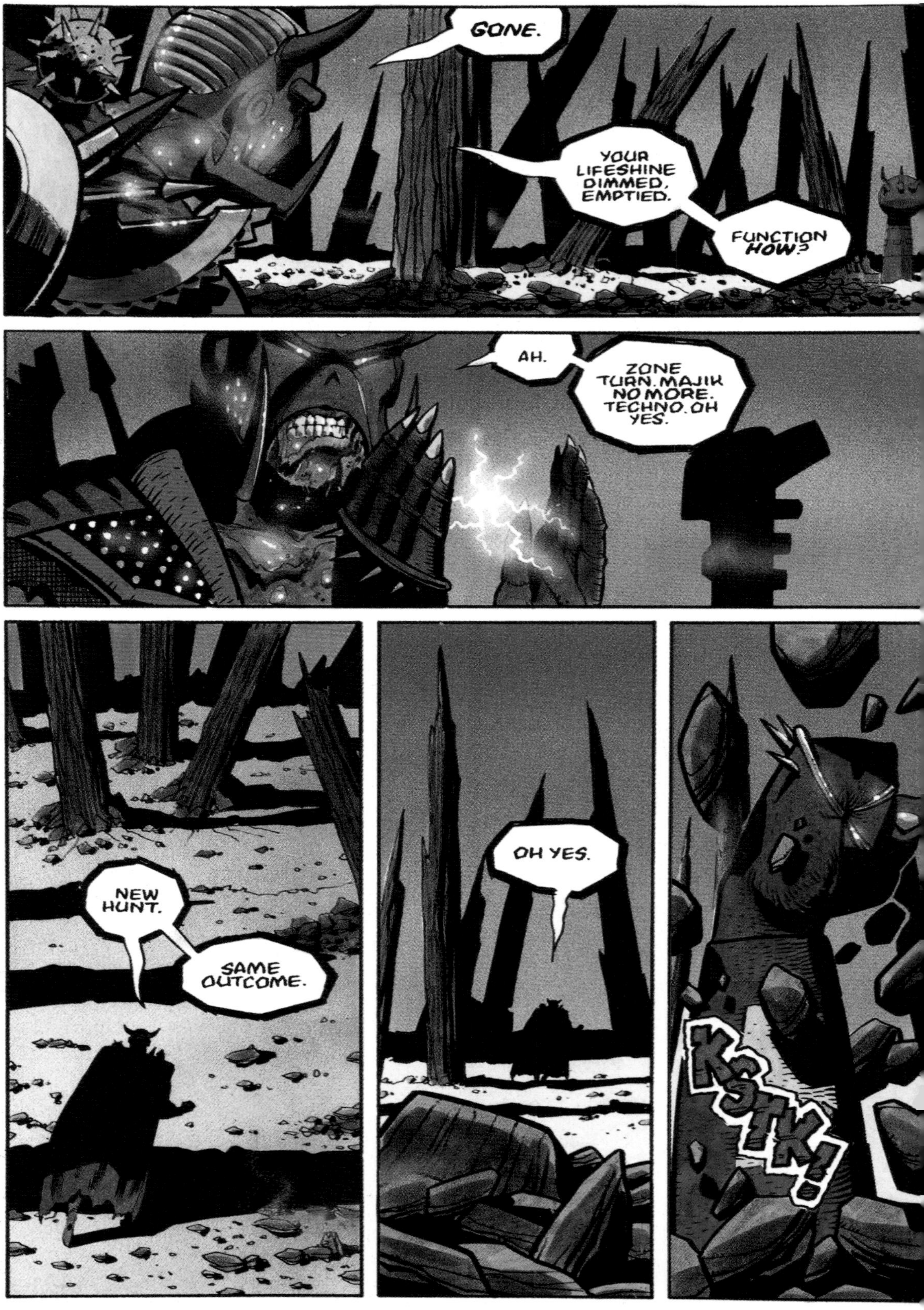
GONE.
YOUR LIFESHINE DIMMED, EMPTIED.
FUNCTION HOW?
AH.
ZONE TURN. MAJIK NO MORE. TECHNO. OH YES.
NEW HUNT.
SAME OUTCOME.
OH YES.
KSTK!

GONE TOO FAR. STUPID.

BUT THE *THRILL*. OH YES. SAND RUNS. TIME TICKS ON. TICK-TICKTICK. FOR PREY--

--FOR ME.

STRONG. STRONGEST. BUT ITS TIME IS LONG PAST.

ANOTHER SHOULD I HAVE TAKEN. BEFORE THE HUNT. OH YES. BUT THE DANGER, THE *THRILL*...

ENOUGH. NOT LOSE. OH NO.

RRT!

GONE MAJIK. BUT COMES TECHNO.

SHK!

AND LUPEX--

FFN!

IRZ

--OF *BOTH* IS MASTER. OH YES.

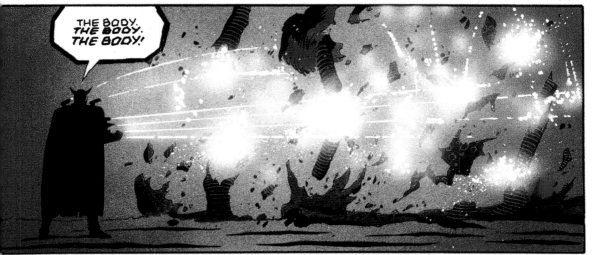

THE BODY. *THE BODY*. *THE BODY!*

123

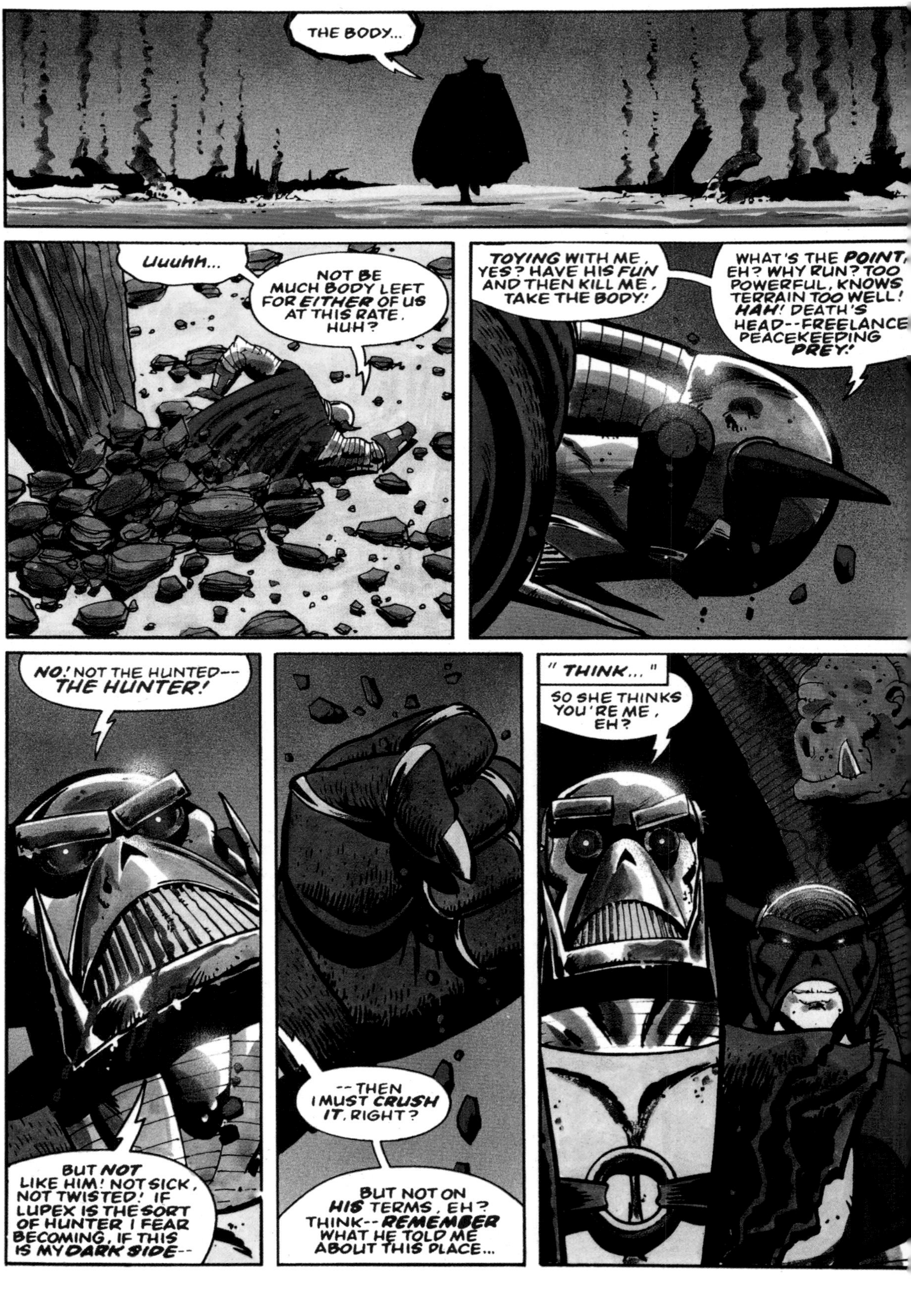
THE BODY...
Uuuhh...
NOT BE MUCH BODY LEFT FOR EITHER OF US AT THIS RATE. HUH?
TOYING WITH ME, YES? HAVE HIS FUN AND THEN KILL ME, TAKE THE BODY!
WHAT'S THE POINT, EH? WHY RUN? TOO POWERFUL, KNOWS TERRAIN TOO WELL! HAH! DEATH'S HEAD--FREELANCE PEACEKEEPING PREY!
NO! NOT THE HUNTED-- THE HUNTER!
BUT NOT LIKE HIM! NOT SICK, NOT TWISTED! IF LUPEX IS THE SORT OF HUNTER I FEAR BECOMING, IF THIS IS MY DARK SIDE--
--THEN I MUST CRUSH IT, RIGHT?
BUT NOT ON HIS TERMS, EH? THINK--REMEMBER WHAT HE TOLD ME ABOUT THIS PLACE...
"THINK..."
SO SHE THINKS YOU'RE ME, EH?

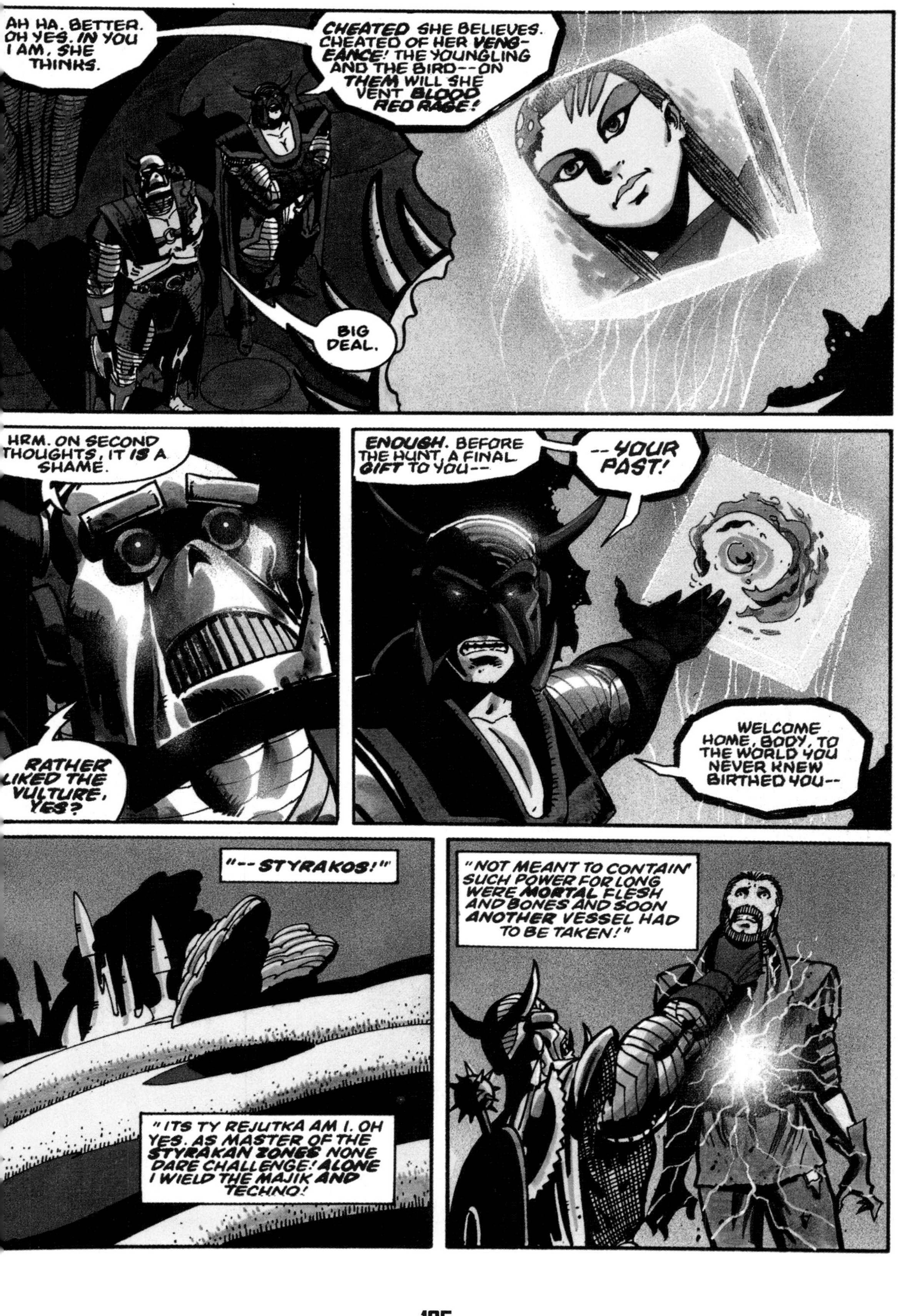
AH HA. BETTER. OH YES. IN YOU I AM, SHE THINKS.
CHEATED SHE BELIEVES. CHEATED OF HER VENGEANCE! THE YOUNGLING AND THE BIRD--ON THEM WILL SHE VENT BLOOD RED RAGE!
BIG DEAL.
HRM. ON SECOND THOUGHTS, IT IS A SHAME.
RATHER LIKED THE VULTURE, YES?
ENOUGH. BEFORE THE HUNT, A FINAL GIFT TO YOU--
--YOUR PAST!
WELCOME HOME, BODY, TO THE WORLD YOU NEVER KNEW BIRTHED YOU--
"--STYRAKOS!"
"ITS TY REJUTKA AM I. OH YES. AS MASTER OF THE STYRAKAN ZONES NONE DARE CHALLENGE! ALONE I WIELD THE MAJIK AND TECHNO!
"NOT MEANT TO CONTAIN SUCH POWER FOR LONG WERE MORTAL FLESH AND BONES AND SOON ANOTHER VESSEL HAD TO BE TAKEN!"

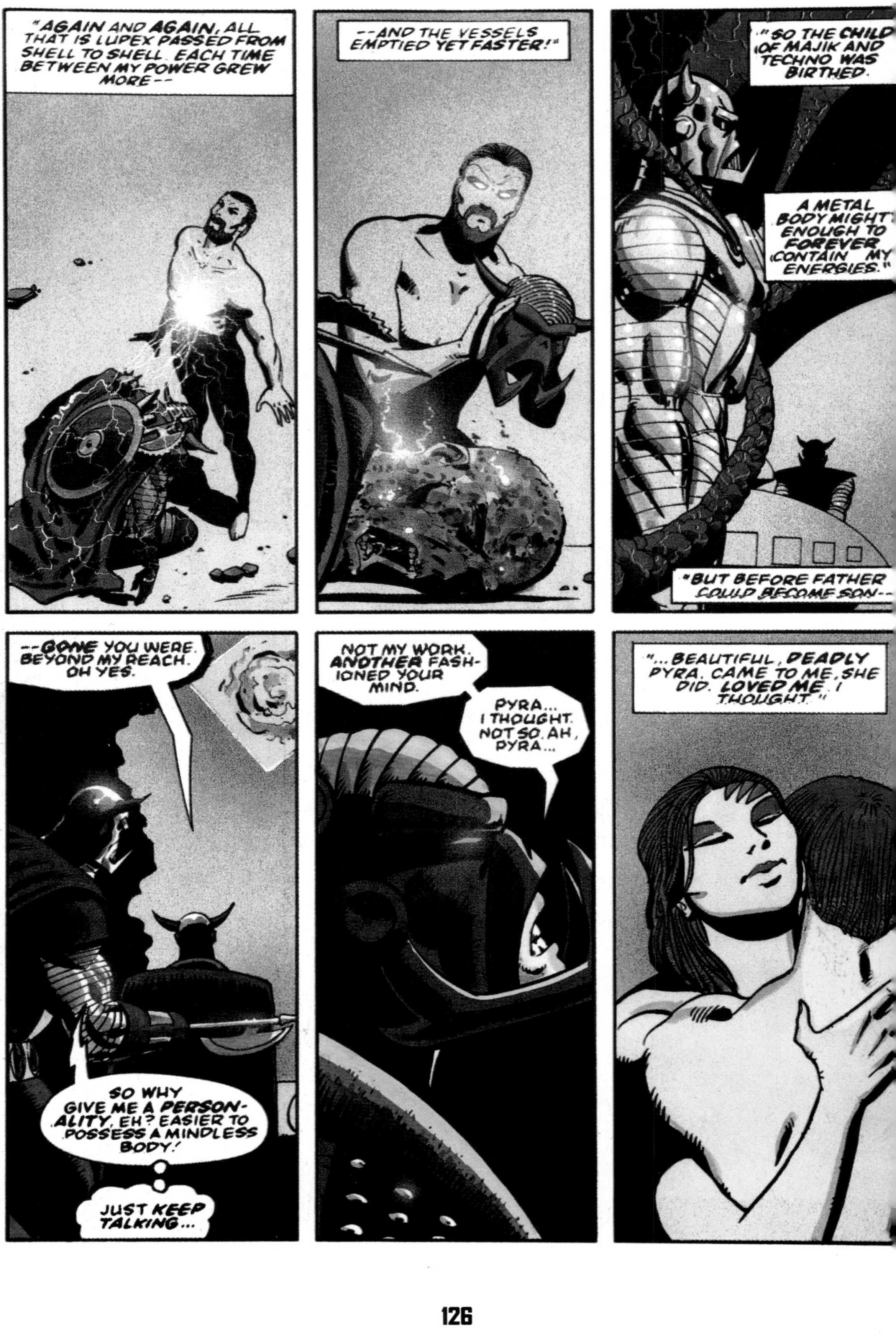
"AGAIN AND AGAIN, ALL THAT IS LUPEX PASSED FROM SHELL TO SHELL. EACH TIME BETWEEN MY POWER GREW MORE--
--AND THE VESSELS EMPTIED YET FASTER!"
"SO THE CHILD OF MAJIK AND TECHNO WAS BIRTHED.
A METAL BODY MIGHT ENOUGH TO FOREVER CONTAIN MY ENERGIES."
"BUT BEFORE FATHER COULD BECOME SON--
--GONE YOU WERE. BEYOND MY REACH. OH YES.
SO WHY GIVE ME A PERSONALITY, EH? EASIER TO POSSESS A MINDLESS BODY!
JUST KEEP TALKING...
NOT MY WORK. ANOTHER FASHIONED YOUR MIND.
PYRA... I THOUGHT. NOT SO. AH, PYRA...
"...BEAUTIFUL, DEADLY PYRA. CAME TO ME, SHE DID. LOVED ME. I THOUGHT."

MY POWER SHE WANTED. SECRETS. CARED NOTHING TAUGHT HER--
"--THE PRICE OF BETRAYAL. OH YES."
REVENGE SHE SEEKS. BUT IF SHE BELIEVES YOU AND I ARE ONE, ANOTHER MUST HAVE STOLEN THE BODY AND--
SKZZAK!
BODY--
YOU TRY MY PATIENCE!
UUNH!

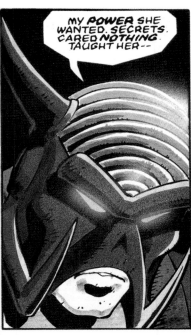

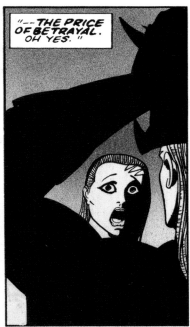

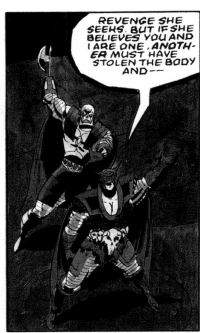

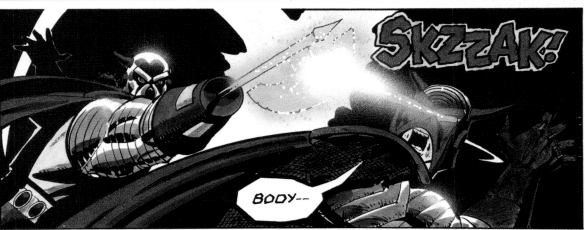

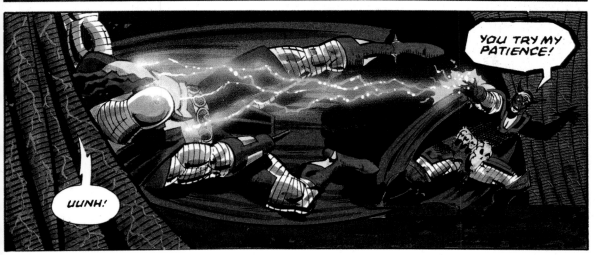

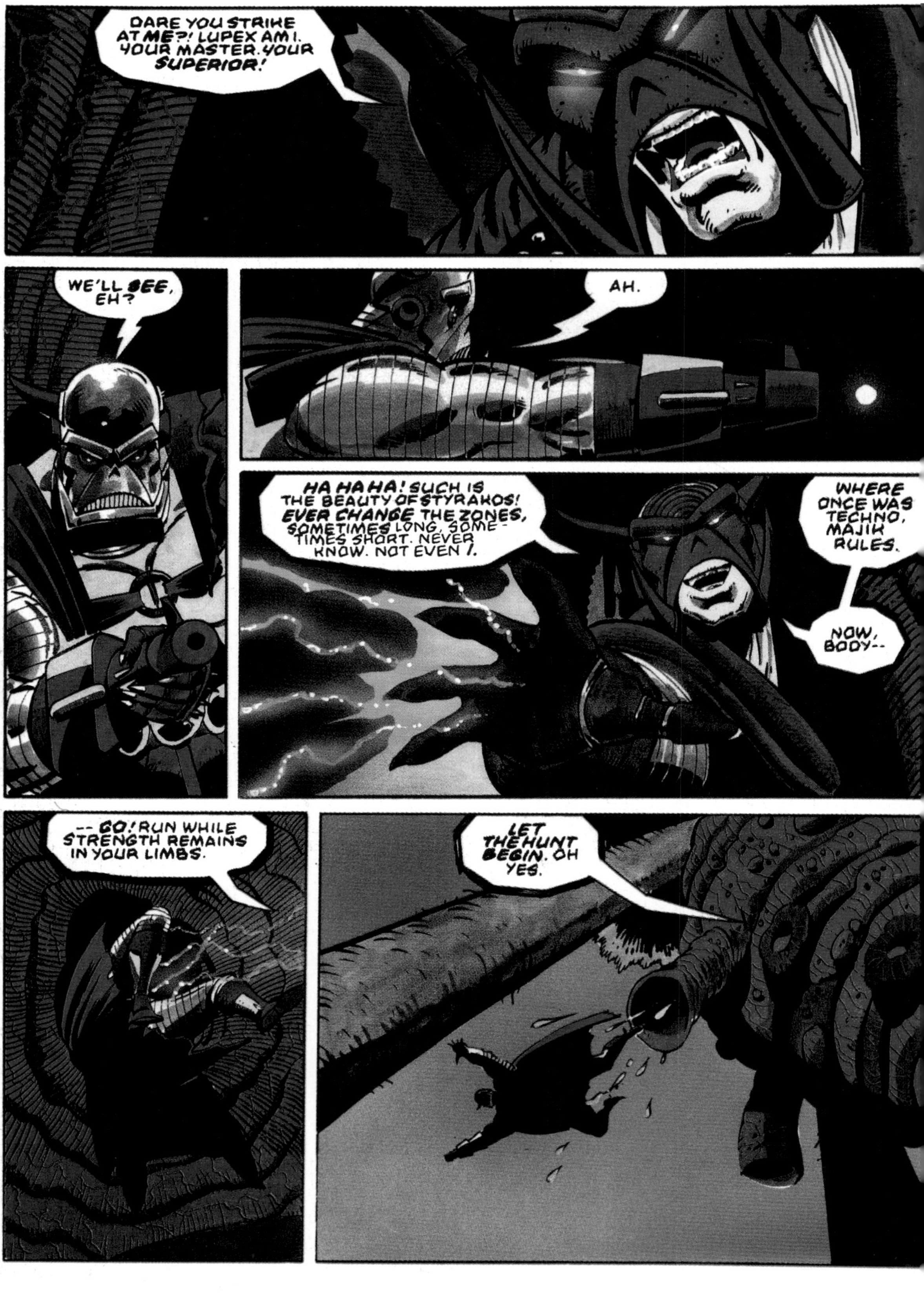
DARE YOU STRIKE AT ME?! LUPEX AM I. YOUR MASTER. YOUR SUPERIOR!
WE'LL SEE, EH?
AH.
HA HA HA! SUCH IS THE BEAUTY OF STYRAKOS! EVER CHANGE THE ZONES, SOMETIMES LONG, SOMETIMES SHORT. NEVER KNOW. NOT EVEN I.
WHERE ONCE WAS TECHNO, MAJIK RULES.
NOW, BODY--
--GO! RUN WHILE STRENGTH REMAINS IN YOUR LIMBS.
LET THE HUNT BEGIN. OH YES.

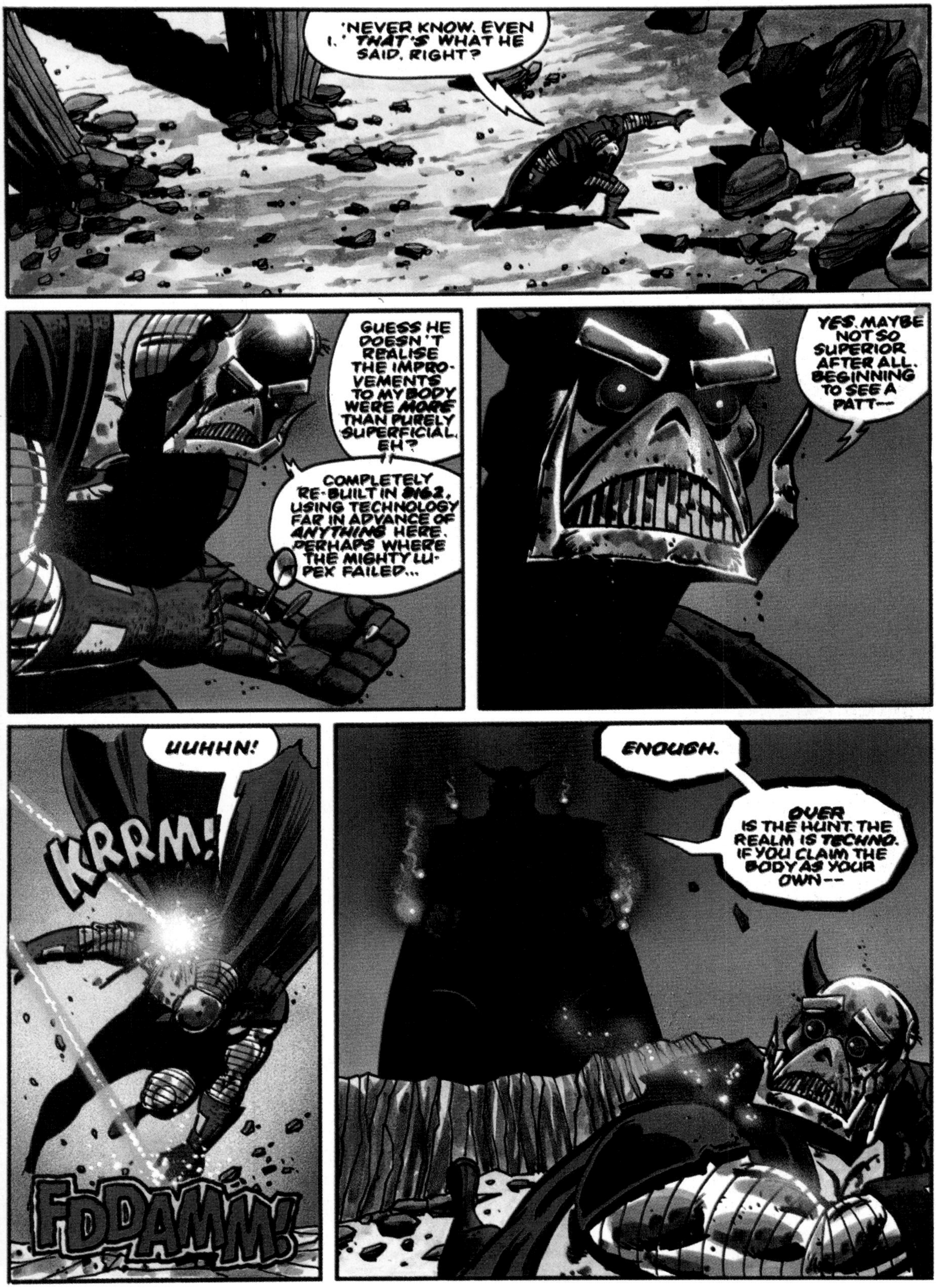
'NEVER KNOW. EVEN I.' THAT'S WHAT HE SAID, RIGHT?
GUESS HE DOESN'T REALISE THE IMPROVEMENTS TO MY BODY WERE MORE THAN PURELY SUPERFICIAL, EH?
COMPLETELY RE-BUILT IN 8162, USING TECHNOLOGY FAR IN ADVANCE OF ANYTHING HERE. PERHAPS WHERE THE MIGHTY LUPEX FAILED...
YES. MAYBE NOT SO SUPERIOR AFTER ALL. BEGINNING TO SEE A PATT--
UUHHN!
KRRM!
FDDAMM!
ENOUGH.
OVER IS THE HUNT. THE REALM IS TECHNO. IF YOU CLAIM THE BODY AS YOUR OWN--

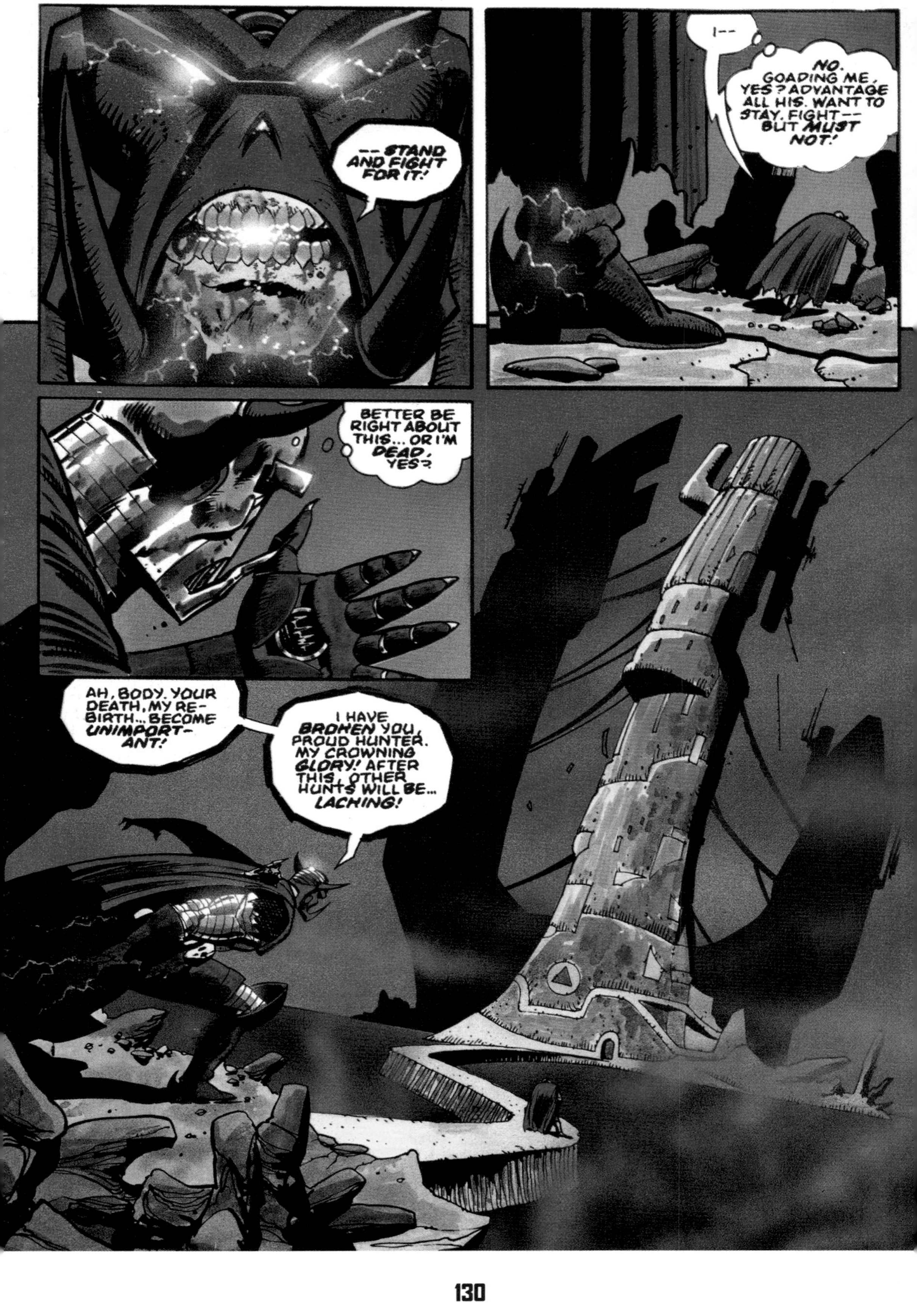
-- STAND AND FIGHT FOR IT!'
I--
NO. GOADING ME, YES? ADVANTAGE ALL HIS. WANT TO STAY, FIGHT-- BUT MUST NOT!'
BETTER BE RIGHT ABOUT THIS... OR I'M DEAD, YES?
AH, BODY. YOUR DEATH, MY RE-BIRTH... BECOME UNIMPORT-ANT!
I HAVE BROKEN YOU, PROUD HUNTER. MY CROWNING GLORY! AFTER THIS, OTHER HUNTS WILL BE... LACKING!

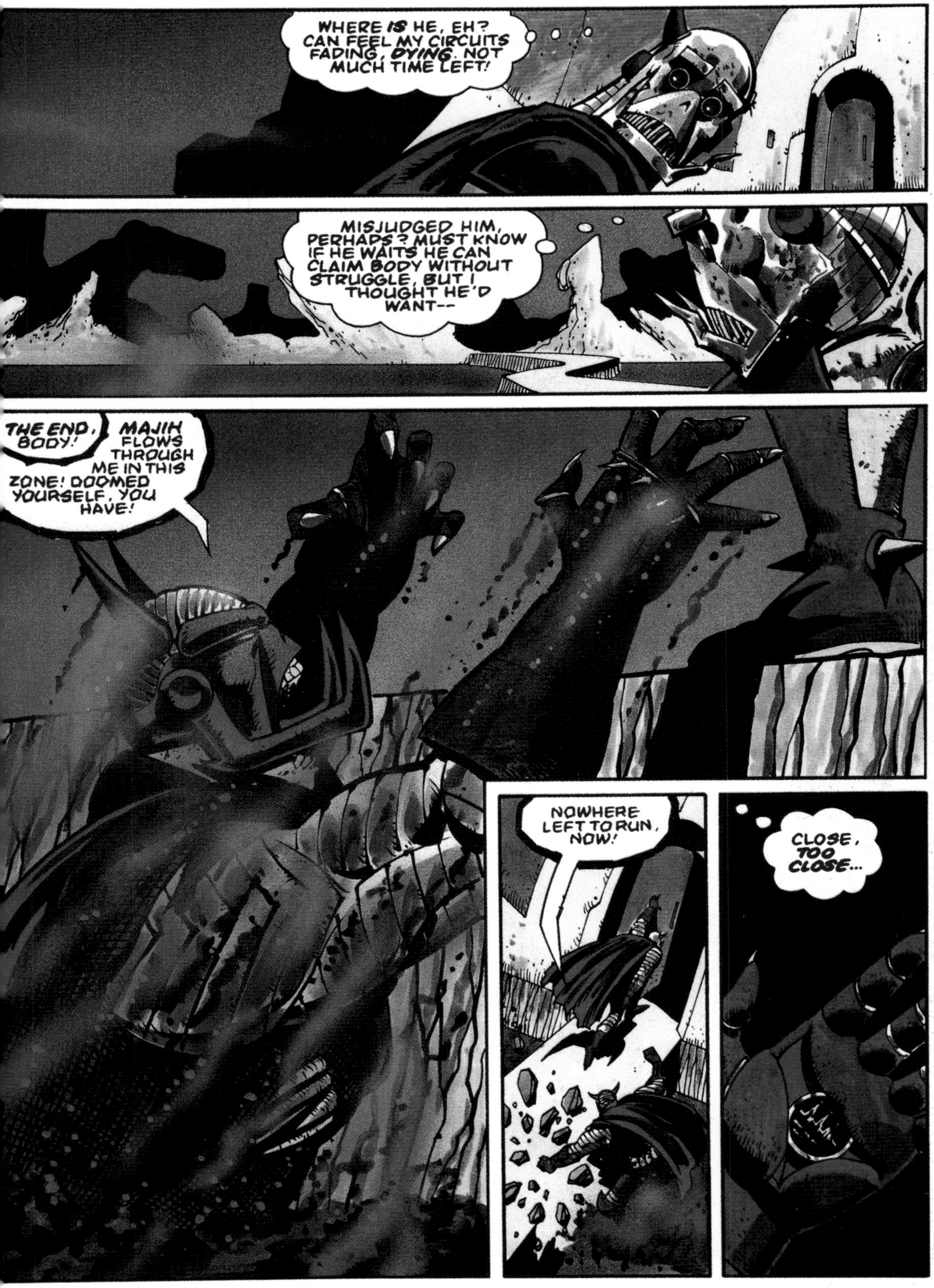
WHERE IS HE, EH? CAN FEEL MY CIRCUITS FADING, DYING. NOT MUCH TIME LEFT!
MISJUDGED HIM, PERHAPS? MUST KNOW IF HE WAITS HE CAN CLAIM BODY WITHOUT STRUGGLE, BUT I THOUGHT HE'D WANT--
THE END, BODY!
MAJIH FLOWS THROUGH ME IN THIS ZONE! DOOMED YOURSELF, YOU HAVE!
NOWHERE LEFT TO RUN, NOW!
CLOSE, TOO CLOSE...

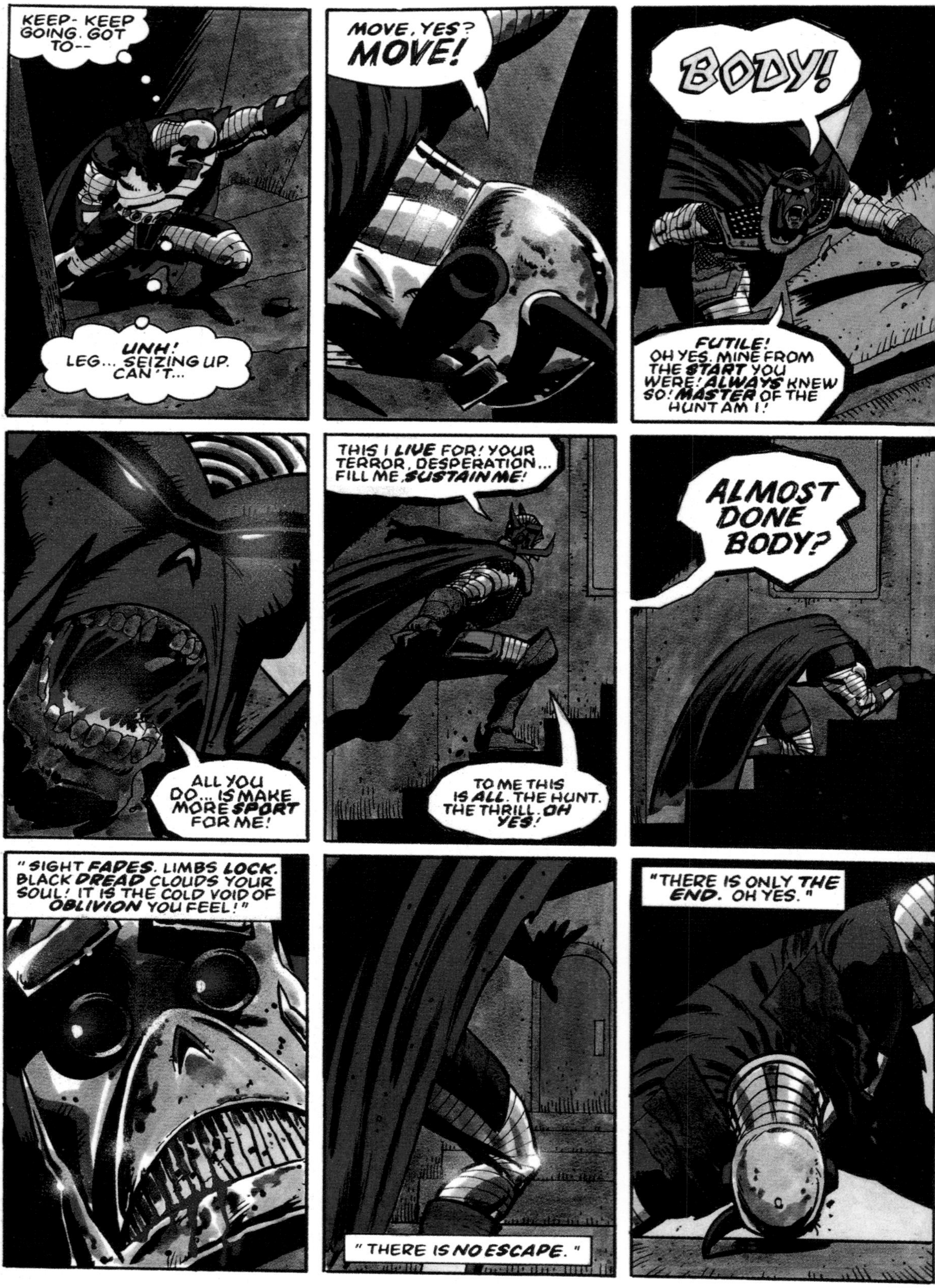
KEEP- KEEP GOING. GOT TO--
UNH! LEG... SEIZING UP. CAN'T...
MOVE, YES? MOVE!
BODY!
FUTILE! OH YES. MINE FROM THE START YOU WERE! ALWAYS KNEW SO! MASTER OF THE HUNT AM I!
ALL YOU DO... IS MAKE MORE SPORT FOR ME!
THIS I LIVE FOR! YOUR TERROR, DESPERATION... FILL ME, SUSTAIN ME!
TO ME THIS IS ALL. THE HUNT. THE THRILL. OH YES!
ALMOST DONE BODY?
"SIGHT FADES. LIMBS LOCK. BLACK DREAD CLOUDS YOUR SOUL! IT IS THE COLD VOID OF OBLIVION YOU FEEL!"
"THERE IS NO ESCAPE."
"THERE IS ONLY THE END. OH YES."

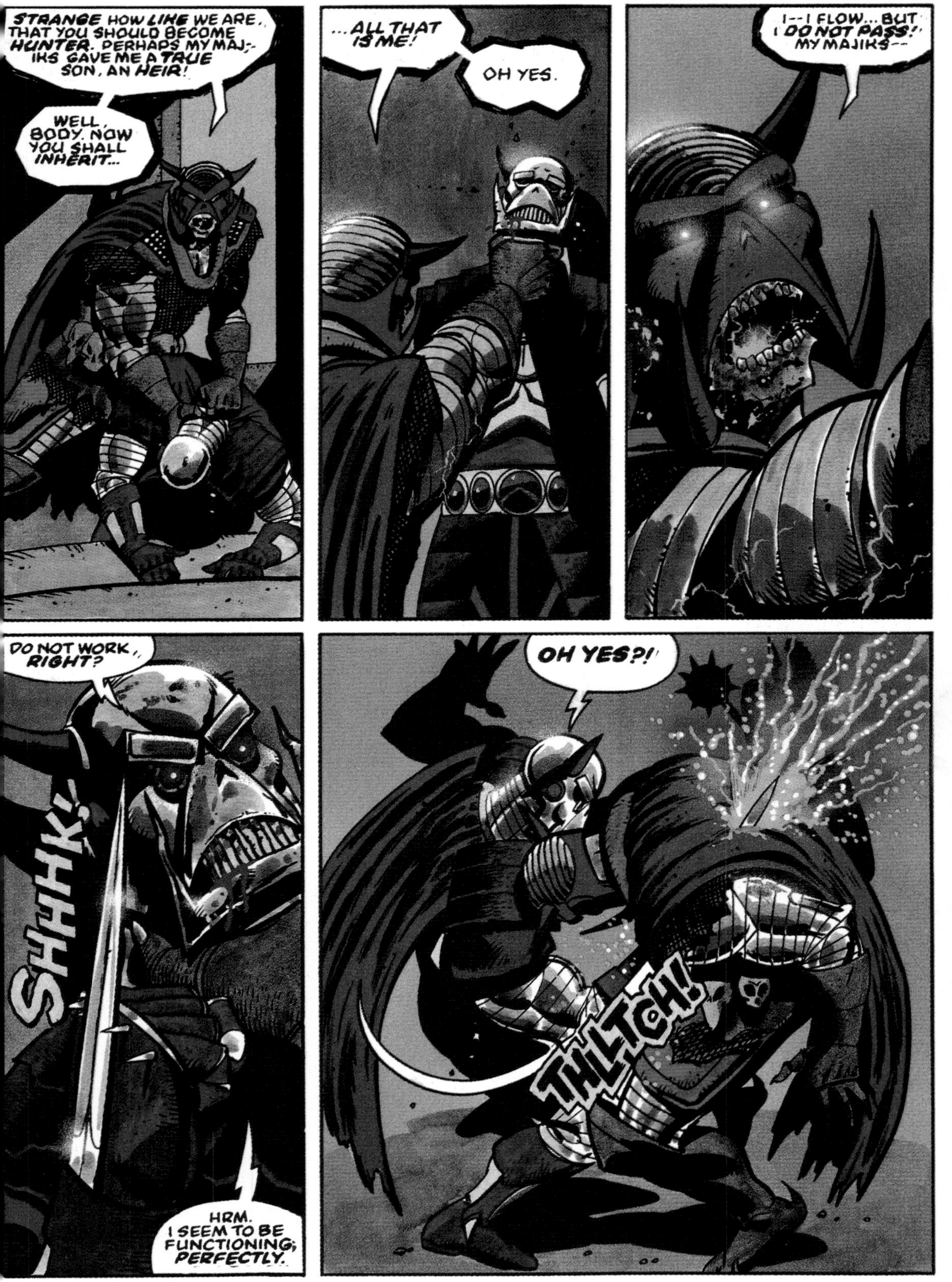

STRANGE HOW LIKE WE ARE, THAT YOU SHOULD BECOME HUNTER. PERHAPS MY MAJ-IKS GAVE ME A TRUE SON, AN HEIR!
WELL, BODY. NOW YOU SHALL INHERIT...
...ALL THAT IS ME!
OH YES.
I--I FLOW... BUT I DO NOT PASS! MY MAJIKS--
DO NOT WORK, RIGHT?
SHHHK!
HRM. I SEEM TO BE FUNCTIONING, PERFECTLY.
OH YES?!
THLTCH!

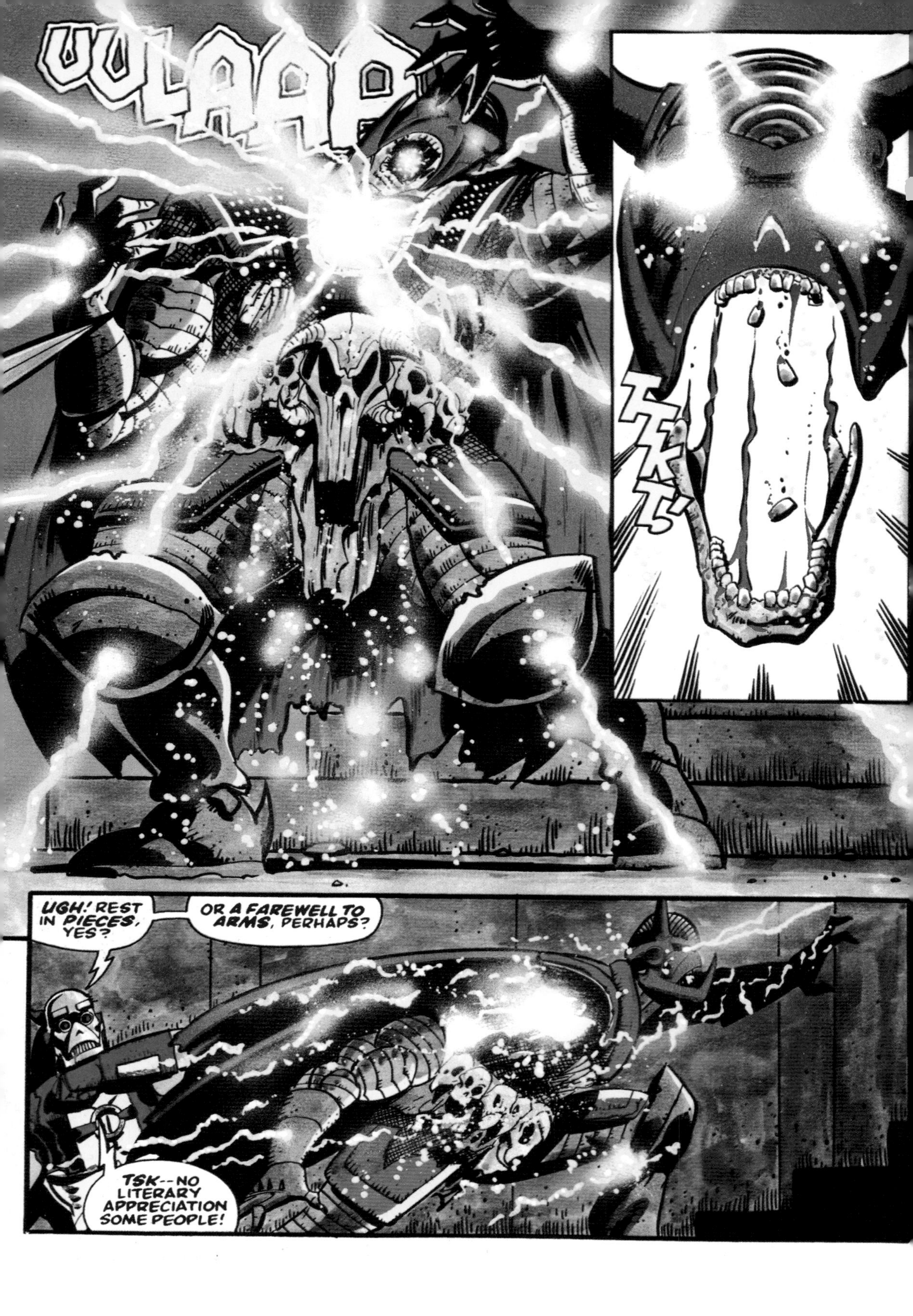
UULAAP
TEKT!
UGH! REST IN PIECES, YES?
OR A FAREWELL TO ARMS, PERHAPS?
TSK--NO LITERARY APPRECIATION SOME PEOPLE!

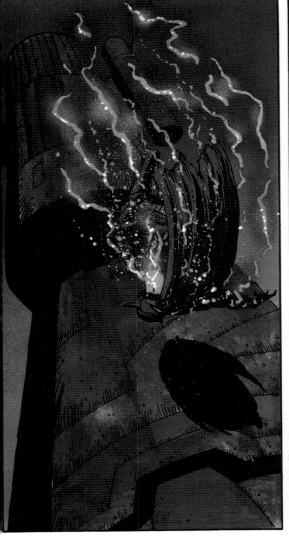

ZONE CHANGE, YES? LED YOU INTO ONE MY ONBOARD COMPUTER CALCULATED WAS ABOUT TO SWITCH FROM MAJIK TO TECHNO!

SO **SURE**, EH? SO SURE OF YOUR OWN **OMNIPOTENCE**, COULD NOT **CONCEIVE** OF SOMEONE SUCCEEDING WHERE YOU FAILED!

STILL ALIVE, HUH? **GOOD!** HOPE DEATH IS A LONG TIME COMING FOR YOU! MORE **SATISFYING** TO SEE YOU SUFFER--

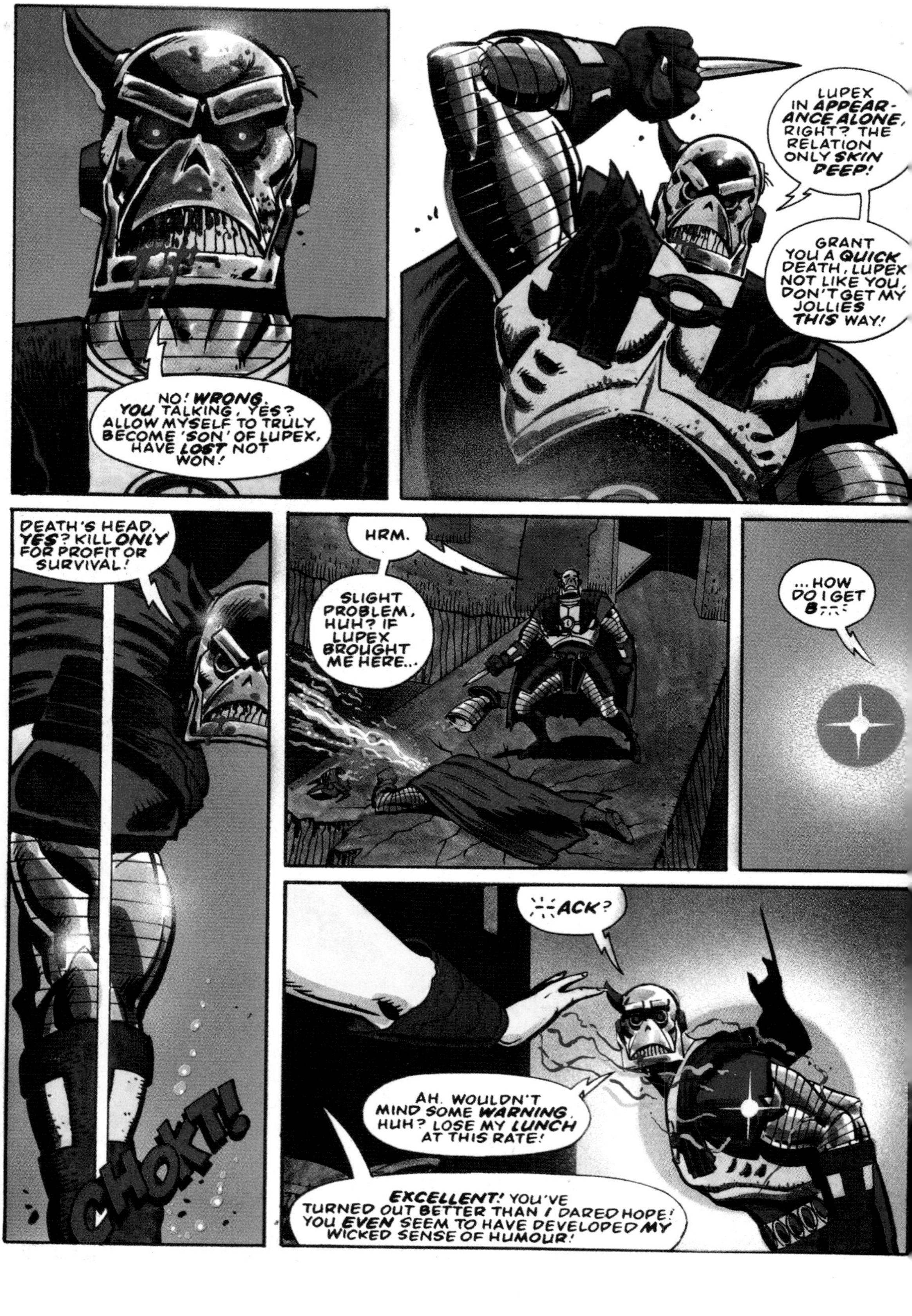
NO! WRONG. YOU TALKING, YES? ALLOW MYSELF TO TRULY BECOME 'SON' OF LUPEX, HAVE LOST NOT WON!
LUPEX IN APPEARANCE ALONE, RIGHT? THE RELATION ONLY SKIN DEEP!
GRANT YOU A QUICK DEATH, LUPEX NOT LIKE YOU, DON'T GET MY JOLLIES THIS WAY!
DEATH'S HEAD, YES? KILL ONLY FOR PROFIT OR SURVIVAL!
CHOKT!
HRM.
SLIGHT PROBLEM, HUH? IF LUPEX BROUGHT ME HERE...
...HOW DO I GET B---
---ACK?
AH. WOULDN'T MIND SOME WARNING, HUH? LOSE MY LUNCH AT THIS RATE!
EXCELLENT! YOU'VE TURNED OUT BETTER THAN I DARED HOPE! YOU EVEN SEEM TO HAVE DEVELOPED MY WICKED SENSE OF HUMOUR!

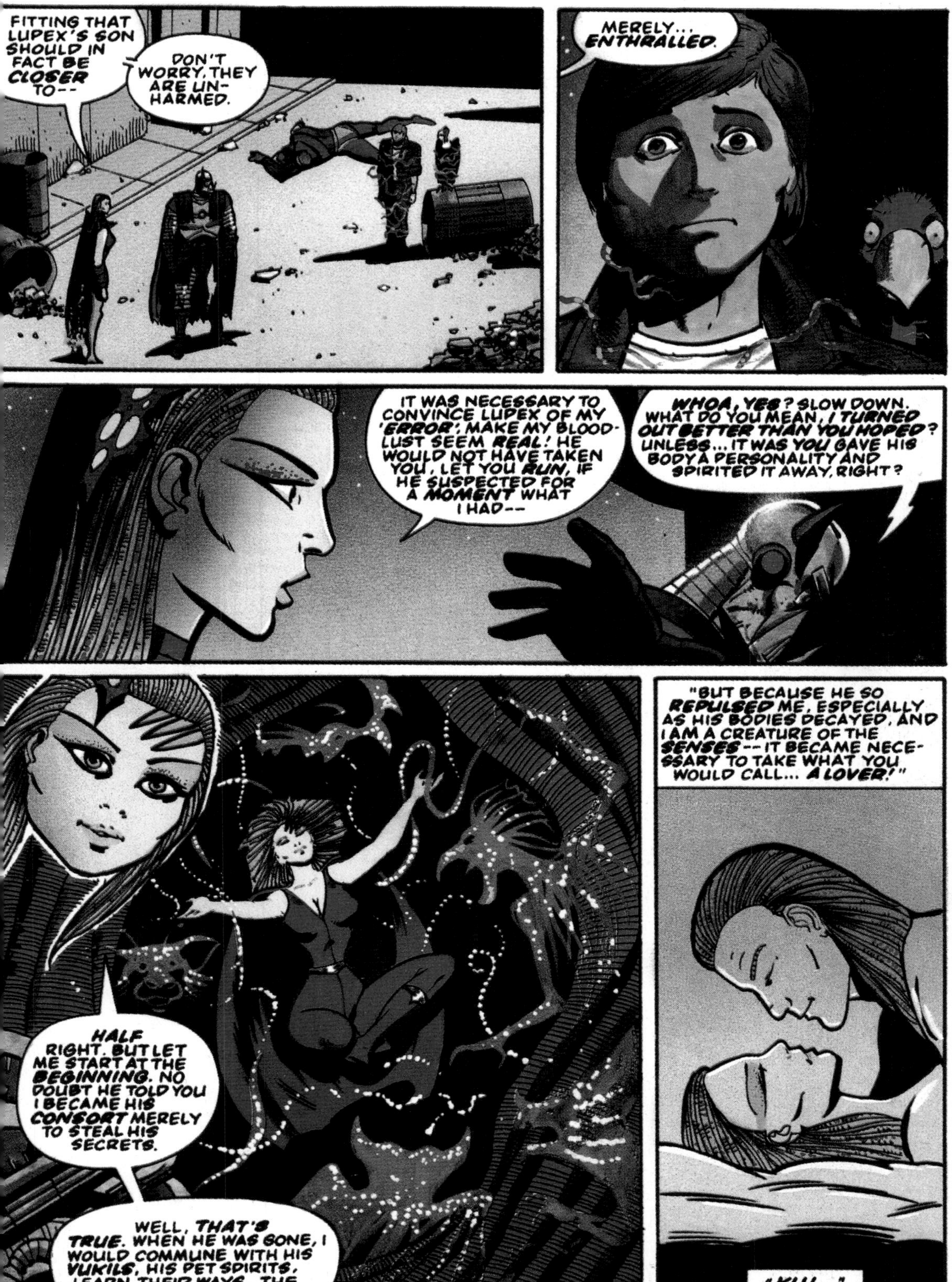
FITTING THAT LUPEX'S SON SHOULD IN FACT BE CLOSER TO--
DON'T WORRY. THEY ARE UN-HARMED.
MERELY... ENTHRALLED.
IT WAS NECESSARY TO CONVINCE LUPEX OF MY 'ERROR'; MAKE MY BLOOD-LUST SEEM REAL! HE WOULD NOT HAVE TAKEN YOU, LET YOU RUN, IF HE SUSPECTED FOR A MOMENT WHAT I HAD--
WHOA, YES? SLOW DOWN. WHAT DO YOU MEAN, I TURNED OUT BETTER THAN YOU HOPED? UNLESS... IT WAS YOU GAVE HIS BODY A PERSONALITY AND SPIRITED IT AWAY, RIGHT?
HALF RIGHT. BUT LET ME START AT THE BEGINNING. NO DOUBT HE TOLD YOU I BECAME HIS CONSORT MERELY TO STEAL HIS SECRETS.
WELL, THAT'S TRUE. WHEN HE WAS GONE, I WOULD COMMUNE WITH HIS VUKILS, HIS PET SPIRITS. LEARN THEIR WAYS. THE ROADS TO POWER!
"BUT BECAUSE HE SO REPULSED ME, ESPECIALLY AS HIS BODIES DECAYED, AND I AM A CREATURE OF THE SENSES -- IT BECAME NECESSARY TO TAKE WHAT YOU WOULD CALL... A LOVER!"
"KLU..."

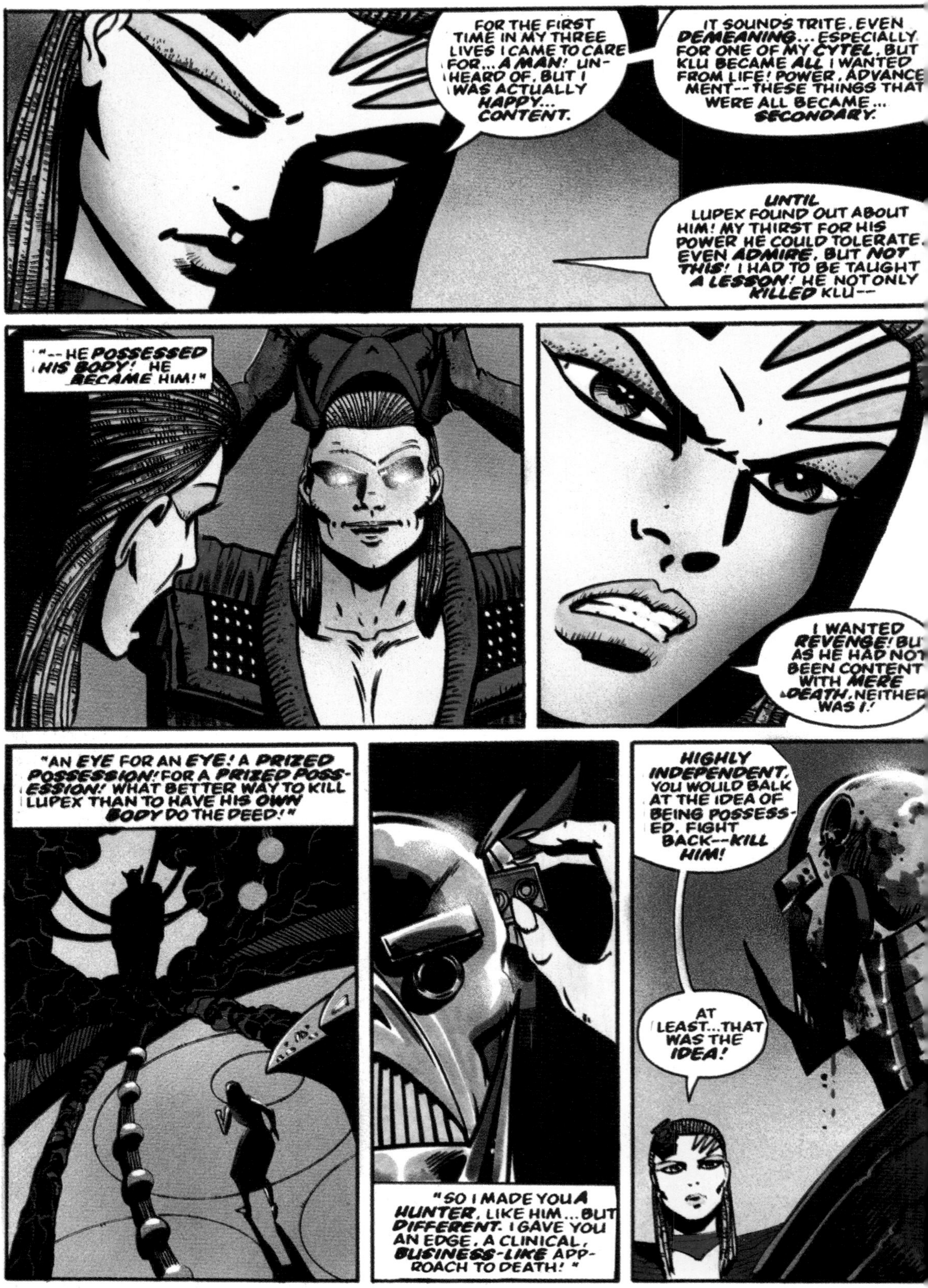
FOR THE FIRST TIME IN MY THREE LIVES I CAME TO CARE FOR... A MAN! UNHEARD OF, BUT I WAS ACTUALLY HAPPY... CONTENT.
IT SOUNDS TRITE, EVEN DEMEANING... ESPECIALLY FOR ONE OF MY CYTEL, BUT KLU BECAME ALL I WANTED FROM LIFE! POWER, ADVANCEMENT--THESE THINGS THAT WERE ALL BECAME... SECONDARY.
UNTIL LUPEX FOUND OUT ABOUT HIM! MY THIRST FOR HIS POWER HE COULD TOLERATE, EVEN ADMIRE, BUT NOT THIS! I HAD TO BE TAUGHT A LESSON! HE NOT ONLY KILLED KLU--
"--HE POSSESSED HIS BODY! HE BECAME HIM!"
I WANTED REVENGE! BUT AS HE HAD NOT BEEN CONTENT WITH MERE DEATH, NEITHER WAS I!
"AN EYE FOR AN EYE! A PRIZED POSSESSION! FOR A PRIZED POSSESSION! WHAT BETTER WAY TO KILL LUPEX THAN TO HAVE HIS OWN BODY DO THE DEED!"
"SO I MADE YOU A HUNTER, LIKE HIM... BUT DIFFERENT. I GAVE YOU AN EDGE, A CLINICAL, BUSINESS-LIKE APPROACH TO DEATH!"
HIGHLY INDEPENDENT, YOU WOULD BALK AT THE IDEA OF BEING POSSESSED, FIGHT BACK--KILL HIM!
AT LEAST... THAT WAS THE IDEA!

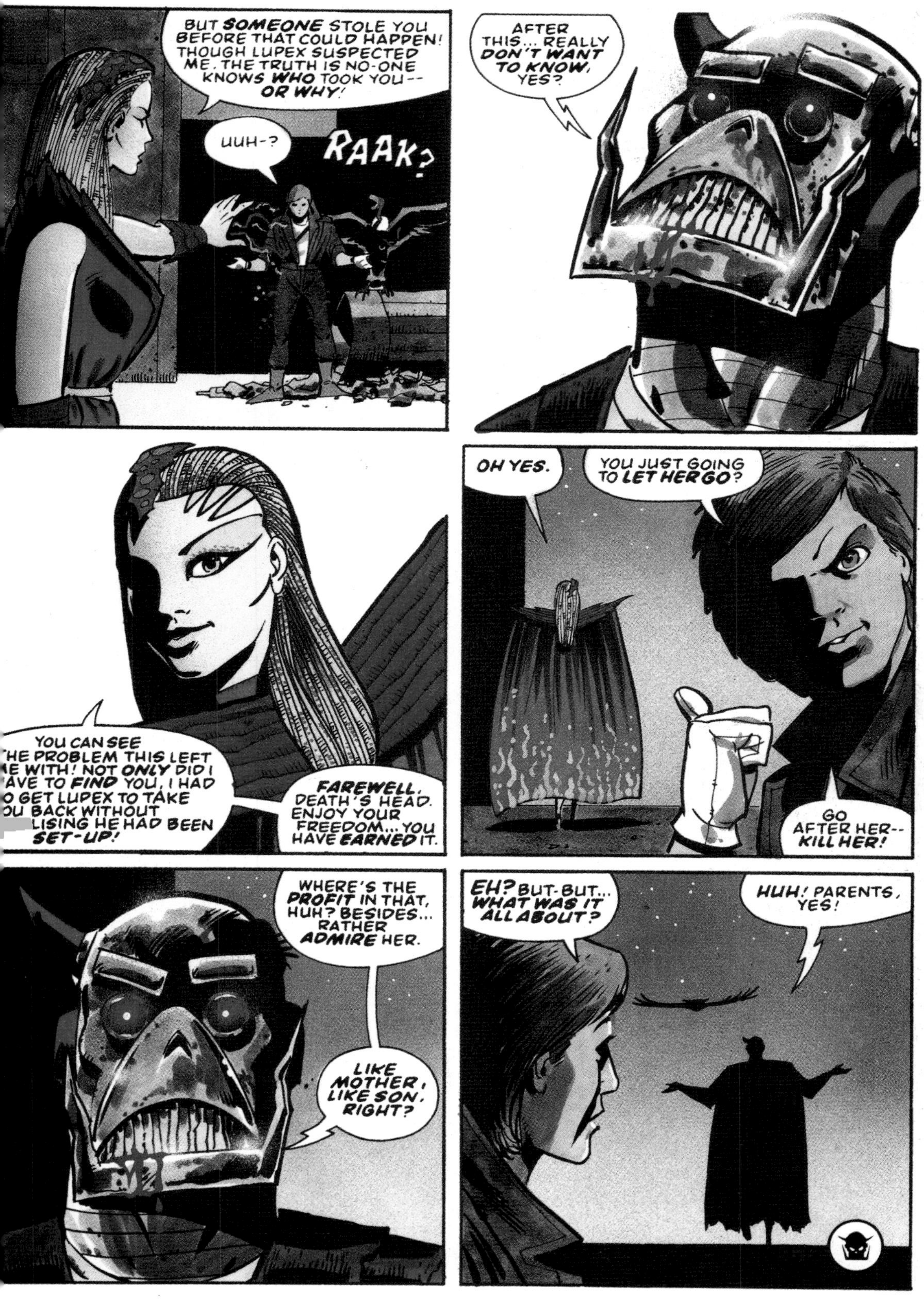
BUT SOMEONE STOLE YOU BEFORE THAT COULD HAPPEN! THOUGH LUPEX SUSPECTED ME. THE TRUTH IS NO-ONE KNOWS WHO TOOK YOU -- OR WHY!
UUH-?
RAAK?
AFTER THIS... REALLY DON'T WANT TO KNOW, YES?
YOU CAN SEE
HE PROBLEM THIS LEFT
E WITH! NOT ONLY DID I
AVE TO FIND YOU, I HAD
O GET LUPEX TO TAKE
OU BACK WITHOUT
LISING HE HAD BEEN
SET-UP!
FAREWELL, DEATH'S HEAD. ENJOY YOUR FREEDOM... YOU HAVE EARNED IT.
OH YES.
YOU JUST GOING TO LET HER GO?
GO AFTER HER-- KILL HER!
WHERE'S THE PROFIT IN THAT, HUH? BESIDES... RATHER ADMIRE HER.
LIKE MOTHER, LIKE SON, RIGHT?
EH? BUT-BUT... WHAT WAS IT ALL ABOUT?
HUH! PARENTS, YES!

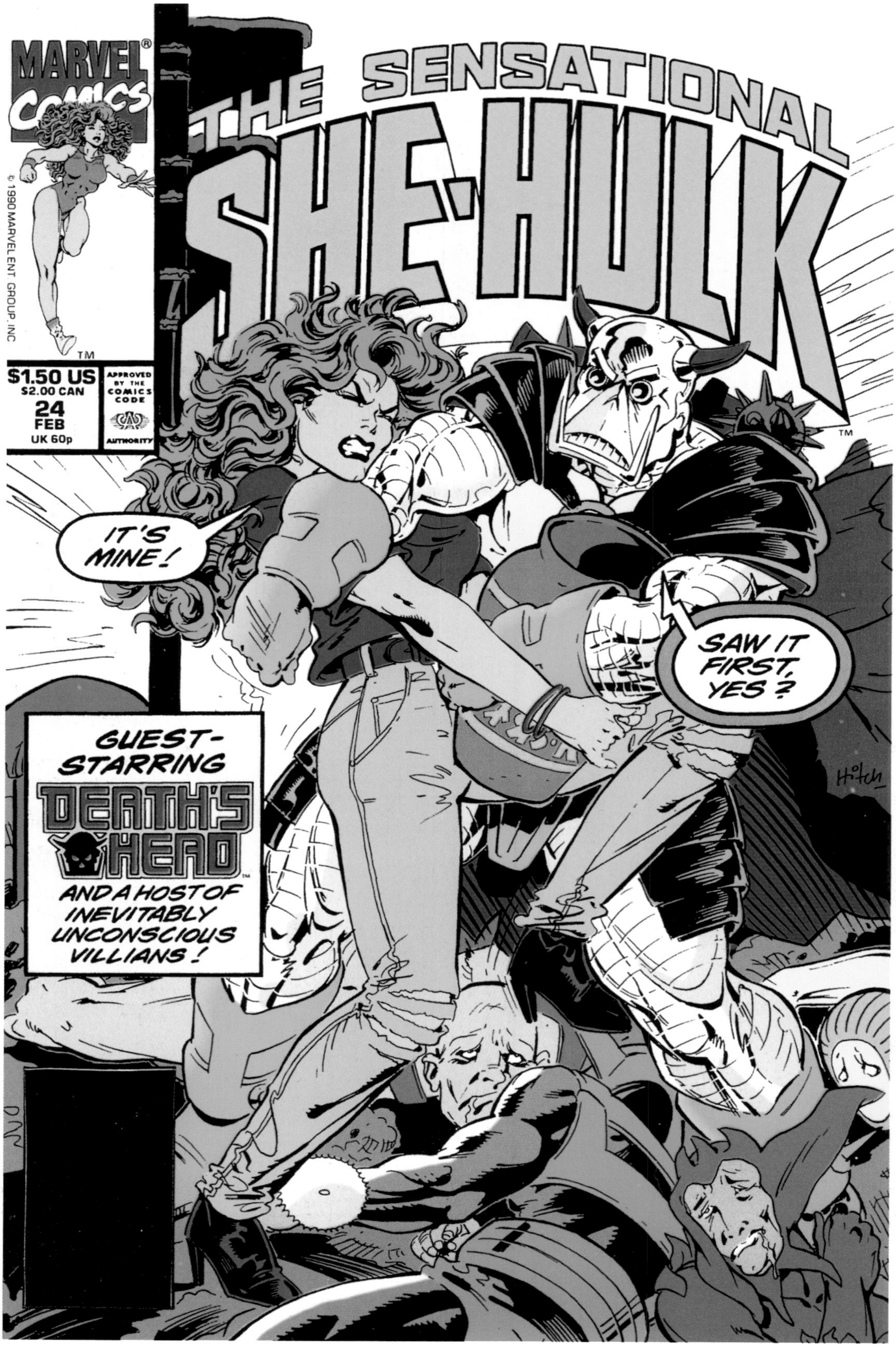
MARVEL® COMICS
THE SENSATIONAL SHE-HULK™
© 1990 MARVEL ENT. GROUP, INC.
$1.50 US
$2.00 CAN
24
FEB
UK 60p
APPROVED BY THE COMICS CODE AUTHORITY
IT'S MINE!
SAW IT FIRST, YES?
GUEST-STARRING
DEATH'S HEAD™
AND A HOST OF INEVITABLY UNCONSCIOUS VILLIANS!
Hitch

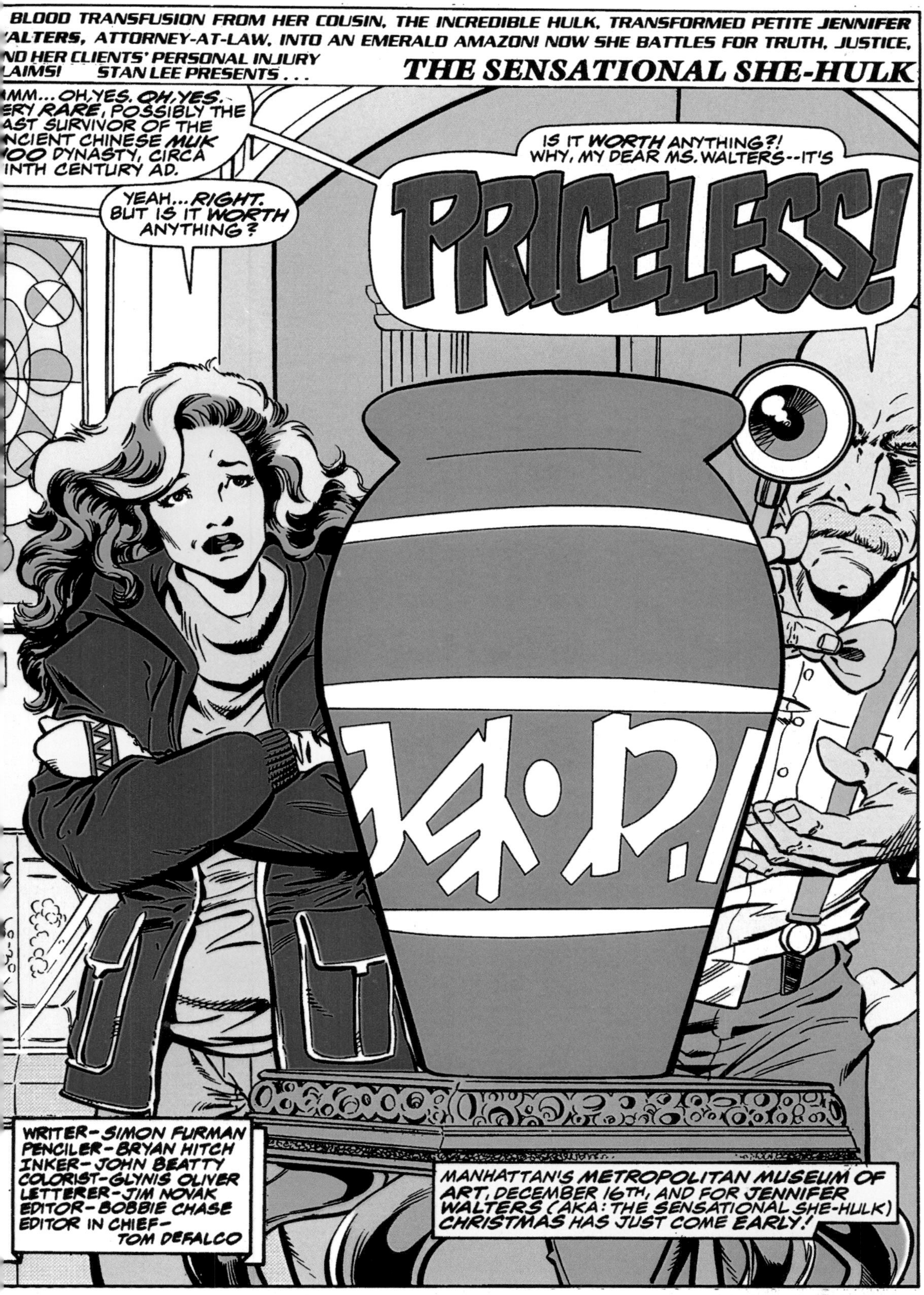
BLOOD TRANSFUSION FROM HER COUSIN, THE INCREDIBLE HULK, TRANSFORMED PETITE JENNIFER WALTERS, ATTORNEY-AT-LAW, INTO AN EMERALD AMAZON! NOW SHE BATTLES FOR TRUTH, JUSTICE, AND HER CLIENTS' PERSONAL INJURY CLAIMS! STAN LEE PRESENTS . . .
THE SENSATIONAL SHE-HULK
MMM... OH,YES. OH,YES. VERY RARE, POSSIBLY THE LAST SURVIVOR OF THE ANCIENT CHINESE MUK WOO DYNASTY, CIRCA NINTH CENTURY AD.
YEAH... RIGHT. BUT IS IT WORTH ANYTHING?
IS IT WORTH ANYTHING?! WHY, MY DEAR MS. WALTERS--IT'S PRICELESS!
WRITER- SIMON FURMAN PENCILER- BRYAN HITCH INKER- JOHN BEATTY COLORIST- GLYNIS OLIVER LETTERER- JIM NOVAK EDITOR- BOBBIE CHASE EDITOR IN CHIEF- TOM DEFALCO
MANHATTAN'S METROPOLITAN MUSEUM OF ART, DECEMBER 16TH, AND FOR JENNIFER WALTERS (AKA: THE SENSATIONAL SHE-HULK) CHRISTMAS HAS JUST COME EARLY!

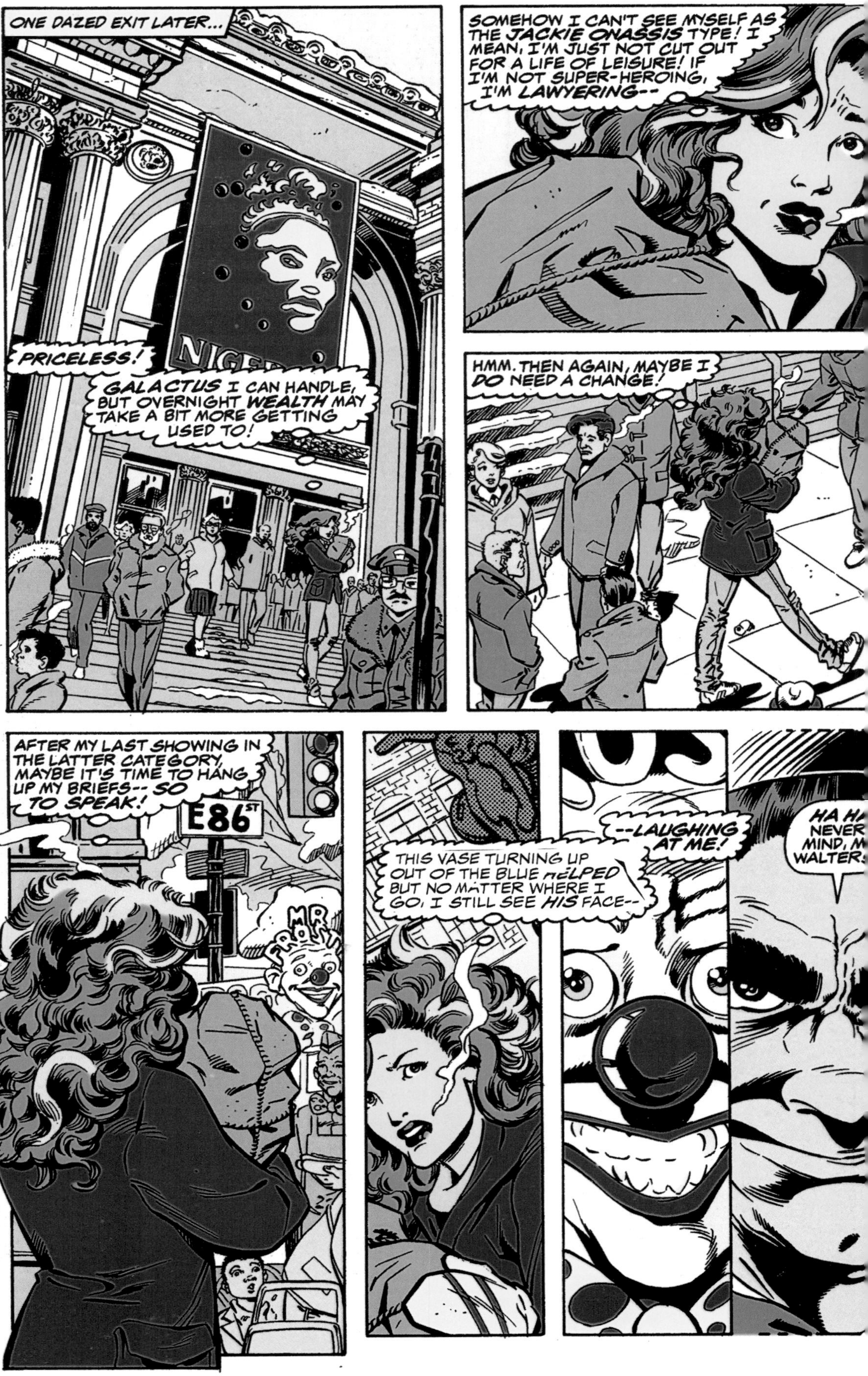
ONE DAZED EXIT LATER...
PRICELESS!
GALACTUS I CAN HANDLE, BUT OVERNIGHT WEALTH MAY TAKE A BIT MORE GETTING USED TO!
SOMEHOW I CAN'T SEE MYSELF AS THE JACKIE ONASSIS TYPE! I MEAN, I'M JUST NOT CUT OUT FOR A LIFE OF LEISURE! IF I'M NOT SUPER-HEROING, I'M LAWYERING--
HMM. THEN AGAIN, MAYBE I DO NEED A CHANGE!
AFTER MY LAST SHOWING IN THE LATTER CATEGORY, MAYBE IT'S TIME TO HANG UP MY BRIEFS-- SO TO SPEAK!
E86 ST
MR FROSTY
THIS VASE TURNING UP OUT OF THE BLUE HELPED BUT NO MATTER WHERE I GO, I STILL SEE HIS FACE--
--LAUGHING AT ME!
HA HA NEVER MIND, M WALTERS

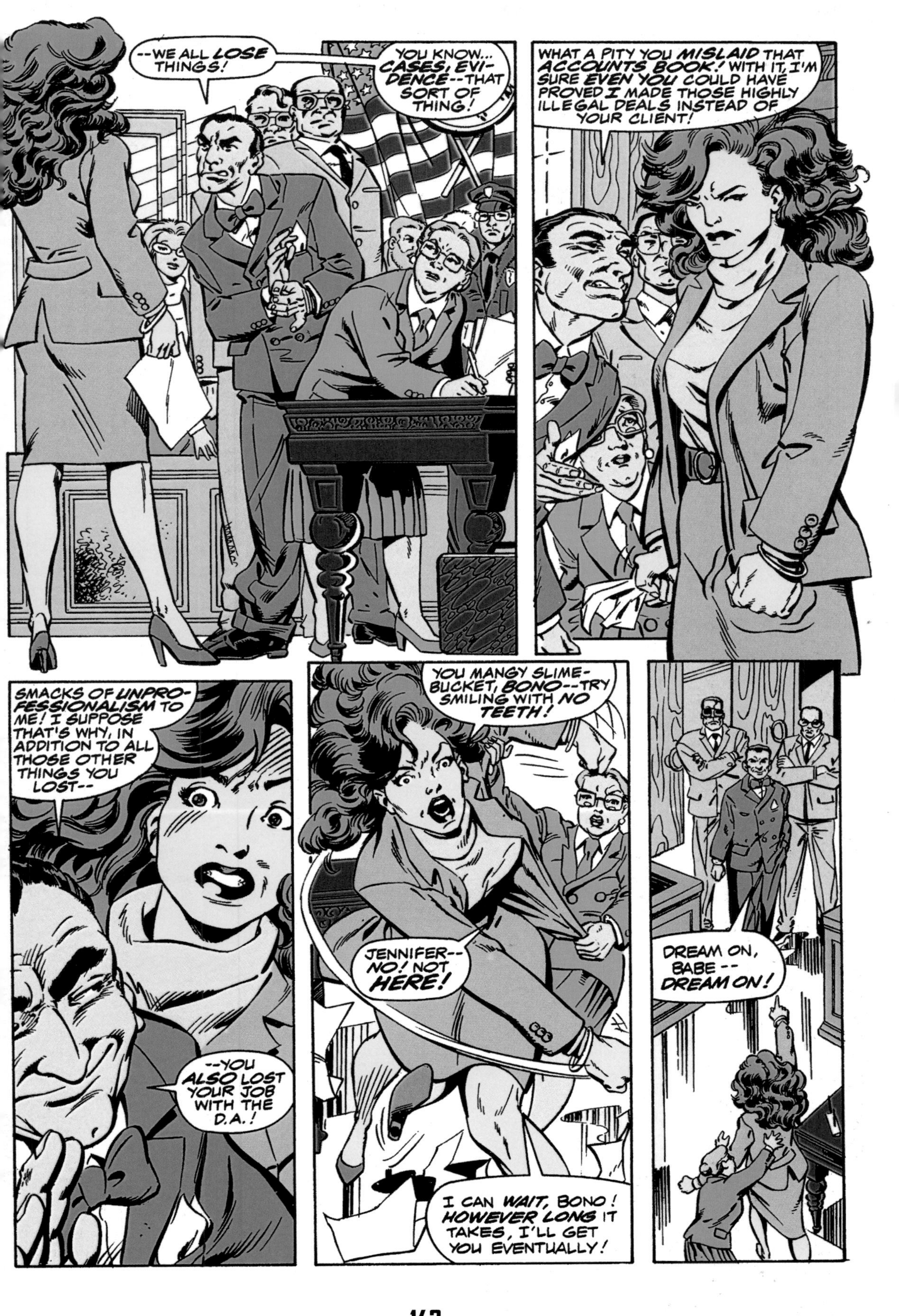
--WE ALL LOSE THINGS!
YOU KNOW... CASES, EVIDENCE--THAT SORT OF THING!
WHAT A PITY YOU MISLAID THAT ACCOUNTS BOOK! WITH IT, I'M SURE EVEN YOU COULD HAVE PROVED I MADE THOSE HIGHLY ILLEGAL DEALS INSTEAD OF YOUR CLIENT!
SMACKS OF UNPROFESSIONALISM TO ME! I SUPPOSE THAT'S WHY, IN ADDITION TO ALL THOSE OTHER THINGS YOU LOST--
--YOU ALSO LOST YOUR JOB WITH THE D.A.!
YOU MANGY SLIME-BUCKET, BONO--TRY SMILING WITH NO TEETH!
JENNIFER-- NO! NOT HERE!
I CAN WAIT, BONO! HOWEVER LONG IT TAKES, I'LL GET YOU EVENTUALLY!
DREAM ON, BABE -- DREAM ON!

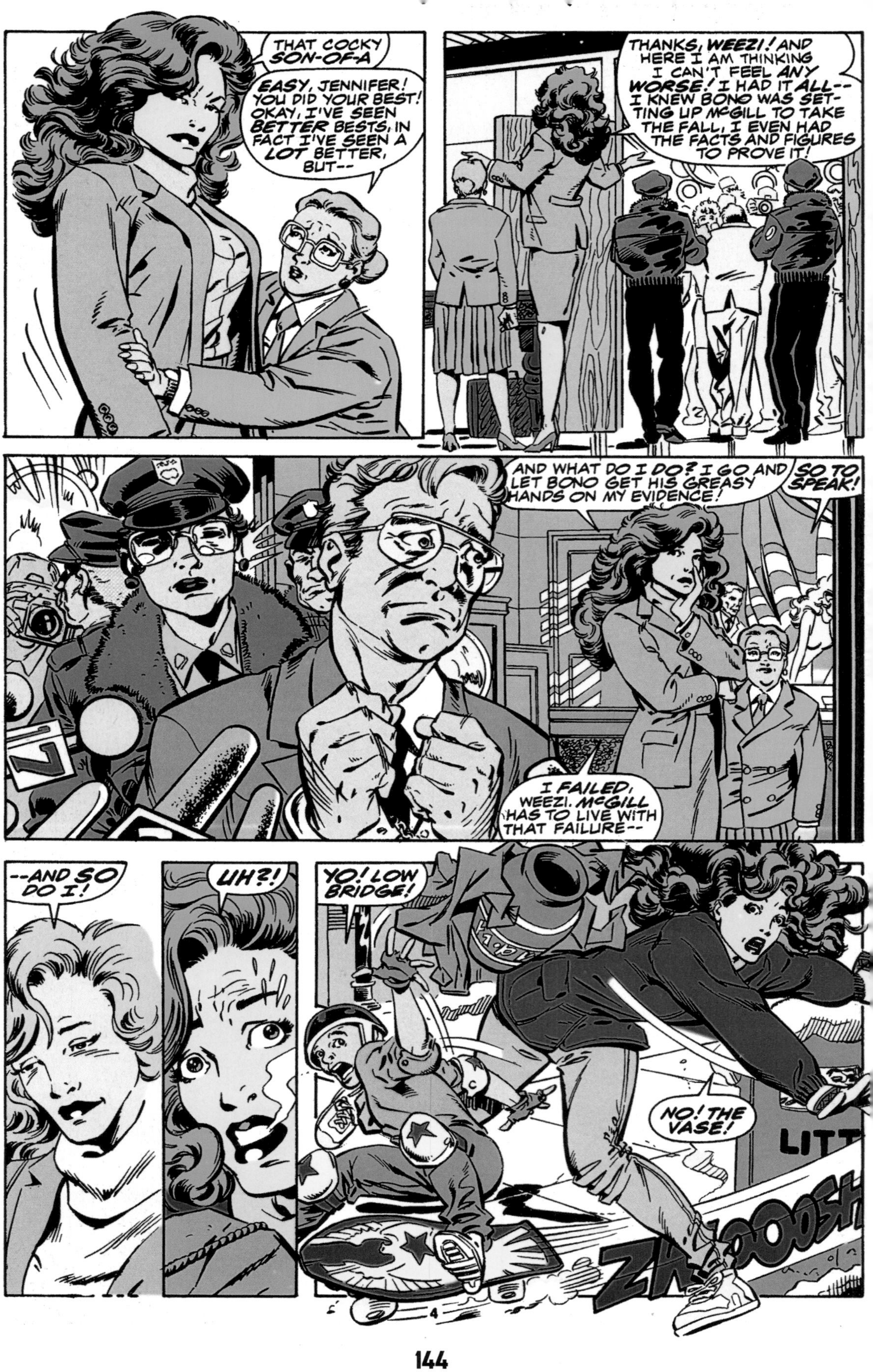
THAT COCKY SON-OF-A
EASY, JENNIFER! YOU DID YOUR BEST! OKAY, I'VE SEEN BETTER BESTS, IN FACT I'VE SEEN A LOT BETTER, BUT--
THANKS, WEEZI! AND HERE I AM THINKING I CAN'T FEEL ANY WORSE! I HAD IT ALL-- I KNEW BONO WAS SETTING UP McGILL TO TAKE THE FALL, I EVEN HAD THE FACTS AND FIGURES TO PROVE IT!
AND WHAT DO I DO? I GO AND LET BONO GET HIS GREASY HANDS ON MY EVIDENCE!
SO TO SPEAK!
I FAILED, WEEZI. McGILL HAS TO LIVE WITH THAT FAILURE--
--AND SO DO I!
UH?!
YO! LOW BRIDGE!
NO! THE VASE!
LITT
ZWOOOSH
4

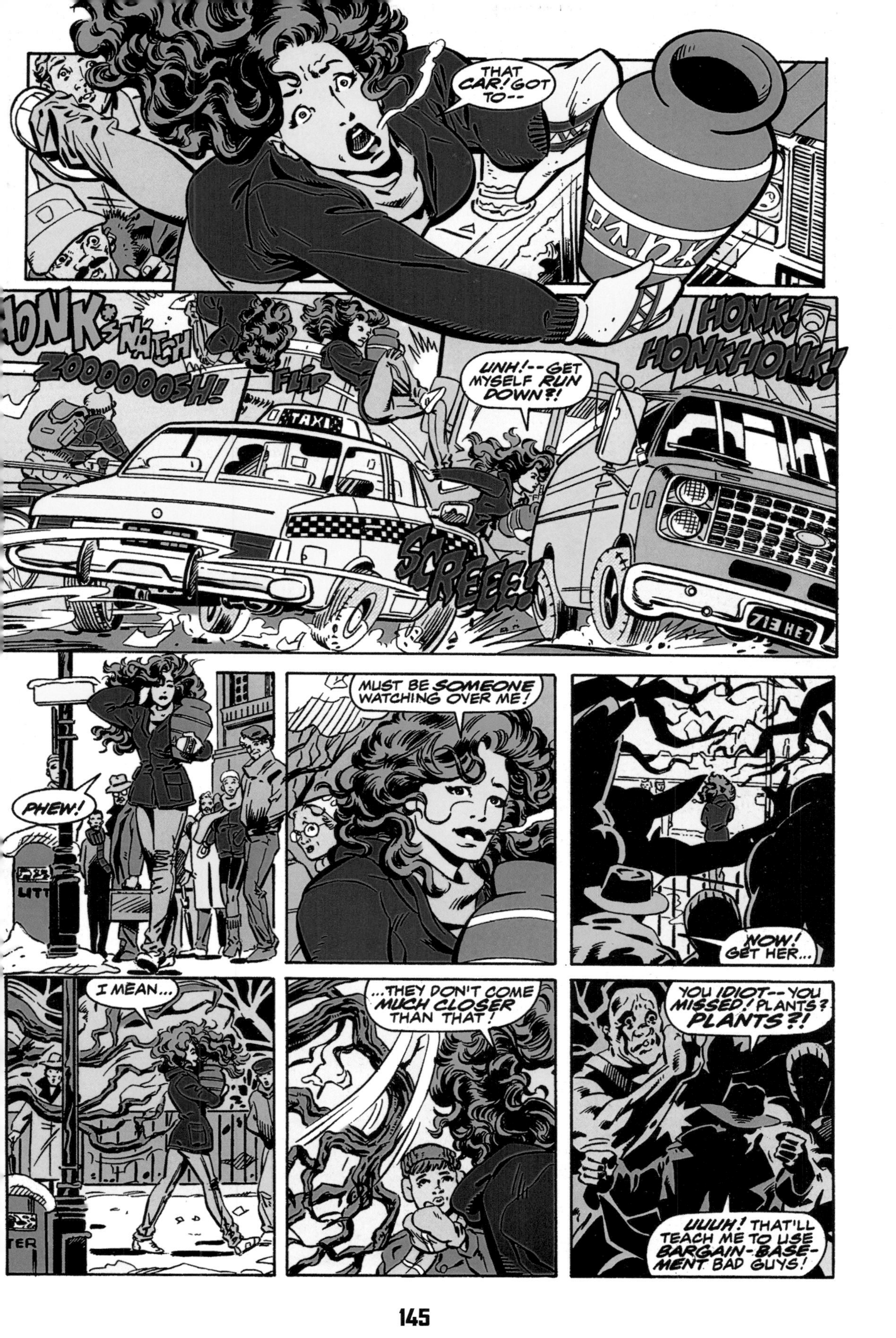
THAT CAR! GOT TO--
HONK SNATCH
ZOOOOOOOSH!
FLIP
TAXI
UNH!--GET MYSELF RUN DOWN?!
HONK! HONKHONK!
SCREEE!
713 HE7
PHEW!
MUST BE SOMEONE WATCHING OVER ME!
NOW! GET HER...
I MEAN...
...THEY DON'T COME MUCH CLOSER THAN THAT!
YOU IDIOT--YOU MISSED! PLANTS? PLANTS?!
UUUH! THAT'LL TEACH ME TO USE BARGAIN-BASEMENT BAD GUYS!

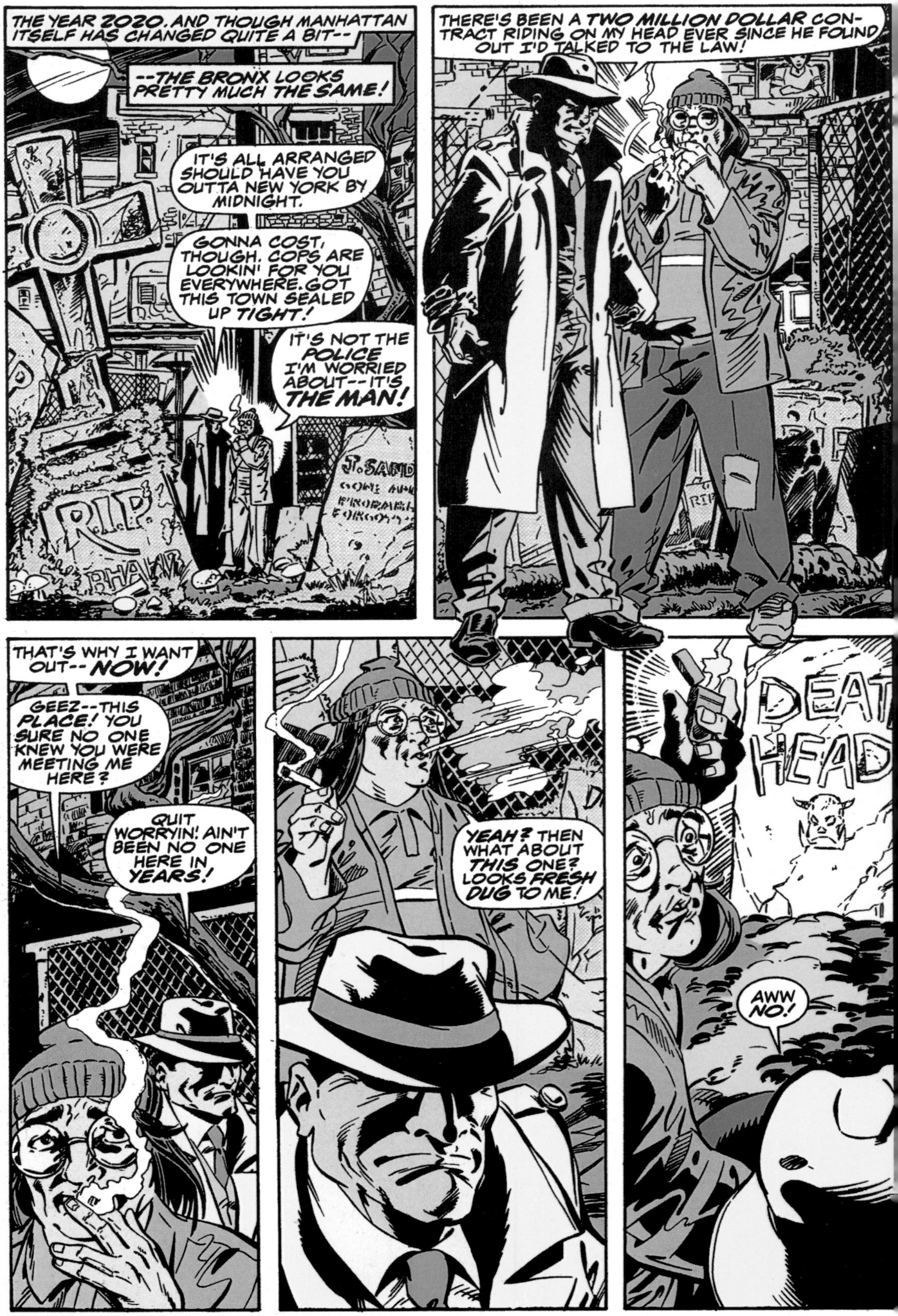

THE YEAR 2020. AND THOUGH MANHATTAN ITSELF HAS CHANGED QUITE A BIT--
--THE BRONX LOOKS PRETTY MUCH THE SAME!
IT'S ALL ARRANGED SHOULD HAVE YOU OUTTA NEW YORK BY MIDNIGHT.
GONNA COST, THOUGH. COPS ARE LOOKIN' FOR YOU EVERYWHERE. GOT THIS TOWN SEALED UP TIGHT!
IT'S NOT THE POLICE I'M WORRIED ABOUT--IT'S THE MAN!
THERE'S BEEN A TWO MILLION DOLLAR CONTRACT RIDING ON MY HEAD EVER SINCE HE FOUND OUT I'D TALKED TO THE LAW!
THAT'S WHY I WANT OUT--NOW!
GEEZ--THIS PLACE! YOU SURE NO ONE KNEW YOU WERE MEETING ME HERE?
QUIT WORRYIN'! AIN'T BEEN NO ONE HERE IN YEARS!
YEAH? THEN WHAT ABOUT THIS ONE? LOOKS FRESH DUG TO ME!
AWW NO!

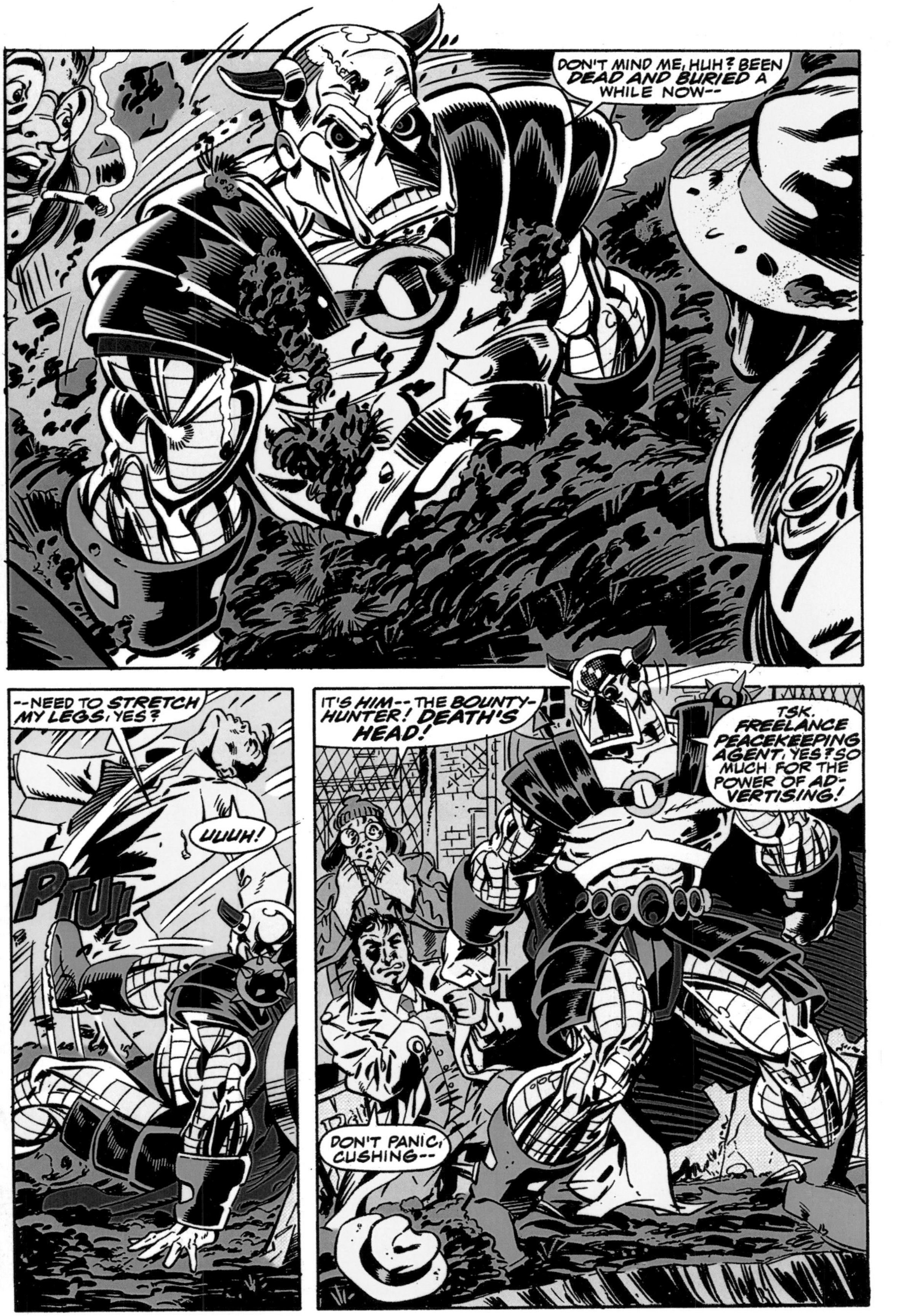
DON'T MIND ME, HUH? BEEN DEAD AND BURIED A WHILE NOW--
--NEED TO STRETCH MY LEGS, YES?
UUUH!
PTUI!
IT'S HIM-- THE BOUNTY-HUNTER! DEATH'S HEAD!
TSK. FREELANCE PEACEKEEPING AGENT, YES? SO MUCH FOR THE POWER OF ADVERTISING!
DON'T PANIC, CUSHING--

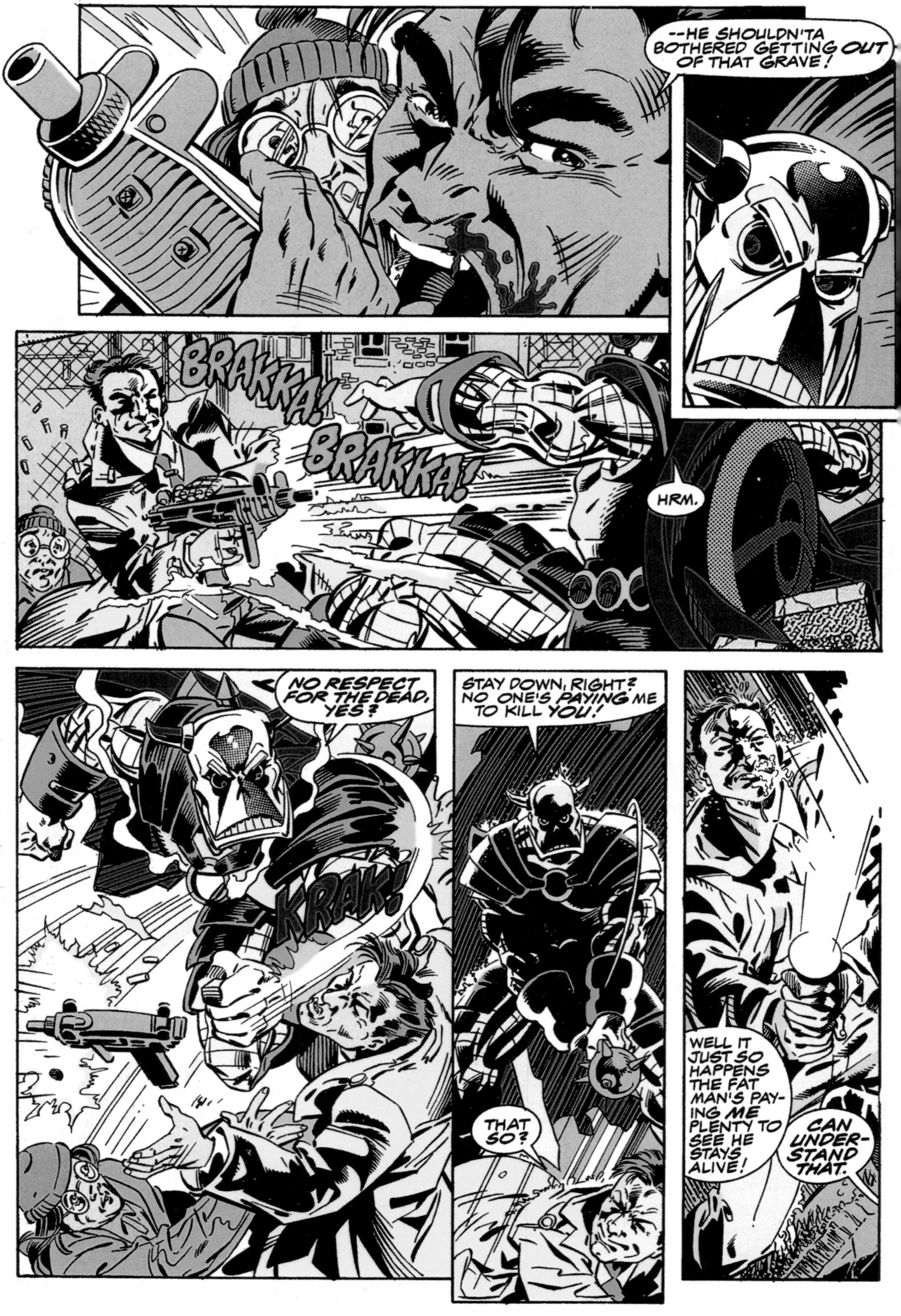
--HE SHOULDN'TA BOTHERED GETTING OUT OF THAT GRAVE!
BRAKKA!
BRAKKA!
HRM.
NO RESPECT FOR THE DEAD, YES?
KRAK!
STAY DOWN, RIGHT? NO ONE'S PAYING ME TO KILL YOU!
THAT SO?
WELL IT JUST SO HAPPENS THE FAT MAN'S PAYING ME PLENTY TO SEE HE STAYS ALIVE!
CAN UNDERSTAND THAT.

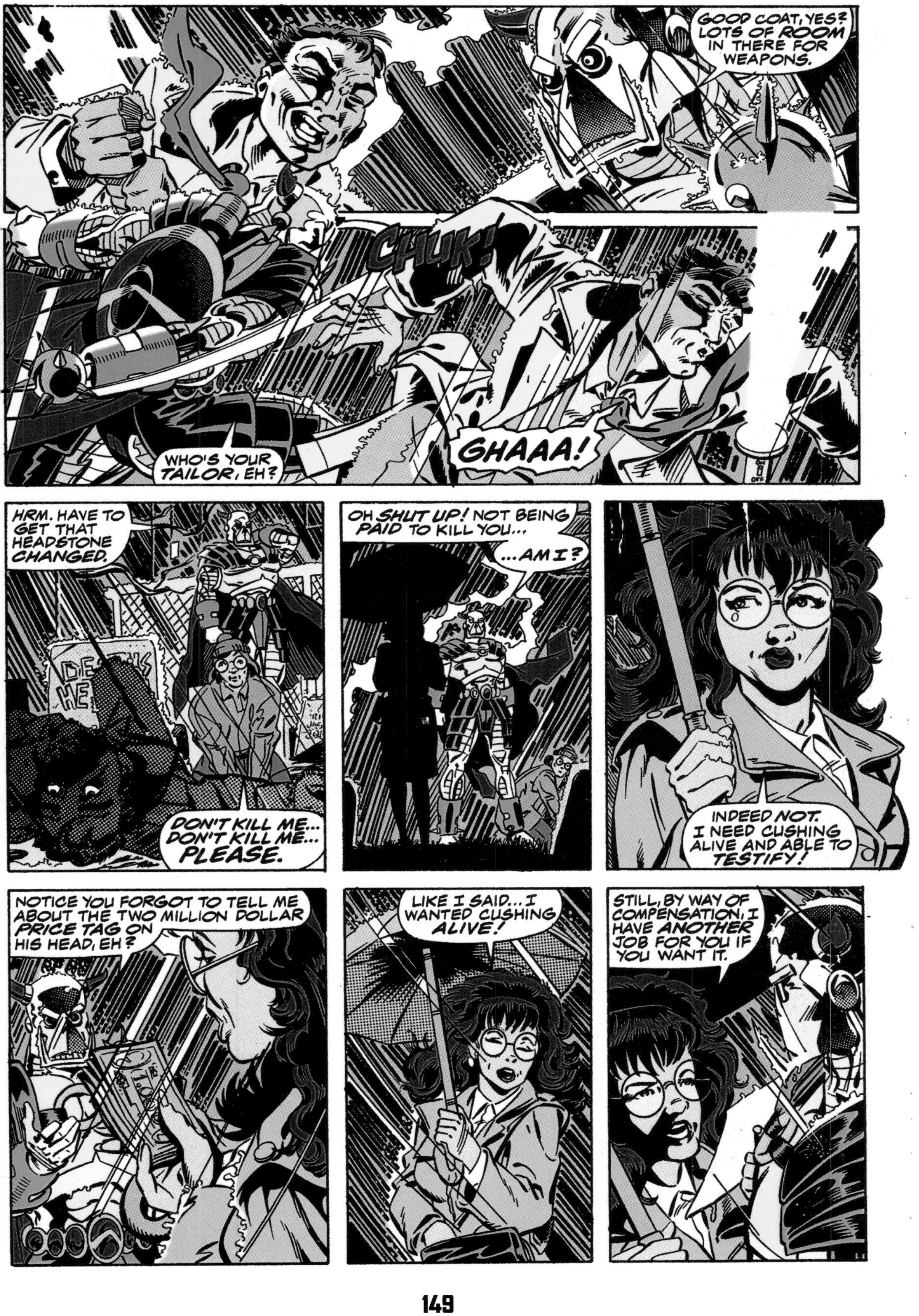
GOOD COAT, YES? LOTS OF ROOM IN THERE FOR WEAPONS.
CHUK!
WHO'S YOUR TAILOR, EH?
GHAAA!
HRM. HAVE TO GET THAT HEADSTONE CHANGED.
DON'T KILL ME... DON'T KILL ME... PLEASE.
OH SHUT UP! NOT BEING PAID TO KILL YOU...
...AM I?
INDEED NOT. I NEED CUSHING ALIVE AND ABLE TO TESTIFY!
NOTICE YOU FORGOT TO TELL ME ABOUT THE TWO MILLION DOLLAR PRICE TAG ON HIS HEAD, EH?
LIKE I SAID... I WANTED CUSHING ALIVE!
STILL, BY WAY OF COMPENSATION, I HAVE ANOTHER JOB FOR YOU IF YOU WANT IT.

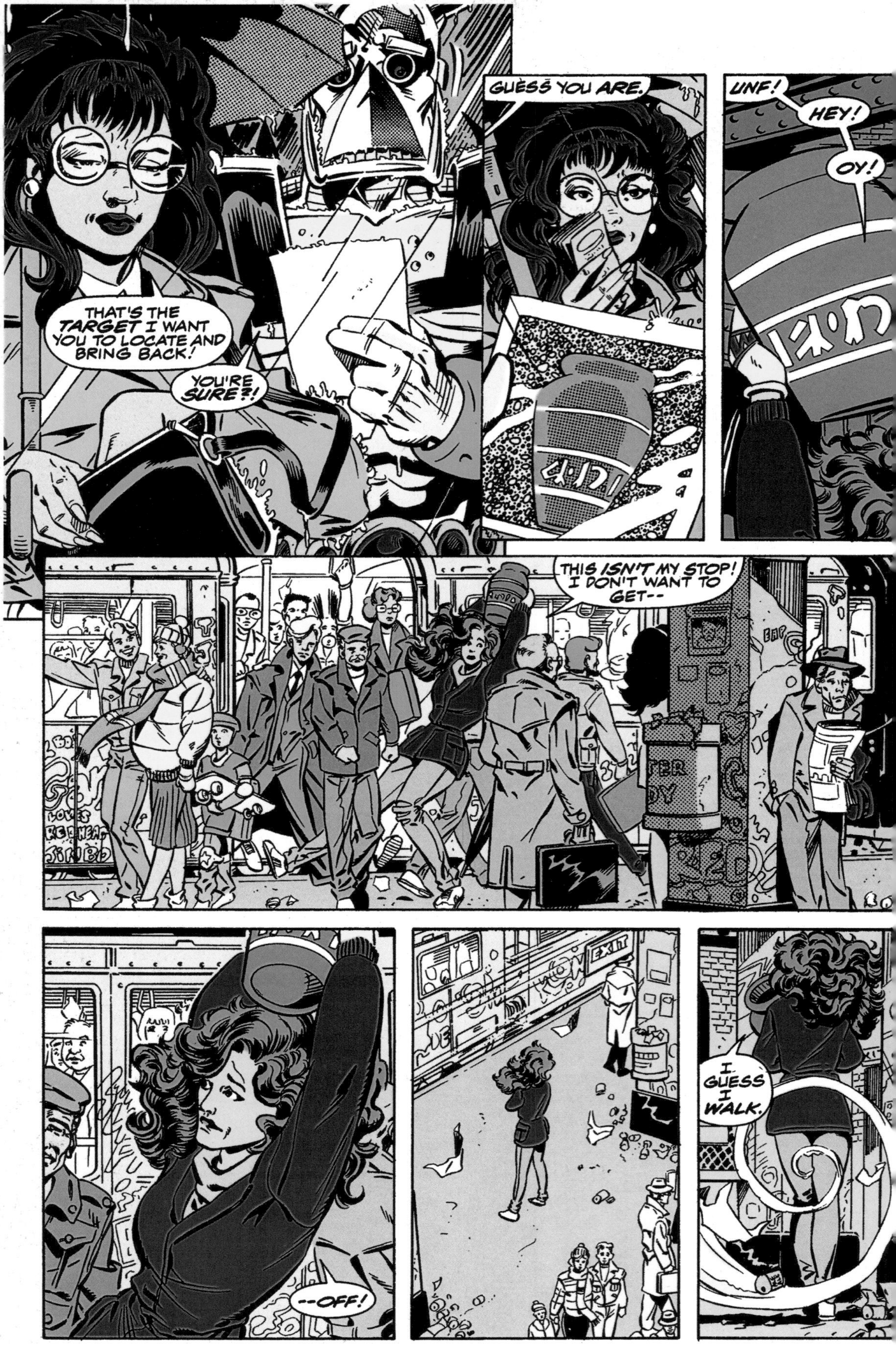
THAT'S THE TARGET I WANT YOU TO LOCATE AND BRING BACK!
YOU'RE SURE?!
GUESS YOU ARE.
UNF!
HEY!
OY!
THIS ISN'T MY STOP! I DON'T WANT TO GET--
--OFF!
EXIT
I GUESS I WALK.

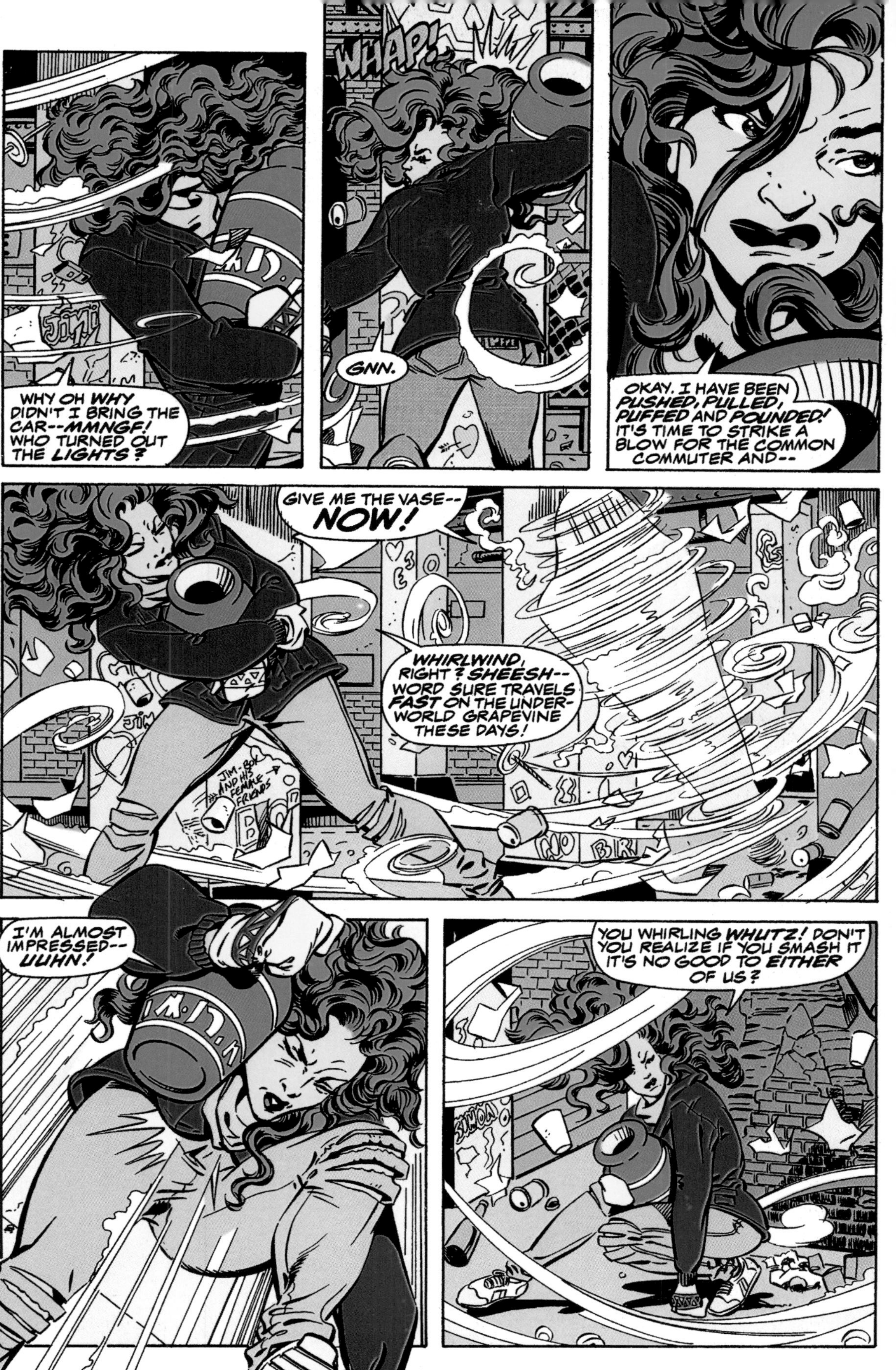

WHY OH WHY DIDN'T I BRING THE CAR--MMNGF! WHO TURNED OUT THE LIGHTS?
WHAP!
GNN.
OKAY. I HAVE BEEN PUSHED, PULLED, PUFFED AND POUNDED! IT'S TIME TO STRIKE A BLOW FOR THE COMMON COMMUTER AND--
GIVE ME THE VASE-- NOW!
WHIRLWIND, RIGHT? SHEESH-- WORD SURE TRAVELS FAST ON THE UNDERWORLD GRAPEVINE THESE DAYS!
JIM-BOB AND HIS FEMALE FRIENDS
I'M ALMOST IMPRESSED-- UUHN!
YOU WHIRLING WHUTZ! DON'T YOU REALIZE IF YOU SMASH IT IT'S NO GOOD TO EITHER OF US?

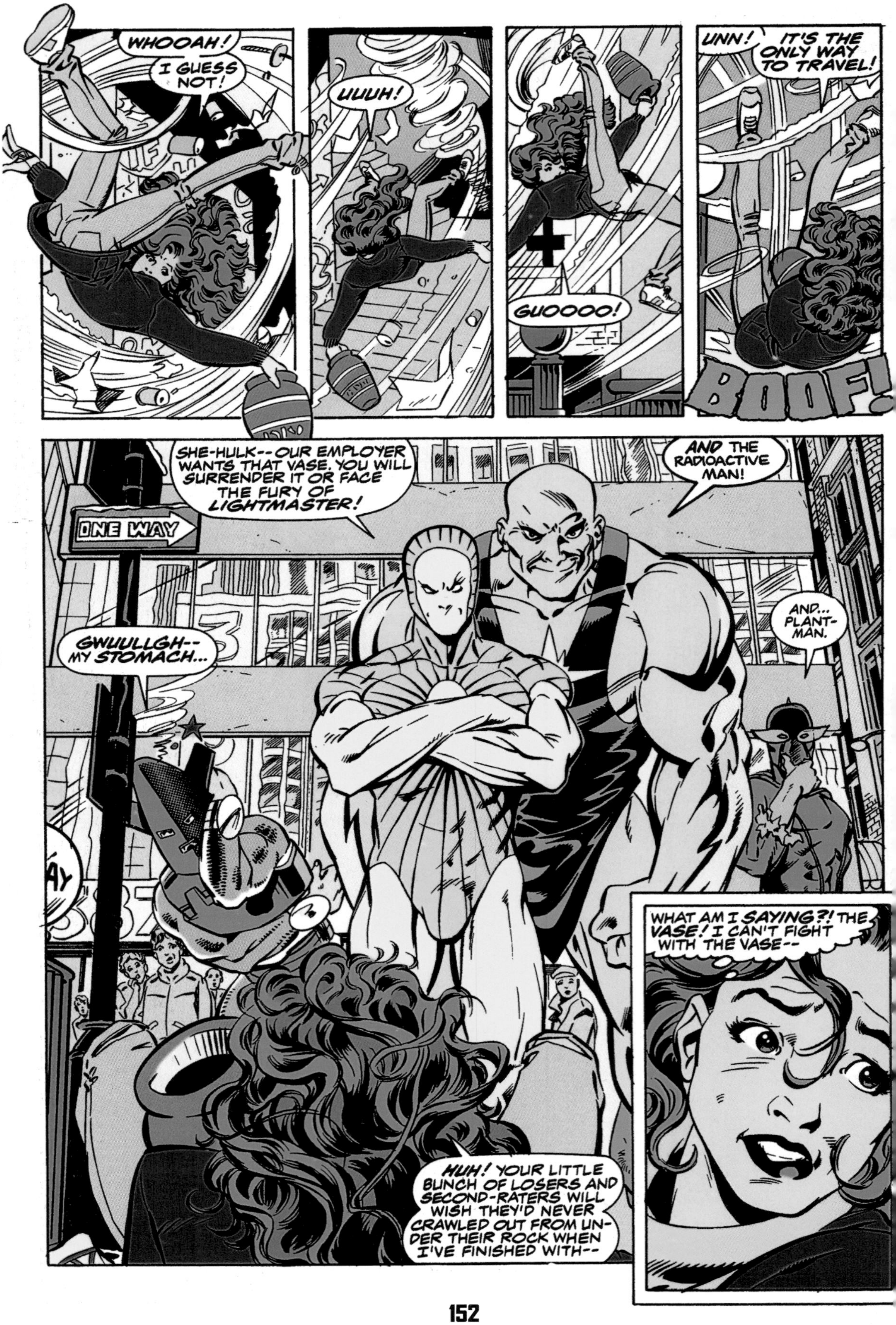
WHOOAH!
I GUESS NOT!
UUUH!
GUOOOO!
UNN!
IT'S THE ONLY WAY TO TRAVEL!
BOOF!
SHE-HULK--OUR EMPLOYER WANTS THAT VASE. YOU WILL SURRENDER IT OR FACE THE FURY OF LIGHTMASTER!
AND THE RADIOACTIVE MAN!
AND... PLANT-MAN.
GWUULLGH--MY STOMACH...
ONE WAY
HUH! YOUR LITTLE BUNCH OF LOSERS AND SECOND-RATERS WILL WISH THEY'D NEVER CRAWLED OUT FROM UNDER THEIR ROCK WHEN I'VE FINISHED WITH--
WHAT AM I SAYING?! THE VASE! I CAN'T FIGHT WITH THE VASE--

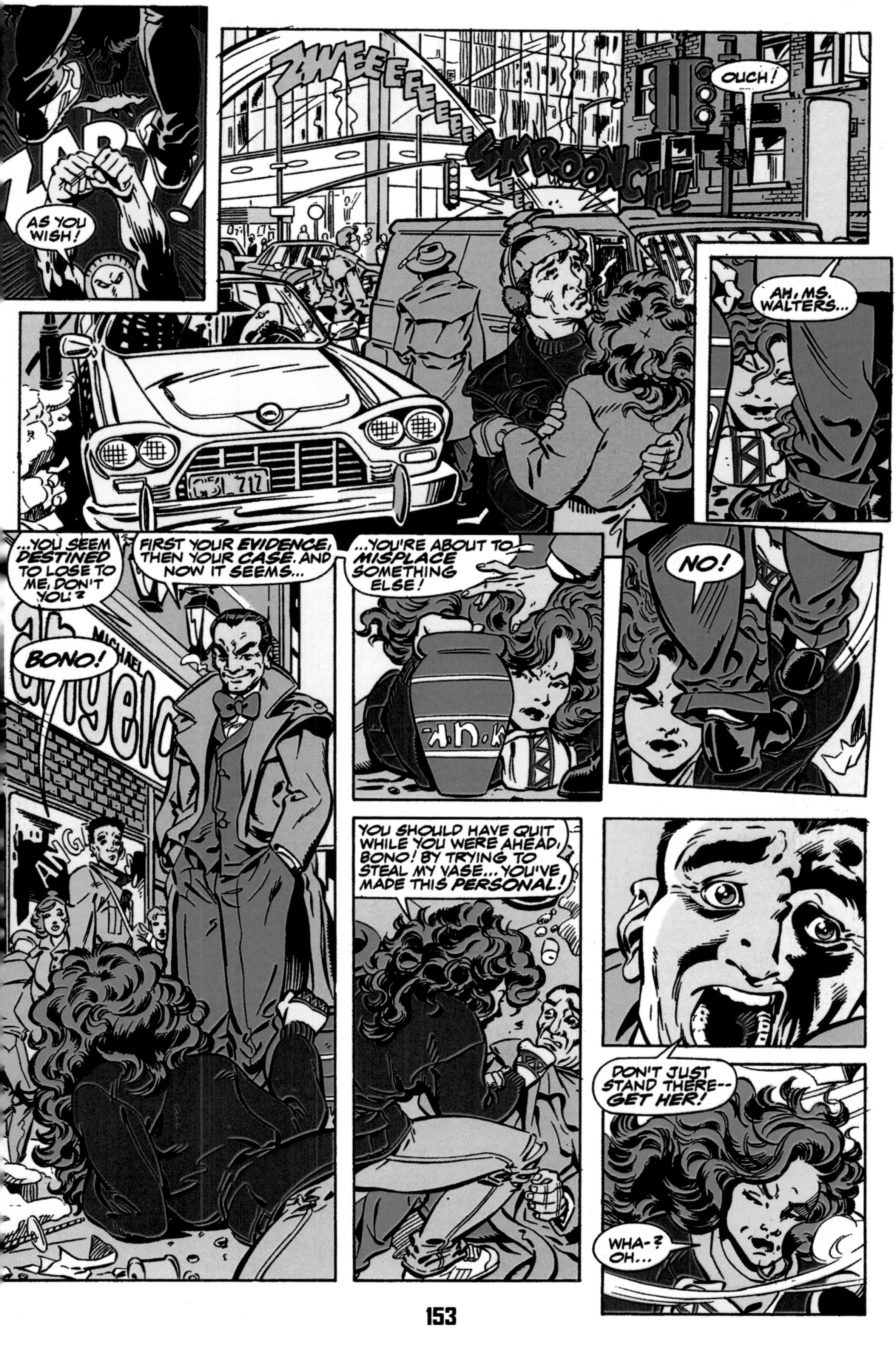
ZAP!
AS YOU WISH!
ZWEEEEEEEEE
SKROONCH!
OUCH!
AH, MS. WALTERS...
...YOU SEEM DESTINED TO LOSE TO ME, DON'T YOU?
FIRST YOUR EVIDENCE, THEN YOUR CASE. AND NOW IT SEEMS...
...YOU'RE ABOUT TO MISPLACE SOMETHING ELSE!
BONO!
MICHAEL ANGELO
NO!
YOU SHOULD HAVE QUIT WHILE YOU WERE AHEAD, BONO! BY TRYING TO STEAL MY VASE... YOU'VE MADE THIS PERSONAL!
DON'T JUST STAND THERE-- GET HER!
WHA-? OH...

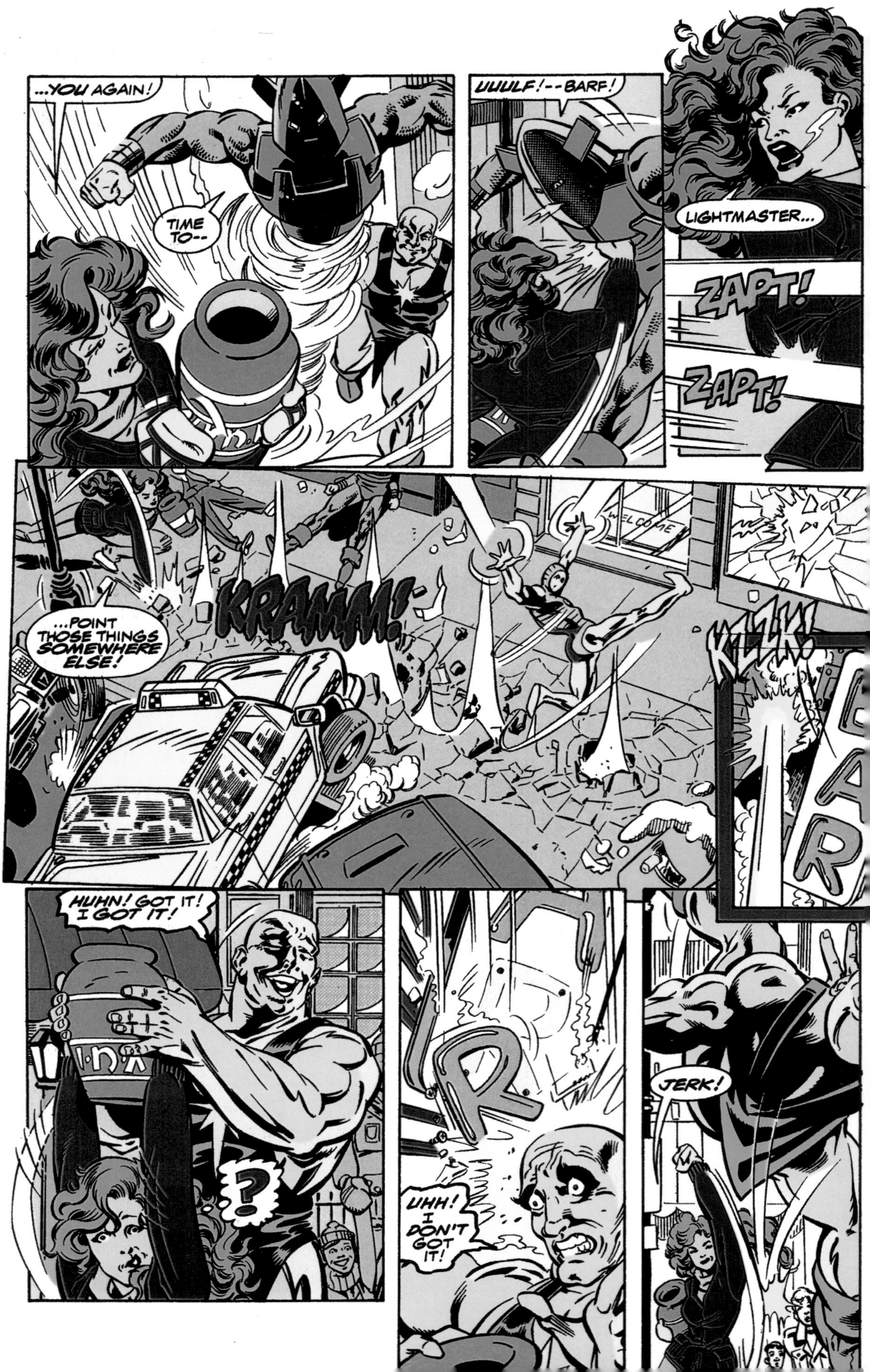
...YOU AGAIN!
TIME TO--
UUULF!--BARF!
LIGHTMASTER...
ZAPT!
ZAPT!
...POINT THOSE THINGS SOMEWHERE ELSE!
KRAMM!
WELCOME
HUHN! GOT IT! I GOT IT!
?
UHH! I DON'T GOT IT!
JERK!

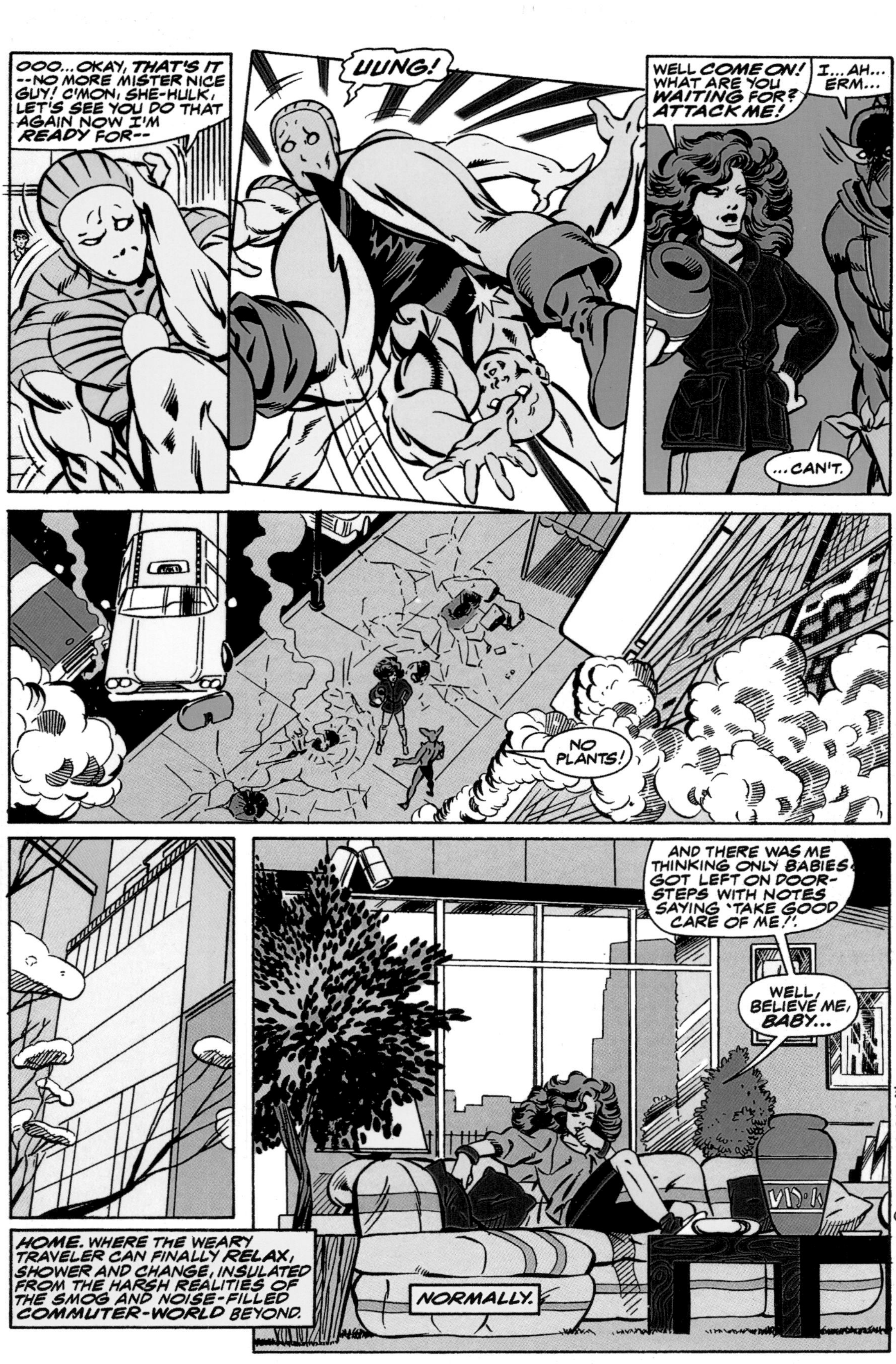
OOO...OKAY, THAT'S IT --NO MORE MISTER NICE GUY! C'MON, SHE-HULK, LET'S SEE YOU DO THAT AGAIN NOW I'M READY FOR--
UUNG!
WELL COME ON! WHAT ARE YOU WAITING FOR? ATTACK ME!
I... AH... ERM...
...CAN'T.
NO PLANTS!
HOME. WHERE THE WEARY TRAVELER CAN FINALLY RELAX, SHOWER AND CHANGE, INSULATED FROM THE HARSH REALITIES OF THE SMOG AND NOISE-FILLED COMMUTER-WORLD BEYOND.
NORMALLY.
AND THERE WAS ME THINKING ONLY BABIES GOT LEFT ON DOOR-STEPS WITH NOTES SAYING 'TAKE GOOD CARE OF ME!'.
WELL, BELIEVE ME, BABY...

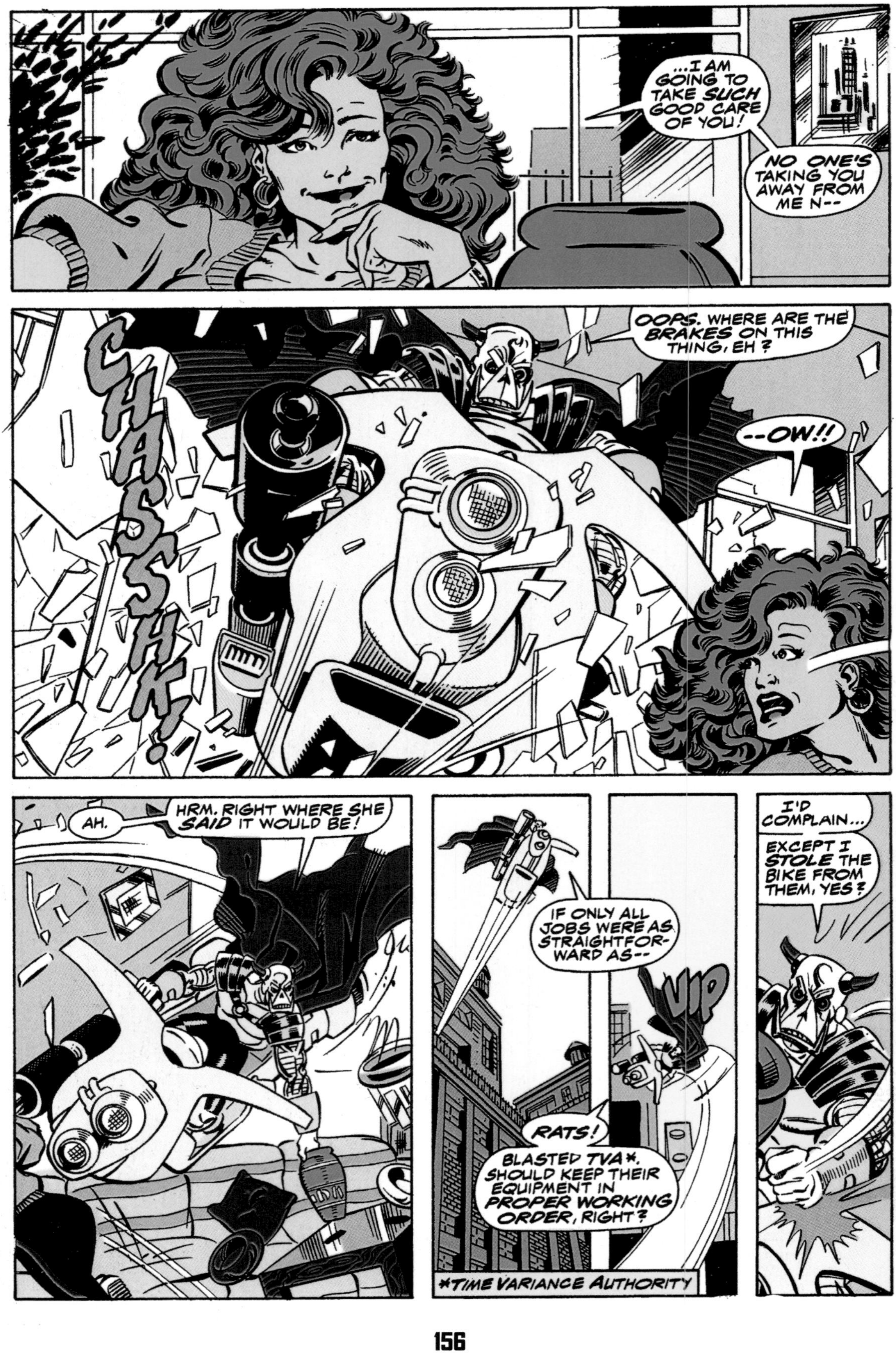
...I AM GOING TO TAKE SUCH GOOD CARE OF YOU!
NO ONE'S TAKING YOU AWAY FROM ME N--
CHASSHK!
OOPS. WHERE ARE THE BRAKES ON THIS THING, EH?
--OW!!
AH.
HRM. RIGHT WHERE SHE SAID IT WOULD BE!
IF ONLY ALL JOBS WERE AS STRAIGHTFORWARD AS--
VIP
RATS!
BLASTED TVA*. SHOULD KEEP THEIR EQUIPMENT IN PROPER WORKING ORDER, RIGHT?
*TIME VARIANCE AUTHORITY
I'D COMPLAIN...
EXCEPT I STOLE THE BIKE FROM THEM, YES?

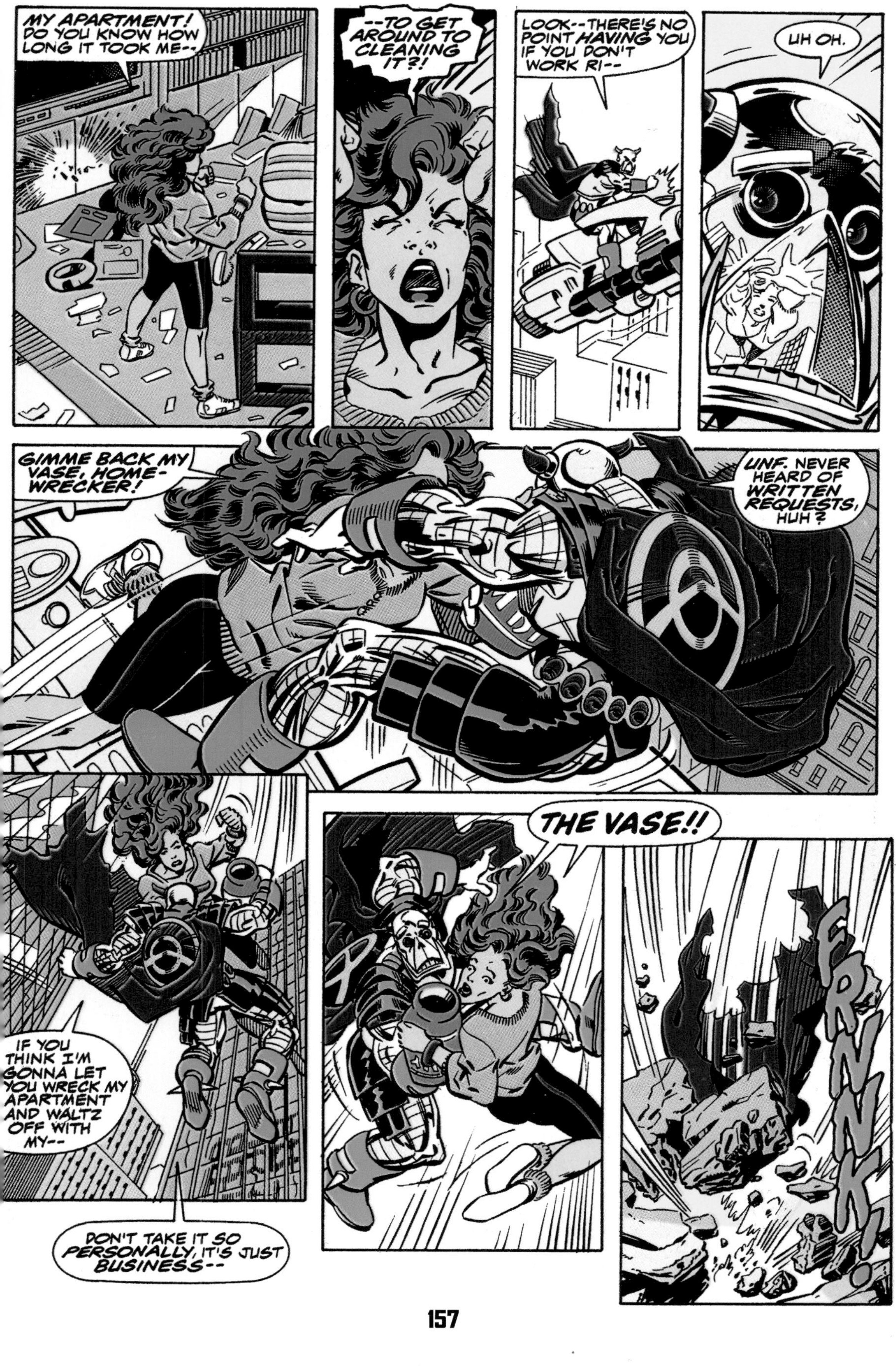
MY APARTMENT! DO YOU KNOW HOW LONG IT TOOK ME--
--TO GET AROUND TO CLEANING IT?!
LOOK--THERE'S NO POINT HAVING YOU IF YOU DON'T WORK RI--
UH OH.
GIMME BACK MY VASE, HOME-WRECKER!
UNF. NEVER HEARD OF WRITTEN REQUESTS, HUH?
IF YOU THINK I'M GONNA LET YOU WRECK MY APARTMENT AND WALTZ OFF WITH MY--
DON'T TAKE IT SO PERSONALLY. IT'S JUST BUSINESS--
THE VASE!!
FRNNK!

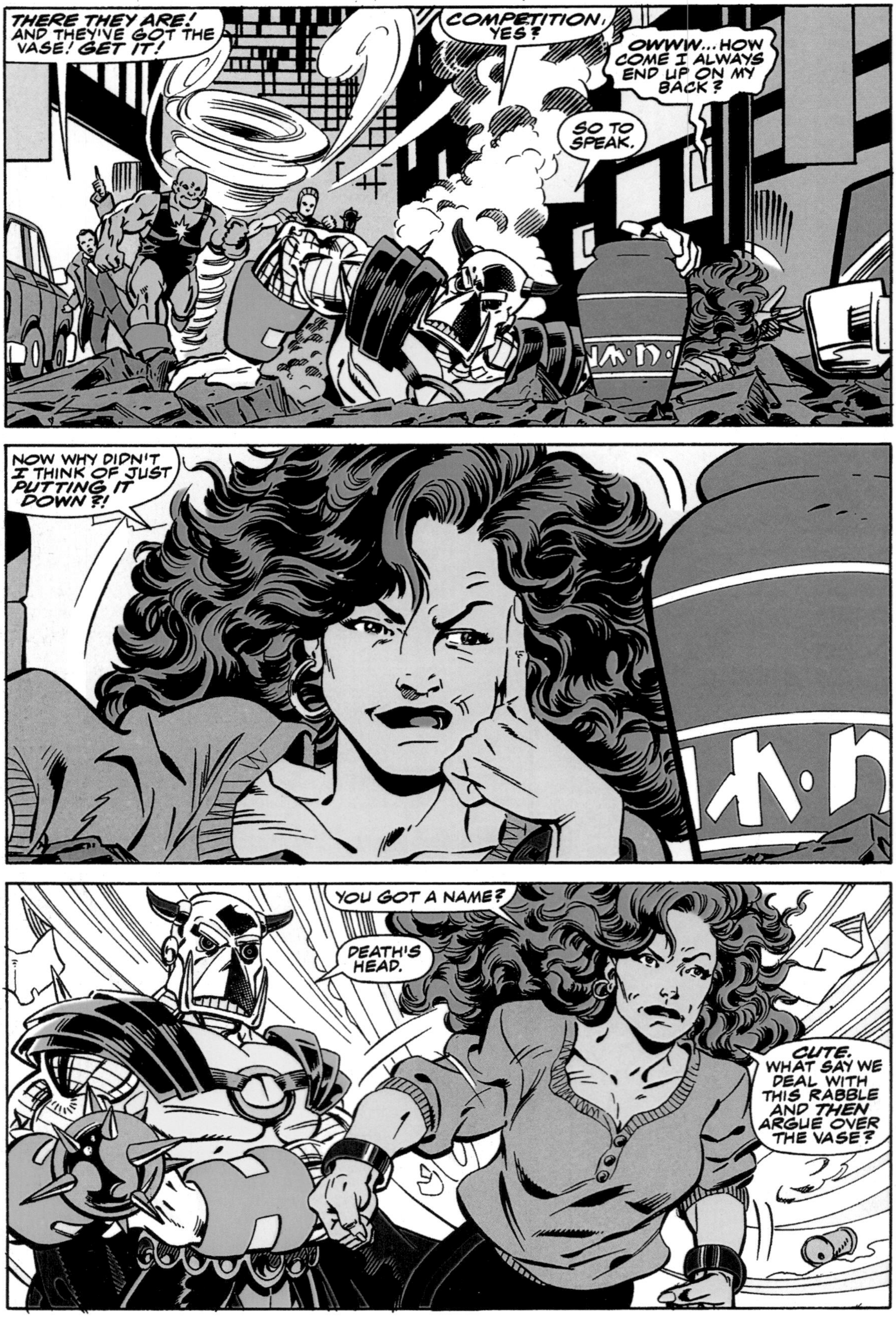
THERE THEY ARE! AND THEY'VE GOT THE VASE! GET IT!
COMPETITION, YES?
OWWW... HOW COME I ALWAYS END UP ON MY BACK?
SO TO SPEAK.
NOW WHY DIDN'T I THINK OF JUST PUTTING IT DOWN?!
YOU GOT A NAME?
DEATH'S HEAD.
CUTE. WHAT SAY WE DEAL WITH THIS RABBLE AND THEN ARGUE OVER THE VASE?

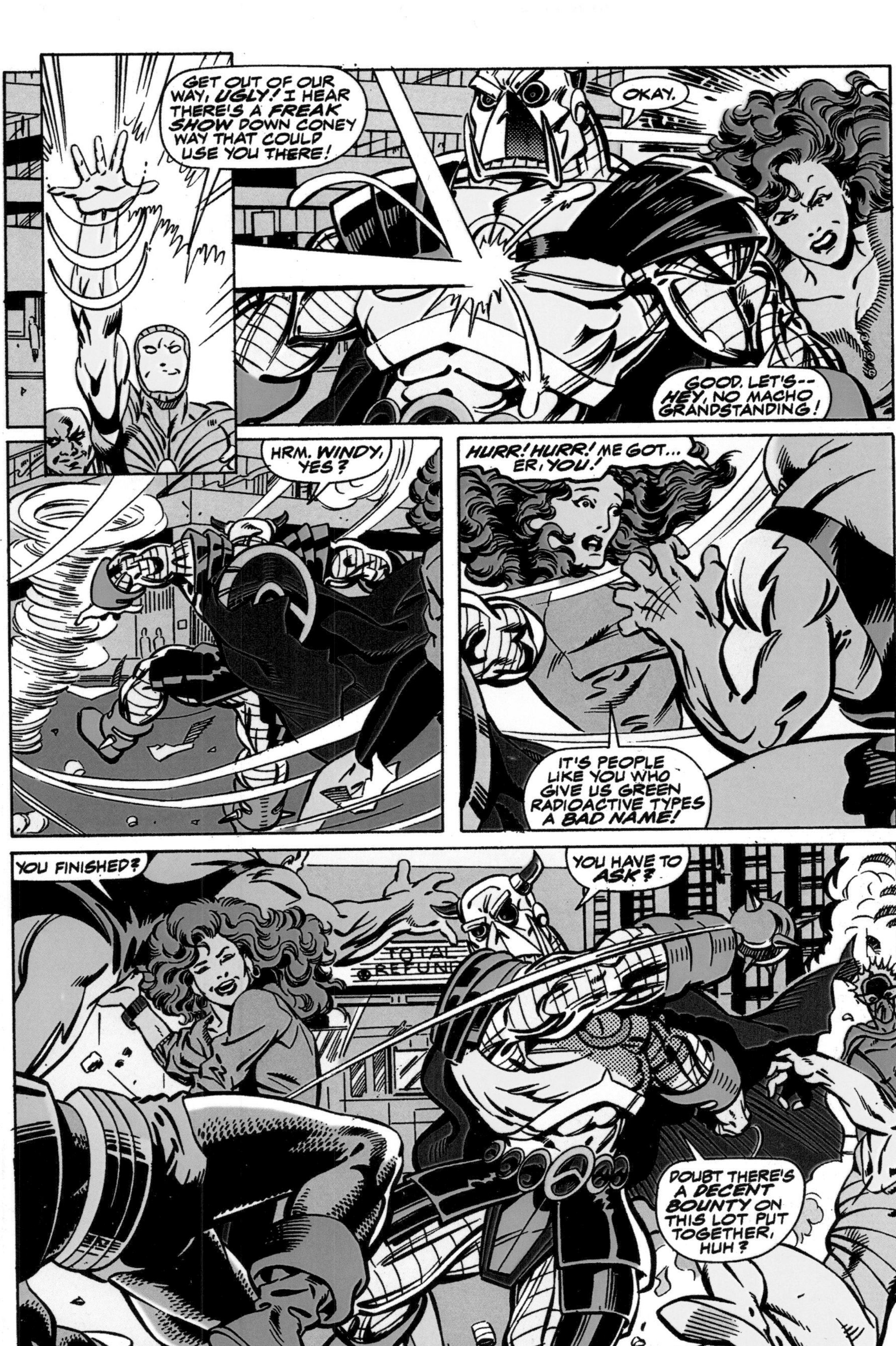
GET OUT OF OUR WAY, UGLY! I HEAR THERE'S A FREAK SHOW DOWN CONEY WAY THAT COULD USE YOU THERE!
OKAY.
GOOD. LET'S-- HEY, NO MACHO GRANDSTANDING!
HRM. WINDY, YES?
HURR! HURR! ME GOT... ER, YOU!
IT'S PEOPLE LIKE YOU WHO GIVE US GREEN RADIOACTIVE TYPES A BAD NAME!
YOU FINISHED?
YOU HAVE TO ASK?
TOTAL REFUND
DOUBT THERE'S A DECENT BOUNTY ON THIS LOT PUT TOGETHER, HUH?

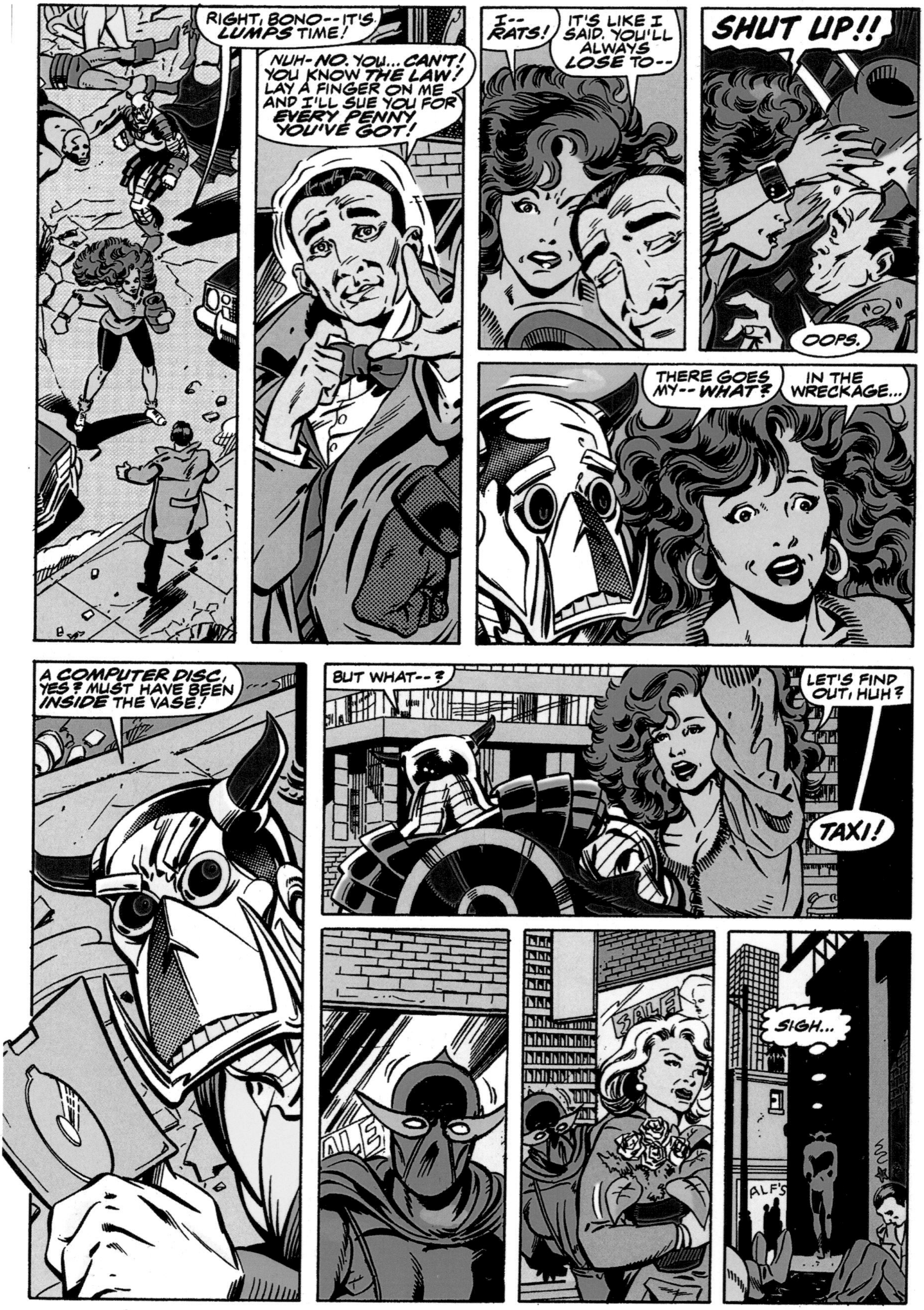
RIGHT, BONO--IT'S LUMPS TIME!
NUH-NO. YOU... CAN'T! YOU KNOW THE LAW! LAY A FINGER ON ME AND I'LL SUE YOU FOR EVERY PENNY YOU'VE GOT!
I-- RATS!
IT'S LIKE I SAID. YOU'LL ALWAYS LOSE TO--
SHUT UP!!
OOPS.
THERE GOES MY--WHAT?
IN THE WRECKAGE...
A COMPUTER DISC, YES? MUST HAVE BEEN INSIDE THE VASE!
BUT WHAT--?
LET'S FIND OUT, HUH?
TAXI!
SALE
SIGH...
ALF'S

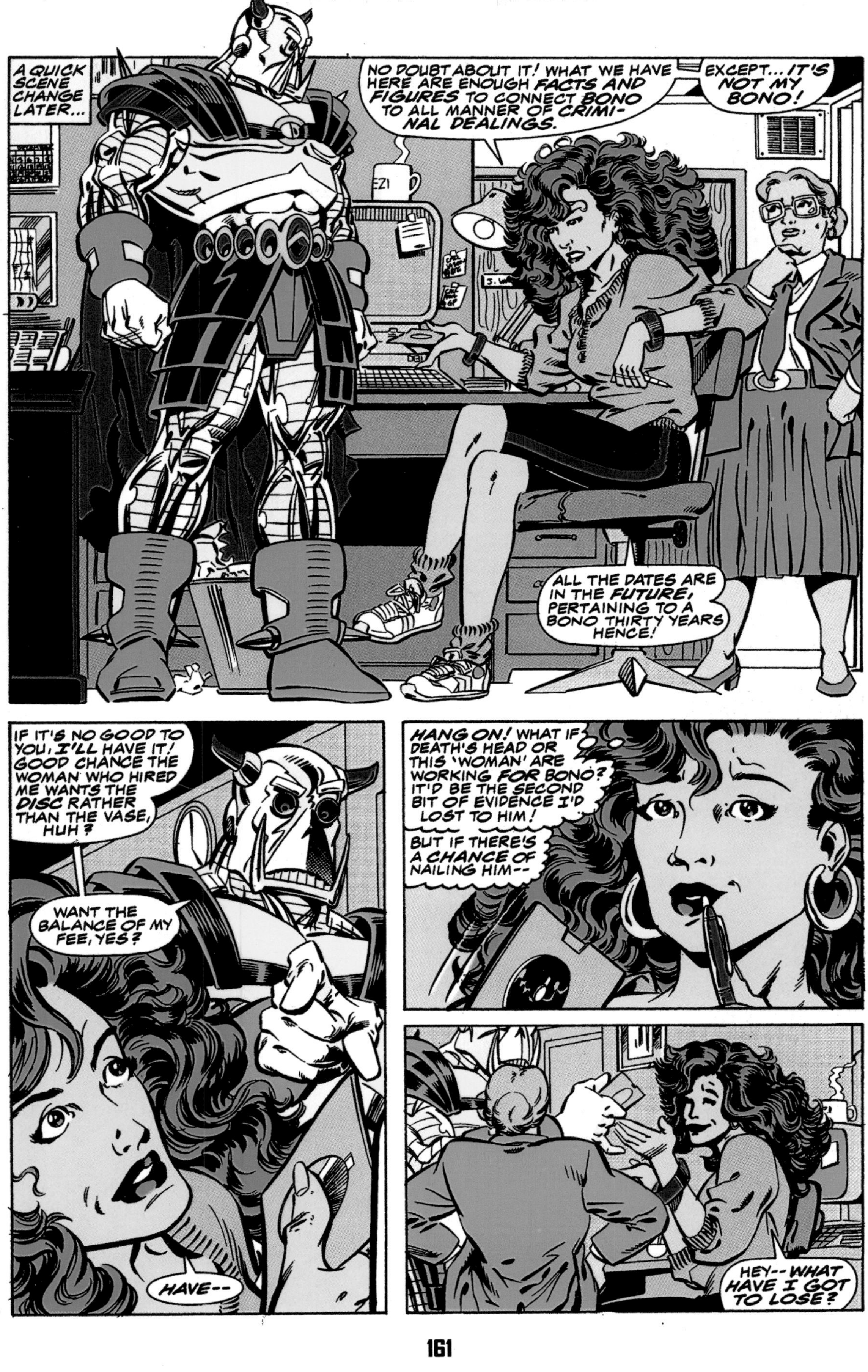

A QUICK SCENE CHANGE LATER...
NO DOUBT ABOUT IT! WHAT WE HAVE HERE ARE ENOUGH FACTS AND FIGURES TO CONNECT BONO TO ALL MANNER OF CRIMINAL DEALINGS.
EXCEPT... IT'S NOT MY BONO!
ALL THE DATES ARE IN THE FUTURE, PERTAINING TO A BONO THIRTY YEARS HENCE!
IF IT'S NO GOOD TO YOU, I'LL HAVE IT! GOOD CHANCE THE WOMAN WHO HIRED ME WANTS THE DISC RATHER THAN THE VASE, HUH?
WANT THE BALANCE OF MY FEE, YES?
HAVE--
HANG ON! WHAT IF DEATH'S HEAD OR THIS 'WOMAN' ARE WORKING FOR BONO? IT'D BE THE SECOND BIT OF EVIDENCE I'D LOST TO HIM!
BUT IF THERE'S A CHANCE OF NAILING HIM--
HEY--WHAT HAVE I GOT TO LOSE?

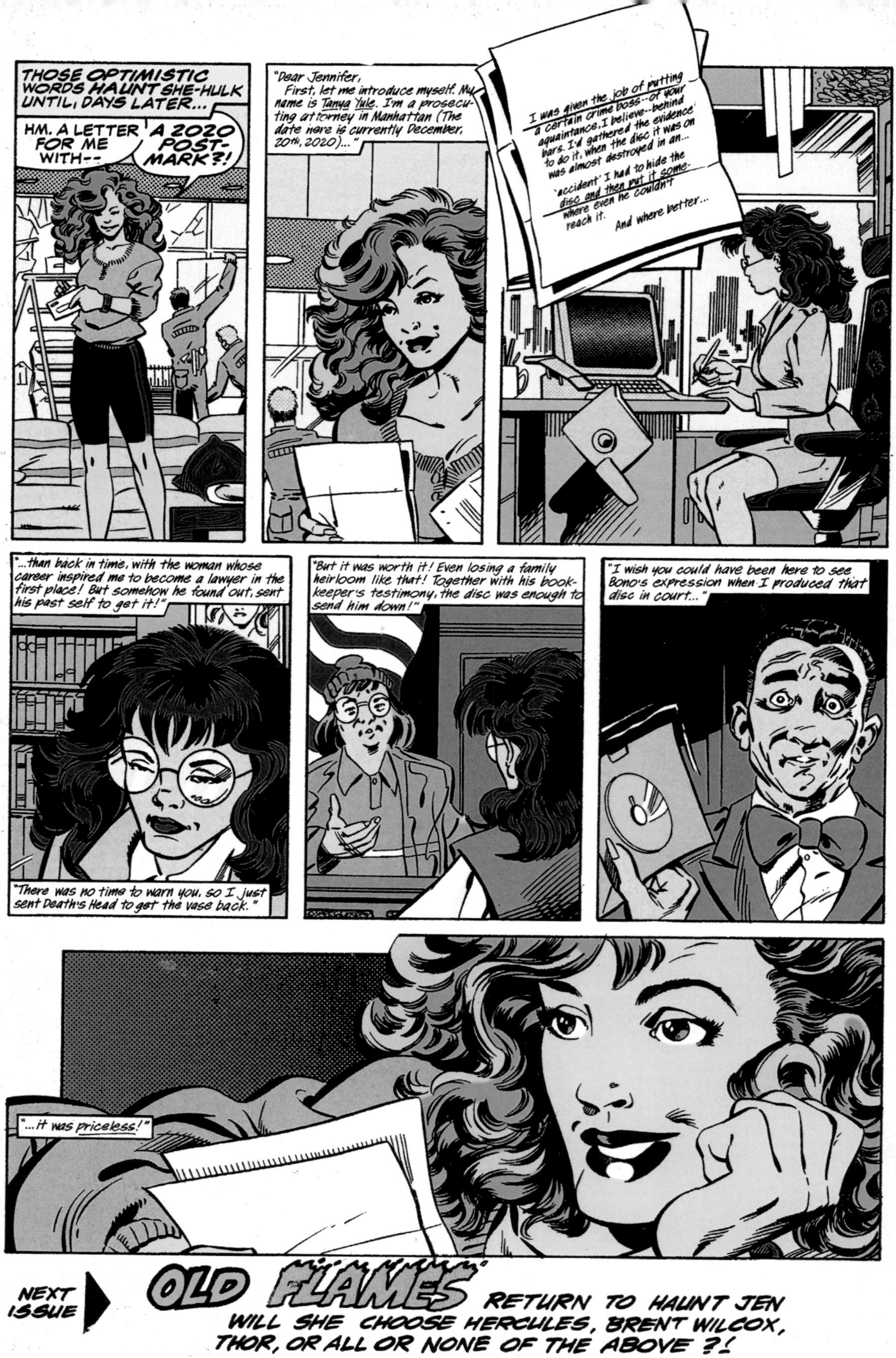

THOSE OPTIMISTIC WORDS HAUNT SHE-HULK UNTIL, DAYS LATER...
HM. A LETTER FOR ME WITH--
A 2020 POST-MARK?!
"Dear Jennifer, First, let me introduce myself. My name is Tanya Yule. I'm a prosecuting attorney in Manhattan (The date here is currently December, 20th, 2020)..."
I was given the job of putting a certain crime boss--of your aquaintance, I believe--behind bars. I'd gathered the evidence to do it, when the disc it was on was almost destroyed in an... 'accident' I had to hide the disc and then put it somewhere even he couldn't reach it. And where better...
"...than back in time, with the woman whose career inspired me to become a lawyer in the first place! But somehow he found out, sent his past self to get it!"
"There was no time to warn you, so I just sent Death's Head to get the vase back."
"But it was worth it! Even losing a family heirloom like that! Together with his bookkeeper's testimony, the disc was enough to send him down!"
"I wish you could have been here to see Bono's expression when I produced that disc in court..."
"...it was priceless!"
NEXT ISSUE
OLD FLAMES RETURN TO HAUNT JEN
WILL SHE CHOOSE HERCULES, BRENT WILCOX, THOR, OR ALL OR NONE OF THE ABOVE ?!

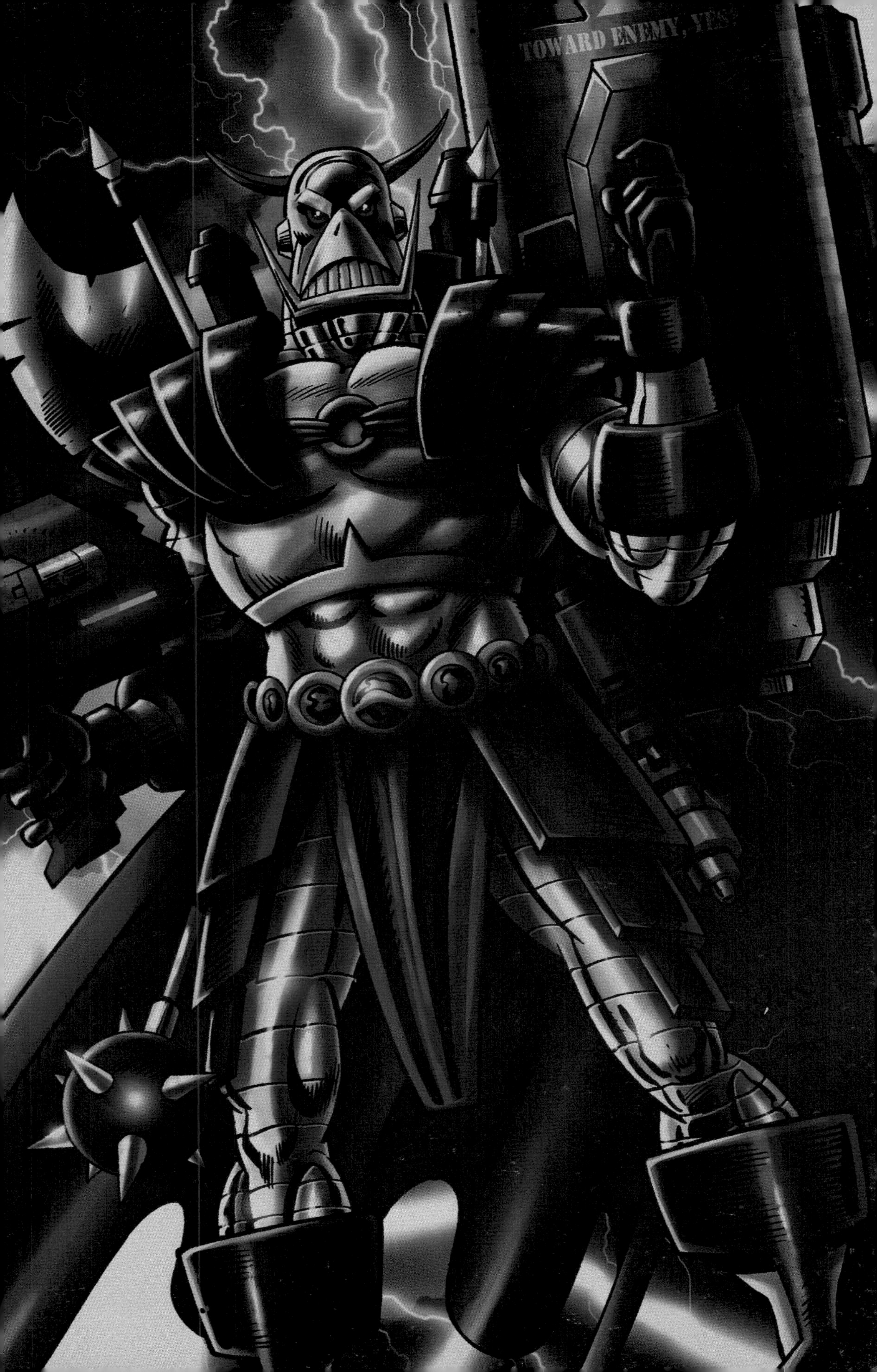
TOWARD ENEMY, YES

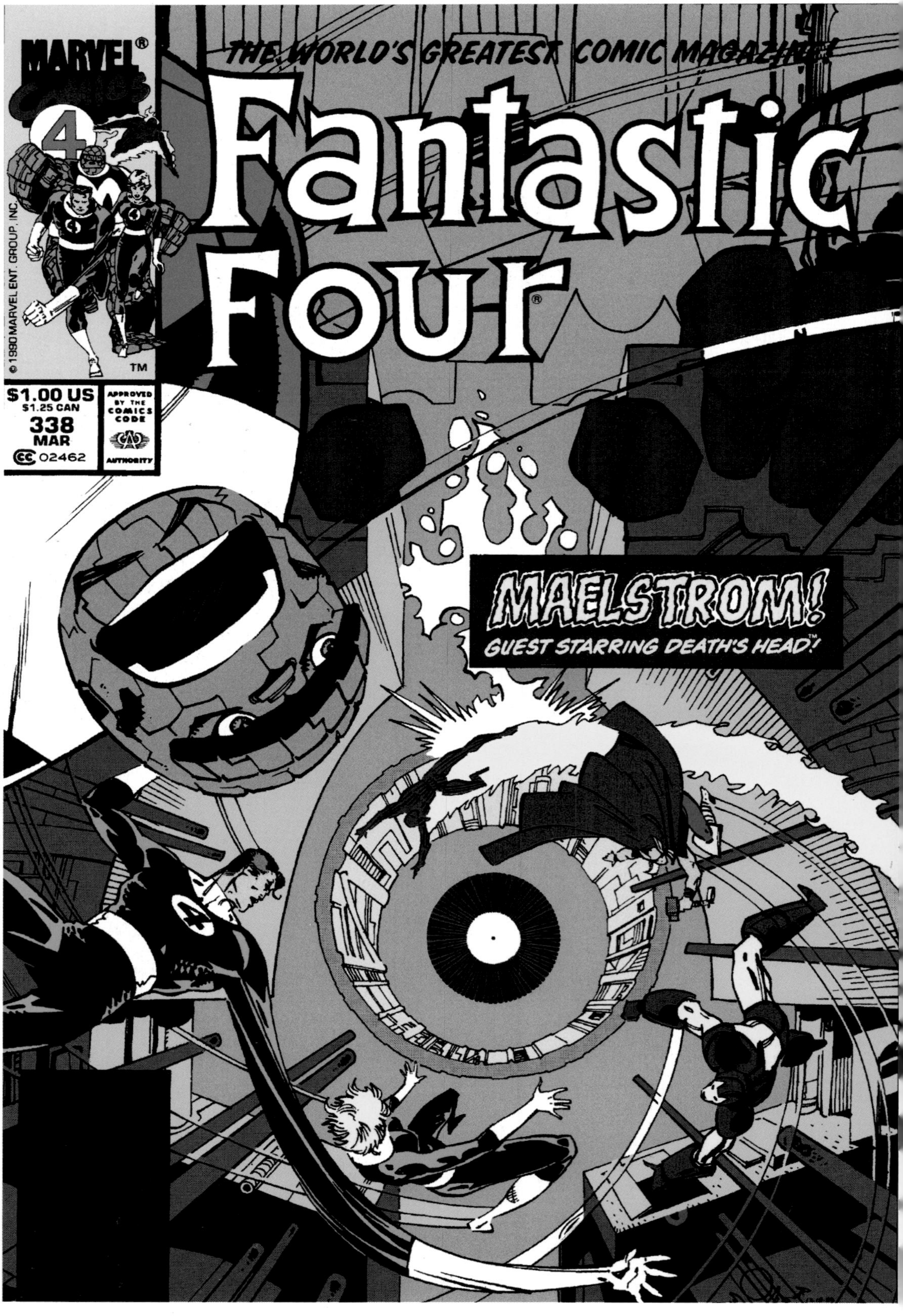
MARVEL COMICS
THE WORLD'S GREATEST COMIC MAGAZINE!
Fantastic Four®
© 1990 MARVEL ENT. GROUP, INC.
TM
$1.00 US
$1.25 CAN
338
MAR
CC 02462
APPROVED BY THE COMICS CODE AUTHORITY
MAELSTROM!
GUEST STARRING DEATH'S HEAD!™

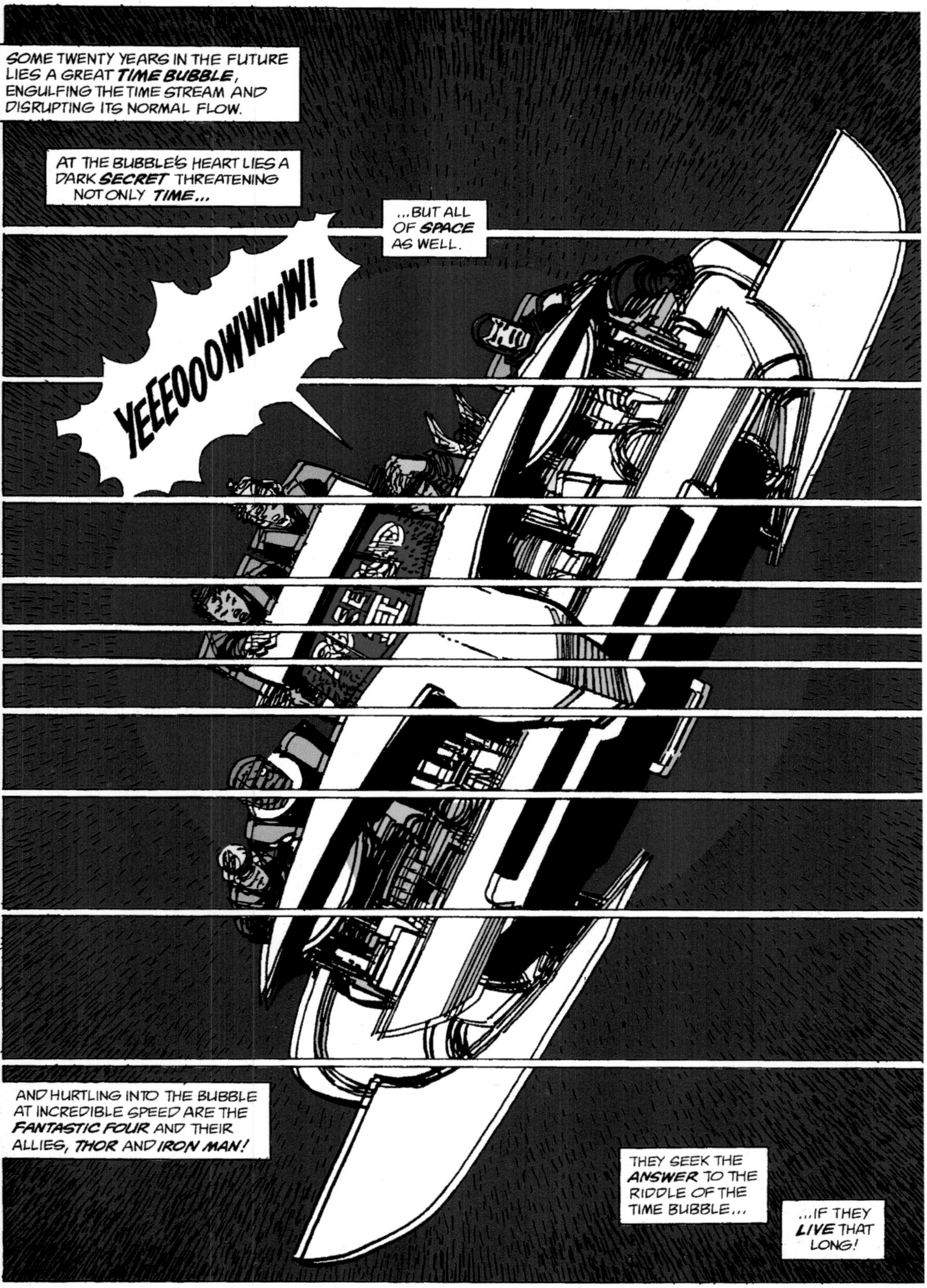
SOME TWENTY YEARS IN THE FUTURE LIES A GREAT TIME BUBBLE, ENGULFING THE TIME STREAM AND DISRUPTING ITS NORMAL FLOW.
AT THE BUBBLE'S HEART LIES A DARK SECRET THREATENING NOT ONLY TIME...
...BUT ALL OF SPACE AS WELL.
YEEEOOOWWWW!
AND HURTLING INTO THE BUBBLE AT INCREDIBLE SPEED ARE THE FANTASTIC FOUR AND THEIR ALLIES, THOR AND IRON MAN!
THEY SEEK THE ANSWER TO THE RIDDLE OF THE TIME BUBBLE...
...IF THEY LIVE THAT LONG!

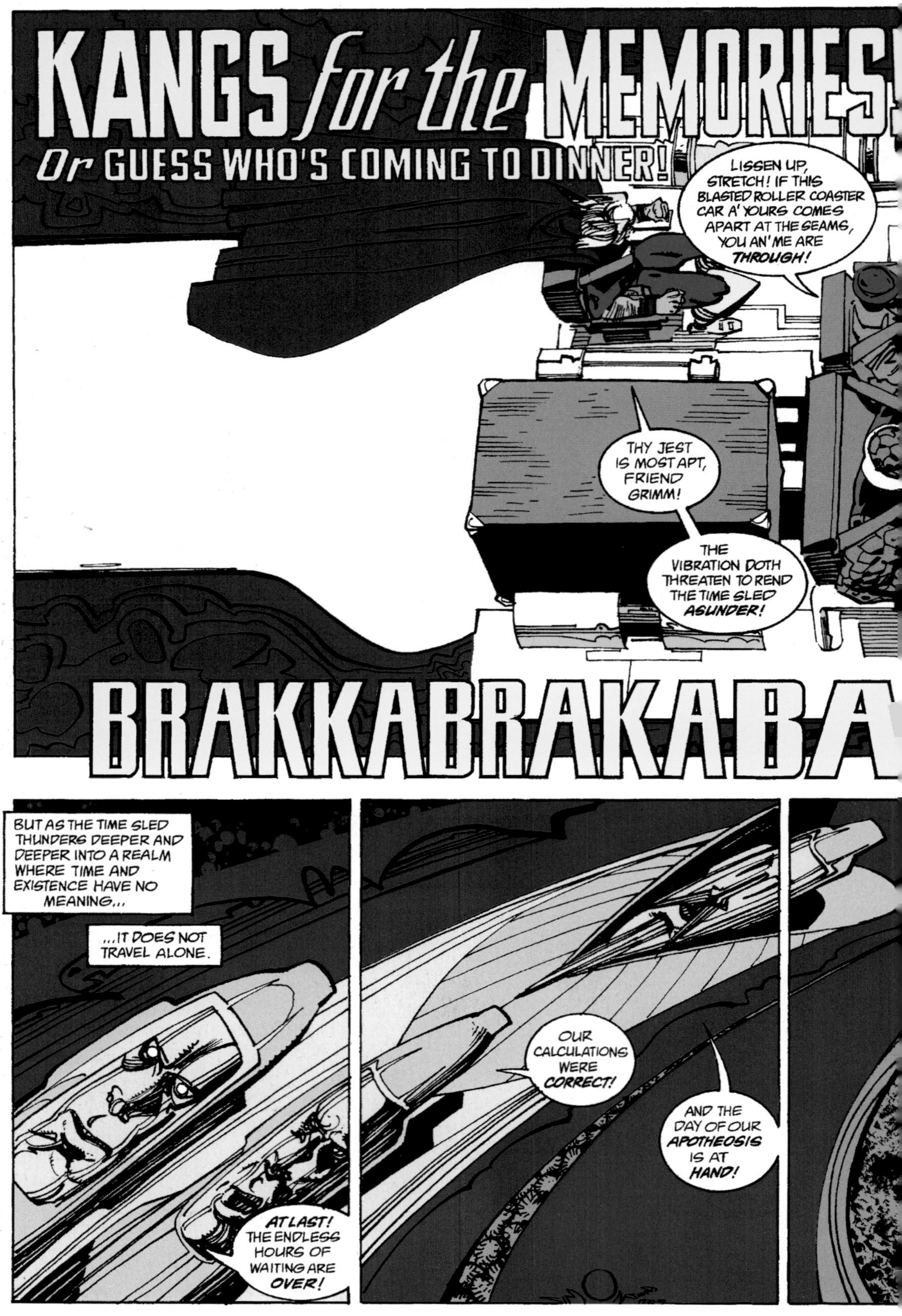
KANGS for the MEMORIES!
Or GUESS WHO'S COMING TO DINNER!
LISSEN UP, STRETCH! IF THIS BLASTED ROLLER COASTER CAR A' YOURS COMES APART AT THE SEAMS, YOU AN' ME ARE THROUGH!
THY JEST IS MOST APT, FRIEND GRIMM!
THE VIBRATION DOTH THREATEN TO REND THE TIME SLED ASUNDER!
BRAKKABRAKABA
BUT AS THE TIME SLED THUNDERS DEEPER AND DEEPER INTO A REALM WHERE TIME AND EXISTENCE HAVE NO MEANING...
...IT DOES NOT TRAVEL ALONE.
AT LAST! THE ENDLESS HOURS OF WAITING ARE OVER!
OUR CALCULATIONS WERE CORRECT!
AND THE DAY OF OUR APOTHEOSIS IS AT HAND!

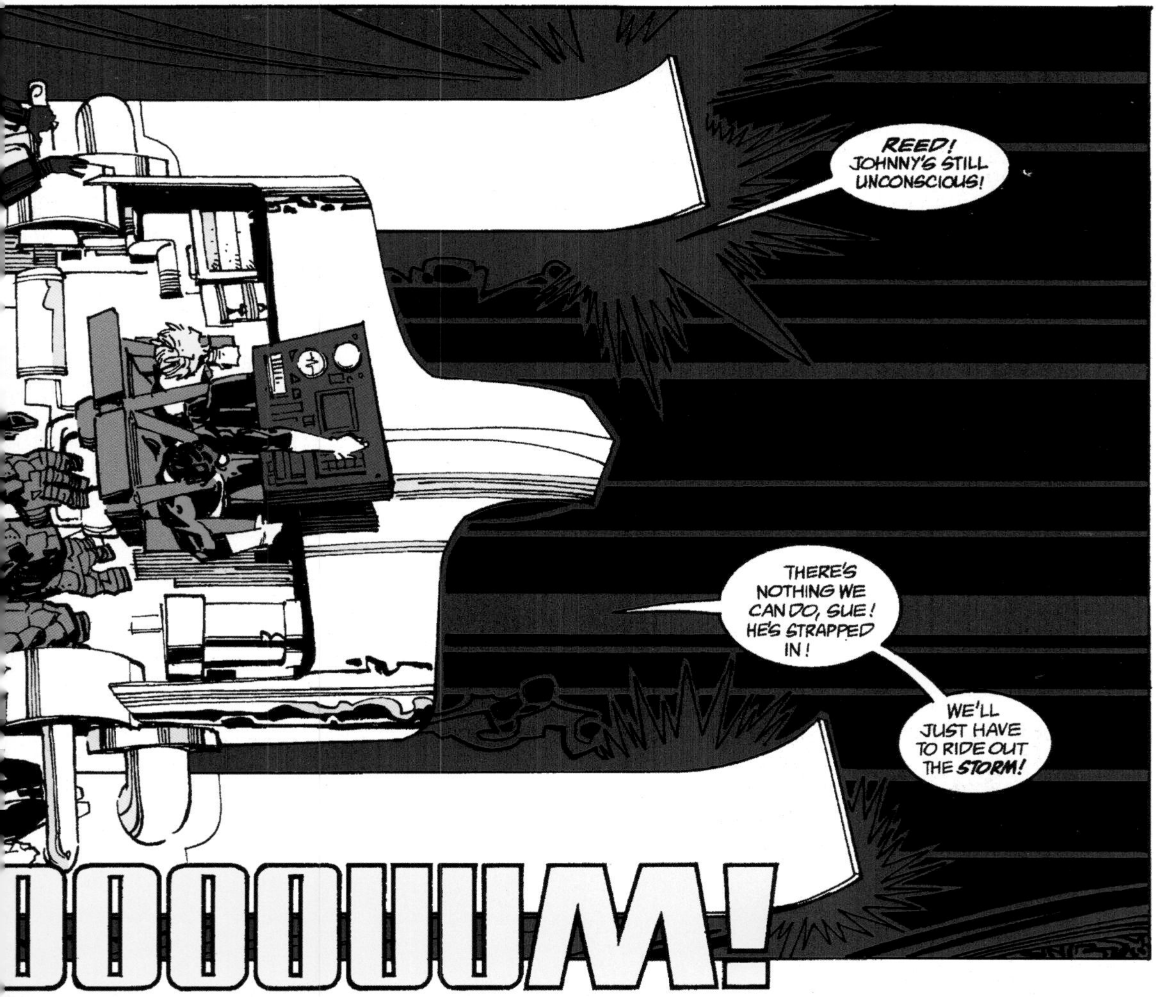
REED! JOHNNY'S STILL UNCONSCIOUS!
THERE'S NOTHING WE CAN DO, SUE! HE'S STRAPPED IN!
WE'LL JUST HAVE TO RIDE OUT THE STORM!
OOOOUUUM!

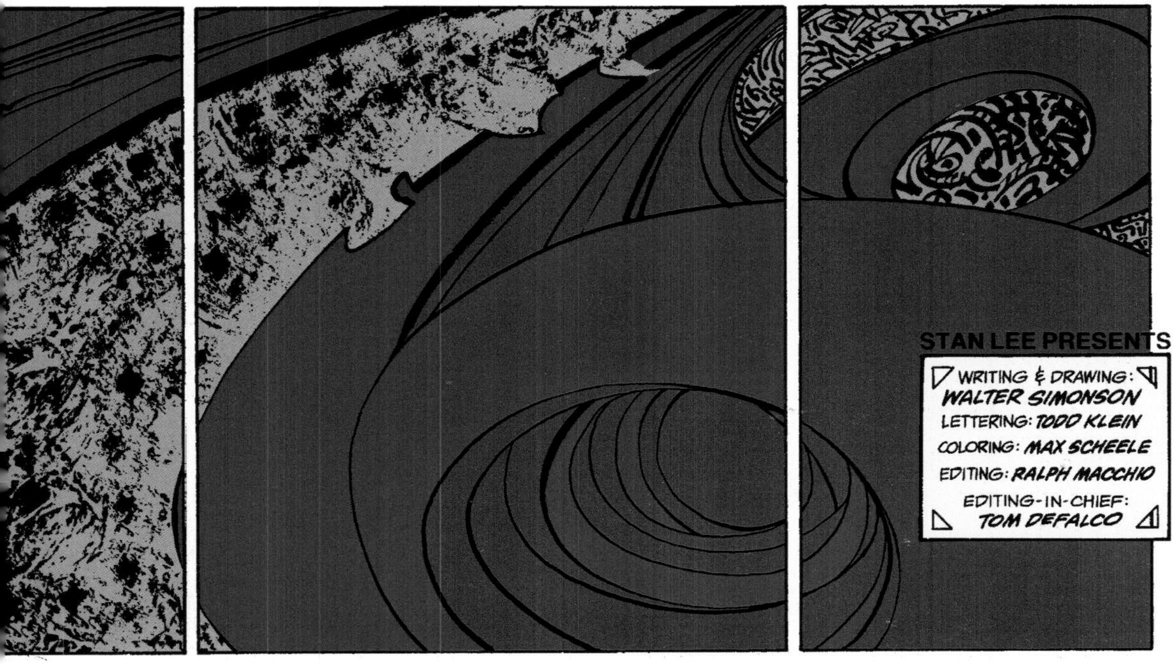
STAN LEE PRESENTS
WRITING & DRAWING: WALTER SIMONSON
LETTERING: TODD KLEIN
COLORING: MAX SCHEELE
EDITING: RALPH MACCHIO
EDITING-IN-CHIEF: TOM DEFALCO

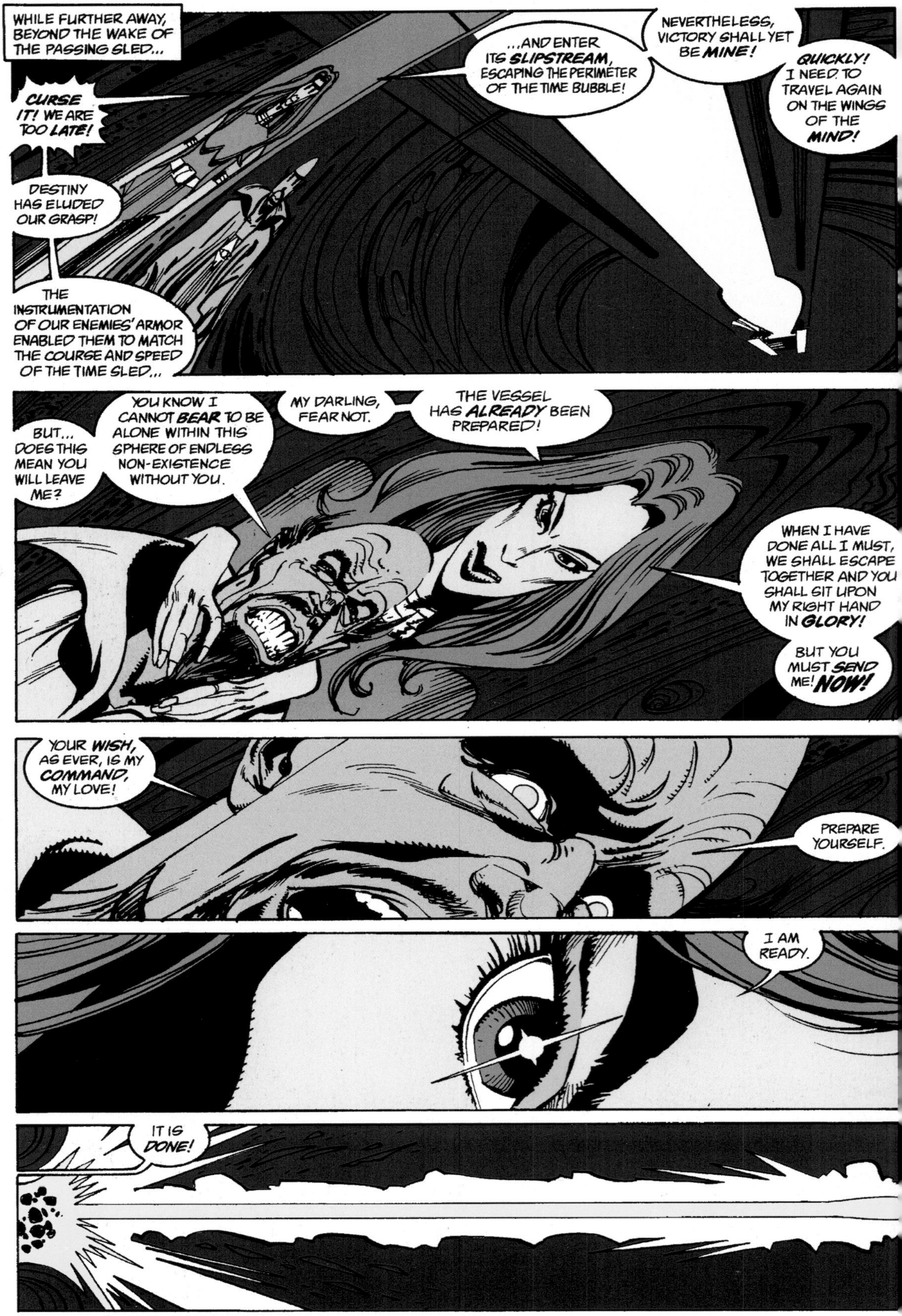
WHILE FURTHER AWAY, BEYOND THE WAKE OF THE PASSING SLED...
CURSE IT! WE ARE TOO LATE!
DESTINY HAS ELUDED OUR GRASP!
THE INSTRUMENTATION OF OUR ENEMIES' ARMOR ENABLED THEM TO MATCH THE COURSE AND SPEED OF THE TIME SLED...
...AND ENTER ITS SLIPSTREAM, ESCAPING THE PERIMETER OF THE TIME BUBBLE!
NEVERTHELESS, VICTORY SHALL YET BE MINE!
QUICKLY! I NEED TO TRAVEL AGAIN ON THE WINGS OF THE MIND!
BUT... DOES THIS MEAN YOU WILL LEAVE ME?
YOU KNOW I CANNOT BEAR TO BE ALONE WITHIN THIS SPHERE OF ENDLESS NON-EXISTENCE WITHOUT YOU.
MY DARLING, FEAR NOT.
THE VESSEL HAS ALREADY BEEN PREPARED!
WHEN I HAVE DONE ALL I MUST, WE SHALL ESCAPE TOGETHER AND YOU SHALL SIT UPON MY RIGHT HAND IN GLORY!
BUT YOU MUST SEND ME! NOW!
YOUR WISH, AS EVER, IS MY COMMAND, MY LOVE!
PREPARE YOURSELF.
I AM READY.
IT IS DONE!

ARRRRGH!
MATCH-HEAD!
THE KID'S HAVING A FIT!
BEN! GET BACK IN YOUR SEAT AND STRAP IN! WE HAVEN'T CLEARED THE TURBULENCE YET!
STUFF IT, MISTER! JOHNNY'S ALMOST PULLIN' HIMSELF OUTA HIS HARNESS! I GOTTA MAKE SURE--
REED! DEAD AHEAD!
I SEE IT, IRON MAN! BRACE, EVERYONE! INITIATING EVASIVE MANEUVERS.
YEEEOOW!
YA WANNA WARN ME NEXT TIME YA DECIDE TO MAKE A U-TURN?
'SIDES, WHAT'S THE BIG DEAL DODGING A BUILDING? IT'S ALL MIRAGES ANYHOW IN THIS LOONY BIN!
IT'S NO MIRAGE THIS TIME, BEN! LOOK! THE CITY'S IMAGE HAS FINALLY STABILIZED!
OH, MY ACHING HEAD! WH-WHERE ARE WE?
JOHNNY! ARE YOU OKAY?
SURE, SIS. I'M FINE. WHAT'S GOING ON?
WE'VE DONE IT, JOHNNY! WE'RE INSIDE THE TIME BUBBLE!
THOU SPEAKEST VERITAS, MRS. RICHARDS. 'TIS TRULY NEW YORK CITY OF THE FUTURE!

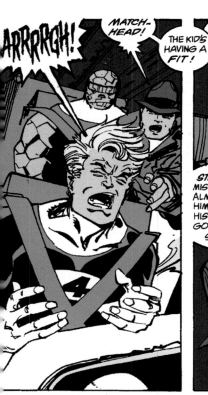

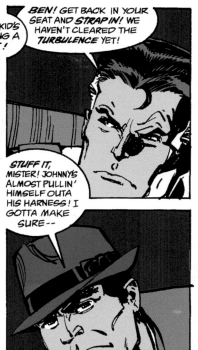

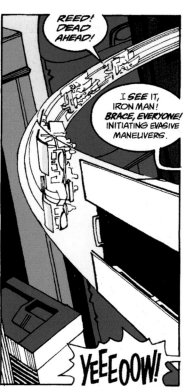

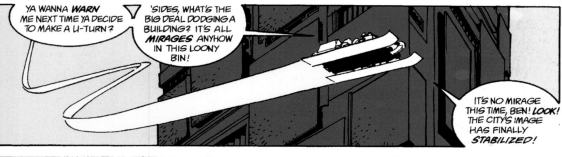

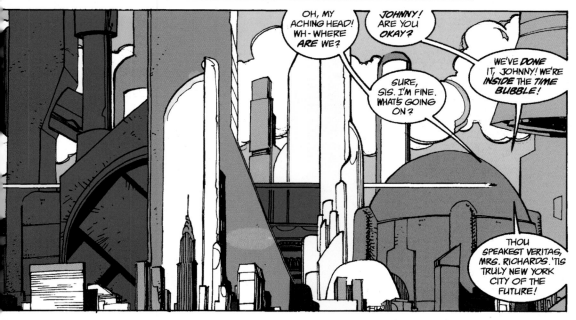

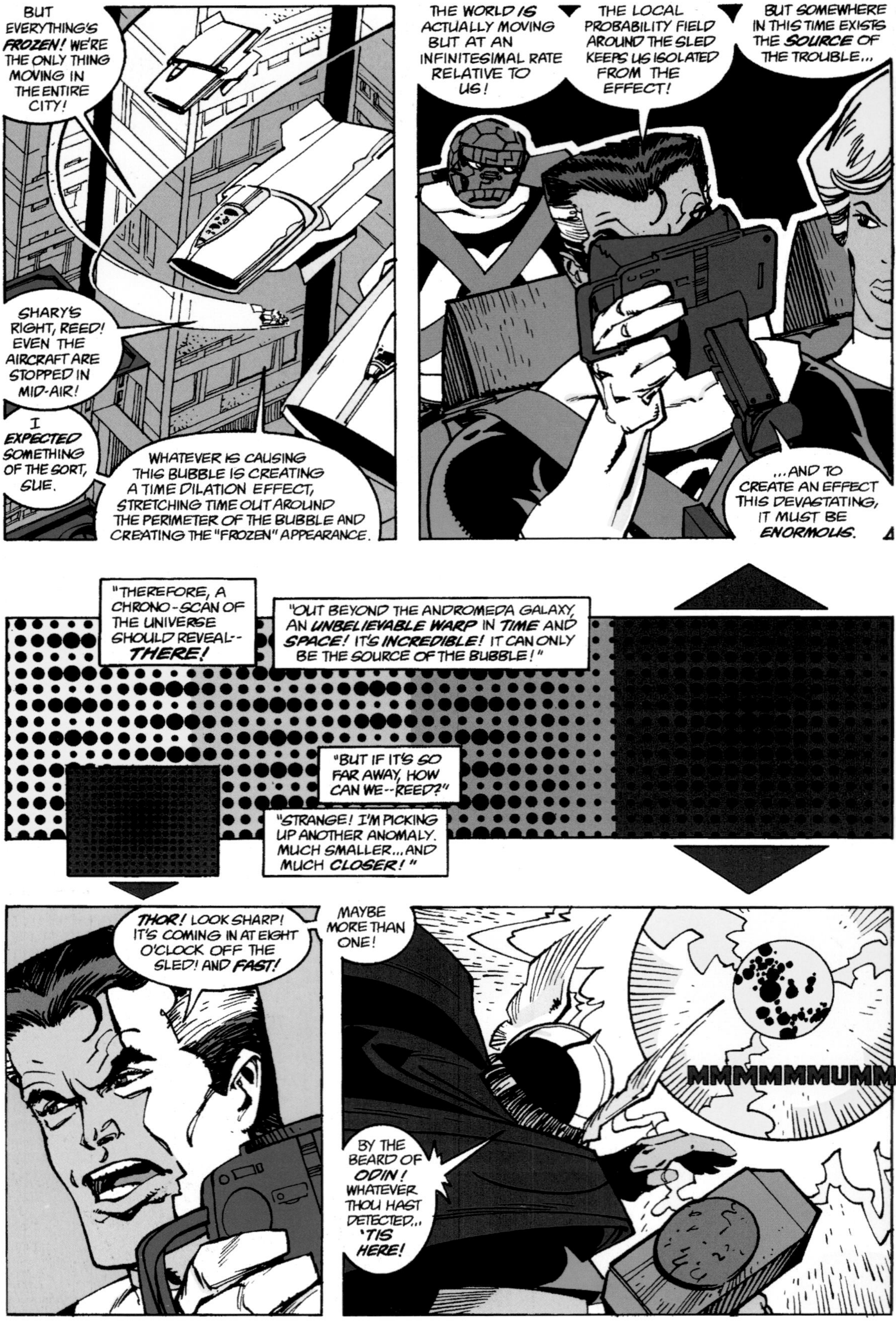

BUT EVERYTHING'S FROZEN! WE'RE THE ONLY THING MOVING IN THE ENTIRE CITY!
SHARY'S RIGHT, REED! EVEN THE AIRCRAFT ARE STOPPED IN MID-AIR!
I EXPECTED SOMETHING OF THE SORT, SUE.
WHATEVER IS CAUSING THIS BUBBLE IS CREATING A TIME DILATION EFFECT, STRETCHING TIME OUT AROUND THE PERIMETER OF THE BUBBLE AND CREATING THE "FROZEN" APPEARANCE.
THE WORLD IS ACTUALLY MOVING BUT AT AN INFINITESIMAL RATE RELATIVE TO US!
THE LOCAL PROBABILITY FIELD AROUND THE SLED KEEPS US ISOLATED FROM THE EFFECT!
BUT SOMEWHERE IN THIS TIME EXISTS THE SOURCE OF THE TROUBLE...
...AND TO CREATE AN EFFECT THIS DEVASTATING, IT MUST BE ENORMOUS.
"THEREFORE, A CHRONO-SCAN OF THE UNIVERSE SHOULD REVEAL-- THERE!
"OUT BEYOND THE ANDROMEDA GALAXY, AN UNBELIEVABLE WARP IN TIME AND SPACE! IT'S INCREDIBLE! IT CAN ONLY BE THE SOURCE OF THE BUBBLE!"
"BUT IF IT'S SO FAR AWAY, HOW CAN WE--REED?"
"STRANGE! I'M PICKING UP ANOTHER ANOMALY. MUCH SMALLER... AND MUCH CLOSER!"
THOR! LOOK SHARP! IT'S COMING IN AT EIGHT O'CLOCK OFF THE SLED! AND FAST!
MAYBE MORE THAN ONE!
MMMMMMMUMM
BY THE BEARD OF ODIN! WHATEVER THOU HAST DETECTED... 'TIS HERE!

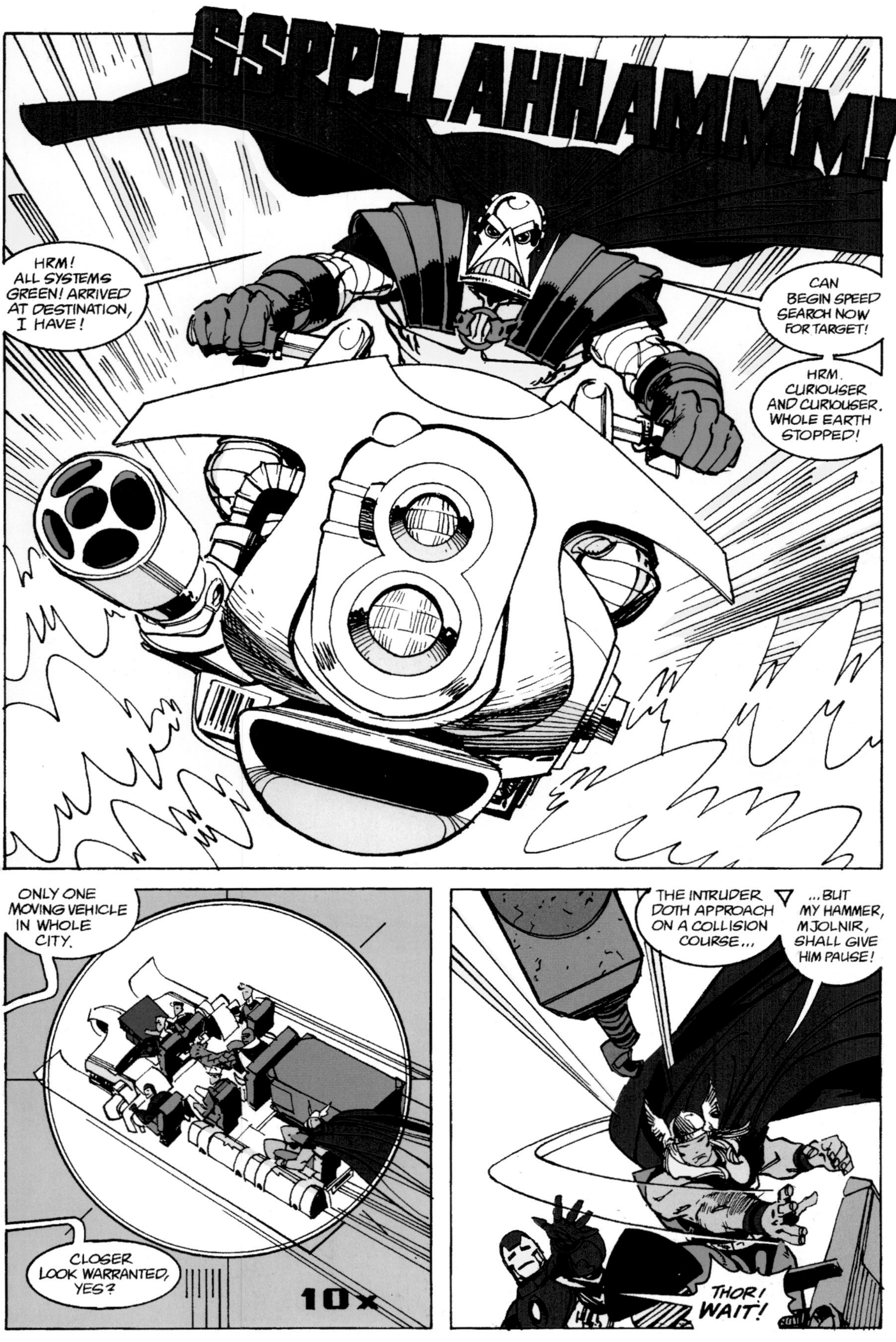
SSPPLLAHHAMMM!
HRM! ALL SYSTEMS GREEN! ARRIVED AT DESTINATION, I HAVE!
CAN BEGIN SPEED SEARCH NOW FOR TARGET!
HRM. CURIOUSER AND CURIOUSER. WHOLE EARTH STOPPED!
ONLY ONE MOVING VEHICLE IN WHOLE CITY.
CLOSER LOOK WARRANTED, YES?
10x
THE INTRUDER DOTH APPROACH ON A COLLISION COURSE...
...BUT MY HAMMER, MJOLNIR, SHALL GIVE HIM PAUSE!
THOR! WAIT!

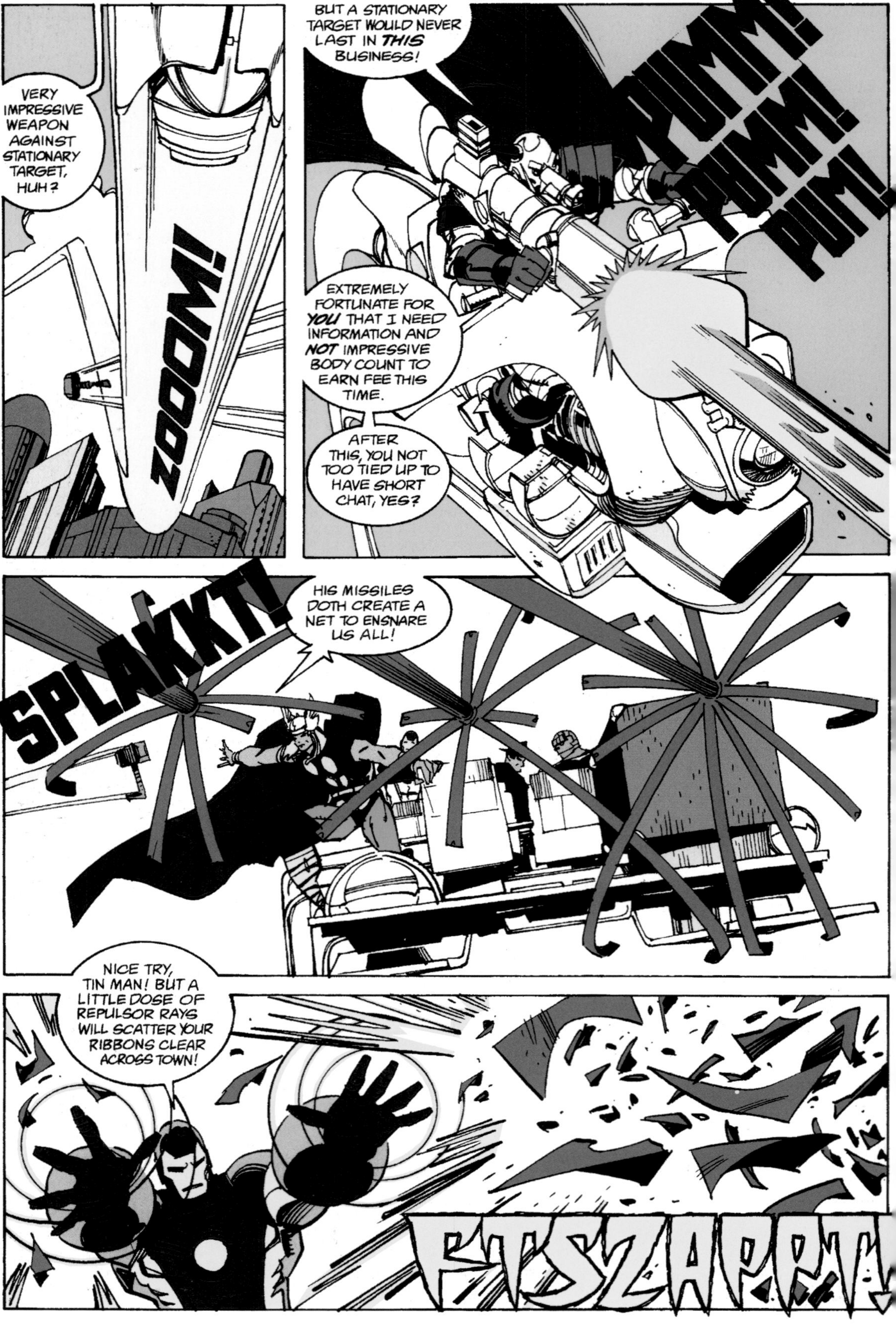
VERY IMPRESSIVE WEAPON AGAINST STATIONARY TARGET, HUH?
ZOOOM!
BUT A STATIONARY TARGET WOULD NEVER LAST IN THIS BUSINESS!
PUM! PUM! PUM!
EXTREMELY FORTUNATE FOR YOU THAT I NEED INFORMATION AND NOT IMPRESSIVE BODY COUNT TO EARN FEE THIS TIME.
AFTER THIS, YOU NOT TOO TIED UP TO HAVE SHORT CHAT, YES?
SPLAKKT!
HIS MISSILES DOTH CREATE A NET TO ENSNARE US ALL!
NICE TRY, TIN MAN! BUT A LITTLE DOSE OF REPULSOR RAYS WILL SCATTER YOUR RIBBONS CLEAR ACROSS TOWN!
FTSZAPPT!

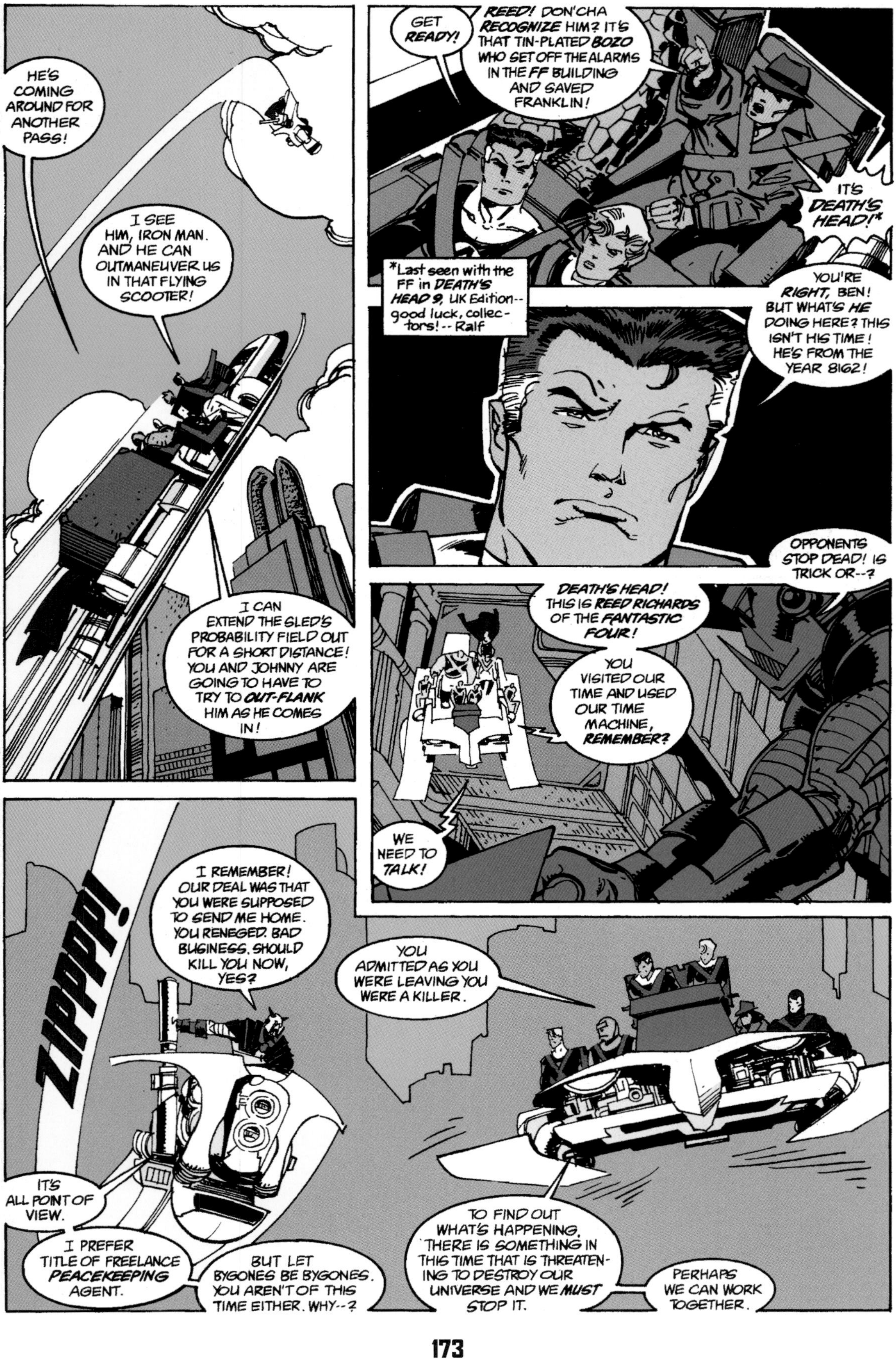
HE'S COMING AROUND FOR ANOTHER PASS!
I SEE HIM, IRON MAN. AND HE CAN OUTMANEUVER US IN THAT FLYING SCOOTER!
I CAN EXTEND THE SLED'S PROBABILITY FIELD OUT FOR A SHORT DISTANCE! YOU AND JOHNNY ARE GOING TO HAVE TO TRY TO OUT-FLANK HIM AS HE COMES IN!
GET READY!
REED! DON'CHA RECOGNIZE HIM? IT'S THAT TIN-PLATED BOZO WHO SET OFF THE ALARMS IN THE FF BUILDING AND SAVED FRANKLIN!
IT'S DEATH'S HEAD!*
*Last seen with the FF in DEATH'S HEAD 9, UK Edition--good luck, collectors!--Ralf
YOU'RE RIGHT, BEN! BUT WHAT'S HE DOING HERE? THIS ISN'T HIS TIME! HE'S FROM THE YEAR 8162!
OPPONENTS STOP DEAD! IS TRICK OR--?
DEATH'S HEAD! THIS IS REED RICHARDS OF THE FANTASTIC FOUR!
YOU VISITED OUR TIME AND USED OUR TIME MACHINE, REMEMBER?
WE NEED TO TALK!
ZIPPPP!
I REMEMBER! OUR DEAL WAS THAT YOU WERE SUPPOSED TO SEND ME HOME. YOU RENEGED. BAD BUSINESS. SHOULD KILL YOU NOW, YES?
YOU ADMITTED AS YOU WERE LEAVING YOU WERE A KILLER.
IT'S ALL POINT OF VIEW.
I PREFER TITLE OF FREELANCE PEACEKEEPING AGENT.
BUT LET BYGONES BE BYGONES. YOU AREN'T OF THIS TIME EITHER. WHY--?
TO FIND OUT WHAT'S HAPPENING. THERE IS SOMETHING IN THIS TIME THAT IS THREATENING TO DESTROY OUR UNIVERSE AND WE MUST STOP IT.
PERHAPS WE CAN WORK TOGETHER.

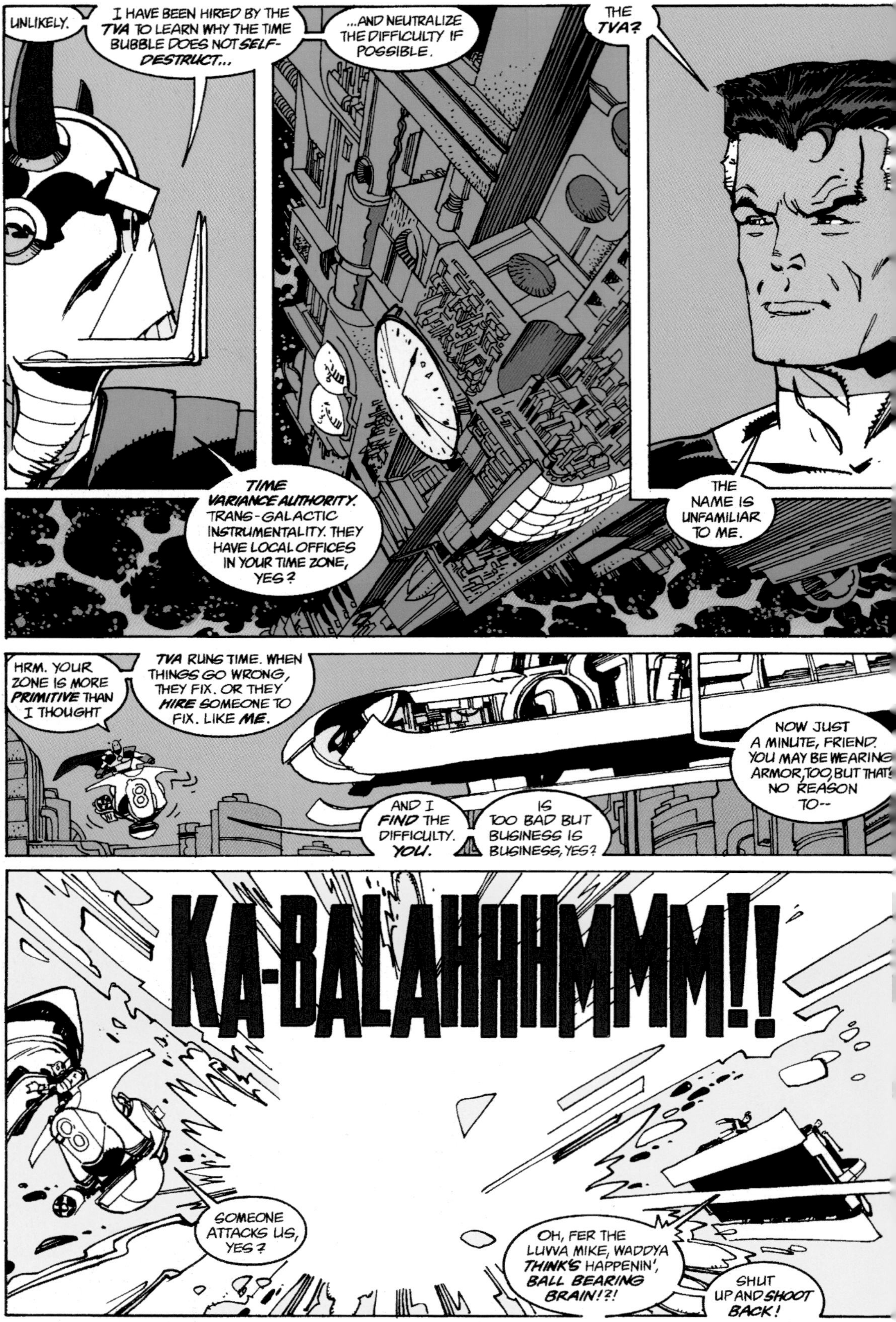
UNLIKELY.
I HAVE BEEN HIRED BY THE TVA TO LEARN WHY THE TIME BUBBLE DOES NOT SELF-DESTRUCT...
...AND NEUTRALIZE THE DIFFICULTY IF POSSIBLE.
THE TVA?
TIME VARIANCE AUTHORITY. TRANS-GALACTIC INSTRUMENTALITY. THEY HAVE LOCAL OFFICES IN YOUR TIME ZONE, YES?
THE NAME IS UNFAMILIAR TO ME.
HRM. YOUR ZONE IS MORE PRIMITIVE THAN I THOUGHT
TVA RUNS TIME. WHEN THINGS GO WRONG, THEY FIX. OR THEY HIRE SOMEONE TO FIX. LIKE ME.
AND I FIND THE DIFFICULTY. YOU.
IS TOO BAD BUT BUSINESS IS BUSINESS, YES?
NOW JUST A MINUTE, FRIEND. YOU MAY BE WEARING ARMOR, TOO, BUT THAT'S NO REASON TO--
KA-BALAHHHMMMM!!
SOMEONE ATTACKS US, YES?
OH, FER THE LUVVA MIKE, WADDYA THINK'S HAPPENIN', BALL BEARING BRAIN!?!
SHUT UP AND SHOOT BACK!

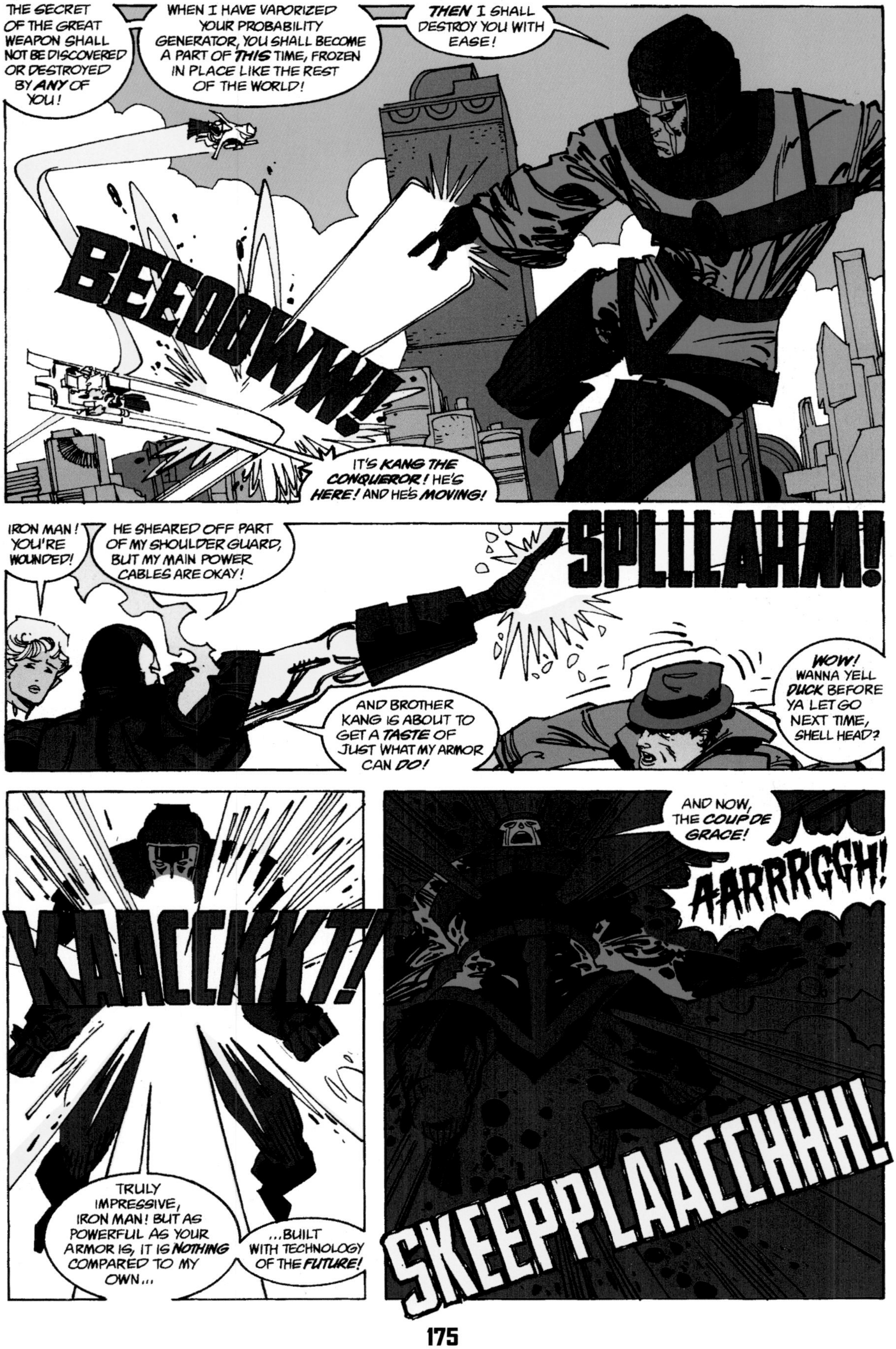
THE SECRET OF THE GREAT WEAPON SHALL NOT BE DISCOVERED OR DESTROYED BY ANY OF YOU!
WHEN I HAVE VAPORIZED YOUR PROBABILITY GENERATOR, YOU SHALL BECOME A PART OF THIS TIME, FROZEN IN PLACE LIKE THE REST OF THE WORLD!
THEN I SHALL DESTROY YOU WITH EASE!
BEEOOWW!
IT'S KANG THE CONQUEROR! HE'S HERE! AND HE'S MOVING!
IRON MAN! YOU'RE WOUNDED!
HE SHEARED OFF PART OF MY SHOULDER GUARD, BUT MY MAIN POWER CABLES ARE OKAY!
SPLLLAHM!
AND BROTHER KANG IS ABOUT TO GET A TASTE OF JUST WHAT MY ARMOR CAN DO!
WOW! WANNA YELL DUCK BEFORE YA LET GO NEXT TIME, SHELL HEAD?
KAACKKKT!
TRULY IMPRESSIVE, IRON MAN! BUT AS POWERFUL AS YOUR ARMOR IS, IT IS NOTHING COMPARED TO MY OWN...
...BUILT WITH TECHNOLOGY OF THE FUTURE!
AND NOW, THE COUP DE GRACE!
AARRRGGH!
SKEEPPLAACCHHH!

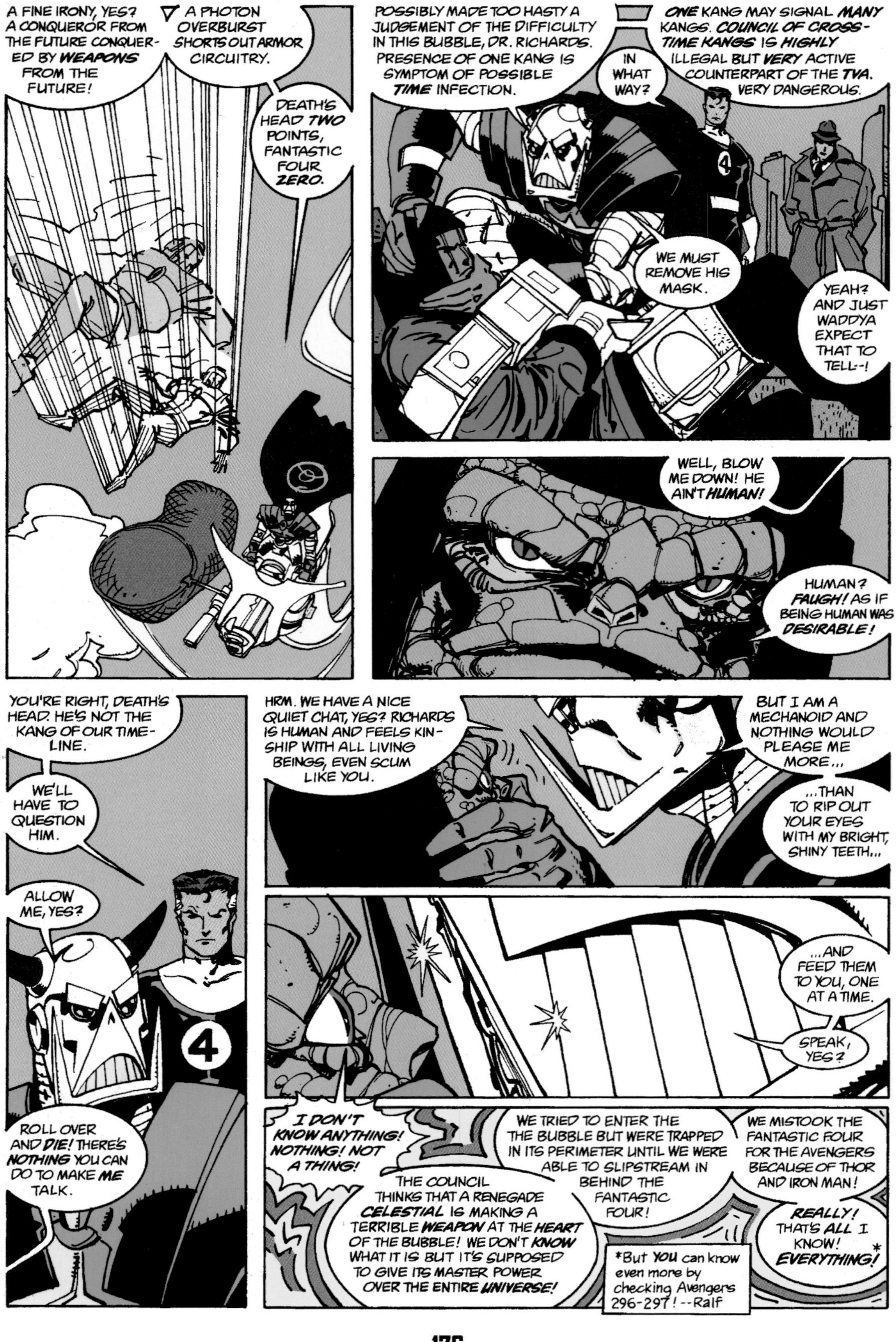
A FINE IRONY, YES? A CONQUEROR FROM THE FUTURE CONQUERED BY WEAPONS FROM THE FUTURE!
A PHOTON OVERBURST SHORTS OUT ARMOR CIRCUITRY.
DEATH'S HEAD TWO POINTS, FANTASTIC FOUR ZERO.
POSSIBLY MADE TOO HASTY A JUDGEMENT OF THE DIFFICULTY IN THIS BUBBLE, DR. RICHARDS. PRESENCE OF ONE KANG IS SYMPTOM OF POSSIBLE TIME INFECTION.
IN WHAT WAY?
ONE KANG MAY SIGNAL MANY KANGS. COUNCIL OF CROSS-TIME KANGS IS HIGHLY ILLEGAL BUT VERY ACTIVE COUNTERPART OF THE TVA. VERY DANGEROUS.
WE MUST REMOVE HIS MASK.
YEAH? AND JUST WADDYA EXPECT THAT TO TELL--!
WELL, BLOW ME DOWN! HE AIN'T HUMAN!
HUMAN? FAUGH! AS IF BEING HUMAN WAS DESIRABLE!
YOU'RE RIGHT, DEATH'S HEAD. HE'S NOT THE KANG OF OUR TIME-LINE.
WE'LL HAVE TO QUESTION HIM.
ALLOW ME, YES?
ROLL OVER AND DIE! THERE'S NOTHING YOU CAN DO TO MAKE ME TALK.
HRM. WE HAVE A NICE QUIET CHAT, YES? RICHARDS IS HUMAN AND FEELS KINSHIP WITH ALL LIVING BEINGS, EVEN SCUM LIKE YOU.
BUT I AM A MECHANOID AND NOTHING WOULD PLEASE ME MORE...
...THAN TO RIP OUT YOUR EYES WITH MY BRIGHT, SHINY TEETH...
...AND FEED THEM TO YOU, ONE AT A TIME.
SPEAK, YES?
I DON'T KNOW ANYTHING! NOTHING! NOT A THING!
THE COUNCIL THINKS THAT A RENEGADE CELESTIAL IS MAKING A TERRIBLE WEAPON AT THE HEART OF THE BUBBLE! WE DON'T KNOW WHAT IT IS BUT IT'S SUPPOSED TO GIVE ITS MASTER POWER OVER THE ENTIRE UNIVERSE!
WE TRIED TO ENTER THE THE BUBBLE BUT WERE TRAPPED IN ITS PERIMETER UNTIL WE WERE ABLE TO SLIPSTREAM IN BEHIND THE FANTASTIC FOUR!
WE MISTOOK THE FANTASTIC FOUR FOR THE AVENGERS BECAUSE OF THOR AND IRON MAN!
REALLY! THAT'S ALL I KNOW! EVERYTHING!*
*But YOU can know even more by checking Avengers 296-297! --Ralf

A LITTLE KNOWLEDGE IS DANGEROUS, HUH?

WHEEZZZZ!

SPRICCH! PAFFFFFF!

SO LIVE HERE IN IGNORANCE! LIZARD MAN PLAY *TORTOISE*, YES? WITHOUT POWER, ARMOR IS JUST *SHELL*.

I THINK WE OUGHT TO KILL HIM HERE AND NOW. WHO KNOWS WHAT A KANG IS CAPABLE OF?

JOHNNY! I'M SURPRISED AT YOU. WITHOUT POWER, THIS KANG IS INEXTRICABLY BOUND TO THIS PLACE, A PRISONER OF THE LOCAL TIME.

HE'S HARMLESS.

4

LET'S GO. WE'VE GOT A LONG ROAD AHEAD OF US.

I DUNNO WHUT YA SAID TO THE LIZARD, BUT NICE GOIN'. REED'S SHARP BUT HE AIN'T *MEAN* ENOUGH FER *SOME* JOBS.

YOU COMIN' WITH US?

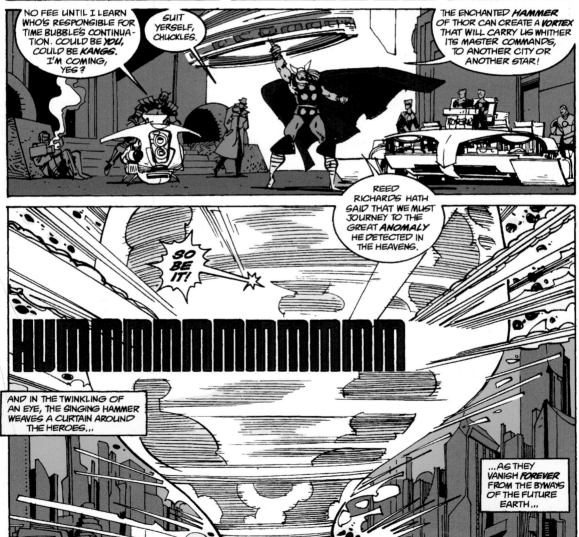

NO FEE UNTIL I LEARN WHO'S RESPONSIBLE FOR TIME BUBBLE'S CONTINUATION. COULD BE *YOU*, COULD BE *KANGS*. I'M COMING, YES?

SUIT YERSELF, CHUCKLES.

THE ENCHANTED *HAMMER* OF THOR CAN CREATE A *VORTEX* THAT WILL CARRY US WHITHER ITS MASTER COMMANDS, TO ANOTHER CITY OR ANOTHER STAR!

REED RICHARDS HATH SAID THAT WE MUST JOURNEY TO THE GREAT *ANOMALY* HE DETECTED IN THE HEAVENS.

SO BE IT!

HUMMMMMMMMMMM

AND IN THE TWINKLING OF AN EYE, THE SINGING HAMMER WEAVES A CURTAIN AROUND THE HEROES...

...AS THEY VANISH *FOREVER* FROM THE BYWAYS OF THE FUTURE EARTH...

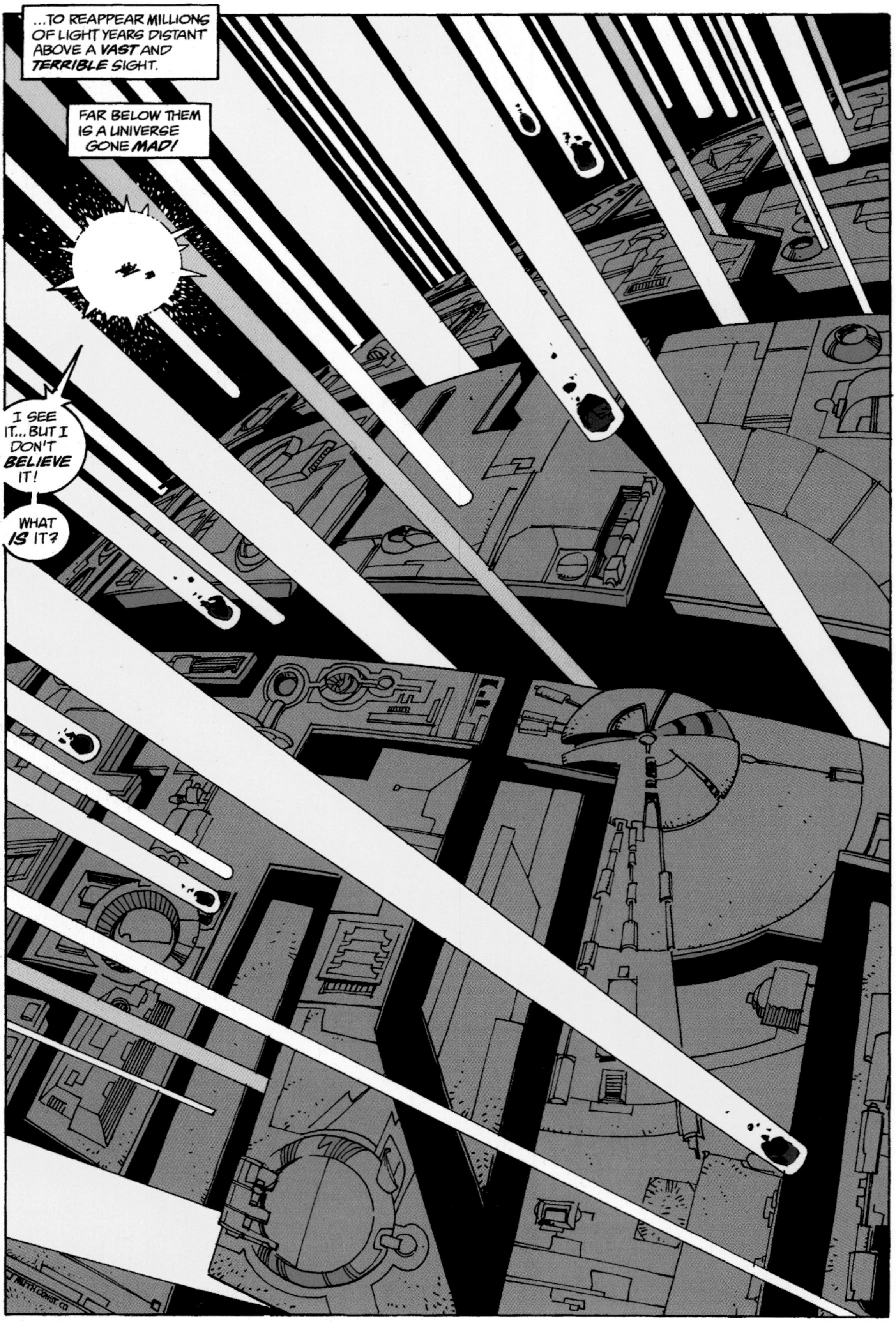
...TO REAPPEAR MILLIONS OF LIGHT YEARS DISTANT ABOVE A VAST AND TERRIBLE SIGHT.
FAR BELOW THEM IS A UNIVERSE GONE MAD!
I SEE IT... BUT I DON'T BELIEVE IT!
WHAT IS IT?

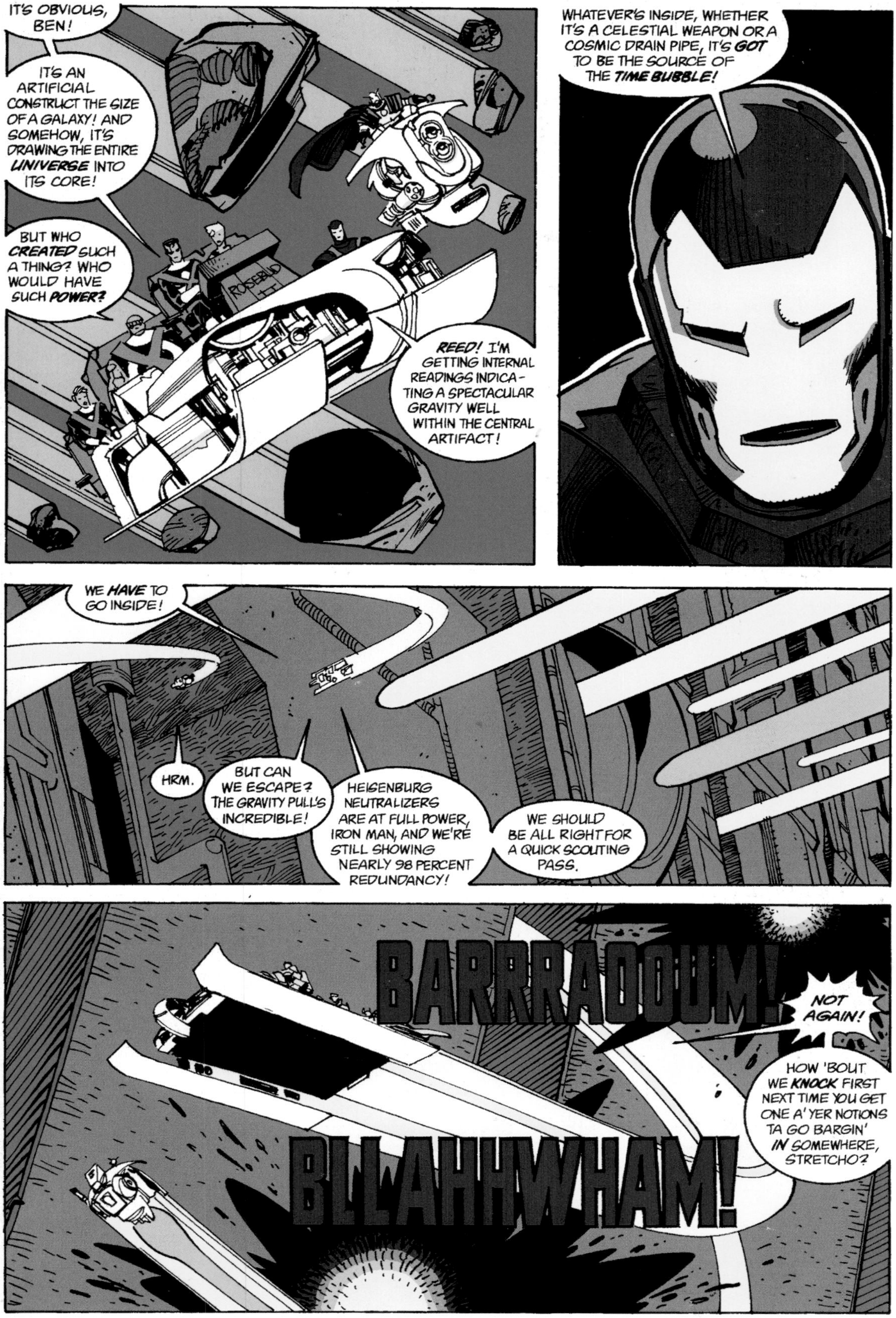
IT'S OBVIOUS, BEN!
IT'S AN ARTIFICIAL CONSTRUCT THE SIZE OF A GALAXY! AND SOMEHOW, IT'S DRAWING THE ENTIRE UNIVERSE INTO ITS CORE!
BUT WHO CREATED SUCH A THING? WHO WOULD HAVE SUCH POWER?
ROSEBUD
REED! I'M GETTING INTERNAL READINGS INDICATING A SPECTACULAR GRAVITY WELL WITHIN THE CENTRAL ARTIFACT!
WHATEVER'S INSIDE, WHETHER IT'S A CELESTIAL WEAPON OR A COSMIC DRAIN PIPE, IT'S GOT TO BE THE SOURCE OF THE TIME BUBBLE!
WE HAVE TO GO INSIDE!
HRM.
BUT CAN WE ESCAPE? THE GRAVITY PULL'S INCREDIBLE!
HEISENBURG NEUTRALIZERS ARE AT FULL POWER, IRON MAN, AND WE'RE STILL SHOWING NEARLY 98 PERCENT REDUNDANCY!
WE SHOULD BE ALL RIGHT FOR A QUICK SCOUTING PASS.
BARRRADOOUM!
NOT AGAIN!
HOW 'BOUT WE KNOCK FIRST NEXT TIME YOU GET ONE A' YER NOTIONS TA GO BARGIN' IN SOMEWHERE, STRETCHO?
BLLAHHWHAM!

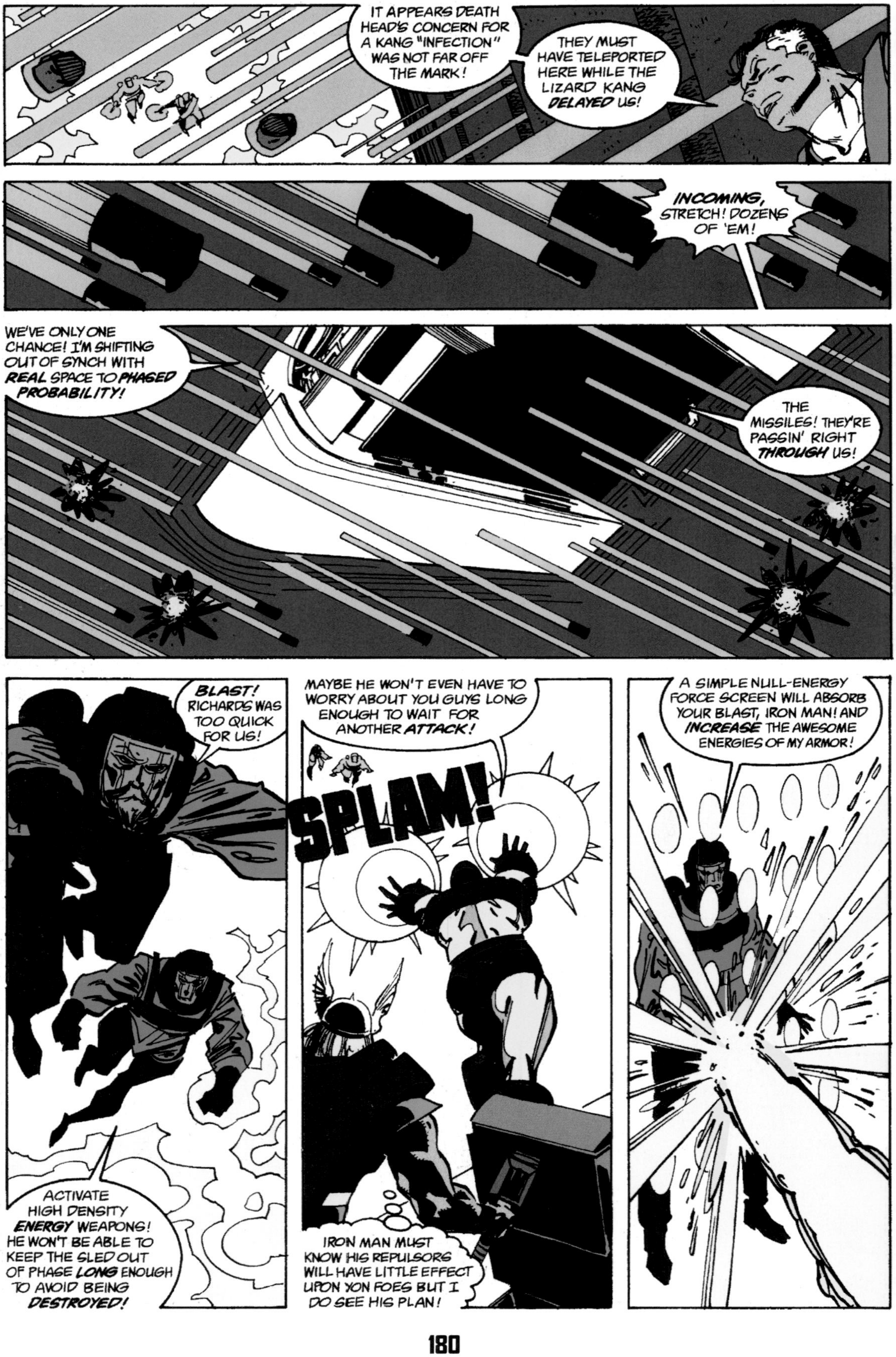
IT APPEARS DEATH HEAD'S CONCERN FOR A KANG "INFECTION" WAS NOT FAR OFF THE MARK!
THEY MUST HAVE TELEPORTED HERE WHILE THE LIZARD KANG DELAYED US!
INCOMING, STRETCH! DOZENS OF 'EM!
WE'VE ONLY ONE CHANCE! I'M SHIFTING OUT OF SYNCH WITH REAL SPACE TO PHASED PROBABILITY!
THE MISSILES! THEY'RE PASSIN' RIGHT THROUGH US!
BLAST! RICHARDS WAS TOO QUICK FOR US!
ACTIVATE HIGH DENSITY ENERGY WEAPONS! HE WON'T BE ABLE TO KEEP THE SLED OUT OF PHASE LONG ENOUGH TO AVOID BEING DESTROYED!
MAYBE HE WON'T EVEN HAVE TO WORRY ABOUT YOU GUYS LONG ENOUGH TO WAIT FOR ANOTHER ATTACK!
SPLAM!
IRON MAN MUST KNOW HIS REPULSORS WILL HAVE LITTLE EFFECT UPON YON FOES BUT I DO SEE HIS PLAN!
A SIMPLE NULL-ENERGY FORCE SCREEN WILL ABSORB YOUR BLAST, IRON MAN! AND INCREASE THE AWESOME ENERGIES OF MY ARMOR!

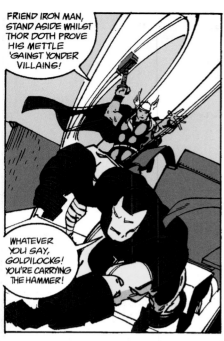

FRIEND IRON MAN, STAND ASIDE WHILST THOR DOTH PROVE HIS METTLE 'GAINST YONDER VILLAINS!

WHATEVER YOU SAY, GOLDILOCKS! YOU'RE CARRYING THE HAMMER!

RICHARDS' ALLIES FIGHT A GOOD FIGHT, YES? THEY *DISTRACT* THE ENEMY WHILE THE REAL DANGER TO THE KANGS REMAINS *UNNOTICED!*

A REVERSED POSITRONIC ENERGY DISPERSER WILL DAMPEN THE TARGET'S SHIELD!

"AND IF MY TIMING IS RIGHT..."

SKRRRRHHHHHMMM

MY FORCE-SCREEN! IT'S DE-ENERGIZING!

OH, NO!

KE-BLAAHMM

"PERFECT, YES?"

181

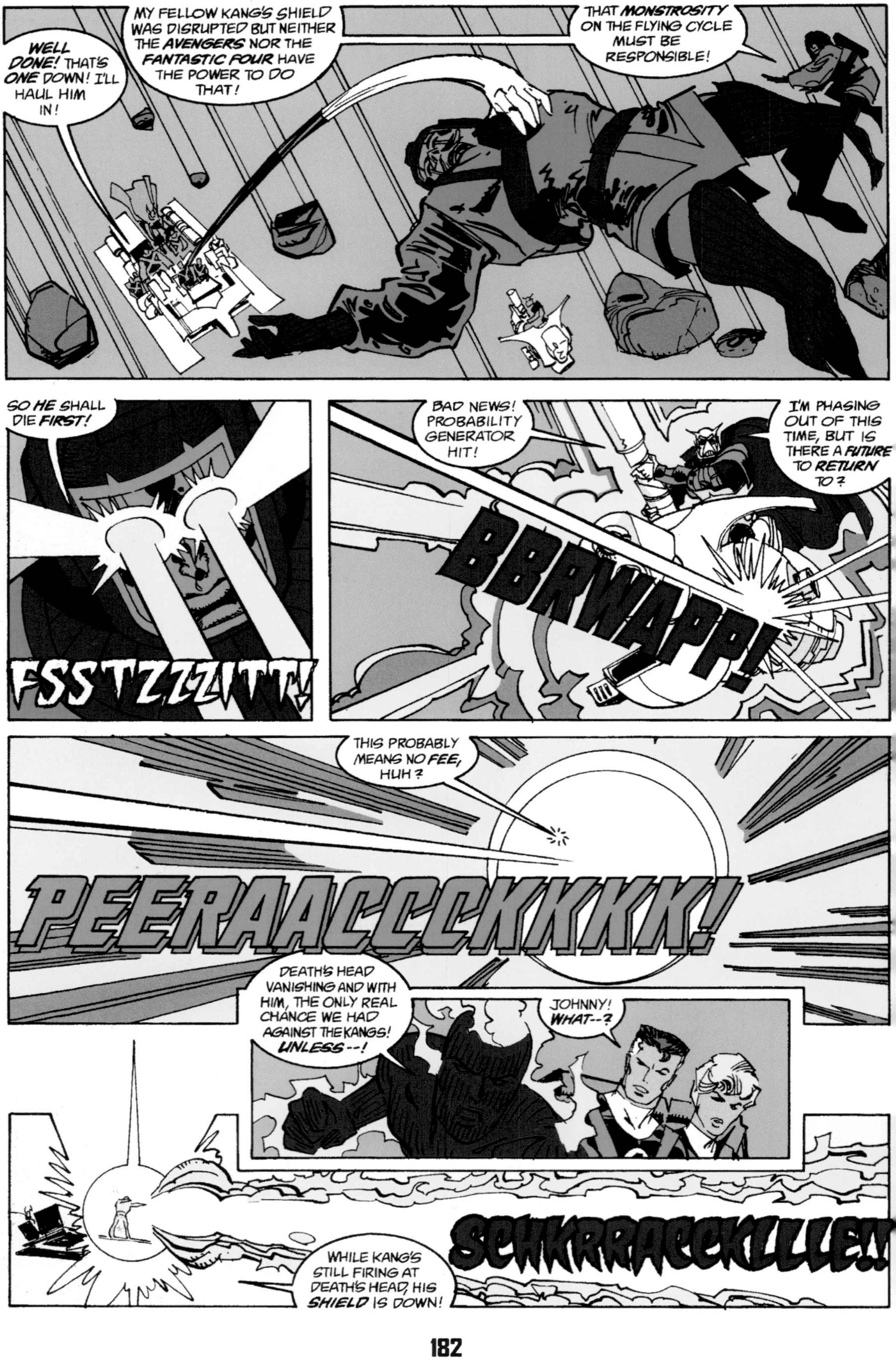
WELL DONE! THAT'S ONE DOWN! I'LL HAUL HIM IN!
MY FELLOW KANG'S SHIELD WAS DISRUPTED BUT NEITHER THE AVENGERS NOR THE FANTASTIC FOUR HAVE THE POWER TO DO THAT!
THAT MONSTROSITY ON THE FLYING CYCLE MUST BE RESPONSIBLE!
SO HE SHALL DIE FIRST!
FSSTZZZITT!
BAD NEWS! PROBABILITY GENERATOR HIT!
I'M PHASING OUT OF THIS TIME, BUT IS THERE A FUTURE TO RETURN TO?
BBRWAPP!
THIS PROBABLY MEANS NO FEE, HUH?
PEERAACCCCKKKKK!
DEATH'S HEAD VANISHING AND WITH HIM, THE ONLY REAL CHANCE WE HAD AGAINST THE KANGS! UNLESS--!
JOHNNY! WHAT--?
SCHKRRACCKLLLE!!
WHILE KANG'S STILL FIRING AT DEATH'S HEAD, HIS SHIELD IS DOWN!

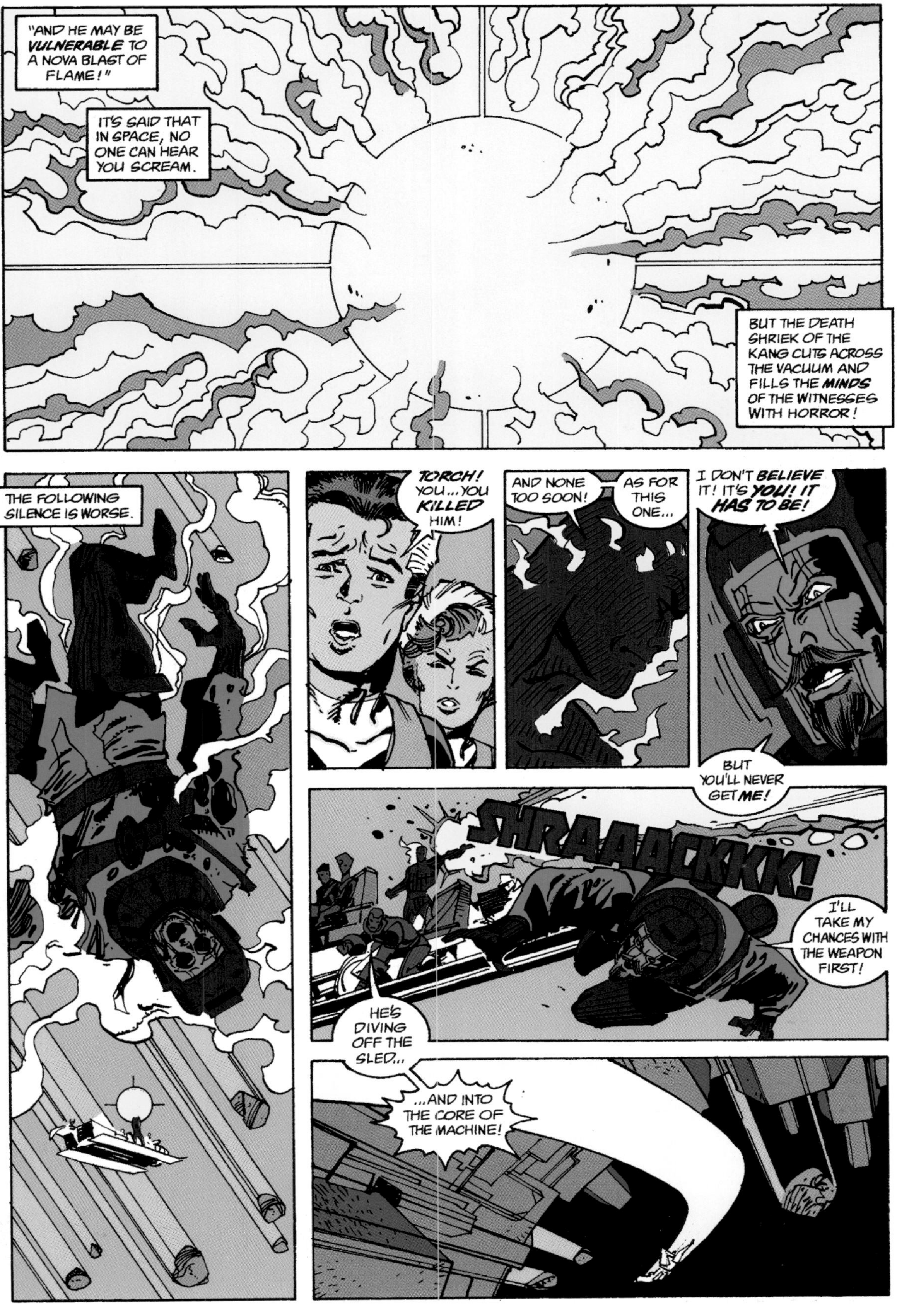
"AND HE MAY BE **VULNERABLE** TO A NOVA BLAST OF FLAME!"
IT'S SAID THAT IN SPACE, NO ONE CAN HEAR YOU SCREAM.
BUT THE DEATH SHRIEK OF THE KANG CUTS ACROSS THE VACUUM AND FILLS THE **MINDS** OF THE WITNESSES WITH HORROR!
THE FOLLOWING SILENCE IS WORSE.
TORCH! YOU... YOU **KILLED** HIM!
AND NONE TOO SOON!
AS FOR THIS ONE...
I DON'T **BELIEVE** IT! IT'S **YOU! IT HAS TO BE!**
BUT YOU'LL NEVER GET **ME!**
SHRAAAACKKKK!
I'LL TAKE MY CHANCES WITH THE WEAPON FIRST!
HE'S DIVING OFF THE SLED...
...AND INTO THE CORE OF THE MACHINE!

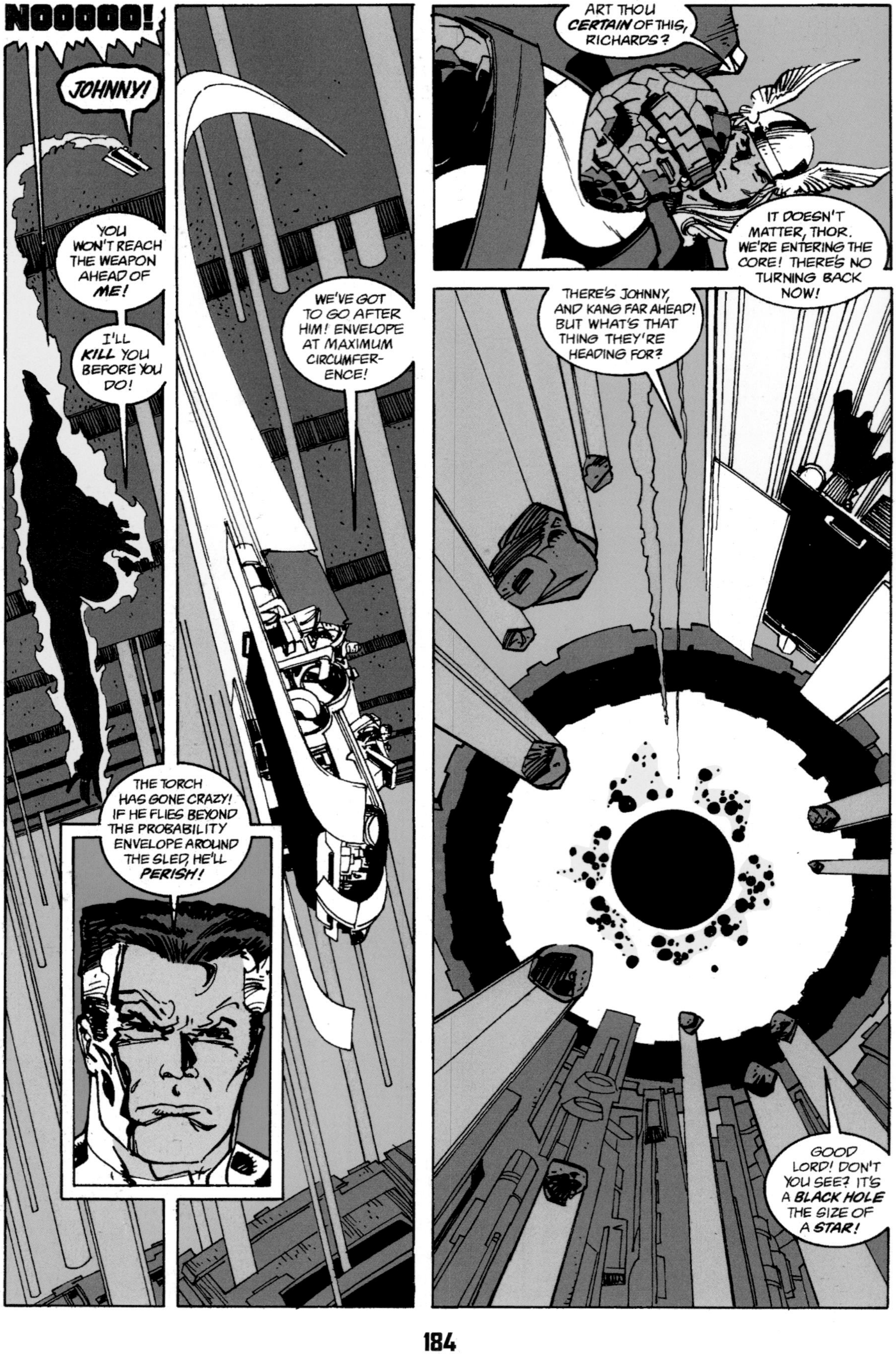
NOOOOO!
JOHNNY!
YOU WON'T REACH THE WEAPON AHEAD OF ME!
I'LL KILL YOU BEFORE YOU DO!
THE TORCH HAS GONE CRAZY! IF HE FLIES BEYOND THE PROBABILITY ENVELOPE AROUND THE SLED, HE'LL PERISH!
WE'VE GOT TO GO AFTER HIM! ENVELOPE AT MAXIMUM CIRCUMFERENCE!
ART THOU CERTAIN OF THIS, RICHARDS?
IT DOESN'T MATTER, THOR. WE'RE ENTERING THE CORE! THERE'S NO TURNING BACK NOW!
THERE'S JOHNNY, AND KANG FAR AHEAD! BUT WHAT'S THAT THING THEY'RE HEADING FOR?
GOOD LORD! DON'T YOU SEE? IT'S A BLACK HOLE THE SIZE OF A STAR!

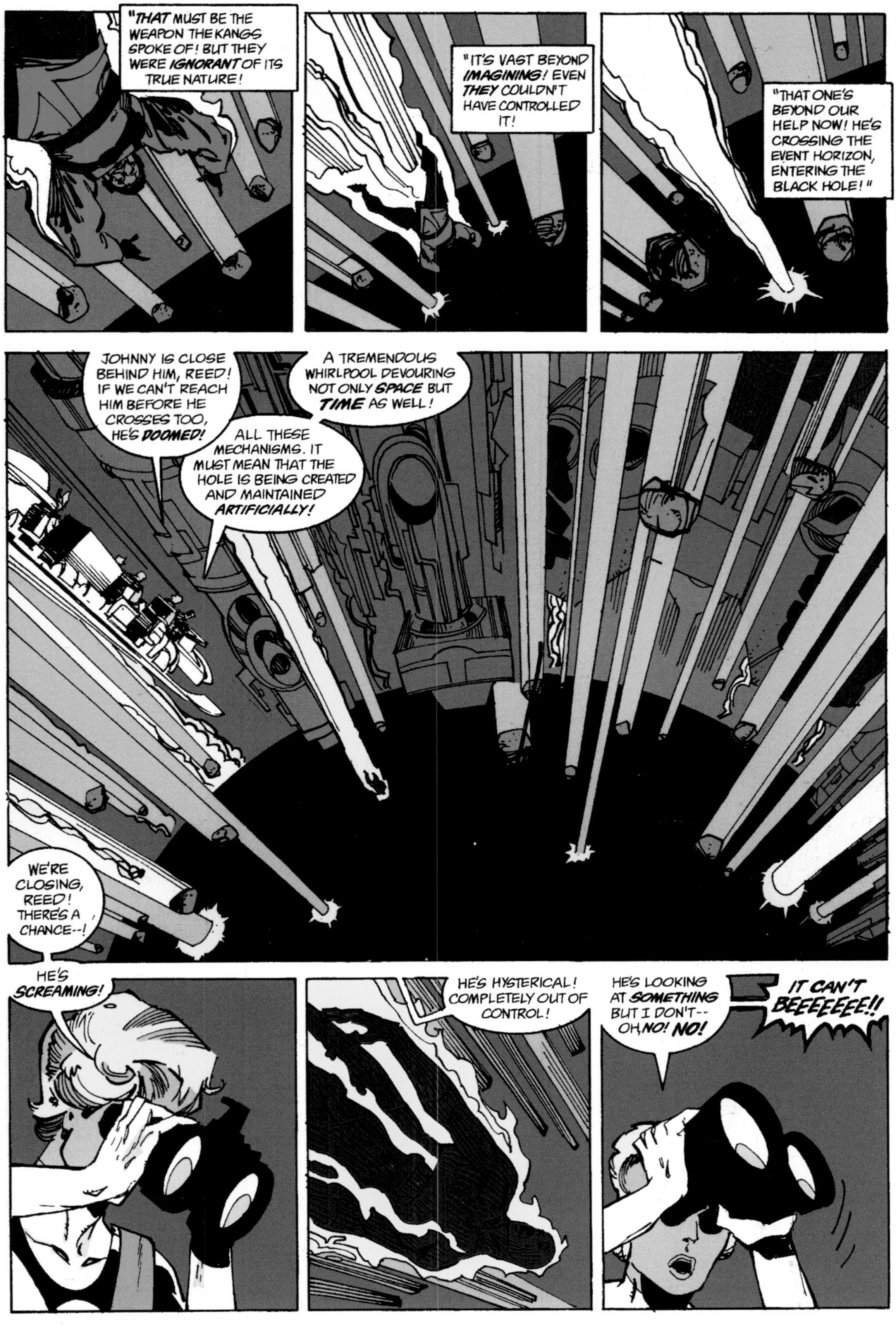
"THAT MUST BE THE WEAPON THE KANGS SPOKE OF! BUT THEY WERE IGNORANT OF ITS TRUE NATURE!
"IT'S VAST BEYOND IMAGINING! EVEN THEY COULDN'T HAVE CONTROLLED IT!
"THAT ONE'S BEYOND OUR HELP NOW! HE'S CROSSING THE EVENT HORIZON, ENTERING THE BLACK HOLE!"
JOHNNY IS CLOSE BEHIND HIM, REED! IF WE CAN'T REACH HIM BEFORE HE CROSSES TOO, HE'S DOOMED!
A TREMENDOUS WHIRLPOOL DEVOURING NOT ONLY SPACE BUT TIME AS WELL!
ALL THESE MECHANISMS. IT MUST MEAN THAT THE HOLE IS BEING CREATED AND MAINTAINED ARTIFICIALLY!
WE'RE CLOSING, REED! THERE'S A CHANCE--!
HE'S SCREAMING!
HE'S HYSTERICAL! COMPLETELY OUT OF CONTROL!
HE'S LOOKING AT SOMETHING BUT I DON'T-- OH, NO! NO!
IT CAN'T BEEEEEEE!!

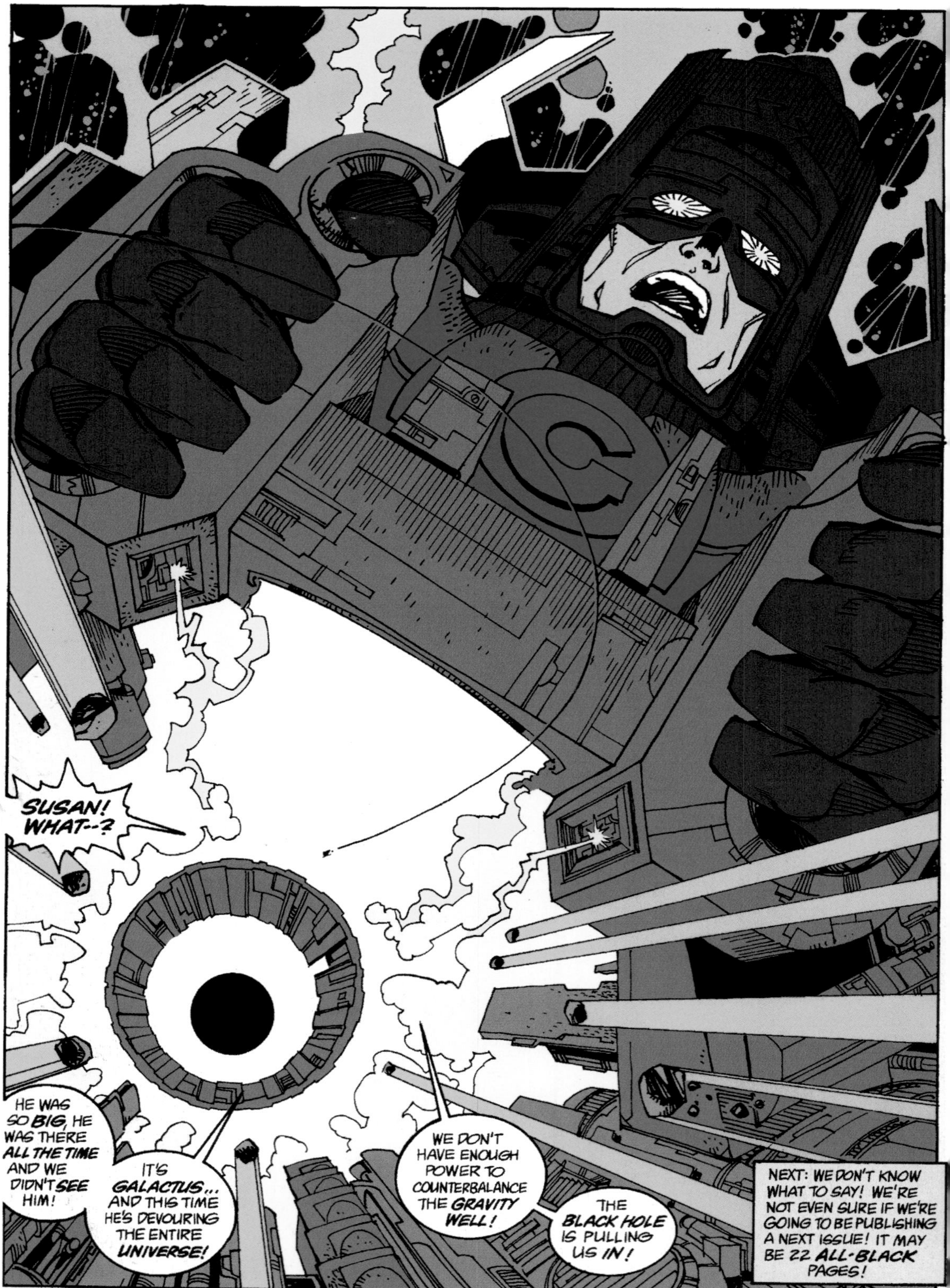
SUSAN! WHAT--?
HE WAS SO BIG, HE WAS THERE ALL THE TIME AND WE DIDN'T SEE HIM!
IT'S GALACTUS... AND THIS TIME HE'S DEVOURING THE ENTIRE UNIVERSE!
WE DON'T HAVE ENOUGH POWER TO COUNTERBALANCE THE GRAVITY WELL!
THE BLACK HOLE IS PULLING US IN!
NEXT: WE DON'T KNOW WHAT TO SAY! WE'RE NOT EVEN SURE IF WE'RE GOING TO BE PUBLISHING A NEXT ISSUE! IT MAY BE 22 ALL-BLACK PAGES!

BE HERE IN 30 FOR

BIGGER THAN A BREADBOX!!! or DINNER IS SERVED!

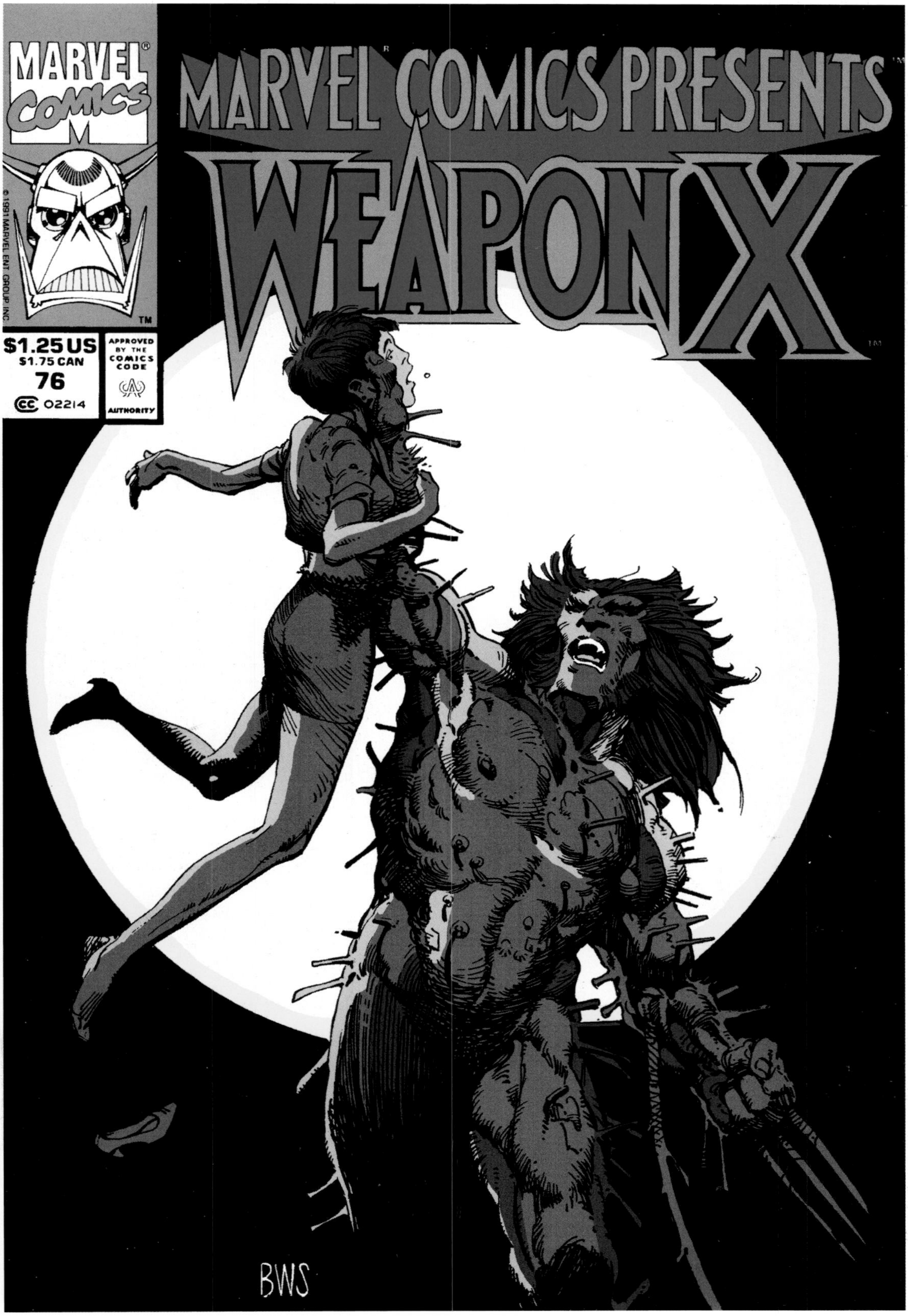
MARVEL COMICS
MARVEL COMICS PRESENTS
WEAPON X
$1.25 US
$1.75 CAN
76
02214
APPROVED BY THE COMICS CODE AUTHORITY
© 1991 MARVEL ENT. GROUP, INC.
BWS

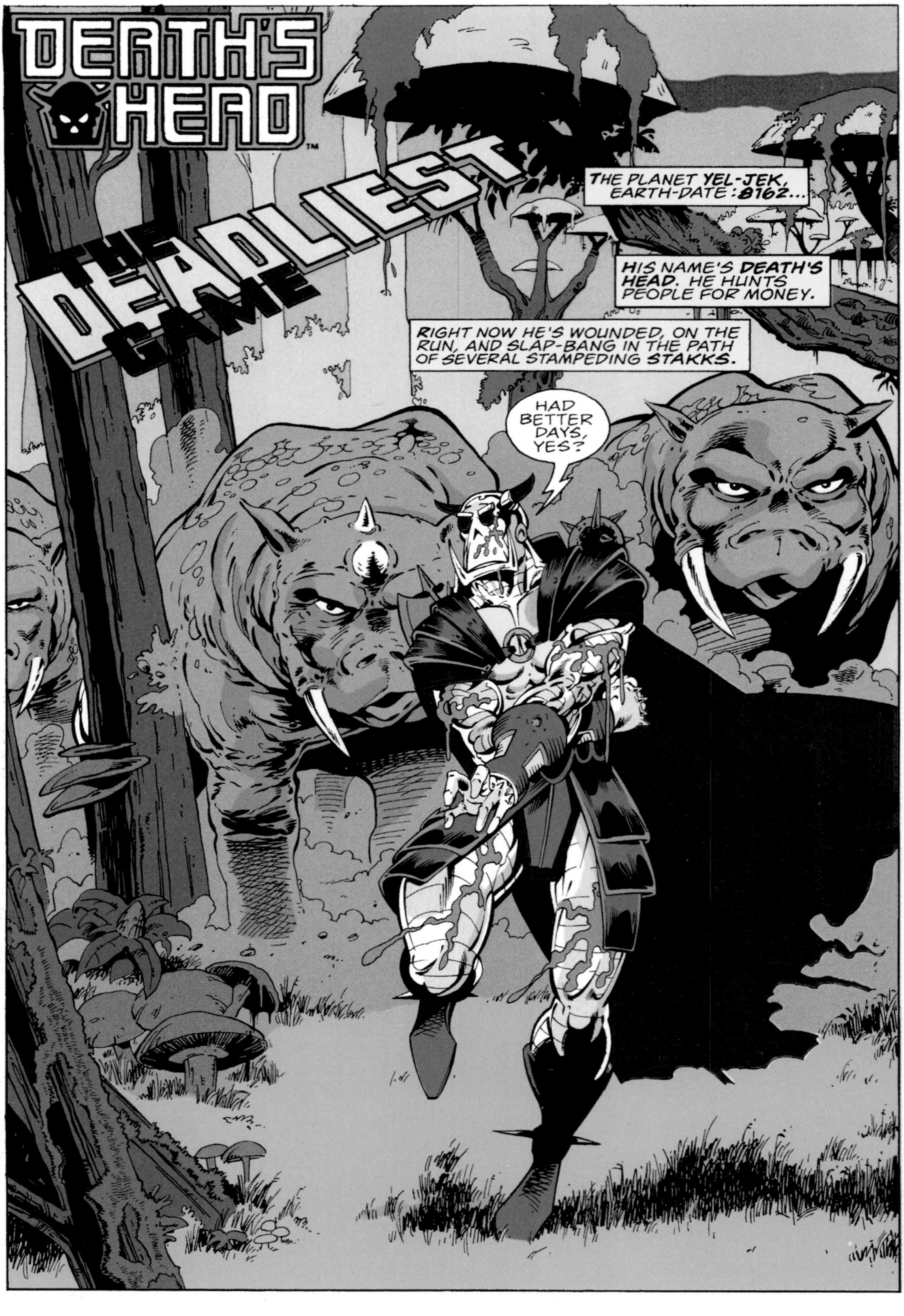
DEATH'S HEAD™
THE DEADLIEST GAME
THE PLANET YEL-JEK, EARTH-DATE: 8162...
HIS NAME'S DEATH'S HEAD. HE HUNTS PEOPLE FOR MONEY.
RIGHT NOW HE'S WOUNDED, ON THE RUN, AND SLAP-BANG IN THE PATH OF SEVERAL STAMPEDING STAKKS.
HAD BETTER DAYS, YES?

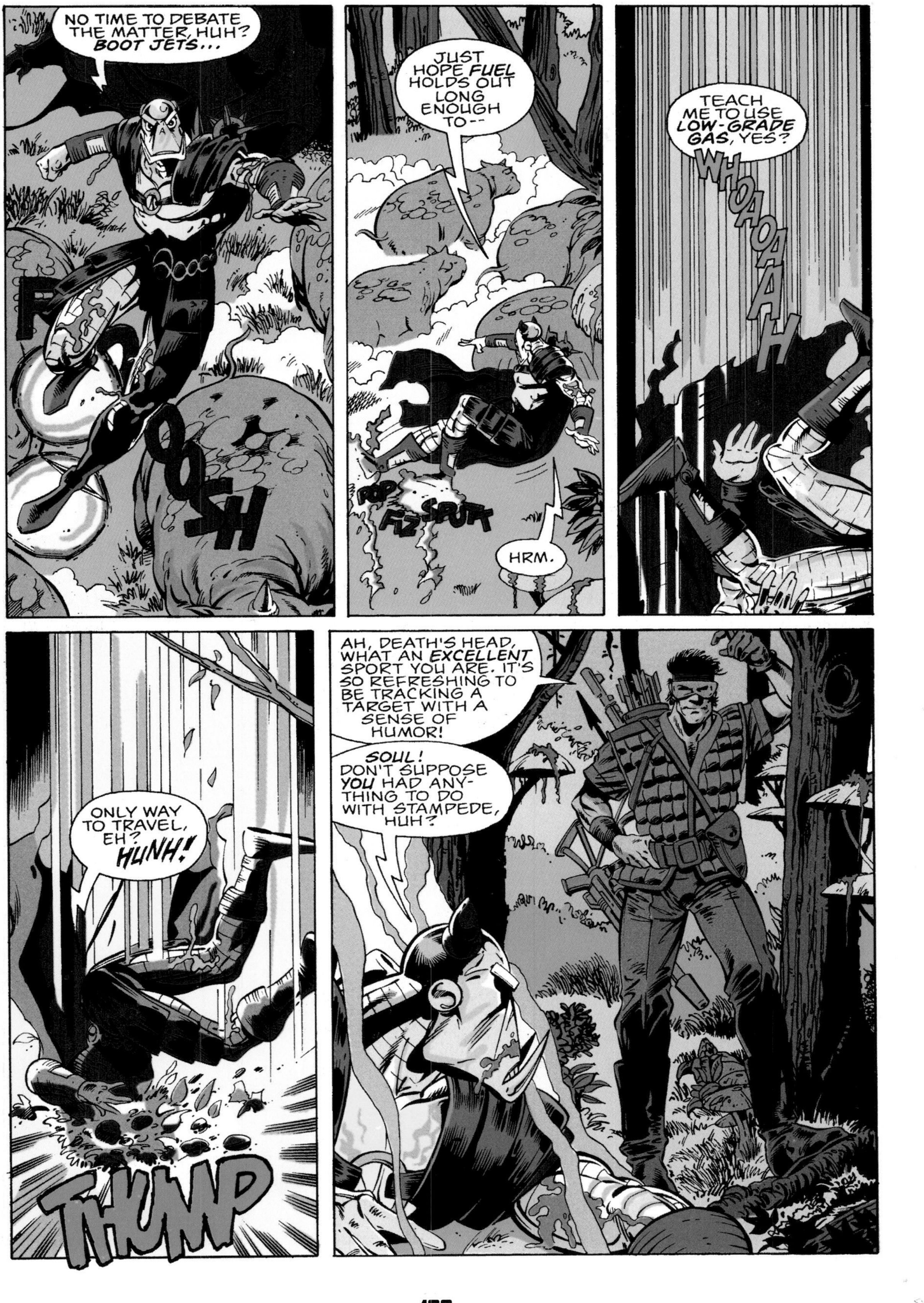
NO TIME TO DEBATE THE MATTER, HUH? BOOT JETS...
FOOOSH
JUST HOPE FUEL HOLDS OUT LONG ENOUGH TO--
POP FIZ SPUTT
HRM.
TEACH ME TO USE LOW-GRADE GAS, YES?
WHOAOAOAH
ONLY WAY TO TRAVEL, EH? HUNH!
THUMP
AH, DEATH'S HEAD, WHAT AN EXCELLENT SPORT YOU ARE. IT'S SO REFRESHING TO BE TRACKING A TARGET WITH A SENSE OF HUMOR!
SOUL! DON'T SUPPOSE YOU HAD ANYTHING TO DO WITH STAMPEDE, HUH?

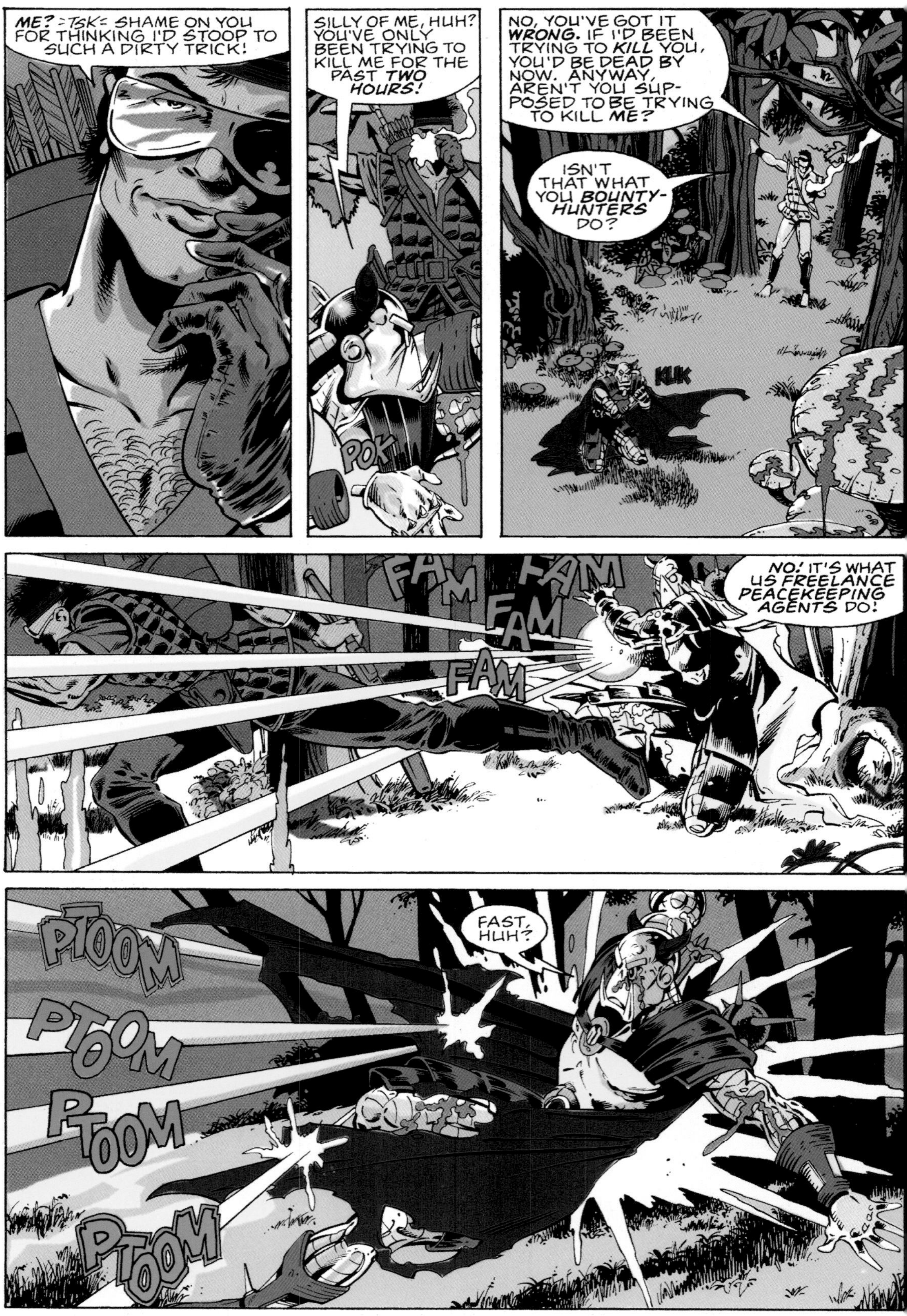
ME? =TSK= SHAME ON YOU FOR THINKING I'D STOOP TO SUCH A DIRTY TRICK!
SILLY OF ME, HUH? YOU'VE ONLY BEEN TRYING TO KILL ME FOR THE PAST TWO HOURS!
POK
NO, YOU'VE GOT IT WRONG. IF I'D BEEN TRYING TO KILL YOU, YOU'D BE DEAD BY NOW. ANYWAY, AREN'T YOU SUPPOSED TO BE TRYING TO KILL ME?
ISN'T THAT WHAT YOU BOUNTY-HUNTERS DO?
KLIK
FAM FAM FAM FAM FAM
NO! IT'S WHAT US FREELANCE PEACEKEEPING AGENTS DO!
PTOOM PTOOM PTOOM PTOOM
FAST, HUH?

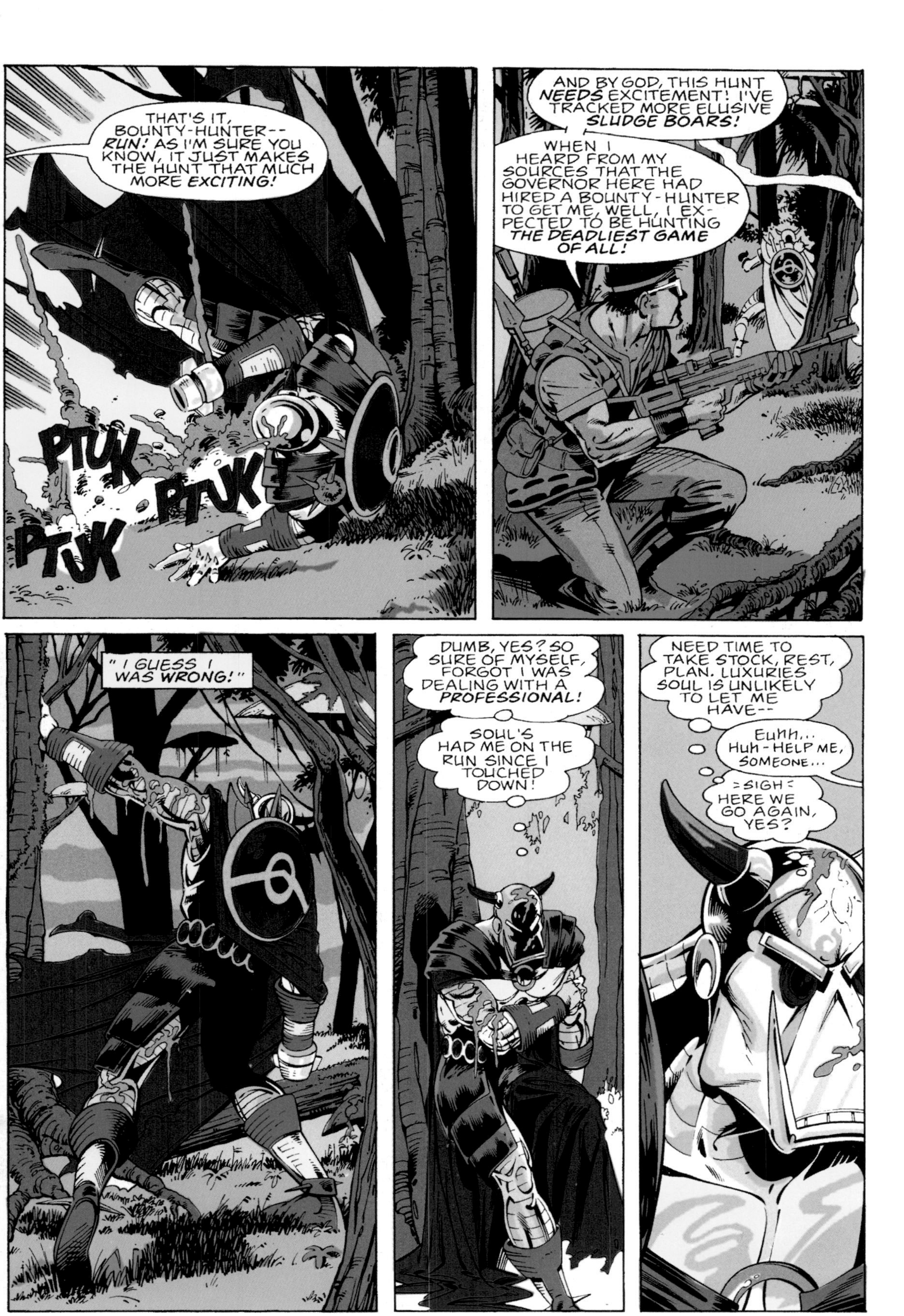
THAT'S IT, BOUNTY-HUNTER-- RUN! AS I'M SURE YOU KNOW, IT JUST MAKES THE HUNT THAT MUCH MORE EXCITING!
PTUK
PTUK
PTUK
AND BY GOD, THIS HUNT NEEDS EXCITEMENT! I'VE TRACKED MORE ELUSIVE SLUDGE BOARS!
WHEN I HEARD FROM MY SOURCES THAT THE GOVERNOR HERE HAD HIRED A BOUNTY-HUNTER TO GET ME, WELL, I EXPECTED TO BE HUNTING THE DEADLIEST GAME OF ALL!
"I GUESS I WAS WRONG!"
DUMB, YES? SO SURE OF MYSELF, FORGOT I WAS DEALING WITH A PROFESSIONAL!
SOUL'S HAD ME ON THE RUN SINCE I TOUCHED DOWN!
NEED TIME TO TAKE STOCK, REST, PLAN. LUXURIES SOUL IS UNLIKELY TO LET ME HAVE--
Euhh... Huh-HELP ME, SOMEONE...
=SIGH= HERE WE GO AGAIN, YES?

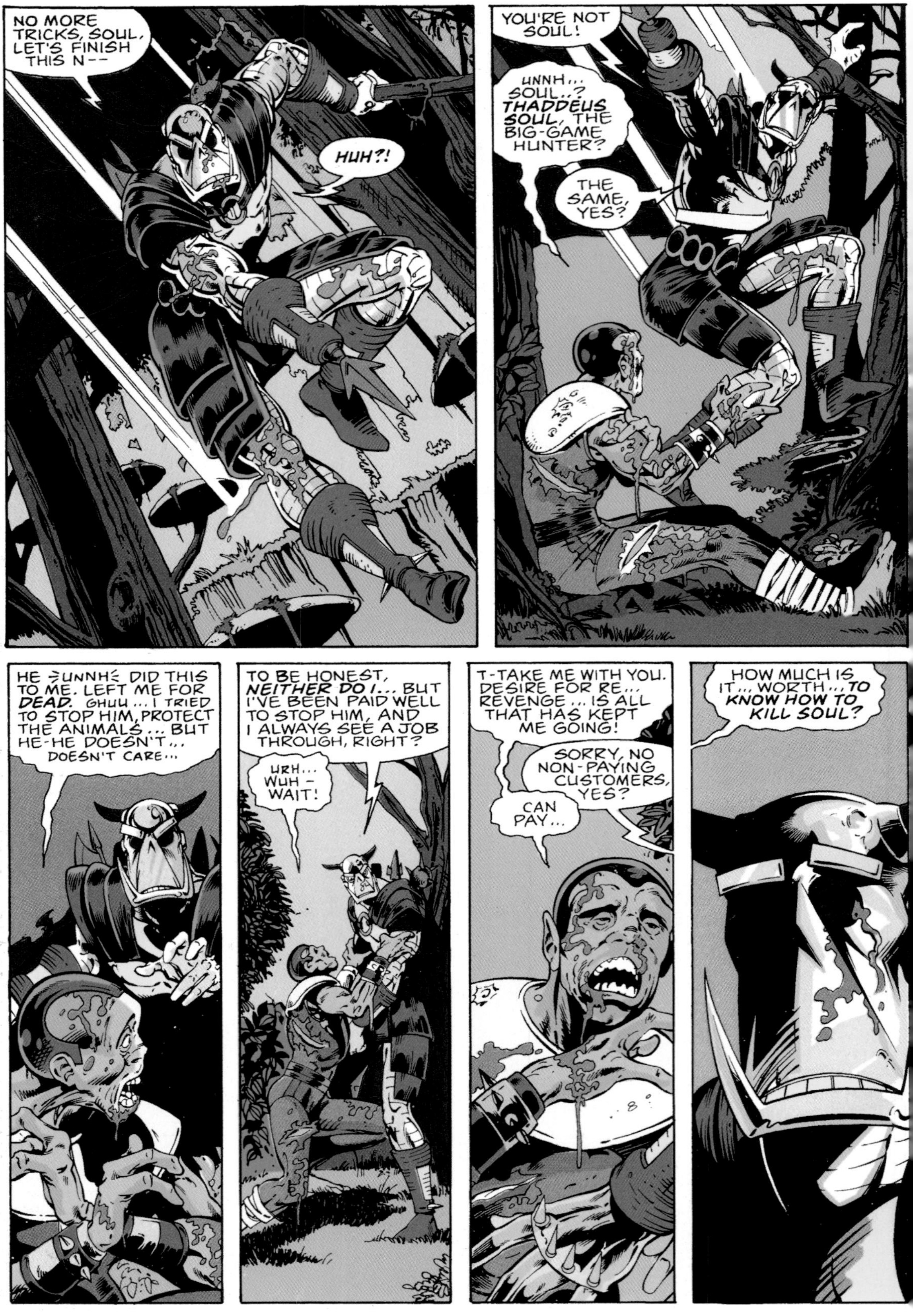

NO MORE TRICKS, SOUL, LET'S FINISH THIS N--
HUH?!
YOU'RE NOT SOUL!
UNNH... SOUL..? THADDEUS SOUL, THE BIG-GAME HUNTER?
THE SAME, YES?
HE UNNH DID THIS TO ME. LEFT ME FOR DEAD. GHUU... I TRIED TO STOP HIM, PROTECT THE ANIMALS... BUT HE-HE DOESN'T... DOESN'T CARE...
TO BE HONEST, NEITHER DO I... BUT I'VE BEEN PAID WELL TO STOP HIM, AND I ALWAYS SEE A JOB THROUGH, RIGHT?
URH... WUH- WAIT!
T-TAKE ME WITH YOU. DESIRE FOR RE... REVENGE... IS ALL THAT HAS KEPT ME GOING!
SORRY, NO NON-PAYING CUSTOMERS, YES?
CAN PAY...
HOW MUCH IS IT... WORTH... TO KNOW HOW TO KILL SOUL?

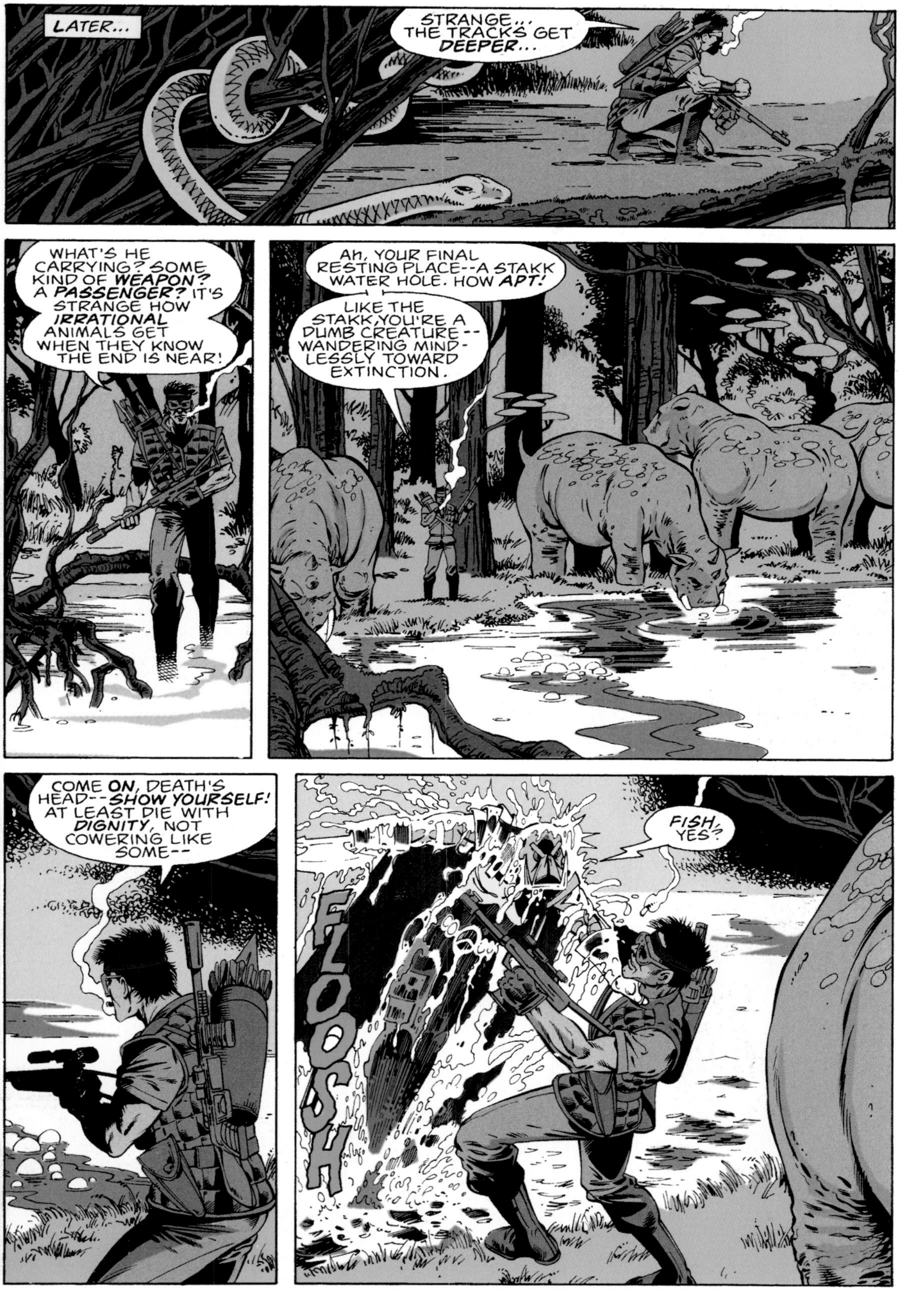

LATER...
STRANGE... THE TRACKS GET DEEPER...
WHAT'S HE CARRYING? SOME KIND OF WEAPON? A PASSENGER? IT'S STRANGE HOW IRRATIONAL ANIMALS GET WHEN THEY KNOW THE END IS NEAR!
AH, YOUR FINAL RESTING PLACE--A STAKK WATER HOLE. HOW APT!
LIKE THE STAKK, YOU'RE A DUMB CREATURE--WANDERING MINDLESSLY TOWARD EXTINCTION.
COME ON, DEATH'S HEAD--SHOW YOURSELF! AT LEAST DIE WITH DIGNITY, NOT COWERING LIKE SOME--
FLOOSH
FISH, YES?

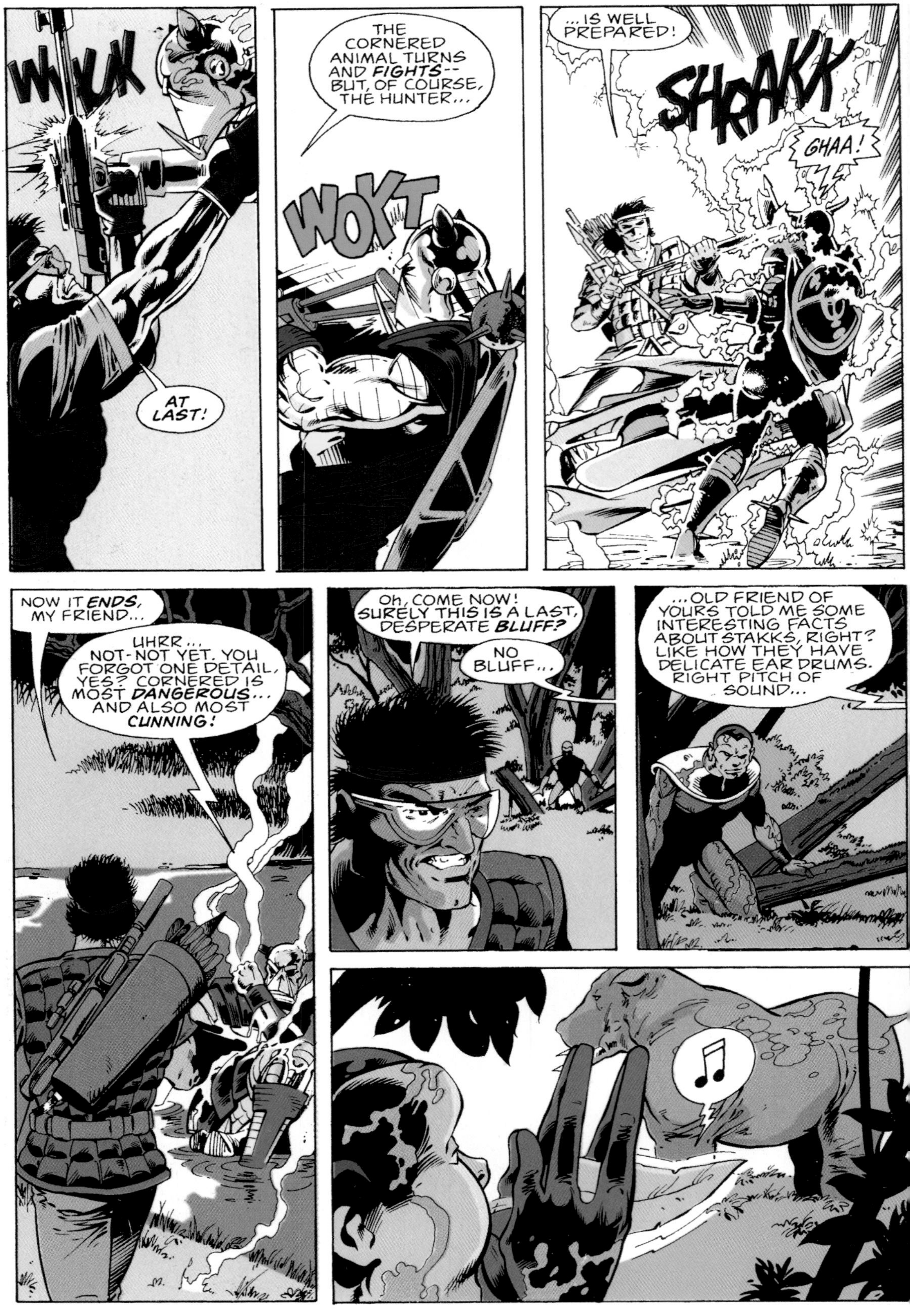
WHUK
AT LAST!
THE CORNERED ANIMAL TURNS AND FIGHTS-- BUT, OF COURSE, THE HUNTER...
WOKT
...IS WELL PREPARED!
SHRAKK
GHAA!
NOW IT ENDS, MY FRIEND...
UHRR... NOT- NOT YET. YOU FORGOT ONE DETAIL, YES? CORNERED IS MOST DANGEROUS... AND ALSO MOST CUNNING!
Oh, COME NOW! SURELY THIS IS A LAST, DESPERATE BLUFF?
NO BLUFF...
...OLD FRIEND OF YOURS TOLD ME SOME INTERESTING FACTS ABOUT STAKKS, RIGHT? LIKE HOW THEY HAVE DELICATE EAR DRUMS. RIGHT PITCH OF SOUND...

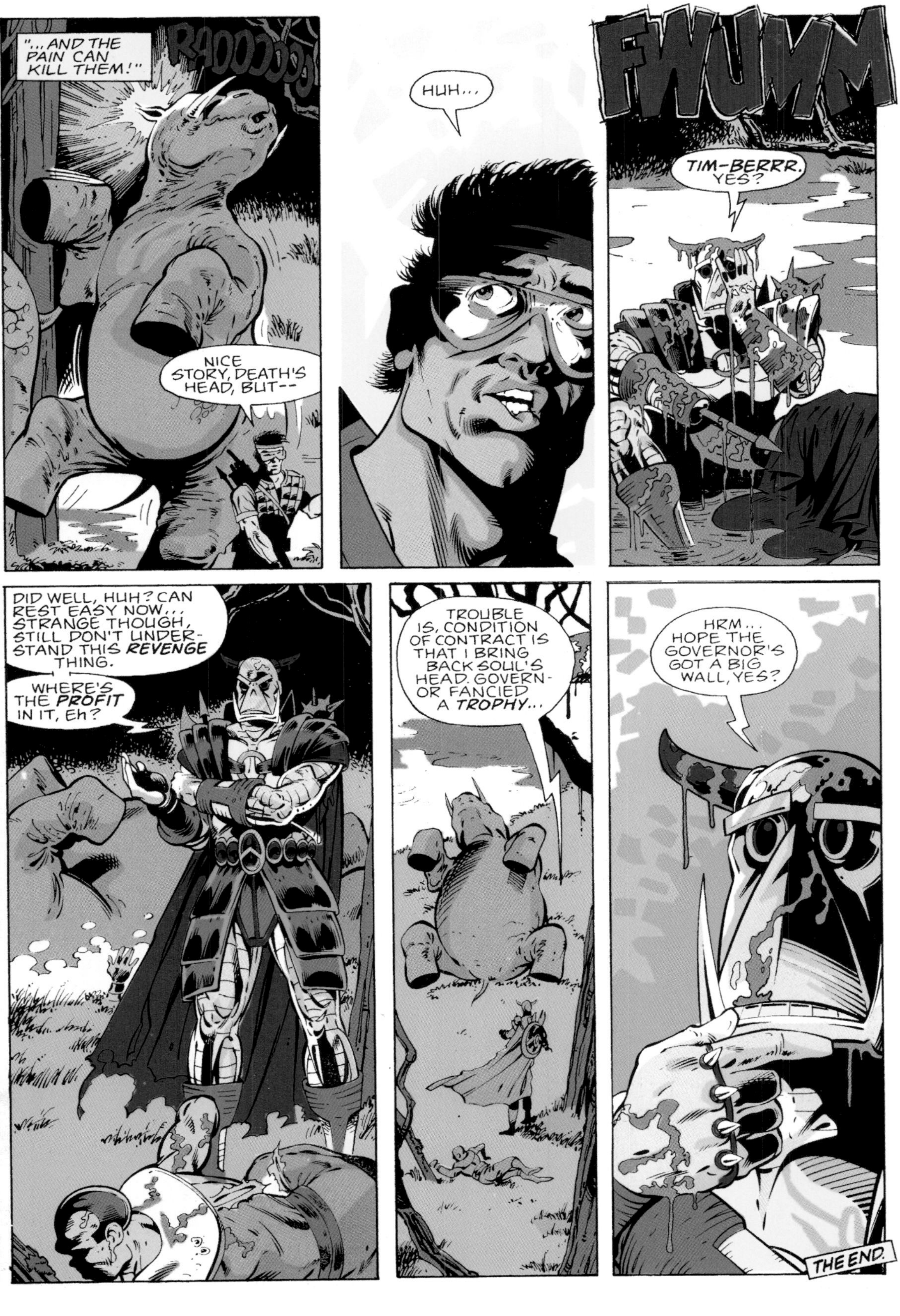
"...AND THE PAIN CAN KILL THEM!"
RADOOOOOO
NICE STORY, DEATH'S HEAD, BUT--
HUH...
FWUMM
TIM-BERRR. YES?
DID WELL, HUH? CAN REST EASY NOW... STRANGE THOUGH, STILL DON'T UNDERSTAND THIS *REVENGE* THING.
WHERE'S THE *PROFIT* IN IT, Eh?
TROUBLE IS, CONDITION OF CONTRACT IS THAT I BRING BACK SOUL'S HEAD. GOVERNOR FANCIED A *TROPHY*...
HRM... HOPE THE GOVERNOR'S GOT A BIG WALL, YES?
THE END.

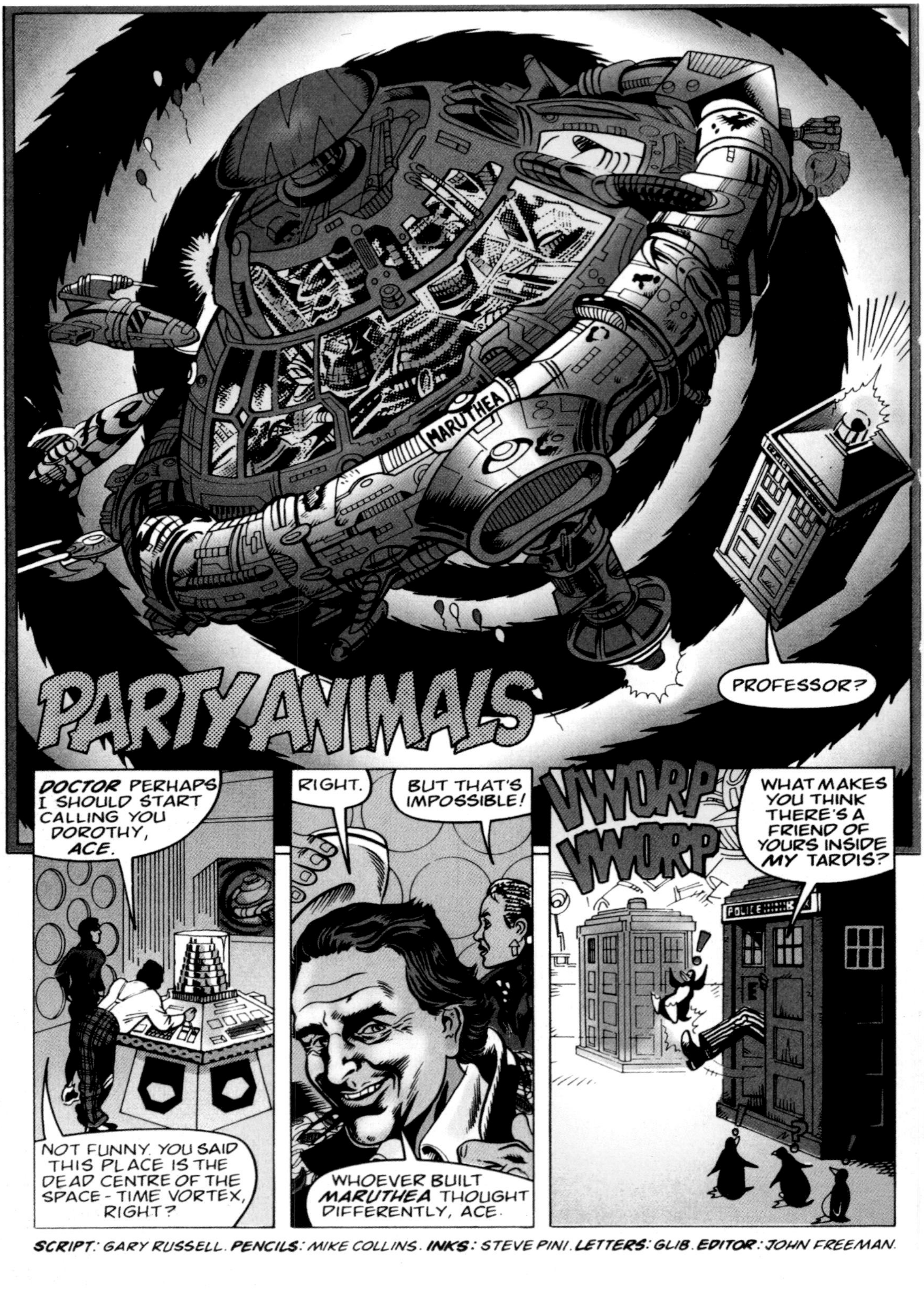
MARUTHEA
PROFESSOR?
PARTY ANIMALS
DOCTOR PERHAPS I SHOULD START CALLING YOU DOROTHY, ACE.
NOT FUNNY. YOU SAID THIS PLACE IS THE DEAD CENTRE OF THE SPACE - TIME VORTEX, RIGHT?
RIGHT.
BUT THAT'S IMPOSSIBLE!
WHOEVER BUILT MARUTHEA THOUGHT DIFFERENTLY, ACE.
VWORP VWORP
WHAT MAKES YOU THINK THERE'S A FRIEND OF YOURS INSIDE MY TARDIS?
POLICE

SCRIPT: GARY RUSSELL. **PENCILS**: MIKE COLLINS. **INKS**: STEVE PINI. **LETTERS**: GLIB. **EDITOR**: JOHN FREEMAN.

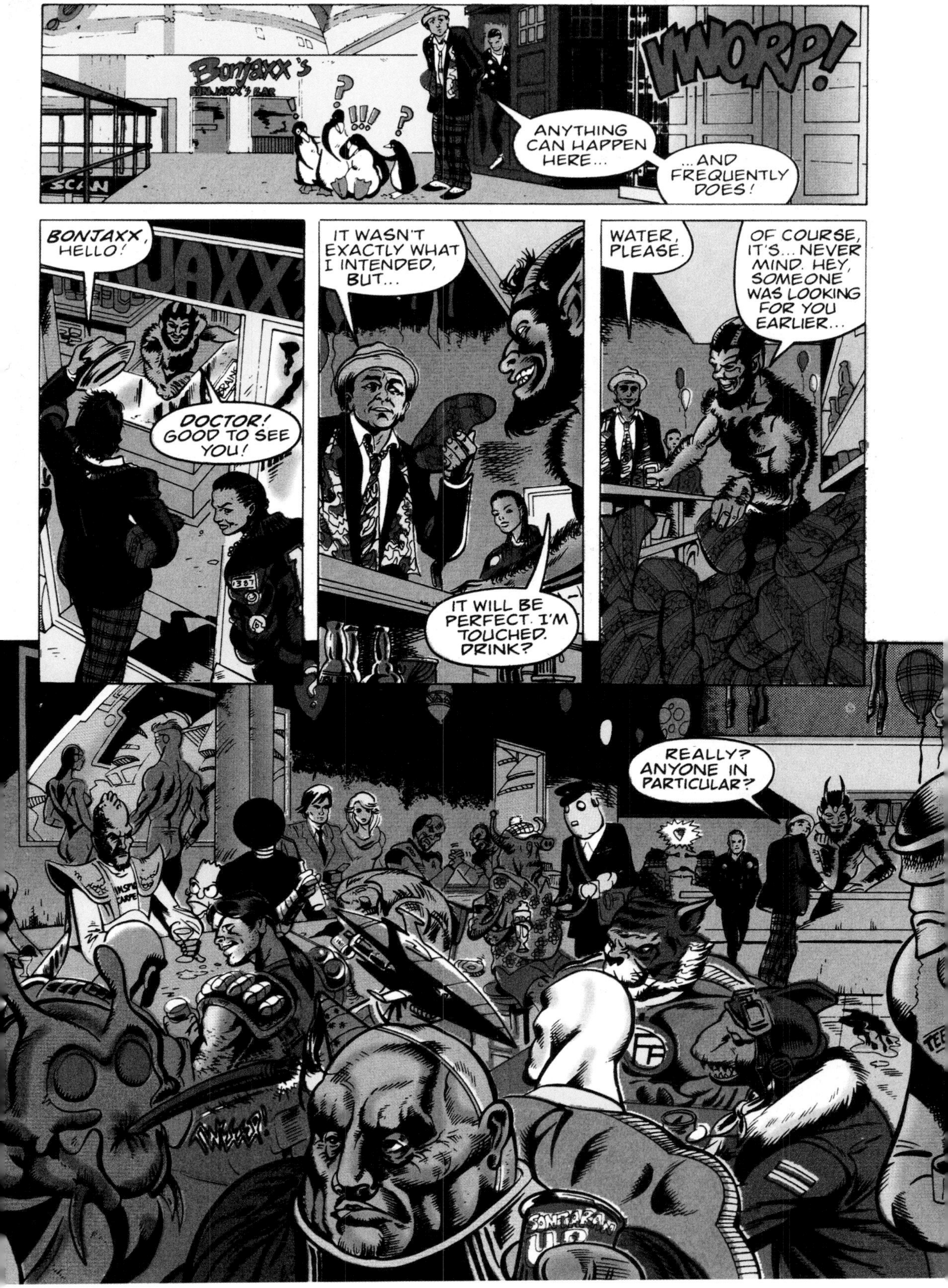
Bonjaxx's
SCAN
VWORP!
?
!!!
?
ANYTHING CAN HAPPEN HERE...
...AND FREQUENTLY DOES!
BONJAXX, HELLO!
DOCTOR! GOOD TO SEE YOU!
IT WASN'T EXACTLY WHAT I INTENDED, BUT...
IT WILL BE PERFECT. I'M TOUCHED. DRINK?
WATER, PLEASE.
OF COURSE, IT'S... NEVER MIND. HEY, SOMEONE WAS LOOKING FOR YOU EARLIER...
REALLY? ANYONE IN PARTICULAR?
SONTARAN UP

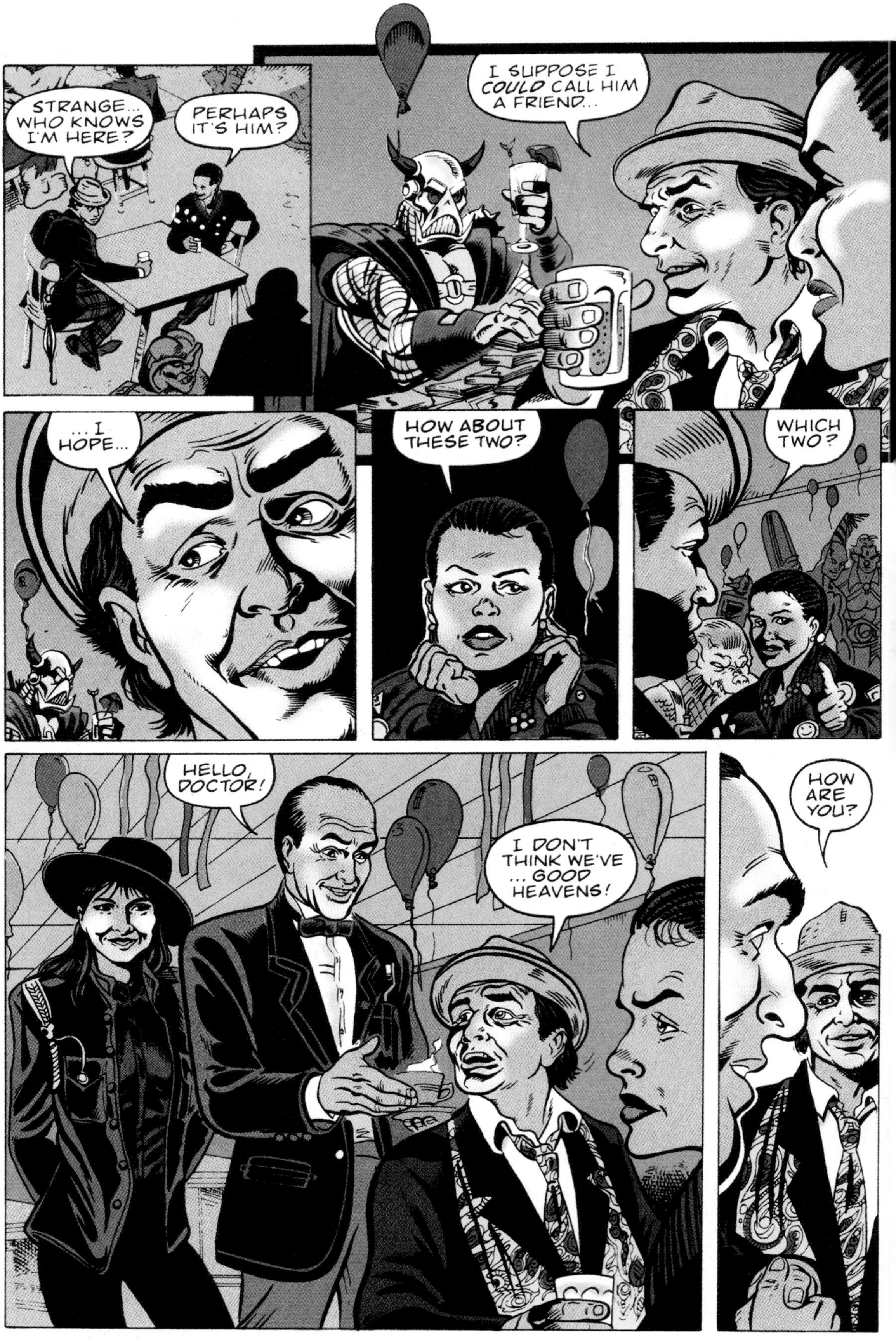
STRANGE... WHO KNOWS I'M HERE?
PERHAPS IT'S HIM?
I SUPPOSE I COULD CALL HIM A FRIEND...
... I HOPE...
HOW ABOUT THESE TWO?
WHICH TWO?
HELLO, DOCTOR!
I DON'T THINK WE'VE ...GOOD HEAVENS!
HOW ARE YOU?

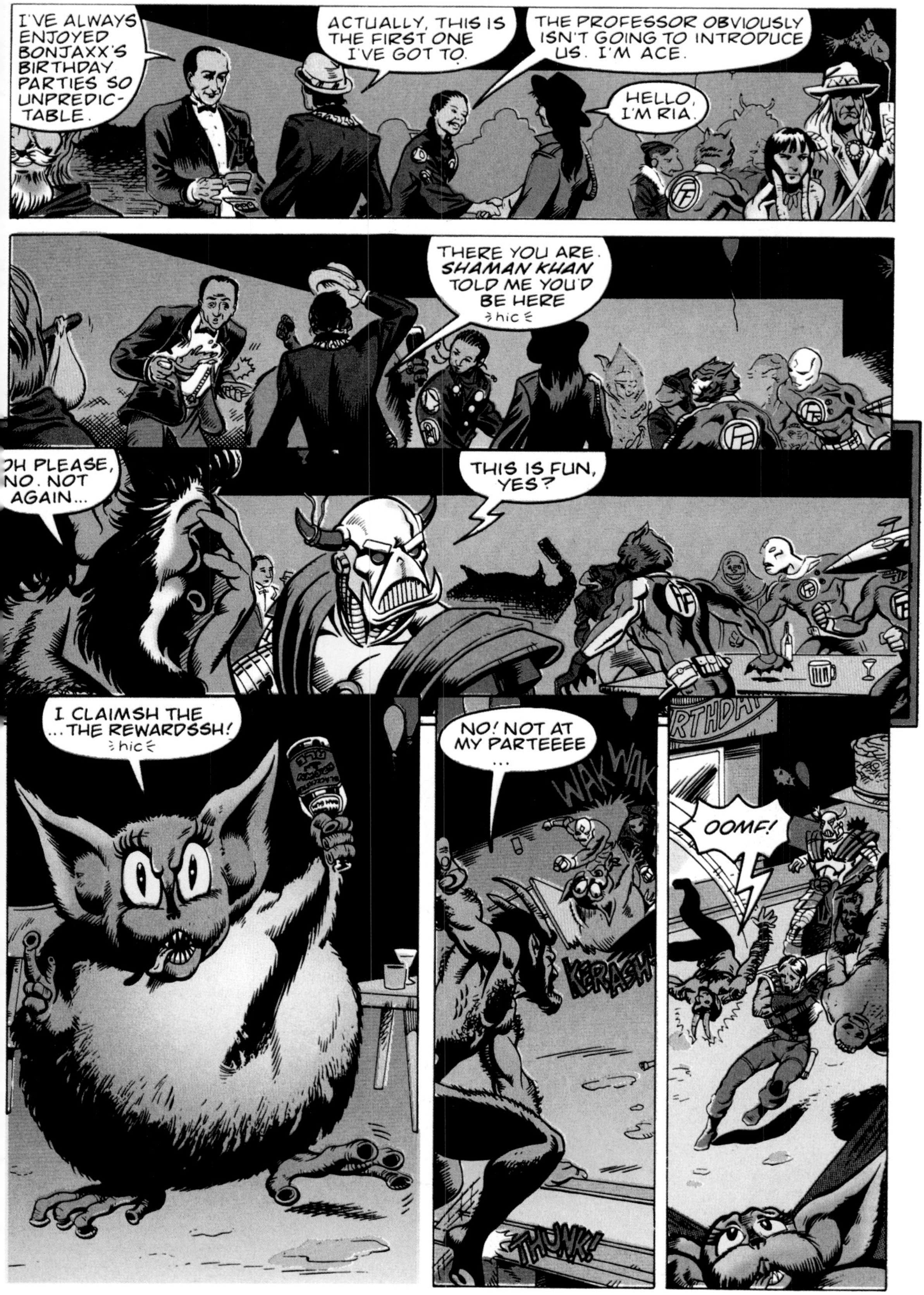
I'VE ALWAYS ENJOYED BONJAXX'S BIRTHDAY PARTIES SO UNPREDIC-TABLE.
ACTUALLY, THIS IS THE FIRST ONE I'VE GOT TO.
THE PROFESSOR OBVIOUSLY ISN'T GOING TO INTRODUCE US. I'M ACE.
HELLO, I'M RIA.
THERE YOU ARE. SHAMAN KHAN TOLD ME YOU'D BE HERE
hic
OH PLEASE, NO. NOT AGAIN...
THIS IS FUN, YES?
I CLAIMSH THE ...THE REWARDSSH!
hic
NO! NOT AT MY PARTEEEE ...
WAKWAK
KERASH
THUNK!
OOMF!

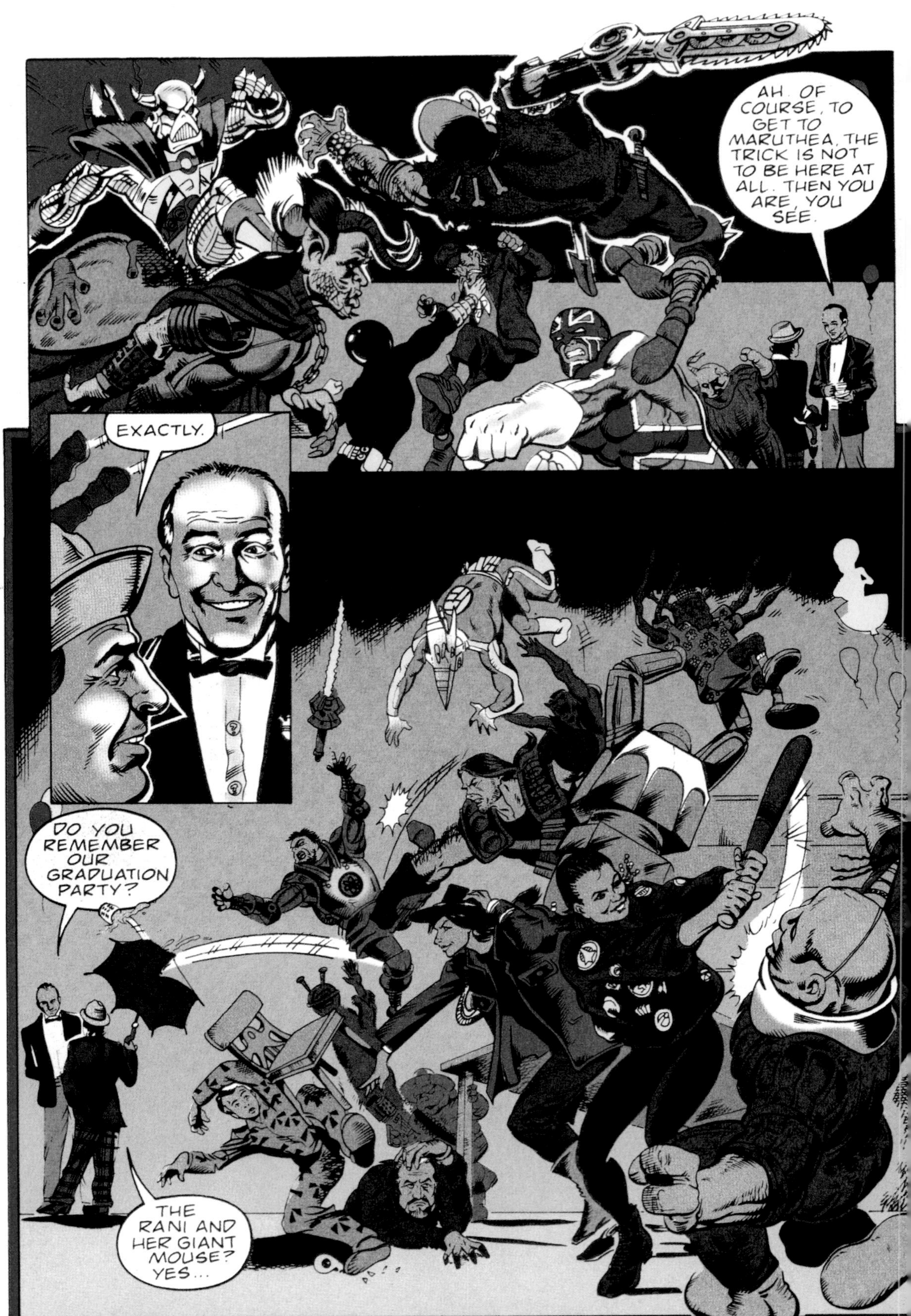
AH. OF COURSE, TO GET TO MARUTHEA, THE TRICK IS NOT TO BE HERE AT ALL. THEN YOU ARE, YOU SEE.
EXACTLY.
DO YOU REMEMBER OUR GRADUATION PARTY?
THE RANI AND HER GIANT MOUSE? YES...

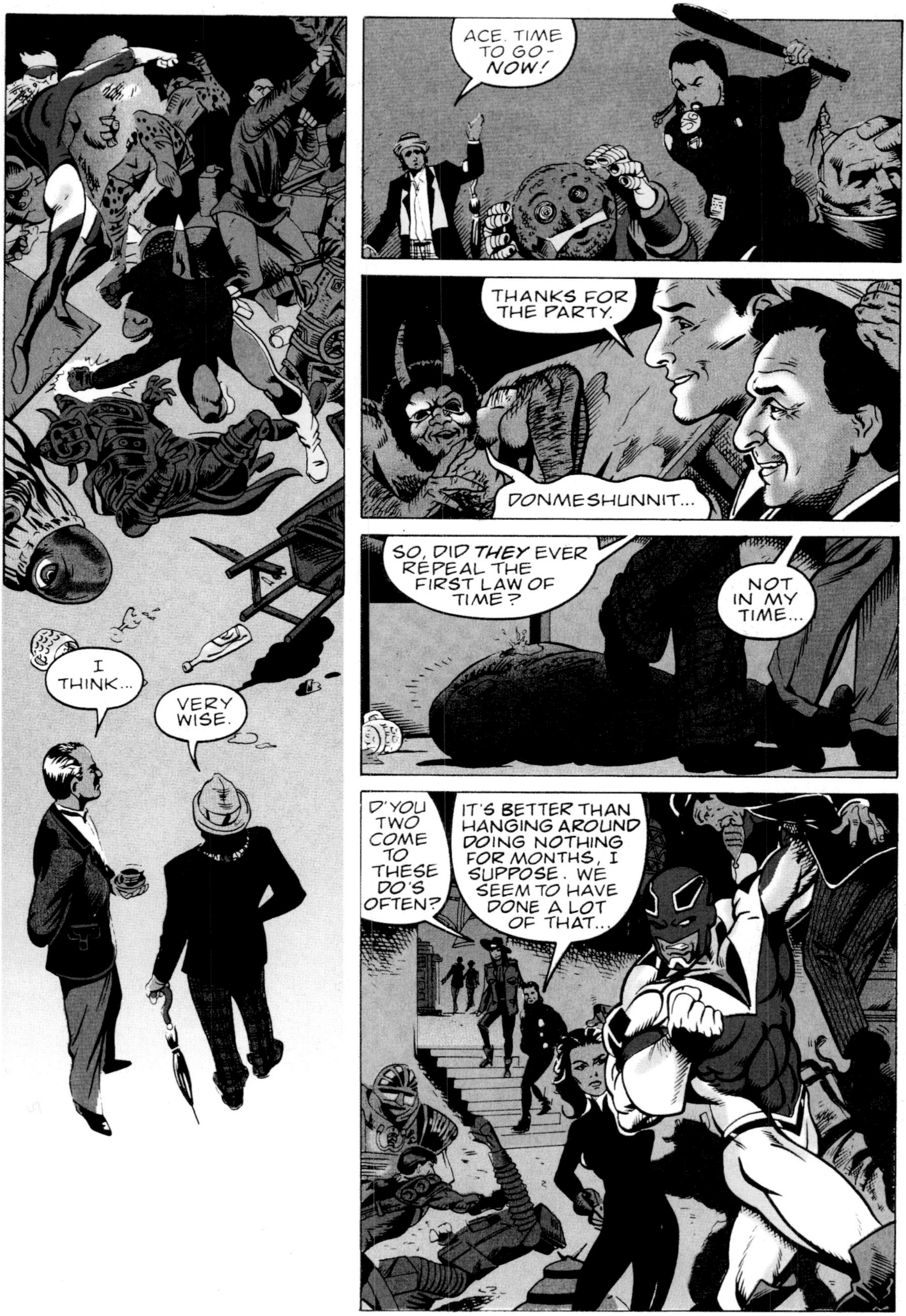
I THINK...
VERY WISE.
ACE. TIME TO GO - NOW!
THANKS FOR THE PARTY.
DONMESHUNNIT...
SO, DID THEY EVER REPEAL THE FIRST LAW OF TIME?
NOT IN MY TIME...
D'YOU TWO COME TO THESE DO'S OFTEN?
IT'S BETTER THAN HANGING AROUND DOING NOTHING FOR MONTHS, I SUPPOSE. WE SEEM TO HAVE DONE A LOT OF THAT...

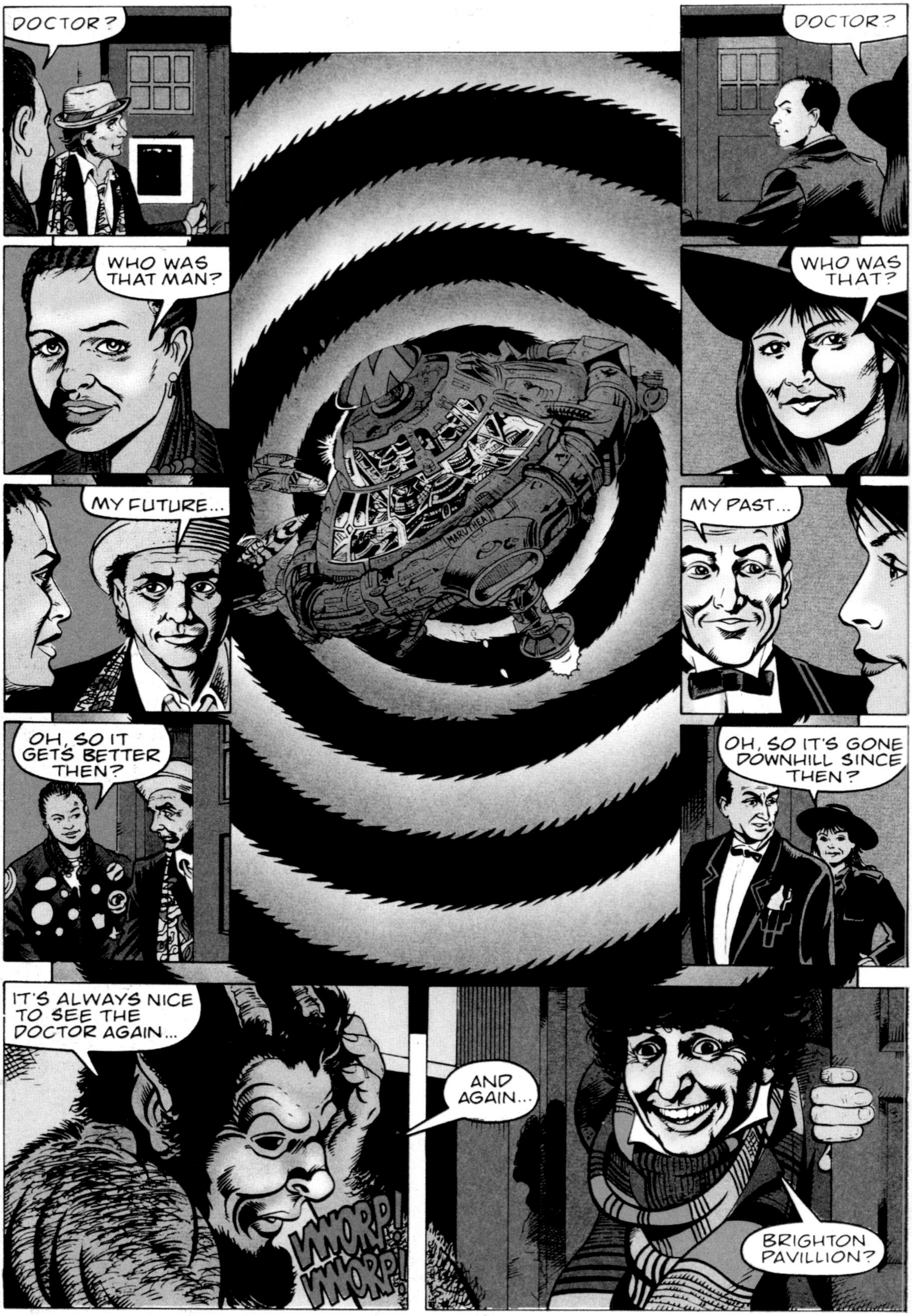
DOCTOR?
DOCTOR?
WHO WAS THAT MAN?
WHO WAS THAT?
MY FUTURE...
MY PAST...
OH, SO IT GETS BETTER THEN?
OH, SO IT'S GONE DOWNHILL SINCE THEN?
MARUTHEA
IT'S ALWAYS NICE TO SEE THE DOCTOR AGAIN...
AND AGAIN...
VWORP! VWORP!
BRIGHTON PAVILLION?

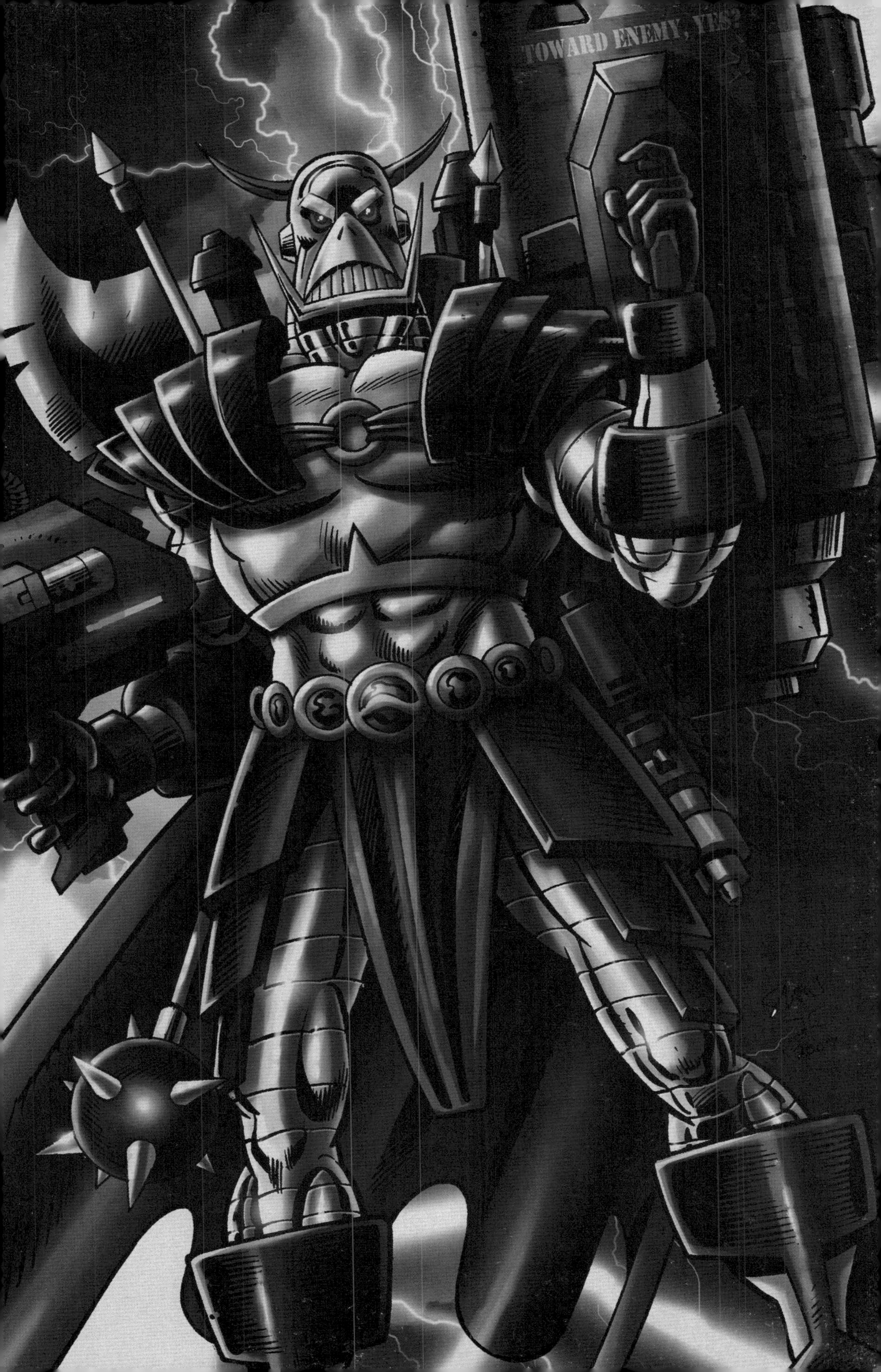
TOWARD ENEMY, YES?

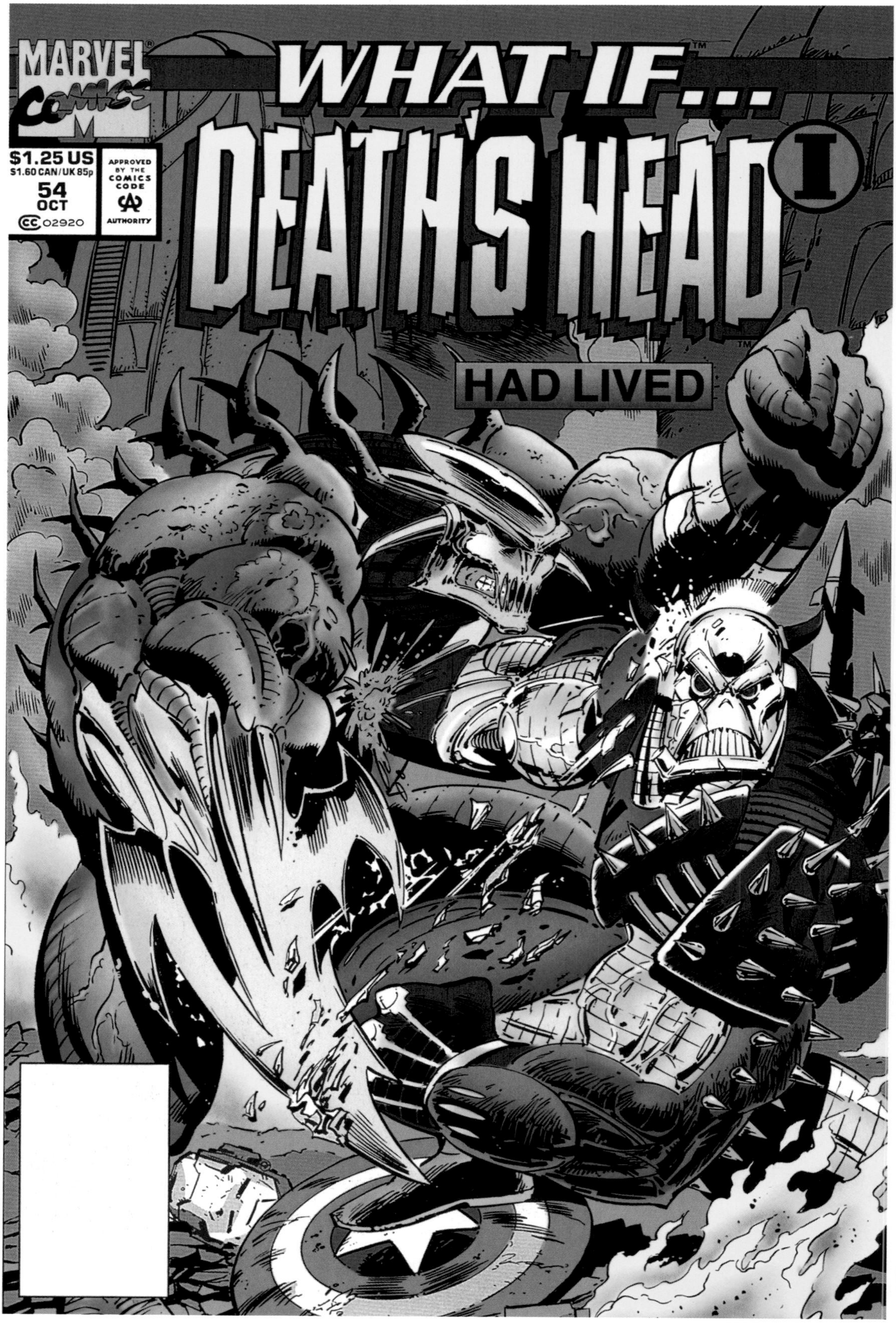
MARVEL COMICS
WHAT IF...
DEATH'S HEAD I
HAD LIVED
$1.25 US
$1.60 CAN/UK 85p
54
OCT
02920
APPROVED BY THE COMICS CODE AUTHORITY

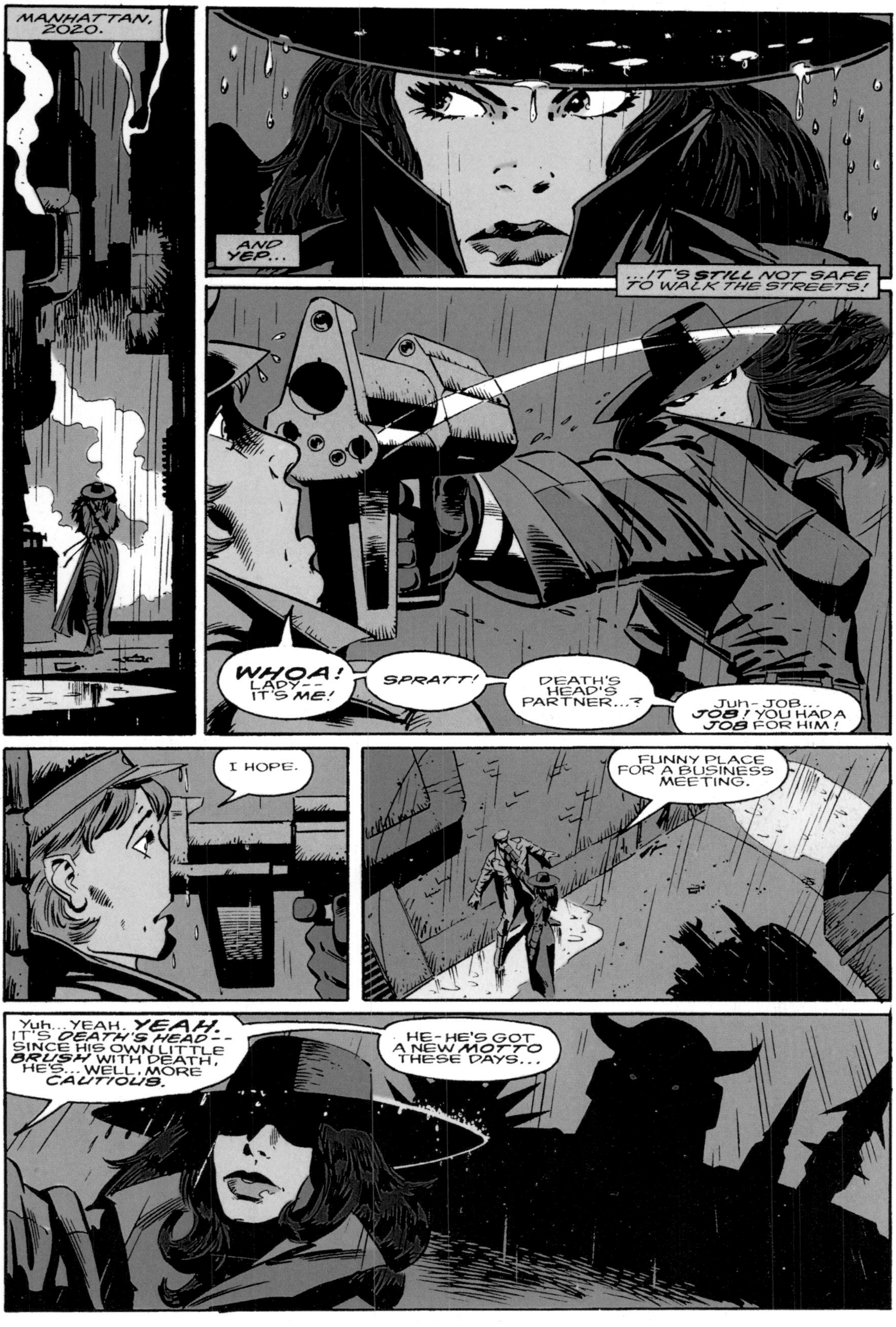
MANHATTAN, 2020.
AND YEP...
...IT'S STILL NOT SAFE TO WALK THE STREETS!
WHOA! LADY-- IT'S ME!
SPRATT!
DEATH'S HEAD'S PARTNER...?
Juh-JOB... JOB! YOU HAD A JOB FOR HIM!
I HOPE.
FUNNY PLACE FOR A BUSINESS MEETING.
Yuh... YEAH. YEAH. IT'S DEATH'S HEAD-- SINCE HIS OWN LITTLE BRUSH WITH DEATH, HE'S... WELL, MORE CAUTIOUS.
HE-HE'S GOT A NEW MOTTO THESE DAYS...

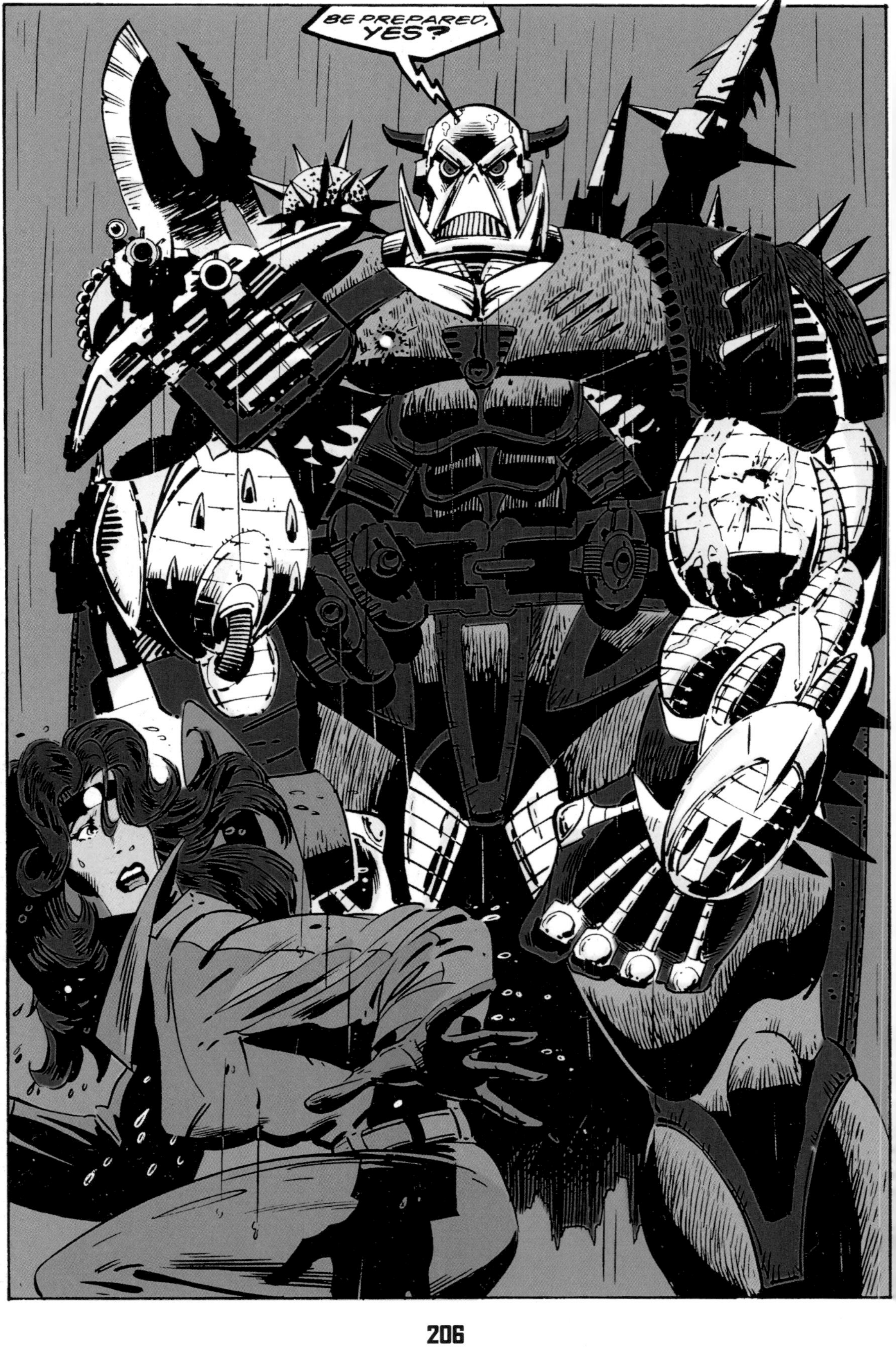
BE PREPARED, YES?

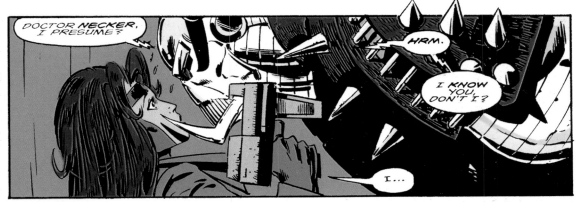

DOCTOR *NECKER*, I PRESUME?

HRM.

I *KNOW* YOU, DON'T I?

I...

I BELIEVE WE HAVE A *MUTUAL* PROBLEM. IN RETURN FOR REMOVING SOMETHING OF A *LIABILITY* TO MY ORGANIZATION, I CAN OFFER YOU ANOTHER CRACK AT THE CYBORG WHO CAME WITHIN A *HAIR'S BREADTH* OF KILLING YOU...

MINION.

YOU WERE *THERE!* WHEN THAT *THING* NEARLY *DISEMBOWELLED* ME! YOU GAVE IT ORDERS!

HO!!

WHAT'S ALL *THIS?* I THOUGHT THE CUSTOMER WAS ALWAYS RIGHT, I THOUGHT THERE WAS NO PROFIT IN REVENGE!

YOU'RE A *BUSINESSMAN,* REMEMBER?

OKAY, I'LL HEAR YOU OUT, BUT *FORGET* ABOUT GETTING EVEN. AS MY..."*PARTNER*" RIGHTLY POINTED OUT--

--REVENGE *DOESN'T PAY* THE *BILLS,* YES?

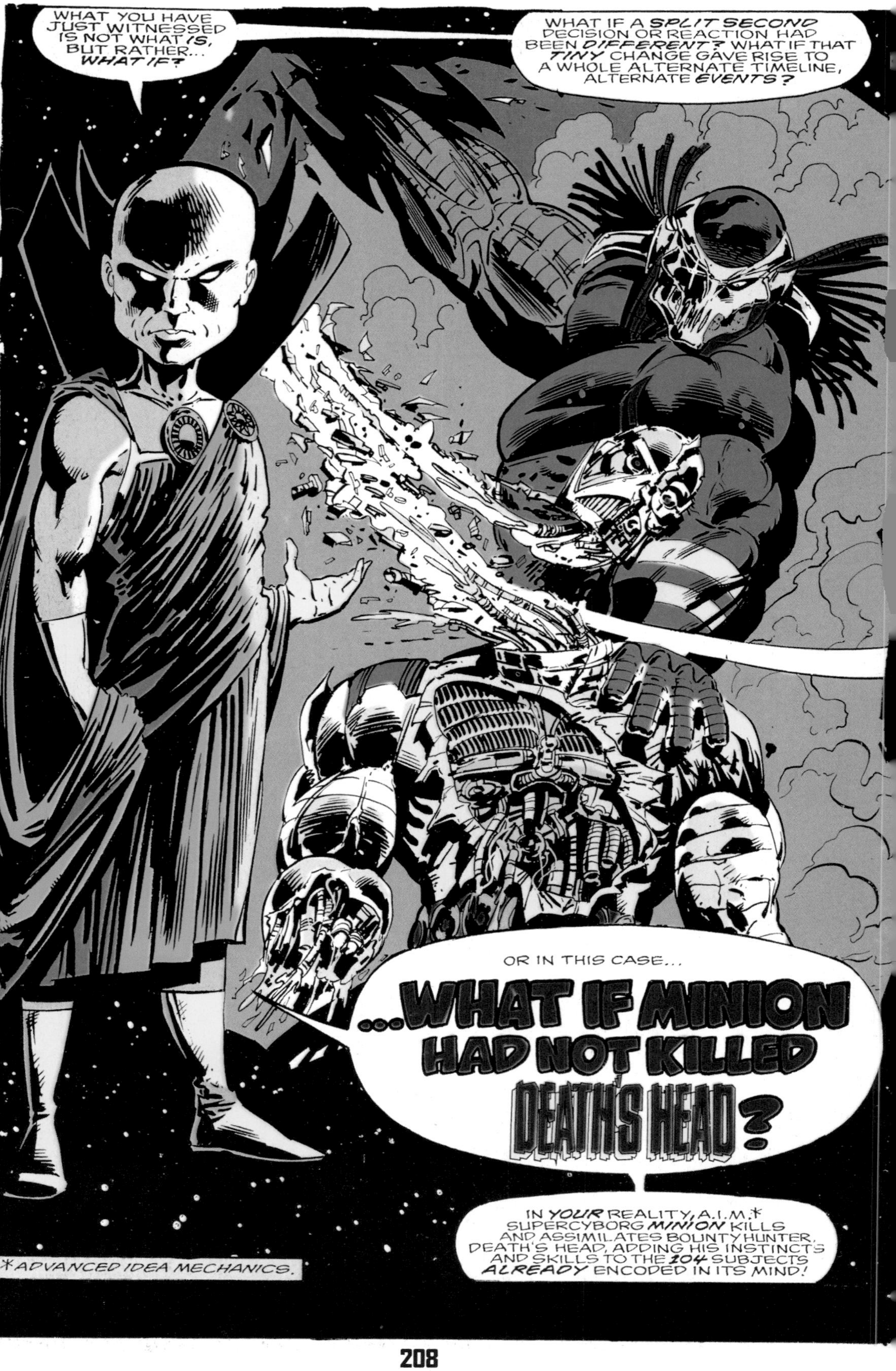
WHAT YOU HAVE JUST WITNESSED IS NOT WHAT IS, BUT RATHER... WHAT IF?
WHAT IF A SPLIT SECOND DECISION OR REACTION HAD BEEN DIFFERENT? WHAT IF THAT TINY CHANGE GAVE RISE TO A WHOLE ALTERNATE TIMELINE, ALTERNATE EVENTS?
OR IN THIS CASE... ...WHAT IF MINION HAD NOT KILLED DEATH'S HEAD?
IN YOUR REALITY, A.I.M.* SUPERCYBORG MINION KILLS AND ASSIMILATES BOUNTY HUNTER, DEATH'S HEAD, ADDING HIS INSTINCTS AND SKILLS TO THE 204 SUBJECTS ALREADY ENCODED IN ITS MIND!
*ADVANCED IDEA MECHANICS.

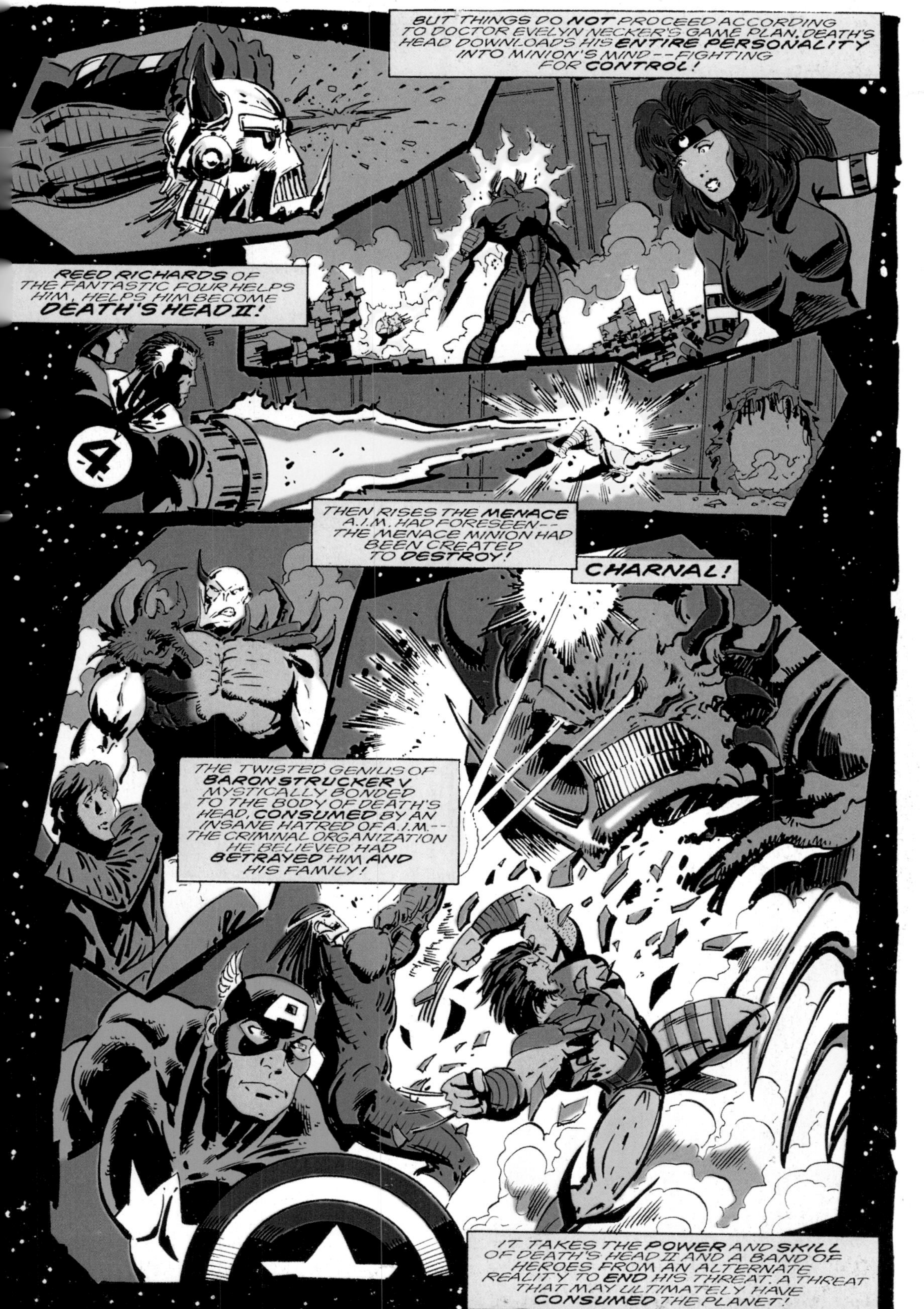
BUT THINGS DO NOT PROCEED ACCORDING TO DOCTOR EVELYN NECKER'S GAME PLAN. DEATH'S HEAD DOWNLOADS HIS ENTIRE PERSONALITY INTO MINION'S MIND -- FIGHTING FOR CONTROL!
REED RICHARDS OF THE FANTASTIC FOUR HELPS HIM, HELPS HIM BECOME DEATH'S HEAD II!
4
THEN RISES THE MENACE A.I.M. HAD FORESEEN -- THE MENACE MINION HAD BEEN CREATED TO DESTROY!
CHARNAL!
THE TWISTED GENIUS OF BARON STRUCKER V MYSTICALLY BONDED TO THE BODY OF DEATH'S HEAD, CONSUMED BY AN INSANE HATRED OF A.I.M. -- THE CRIMINAL ORGANIZATION HE BELIEVED HAD BETRAYED HIM AND HIS FAMILY!
IT TAKES THE POWER AND SKILL OF DEATH'S HEAD II AND A BAND OF HEROES FROM AN ALTERNATE REALITY TO END HIS THREAT. A THREAT THAT MAY ULTIMATELY HAVE CONSUMED THE PLANET!

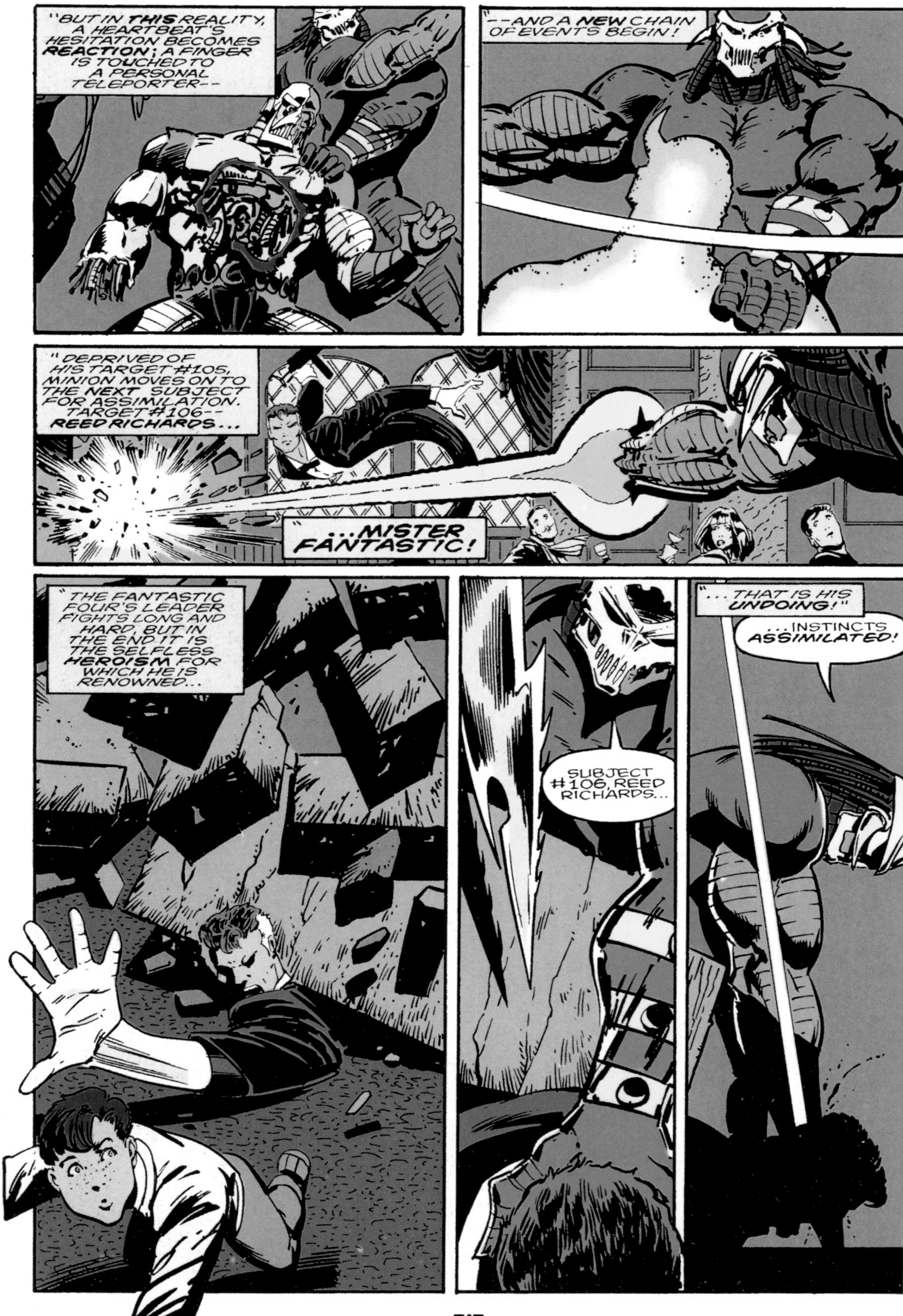
"BUT IN THIS REALITY, A HEARTBEAT'S HESITATION BECOMES REACTION; A FINGER IS TOUCHED TO A PERSONAL TELEPORTER--
--AND A NEW CHAIN OF EVENTS BEGIN!
"DEPRIVED OF HIS TARGET #105, MINION MOVES ON TO THE NEXT SUBJECT FOR ASSIMILATION. TARGET #106-- REED RICHARDS...
"...MISTER FANTASTIC!
"THE FANTASTIC FOUR'S LEADER FIGHTS LONG AND HARD, BUT IN THE END IT IS THE SELFLESS HEROISM FOR WHICH HE IS RENOWNED...
SUBJECT #106, REED RICHARDS...
"...THAT IS HIS UNDOING!"
...INSTINCTS ASSIMILATED!

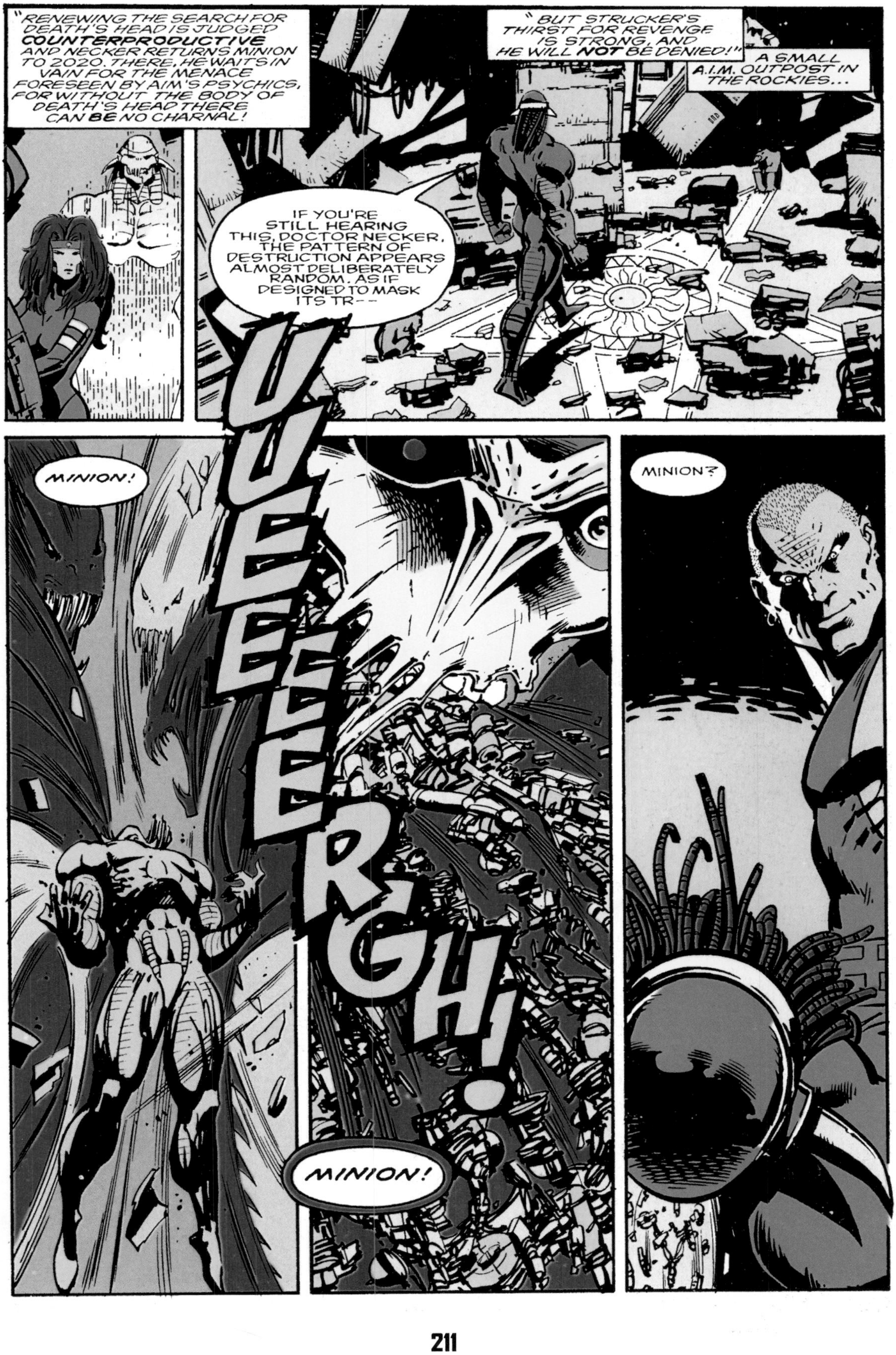
"RENEWING THE SEARCH FOR DEATH'S HEAD IS JUDGED COUNTERPRODUCTIVE AND NECKER RETURNS MINION TO 2020. THERE, HE WAITS IN VAIN FOR THE MENACE FORESEEN BY AIM'S PSYCHICS, FOR WITHOUT THE BODY OF DEATH'S HEAD THERE CAN BE NO CHARNAL!
"BUT STRUCKER'S THIRST FOR REVENGE IS STRONG, AND HE WILL NOT BE DENIED!"
A SMALL A.I.M. OUTPOST IN THE ROCKIES...
IF YOU'RE STILL HEARING THIS, DOCTOR NECKER, THE PATTERN OF DESTRUCTION APPEARS ALMOST DELIBERATELY RANDOM. AS IF DESIGNED TO MASK ITS TR--
UUEEEERGH!
MINION!
MINION!
MINION?

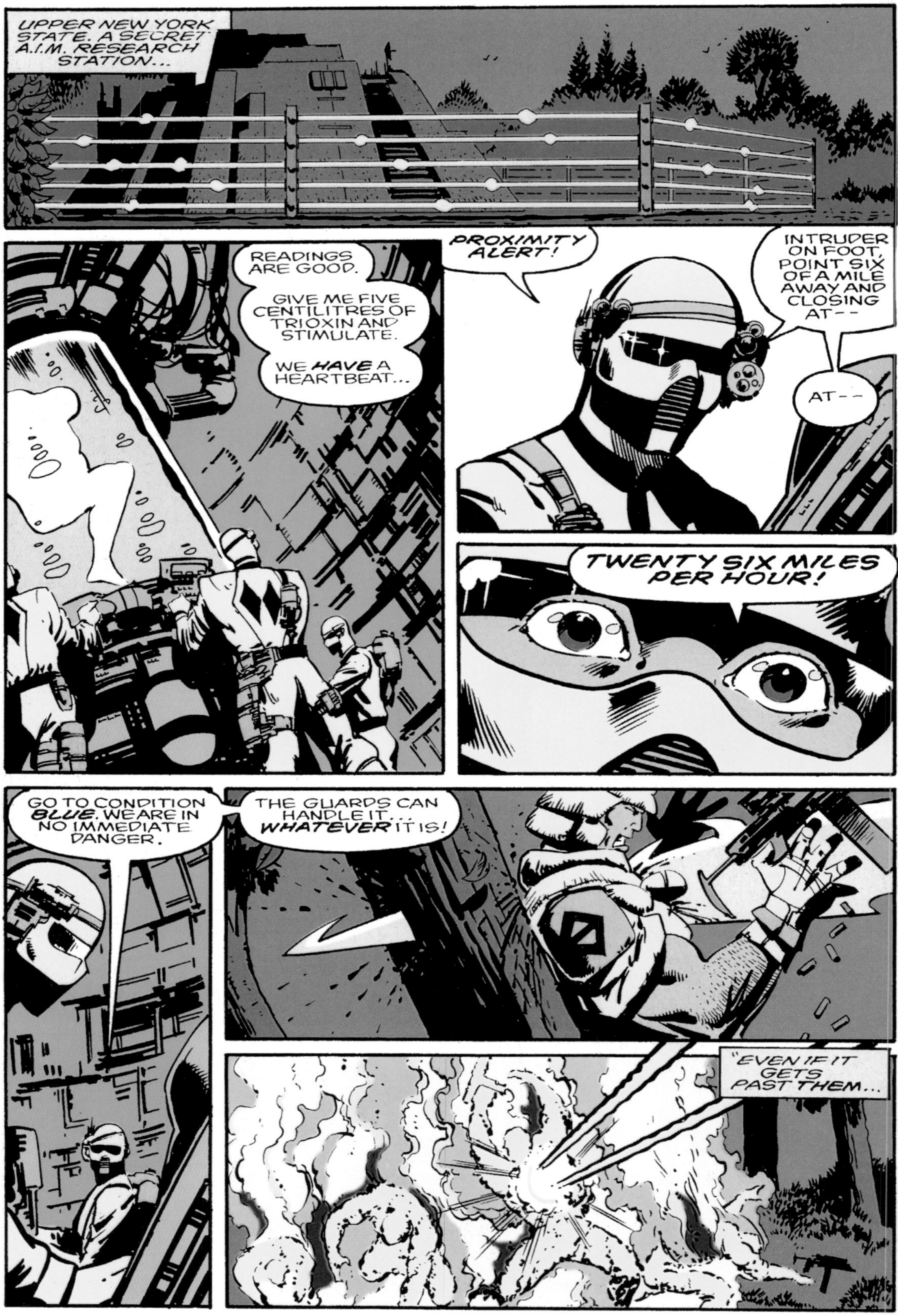
UPPER NEW YORK STATE. A SECRET A.I.M. RESEARCH STATION...
READINGS ARE GOOD.
GIVE ME FIVE CENTILITRES OF TRIOXIN AND STIMULATE.
WE HAVE A HEARTBEAT...
PROXIMITY ALERT!
INTRUDER ON FOOT, POINT SIX OF A MILE AWAY AND CLOSING AT--
AT--
TWENTY SIX MILES PER HOUR!
GO TO CONDITION BLUE. WE ARE IN NO IMMEDIATE DANGER.
THE GUARDS CAN HANDLE IT... WHATEVER IT IS!
"EVEN IF IT GETS PAST THEM...

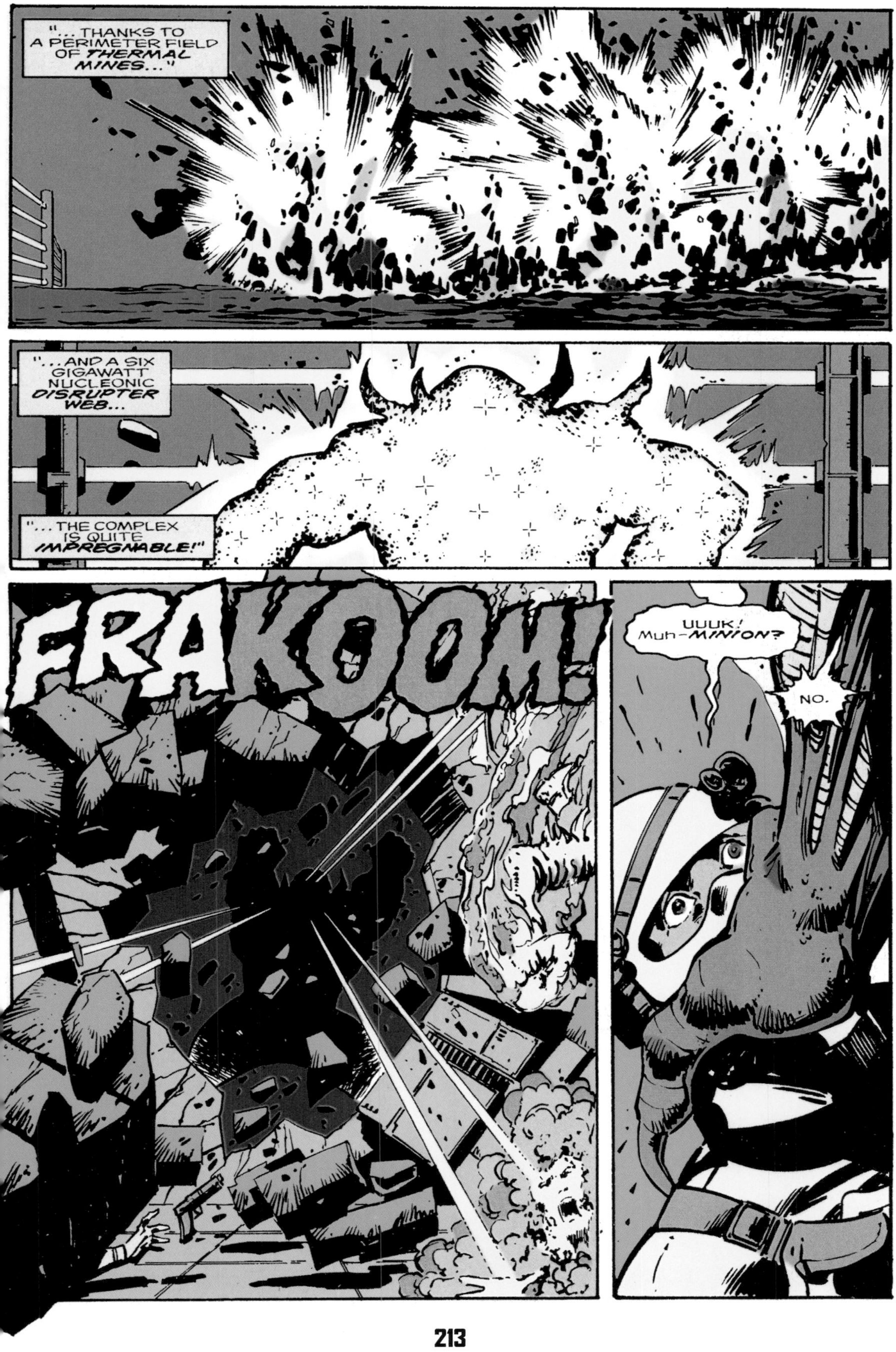

"... THANKS TO A PERIMETER FIELD OF THERMAL MINES..."
"... AND A SIX GIGAWATT NUCLEONIC DISRUPTER WEB...
"... THE COMPLEX IS QUITE IMPREGNABLE!"
FRAKOOM!
UUUK! Muh-MINION?
NO.

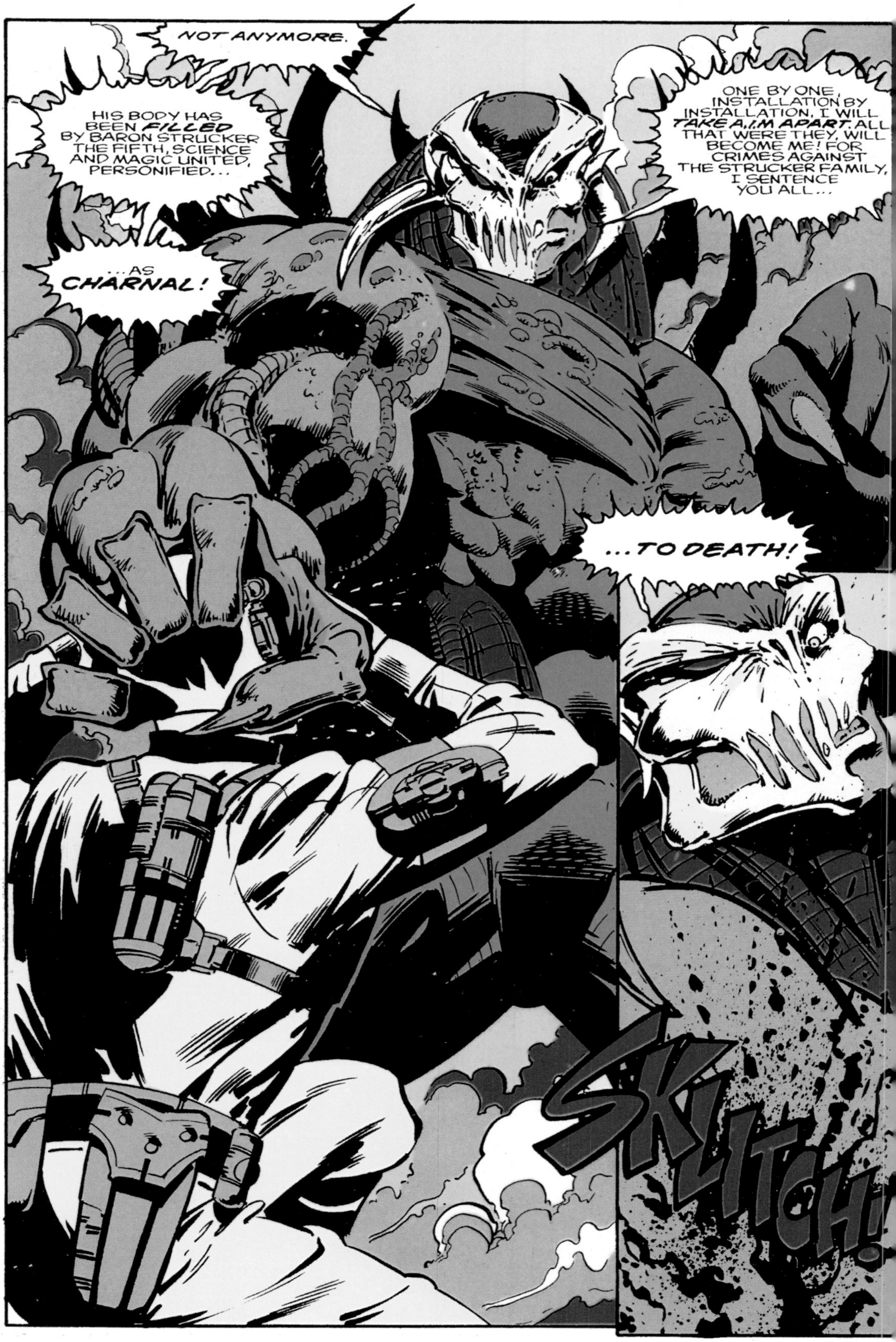
NOT ANYMORE.
HIS BODY HAS BEEN FILLED BY BARON STRUCKER THE FIFTH, SCIENCE AND MAGIC UNITED, PERSONIFIED...
...AS CHARNAL!
ONE BY ONE, INSTALLATION BY INSTALLATION, I WILL TAKE A.I.M APART. ALL THAT WERE THEY, WILL BECOME ME! FOR CRIMES AGAINST THE STRUCKER FAMILY, I SENTENCE YOU ALL...
...TO DEATH!
SKLITCH!

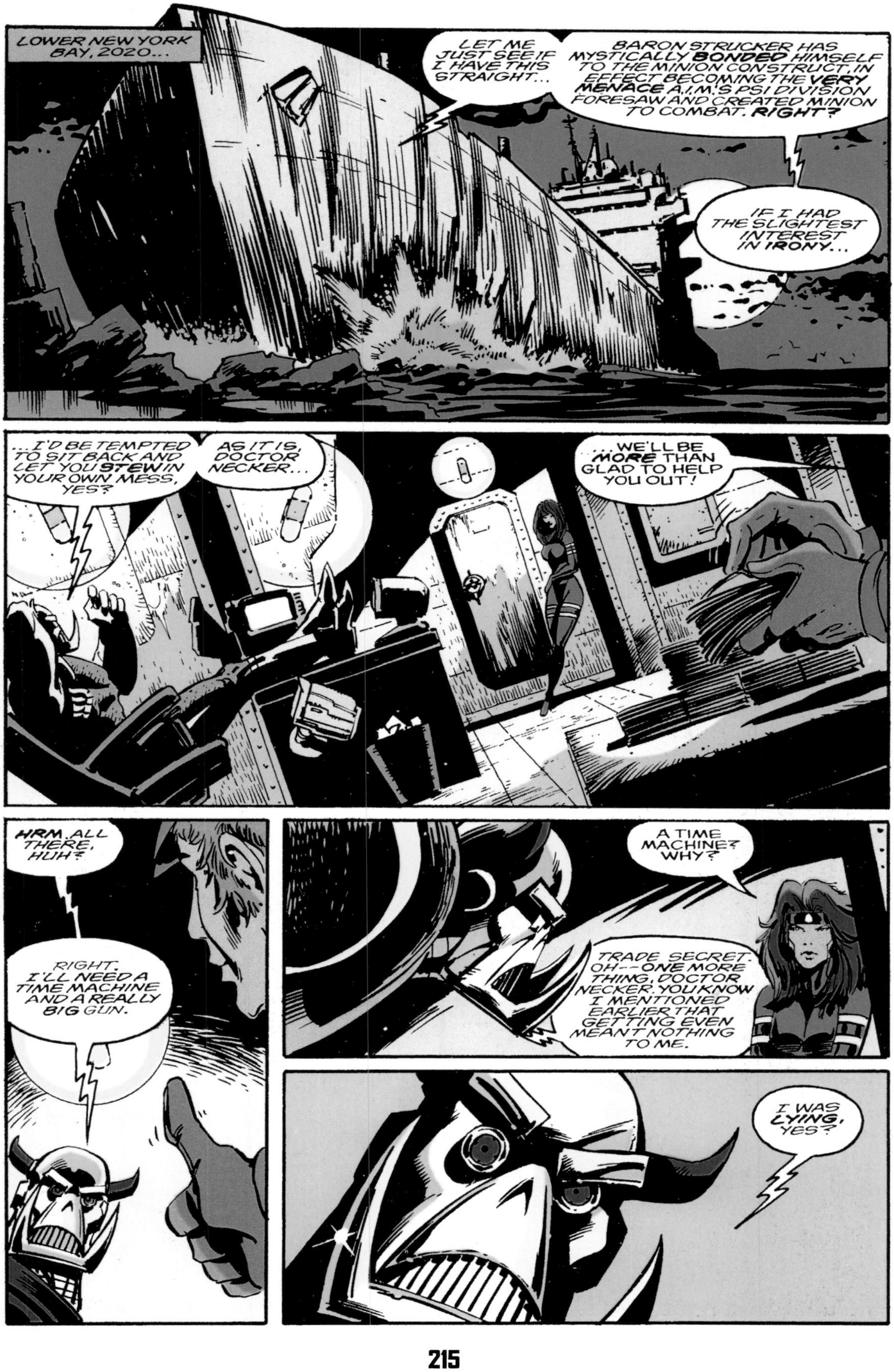
LOWER NEW YORK BAY, 2020...
LET ME JUST SEE IF I HAVE THIS STRAIGHT...
BARON STRUCKER HAS MYSTICALLY BONDED HIMSELF TO THE MINION CONSTRUCT, IN EFFECT BECOMING THE VERY MENACE A.I.M.'S PSI DIVISION FORESAW AND CREATED MINION TO COMBAT. RIGHT?
IF I HAD THE SLIGHTEST INTEREST IN IRONY...
...I'D BE TEMPTED TO SIT BACK AND LET YOU STEW IN YOUR OWN MESS, YES?
AS IT IS, DOCTOR NECKER...
...WE'LL BE MORE THAN GLAD TO HELP YOU OUT!
HRM. ALL THERE, HUH?
RIGHT. I'LL NEED A TIME MACHINE AND A REALLY BIG GUN.
A TIME MACHINE? WHY?
TRADE SECRET. OH--ONE MORE THING, DOCTOR NECKER. YOU KNOW I MENTIONED EARLIER THAT GETTING EVEN MEANT NOTHING TO ME.
I WAS LYING, YES?

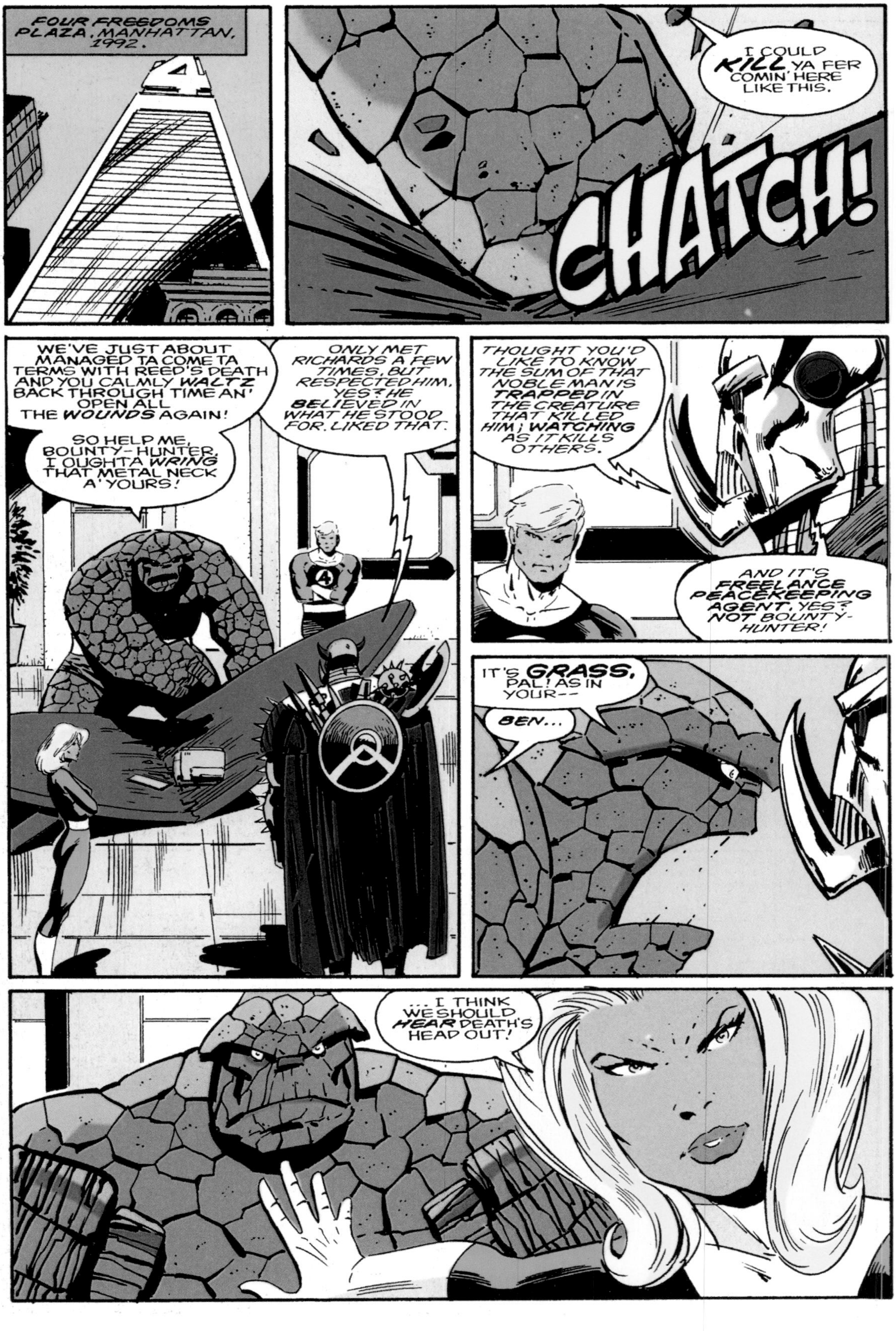
FOUR FREEDOMS PLAZA, MANHATTAN, 1992.
I COULD KILL YA FER COMIN' HERE LIKE THIS.
CHATCH!
WE'VE JUST ABOUT MANAGED TA COME TA TERMS WITH REED'S DEATH AND YOU CALMLY WALTZ BACK THROUGH TIME AN' OPEN ALL THE WOUNDS AGAIN!
SO HELP ME, BOUNTY-HUNTER, I OUGHTA WRING THAT METAL NECK A' YOURS!
ONLY MET RICHARDS A FEW TIMES, BUT RESPECTED HIM, YES? HE BELIEVED IN WHAT HE STOOD FOR. LIKED THAT.
THOUGHT YOU'D LIKE TO KNOW THE SUM OF THAT NOBLE MAN IS TRAPPED IN THE CREATURE THAT KILLED HIM; WATCHING AS IT KILLS OTHERS.
AND IT'S FREELANCE PEACEKEEPING AGENT, YES? NOT BOUNTY-HUNTER!
IT'S GRASS, PAL! AS IN YOUR--
BEN...
...I THINK WE SHOULD HEAR DEATH'S HEAD OUT!

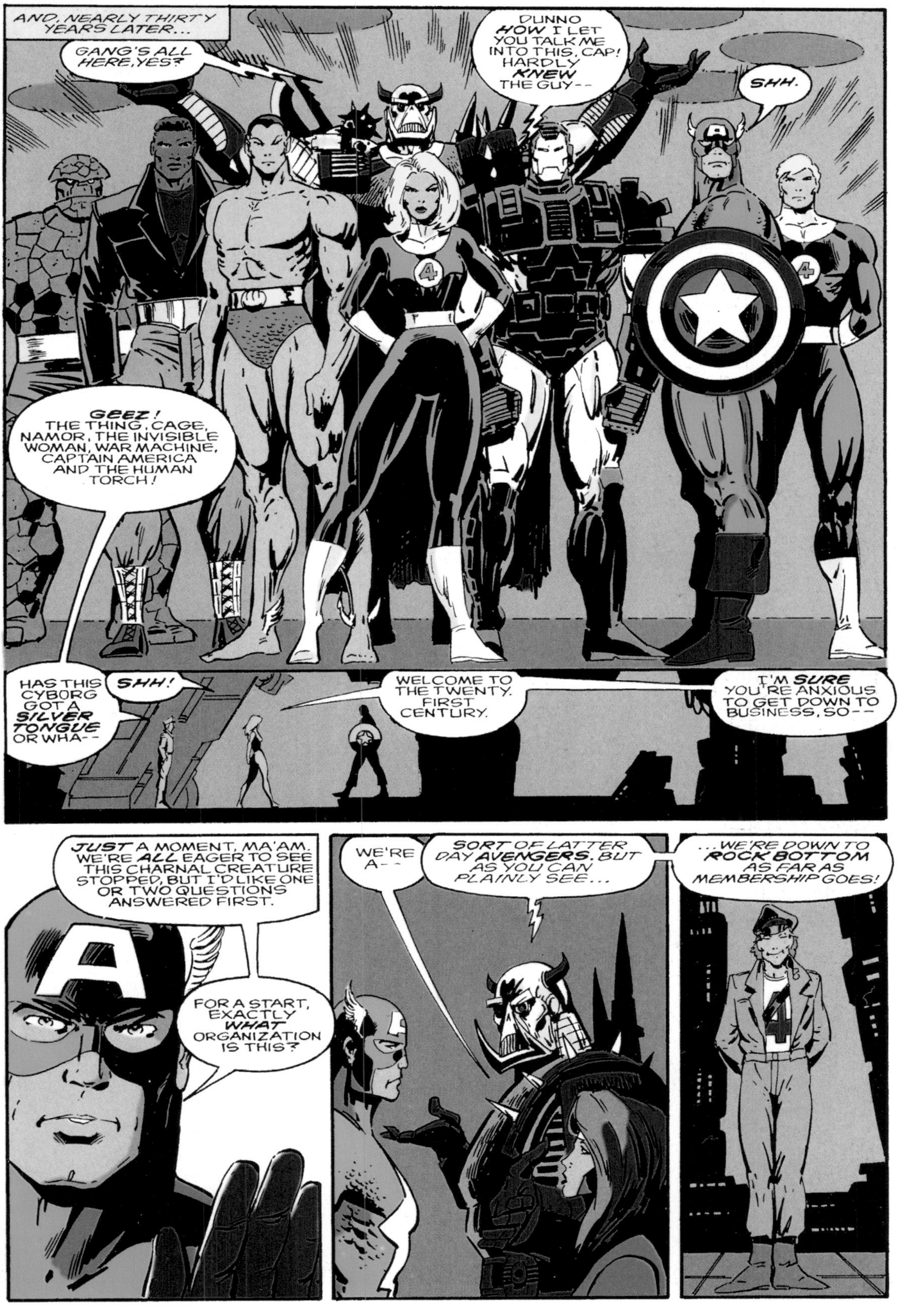

AND, NEARLY THIRTY YEARS LATER...
GANG'S ALL HERE, YES?
DUNNO HOW I LET YOU TALK ME INTO THIS, CAP! HARDLY KNEW THE GUY--
SHH.
GEEZ! THE THING, CAGE, NAMOR, THE INVISIBLE WOMAN, WAR MACHINE, CAPTAIN AMERICA AND THE HUMAN TORCH!
HAS THIS CYBORG GOT A SILVER TONGUE OR WHA--
SHH!
WELCOME TO THE TWENTY-FIRST CENTURY.
I'M SURE YOU'RE ANXIOUS TO GET DOWN TO BUSINESS, SO--
JUST A MOMENT, MA'AM. WE'RE ALL EAGER TO SEE THIS CHARNAL CREATURE STOPPED, BUT I'D LIKE ONE OR TWO QUESTIONS ANSWERED FIRST.
FOR A START, EXACTLY WHAT ORGANIZATION IS THIS?
WE'RE A--
SORT OF LATTER DAY AVENGERS. BUT AS YOU CAN PLAINLY SEE...
...WE'RE DOWN TO ROCK BOTTOM AS FAR AS MEMBERSHIP GOES!

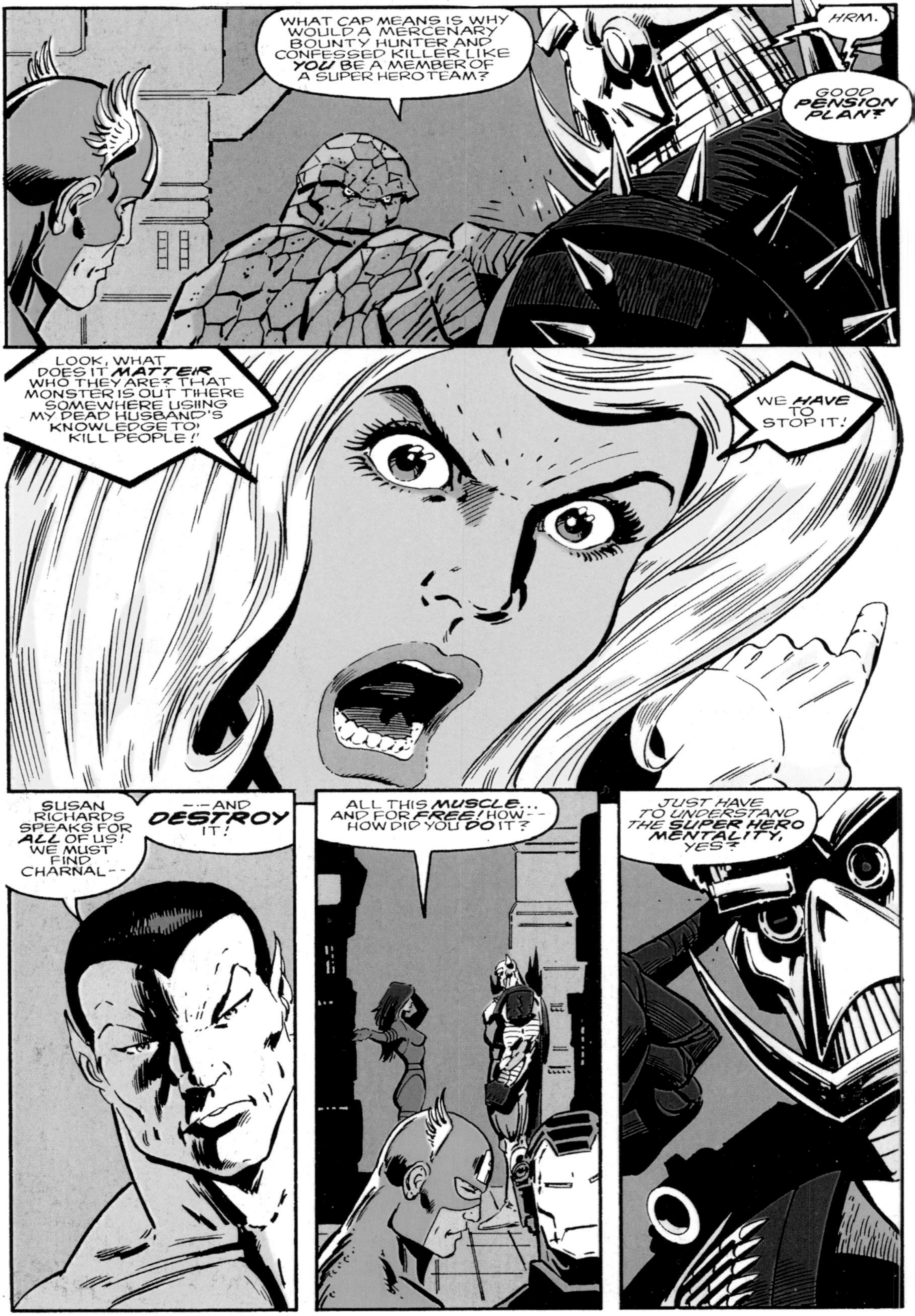
WHAT CAP MEANS IS WHY WOULD A MERCENARY BOUNTY HUNTER AND CONFESSED KILLER LIKE YOU BE A MEMBER OF A SUPER HERO TEAM?
HRM.
GOOD PENSION PLAN?
LOOK, WHAT DOES IT MATTEIR WHO THEY ARE? THAT MONSTER IS OUT TIHERE SOMEWHERE USIING MY DEAD HUSBAND'S KNOWLEDGE TO! KILL PEOPLE!
WE HAVE TO STOP IT!
SUSAN RICHARDS SPEAKS FOR ALL OF US! WE MUST FIND CHARNAL--
--AND DESTROY IT!
ALL THIS MUSCLE... AND FOR FREE! HOW-- HOW DID YOU DO IT?
JUST HAVE TO UNDERSTAND THE SUPER HERO MENTALITY, YES?

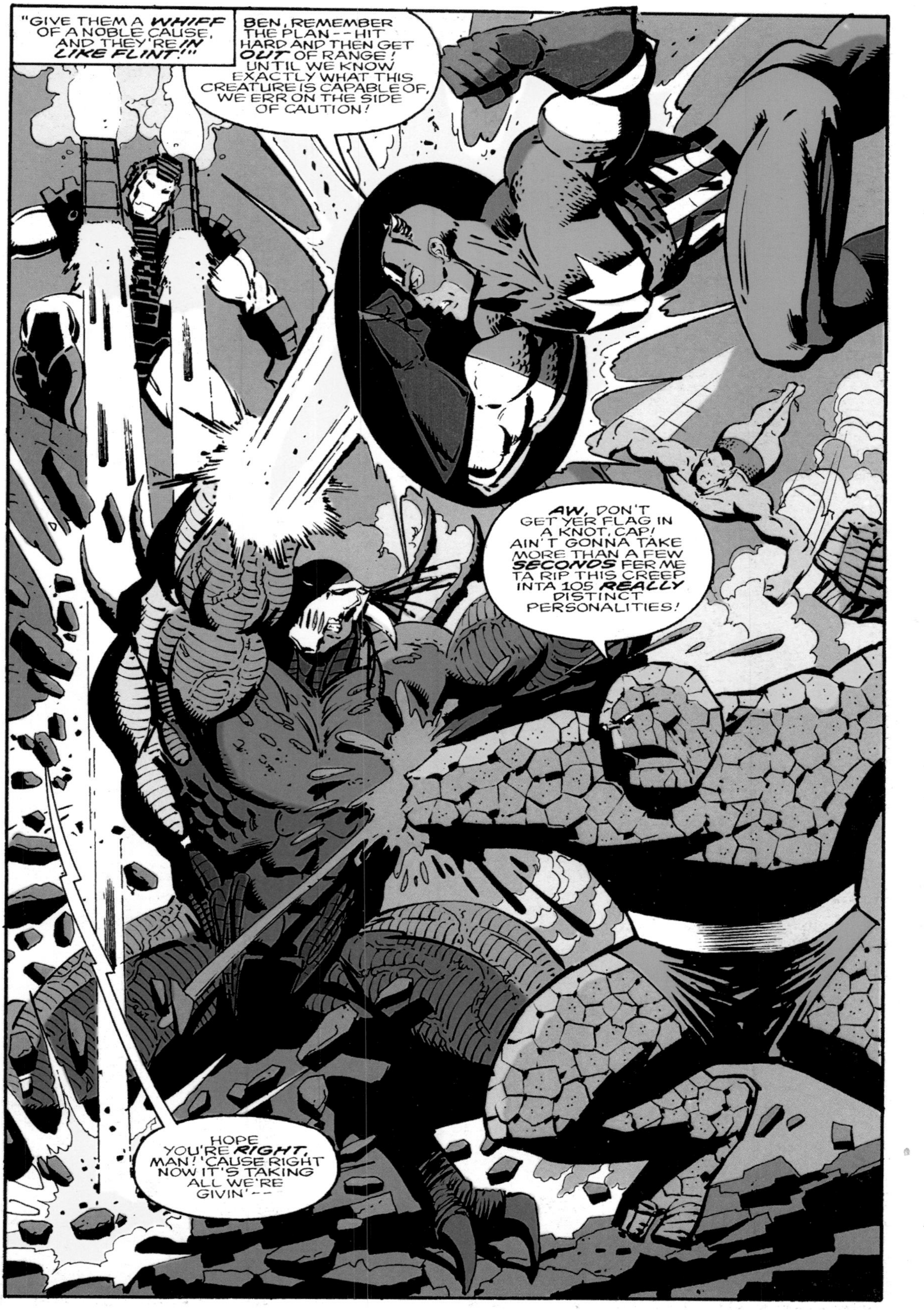
"GIVE THEM A WHIFF OF A NOBLE CAUSE, AND THEY'RE IN LIKE FLINT!"
BEN, REMEMBER THE PLAN--HIT HARD AND THEN GET OUT OF RANGE! UNTIL WE KNOW EXACTLY WHAT THIS CREATURE IS CAPABLE OF, WE ERR ON THE SIDE OF CAUTION!
AW, DON'T GET YER FLAG IN A KNOT, CAP! AIN'T GONNA TAKE MORE THAN A FEW SECONDS FER ME TA RIP THIS CREEP INTA 105 REALLY DISTINCT PERSONALITIES!
HOPE YOU'RE RIGHT, MAN! 'CAUSE RIGHT NOW IT'S TAKING ALL WE'RE GIVIN'--

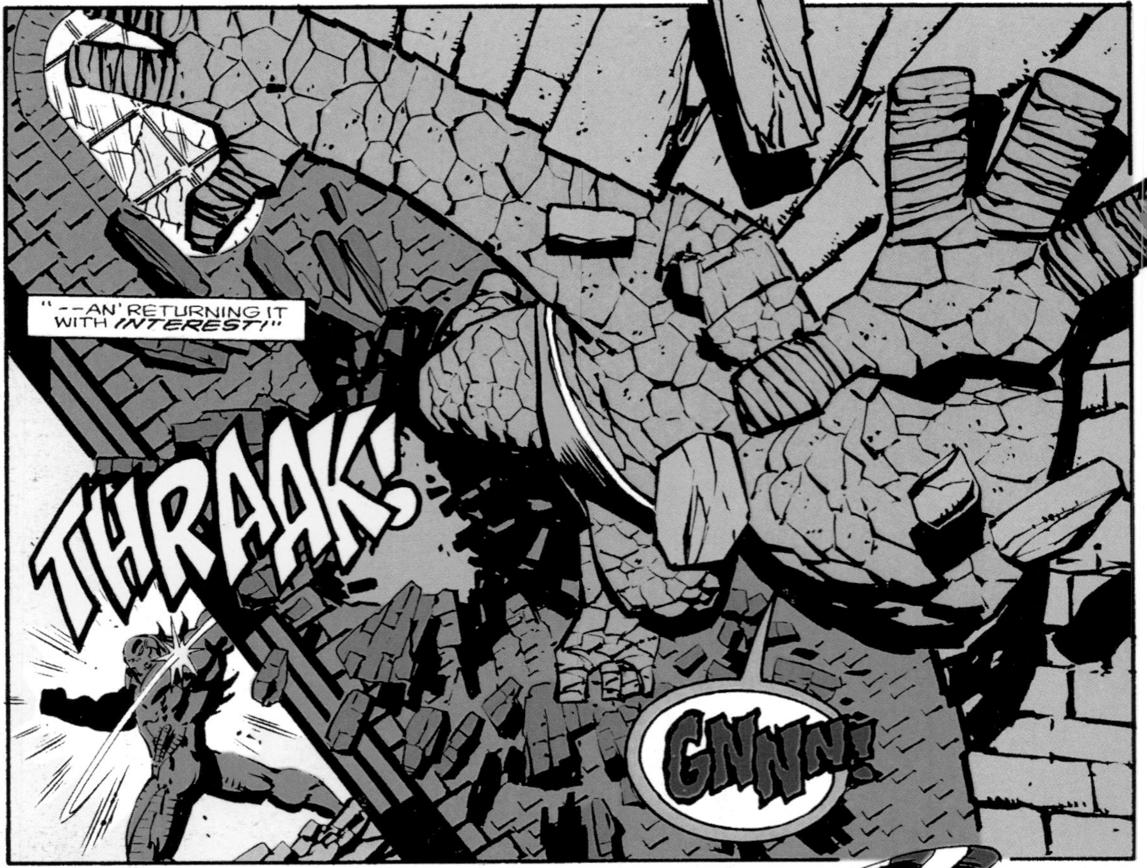
"--AN' RETURNING IT WITH INTEREST!"
THRAAK!
GNNN!

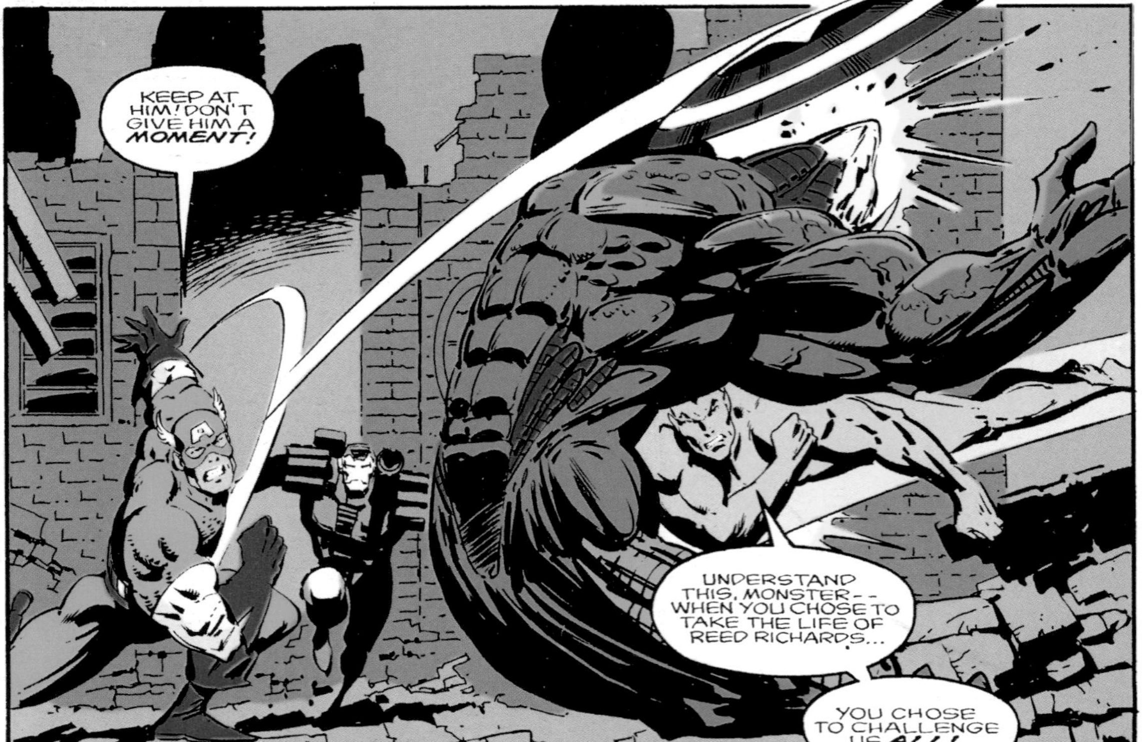
KEEP AT HIM! DON'T GIVE HIM A MOMENT!
UNDERSTAND THIS, MONSTER-- WHEN YOU CHOSE TO TAKE THE LIFE OF REED RICHARDS...
YOU CHOSE TO CHALLENGE US ALL!

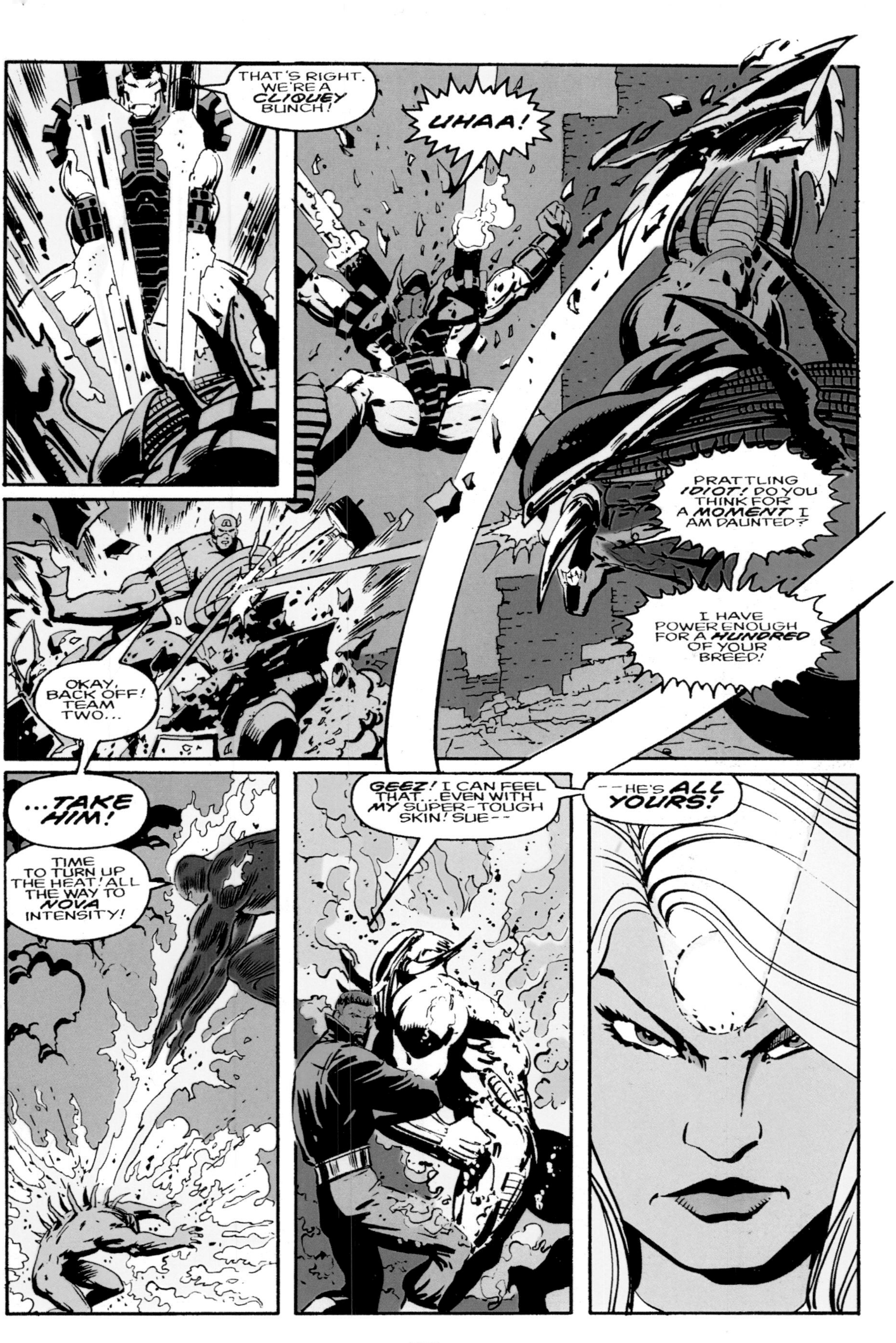
THAT'S RIGHT. WE'RE A CLIQUEY BUNCH!
UHAA!
PRATTLING IDIOT! DO YOU THINK FOR A MOMENT I AM DAUNTED?
I HAVE POWER ENOUGH FOR A HUNDRED OF YOUR BREED!
OKAY, BACK OFF! TEAM TWO...
...TAKE HIM!
TIME TO TURN UP THE HEAT! ALL THE WAY TO NOVA INTENSITY!
GEEZ! I CAN FEEL THAT... EVEN WITH MY SUPER-TOUGH SKIN! SUE--
--HE'S ALL YOURS!

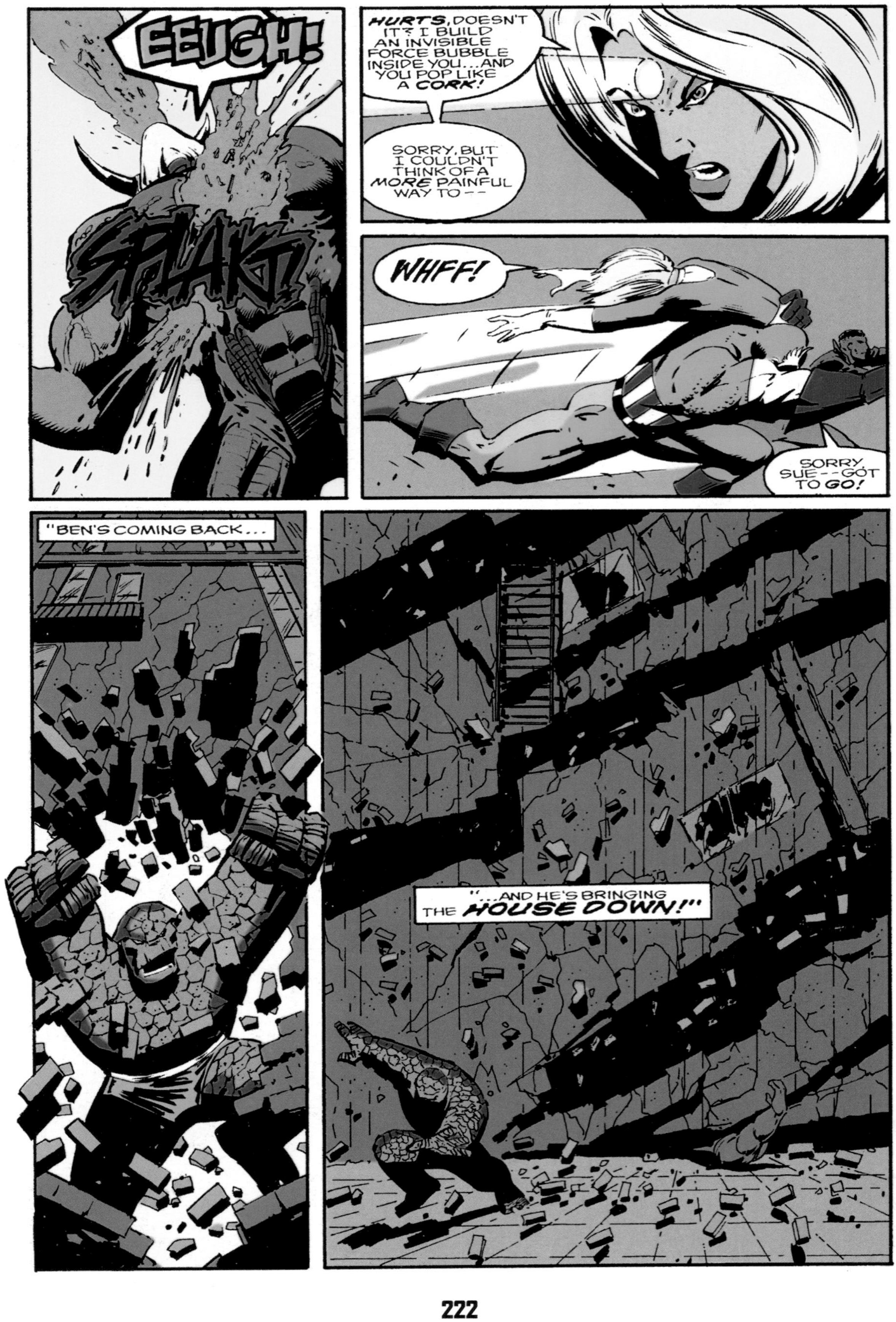
EEUGH!
SPLAK!
HURTS, DOESN'T IT? I BUILD AN INVISIBLE FORCE BUBBLE INSIDE YOU...AND YOU POP LIKE A CORK!
SORRY, BUT I COULDN'T THINK OF A MORE PAINFUL WAY TO--
WHFF!
SORRY, SUE--GOT TO GO!
"BEN'S COMING BACK...
"...AND HE'S BRINGING THE HOUSE DOWN!"

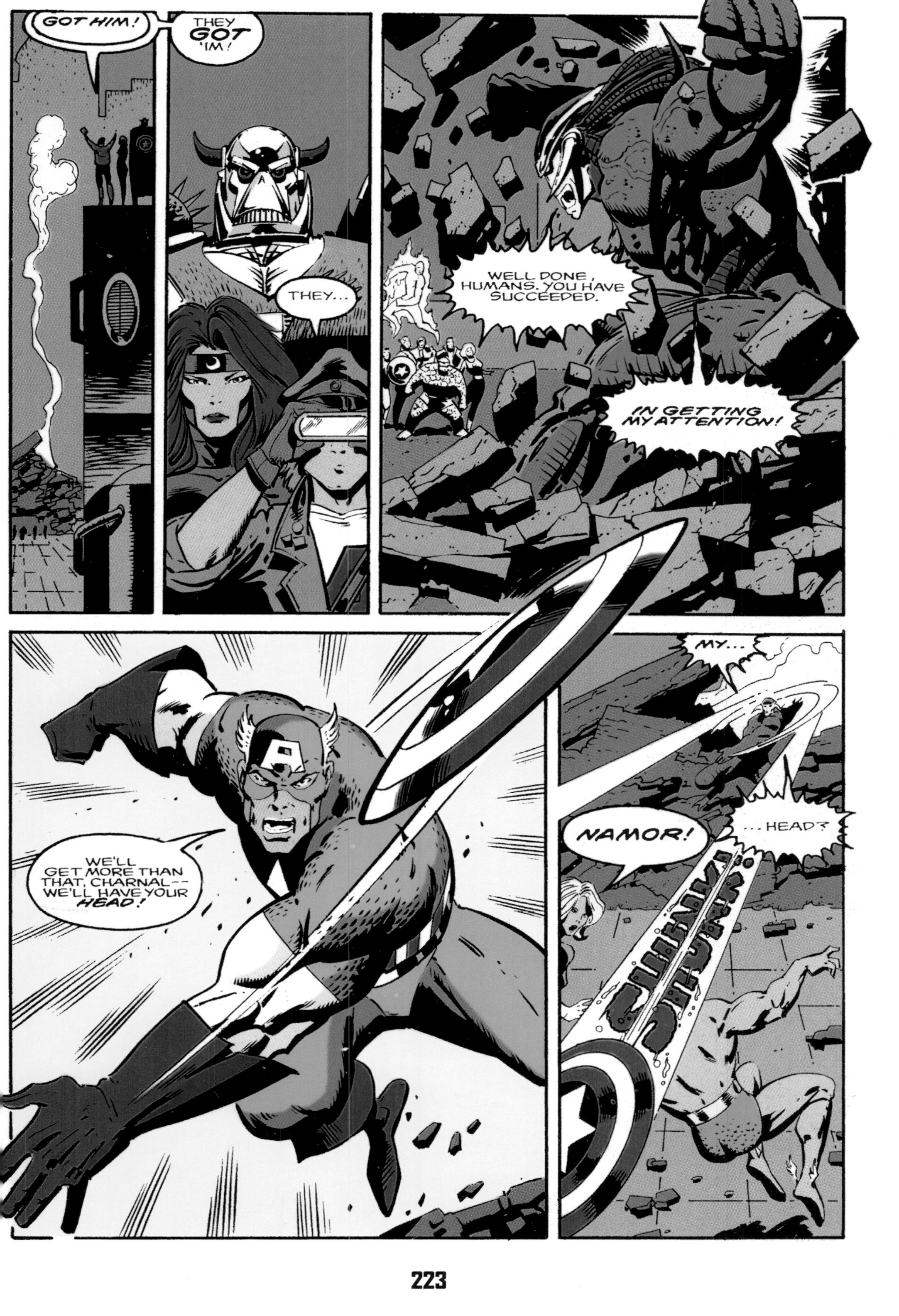
GOT HIM!
THEY GOT 'IM!
THEY...
WELL DONE, HUMANS. YOU HAVE SUCCEEDED.
IN GETTING MY ATTENTION!
WE'LL GET MORE THAN THAT, CHARNAL-- WE'LL HAVE YOUR HEAD!
MY...
NAMOR!
...HEAD?
SHUNK!

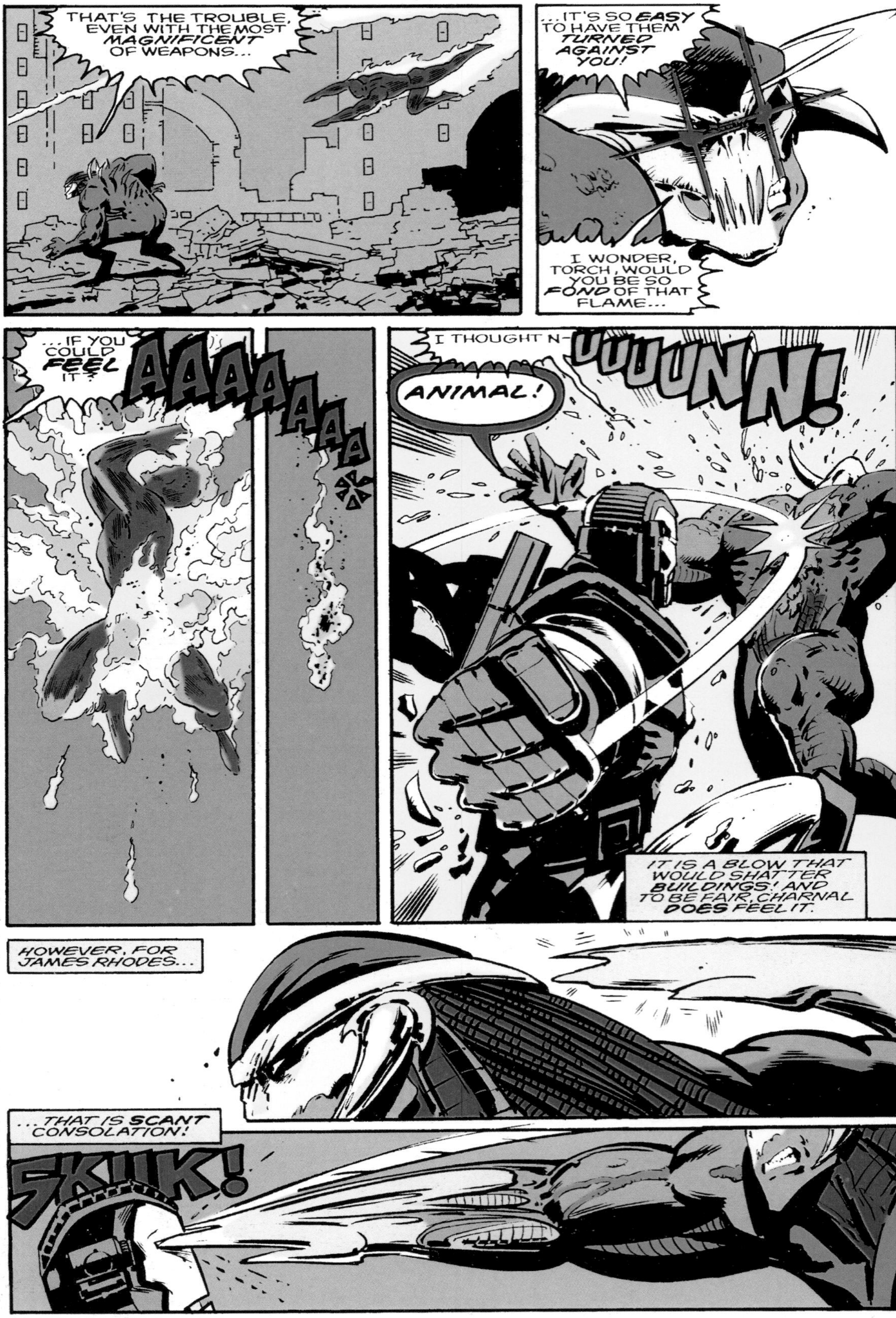

THAT'S THE TROUBLE. EVEN WITH THE MOST MAGNIFICENT OF WEAPONS...
...IT'S SO EASY TO HAVE THEM TURNED AGAINST YOU!
I WONDER, TORCH, WOULD YOU BE SO FOND OF THAT FLAME...
...IF YOU COULD FEEL IT?
AAAAAAAAAA
I THOUGHT N-
UUUUNN!
ANIMAL!
IT IS A BLOW THAT WOULD SHATTER BUILDINGS! AND TO BE FAIR, CHARNAL DOES FEEL IT.
HOWEVER, FOR JAMES RHODES...
...THAT IS SCANT CONSOLATION!
SKUK!

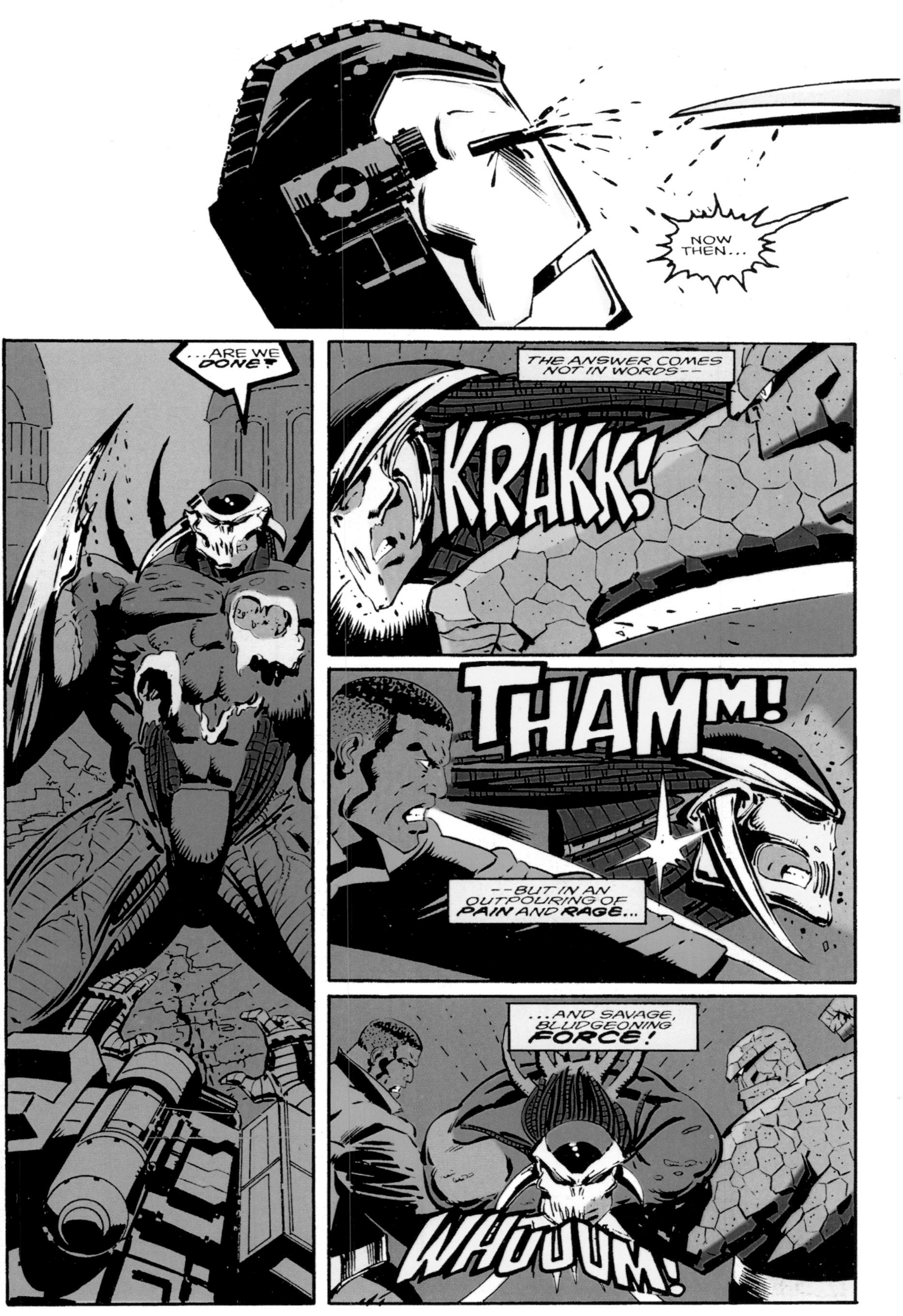
NOW THEN...
...ARE WE DONE?
THE ANSWER COMES NOT IN WORDS--
KRAKK!
THAMM!
--BUT IN AN OUTPOURING OF PAIN AND RAGE...
...AND SAVAGE, BLUDGEONING FORCE!
WHOOOM!

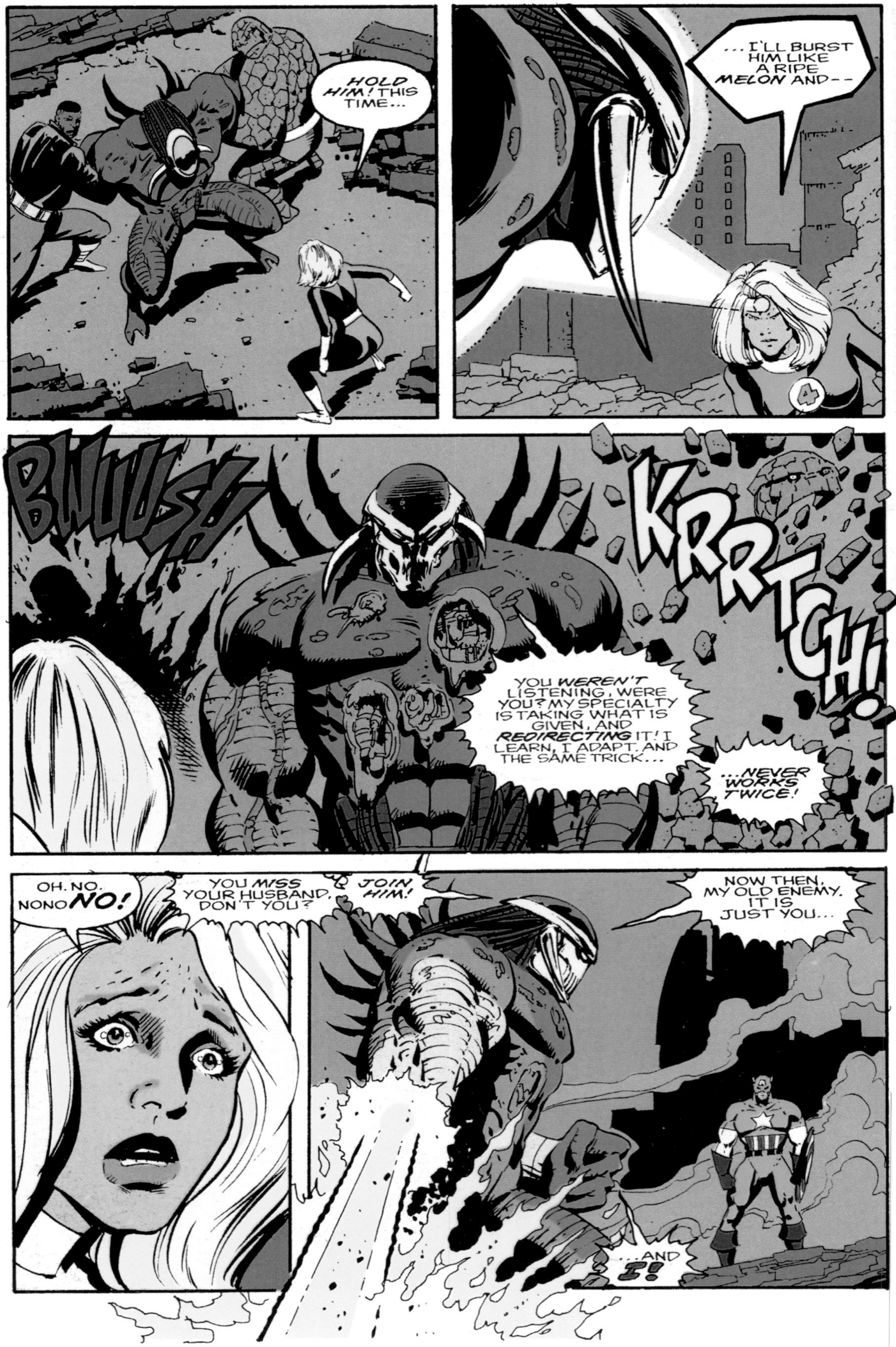
HOLD HIM! THIS TIME...
...I'LL BURST HIM LIKE A RIPE MELON AND--
BWUUSH
KRRTCH!
YOU WEREN'T LISTENING, WERE YOU? MY SPECIALTY IS TAKING WHAT IS GIVEN, AND REDIRECTING IT! I LEARN, I ADAPT, AND THE SAME TRICK...
...NEVER WORKS TWICE!
OH. NO. NONONO NO!
YOU MISS YOUR HUSBAND, DON'T YOU?
JOIN HIM!
NOW THEN, MY OLD ENEMY. IT IS JUST YOU...
...AND I!

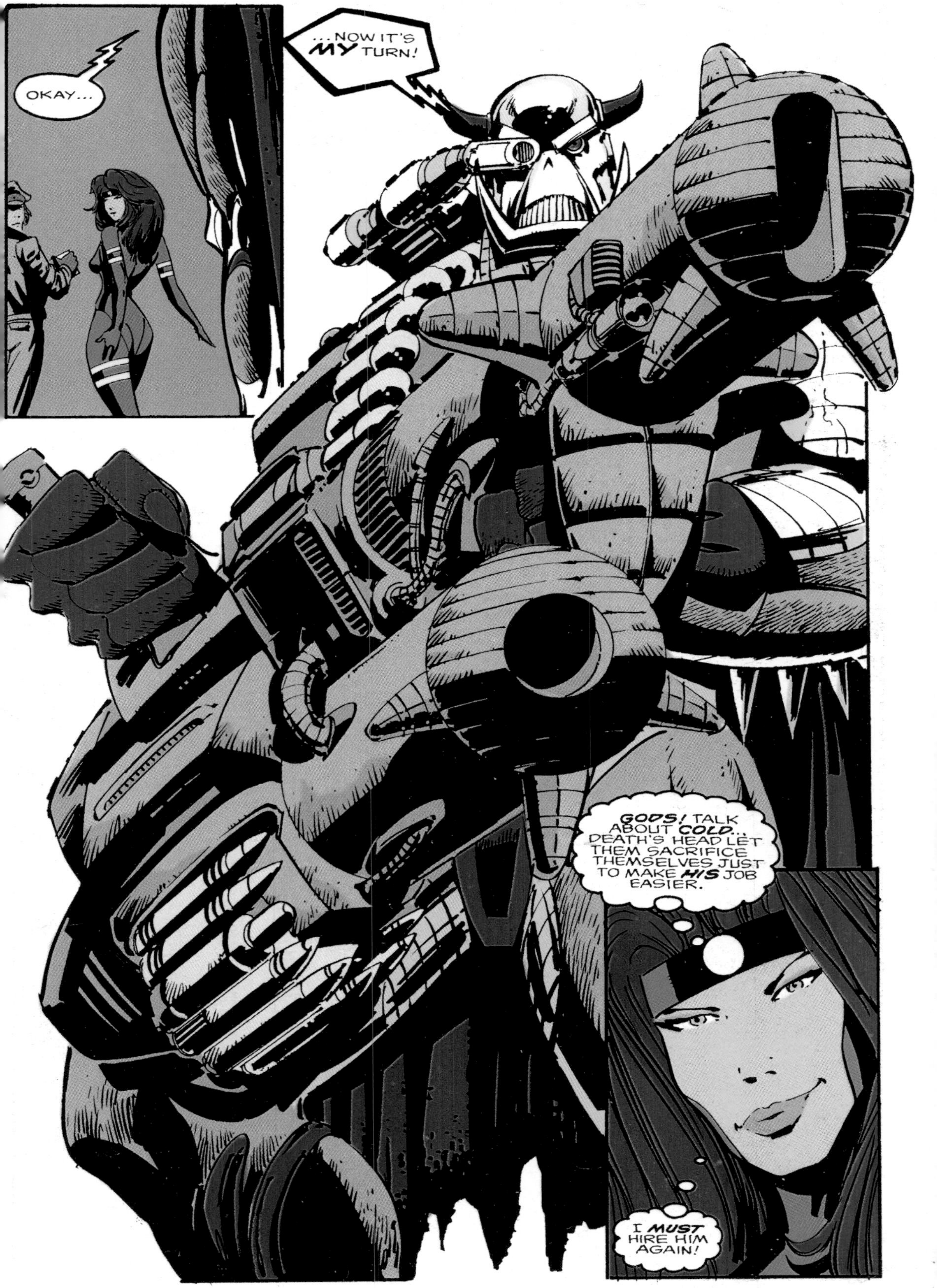
OKAY...
...NOW IT'S MY TURN!
GODS! TALK ABOUT COLD... DEATH'S HEAD LET THEM SACRIFICE THEMSELVES JUST TO MAKE HIS JOB EASIER.
I MUST HIRE HIM AGAIN!

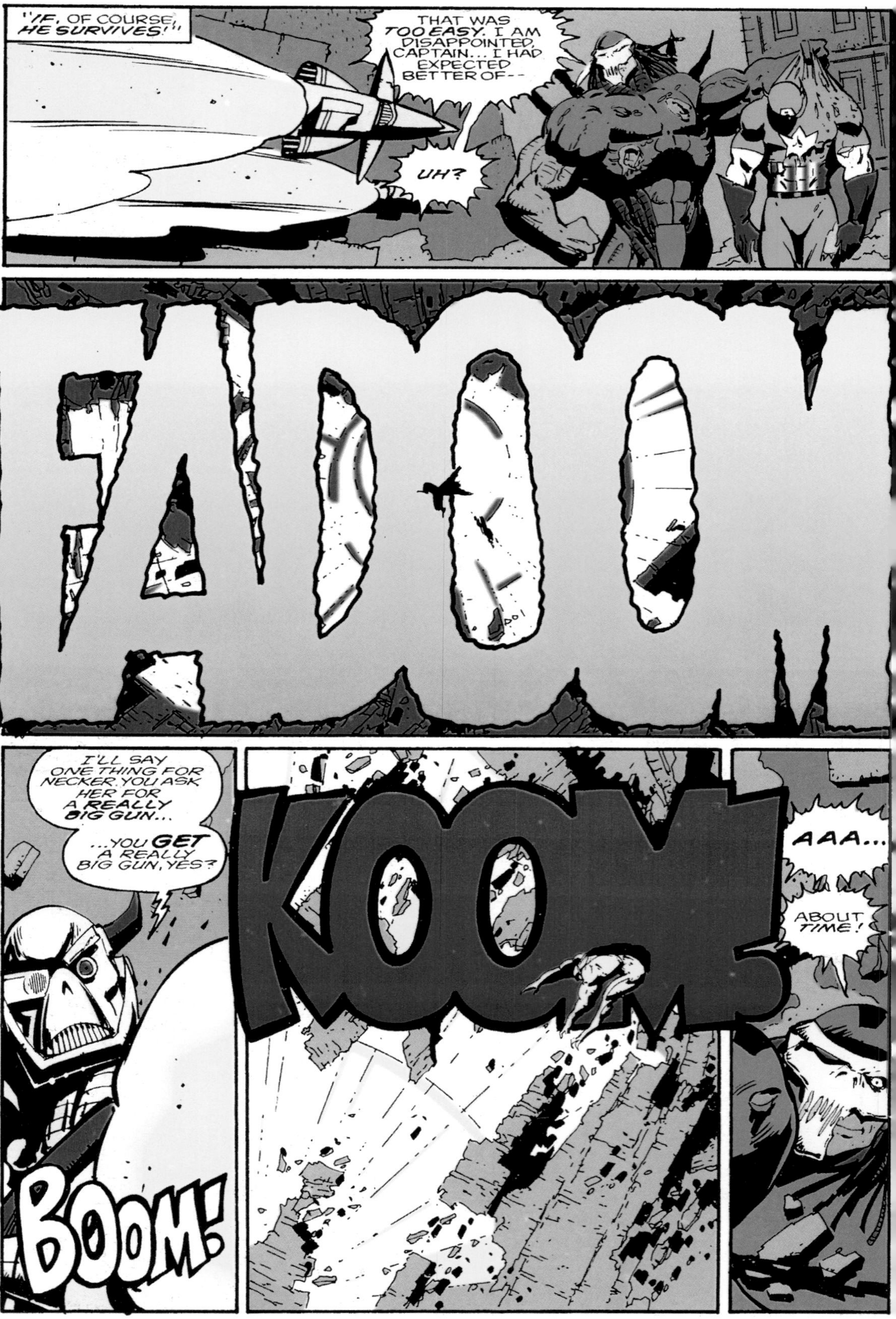
"IF, OF COURSE, HE SURVIVES!"
THAT WAS TOO EASY. I AM DISAPPOINTED, CAPTAIN... I HAD EXPECTED BETTER OF--
UH?
I'LL SAY ONE THING FOR NECKER. YOU ASK HER FOR A REALLY BIG GUN...
...YOU GET A REALLY BIG GUN, YES?
BOOM!
KOOM!
AAA...
ABOUT TIME!

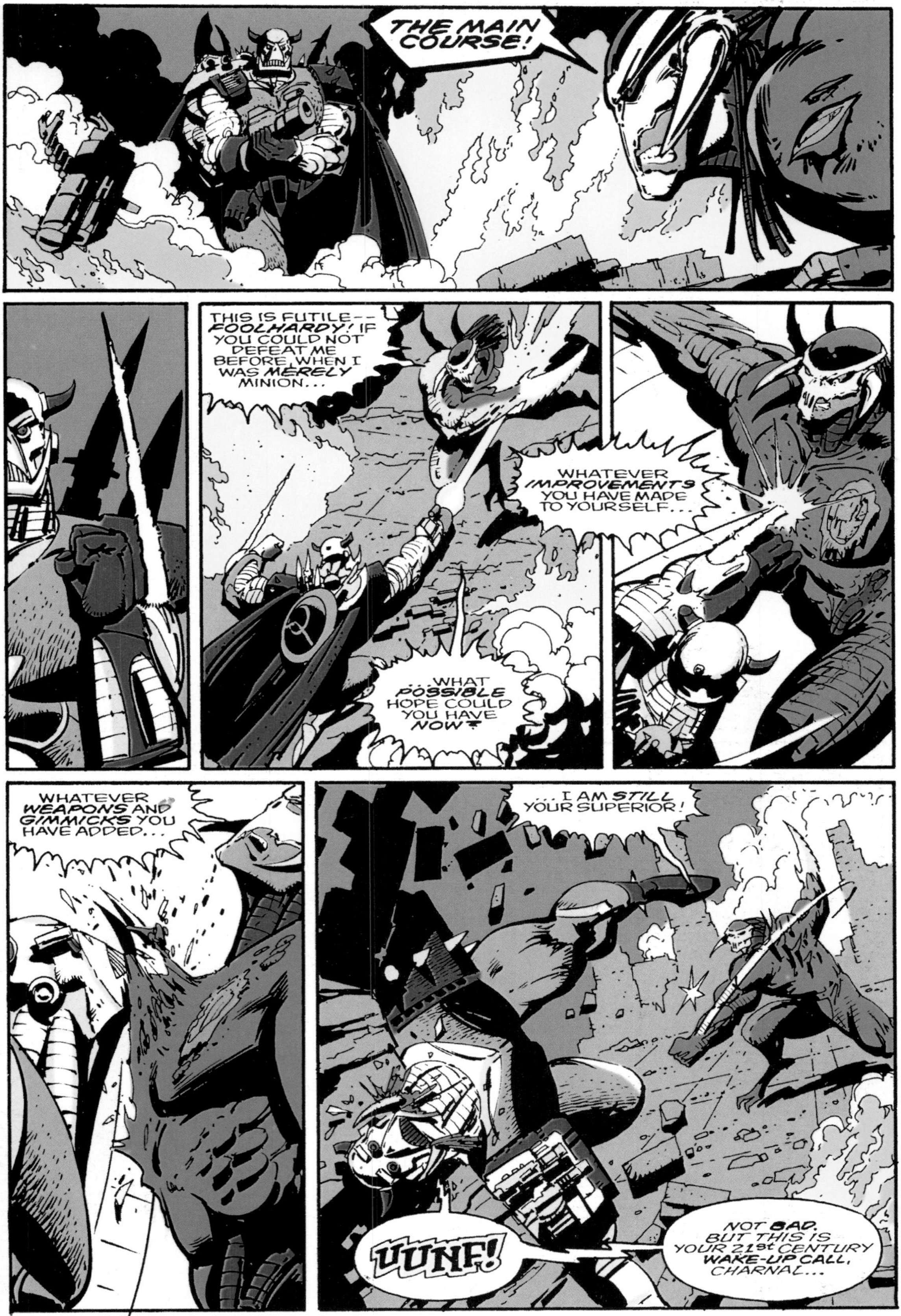

THE MAIN COURSE!
THIS IS FUTILE-- FOOLHARDY! IF YOU COULD NOT DEFEAT ME BEFORE, WHEN I WAS MERELY MINION...
WHATEVER IMPROVEMENTS YOU HAVE MADE TO YOURSELF...
...WHAT POSSIBLE HOPE COULD YOU HAVE NOW?
WHATEVER WEAPONS AND GIMMICKS YOU HAVE ADDED...
...I AM STILL YOUR SUPERIOR!
UUNF!
NOT BAD. BUT THIS IS YOUR 21st CENTURY WAKE-UP CALL, CHARNAL...

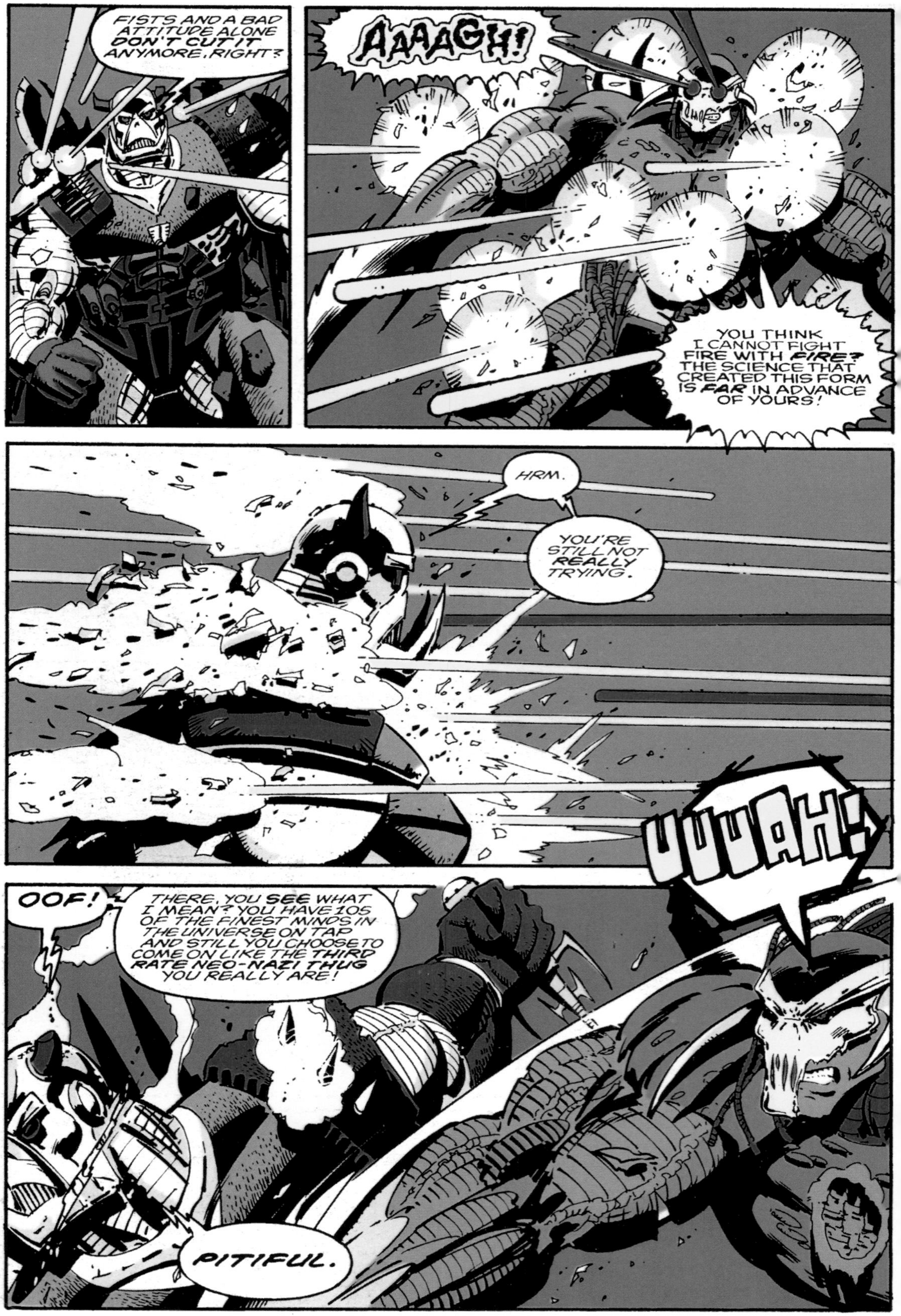
FISTS AND A BAD ATTITUDE ALONE DON'T CUT IT ANYMORE, RIGHT?
AAAAGH!
YOU THINK I CANNOT FIGHT FIRE WITH FIRE? THE SCIENCE THAT CREATED THIS FORM IS FAR IN ADVANCE OF YOURS!
HRM.
YOU'RE STILL NOT REALLY TRYING.
UUUAH!
OOF!
THERE, YOU SEE WHAT I MEAN? YOU HAVE 105 OF THE FINEST MINDS IN THE UNIVERSE ON TAP AND STILL YOU CHOOSE TO COME ON LIKE THE THIRD RATE NEO-NAZI THUG YOU REALLY ARE!
PITIFUL.

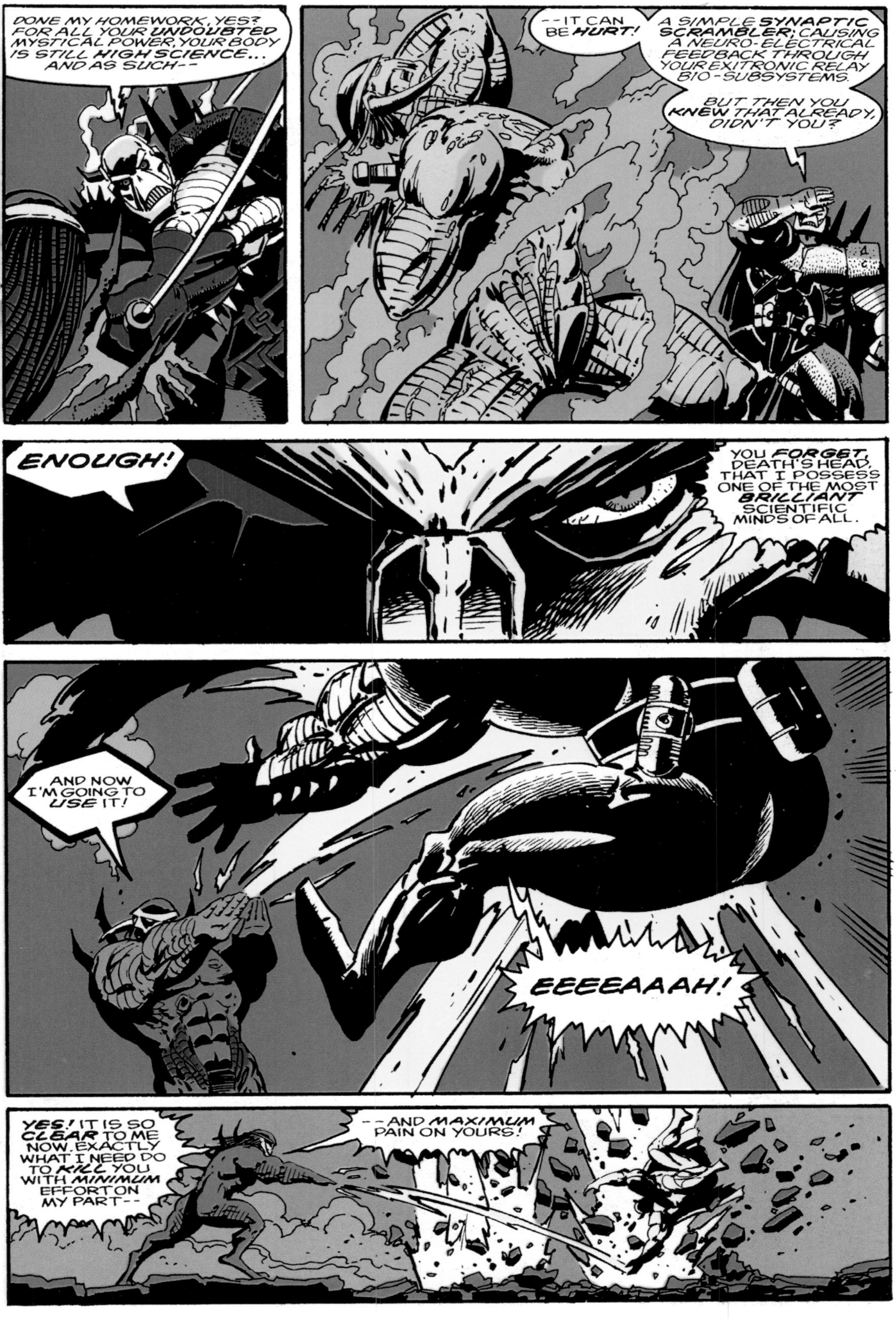
DONE MY HOMEWORK, YES? FOR ALL YOUR UNDOUBTED MYSTICAL POWER, YOUR BODY IS STILL HIGH SCIENCE... AND AS SUCH--
--IT CAN BE HURT!
A SIMPLE SYNAPTIC SCRAMBLER: CAUSING A NEURO-ELECTRICAL FEEDBACK THROUGH YOUR EXITRONIC RELAY BIO-SUBSYSTEMS.
BUT THEN YOU KNEW THAT ALREADY, DIDN'T YOU?
ENOUGH!
YOU FORGET, DEATH'S HEAD, THAT I POSSESS ONE OF THE MOST BRILLIANT SCIENTIFIC MINDS OF ALL.
AND NOW I'M GOING TO USE IT!
EEEEAAAH!
YES! IT IS SO CLEAR TO ME NOW. EXACTLY WHAT I NEED DO TO KILL YOU WITH MINIMUM EFFORT ON MY PART--
--AND MAXIMUM PAIN ON YOURS!

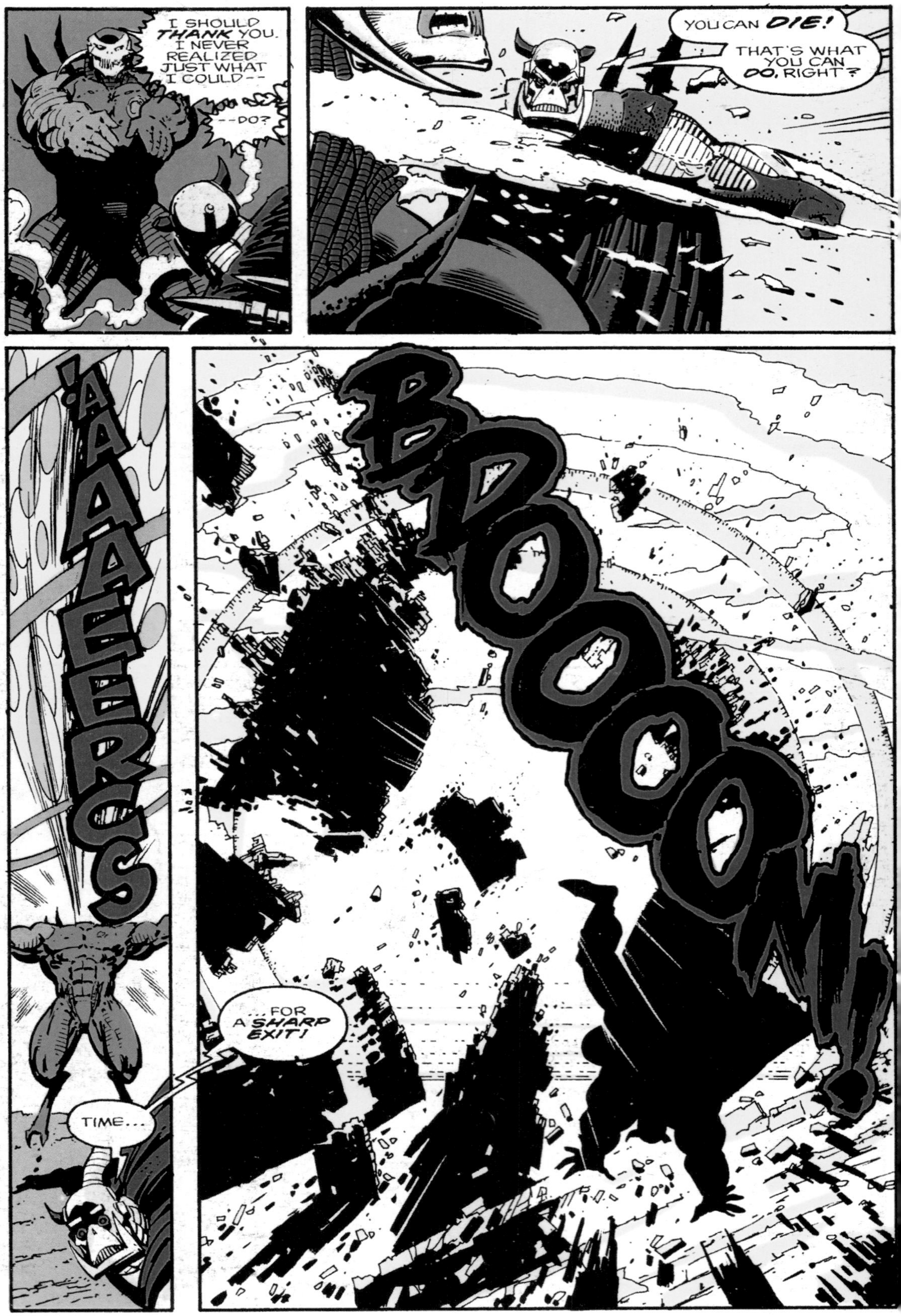
I SHOULD THANK YOU. I NEVER REALIZED JUST WHAT I COULD--
--DO?
YOU CAN DIE!
THAT'S WHAT YOU CAN DO, RIGHT?
AAAAEERGS!
BDOOOOOM!
TIME...
...FOR A SHARP EXIT!

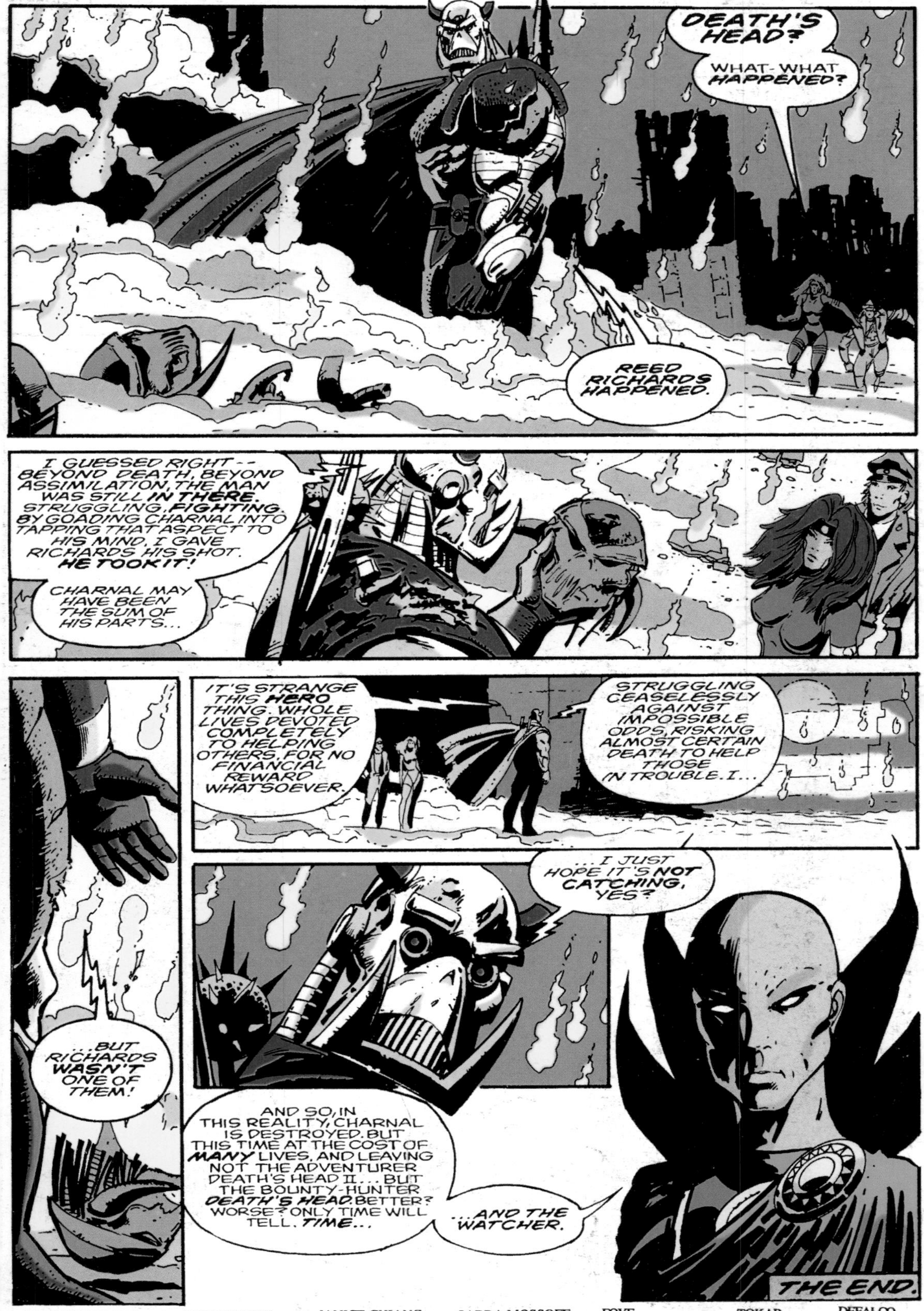
DEATH'S HEAD?
WHAT- WHAT HAPPENED?
REED RICHARDS HAPPENED.
I GUESSED RIGHT -- BEYOND DEATH, BEYOND ASSIMILATION, THE MAN WAS STILL IN THERE. STRUGGLING, FIGHTING. BY GOADING CHARNAL INTO TAPPING THAT ASPECT TO HIS MIND, I GAVE RICHARDS HIS SHOT. HE TOOK IT!
CHARNAL MAY HAVE BEEN THE SUM OF HIS PARTS...
...BUT RICHARDS WASN'T ONE OF THEM!
IT'S STRANGE THIS HERO THING. WHOLE LIVES DEVOTED COMPLETELY TO HELPING OTHERS, FOR NO FINANCIAL REWARD WHATSOEVER.
STRUGGLING CEASELESSLY AGAINST IMPOSSIBLE ODDS, RISKING ALMOST CERTAIN DEATH TO HELP THOSE IN TROUBLE. I...
...I JUST HOPE IT'S NOT CATCHING, YES?
AND SO, IN THIS REALITY, CHARNAL IS DESTROYED. BUT THIS TIME AT THE COST OF MANY LIVES, AND LEAVING NOT THE ADVENTURER DEATH'S HEAD II... BUT THE BOUNTY-HUNTER DEATH'S HEAD. BETTER? WORSE? ONLY TIME WILL TELL. TIME...
...AND THE WATCHER.
THE END.

SIMON FURMAN WRITER | GEOFF SENIOR ARTIST | JANICE CHIANG LETTERER | SARRA MOSSOFF COLORIST | FOYE ASST. EDITOR | TOKAR EDITOR | DEFALCO CHIEF

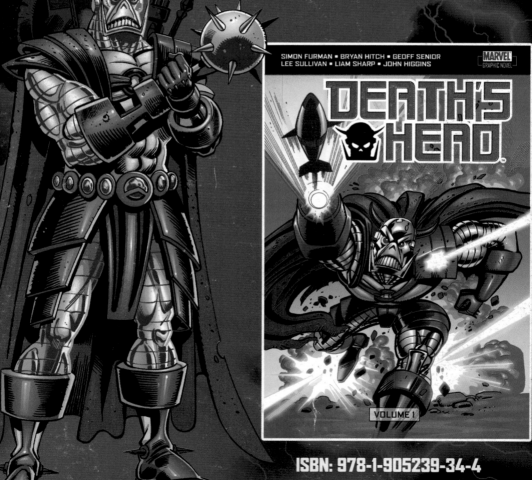